Netherlands

"Holland is a dream. A dream in a haze of smoke and gold, in the daylight more of smoke, but golden in the evening."

Albert Camus,
1956

The Netherlands has preserved numerous interesting monuments from its rich past in which economic prosperity went hand in hand with a rich culture. A large number of often carefully renovated monuments and the widely divergent collections of many museums attest to a captivating and rather eventful history. Not only the spectacular buildings and bridges but also the fact that large cities as well as small towns have museums, parks or art galleries where paintings or sculptures of modern-day artists can be admired, are evidence that the Netherlands is interested in modern art. The landscape is quite varied despite the relatively small area of the country: vast grassy meadows in the north, dunes with interesting flora and fauna along a large part of the coastline and on the Wadden, fertile hilly country with meandering brooks in the southern part of Limburg province etc. Human intervention is often quite clearly visible beyond the borders of nature reserves. Imposing works such as the IJsselmeer dam, the East and South Flevoland polders, the port of Rotterdam and the Delta works characterise the landscape of the Netherlands, a country which has adapted itself to modern-day needs throughout the ages.

Contents

Key

	Sight	Seaside Resort	Winter Sports Resort	Spa
Worth a journey	★★★	� � �	✻✻✻	♆♆♆
Worth a detour	★★	� �	✻✻	♆♆
Interesting	★	�	✻	♆

Tourism

⊘	Admission Times and Charges listed at the end of the guide	►►	Visit if time permits
◉ ➡	Sightseeing route with departure point indicated	AZ B	Map co-ordinates locating sights
⛪⛪⛪⛪	Ecclesiastical building	🛈	Tourist information
✡ ☪	Synagogue – Mosque	⚰ ⁙	Historic house, castle – Ruins
⬒	Building (with main entrance)	⌣ ☆	Dam – Factory or power station
■	Statue, small building	☆ ⌒	Fort – Cave
✝	Wayside cross	⛏	Prehistoric site
◎	Fountain	▼ ᙍ	Viewing table – View
●━━■	Fortified walls – Tower – Gate	▲	Miscellaneous sight

Recreation

🏇	Racecourse	🏃	Waymarked footpath
⛸	Skating rink	◆	Outdoor leisure park/centre
≋ ▦	Outdoor, indoor swimming pool	🎭	Theme/Amusement park
⛵	Marina, moorings	⅄	Wildlife/Safari park, zoo
⛺	Mountain refuge hut	❀	Gardens, park, arboretum
▫▪▫▪▫	Overhead cable-car	◔	Aviary, bird sanctuary
🚂	Tourist or steam railway		

Additional symbols

══ ══	Motorway (unclassified)	✉ ☏	Post office – Telephone centre
❶ ❶	Junction: complete, limited	⬓	Covered market
▭▭	Pedestrian street	⋅✗⋅	Barracks
ɪ══ɪ	Unsuitable for traffic, street subject to restrictions	△	Swing bridge
▥▥▥	Steps – Footpath	℧ ✗	Quarry – Mine
🚆 🚌	Railway – Coach station	🅱 🅵	Ferry (river and lake crossings)
▫┼┼┼┼▫	Funicular – Rack-railway	🛥	Ferry services: Passengers and cars
━━● ◉	Tram – Metro, Underground	🛥	Foot passengers only
Bert (R.)...	Main shopping street	③	Access route number common to MICHELIN maps and town plans

Abbreviations and special symbols

G	Police station (Marechaussee)	**POL.**	Police station (Politie)
H	Town hall (Stadhuis)	**T**	Theatre (Schouwburg)
J	Law courts (Gerechtshof)	**U**	University (Universiteit)
M	Museum (Museum)	❸	Hotel
ℙ	Provincial capital (Hoofdplaats provincie)	⬌	Landing stage
P	Provincial council (Provinciehuis)	🏛	Outstanding frontage
		ℙℝ	Park and Ride

Using this guide

This guide contains a wealth of information. You can find:

● **Thematic maps** to help you plan your route; the **map of principal sights** situates the major attractions whereas the **map of touring programmes** recommends a number of excursions to sights which should not be missed.

● An **introduction** to get a general picture of the geographical, historical and cultural background of the country to fully enjoy your trip.

● **Sights** section: an alphabetical summary of the principal tourist sights. The clock ⊙ symbol placed after the name of a sight refers to the **Admission times and charges** chapter indicated at the end of this guide.

● Cross-references to the Michelin road **map 908** of the Netherlands and the Michelin tourist **maps 210** and **211**. These cross-references appear in blue print under the name of each sight.

● The **Out and about** section for a number of cities with a selection of hotels, restaurants and cafes, and a wealth of practical information (guided tours, boat trips, stores, markets and festivals).

● **Practical information** including general information (formalities, transport, recreational facilities), calendar of events, a bibliography and the admission times and charges of sights.

● An alphabetical **index** to quickly find towns, regions, sights, historic figures or other subjects in the guide.

We appreciate comments and suggestions from our readers. Write to us at the address shown on the inside front cover or at our website: **www.michelin-travel.com**.

Have a pleasant journey!

Morand-Grahame/HOA QUI

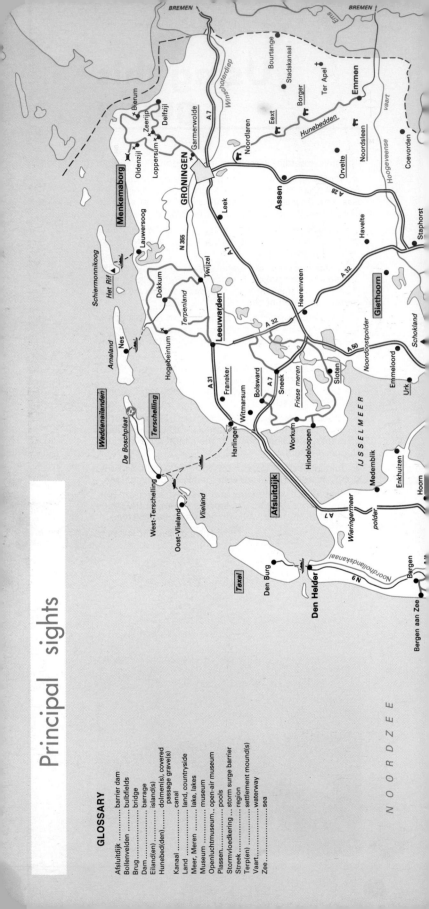

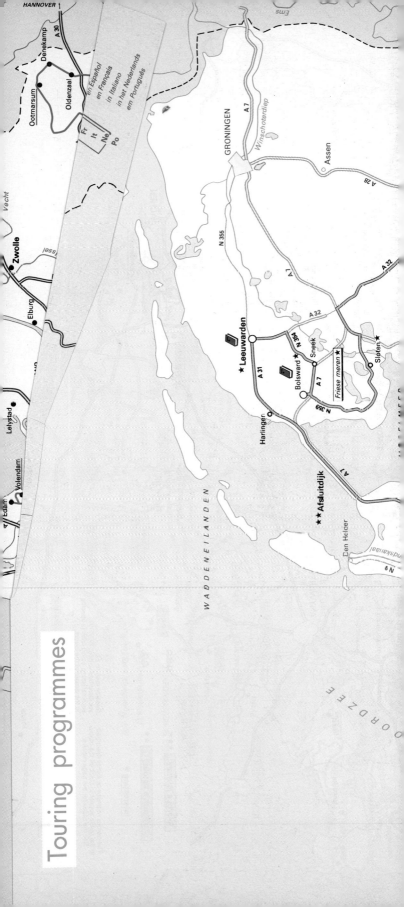

Touring programmes

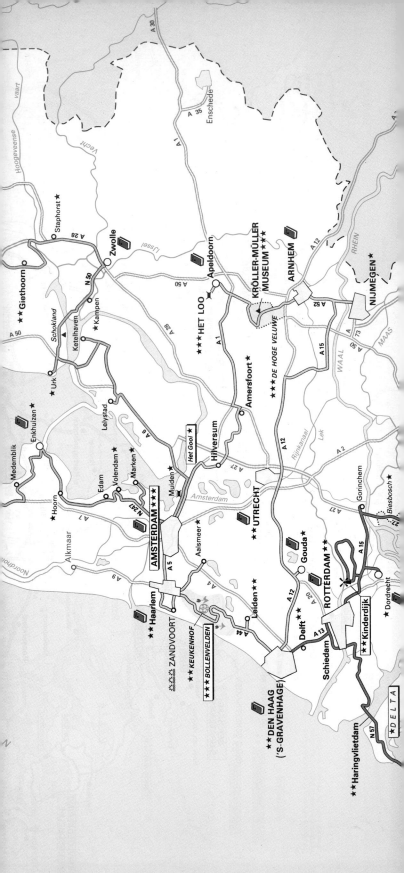

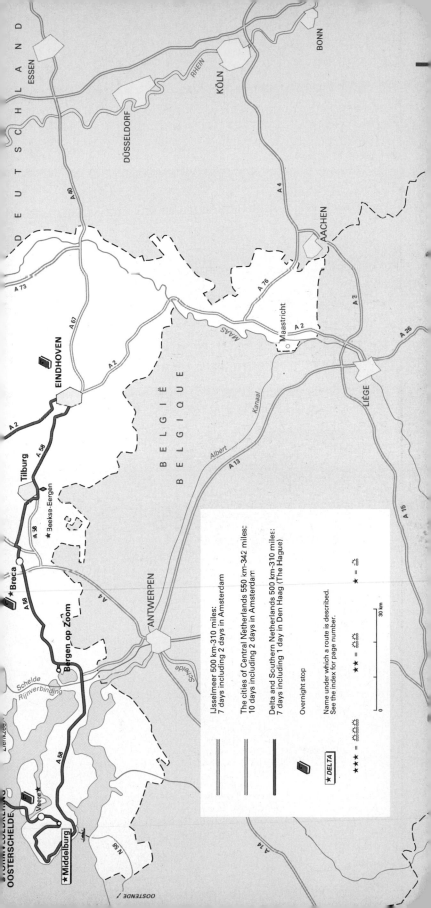

Introduction

Description of the country

The area of the Netherlands, which includes huge stretches of water such as the IJsselmeer and the Waddenzee, is 41 863km²/16 163sq mi, of which 9 896km²/3 820sq mi is reclaimed land. The longest distance from one end of the country to the other is 310km/193mi, ie from Rottum Island in the north of the province of Groningen to the south of Limburg.

The Netherlands has a total population of 15 567 107 (1997 census). With a density of 459 persons per km² or 1 187 per sq mi, it is one of the most densely populated countries in the world (the United Kingdom, by comparison, has a density of 236 per km² or 612 per sq mi). The population distribution is very uneven, and the highest densities are in the provinces of Noord- and Zuid-Holland. Together with the province of Utrecht these form the **Randstad**, a large conurbation encompassing the country's four main cities: Amsterdam, The Hague, Rotterdam and Utrecht.

Agriculture in the Netherlands is highly intensive and productive, but represents only a small percentage of the gross national product. Stock raising is well suited to the fertile reclaimed areas. Industry, especially chemicals, metallurgy and food processing, is concentrated within the Randstad area, the Twente, Noord-Brabant and Limburg. The Netherlands relies heavily on imported raw materials and the export of its manufactured goods. Because of its privileged geographical location trade, especially goods in transit between Europe and the rest of the world, plays an important role in the Dutch economy.

Holland and the Netherlands – Over the years the name **Holland** has come to designate the whole of the Netherlands. In fact, this old province, separated since 1840 into Noord-Holland and Zuid-Holland, supplanted the other regions of the United Provinces in the 17C due to its economic prosperity and political supremacy. Napoleon I ratified the primacy of Holland by creating the short-lived kingdom of Holland in 1810.

In fact, as early as the late Middle Ages the plains stretching from Friesland to Flanders were called **Lage Landen** or **Nederlanden** (Low Countries). In 1581 the United Provinces of the Netherlands (Verenigde Provinciën der Nederlanden) came into being. In 1815 this was still the name used when William I became ruler of the kingdom, which included part of Belgium. The name has remained unchanged – Netherlands – despite the secession of Belgium in 1830. Queen Beatrix has the title of Queen of the Netherlands (Koningin der Nederlanden). The country now has 12 provinces.

Climate – A cloudy sky pierced by a few timid rays of sunshine or a misty horizon are typical of the climate, and were beautifully captured by the landscape artists of the 17C.

The oceanic climate is humid and cool. An average of 750mm/30in of rain falls each year, spread over more than 200 days. The temperature is fairly cool in summer without being too harsh in winter. Winters are warmer than in the past, as proved by Avercamp's delightful 17C skating scenes; in 1795, too, the town of Den Helder fell after the French took advantage of the fact that the Dutch fleet was frozen into the ice.

The westerly winds are often strong, and many of the farmhouses are protected by a screen of poplar trees.

A "LOW COUNTRY"

The name Netherlands is very apt (*land* means country, *neder* means low). The sea is a constant threat, since more than one third of the country is

below sea level. Without the protection of dunes and dikes more than half the country would be under water during surge tides or when the rivers are in spate. The lowest point, 6.5m/21ft below sea level, is at Alexanderpolder, near Rotterdam. There is a marked difference between east and west. The west of the country is a low-lying plain with an altitude of less than 5m/16ft. This is the most densely populated area. In the east, on the other hand, the Veluwe hills rise to a height of 106m/348ft at Zijpenberg to the northeast of Arnhem, and **Drielandenpunt** (321m/1 053ft), at the junction of the Dutch, Belgian and German frontiers, is the highest point. The Netherlands represents a depressed area of the earth's crust which has subsequently been infilled by depositions of sands and morainic material during the Quaternary Era, and then by alluvial deposits from the River Rhine and River Meuse.

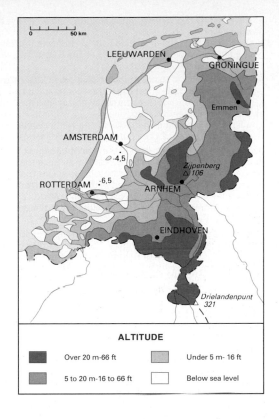

ALTITUDE

Over 20 m-66 ft

Under 5 m- 16 ft

5 to 20 m-16 to 66 ft

Below sea level

A land of water – The land above sea level represents only five-sixths of the total area. The country is crisscrossed by a network of rivers, whose estuaries form an immense delta. In addition, the large freshwater lake, the IJsselmeer, created by the Zuiderzee Project, covers an area of 120 000ha/296 400 acres. Elsewhere ponds, small lakes, canals, streams and ditches abound, especially in Friesland, whose flag has water lily leaves as its emblem.
The percentage of land above sea level increases with the altitude from west to east. In the east the land is relatively well drained, while water tends to accumulate in the low-lying plains and polders of the west.

LANDSCAPE

Apart from a few hilly regions, the Netherlands consists of an immense plain with little diversity of soil, resulting in a corresponding lack of variety in the landscape. The polder lands are the result of man's determined intervention throughout the ages, but they also give a somewhat monotonous appearance to the countryside. However, they are one of the quintessential aspects of the country and their peacefulness, light and colour give the landscape a poetic dimension.

Vast sandy tracts – Sand covers 43% of the territory with the main areas in the south and the east, notably the **Kempenland** of Noord-Brabant, which is a continuation of the Belgian Kempenland, the **Veluwe** and the north of the provinces of Overijssel and Drenthe. In addition to agricultural land there are moorlands of heather, broom and gorse and forests (in the vicinity of Breda and the pines of the Veluwe). The great Scandinavian glaciers left tracts of **morainic material** with their tell-tale erratics in the undulating Utrechtse Heuvelrug and the Veluwe. The glaciers were also responsible for deflecting the course of the Rhine and Meuse rivers westwards. There are several areas of **marshland** (De Peel and Biesbosch) and lakes, for example in the south of Friesland. Unlike those in the province of Holland, these have not been reclaimed due to the infertility of their sandy soil.

Dunes – Coastal currents have caused offshore sand bars to form along the coast. The coastal sand dunes are of the utmost importance, as they provide protection against the high tides. Marram grass is planted to stabilise the dunes, which are carefully monitored by local authorities. Public access is restricted in certain sectors to prevent further erosion and damage to this fragile ecosystem. In some cases the chain of dunes is strengthened by a dike. The dunes also act as reservoirs for the rainwater which then filters down to the water table.

15

The vast sandy beaches beyond the dunes and dikes are a valuable asset for the local seaside resorts.

In the north, the Wadden Islands form an important offshore barrier. They are lashed on the north and west by the waves of the North Sea, with the calmer waters of the Waddenzee on the landward side.

Alluvial deposits – Marine deposited clays cover 28% of the country, especially in the Delta area, around the great coastal estuaries and bays, and in those which have been reclaimed as polders such as the Lauwerszee and the Middelzee, which once reached as far inland as Leeuwarden.

The **fluvial clays** which cover 10% of the Netherlands are associated with the many rivers in the centre of the country and the Meuse Valley, to the south of Venlo.

Peat bogs – In the Netherlands there are two types of peat bog. The first has formed in the lagoons on top of marine sediments. Once the peat was extracted, lakes then formed which were drained and used for agricultural purposes.

In the upland region peat formed in the marshy areas; here again it was used for fuel and the land was then given over to agriculture. The provinces of Groningen and Drenthe were known for the **peat colonies** *(veenkoloniën)* which flourished from the 16C to the 19C.

Limestone plateau – The limestone landscapes of southern Limburg provide a sharp contrast to the rest of the country. Some parts of the bedrock are silt-covered (loess) as in the Hesbaye region of Belgium, while others appear as rocky outcrops more akin to the ancient (Hercynian) Ardennes Massif, again in Belgium.

All mining activity has now ceased in the Limburg coalfields, which are a continuation of the coal seams of Kempenland in Belgium.

THE FIGHT AGAINST THE SEA

The history of the Netherlands tells of man's continuous struggle with the elements, against the sea, storm surges and rivers in spate.

The first dunes were formed to the south of Haarlem around 5 BC, and by AD 1000 a sand bar stretched from the Scheldt to the Eems. The bar was breached at several points, creating the chain of islands now known as the Wadden Islands, and the sea inundated the peat bogs lying inland to form the **Waddenzee**.

First steps: terps and dikes – Around 500 BC the **Frisians**, the earliest inhabitants of the coastal areas, were already engaged in their struggle with the sea. They built artificial mounds or **terps** to protect their settlements from the encroaching water. As early as AD 1200 they were building dikes and had drained a few areas of land – the very first polders – between Leeuwarden and Sneek.

During the 13C there were at least 35 great floods, and large tracts of land were inundated, creating the Dollard and **Lauwerszee** in the north and the **Zuiderzee**, now IJsselmeer, in 1287.

Windmills: the first polders – In the 14C **windmills** were being used to drain lakes and marshes. By the 15C the rivers of Zeeland had already carved out an intricate network of peninsulas and islands, and the coastal dunes were crumbling under the assaults of the waves. The overall lack of protection was responsible for the catastrophic **St Elizabeth Flood**. Following this disaster, windmills were increasingly used in the threatened low-lying areas. Thus in Noord-Holland small **polders** appeared in Schagen in 1456 and in Alkmaar in 1564. Many of the coastal dikes of the time were the work of **Andries Vierlingh** (1507-79).

The creation of a polder

A polder is defined as land reclaimed from the sea, a lake or marshland. The area is enclosed with dikes and then pumping begins to regulate the water level. The method has been the same since earliest times despite various technological developments; windmills were replaced first by steam and then by diesel engines or electrically operated pumps.

The coastal or riverside peatbogs, lying above sea level, necessitate the creation of a simple polder where all the surplus water is returned directly to the sea or the river via locks at low tide. However, when the polder lies below sea level, the water needs to be pumped into diversion canals (lodes) and thence to the sea.

A more complex type of polder is required when draining a lake. The lake is surrounded by a dike and then a canal, which also encircles the ring dikes of neighbouring polders. The polder itself is crisscrossed with small canals linked to each other by collector canals. When the water level reaches a set height, the pump (formerly the windmill) forces the water back into the collector canals towards the peripheral canal and a network of lakes or canals serving as a temporary reservoir. The water is then discharged into the rivers and the sea, either directly or by pumping; the water level has to be constantly monitored and controlled.

When the lake to be drained was fairly deep, then a number of **windmills** (known as a gang) were required to pump the water out of the polder. The best example of this are the windmills at **Kinderdijk**.

17C: a series of polders – In the 17C, much of the draining of inland tracts of water was carried out by **Jan Adriaensz Leeghwater** (his name means low water). Leeghwater supervised the successful draining of the **Beemstermeer** to the north of Amsterdam in 1612 with the help of 40 windmills. The success of this initial project encouraged the Dutch to continue reclamation work, and they built the polders of **Purmer** in 1622 and **Wormer** in 1626.

In 1631 the town of Alkmaar started reclaiming the **Schermermeer** in accordance with Leeghwater's instructions. This time 50 windmills were used and the work was completed in 1635. Another of Leeghwater's projects was the draining of Haarlem Lake. As early as 1667, Hendrik Stevin proposed a project to drain the Zuiderzee "to evacuate the violence and poison of the North Sea". The project was only completed in the 20C.

In the 18C autonomous water boards **(waterschappen)** were invested with the responsibility for building, maintaining and monitoring the country's dikes, canals and locks. These bodies still exist, but since 1798 they have been assisted by the Ministry of Transport and Waterways. Steam power was introduced just before 1800, and this proved capable of pumping water over high dikes, thus replacing several rows or gangs of windmills. Pumping operations no longer depended on the vagaries of wind power.

The ambitious projects of the 19C and 20C – The most spectacular period of land reclamation began in 1848 with the draining of **Haarlem Lake** which was completed four years later. Three large pumping stations were built, including that of Cruquius, which has now been converted into a museum *(see HAARLEM, outskirts)*.

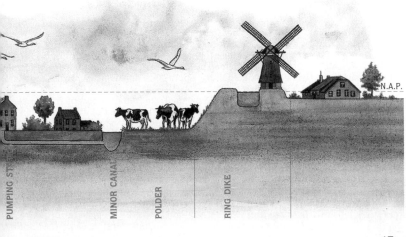

THE FIGHT AGAINST THE SEA

| ■ Polders: 14-18C | Polders: 19C to the present | ∧∧ Dike: coastal or fluvial |

After the great floods of 1916 it was the turn of the Zuiderzee itself. This great arm of the sea was closed off by the barrier dam or **Afsluitdijk** in 1932, creating the outer Waddenzee and an inland freshwater lake now known as the **IJsselmeer**. Once enclosed, work began on draining several polders around the edge (Wieringermeer, Noordoost, Zuidelijk Flevoland and Oostelijk Flevoland). The fifth polder **(Markerwaard)** was abandoned in 1986.

Other polders reclaimed in the 19C and 20C are the Prins Alexander Polder (1872) near Rotterdam and the Lauwersmeer Polder.

The most recent disaster occurred during the night of 31 January 1953, when gale force winds swept landwards at high tide. 1 865 people died and 260 000ha/642 200 acres were inundated. The success of the Zuiderzee Project encouraged engineers to find a similar way of protecting the islands of Noord-and Zuid-Holland. The outcome was the **Delta Plan**, work on which began in 1954. This vast project was not completed until 1998, with the building of the storm surge barrier in the Nieuwe Waterweg.

Conquering the sea – Since the 13C about 7 050km²/2 745sq mi have been reclaimed from the sea. Coastal dikes have been responsible for creating 4 000km²/2 400sq mi, the IJsselmeer for another 1 650km²/644sq mi and a further 1 400km²/546sq mi has been reclaimed by other means. These figures do not include land which was flooded during military operations and which was subsequently reclaimed.

However, at the dawn of the 21C, some parts of the Dutch landscape may undergo a radical change. New EU farming regulations, the surplus of floral and market garden products, and the critical level of pollution – partly caused by large-scale pig breeding – led the Dutch government to pass a bill in 1993 stipulating that one tenth of arable land should be left fallow.

NATURE CONSERVATION

In this highly industrialised and densely populated country, certain groups are very active in the protection of the environment. The Nature Conservation Society (Vereniging tot Behoud van Natuurmonumenten) is a private organisation which acquires and preserves unspoilt coastal and rural areas. The Society currently manages 150 sites **(natuurmonumenten)** covering a total area of 46 000ha/113 620 acres of varied habitats, including woodlands, moors, dunes and marshes. In general visitors are welcome to the reserves, and some have visitor centres, nature trails and bird hides, but there are usually restrictions.

State-owned forests and woodlands are managed by the Forestry Commission (Staatsbosbeheer). Recreation is encouraged and the facilities include picnic sites, nature trails and camp sites.

Birds

The great variety of habitats provided by the Netherlands' seasides, hills, waters and woodlands attracts many bird species, both native and migratory *(illustrations: see WADDENEILANDEN)*. One of the most common species is the **lapwing** with its plaintive peewit cry, which is almost considered the national bird. This plump little bird is about 30cm/12in in length, with lustrous bronze plumage, and prefers grassy areas, especially in Friesland. Its eggs are considered a delicacy, but plans are afoot for a ban on their sale, and Queen Juliana ended the tradition whereby the first lapwing's egg to be found each year is given to the queen.

The seashores are home to **terns**, **seagulls** and other **gulls**, particularly the black-headed gulls, which often nest inland. Colonies of **oyster catchers**, a small black and white wader, nest along the shores while the **grey heron** can be seen along the canals. The **spoonbill** is rarer but can be seen in shallow estuaries, while the **white stork** is protected to prevent its extinction.

All sorts of **ducks** abound in the canals, ponds and marshes: the wild duck or mallard and the sheldrake with multicoloured plumage are the most common.

The country's numerous **nature reserves** provide protection for a variety of species and their coastal and inland habitats. The reserves provide safe breeding and feeding grounds and facilities for scientific study. Public access is limited and usually prohibited during the breeding season (April to August).

Historical table and notes

Prehistory

BC 30000	Earliest traces of human settlement in the east of the country.
4500	Agriculturalists settle in Limburg; their pottery belongs to the Spiral Meander Ware culture.
3000-2000	The megalithic Hunebed culture flourishes in the Drenthe area.
2200	A nomadic people settles to the north of the great rivers; stroke ornamented pottery ware.
2000	Bell-Beaker civilization, notably in the Drenthe. New settlements in the alluvial areas of the delta.
1900	Bronze Age. The dead are buried in burial mounds.
800	In the east the people incinerate their dead and bury them in urnfields.
750-400	First Iron Age: Hallstatt Period. First **terps** are built in Friesland and the Groningen area.
450	South of the great rivers, Second Iron Age: the La Tene Period.
300	Germanic and Celtic tribes arrive in the area south of the Rhine.

Romans – Vikings

57-51	South of the Rhine, **Caesar** defeats the Menapii and Eburones, Celtic tribes belonging to the Roman province of Gallia Belgica.
12	The Germanic tribe, the **Batavi** settle on the banks of the great rivers.
AD 69-70	Batavian uprising against the Roman garrisons.
3C	Incursions by Germanic tribes: the **Franks** settle on the banks of the Rhine. At this time the main tribes occupying the territory are the Franks, **Saxons** and **Frisians**.
Late 3C	The area south of the Rhine belongs to the Roman province of Germania Secunda (capital: Cologne).
4C	Power struggle between the Salian Franks and the Romans.
382	St Servatius transfers his bishopric from Tongeren to Maastricht and the region's gradual conversion to Christianity begins.
Early 6C	The Merovingian kingdom under Clovis (465-511) extends from the north of Gaul to the Rhine.

561	The Merovingian kingdom is divided into Neustria (west of the river Scheldt) and Austrasia (east of the Scheldt; the present Netherlands).
Late 7C	The Northumbrian missionary **Willibrord** evangelises Friesland.
800	**Charlemagne** is crowned Emperor of the West, a territory which covers the whole of the country and is centred on Aachen.
834	First of the **Viking** raids at Dorestad.
843	**Treaty of Verdun**. The Carolingian Empire is divided into three kingdoms: Germania, Francia and, between the two, a Middle Kingdom stretching from the North Sea to the Mediterranean and including the present-day Netherlands. The Middle Kingdom (Lotharingia) was short-lived and Lothair II received only the northern part.
879-882	Viking invasions: from their base in Utrecht they make raids into the surrounding countryside.
925	The German king, Henry I, the Fowler, annexes **Lotharingia**.
959	Lotharingia is divided into Upper Lotharingia (Lorraine) and Lower Lotharingia, covering nearly all the present country.

Counties and Duchies

10C	Bishop Balderic (919-976) extends the **See of Utrecht**.
Early 11C	The **Duchy of Brabant** is founded by Lambert, Count of Louvain.
11C	Creation of the county of Gelderland.
Late 11C	The county of **Holland** is extended at the expense of the county of Flanders (in Zeeland) and the See of Utrecht.
Early 13C	Zutphen and Veluwe become part of the county of Gelderland.
Late 13C	**Floris V**, Count of Holland conquers West-Friesland.
1323	Zeeland passes from Flanders to Holland.
1350	Start of the civil war between the **Hooks** (*Hoeken* – backed by Margaret of Bavaria) and the **Cods** (*Kabeljauwen* – backed by her son William V).

Consolidation of Burgundian power

Late 14C	The Duchy of Burgundy is extended northwards when **Philip the Bold** acquires Limburg and certain rights over Brabant.
1428	Philip the Good deposes **Jacoba** and makes himself ruler of Holland and Zeeland.
1473	**Charles the Bold** acquires Gelderland; the only territory not in Burgundian hands is Friesland.

The Habsburgs

1477	Death of Charles the Bold; his daughter and heir Mary of Burgundy marries Maximilian of Austria, one of the Habsburgs. Mary is forced to sign the Great Privilege, a charter conferring far-reaching local powers.
1494	Philip the Fair, their son, inherits the Low Countries when Maximilian is elected Holy Roman Emperor.
1515	Charles I of Spain, son of Philip the Fair, inherits the Low Countries. In 1516 he becomes King of Spain, and then in 1519 Emperor of Germany as **Charles V**. He adds **Friesland** to the Low Countries in 1523; the See of Utrecht in 1527; Overijssel in 1528; and takes Groningen and Drenthe by force in 1536.
1543	The Duke of Gelderland cedes his dukedom to Charles V, who thus rules over nearly the whole of Europe.
1548	Charles V groups the 17 provinces of the Low Countries and the Franche-Comté into the independent Burgundian Kreis.

The Spanish Netherlands

1555	Charles V abdicates his claim to the Low Countries in favour of his son Philip II, soon to become King of Spain.
1555-1579	The **Revolt of the Netherlands**; the rise of Protestantism.
1566	The **Breda Compromise** also known as the Compromise of the Nobility; The Beggars protest against the Inquisition. The **Iconoclasm**, involving riots and destruction of Church property.
1567	The Duke of Alva is appointed Governor of the Low Countries.

William the Silent (detail of a stained-glass window in the Sint-Janskerk), Gouda

1568	**William the Silent** raises an army; beginning of the Eighty Years War.
1572	**Capture of Brielle** by the Sea Beggars; Vlissingen and Enkhuizen follow.
1579	**Union of Arras** is signed by Catholic Hainaut, Artois and Douai, pledging allegiance to Philip; in reply the northern Protestant provinces form an essentially military alliance and sign the **Union of Utrecht**.

The United Provinces

1581	Creation of the **Republic of the United Provinces**, a federation of seven provinces, independent of Spanish rule; Philip II is deposed.
1584	William the Silent is assassinated in Delft.
1585	His second son, Maurice of Nassau, succeeds his father as Stadtholder of Holland and Zeeland. He becomes the undisputed leader of the United Provinces in 1618 on the death of his elder brother.
1596	Cornelis de Houtman establishes trading relations with Java.
1598	Edict of Nantes.
1602	**Dutch East India Company** founded to trade with Asia.
1609-21	**Twelve Years Truce** with Spain. Henry Hudson sails up the river named after him in his ship the *Half Moon*, while on a voyage for the Dutch East India Company.
1614	The name New Netherland is first used for the colony founded in the New World.
1618	**Synod of Dort**. Reprobation of the Remonstrants.
1619	Founding of Batavia (Jakarta) in the Dutch East Indies.
1620	The Pilgrim Fathers arrive on the *Mayflower* and establish Plymouth Colony.
1621	Founding of the **Dutch West India Company** to trade with America. Renewal of hostilities with Spain.
1624-54	Colonisation of northeast Brazil.
1625	The Dutch trading post on Manhattan Island is called Nieuw Amsterdam.
1626	Peter Minuit of the Dutch West India Company buys Manhattan from the Indians for the equivalent of $24.
1634	Dutch West India Company establishes a trading post in Curaçao in the Antilles.
1648	Treaty of Westphalia ends the Thirty Years War, also called the Eighty Years War. In the **Peace of Munster** Philip IV of Spain recognises the independence of the United Provinces.
1651	The English Navigation Act augurs ill for Dutch trade.
1652	Jan van Riebeeck founds the Cape Colony.

1652-54	**First Anglo-Dutch War**: commercial and colonial rivalry lead to what is essentially a war at sea; the Dutch fleet is commanded by Admiral Tromp *(see BRIELLE)*.
1653-72	Stadtholderless period: the statesman **Johan de Witt** *(see DORDRECHT)* governs as Grand Pensionary.
1658-1795	Colonisation of Ceylon (Sri Lanka).
1664	The English seize New Netherland and rename its capital New York after the Duke of York, later James II.
1665-7	**Second Anglo-Dutch War**. Admiral de Ruyter earns distinction as commander of the Dutch fleet. Under the **Treaty of Breda**, Dutch Guiana (Suriname) is ceded to the Dutch in exchange for control of New Netherland.
1667-8	War of Devolution led by Louis XIV; Treaty of Aachen.
1672	**William III** becomes Stadtholder of Holland and Zeeland.
1677	William marries Mary, the daughter of James II.
1672-8	War with France.
1678-1679	Peace of Nijmegen
1685	Revocation of the Edict of Nantes.
1688	Glorious Revolution: British crown offered jointly to William and Mary following the flight of James II.
1689	William becomes King of England.
1701-13	Spanish War of Succession: alliance of several countries, including the United Provinces, against Louis XIV. **Treaty of Utrecht**.
1702	Stadtholder William III dies without an heir. The title of Prince of Orange passes to the Frisian stadtholder, Jan Willem Friso.
1702-47	Stadtholderless period.
1747	**William IV**, the son of Jan Willem Friso, is the first elected Stadtholder of the United Provinces.
1751-95	**William V**, William IV's son, is Stadtholder.

French domination

1795	A French army under General Pichegru overruns the country; William V flees to England; the United Provinces become the **Batavian Republic** (1795-1806).
1806	**Louis Bonaparte** becomes King of the **Kingdom of Holland** with Amsterdam as the capital.
1810-13	Louis Bonaparte abdicates; the country becomes part of the **French Empire** under Napoleon.

Union with Belgium

Dec. 1813	William VI of Orange, son of William V, becomes the last Stadtholder of the Netherlands.
1815	Battle of Waterloo and the fall of Napoleon. The Congress of Vienna recognises William VI, Prince of Orange, as the King of the Netherlands (including Belgium) under the name **William I**. In addition, he becomes Grand Duke of Luxembourg. The Western seaboard of New Guinea is colonised.
1830	Brussels Revolution leads to Belgium's independence.

Kingdom of the Netherlands: an independent kingdom

1831	Parts of Limburg and Brabant are ceded to Belgium but William I only ratifies the treaty in 1839.
1890-1948	Reign of **Queen Wilhelmina** (b 1880).
1932	Zuiderzee Project.
May 1940	The country is invaded by the German army. The Queen and her family leave for London.
5 May 1945	German army surrenders, and the Queen returns.
1948	Queen Wilhelmina abdicates in favour of her daughter **Juliana** (b 1909). Economic Union of Benelux.
Dec. 1949	Independence of the Dutch East Indies which become the Republic of **Indonesia**.
1954	Autonomy of Dutch Guiana or Suriname and the archipelago of the Dutch Antilles.

1957	The Netherlands joins the EEC.
1960	The **Benelux** economic union comes into effect.
Nov. 1975	Dutch Guiana becomes independent as the Republic of **Suriname**.
30 April 1980	Queen Juliana abdicates in favour of her daughter **Beatrix**.
1986	Flevoland becomes the 12th province.
1987	Inauguration of the Oosterschelde storm-surge barrier.
1992	**Treaty of Maastricht** signed by the 12 EC members.
1998	Completion of the Delta Plan.

TIES BETWEEN THE BRITISH AND THE DUTCH

The Netherlands and Britain were two small seafaring nations with a strong Protestant tradition, in an otherwise predominantly Catholic world. They were linked politically, religiously, commercially, intellectually and artistically long before William III's reign, though it was during his time that their friendship reached its peak. **William III, Prince of Orange**, was the nephew and son-in-law of King James II (1685-8) of England, and Stadtholder of the United Provinces. He married Mary, James' daughter, in 1677. James set about establishing Catholicism, which created nationwide unrest and dissent. The British wrote to William in June 1688 asking him to restore peace and unity to the country. William landed in October 1688, James abdicated, and Mary, the nearest Protestant claimant to the throne, was crowned jointly with William in April 1689. During their reign (1689-1702), a vogue for all things Dutch developed. Political decisions were closely linked to commercial interests, and the Dutch, English and Scots had been exchanging naval techniques and trading together for years, in areas such as the wool and shipbuilding industries.

Once commercial links had been established between the two countries, Dutch goods and influences began appearing in Britain. These included bricks and gables, sash windows, Dutch-style gardens, marine painting and portraits, and interior decoration. Dutch influence reached its peak during William and Mary's reign with the transformation of Hampton Court and Kensington Palace, where the influence of their Dutch residence, Het Loo, is apparent. They employed Grinling Gibbons to do carvings, Daniel Marot as their architect and interior decorator, and Sir Godfrey Kneller to paint portraits; all were in some way connected with the Netherlands. Many stately homes, such as Belton, Ashdown and Easton, contained Dutch-style decorative features including carvings, tulip vases, lacquerware cabinets, and upholstered cabriole-legged chairs, and reflected Mary's great love of porcelain and William's for gardens.

The Dutch tradition of religious tolerance and freedom of expression also attracted political and religious refugees from Britain. With the reign of William and Mary, a wave of tolerance spread through Britain, rendering exile to the Netherlands unnecessary.

OVERSEAS EXPANSION

In the middle of the 16C, Amsterdam traders went to Antwerp to obtain goods brought back from the Indies by Portuguese ships. Since the mouth of the Scheldt was cut off by the Sea Beggars, the traders started sailing to Lisbon in 1580, the same year that Philip II of Spain invaded Portugal. In 1585 he placed an embargo on Dutch trade in Spain and Portugal. The Dutch merchants, forced to handle shipments themselves, clashed with the Spanish, Portuguese and above all the English, who were fearsome competitors in the overseas markets.

The route to the East – While looking for a passage to India from the north of Europe, **William Barents** *(see WADDENEILANDEN, Terschelling)* discovered Novaya Zemlya in 1594 and Spitsbergen in 1596. In the same year, **Cornelis de Houtman** landed in **Java**. Jacob van Neck conquered the island of Mauritius in 1598. After the establishment of Batavia (now Jakarta) by **Jan Pieterszoon Coen** *(see HOORN)* in 1619, Java became a Dutch colony. In 1641, Malacca was wrested from the Portuguese, and in the following year the explorer Abel Jansz Tasman, an explorer working for the East India Company, discovered the islands of Tasmania and New Zealand. Australia was first mapped by Dutch cartographers, who called it Nieuw-Holland. Jan Anthonisz van Riebeeck established the Cape Colony (South Africa) in 1652, and Ceylon was occupied in 1658.

The East India Company – To coordinate the large number of trading companies sailing to the East, Johan van Oldenbarnevelt founded the **United East India Company** or **VOC** *(see AMSTERDAM)* in 1602. The Company obtained a monopoly over shipping and trade to the east of the Cape of Good Hope and west of the Strait of Magellan, and very soon became the biggest trading company of the 17C, with trading posts all over Asia.

From these settlements, the VOC brought back costly spices (nutmeg, pepper, cinnamon, saffron, ginger and cloves) and Chinese porcelain; these were largely replaced by tea, coffee, silk and cotton from the 18C onwards. The journey from the Netherlands to Java took eight months, and to coordinate all these expeditions a

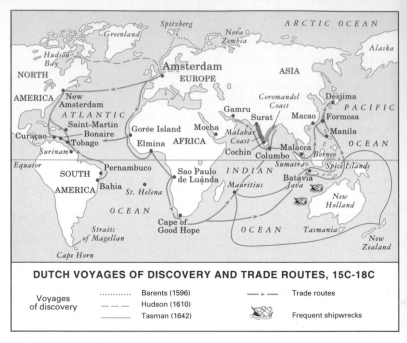

DUTCH VOYAGES OF DISCOVERY AND TRADE ROUTES, 15C-18C

Voyages of discovery	.... Barents (1596)	——▸—— Trade routes
	– – – Hudson (1610)	
	———— Tasman (1642)	Frequent shipwrecks

central administration was set up in **Batavia**. Here, all products from Sumatra, Borneo, the Moluccas, and also India, China, Japan and Persia, were centralised for transportation to the home country. Here, they played a major part in creating the prosperity that was the Golden Age. The VOC was finally disbanded in 1789.

The Americas – In the 17C, Dutch trade also turned towards the New World. The first expedition was that of **Hudson** (*see AMSTERDAM*) in 1609; Amsterdam merchants established a factory in **Suriname** in 1613, and **Willem Schouten** (*see HOORN*) discovered Cape Horn in 1616.

The **Dutch West India Company (WIC)**, created in 1621, traded both with Africa and the Americas; the commodities included slaves. It set up trading posts on the coasts of both continents, and also conquered many islands in the Caribbean: Bonaire, Tobago, **Curaçao**, Sint-Maarten and the other Antilles.

In **Brazil**, **Johan Maurits van Nassau** (1604-79) was appointed governor-general (1636-44). He was a great patron of the arts and sciences, and assembled a team of academics and artists who documented the country in great detail.

The WIC concentrated mainly on southern America, but in 1624 it established a settlement known as **Nieuw Amsterdam** on the east coast of North America, and the Dutch colonialist **Peter Stuyvesant** became its governor shortly afterwards. Under his rule, Nieuw-Amsterdam developed rapidly, but in 1664 it was taken by the English and renamed New York.

Many of the Dutch conquests in Asia and America were only temporary. However, they succeeded in establishing lasting settlements in Indonesia, Guiana and the Caribbean; the **Netherlands Antilles** and Aruba still form part of the Kingdom of the Netherlands.

Language and literature

Language – The Dutch language is spoken by about 20 million people throughout the world: in the Netherlands itself, in part of Belgium, and in the Netherlands Antilles and Surinam. Dutch is one of the western branches of the Germanic family of languages, and resembles both German and English. Frisian is not a dialect of Dutch, but a language in its own right. It was only on 29 January 1993 that Dutch was recognised by law as being the official national language, and Frisian was accorded the status of the second governmental language.

Literature: the Middle Ages – Although most literature until the Middle Ages was written in Latin, a number of mystical works were published in Dutch during the 13C, by authors including Jan van Ruusbroeck and Hadewych. Other works written in Dutch were those of the Flemish poet Jacob van Maerlant, the anonymous animal epic **Reynard the Fox**, the miracle play **Mariken van Nieumeghen**, the morality play **Elckerlyc** (Everyman) and the works of Thomas à Kempis.

16C-17C – The great 16C and 17C humanists wrote in Latin; they included **Erasmus**, **Jansenius** (1585-1638), the theologian Hugo de Groot or **Grotius**, and the jurist and Jewish philosopher **Spinoza** (1634-1677). The country, and especially Amsterdam, became known for its liberal attitude; many foreign scholars and philosophers, such as John Locke, Descartes and Pierre Bayle, sought shelter in the Netherlands and found freedom to publish. The two great figures in Dutch literature of the period were the poet and historian **PC Hooft** (1581-1647), and the poet and dramatist **Joost van den Vondel** (1587-1679); both belonged to the **Muiderkring**, a circle of artists, writers and musicians founded by Hooft.

18C – The Age of Enlightenment – The Dutch presses continued to print the uncensored works of great foreigners, including such prophets of enlightenment as Voltaire and Diderot, but for Dutch literature this was a period of decline.

19C – **Eduard Douwes Dekker**, known under the pseudonym of **Multatuli** (1820-87), gained an international reputation with his novel *Max Havelaar* (1860), a satire on colonial life in the Dutch East Indies. **Louis Couperus** (1863-1923) was an important novelist of the 1880 literary revival, and is best known for *Eline Vere* (1889), dealing with contemporary life in The Hague, and *Old People and the Things That Pass* (1906).

20C – Other writers of the early 20C include the historian **Johan Huizinga** (1872-1945), known for the lively style of his book *The Waning of the Middle Ages*, the prolific novelist **Simon Vestdijk** who wrote several works on middle-class provincial life, and **Simon Carmiggelt** (1913-87).

The postwar generation included Willem Frederik Hermans (1921-1995), **Gerard Reve** (b 1923), **Cees Nooteboom** and Harry Mulisch (b 1927). The prevalence of the war theme in postwar Dutch literature is evident in Jeroen Brouwer's *Sunken Road* (1981), Willem Frederik Hermans' controversial novels, including *The Tears of the Acacias* and *The Dark Room of Damocles*, Gerrit Kouwenaar's *I Was Not a Soldier* (1951) and Harry Mulisch's *The Assault*. Two other important figures are the poet **Ida Gerhardt** (b 1905) and **Hella Haasse** (b 1918), renowned for her historical novels.

The new avant-garde or Revisor writers reacted against realism: they included Dirk Ayelt Kooiman *(A Romance)*, Doeschka Meijsing *(Tiger, Tiger!)*, Frans Kellendonk *(Letter and Spirit)* and Nicholas Matsier *(The Eternal City)*.

The **Raster** writers formed an even more influential group named after the literary magazine of the same name. These representatives of alternative prose were a less homogeneous group and represented several generations. The Flemish writers Louis Paul Boon and Hugo Claus influenced their younger compatriots.

Other writers remained outside the mainstream of Dutch literature: the traditional realist storyteller Maarten 't Hart, Jeroen Brouwers, Joost Zwagerman *(Gimmick)*, who portrayed a tarnished image of the Amsterdam art world, and Willem Jan Otten. The old guard produced bestselling works such as Hugo Claus's much-acclaimed *The Sorrow of Belgium* (1983) and Harry Mulisch's *The Discovery of Heaven*. Kellendonk's very topical *Mystic Body* caused considerable controversy when it was published in 1986.

Frisian literature – The highly gifted poet Gysbert Japicx is the first to use the Frisian language in literature; a literary prize named after him is awarded in Bolsward every two years.

ABC of architecture

RELIGIOUS ARCHITECTURE

'S-HERTOGENBOSCH – Ground plan of St.-Janskathedraal (1380-1580)

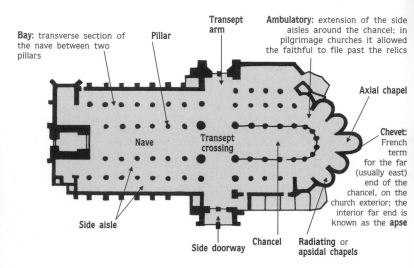

Bay: transverse section of the nave between two pillars

Pillar

Transept arm

Ambulatory: extension of the side aisles around the chancel; in pilgrimage churches it allowed the faithful to file past the relics

Axial chapel

Nave

Transept crossing

Chevet: French term for the far (usually east) end of the chancel, on the church exterior; the interior far end is known as the **apse**

Side aisle

Side doorway

Chancel

Radiating or **apsidal chapels**

HAARLEM – Grote of St.-Bavokerk (Chancel)

The inclusion of an ambulatory and the length of the chancel are unusual in a Gothic church in the Netherlands, suggesting French influence. The architect chose cedar wood for the stellar vaulting.

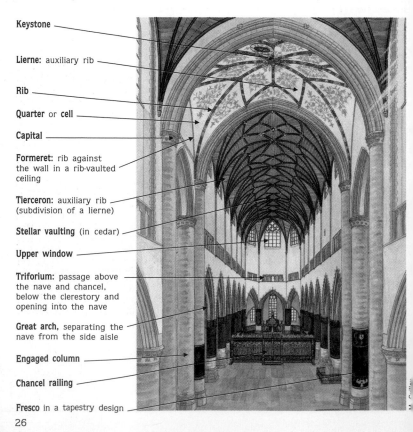

Keystone

Lierne: auxiliary rib

Rib

Quarter or **cell**

Capital

Formeret: rib against the wall in a rib-vaulted ceiling

Tierceron: auxiliary rib (subdivision of a lierne)

Stellar vaulting (in cedar)

Upper window

Triforium: passage above the nave and chancel, below the clerestory and opening into the nave

Great arch, separating the nave from the side aisle

Engaged column

Chancel railing

Fresco in a tapestry design

AMSTERDAM – Westerkerk (1619-31)

The Westerkerk is the last and most imposing of the three Mannerist churches built by Hendrik de Keyser commissioned by the city of Amsterdam. The two churches which predate it are the Zuiderkerk and the Noorderkerk.

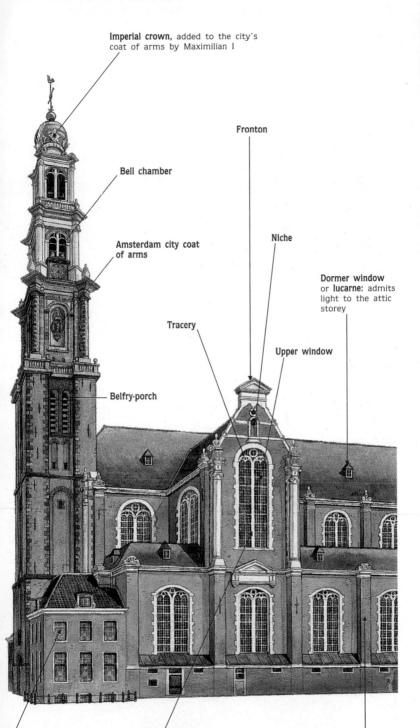

Imperial crown, added to the city's coat of arms by Maximilian I

Bell chamber

Amsterdam city coat of arms

Fronton

Niche

Dormer window or **lucarne:** admits light to the attic storey

Tracery

Upper window

Belfry-porch

Window (late 18C)

Mullion: vertical element dividing a window opening

Buttress: external support for a wall, built against it or projecting from it

M. Guillou

MILITARY ARCHITECTURE

AMERSFOORT – Koppelpoort (c1400)

This fortified gateway is a remnant of the second enceinte around Amersfoort. It is a unique combination of a town and water gate; the latter houses a double fulling mill.

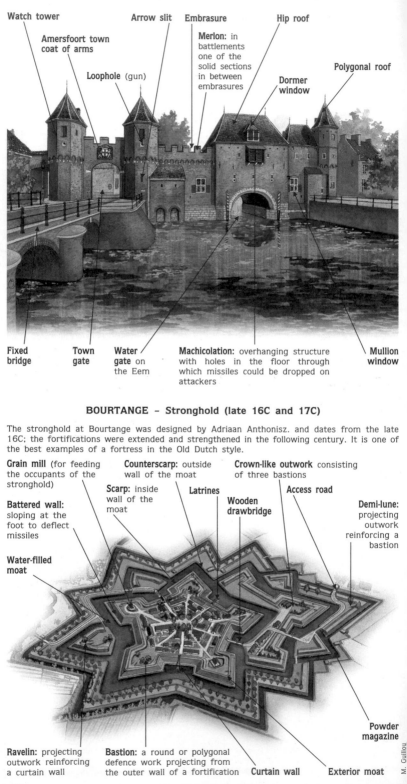

Watch tower

Amersfoort town coat of arms

Arrow slit **Embrasure**

Merlon: in battlements one of the solid sections in between embrasures

Hip roof

Loophole (gun)

Dormer window

Polygonal roof

Fixed bridge

Town gate

Water gate on the Eem

Machicolation: overhanging structure with holes in the floor through which missiles could be dropped on attackers

Mullion window

BOURTANGE – Stronghold (late 16C and 17C)

The stronghold at Bourtange was designed by Adriaan Anthonisz. and dates from the late 16C; the fortifications were extended and strengthened in the following century. It is one of the best examples of a fortress in the Old Dutch style.

Grain mill (for feeding the occupants of the stronghold)

Counterscarp: outside wall of the moat

Crown-like outwork consisting of three bastions

Scarp: inside wall of the moat

Latrines

Wooden drawbridge

Access road

Battered wall: sloping at the foot to deflect missiles

Demi-lune: projecting outwork reinforcing a bastion

Water-filled moat

Powder magazine

Ravelin: projecting outwork reinforcing a curtain wall

Bastion: a round or polygonal defence work projecting from the outer wall of a fortification

Curtain wall

Exterior moat

M. Guillou

28

AMSTERDAM – 18C merchant's house

The beautiful town houses along the canals of Amsterdam were built on pilotis (free-standing piles). Those commissioned by merchants in the 18C consist of a "downstairs", where the domestic staff were housed, an "upstairs", where the merchant and his family lived, and a loft in which merchandise was stored.

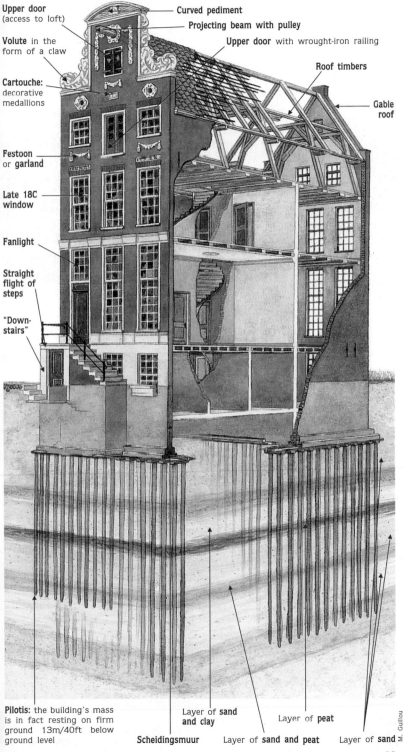

Upper door (access to loft)

Curved pediment

Projecting beam with pulley

Volute in the form of a claw

Upper door with wrought-iron railing

Roof timbers

Cartouche: decorative medallions

Gable roof

Festoon or **garland**

Late 18C window

Fanlight

Straight flight of steps

"Downstairs"

Pilotis: the building's mass is in fact resting on firm ground 13m/40ft below ground level

Layer of **sand and clay**

Layer of **peat**

Scheidingsmuur

Layer of **sand and peat**

Layer of **sand**

M. Guillou

HILVERSUM – Town Hall (1927-31)

Hilversum town hall won international renown for architect WM Dudok. Giant cuboid forms sit on top of or next to one another, giving rise to a harmonious interplay of vertical and horizontal lines. A tall clock tower overlooks the complex.

Roof overhang, designed to accentuate the horizontal and create a play of light and shade

Tall, thin brick; bricks with this dimension (24 x 11.5 x 4.5cm/9.4 x 4.5 x 1.8in) came to be known as "Hilversum format"

WM Dudok's **office** with a large corner window

Tower

Gallery

Tall, narrow **windows,** surmounted by a small projecting roof; the openings are reminiscent of those in a bell tower

Row of small windows directly beneath the roof, making it seem to be floating in thin air

Canopy

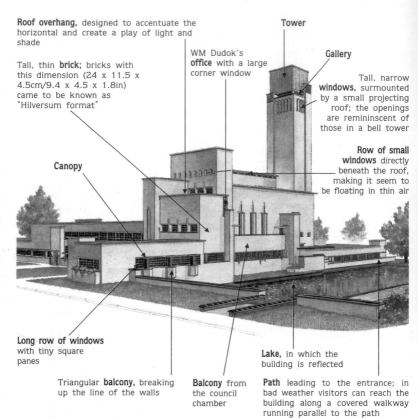

Long row of windows with tiny square panes

Lake, in which the building is reflected

Triangular **balcony,** breaking up the line of the walls

Balcony from the council chamber

Path leading to the entrance; in bad weather visitors can reach the building along a covered walkway running parallel to the path

ROTTERDAM – Erasmusbrug (1996)

This 802m/2 630ft long single pylon bridge is the work of Ben van Berkel. It was inaugurated in 1996 and consists of two approach ramps joined in the middle by a fixed metal cable bridge and a steel bascule bridge.

Cable

Pylon (139m/456ft high); this has give the bridge its nickname "The Swan"

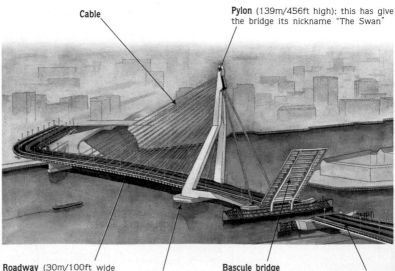

Roadway (30m/100ft wide and 2.3m/7.5ft thick)

Pillar

Bascule bridge in steel

Approach ramp

M. Guillou

The Arts

ARCHITECTURE AND SCULPTURE

Over the centuries, the Netherlands has made a major contribution to Western art. Sculpture occupies a relatively modest place in the Dutch artistic heritage, perhaps due to a shortage of materials until the 20C, and so does music. But the country's architecture has been outstanding during some periods of its history, and its paintings, too, make the Netherlands a place of pilgrimage and inspiration.

Romanesque art and architecture

Examples of Romanesque art and architecture can be seen throughout the country.

Rhenish-Mosan art – This developed in the Meuse Valley and in particular at Maastricht, which belonged to the diocese of Liège. The style is very similar to that of the Rhine Valley; hence its name.

Maastricht was an important town in the Roman Era and then a place of pilgrimage where the relics of St Servatius, who died in 384, were venerated. The town has some magnificent buildings, such as the Sint-Servaasbasiliek and the Onze Lieve Vrouwebasiliek.

In its early days, Mosan art borrowed a great deal from **Carolingian architecture**. Apart from the Sint-Nicolaaskapel at Nijmegen, whose shape imitated the octagonal basilica of Charlemagne in Aachen Cathedral, Carolingian churches usually have two chancels, an imposing westwork, and a court chapel. Inside, there is a flat wooden ceiling and square pillars.

Construction of the **Sint-Servaasbasiliek** began in about 1000, starting with a westwork with two large towers decorated with Lombard arcading. The **Onze Lieve Vrouwebasiliek**, dating from the same period, also has a massive westwork, flanked by round turrets *(photograph: see MAASTRICHT)*. The Sint-Amelbergakerk at **Susteren**, built in the second half of the 11C, is very plain.

In the 12C, Mosan architecture mellowed and became more decorative, and sculpture started appearing on the capitals, low reliefs and portals. It was during this period that both the Sint-Servaasbasiliek and the Onze Lieve Vrouwebasiliek were altered, and the chancel of the latter, viewed from the nave, is one of the most beautiful Romanesque achievements in the country. The original trefoiled plan of **Rolduc Abbey** in Kerkrade also shows a Rhenish influence.

The Onze Lieve Vrouwe Munsterkerk at **Roermond**, although restored, retains some Rhenish-Mosan characteristics. The crypts of these Romanesque churches are often very beautiful.

Other centres – Utrecht, which was an important bishopric in the Middle Ages, became a centre of Romanesque church architecture at an early stage. However, apart from the Pieterskerk, a beautiful example of the local style dating from 1148, there are only a few remains of the fine Romanesque buildings erected by Bishop Bernulphus. Among the churches in the diocese of Utrecht, the Grote Kerk at **Deventer** has preserved the remains of a double transept and a westwork (c 1040) which links it to Mosan churches.

At **Oldenzaal**, the great Sint-Plechelmus-basiliek is later (early 12C) and has a nave with groined vaulting supported by powerful pillars.

Beginning in the mid 12C, regional versions of the Romanesque style appeared in **Friesland** and in the **province of Groningen**, where **brick decoration** was used on the outside walls of village churches *(see GRONINGEN and LEEUWARDEN: Excursions)*; inside, there are often the remains of frescoes.

Gothic architecture

Gothic architecture appeared in the Netherlands during the 14C and 15C. Many churches, and some town halls, date from this period.

Churches – Noord-Brabant, a province where the majority of the inhabitants are Catholic, has most of the large churches and **cathedrals** in the country. These were built in the **Brabant Gothic style**, which resembles Flamboyant Gothic and is found in many buildings in Belgium. Their exteriors have many openwork gables and crocket spires, tall windows, flying buttresses, and a tall belfry porch on the west side, while the interiors have a slender central nave with pointed vaulting resting on round columns with crocket capitals and a triforium.

The Grote Kerk in **Breda** *(illustration: see BREDA)* is a typical example of Brabant Gothic, as is the Sint-Janskathedraal in **'s-Hertogenbosch** *(illustration: see ABC of architecture and 'S-HERTOGENBOSCH)*, which was begun in the 14C and is one of the most beautiful pieces of architecture in the country, as well as being the largest. Unlike other buildings, its vaults rest not on columns but on a cluster of small columns without capitals.

Brabant Gothic influenced the style of many other churches in the country. In Noord-and Zuid-Holland, the stone vault was rare and churches had flat or barrel-vaulted wooden ceilings; the only exception is the Grote Kerk in Dordrecht. Other beautiful Gothic buildings include the Hooglandse or Sint-Pancraskerk in Leiden, the Grote Kerk in Alkmaar, the Nieuwe Kerk in Amsterdam, the Sint-Janskerk in Gouda, and the Sint-Bavokerk in Haarlem (*illustration: see ABC of architecture*).

The cathedral in Utrecht unfortunately did not survive the great storm of 1672, but its elegant bell-tower, the **Domtoren**, still stands, and influenced many other bell-towers around the country, including that of Amersfoort. In the same diocese, the Gothic Sint-Nicolaaskerk in Kampen is also interesting.

Vaults of the Sint-Janskathedraal, 's-Hertogenbosch

Town halls (Stadhuizen) – Two town halls in the Flamboyant Gothic style are particularly remarkable. That of **Gouda** is delightful, its façade a mass of pinnacles and slender spires. The town hall in **Middelburg** (*photograph: see MIDDELBURG*) is more sumptuous; it was built by Belgian architects and shows the influence of Brussels town hall.

Sculpture – Although this is not as abundant as in Belgium, there are some interesting 15C and early 16C woodcarvings.

The groups by **Adriaen van Wesel** (late 15C) displayed in the Rijksmuseum in Amsterdam are carved with a remarkable sense of composition and a great strength of expression.

The **Brabant altarpieces** are triptychs in the Flamboyant style, with a carved central panel showing very lively scenes full of comic detail. This is flanked by two painted panels. The altarpieces can be seen at the Sint-Janskathedraal in 's-Hertogenbosch and the Onze Lieve Vrouwe Munsterkerk in Roermond.

There are some fine examples of **choir stalls**, often carved with satirical themes, in churches including the Martinikerk in Bolsward and the Grote Kerk in Breda.

The Renaissance and Mannerism

The Renaissance reached the Netherlands at a relatively late stage, and its pure Italian form appears hardly at all. However, Mannerism (a transitional form between Renaissance and Baroque) flourished, particularly in Holland.

Architecture – This was not influenced by the Renaissance until the mid 16C. The style was brought here by Italian artists such as **Thomas Vincidor da Bologna**, who designed Breda Castle (begun in 1536); it was then taken up by local architects.

In fact, Renaissance elements were used without making major architectural changes, and the traditional Gothic plan was often retained. They were mainly apparent in details, such as shell-shaped window tympana, dormer windows overburdened with pinnacles and blind arcading, and octagonal turrets.

Hans Vredeman de Vries (1527-c 1603) was a great advocate of Renaissance decoration applied to architecture, but did not do much work in his own country. His theoretical writings had an important influence on the architecture of the Low Countries.

The Fleming **Lieven de Key** worked a great deal in Haarlem, where he was the municipal architect. The old meat market, or Vleeshal (1603), is his finest work.

Hendrick de Keyser (1565-1621) was both a sculptor and architect. He built several churches, mainly in Amsterdam including the Zuiderkerk and Westerkerk (*illustration, see ABC of architecture*); large town houses (Huis Bartolotti) and, in Hoorn, the weigh house (Waag). De Keyser's Mannerist style, like that of Lieven de Key, also contained Baroque elements; his buildings were more monumental, with an imposing feeling of line.

Lescourret/PIX

Renaissance influences were particularly apparent in **Friesland**, where the penchant for geometric decoration and playful, picturesque detail which was already apparent in Romanesque churches spread to many other buildings.

The new style was used in town halls, such as those of Franeker and Bolsward, law courts (the Kanselarij in Leeuwarden), and town gateways (the Waterpoort in Sneek; *illustration: see SNEEK*). The east and west of the country were less affected by these influences, though the weigh house in Nijmegen is a good example of the Renaissance style.

Sculpture – Increasing numbers of **funerary monuments** were made in the Italian Renaissance style.

Thomas Vincidor da Bologna made the tomb of Engelbert II of Nassau in Breda; the four Romanesque figures at the corners and the materials in contrasting colours reflect the new style.

Hendrick de Keyser continued this trend in the early 17C with the tomb of William the Silent in Delft. He also designed the bronze statue of Erasmus in Rotterdam.

In **Friesland**, the Renaissance style was expressed in woodwork. Some churches, such as the Martinikerk in Bolsward and the Grote Kerk in Dokkum, have **pulpits** whose panels are carved with symbolic scenes.

The remarkable 17C choir stalls of Dordrecht's Grote Kerk are also inspired by the Renaissance, and the magnificent stained glass of the Sint-Janskerk in Gouda is one of the finest examples of Renaissance art.

The Golden Age: 17C

In the middle of the century, the playful ornamentation of Mannerism began to disappear. Architecture became dominated by symmetry and proportion, although this was much more restrained in the Netherlands than the Baroque style of other countries, and is sometimes called **Classicism**.

Mauritshuis, The Hague

Architecture and sculpture – One of the most famous architects of the Golden Age was **Jacob van Campen** (1595-1657), designer of **Amsterdam's town hall** (1648), which subsequently became the royal palace. This is square in shape, with severe lines barely softened by the slightly projecting facade, sculpted pediments and small tower. It is a majestic work which greatly influenced architecture throughout the country. **Pieter Post** (1608-69), who built the royal palace (Huis ten Bosch) and the Mauritshuis in The Hague based on plans by Van Campen, and the town hall in Maastricht, continued this trend. **Jacob Roman** built Het Loo Palace in Apeldoorn in a similar style in 1685.

The style reflects a period of great prosperity in the Netherlands, and is also apparent in the **town houses** along Amsterdam's main canals *(illustration: see AMSTERDAM)*. One of the most beautiful examples of this stately architecture is the Trippenhuis built by **Justus Vingboons** (c 1620-98), who worked a great deal with his brother Philips. Many of the Protestant **churches** of this period are circular, often with a dome; one example is the Nieuwe Kerk, or Ronde Lutherse Kerk, in Amsterdam (1671).

In the south of the country, some buildings were constructed using the more extravagant Baroque style; one example is the Jezuït-enkerk in Maastricht.

33

18C and 19C

The French-born architect and decorative designer **Daniël Marot** (1661-1752) built a number of elegant town houses in The Hague, including no 34 Lange Voorhout (1736). From now on, the French influence and the Louis styles predominated; the Rococo or Louis XV style was mainly apparent in the external sculpture, and in the grilles and imposts used to decorate the doors, though it also appeared in stucco interior decoration.

In the early 19C, architects began once again to seek their inspiration in the past; first ancient Greece and Rome (neo-Classicism), and later the Middle Ages and Renaissance (neo-Gothic and neo-Renaissance). In Eclecticism, these stylistic elements were used together.

One of the most important architects in this period, **PJH Cuypers** (1827-1921), introduced a form of neo-Gothic to his buildings, which included the Rijksmuseum and the central railway station in Amsterdam, and carried out radical restorations of several medieval buildings such as the Kasteel De Haar.

Although the architecture of earlier eras provided such a major source of inspiration for that of the 19C, it was also during this period that new materials such as cast iron and steel were first used *(see below, Industrial heritage)*.

20C

During the 20C, architecture has experienced something of a renaissance in the Netherlands, and there has also been a renewed interest in sculpture.

Architecture – **HP Berlage** (1856-1934), who built Amsterdam's Stock Exchange (1897-1903), was the precursor of Rationalism, an architectural movement which placed a great deal of emphasis on materials and function. **KPC de Bazel** (1869-1923) worked in a similar way with his building for Algemene Bank Nederland in Vijzelstraat, Amsterdam.

The **Amsterdam School** (c 1912-23) strove for a less austere architecture than that of Berlage, and **Michel de Klerk**, **Peter Kramer** and **JM van der Mey** were the great masters of urban renewal; their work made expressionistic use of brick. WM Dudok stood slightly apart from the Amsterdam School; he was influenced by Frank Lloyd Wright and is best known as the designer of the town hall in Hilversum *(illustration: see ABC of architecture)*.

At the same time, the **De Stijl movement** was being founded by the painters **Piet Mondriaan** and **Theo van Doesburg** and the architect **JJP Oud**. Architects such as **Gerrit Rietveld** (who also designed furniture), J Duiker and B Bijvoet also gained their inspiration from the movement, using concrete skeletons and superimposing and juxtaposing cube-shaped spaces to form a whole. This was known as Het Nieuwe Bouwen (New Building) or Functionalism, and was at its height from 1920-1940. One of the highlights of this style is the Van Nelle factory in Rotterdam by the architects Brinkman and Van der Vlugt, a masterpiece in steel, glass and concrete.

Around 1950, particularly during the rebuilding of **Rotterdam**, urban planners began taking more account of local people's needs. The Lijnbaan (1952-4), designed by JH Van den Broek and **JB Bakema**, was the first pedestrian precinct in Europe. The Forum generation, as it was called, also included Aldo van Eyck (who built the Burgerweeshuis and Moederhuis in Amsterdam), Herman Hertzberger (responsible for the Vredenburg in Utrecht and the VROM building in The Hague), and Piet Blom, the architect of the famous cube-shaped apar-

Ph. Lau/EUREKA SLIDE

Amsterdam – Spaarndammerplantsoen (M. de Klerk)

tments and the building known as Het Potlood, both in Rotterdam. Wim Quist built the Willemswerf, a dock in the same city, and various museums including the Museum Beelden aan Zee, the Seaside Sculpture Museum in The Hague.

Rem Koolhaas (b 1944) is one of the country's leading contemporary architects. He established a firm of international architects, Office for Metropolitan Architecture, in Rotterdam in 1975. Koolhaas has become famous in the Netherlands for buildings such as the Nederlands Danstheater in The Hague and the Museumpark and Kunsthal in Rotterdam. He has also gained an international reputation for work such as his urban plan for the French city of Lille.

The local environment and traditional building styles play an important part in the work of Jo Coenen, whose most important project has been the Nederlands Architectuurinstituut in Rotterdam. Finally, among the younger generation of architects, Ben van Berkel (b 1957) designed Rotterdam's Erasmusbrug, or Erasmus Bridge, completed in 1996.

Sculpture – Most Dutch towns and cities have used sculpture in a wide variety of materials to enliven their pedestrian precincts and parks. Many modern buildings have façades decorated with mosaics, coloured ornamentation or bronze figures. Well-known examples include the statue of Bartje in Assen *(Illustration: see ASSEN)* and The Bear Cubs in Rotterdam.

> The Netherlands has a leading international reputation for modern architecture and urban planning. Top Dutch and foreign architects have worked on such major projects as the Resident and Kop van Zuid developments in The Hague and Rotterdam respectively. The latter, in particular, is an absolute must for visitors interested in contemporary architecture, and more new projects are in progress there. A number of museums are also important works of architecture in their own right; they include the Groninger Museum in Groningen, the Bonnefantenmuseum in Maastricht and the New Metropolis in Amsterdam.

Mari Andriessen (1897-1979) was one of the greatest Dutch sculptors of the 20C. He created the statue of a docker near the Portuguese Synagogue in Amsterdam, the monument in the Volkspark in Enschede, and the statue of Queen Wilhelmina in the Wilhelminapark in Utrecht.

Other leading contemporary sculptors are **the Fortuin** duo (b 1959) and **O'Brien** (1951-88), whose light, elegant compositions feature wooden slats wrapped in paper or silk.

Carel Visser (b 1928) was one of the first Dutch sculptors to work in metal, and made collage sculptures, including a wide variety of found objects. His recent work is more detailed and intricate.

Henk Visch (b 1950) is mainly known for his figurative sculptures, often consisting of contemplative human or animal figures with poetic titles.

Groninger Museum (1995), designed by the Coop Himmelb

MILITARY ARCHITECTURE

All over the Netherlands there are the remains of fortifications built over the centuries to defend the country against invasion. Some are no more than barely visible bumps in the ground; others have been beautifully restored.

The early stages: earthworks, fortresses and castles – In the Middle Ages, defensive works initially consisted of walls of earth surrounded by a ditch and a ring of stakes; later on, castles and fortresses were built. Some of the finest examples are the fortress in Leiden, the **Muiderslot** and the **Slot Loevestein**.

Stone walls, towers and gateways – As towns began to develop, so earthworks were replaced by stone walls with towers and impressive gateways. Parts of these walls can still be seen in Amersfoort *(illustration: see ABC of architecture)* and **Elburg**. Typical features included machicolations and parapet walks along the tops of walls and towers, and crenels and other holes through which stones and burning pitch could be thrown.

New weapons – The walls of fortified towns were not able to withstand the cannons introduced in the early 15C, and so the high walls and towers were lowered and provided with moats or earthworks which could not be breached by these weapons. The **Spanjaardsgat** in Breda is an example of this kind of construction.

Breda – the Spanjaardsgat

The next step was to build bigger towers, but not as high, known as **roundels**; a fine example of these is **De Vijf Koppen** in Maastricht. However, their round shape was not very practical, since there was not enough room for armaments at the top and there was a blind spot straight in front of the roundel which could not be fired at from inside.

Bastions – In the early 16C, Italian engineers developed the bastion, a five-sided projecting fortification intended to overcome the drawbacks of roundels. This new structure was soon adopted in the Netherlands; the **Zonnenburg** bastion in Utrecht is a good example.

The Old Dutch System – During the Eighty Years War, a variety of Italian-inspired changes resulted in the development of a new form of defence known as the Old Dutch System.

The Flemish engineer **Simon Stevin** (1548-1620) developed the theoretical basis for this system. The fortifications were made of earth, so that cannon-balls would simply become lodged in them, and were nearly always surrounded by a ditch in which small islands known as demilunes were built to protect the bastions and keep invaders away from the ramparts.

The leading builder of fortifications at this time was Adriaan Anthonisz (c 1543-1620), who worked on nearly 30 towns and forts around the country. The best-preserved examples of these are at Willemstad, Heusden, and Bourtange *(illustration: see ABC of architecture)*.

The New Dutch System – Further advances continued to be made. Naarden, whose fortifications are better preserved than any other in the country, was built using the so-called **French System**, with larger bastions and a double ring of defences. In 1685, **Colonel Menno van Coehoorn** (1641-1704) designed the New Dutch System exemplified by Hellevoetsluis and Bergen op Zoom. This had large bastions placed close together, making the walls between them (known as curtain walls) shorter and shorter, eventually resulting in the **tenaille system** of star-shaped fortifications formed by a succession of bastions with no curtain walls. An example of this system is the ruined **Linie van Doesburg**.

Lines and citadels – The development of longer-range artillery meant that fortifications had to be built at increasing distances from the towns they were built to defend. Forts were built in a circle around the fortifications, as in the **Nieuwe Hollandse Waterlinie** (1840-1860) around Utrecht. The main purpose of these water lines was to flood the land to a depth of about 40cm/16in to slow the enemy down; this was done using a system of sluices and quays. Forts were built in places which could not be flooded, such as the huge fort at Rijnauwen, near Bunnik.
The circle of some 40 forts that form the **Amsterdam Citadel**, built between 1883 and 1914, is an average of 12km/8mi from the capital; one is the island fort of **Pampus** in the IJsselmeer. This famous citadel has been a UNESCO world heritage site since 1996. The earlier citadel of **Den Helder** was built by Napoleon in 1811.

The modern period – After the First World War, defensive lines of concrete bunkers were built; the best-known are the Grebbelinie and the bunkers on the Afsluitdijk near **De Oever** and **Kornwerderzand** (now a museum). The most prominent Second World War fortifications in the Netherlands are the long series of bunkers along the coast, which formed part of the German **Atlantikwall**. The most recent are the Rijn-IJssellinie, built in 1951 as part of NATO defences. These consist of mobile dams to control water levels in the floodplains of the Nederrijn, Waal and Gelderse IJssel. The project was cancelled in 1954 as a result of changes in NATO's strategic plans.

INDUSTRIAL HERITAGE

The **Industrial Revolution** did not take place in the Netherlands until the end of the 19C. **Factories** were built, steam power began to be used, and iron and steel were used in the construction of machinery and buildings. But as far back as the 17C, the Netherlands had Europe's biggest industrial area, the **Zaanstreek** *(see ZAANSTREEK)*, where nearly 1 000 windmills were used to manufacture paper, dye and foodstuffs.

Factories and machines – The first factories were built in Twente and Noord-Brabant, making such products as cotton and wool. Many of these were subsequently demolished, but some have been put to new uses, such as the 19C Mommers wool factory in Tilburg, which is now the **Nederlands Textielmuseum**, and the **Jannink spinning mill** in Enschede, also a museum.
In the early 20C, the use of concrete enabled larger factories to be built, such as the **Wiebengahal** of the former Sphinx Céramique factory in Maastricht, now part of the Bonnefantenmuseum. Rotterdam's **Van Nelle factory** (1926-30) successfully combined modern materials including steel, glass and concrete.
There are collections of steam-powered industrial machinery in the **Nederlands Stoommachinemuseum** in Medemblik and the **Techniekmuseum** in Delft.

Workers' housing – Examples of whole districts built specially to house workers include the Agnetapark in Delft and Philipsdorp in Eindhoven. Many miners' communities remain in Zuid-Limburg; one example is De Hopel in Kerkrade.

Minerals – There are still some impressive limekilns to be seen here and there; these were bottle-shaped structures used to burn shells to make lime. There are three fine examples in the Zuiderzeemuseum in Enkhuizen.
There are some fascinating remains of Zuid-Limburg's coal industry, including the Nulland pit in Kerkrade and the Oranje Nassau mine in Heerlen. The reconstructed mine at Valkenbrug gives a first-hand view of how coal was dug.

Stations – The oldest surviving railway station in the Netherlands is the neo-Gothic building at Valkenburg, dating from 1853. Amsterdam's Central Station was designed by PJH Cuypers (1827-1921), and the elegant Art Nouveau station at Haarlem is by the architect Margadant. The enormous iron roofs of such stations as 's-Hertogenbosch and The Hague were a major technological innovation, added later on in most cases.
The history of railways is chronicled in the **Nederlands Spoorwegmuseum** in Utrecht.

Ports – Amsterdam still has a 19C wharf with cast iron roofs, **'t Kromhout**, where old boats are now restored. In Rotterdam, which was largely destroyed in 1945, there are still some old warehouses such as the **Vrij Entrepot De Vijf Werelddelen** (now a shopping and entertainment centre). The former headquarters of the **Holland-Amerika shipping line** (1901) on Wilhelmskade has been converted into an elegant hotel. **De Hef**, an old lifting railway bridge, is on permanent display in the raised position.

Ph. Gajic/MICHELIN

De Cruquius steam pumping station

Steam-operated pumping stations – The first time that steam pumping stations were used was in the draining of the Haarlemmermeer lake *(see p 16, The fight against the sea)*. One of these was the **Cruquius**, near Heemstede, which is now a museum.

These stations were used in increasing numbers in the second half of the 19C; they included the **Vier Noorder Koggen** (now the Nederlands Stoommachinemuseum), and the **Ir Lely station** at Medemblik, the **Mastenbroek** in Genemuiden, and the steam pumping station near **Halfweg**, now a museum. The **Ir Wouda steam pumping station** just outside Lemmer is the largest in Europe; this highly impressive structure was built in 1917.

Water towers and lighthouses – The oldest water tower in the country is in **Rotterdam**, and dates from 1873. The oldest lighthouse, the **Brandaris** on the island of Terschelling, was built in 1594. Both types of structure tended to reflect the architectural fashions of the time, so the **Breda** water tower is neo-Gothic, that of **Schimmert** is built in the style of the Amsterdam School, and **Aalsmeer's** is in the Art Deco style. The brick lighthouse at **Haamstede** is depicted on the 250fl banknote.

The **Waterleidingmuseum**, situated in Utrecht's oldest water tower, describes the history of the mains water supply in the Netherlands.

PAINTING

Dutch painting was initially very similar to that of Flanders, and was later influenced by Italian art. It reached its peak in the 17C, reflecting the country's increasing prosperity.

Primitives

One of the greatest of all Dutch artists was **Hieronymus Bosch**, who was active in 'S-Hertogenbosch in the late 15C. His work was extraordinarily imaginative for its time *(illustration: see 'S-HERTOGENBOSCH)*. Although his vision of a world dominated by the spectre of sin was a medieval one, his realism presaged that of 17C painting, and his work has many features of modern Surrealism.

Other artists had more in common with the Flemish primitives. One of these was **Geertgen tot Sint Jans**, the painter of a delicate and serene *Adoration of the Magi*, with a landscape background, which is now in the Rijksmuseum.

Cornelis Engebrechtsz. painted lively, colourful scenes full of people; a number of his works can be seen in the Stedelijk Museum De Lakenhal in Leiden. Another of the Dutch primitives was **Jan Mostaert**.

Renaissance

Jan van Scorel, a pupil of **Jacob Cornelisz van Oostsanen** (c 1470-1533), introduced the Renaissance to the Northern Netherlands when he returned from Rome in 1524. He was the first Dutch painter to be influenced by Italian art, and painted portraits of great sensitivity, such as the *Portrait of a Young Scholar* in the Museum Boigmans-Van Beuningen in Rotterdam, as well as rather Mannerist religious pictures. His pupil **Maarten van Heemskerck** also painted subtle portraits and religious scenes.

Lucas van Leyden, a pupil of Cornelis Engebrechtsz., was also influenced by the Renaissance. He painted large, carefully composed canvases such as the *Last Judgement* in the Stedelijk Museum De Lakenhal in Leiden, and the *Adoration of the Golden Calf* (c 1525) in the Rijksmuseum in Amsterdam.

Pieter Aertsen (c 1509-75) was not at all influenced by Italian art. This great Amsterdam artist, who also lived in Antwerp for a time, painted subtle landscapes and interior scenes with still-life paintings in the background.

Antoon Mor became famous under the Spanish name of Antonio Moro, since he was the court painter to Charles V and Philip II of Spain. He later worked at the English court, and died in Antwerp.

Museum Boijmans Van Beuningen, Rotterdam

The Assumption of the Virgin Mary, Geertgen tot Sint Jans

The Golden Age

The 17C may have been dominated by such great figures as Rembrandt, Hals, Vermeer and Ruisdael, but it had many other highly talented artists. While the Flemish continued to paint large numbers of religious scenes, Dutch art was more secular and varied, since much of it was painted for well-off middle-class homes. It also provides a remarkable record of the daily life of the period.

Group portraits – During the Golden Age, there was a considerable demand for group portraits from bodies such as guilds, companies of the civic guard, groups of surgeons, and the governing bodies of almshouses. **Bartholomeus van der Helst** painted many traditional, formal portraits of wealthy citizens and members of the House of Orange, as well as numerous group portraits. **Frans Hals** had the nonconformist style that came with genius. Most of his large group portraits are in the Frans Hals Museum, in his home town of Haarlem. He also painted striking and lively individual portraits, such as *The Merry Drinker*, now in the Rijksmuseum.

Rembrandt and his pupils – **Rembrandt** also painted group portraits such as the famous *The Anatomy Lesson of Doctor Tulp* which is in the Mauritshuis in The Hague, but the best-known example is the *Night Watch*, in the Rijksmuseum. This museum has an excellent collection of Rembrandt's work, notably Biblical scenes, portraits and self-portraits, with brightly lit, solemn figures against dark backgrounds.

Rembrandt had a number of pupils: **Gerard Dou**, who did chiaroscuro genre paintings; **Ferdinand Bol**, one of the closest to Rembrandt in style; **Nicolaes Maes** who used warm colours to paint calm interior scenes; **Samuel van Hoogstraten**; **Aert van Gelder**; **Carel Fabritius** (1622-54), who died young, but was the most gifted of all; and **Philips Koninck**, who was mainly a landscape painter.

Landscape and seascape painters – Although Rembrandt produced many landscape drawings and etchings, he painted few landscapes. Many artists specialised in this genre. Early 17C landscape artists included **Hercules Seghers** (1589-1638), **Salomon van Ruisdael** and **Jan van Goyen**. They painted luminous, serene compositions with wide horizons, still rivers, sunlight filtering through the clouds, and silhouetted trees, churches and windmills. The greatest landscape painter of the time, **Jacob van Ruysdael**, had a penchant for romantic scenes.

Meindert Hobbema painted tall trees with vivid green sunlit foliage, while **Cornelis van Poelenburgh** preferred Italian-style landscapes and sunsets.

Sometimes landscapes were a pretext to depict human figures, as with **Aelbert Cuyp**; elsewhere, they included shepherds and their flocks in the case of **Nicolaes Berchem**, cows and horses in the case of **Paulus Potter**, and horses and their riders in the paintings of **Philips Wouwerman**.

Hendrick Avercamp was slightly different, his paintings were similar to miniatures, with subtle colours bringing to life the picturesque world of ice-skaters.

Aert van der Neer (1603/4-77) also painted winter scenes and rivers by moonlight. Willem van de Velde the Elder, and more especially his son Willem the Younger, were remarkable marine painters, as were Ludolf Bakhuizen (1631-1708), Jan van de Cappelle (1626-79) and the Ghent painter Jan Porcellis (1584-1632).

Pieter Saenredam (1597-1665) and Emanuel de Witte (c 1617-92) whose work was highly appreciated during their lifetime, depict church interiors in carefully studied compositions. Job Berckheyde (1630-93) and his younger brother Gerrit (1638-98) were also painters of architecture.

A Black Squall, Willem van de Velde the Younger

Rijksmuseum, Amsterdam

Genre pieces

Apart from some of Rembrandt's pupils, many other painters specialised in domestic interiors. Gerard Terborch, Frans van Mieris the Elder and Gabriel Metsu recreated domestic scenes with delicate brushwork, while Pieter de Hooch, a remarkable colourist and virtuoso of perspective, depicted the daily lives of the wealthy.

Vermeer was neglected for a long period, but is now regarded as one of the greatest of all artists. He mainly painted interior scenes, which were realistic but extraordinarily poetic. Although simple in appearance, they make highly sophisticated use of colours, composition and light.

Adriaen van Ostade was a painter of rollicking peasant scenes, and was influenced by the Flemish artist Adriaen Brouwer. Van Ostade's pupil Jan Steen painted similarly cheerful and humorous pictures, though with a moral message.

In Utrecht, the Italian influence which was widespread in the 16C made itself felt in the work of Abraham Bloemaert. One of his pupils, Hendrick Terbrugghen, introduced "Caravaggism" to the Netherlands along with Gerard van Honthorst. Their work is characterised by strong light-dark contrasts, half-length portraits of ordinary people, and people playing music. Judith Leyster, the wife of the painter Jan Molenaer and a pupil of Frans Hals, was also clearly influenced by Caravaggio.

Still-life

The tradition of still-life painting had its origins in Flanders, in the work of artists such as Fyt and Snyders. It was taken up in Haarlem by Pieter Claesz and Willem Claesz Heda. Their favourite subject was a table covered with the remains of a meal, and glasses and dishes reflecting the light. Their paintings were less crowded than those of their Flemish predecessors, with flatter colours and strictly geometrical compositions.

Still-life with Cheeses, Floris Claesz van Dijk, Rijksmuseum, Amsterdam

The works of **Willem Kalff** (1619-93), **Abraham van Beyeren** (1620/1-1690) and **Jan Davidsz de Heem** were more colourful and Baroque.

Drawings and prints – 17C painters also produced very large numbers of drawings and prints, particularly etchings, and Rembrandt excelled in this form of art (*illustration: see Admission times and charges*).

18C, 19C and 20C

In the 18C, a decline set in. One notable exception was **Cornelis Troost** (1697-1750), an Amsterdam painter whose work was inspired by the theatre, and evokes Watteau and Hogarth. **Jacob Wit** (1695-1754) was known for his *grisailles* (in Dutch: *witjes*), which were popular forms of household decoration among the wealthy. **Wouter Johannes van Troostwijk** (1782-1810) immortalised the streets of Amsterdam in his paintings.

In the 19C, with **The Hague School** led by **Jozef Israëls** (1824-1911), Dutch art enjoyed a rebirth. Nature, beaches, dunes and the lives of fishermen provided an inexhaustible source of inspiration for the artists of this school (*illustration: see The HAGUE*).

JB Jongkind (1819-91) was a precursor of the Impressionists, and his paintings were full of light and atmosphere. This was also true of **George Hendrick Breitner** (1857-1923), who is known for his pictures of horsemen and of old Amsterdam (*illustration: see AMSTERDAM*).

Isaac Israëls (1865-1934), the son of Jozef, painted beach scenes and numerous portraits.

Vincent van Gogh was the greatest figure of the late 19C. His early paintings were sombre, but under the influence of Impressionism his canvases became lighter and more colourful. From 1886 onwards he worked mainly in Paris and near Arles in Provence. Many of his masterpieces can be seen in the Kröller-Müller Museum, near Arnhem, and the Rijksmuseum Vincent Van Gogh in Amsterdam.

Jan Theodoor Toorop, known as **Jan Toorop** (1858-1928), was born in Java. He began his career as an Impressionist, before turning to Symbolism, a movement in which he held an important place in Europe along with **Johan Thorn Prikker** (1868-1932). Later, Toorop briefly allied himself with the pointillists and divisionists, and also took an interest in the Art Nouveau movement, painting a large number of posters in this style.

Piet Mondriaan (*illustration: see AMERSFOORT*) was one of the greatest innovators of his time. He was the driving force behind the De Stijl movement and its magazine of the same name, along with **Theo van Doesburg** and **JJP Oud**. In so doing, he helped to found the constructivist movement.

One of the most intriguing artists of the inter-war period was **Herman Kruyder** (1881-1935), whose work is highly enigmatic.

Jan Wiegers (1893-1953) was the leader of the Expressionist movement **De Ploeg** (The Plough), characterised by dramatic contrasts in colour; despite their distinctive style, Wiegers' paintings were clearly influenced by the German artist,

Counter-composition of Dissonants XVI (1925), Theo van Doesburg
Haags Gemeentemuseum, The Hague

Ernst Kirchner. **Hendrik Werkman** (1882-1945) is now regarded as the most important member of De Ploeg; he introduced radical innovations in woodcuts and typography.

After a brief Expressionist period, **Charley Toorop** (1891-1955), the daughter of Jan Toorop, subsequently adopted a realist style of painting.

Kees van Dongen *(illustration: see ROTTERDAM)* became a famous artist in Paris.

The main exponents of **magic realism** (or new objectivity) in the Netherlands were **Raoul Hynckes** (1893-1973), **Pyke Koch** (1901-91) and **Carel Willink** (1900-83). Their strange, near-photographic Realism, tinged with Surrealism, influenced many young artists. One of their contemporaries was MC Escher (1898-1972), the Netherlands' leading graphic artist, whose ingenious play on spaces and dimensions became world-famous.

The international group of experimental artists **Cobra** was named from the initial letters of Copenhagen, Brussels and Amsterdam. Its main members were the Dane Asger Jorn, the Belgian artist Dotremont and three Dutchmen, **Karel Appel** (b 1921; *illustration: see EINDHOVEN*), **Constant** (b 1920) and **Corneille** (b 1922) The movement advocated free, spontaneous creation, often inspired by children's drawings. Constant is also known for his plans of a futuristic city, New Babylon (1956).

The year 1961 saw the creation of the Dutch group **Nul** (Zero) whose three principles were impersonality, detachment and objectivity. Its most important representative was **Jan Schoonhoven** (1914-94), best-known for his monochrome reliefs.

During the 1970s, **Jan Dibbets** (b 1944) and **Ger van Elk** (b 1941) used photography as a means of expression; Dibbets turned reality into abstraction by creating trick montages characterised by a strong sense of perspective.

Rob van Koningsbruggen (b 1948) uses unconventional techniques to produce his quasi-monochrome pictures: he takes canvases painted in black, white or primary colours and rubs one or more unpainted canvases over them.

The leading artistic figures of the 1980s were **Rob Scholte** (b 1955) and **Marlene Dumas** (b 1953) who, despite their different styles, both draw inspiration from the visual imagery generated by newspapers, magazines and other media.

Belvédère (1958), MC Escher

EVERYDAY OBJECTS AND ORNAMENTS

From sandstone and majolica... – The majolica technique was brought to Antwerp and other parts of Northern Europe by Italian potters in the 16C. After the fall of Antwerp in 1585, many potters moved to the Netherlands and settled in towns such as Middelburg, Delft, Leiden, Amsterdam and Haarlem, where majolica production subsequently flourished. Very soon, this technique replaced the traditional Rhine sandstone pottery.

...to Delftware – In the early 17C, large quantities of **Chinese eggshell porcelain** were imported by the United East India Company. These damaged the domestic market and bankrupted many potters. Some majolica-makers switched to making tiles or domestic objects not made by the Chinese, such as mustard pots and apothecaries' jars, often imitating oriental styles of decoration.

Others tried to discover the secret of eggshell porcelain, but initially they had no success. However, a few manufacturers in **Delft** and **Haarlem** did manage to make a better-quality product than traditional majolica to compete with porcelain from the Far East. This new technique, called **faience**, used a different mixture of clays to make thinner ceramics. The lead glaze was replaced by a white tin glaze closely resembling white porcelain, and the pieces were decorated with both Chinese and Dutch motifs; Italian-inspired decoration was also popular.

When imports of Asian porcelain declined around 1650 as the result of a civil war in China, Delftware enjoyed a huge success. Delft potters responded quickly to the gap in the market, and specialist faience factories began producing on a larger scale *(see DELFT)*.

Frisian majolica – In the second half of the 17C, **Makkum** *(see MAKKUM)* and **Harlingen** became the centres of Frisian majolica production, consisting mainly of tiles and tableware. This bore considerable similarities to the tin-glazed pottery produced in Delft, but was simpler in style and less imitative of Chinese porcelain. Also, the Frisian pieces rarely bore a manufacturer's mark; most were inscribed with the name of the client for whom they were made. Plates made in the **port of Lemmer** were particularly distinctive: they were inscribed with sayings or simple decorations on a white tin glaze. The **Tichelaar factory** in Makkum was established in the late 17C and is still in operation.

Dutch porcelain – True porcelain was first successfully produced in the German town of Meissen in the early 18C, and other West European countries began making it shortly afterwards. Porcelain was made in the Netherlands only for a short period of about 50 years, mainly in imitation of the German variety. The typically Dutch **porcelain cabinet** was designed to display and protect these costly objects; it consisted of a tall, flat display case on a base.

The first factory was established in **Weesp**, producing Rococo forms with multicoloured decoration, but this closed 10 years later due to financial problems. Its equipment and stock were acquired by a priest in Loosdrecht to provide jobs for poor people in his area, and the **Loosdrecht** factory produced beautifully painted tableware and ornaments between 1774 and 1784. The blue and enamelled decoration consisted mainly of bouquets of flowers, tendrils, landscapes and birds. After the priest's death, the factory moved to **Ouder-Amstel**, where it produced its own Louis XVI-style designs, including townscapes, landscapes and flowers, between 1784 and 1809. In that year it moved to **Nieuwer-Amstel** and continued making Empire-style porcelain until it closed in 1814.

Hague porcelain was made in The Hague from 1776 to 1790, using porcelain imported mainly from Ansbach and Tournai and painted with garlands of flowers, landscapes, arbour scenes, birds and butterflies.

Dutch porcelain was of reasonably high quality, but high production costs and a limited market meant that large-scale production was not possible.

Dutch Art Nouveau – In the second half of the 19C, Petrus Regout's factory in **Maastricht** made mainly white dinner services, sometimes with printed decoration; these were strongly influenced by, and sometimes copied from, Wedgewood and other British manufacturers.

Art Nouveau did not become widespread in the Netherlands until the end of the 19C. The **Rozenburg** Delftware factory in The Hague made pottery with stylised, often fanciful flower and plant motifs. The designer **TAC Colenbrander** was a great innovator who devised some highly imaginative forms and decorations. Another very successful product of the Rozenburg factory, under **JJ Kok**, was **eggshell porcelain** with very fine, naturalistic decoration.

In Gouda, too, brightly coloured ceramics were made between 1900 and 1930; these were decorated mainly with leaf and flower motifs.

Modern ceramics – Despite increasing industrialisation at the beginning of the 20C, smaller-scale production of stoneware and earthenware has continued, and ceramics have become unique works of art. Leading modern Dutch ceramists include Chris Lannooy, Bert Nienhuis, WC Brouwer, Johan van Loon and Jan van der Vaart.

Window pane (c 1625)

Vase, Chris Lanooy (1927)

Haarlem dish (c 1660)
and Delft water jug (c 1650-1670

Porcelain candle-holder,
Rozenburg Den Haag (1920)

Dish of Italian inspiration,
Haarlem (c 1660)

Porcelain soup tureen, Loosdrecht (c 1780)

ke majolica, tiles arrived in the Netherlands in the 16C via Italy and Flanders. They ■ere initially used as **floor tiles**, but the thin tin glaze was easily damaged, and soon ▪all tiles were being made instead.

number of tile factories grew up in various towns around 1600. Wall tiles were ▪itially painted in bright colours and decorated with geometric motifs, animals and ▪uit. Later, under the influence of Chinese porcelain, they were often decorated ▪ntirely in blue.

▪fter 1750, the demand among townspeople for painted tiles tailed off almost to ▪othing; they preferred to decorate their walls with expensive fabrics. In the ▪ountryside, however, they remained a popular form of decoration, colourfully ▪ainted with birds, animals, flowers, plants and other subjects.

▪utch tiles bore a huge variety of motifs: pictures of craftsmen and women, Cupids, ▪naginary sea creatures, children playing, soldiers and ships. Later on in the 18C, ▪iblical and **pastoral scenes** became increasingly popular.

▪fter 1800, however, interest declined as people began using wallpaper, and also ▪achine-produced tiles from England.

ile pictures – Huge tile pictures were made in the Netherlands from about 1620 ▪ntil well into the 18C. These were placed either against the back of a fireplace or ▪ other positions such as in **passageways**, on **walls** or above the **hearth**. They included ▪eautifully painted vases of flowers; in the 18C, a wider variety of motifs was ▪roduced, including scenes from rural life, allegorical pictures, naval battles, ▪ownscapes, dogs and parrots.

ile pictures enjoyed a small-scale revival at the beginning of the 20C; they were made ▪ainly for commercial purposes such as **shop interiors** or **advertising** on the outsides of ▪uildings.

urniture

▪ach particular era of history had its own national style of furniture, but there have ▪lways been distinctive local forms as well.

Middle Ages and Renaissance – The Late Gothic period produced carved oak chests, ▪redence tables (small side-tables with shelves), and dressers decorated with pointed ▪rches and letterbox motifs.

▪rom 1550 onwards, the Italian Renaissance inspired credence tables with carved ▪anels depicting medallions and grotesques, and heavy tables in the Flemish style ▪bolpoottafels) with turned feet widening into vase-like shapes. These tables first had ▪ectangular struts but later were characterised by their H-shaped crossbars; later ▪till, from 1650 onwards, the crossbars were shaped like two forks. Elegant stools ▪ith highly decorated backs and divergent legs were also a feature of the Renaissance ▪eriod.

Chests in the Golden Age – The most beautiful items of furniture from the late 16C ▪nd the Golden Age were linen chests.

▪he **Dutch chest** (Hollandse kast) was perhaps the most common kind. It had very ▪aried decoration: lion's heads, caryatids, friezes of foliated scrolls and grotesque ▪nasks, and flat panels later replaced by geometric relief ornamentation. The chest ▪ad a wide plinth, four doors (those below usually divided into two panels) and a heavy ▪ornice decorated with a frieze of plants. Its uprights consisted of fluted pilasters, ▪nd subsequently columns: it was then called a columned chest (kolommenkast).

Bombé chest

Dutch chest

45

After photo Gemeente-Archief

Zeeland chest

By the second half of the 17C magnificent and imposing chests in various kinds of wood were being made, known as **bombé chests** (*kussenkast*) because of the bulging shape of their panels, usually veneered with ebony. The chest rested on enormous ball feet. A set of five Delft vases, some of them pot-bellied, would often be placed on the cornice.

The **Zeeland chest** (*Zeeuwse kast*) was wider than it was high, with four or five doors and little relief, but with very fine Renaissance decoration similar to that of the Dutch chest.

Frisian chests had two doors. The panels had carved decorations between the uprights, which consisted of engaged columns similar to those of columned chests. The cornice was very thick and decorated with a finely carved frieze.

In the **Gelderland**, chests had two large doors with relief designs on the panels and fluted uprights, precious wood inlays, and a projecting cornice, simply decorated with gadrooning (convex curves).

Utrecht chests, which in fact were made in the province of Holland, were similar to those of the Gelderland: the panels were topped by an arch outlined with ebony inlay.

Both town and country-dwellers usually slept in box-beds, with wooden panels matching the style of the room.

Another common feature of 17C Dutch interiors were yellow copper chandeliers; these are also widely found in churches.

Marquetry and inlaid work – In the 17C and 18C, marquetry and inlays of ebony, tortoiseshell, metal and ivory became increasingly popular. Both in the Netherlands and in Flanders, they were used on inkstands and cabinets with numerous drawers used to store precious objects.

The *sterrekabinet* was inlaid with ivory motifs or with marquetry depicting stars (*sterren*) enclosed in circles or ovals.

18C and 19C chests – The Louis XV style, imported by the French Huguenots after the Revocation of the Edict of Nantes (1685), was very much in vogue in the 18C, though it was freely adapted. **18C cabinets** had two doors and a base with drawers,

Frisian chest

which in the middle of the century acquired a characteristic bulge, and undulating cornices on their tops. Inlays and marquetry remained popular during this period, and the English style made its presence increasingly felt as the two countries developed closer trade links.

At the end of the 18C, the influence of the more austere Louis XVI style became apparent; this was much more faithfully reproduced.

In the 19C, the Empire style became popular following the arrival in the Netherlands of King Louis Napoleon and his wife Hortense, both of whom were very fond of Parisian fashions.

Painted furniture – Several localities in the north of the country specialised in the production of painted furniture in the 18C. This was mainly made by fishermen in the Zuiderzee ports during the months when they did not fish, and they used methods they had seen during their travels in the Baltic or the East.

This furniture was elaborately carved, and painted in bright colours in a style reminiscent of naive popular art. Many different objects were painted in this manner: chests, dressing tables, box-beds, cradles, chairs, and even children's wooden satchels. There are fine collections of this form of furniture in the Zuiderzee museum in Enkhuizen, the Hidde Nijland Stichting in Hindeloopen, and the Openluchtmuseum in Arnhem.

After photo Rijksmuseum

18C cabinet

Clocks

After the famous scholar Christiaan Huygens invented the pendulum clock in 1656, clocks became a great deal more accurate, and **long-case** or **grandfather clocks** became increasingly popular in well-off households. These had a tall ornamented plinth containing the weights and pendulum, with the mechanism contained in a case above this and an arched pediment at the top. The dial was often painted with pictures of the night sky and moving human figures or boats; some showed the month, the day of the week, the date and the phase of the moon as well as the time.

Amsterdam was a great clockmaking centre in the 18C, and wall clocks in the Louis XV style were also popular.

The provinces of Friesland, Groningen and Drenthe had their own distinctive form of clocks known as **stoeltjesklokken**. These had ornate openwork decoration, similar to that of the painted furniture described above, and the mechanism rested on a console. Zaandam clocks were more elegant.

Gold and silverware

Romanesque period – As elsewhere, in the bishopric of Louvain in Belgium, the **gold and silversmiths of the Maasland** produced many masterpieces. The **shrine** of St Servatius in the Sint-Servaaskerk in Maastricht, for example, is made of copper gilt decorated with enamel and precious stones, with depictions of Christ, St Servatius and the apostles around it.

A number of museums in Utrecht contain examples of **gold and silverware** that reflect the prosperity of bishops in the region during the Romanesque period; they include monstrances, pyxes, shrines, processional crosses, and books decorated with chasing.

The Golden Age – In the 16C, and even more so in the 17C, it was a common practice among town councils, guilds and well-off ordinary people to commission finely engraved and chased silver objects to commemorate particular events. Most museums have collections of these items; they include large metal goblets, dishes, water jugs, **nautilus-shell cups** (made with a nautilus shell on a silver base), chains of office and other ceremonial items. The most famous silversmiths were the **Van Vianen brothers**.

Many Protestant churches also owned silver Communion chalices.

Many beautiful brandy bowls were made during this period. They were oval in shape, with two handles, and were highly decorated. The brandy was poured out using a special ornamented silver spoon.

The shrine of St Servatius

Stichting Schatkamer St.-Servaas

MUSIC

Music has always held a very important place in the lives of the Dutch, and has been played at home, in churches and in the street since time immemorial.

Musicians – One famous Renaissance musician was **JP Sweelinck** (1562-1621), organist for the Oude Kerk in Amsterdam, and composer of vocal and instrumental works. During the same period, the poet and diplomat **Constantijn Huygens** (1596-1687) composed a number of pieces of music, as well as writing about the subject.

In the 19C, the composer and conductor **Johannes Verhulst** (1816-91) made an important contribution to music in the Netherlands, as did **Richard Hol** (1825-1904), a conductor, pianist and composer of cantatas and symphonies.

One of Hol's students was **Johan Wagenaar** (1862-1941), an organist who compose works in his own very distinctive style. Wagenaar in turn taught the composer **Willer Pijper** (1894-1947), who was also known for his essays on music.

Today, the Netherlands has two of the world's leading orchestras: the Roya Concertgebouw Orchestra in Amsterdam, and the Residentie Orchestra in Th Hague.

The first conductor of the Concertgebouw Orchestra was **Willem Mengelberg** (187 1951), who had a particular interest in the works of contemporary composers suc as Mahler. Under his leadership, the orchestra became known for its exceptionall high standard of performance, and he was succeeded by Eduard van Beinum, Bernar Haitink and Riccardo Chailly.

Ph. Gajic/MICHELIN

The organ case, Grote Kerk, Haarlem

Organs – This instrument wa first developed in Byzantium imported into Western Europ in the 9C, and played a important part in Catholic wor ship from the 12C onwards Organs were originally mad by monks.

The instrument was also use in people's homes from a early stage, and therefore es caped the destruction wrough by the Iconoclasm of the 16C However, organ music was a first condemned by the Calvir ist religion, and it was only i the mid 17C that it spread int Protestant churches.

Numerous instruments wer made during this and the fo lowing century. The sons of th famous German organ builde **Arp Schnitger**, who had moved t Groningen, perfected the ins trument in the Netherland and built the great organ i **Zwolle**'s Grote Kerk. The im pressive 18C organ of the Sint Bavokerk in **Haarlem**, built b **Christiaan Müller**, is one of th best-known in the country.

Most of the organ cases dat from the Baroque Era, and ar sumptuous achievement with statues and carving above the pipes.

Where regular organ concerts are held, this is mentioned under the heading fo the locality in this guide.

Mechanical organs – The cheerful sound of the mechanical organ or *pieremen* is a familiar one in the streets of the Netherlands, along with that of th carillon.

The first such instrument was a **barrel organ**, probably invented by an Italian in the 18C A barrel covered in pins and turned by a handle raises levers which admit air to a se of organ pipes. Wheeled organs of this kind became widespread in 19C Europe.

In 1892, Gavioli built the first mechanical organ to use a **perforated paper roll** instea of a barrel. Turning the handle moves a continuous sheet of perforated paper acros a keyboard. The organ's repertoire was almost unlimited, since the paper rolls wer interchangeable.

The mechanical-organ builder **Carl Frei** established a business in Breda in 1920, bu most of the instruments were imported from abroad, from Belgium (Mortier) an France (Gasparini and Limonaire Frères).

At the end of the 19C, the dance hall organ became popular; this was an impressiv instrument with a beautifully ornamented front. The beginning of the 20C saw th introduction of the fairground organ, which produced loud music intended to b heard above the hubbub of the fair. Finally, in 1945, an electric dance hall orga appeared, with many built-in automatic instruments imitating the sound of a fu orchestra.

The Museum van Speelklok tot Pierement (Museum of Mechanical Music) in Utrech has an interesting collection of mechanical organs.

Carillons – Countless churches and town halls in the Netherlands have carillons These are believed to have been first used in the 15C, and are operated by barrels i a similar way to mechanical organs.

In the 17C, **François and Pierre Hemony**, famous bell-founders from Lorraine, played a very important role in the development of the carillon in the Netherlands. Of the many carillons they made, the best-known are those of the Onze Lieve Vrouwe Toren in Amersfoort, the Martini Toren in Groningen and the Domtoren in Utrecht.

In 1941, a bell-founder in Heiligerlee, in Groningen province, invented an **electro-magnetic system** to replace the barrel.

In 1953, the Netherlands Carillon School was established in Amersfoort.

The town of Asten has an interesting National Carillon Museum *(see **EINDHOVEN**: Excursions)*. Details of carillon concerts are given in the descriptions of individual towns and at the end of the guide.

Traditions and folklore

COSTUMES

In the past, the Netherlands had a great variety of local costumes. Today, apart from Marken and Volendam where many people wear traditional costume during the tourist season, there are few places where it is regularly worn, and then it is mostly confined to women.

However, those which are still worn are exceptionally interesting, both in terms of their variety and originality, and in their partly symbolic use of colours and motifs.

Women's costumes – In spite of their variety, there are common features shared by all women's costumes. They consist of a skirt, an apron and a jacket done up at the front, usually with short sleeves. Over the jacket some women wear a stiff bodice or a shawl. The costume worn on Sundays is always more elegant than that of other days, and on Whit Sunday in particular, women usually dress up in their finest clothes and jewellery.

Caps – Although many foreigners immediately think of the typical Volendam lace cap, there is a wide variety of other forms of cap throughout the country.

Those worn on the island of South Beveland, particularly on weekly market days in Goes, are particularly eye-catching. Cap brooches are widely worn; these are usually made of silver, and have ornamented ends which vary from one place to another. In Scheveningen, they are oval and decorated with filigree; in Walcheren, Axel and Arnemuiden they are spiral-shaped, and those of Urk bear the figures of animals' heads. Two gold pins with pearl heads are used to hold the brooch in place.

The lacework on all these caps is exceptionally beautiful.

Morand-Grahame/HOA QUI

Woman in Middelburg costume

Men's costumes – Nowadays, these are worn only in a few ports, such as Urk, Volendam and in South Beveland. They are nearly always black, whereas in the past brighter colours were worn. The costume consists of a jacket, often double-breasted, and wide trousers or, around the Zuider zee, knickerbockers. The shirt, which is rarely visible, is made of brightly coloured cotton with a striped or checked pattern, and has a straight collar with two gold buttons. These are the costume's only ornaments, except in Zuid-Beveland, where two attractive chased silver buckles are used to hold up the trousers.

Men also wear a small cotton scarf knotted round the neck, and a black hat; this is often a simple cap, but in Urk it resembles a kepi, and a round hat is worn in Zeeland. Wooden clogs are usually worn as well.

Fabrics – Women's jackets and shawls, and also men's shirts worn under their black jackets, were made out of traditional, brightly coloured textiles patterned with stripes, checks, or flowers; the latter were most often **chintz**.

From the 17C onwards, the Dutch East India Company imported enormous quantities of chintz from the East. This cotton cloth was hand decorated with a coloured pattern, using a special technique, and its suppleness, lightness and bright colours and designs made it hugely popular in the Netherlands. It was used for interior decoration in the form of bedspreads, curtains and wall hangings, and to make clothes of all kinds. The women of Hindeloopen in Friesland used chintz to make the traditional jacket known as the *wentke*, and elsewhere women replaced their plain jackets with brightly coloured chintz.

In the late 17C, chintz began to be machine made in the Twente.

Where to see local costumes – The main centres where costumes are worn daily by local men, women and children are **Volendam** and **Marken**, but this is less common in winter than in summer. In **Staphorst** and the neighbouring village of **Rouveen**, women and girls wear traditional clothes every day, as do some female inhabitants of **Bunschoten** and **Spakenburg**.

On the islands of **Walcheren** and **Zuid-Beveland** in Zeeland, a number of women still retain a strong allegiance to their costume, to the extent that in 1975 they strongly protested against a law requiring motorcyclists to wear crash helmets.

Other places where costumes are still sometimes worn are **Scheveningen**, **Urk**, and various towns and villages in Overijssel such as Rijssen, Dalfsen, and Raalte. These are brought out for special occasions such as church services, market days, and festivals *(see Practical information)*.

More details of local costumes can be found under the headings for individual places in the guide. In addition, various Dutch museums have departments devoted to costumes from a particular area or areas.

FARMHOUSES

The lovely farmhouses which are scattered over the countryside are part of the country's familiar landscape. They are largest in the polder areas.

Frisian farmhouses – These buildings with huge roofs can be seen all over Friesland, in areas which were formerly part of Friesland such as the north of the province of Noord-Holland, and in the province of Groningen.

Pyramid-roofed farmhouses *(Stolpboerderijen)* – There are many of these in the north of the province of Noord-Holland. Their enormous pyramid-shaped roofs are reminiscent of haystacks, and the stables, barn and living quarters are all under one roof. On one side of the roof, the thatch is partially replaced by tiles forming a decorative pattern. Sometimes, in the more elaborate farmhouses, the façade has a richly decorated brick pediment. Similar buildings which are rectangular rather than square are found in southern Friesland.

Head-neck-trunk farmhouses *(Kop-hals-rompboerderijen)* can be seen in the north of Friesland and the province of Groningen.

These are made up of three parts: the living quarters (the head), are linked by a narrow section (the neck), to a large building (the trunk), which includes the cowshed, barn, and in some cases a stable.

Traditionally, the living quarters have a tiled roof, whereas the barn is thatched. This kind of farmhouse is often built on a mound *(see LEEUWARDEN, Excursions)*.

At either end of the ridge of the barn roof, there is an ornamental triangular board with holes in it, which were placed there to allow owls to fly in and out of the building, nest in the hay and catch mice *(illustration: see Admission times and charges)*. The boards are often decorated with carved wooden motifs depicting two swans.

Head-neck farmhouses *(Kop-rompboerderijen)* – These are found in the same areas as Head-neck-trunk farmhouses, and are similar to them except that, although the living quarters have a tiled roof, there is also some living accommodation in the thatched section. Sometimes, the back of the house gradually widens out to form the barn; this is also the case with Oldambt farmhouses.

Oldambt farmhouses – These are named after the region of Oldambt, in the east of Groningen province, where they were first built. They can now be seen all over the province, and have staggered side walls which merge into those of the barn.

The tall, wide living quarters often have stucco mouldings around the front door, making the building look very elegant, though in most cases the entrance is at the side. There are small windows in the attic, and the living quarters have a tiled roof, while the barn is usually thatched.

Sometimes, a second or even a third barn would be attached to the first to cope with large harvests.

Hall-houses *(Hallehuizen)* – These are the most widespread type found in the Netherlands, particularly in the provinces of Drenthe, Overijssel, Gelderland and Utrecht; they can also be seen in Zuid-Holland and in the Gooi (Noord-Holland). Inside, the ceiling rests on two rows of piles connected by crossbeams, similar to the pillars of a church. These divide the interior into a wide central nave and two narrower side aisles.

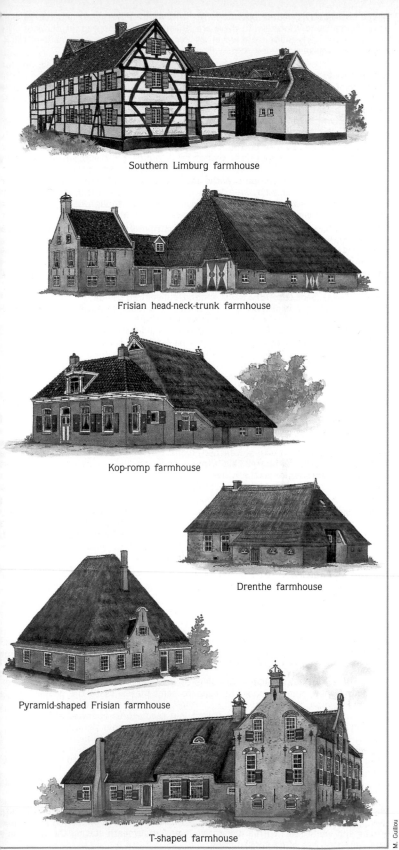

Southern Limburg farmhouse

Frisian head-neck-trunk farmhouse

Kop-romp farmhouse

Drenthe farmhouse

Pyramid-shaped Frisian farmhouse

T-shaped farmhouse

M. Guillou

Twente farmhouses (*Twentse boerderijen*) – In Twente (Overijssel) and the east of Gelderland around Winterswijk, there are still some half-timbered farmhouses. The walls were formerly made from woven wicker and clay, but are now made of brick. The buildings have two-sided roofs with wooden gable ends.

The open house (*Losse hoes*) – These have unfortunately almost disappeared, but can still be found in Twente. Hall-houses derived from this kind of building.

The interior consisted of one large room with no partitions: the family and cattle shared the same space, and the hay was stored on the beams beneath the roof. The room had an open fire.

A separate living area for the parents was sometimes built onto the side of the house.

Drenthe farmhouses (*Drentse boerderijen*) – These are elongated in shape, with a usually thatched four-sided roof to both the house and the barn and stable section. At the back of the building, the roof has a section taken out of it to create sufficient height for the stable doors, so that hay carts can pass through. From the 18C onwards some farmhouses in southwest Drenthe and to the north of Overijssel had the stable doors at the back replaced by side doors in order to increase the space in the barn. Examples of this style can be found in Wanneperveen, though here, because the houses were set close together, the doors were placed at the corners.

T-shaped farmhouses (*T-huizen*) – In Gelderland (particularly in the Achterhoek and IJssel areas), in the provinces of Utrecht and Zuid-Holland, and in Gooi (Noord-Holland), the house is set crosswise to the barn, creating a T shape. This design owes its existence to the prosperity of farmers in the fertile areas along the main rivers, who extended their houses out to either side, creating a church-like transept. Carts entered through the back of the building, which had a single long roof.

In the Veluwe, there is often a haystack and a sheepfold beside the farmhouse, but in the Gooi the hay was heaped up at the back of the house because the entrance was on the long wall, though haystacks became more common in the 19C.

In the provinces of Utrecht, and near Woerden in Zuid-Holland, cheesemaking farms had a dairy and cheese storage area in the basement of the house.

Local variations on the hall-type farmhouse can also be seen in Staphorst, Giethoorn and Lopikerwaard, in the province of Utrecht. They also exist in the Krimpenerwaard and Alblasserwaard in Zuid-Holland, where the living quarters have a raised floor because of the risk of floods.

Transverse farmhouses (*Dwarshuizen*) – These farmhouses have their longest side at the front, and the rooms are side by side, with the living quarters set at right angles to the barn. They can be seen in Limburg and in the eastern part of Noord-Brabant.

Limburg – This is the only province in the Netherlands where farmhouses have a square enclosed courtyard, which is reached from the outside via a large gateway immediately beside the house. This layout evolved gradually; it originally consisted of a barn at right angles to the house.

In southern Limburg, some of the buildings often have black and white half-timbered walls.

Noord-Brabant – This province has a distinctive long-fronted style of farmhouse with the doors and windows facing the road and a long thatched or tiled roof.

Because these farmhouses often provided limited space, a Flemish barn would often be built beside them, with wooden walls and a thatched roof which was arched above the doors.

Zeeland – Here, the various buildings were kept separate. The largest was the wooden barn, which had tarred walls and white door and window frames.

WINDMILLS

There are still some 950 windmills in the Netherlands, and they are one of the most distinctive features of the landscape. Some overlook the old walls of towns and dykes; others stand at the entrances to villages or beside lakes. The most famous group of windmills is at Kinderdijk.

The language of windmills – The sails of a windmill turn anticlockwise. When stationary, their position could be used to send messages to the people of the surrounding area, as follows:
– two vertical sails (+): windmill is at rest, but ready to be operated again.
– two diagonal sails (x): polder windmill, at rest for a longer period.
– upper sail just to the right of vertical (⅄): a sign of celebration.
– upper sail just to the left of vertical (⅄): a symbol of mourning.
When a wedding took place, the sails would be abundantly decorated with garlands and symbolic motifs.
During the last war, windmill sails were used to send pre-arranged warning signals to members of the resistance and to people in hiding.

Windmill decorations – Many wooden windmills are painted green with white edging. The windshaft, where the sails cross, is often painted with a red and yellow or blue and white star, with a decorative board underneath stating the windmill's name and the date of its construction.

Stage mill

Hollow post mill

Mill with rotating cap

Post mill

Tjasker

M. Guillou

Winter in Kinderdidjk

Main types of windmills – There are two main kinds of windmills: polder mills and industrial mills.

Polder mills were used for drainage purposes, and there are none in the east of the country, where the height above sea level ensures natural drainage of water.

Industrial mills, of which there are still about 500, were used for a wide variety of purposes, such as milling wheat, extracting oil, hulling rice and peppercorns, and sawing wood. Some of these are still in use.

The oldest type of windmill: the post-mill – Originally, the only mills in the Netherlands were the watermill and the horse-powered treadmill. The first windmills appeared in the mid 13C, and may have derived from the stone-built ones used in Persia to mill corn. The body and sails rotate round a heavy fixed wooden post made out of a tree trunk, so that the mill is always facing into the wind. When the sails turn, they rotate the grindstones inside. Outside, on the side opposite the sails, a tail pole joined to the post and operated by a wheel enables the windmill to be turned round. The ladder fixed to the main body of the windmill also turns with it. Few windmills of this type remain in the country.

The first polder mills – The first windmill used for drainage, in about 1350, was a post-mill adapted specifically for the purpose by replacing the solid central post with a hollow one, through which the driveshaft was placed. This was known as a **hollow post mill**; the earliest known example dates from 1513. This had a smaller tower and a larger base to allow space for a scoop, resembling a paddle-wheel, which was used to lift the water. In most cases, however, the scoop was on the outside and the base was used as living accommodation, particularly in Zuid-Holland.

The **sleeve windmill** *(kokermolen)* was easier to turn into the wind: the wooden spindle was replaced by a sleeve, around which the sails and the top part of the windmill rotated. In Friesland, there is a smaller version of the hollow post-mill known as the **spinnekop** (spider's head) because it looks like a spider from a distance. The **weidemolentje** of Noord-Holland is even smaller.

In Friesland and Overijssel, there are still a few examples of the **tjasker**, a simply constructed windmill with a tilted spindle, whose windshaft is connected direct to the device which draws up water.

Mills with rotating caps – Turning the whole windmill into the wind was heavy work, and the Dutch invention of the **smock mill** represented a major improvement. This had a small rotating cap and sails on a large fixed tower. The wheel used to turn the cap and sails was usually on the outside, though there was also a form in Noord-Holland where the wheel was inside the mill, making it larger.

These mills were built of wood. They often had a **thatched roof** and an octagonal shape, in which case the base was made of stone. Sometimes, the wooden frame was clad in brick, giving it a truncated cone shape.

Industrial mills – *(Illustration: see* **ZAANSTREEK***).* In the 16C, the windmill was adapted for industrial purposes.

The first oil windmill began operation in Alkmaar in 1582. In 1592, Cornelis Corneliszoon of Uitgeest (Noord-Holland) built the first **sawmill**, which subsequently underwent many improvements and resulted in the first post-mill used for sawing, which rotated on its base.

Next, **hulling mills** were built to hull first barley and then, when the Dutch began trading in the Far East, rice. The first of these was built in 1639 in Koog aan de Zaan.

Paper mills were first used in about 1600, and became more widespread in 1673 when French paper manufacturers relocated to the **Zaanstreek**. It was here that the greatest concentration could be found until the 19C; they were specially built for making paper and sawing wood for boatbuilding. Most of the other different types of windmills developed in this area; they included tobacco snuffmills, hemp mills for making ropes, tanning mills for leather, spice mills mainly for mustard, and fulling mills for textiles. Most of these were very tall, with a balcony around the side and a workshop at the bottom.

Tower mills – Industrial windmills were often built in towns, and had to be several storeys high if they were to catch the wind. Because they were so tall, the sails could not be set from the ground, and so this was done from a balcony halfway up the windmill; the miller's accommodation and the storage area were below this. Alternatively, instead of a balcony, an earth wall was built around the windmill and served the same purpose.

CPA STOCKI-OA QUI

Most tower mills were made of stone and in a truncated cone shape. In Groningen province, they had octagonal bases made of brick, and in the Zaanstreek there was a workshop in the wooden base.

TRADITIONAL SPORTS

Many sports from olden times are being kept alive, and in some cases are highly popular.

Archery is one such example; it is particularly widely practised in **Limburg**, and dates from a time when citizens felt it necessary to arm themselves against possible enemies. Members of a large number of local societies or guilds of archers congregate at an annual gathering, the Oud Limburgs Schuttersfeest (Old Limburg Archers' Festival), and give a colourful demonstration of their sport. The town or village which wins the event becomes the host for the following year.

In Friesland, **kaatsen** is a traditional ball game similar to fives, with six players divided into two teams, and the **skûtsjesilen** are spectacular annual regattas using traditional boats called *skûtsjes (see SNEEK)*.

Pole-vaulting (known as *ljeppen* in Frisian) is another equally exciting traditional sport. It originates from the time when people hunting birds' eggs in the fields used to cross the many canals with the help of a long pole.

In the Zeeland town of Middelburg, the sport of **ringrijderijen** has been revived. This is a tournament where riders on horseback gallop past and try to place their lances through a ring.

Skating was not only a traditional sport and pastime, but also a practical means of transport in the harsh winters of years gone by. The delightful winter scenes of the 17C Dutch master Hendrick Avercamp show how popular skating was at the time, and how sleighs were also used on the ice.

> A few proverbs about windmills:
> *Hij heeft een klap van de molen gehad*
> He was struck by a windmill (He's a little crazy)
> *Hij loopt met molentjes*
> His mind runs on little windmills (He's rather simple-minded)
> *Dat is koren op zijn molen*
> It's grain for his windmill (It's all grist to the mill)

Another activity that Avercamp portrayed in his paintings is **kolf**. This game was also played on ice with a club *(kolf)* and ball, and the aim was to hit a pole stuck into the ice. This game has been a subject of controversy between the Dutch and the Scots for centuries. The Dutch claim that it was the origin of the game of golf. However, the Scots claim that the early ball-and-stick version of golf was already being played on the sandy links of Scotland in 1457, when an Act of the Scottish Parliament was passed requiring that "futeball and the golfe be utterly cryit down" in favour of church attendance and archery practice *(see the Michelin Green Guide Scotland)*.

Zandhoek, Amsterdam Ph. Gajic/MICHELIN

Sights

AALSMEER★

Noord-Holland
Population 22 284
Michelin maps 908 F 5 and 211 N 9

Aalsmeer, a centre for growing flowers under glass, is on the edge of Haarlemmer meerpolder *(see HAARLEM)*, reclaimed land crisscrossed with canals and the large lake, the **Westeinder Plas**. The town is mainly known as the home of the world's largest flower auction, where most Dutch florists buy their flowers and, thanks to the proximity of Schiphol airport, foreign buyers as well. About 80% of sales are exported.

Around 9 billion cut flowers were sold in the Netherlands in 1990, of which 1 billion were carnations and 2 billion were roses; 750 million potted plants were also sold. The *Bloemencorso* is a famous annual procession of floral floats from Aalsmeer to Amsterdam and back *(see Calendar of events)*.

SIGHTS

★★ **Bloemenveiling** ⊘ – The flower auction takes place in a huge building (902 972sq yd/755 000m²) decorated with a red tulip, the headquarters of the Aalsmeer Flower Auction, the **VBA** (Verenigde Bloemenveilingen Aalsmeer).

Inside, **walkways** enable visitors to watch the activity in the market and the auction itself.

Part of the hall is reserved for the arrival of cut flowers, which takes place the day before or early in the morning. The flowers are packed and loaded onto trucks elsewhere.

In the centre of the hall, four amphitheatres have been designed for the selling of cut flowers. The retail buyers sit in tiers facing dials linked to a computer. A trolley carrying flowers in bunches is brought to the foot of each dial.

On the dial a number indicates the currency, the number of the trolley and the quantity of flowers it contains. The first buyer to push a button in front of him or her interrupts the countdown from 100 to 0, stops the auction and thus fixes the price.

The successful bidder's number then appears on the dial as well as the number of bunches bought. Pot plants are sold in another part of the building which is not visible from the visitors' walkway.

Selling flowers at the VBA

Westeinder Plas – This large lake is one of the most popular water sports centres near Amsterdam. The road which runs round it via Kudelstaart provides lovely **views**.

The chapter on art and architecture in this guide gives an outline of artistic creation in the region, providing the context of the buildings and works of art described in the Sights section.

This chapter may also provide ideas for touring.

It is advisable to read it at leisure/before setting out.

ALKMAAR★

Noord-Holland

Population 93 004
Michelin maps 908 F 4 and 210 N 7

The historic town of Alkmaar is best-known for its picturesque weekly cheese market.
Inside its surrounding moat, occupied partly by the Noordhollandskanaal, the old town has more or less preserved its 17C plan and a number of old façades. The old fortifications have been transformed into a garden. Alkmaar is now the main market town for the agricultural regions of the Noord-Holland peninsula.

HISTORICAL NOTES

Alkmaar was founded in the 10C in the middle of marshes and lakes. Its name derives either from *elk meer* or "each lake", or from *alken meer* or "auk lake", after the name of the bird which lived in the marshes.

The siege of Alkmaar – During the Eighty Years War, which began in 1568, Alkmaar was besieged in August 1573 by 16 000 Spaniards commanded by Don Federico of Toledo, the son of the Spanish governor, the Duke of Alba.
Heavy autumn rain flooded the surrounding countryside and forced the assailants to withdraw on 8 October, after a seven-week siege. Alkmaar was therefore the first town to resist the Spanish, and for centuries it has been said that victory began in Alkmaar.

Boat trips ⊘ – Tours on offer include Alkmaar's canals as well as excursions to Amsterdam and the Zaanstreek.

Cheese porters

★★ KAASMARKT ⊘ *30min*

This traditional market, known since the early 17C, is held on Waagplein every Friday in summer. Early in the morning, loads of cheese from Edam or Gouda are carefully piled up. At 10am the buyers start tasting and comparing the different cheeses and haggling; they then seal their agreement with the seller with a vigorous gesture of the hand.
Next, the famous **cheese porters** (*kaasdragers*), wearing the traditional white clothes and straw hats take over; the porters belong to an ancient guild, which is divided into four companies each identified by a different colour (green, blue, red and yellow) and consisting of six porters and a weigher or stacker (*tasman*). Once a batch of cheese is sold, it is placed on a stretcher in the company's colour. The porters then run with the load (weighing up to 160kg/353lb) to the weigh house, where the *tasman* officiates. Finally, the cheese is taken to the trucks.

ADDITIONAL SIGHTS

Waag – The weigh house is the former Chapel of the Holy Ghost, built at the end of the 14C and converted in 1582. On the east side, the chancel has been replaced by a Renaissance building with a finely worked gable, which since the 19C has been decorated with a painting on Auvergne lava, representing trade and industry.

The tower, which was built at the end of the 16C, was modelled on that of the Oude Kerk in Amsterdam and has a **carillon** and working models of jousting knights every hour.

Hollands Kaasmuseum ⊙ – *In the Waag*. Visit starts on the second floor. The Dutch Cheese Museum includes a collection of tools and other objects, such as decorative carved wooden cheese moulds, illustrating the history and making of cheese and butter. The display on the first floor shows how cheese is made on farms and in dairies, and explains the importance of dairy products to the Dutch economy.

Nederlands Biermuseum De Boom ⊙ – *Houttil 1*. A beer museum in a 17C brewery chronicling the history of brewing. There is a tasting area in the cellar.

Huis met de Kogel – This building, the house with the cannon-ball, overlooks the canal and has a corbelled wooden façade. Embedded in the gable is a Spanish cannon-ball from the battle of 1573.

From the neighbouring bridge there is a fine **view** of the weigh house.

Mient – On this square and along the canal, there are numerous old façades. To the south is the fish market, Vismarkt.

Langestraat – This pedestrian precinct is the town's main shopping street.

Stadhuis ⊙ – The town hall's charming Gothic façade with its flight of steps is flanked by an elegant octagonal tower with streaks of white limestone. The adjoining building is 17C. The town hall has a collection of porcelain.

Grote Kerk or Sint-Laurenskerk ⊙ – This Protestant church is a beautiful edifice, with three naves, a transept and an ambulatory dating from the late 15C and early 16C. It was built by members of the Keldermans family, famous architects from Mechelen in Belgium.

The imposing interior has wooden vaults with beautiful 17C chandeliers. A plain triforium runs above the large formeret arcades. Under the chancel vault there is a painting, the *Last Judgment*, by **Cornelis Buys** (15C-16C), known as the Master of Alkmaar.

The **great organ case**★, made in 1645 by Jacob van Campen, is decorated with panels depicting the Triumph of King Saul. The **small organ**★ on the north side of the ambulatory dates from 1511; it is one of the country's oldest such instruments. The consistory, the room where the ministers met to discuss church affairs, has kept its original aspect.

On the south side of the transept there is a memorial brass to Pieter Palinc and his wife Josina van Foreest. Over 1 700 gravestones are embedded in the floor. The church also contains the memorial tomb of Count Floris V, who was assassinated in 1296. Since 1996, the building has been used for events such as organ concerts, exhibitions, trade fairs and conferences.

Stedelijk Museum ⊙ – The municipal museum occupies the Nieuwe Doelen, a 17C building which used to house the Archers' Guild. There are several interesting collections pertaining to the history of the town: 16C and 17C paintings, including a great many portraits of companies of the civic guard (*schuttersstukken*), and works by Maerten van Heemskerk, Pieter Saenredam, Gerard van Honthorst, Willem van de Velde the Elder and Allart van Everdingen. The museum also has a collection of silver and pewter, and an interesting display of toys dating from around 1900 in the basement. Changing exhibitions from the museum's collection of modern art are held, including works from the Bergen School (*see below*), and there is a display of statues and memorial stones in the garden.

EXCURSIONS

The dunes – *Round tour of 35km/22mi – about 1hr 30min. Leave Alkmaar via Scharlo.*

Bergen – Also known as Bergen-Binnen (*binnen*: inner) as opposed to the neighbouring seaside town, Bergen is an agreeable holiday resort where substantial villas stand in rows along tree-lined avenues. It has a popular university located in the former manor house of the lords of Bergen.

The **Bergen School** of artists was founded around 1915; its members played an important part in propagating the influence on Dutch art of artists such as Cézanne and Le Fauconnier. The **Museum Kranenburgh** ⊙ (*Hoflaan 26*) contains work by artists including Leo Gestel, Matthieu and Piet Wiegman and Charley Toorop.

Bergen still attracts numerous artists, whose work is exhibited in a space behind the Kunstenaarscentrum *Bergen (on Plein)* and in open-air markets in the summer.

The entrance to the **Noord-Hollands Duinreservaat** ⊙ is at the junction with the Egmond road. This is a nature reserve of 4 760ha/11 757 acres owned by the provincial water company, and a large number of bird species nest in the dunes.

ALKMAAR

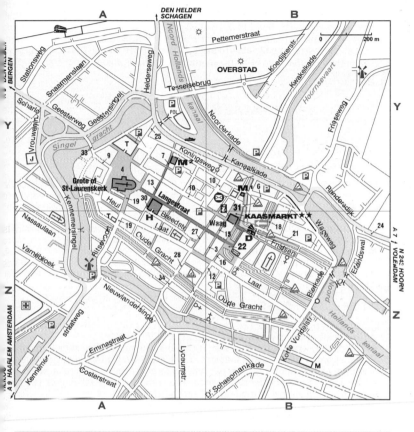

Bergen aan Zee – The coast at this resort, founded in 1906, is lined with high dunes dotted with villas. From the promenade, there is an extensive view over the desolate landscape of dunes, with trees lining the horizon.
The **Zee Aquarium Bergen aan Zee** ⊙ has a collection of colourful exotic fish and crustaceans and large displays of shellfish and sea anemones. The marine aquarium is also home to one of four sperm whales stranded on the Frisian island of Ameland in November 1997.

Egmond aan de Hoef – This village is set in the bulb field area to the south of Alkmaar. To the east, on the Alkmaar road and beyond the church, the ruins of the moated **Slot van Egmond** can be seen. One of its better known owners was the famous Count of Egmond executed in 1568 in Brussels *(see DELFT)*.

Egmond aan Zee – This small seaside resort is in the middle of the dunes. At the foot of the lighthouse a statue of a lion symbolises the heroism of **Lieutenant Van Speijk**, who on 5 February 1831 blew up his gunboat with all on board near Antwerp, rather than surrender to the Belgians.
Return to Egmond aan de Hoef.

Egmond-Binnen – The famous **abbey** of Egmond was destroyed by the Beggars in 1572 and was only rebuilt in 1935.

Return to Alkmaar.

Graft-De Rijp – *17km/11mi to the southeast via Nieuwe Schermerweg.*
These two localities merged in 1970. **Graft** has kept its beautiful town hall buil
in 1613, with crow-stepped gables. **De Rijp** was an important centre for herrin
fishing and whaling in the 16C and 17C. It has a town hall dating from 1630 an
designed by **Jan Adriaensz Leeghwater** (1575-1650), the famous hydraulic enginee
who was born in De Rijp. There are also a number of houses built in the regiona
style with wooden gables. The Dutch Reformed church or Hervormde Kerk ha
17C stained-glass windows.

Broek op Langedijk – *8km/5mi north of Alkmaar via N 245 towards Schagen*
This is the home of Europe's oldest "drive-through" vegetable auction, the **Broeke
Veiling** ○. From 1887 to 1973, market gardeners from the "Kingdom of th
Thousand Islands", as the watery surrounding area is called, transported thei
produce to auction by boat. Instead of wasting time loading and unloading them
they would simply moor at the water's edge. In 1903, the system was change
so that they were actually able to sail into the auction room! Today, visitors ca
buy vegetables themselves using an auction clock, or enjoy a boat tour throug
the fields.

AMERSFOORT★

Utrecht
Population 117 933
Michelin maps 908 H 5 and 211 R 10
Plan of the conurbation in the current Michelin Red Guide Benelux

Amersfoort stands at the confluence of two waterways which form the navigabl
River Eem in the Gelderse Vallei. In the surrounding area, woodland and moorlan
cover the poor glacial soils while the hills to the south, the **Utrechtse Heuvelrug**, ar
moraines deposited by the Scandinavian ice sheets.
Amersfoort is a delightful medieval town encircled by a double ring of canals. Th
whole of the town centre is a protected architectural area.
In the modern northern suburb of **Kattenbroek**, there are a number of building
designed by leading contemporary architects, including Ashok Bhalostra, Babe
Gallis, Jan de Graaf, Leo Heijdenrijk, Jan Poolen, Rudy Uytenhaak and Ka
Oosterhuis.

HISTORICAL NOTES

The town grew up around its 12C castle, and in 1259 it was granted civic rights. Th
first town wall, with its girdle of canals, dates from the 13C.
Amersfoort prospered in the 15C and 16C thanks to its thriving trade in wool an
cloth and to a growing brewing industry. A second town wall was built c 1400 an
reinforced by a ring of canals, now partially replaced by the wide circular boulevard
the Stadsring. The Koppelpoort and other foundations at the far end of the mai
street, Kamp, are all that remain of the second city wall.
The town's main industries are metallurgy, engineering, chemicals, food processing
printing, building and the service sector. The town has expanded far beyond it
medieval centre.
Amersfoort is also home to the Netherlands Carillon School.

Johan van Oldenbarnevelt – Amersfoort was the birthplace of **Johan van Oldenbarnevel**
(1547-1619), the **Grand Pensionary** or political leader of Holland, the most importan
of the United Provinces. Oldenbarnevelt was one of the founding figures of th
independent Netherlands, and strove constantly to achieve peace and prosperity. H
was responsible for the Twelve Years Truce with Spain in 1609, and was one of th
founders of the Dutch East India Company in 1602. Unfortunately, he clashed wit
Prince Maurits of Nassau, the son of William the Silent and Stadtholder from 158
onwards, who had him imprisoned in 1618. Oldenbarnevelt was beheaded in Ma
1619.

★OLD TOWN *4hr*

The recommended itinerary follows the line of the first town wall, where th
famous **Muurhuizen**★, or wall houses, were built in the 15C. These houses are
distinctive feature of Amersfoort, and are so called because they are built into th
town wall.

De Amersfoortse Kei – A park on the Stadsring is the final resting place of thi
enormous **glacial boulder** weighing 9t. It was originally found in a nearby wood
where it had been deposited by the Scandinavian ice sheet. In 1661 it was move
to the Varkensmarkt in the centre of town before it was finally transferred to it
present-day site.

Varkensmarkt – This was the site of the pig market. From the bridge over the canal there is a lovely view to the left over the tree-shaded canal to the tower, Onze-Lieve-Vrouwe Toren.

Krankeledenstraat – There are numerous old houses in this street; note in particular the late Gothic **Kapelhuis** or chapel house.

★ **Onze-Lieve-Vrouwe-Toren** ⊘ – This beautiful 15C Gothic tower dedicated to Our Lady stands 98.33m/324ft high in a large, peaceful square, Lieve Vrouwekerkhof. The brick tower has an octagonal upper storey crowned by an onion-shaped dome and is all that remains of a church destroyed in 1787 by an explosion at a gunpowder mill. The carillon was made by François Hemony *(see Introduction: Music)*.

There is an attractive old house on the corner of Lieve Vrouwestraat.

A flower market is held every Friday morning on Lieve Vrouwekerkhof.

Take the small footbridge to cross the canal, the Lange Gracht, which divides Amersfoort in two.

Hof – This spacious square is still bordered by some old houses (eg no 24) and is the scene of a lively market on Friday mornings and Saturdays.

Sint-Joriskerk ⊘ – The Romanesque church of St George, dating from 1243, was destroyed by fire in 1370. It was rebuilt and then extended in 1534.

The porch tower, a few superimposed arcades, and traces of a fresco depicting St George on the west wall are all that remain of the original building.

A finely sculpted sandstone **rood screen**, in the late 15C Gothic style, separates the nave from the chancel. The capitals and consoles in the chancel depict people (monks and angels) and animals (lions and stags). Against the wall, not far from the rood screen, is a memorial to **Jacob van Campen** (1595-1657), the architect of Amsterdam's old town hall, now the Royal Palace. Other items worthy of attention include the 14C baptismal font beside the pulpit and a jack o'the clock (Klockman) dated 1724 and now connected to a 15C clock.

In an annexe is a 17C surgeons' room *(chirurgijnskamer)*.

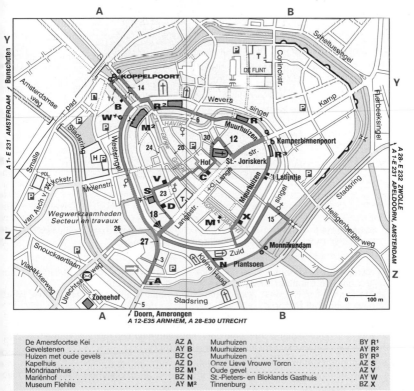

AMERSFOORT

Piet Mondriaan and De Stijl

Pieter Cornelis Mondriaan was born in Amersfoort in 1872. After experimenting with many different forms of painting, and a stay in Paris (1911-14) where he discovered the Cubism of Picasso, Braque and Léger, Mondriaan returned to Amersfoort to look after his sick father.

During the First World War, he came into contact with artists such as Bart van der Leck, Theo van Doesburg *(illustration: see Introduction, Art)* and JJP Oud, with whom he founded the abstract art movement called **De Stijl** (The Style). He passionately expounded his theories in the art periodical of the same name.

From then on, his painting abandoned all subjectivity and he used vertical and horizontal lines and the three primary colours, red, blue and yellow, together with neutral blacks, whites and greys.

Mondrian unremittingly pursued his experimentation in this genre, which is known as neo-Plasticism. After a second period in Paris from 1919 to 1938, he moved to New York in 1940, and died there four years later.

Mondriaan is regarded as one of the founders of geometric abstraction. His last, unfinished painting, *Victory Boogie Woogie*, was bought by The Dutch National Art Collections Fund in September 1998 for 80 million guilders, making it one of the 10 most expensive artworks ever. The painting was given to the Gemeentemuseum Den Haag, which owns the world's largest collection of works by Mondriaan.

His influence can also be seen in architecture; buildings designed by **Gerrit Rietveld** (1888-1964), such as the 1959 **Zonnehof** and the Rietveld Schröder-huis in Utrecht *(illustration: see **UTRECHT**)* are directly inspired by his theories.

Selfportrait (1919), Piet Mondriaan

Collectie Haags Gemeentemuseum

Groenmarkt – Several of the lovely old houses here have been restored, in particular those near the adjoining square, Appelmarkt.

Follow Langestraat to Kamperbinnenpoort.

Kamperbinnenpoort – This 13C brick gateway with its octagonal turrets stood just outside the inner town wall on the road to Kampen.
In the street to the west are some of the smaller wall houses, **Muurhuizen**, which have been well restored.

Bloemendalse Binnenpoort to the left leads to Havik.

Havik – This is Amersfoort's old port, situated near the ford where the town was founded (Amersfoort means ford on the Amer).

Return to Bloemendalse Binnenpoort.

There are some interesting and quite impressive **Muurhuizen**★ between nos 217 and 243.

★ **Koppelpoort** ⊙ – *(Illustration: see Introduction, ABC of architecture)*. This beautiful double gate, built c 1400, includes a fortified bridge or watergate over the Eem, a double treadmill in the centre and the gateway proper, flanked by polygonal towers. The Bag-Carriers' Guild used this as their meeting place and today it is occupied by a **puppet theatre** ⊙.
In **Kleine Spui**, no 8 sports two facing-stones, one of which depicts a sailing ship.

Museum Flehite ⊙ – This museum's collections cover the history, archeology and decorative arts of the town and the Flehite area (the eastern part of the province of Utrecht). There is also a section devoted to the famous local figure of Johan van Oldenbarnevelt *(see above)*, and the museum holds temporary exhibitions.
Opposite the museum, on the Westersingel, is the chapel of the **Sint-Pieters- en Bloklands Gasthuis**, with the restored **Mannenzaal** ⊙ behind it. This almshouse was built in 1530, and until 1907 the sick and poor of Amersfoort could stay here at the expense of local benefactors, sleeping in one of the wooden curtained beds.
Return to the Varkensmarkt via the Westsingel, the last part of which is pedestrianised. Cross the square and turn right a little further on, to reach the town walls.

Mariënhof – It is a beautifully restored 16C convent now housing the **Culinair Museum** ⊙. This attractive display of large and small cooking utensils, cutlery, majolica, pewter, silver, Meissen and Loosdrecht porcelain, earthenware and many other objects, illustrates Dutch eating and drinking habits from prehistoric times to the present day. The museum also has a herb garden, a culinary shop and two restaurants.

Plantsoen – A garden has been laid out on the site of the ramparts, leading to the Monnikendam.

Monnikendam – This graceful watergate (1430) formed part of the outer fortifications, and overlooks the leafy gardens of patrician houses.

Take Herenstraat back to Zuidsingel and follow this to the left.

The lovely shaded **canal**, the Zuidsingel, runs beside the gardens of the wall-houses. Cross the canal back to the wall houses. The bridge over the Kortegracht is in a very picturesque location, with a view of another wall house, **Tinnenburg**.

Mondriaanhuis ⊙ – The restored and modernised house on the Korte Gracht where Piet Mondrian *(see above)* was born has a permanent retrospective of his work. This follows the main phases in the artist's career, from the time when he painted pictures from nature to his neo-Plastic phase, in which line and colour were equally important. There is a particularly interesting reconstruction of the studio in Paris where Mon-

Monnikendam

drian worked from 1921 to 1936; he adapted this five-sided room to suit his own ideas of how spaces and surfaces should be divided up, using panels in primary colours where necessary.

't Latijntje – Also known as the Dieventoren or the Plompetoren, the 13C tower on the right is a relic of the first town wall. Past this tower, there is a very fine series of **Muurhuizen**★ on the right before you reach Langestraat.

EXCURSIONS

Dierenpark Amersfoort – *3km/2mi to the west. Leave Amersfoort via Van Asch Van Wijckstraat.* Surrounded by woodland, Amersfoort's zoo features animals from all over the world. Other attractions include a unique Japanese garden made from 200t of rock, an "ark" whose crow's-nest gives a spectacular view of a savanna landscape, and an exciting adventure playground.

* **Bunschoten** – *12km/8mi to the north via N 199. Leave Amersfoort via Amster damseweg.* Bunschoten forms a single built-up area with **Spakenburg**, a small por on the edge of the freshwater Eemmeer, where eels are caught.

The two villages run along a street for more than 2km/1mi, which divides in the north to form the quays of a canal. The canal then widens into a dock where ol boats, typical of the Zuiderzee, are sometimes moored.

The two villages are famous for the fact that some women and girls still wear the **traditional costume★**. The skirt is long, black and covered with a black apron. The distinctive feature of the costume is the stiff, flowered panels, often of chintz on either side of the tartan band which marks the centre of the bodice. Widow wear a violet or black bodice for the rest of their lives unless they remarry. Unde this, they wear a black shirt with short check sleeves. In the winter, some wome wear a cotton overblouse with long sleeves.

A small white crocheted bonnet is perched on the back of the head.

These costumes can be seen on Saturday afternoons when the market is being held, and on the last two Wednesdays of July and the first two Wednesdays of August (known as Spakenburg Days), when handicrafts are on sale in the marke place and around the port.

The **Museum 't Vurhuus** gives a picture of everyday life in Bunschoten-Spakenburg It includes old shops, a herring smoke-house, a farmhouse and a fisherman's house.

The hills and heathlands of Utrecht Province – *41km/26mi to the south – abou 3hr 30min. Leave Amersfoort to the south via Arnhemsestraat.*

The road crosses the heathland known as the **Leusder Heide** and the woodlands o the Utrechtse Heuvelrug.

Turn right at the Utrecht-Woudenberg junction of N 227.

Piramide van Austerlitz (Austerlitz Pyramid) – In 1804, Napoleon ordered his unemployed troops to build a sand pyramid here. Hidden under vegetation, it was discovered and restored in 1894, and a flight of steps and a small memorial were added.

Doorn – *See DOORN.*

Wijk bij Duurstede – This small town on the River Lek is on the site of **Dorestad**, a great trading centre which was abandoned after its destruction by the Vikings in 863 The town developed again in the 15C after the Bishop of Utrecht chose it as his residence.

Marktplein, the market square, is overlooked by the church with its incomplete square tower and the town hall (1662).

In an adjoining street *(Volderstraat 15)* is a small museum, the **Museum Dorestad** ⊙ which traces the history of the town and the excavations on the site of Dorestad Beside the Lek is a **windmill** (Molen Rijn en Lek) with an arched base, which some believe to be that depicted by Jacob van Ruysdael in one of his pictures, now in the Rijksmuseum. Others believe the picture shows the mill that once stood in the town centre.

On the outskirts of town, the ruined moated castle, **Kasteel Duurstede**, still has the remains of a square keep and a 15C round tower. The grounds were laid out in 1852 and are now a listed monument.

Amerongen – A peaceful place in the area between the Rhine and the Utrechtse Heuvelrug, where tobacco was formerly cultivated; typical wooden tobacco-drying sheds can still be seen here and there. The Gothic **church** has a tall 16C tower with limestone courses. On the square, with its lovely restored rustic houses, an oak tree was planted in 1898 in honour of Queen Wilhelmina's coming of age. The **Amerongs Historisch Museum** ⊙ is housed in an old tobacco-drying shed and gives an insight into the history of tobacco growing in the area.

Not far away, in Drotestraat, stands the famous castle, **Kasteel Amerongen** ⊙. The first castle was built on the foundations of a medieval fortress dating from 1286. After it was destroyed by the French army in 1673, its owner Godard van Reede had a new castle built on the same site. It was finished in 1684: an oblong brick construction circled by double moats, a marvel of simplicity and elegance. Kaiser Wilhelm II of Germany lived here from 1918 to 1920, before abdicating and moving to Doorn.

The rooms inside feature splendid furniture, tapestries and paintings (17C-19C), and the grounds are open to the public.

North of **Leersum**, on the Maarsbergen road, the Het Leersumse Veld nature reserve is situated on the heathlands of an old glacial moraine. The lakes, the **Leersumse Plassen** ⊙, are favourite breeding grounds with seagulls.

The star ratings are allocated for various categories : regions of scenic beauty with dramatic natural features, cities with a cultural heritage-elegant resorts and charming villages, ancient monuments and fine architecture, museum and picture galleries.

AMSTERDAM★★★

Noord-Holland
Population 715 148
Michelin maps 908 F 4 folds 27 and 28 (inset),
210 J 8 and folds 19 and 20 (inset) and 211 J 8 – Local map see IJSSELMEER
Plan of the conurbation in the current Michelin Red Guide Benelux

Amsterdam, the biggest city in the Netherlands, lies on the banks of two rivers, the IJ and the Amstel. One of the best ways of getting to know this unique metropolis is by strolling along the picturesque canals with their narrow brick houses, some of them gradually sinking because they are built on piles to cope with the marshy subsoil. The numerous houseboats moored on the canals reflect the difficulty of building new housing in the old city centre. The lack of tall buildings and wide roads gives Amsterdam a small-town atmosphere, and another of its most striking features is the dominance of the bicycle as a means of transport. Hiring a bike is the ideal way of exploring the city's byways.

Apart from its international importance as a port, Amsterdam is a city of great cultural wealth, including major exhibitions in the Rijksmuseum and the Stedelijk Museum, numerous art galleries in and around Nieuwe Spiegelstraat, concerts by the world-famous Concertgebouw Orchestra, the Hollandfestival of theatre, music and other genres, the Prinsengrachtfestival outside the Pulitzerhotel in summer, and the Uitmarkt, heralding the beginning of the new theatre season.

The city has some of the best night life in the world: cosy "brown cafés", trendy alternative bars, discos, nightclubs, and of course the infamous red-light district, the Walletjes.

Amsterdam is a very outward-looking and tolerant city. As elsewhere in the Netherlands, many coffee shops sell soft drugs quite legally.

HISTORICAL NOTES

Legend has it that Amsterdam was founded by two Frisian fishermen, who landed on the shores of the Amstel in a small boat with their dog. The boat and the dog were depicted on the city seals in the 15C.

In fact, the first documented mention of the city dates from 1275, when Count Floris V of Holland granted toll privileges to this herring-fishing village, situated on two dikes joined by a dam, at the mouth of the River Amstel.

Amsterdam developed in stages round the original village centre, the present-day Dam square. It was awarded its city charter in about 1300, and was annexed by William III to the county of Holland in 1317.

In 1345, following a miracle in which a Eucharistic host was left undamaged in a fire, Amsterdam became a place of pilgrimage. In 1428 the town, together with the county of Holland, passed into the hands of the Duke of Burgundy, Philip the Good.

The imperial crown shown on the city's coat of arms was granted in 1489 by Emperor Maximilian for the support given by the city to the Burgundian-Austrian monarchs.

The beginning of prosperity – A period of great affluence began in the late 16C. After Antwerp had been pillaged by the Spanish in 1576, the town's rich merchants took refuge in Amsterdam, bringing their diamond industry with them. Once Amsterdam had been freed from Spanish rule by the Union of Utrecht in 1579, the town became very prosperous, not least because of the large-scale influx of immigrants.

Later, at the end of the 16C, the Marranos arrived from Spain and Portugal; these were Jews who had been forcibly converted to Catholicism but continued to practise their own religion in secret. The authorities granted them extensive privileges in order to encourage their trading activities.

The Golden Age (17C) – This century marked the height of Amsterdam's powers. Following in the wake of the Portuguese, the Dutch began a period of overseas expansion, and only a few years later their sailing ships were trading all over the Far East. In 1602 they founded the East India Company (Verenigde Oostindische Compagnie, or VOC), followed in 1621 by the West India Company. A Dutch settlement was established at Nieuw Amsterdam; this was later renamed New York by the British.

The Wisselbank, created in 1609, was one of Europe's first banks, and the Stock Exchange was built between 1608 and 1611 by Hendrick de Keyser.

In 1610 it was decided to build the three main canals, the Herengracht, Keizersgracht and Prinsengracht, and these were soon lined with the mansions of wealthy merchants. The town was surrounded with a high wall on which a number of windmills were built.

Rembrandt, who was born in Leiden, came to live in Amsterdam in 1630, and was buried in the Westerkerk in 1669.

In 1648, when the Treaty of Münster ended the Eighty Years War with Spain, the independence of the United Provinces was officially recognised.

Amsterdam in winter

The growth of navigation led to an increased demand for maps and globes, and their manufacture became one of Amsterdam's specialities. The city acquired a leading reputation in this area, partly as a result of the work of famous geographers such as Hondius, who published a new edition of Mercator's famous atlas in 1605.

The Revocation of the Edict of Nantes in France in 1685 resulted in the arrival of a large number of Huguenots, who contributed to the city's prosperity. By the end of the 17C, however, Dutch maritime power was on the decline, as was textile manufacturing.

French occupation – Such was Amsterdam's accumulated wealth that for a long time it withstood the effects of the economic decline of the 18C. Although the city had contrived to repel an attack by Louis XIV's troops in 1672 by opening the locks which protected it, it could do nothing in 1795 against Pichegru's army. In 1806, Napoleon made his brother, Louis Bonaparte, King of Holland. Louis settled in Amsterdam, which became the capital of the kingdom.

The country became a part of France in 1810, and was decreed by Napoleon to be the third city of the French Empire and seat of the local government of the Zuiderzee *département*. However, Amsterdam was seriously hit by Napoleon's blockade of Britain, the Continental System, which ruined its trade.

In November 1813, the population revolted and recognised the Prince of Orange, William I, as their sovereign on 2 December.

Economic reawakening – It was only in the second half of the 19C that the city emerged from a long period of economic lethargy. The city walls were demolished in the 19C, though the Singelgracht still marks the boundary of the city centre. The opening of the Noordzeekanaal in 1876 provided a major boost to overseas trade, and the Centraal Station was built in 1889. The diamond industry also began to flourish again.

Amsterdam in the 20C – In 1903 the new Stock Exchange by **Berlage** was completed, marking the beginning of a new era of architecture.

Shortly before the First World War, the city began expanding and new suburbs were built. The **Amsterdam School** of architecture developed a new style of building, exemplified by the Scheepvaarthuis, mainly after the First World War. The central figure of this movement was **Michel de Klerk**. He, along with **Peter Kramer** and **JM van der Mey**, designed a great deal of local authority housing, particularly to the south of **Sarphatipark** and to the west of **Spaarndammerstraat** *(illustration: see Introduction, Art)*. They tried to break the monotony of façades by using asymmetry and differences in level, and to reduce the severity of straight lines by introducing sections of curving walls.

The last war hit the city badly. Under the five-year German occupation, nearly 80 000 Jews were deported to concentration camps; only 5 000 survived.

P. van Rie/EXPLORER

Post-war period – Since the war, Amsterdam has staged a magnificent recovery from its ordeal. It is now a major industrial city, part of the huge **Randstad conurbation**. Its industries include medical technology, metals, printing, food and of course tourism.

The city also hosts many international congresses.

The **RAI**, on Europaplein, is a large congress and exhibition centre, and the **World Trade Centre Amsterdam** near the Station Zuid was inaugurated in 1985.

The canal from Amsterdam to the Rhine (Amsterdam-Rijnkanaal), completed in 1952, has contributed to the development of the port and made it possible for ships to sail to countries in Eastern Europe.

The completion of a road tunnel under the IJ in 1968 improved communication between the old city and the area to the north of the port; the first Metro line was opened in 1976, and the rail link to Schiphol Airport was inaugurated in 1988.

The town has seen the development of such modern suburbs as **Buitenveldert** to the south and **Bijlmermeer** to the southeast. However, the housing problem remains acute, and the city is continuing to expand. Another typical feature of the city are the 2 400 picturesque houseboats lining 36km/22mi of quays. Amsterdam has two universities and numerous higher educational institutions.

ACCOMMODATION

The **Michelin Red Guide Benelux** gives a detailed list of hotels in each area. The following hotels have been selected for their facilities, location, character or value for money.

They have been divided into three categories:
– **Budget hotels**: Small, simple but comfortable hotels charging less than 150fl for a room.
– **Our selection**: Pleasant hotels with their own distinctive charm, costing between 195fl and 325fl per night.
– **Something special**: Very comfortable and well located luxury hotels with prices to match.

Hotels

BUDGET HOTELS

Amstel Botel – *Oosterdokskade 2-4, 1011 AE Amsterdam.* ☎ *(020) 626 42 47, Fax (020) 626 42 47. 176 rooms.* This former cruise ship is moored close to the Centraal Station, and is modern and comfortable.

Arena Budget Hotel – *'s Gravesandestraat 51, 1092 AA Amsterdam, ☎ (020) 694 74 44, Fax (020) 663 26 49. 600 beds.* This hotel is a bit like a youth hostel, with rooms sleeping two to eight people, all with their own shower and toilet. The hotel also has a café-restaurant with a terrace, a garden, and a concert venue.

Hotel Aalders – *Jan Luijkenstraat 13-15, 1071 CJ Amsterdam, ☎ (020) 662 01 16, Fax (020) 673 46 98. 53 rooms.* Close to the Stedelijk Museum, the Van Gogh Museum and the Rijksmuseum.

Nicolaas Witsen – *Nicolaas Witsenstraat 4, 1017 ZH Amsterdam, ☎ (020) 623 61 43, Fax (020) 620 51 13. 31 rooms.* Walking distance from the main museums and the busy area around Rembrandtplein and Leidseplein.

Hotel Piet Hein – *Vossiusstraat 53, 1071 AK Amsterdam, ☎ (020) 662 72 05, Fax (020) 662 15 26. 36 rooms.* Near Vondelpark and the major museums.

OUR SELECTION

Ambassade – *Herengracht 341, 1016 AZ Amsterdam, ☎ (020) 626 23 33, Fax (020) 624 53 21. 46 rooms.* This stylish hotel is superbly located in a group of 17C houses on the Herengracht, close to the tourist centre.

Canal House Hotel – *Keizersgracht 148, 1015 CX Amsterdam, ☎ (020) 622 51 82, Fax (020) 624 13 17. 26 rooms.* This very elegant 17C hotel is full of antiques; each room is furnished differently.

The dining room, Hotel Canal House

La Casaló – *Amsteldijk 862, 1079 LN Amsterdam, ☎ (020) 642 36 80, Fax (020) 644 74 09. 4 rooms.* Each of the rooms in this floating hotel is in a different style: Dutch, oriental, African and Caribbean. You can have breakfast outside in fine weather.

Toro – *Koningslaan 64, 1075 AG Amsterdam, ☎ (020) 673 72 23, Fax (020) 675 00 31. 22 rooms.* This early 20C villa on the edge of Vondelpark has a pleasant atmosphere and an attractive lake view from the terrace.

SOMETHING SPECIAL

American – *Leidsekade 97, 1017 PN Amsterdam, ☎ (020) 624 53 22, Fax (020) 625 32 36. 185 rooms.* This hotel was recently renovated; its magnificent Art Deco-style brasserie is frequented mainly by politicians and leading figures in the arts.

Amstel – *Prof. Tulpplein 1, 1018 GX Amsterdam, ☎ (020) 622 60 60, Fax (020) 622 58 08. 62 rooms.* This luxury hotel on the banks of the Amstel has one of the Netherlands' most famous restaurants, La Rive. It also boasts a fitness club complete with pool, jacuzzi, sauna, gymnasium and steam room.

Europe – *Nieuwe Doelenstraat 2, 1012 CP Amsterdam, ☎ (020) 531 17 77, Fax (020) 531 17 78. 96 rooms.* This famous hotel is close to the historic centre of Amsterdam. The Excelsior restaurant, known for its outstanding wine cellar, has a unique view of the Amstel. The hotel also has a heated indoor pool, a solarium and a fitness club.

Pulitzer – *Prinsengracht 315-331, 1016 GZ Amsterdam*, ☎ *(020) 523 52 35, Fax (020) 626 26 46. 230 rooms*. This magnificent hotel was created from 24 17C and 18C houses. It has a restaurant, De Goudsbloem, and a piano bar and café.

The Grand – *Oudezijds Voorburgwal 197, 1012 EX Amsterdam*, ☎ *(020) 555 31 11, Fax (020) 555 32 22. 155 rooms*. The former Prinsenhof has been superbly restored, and the luxurious Art Deco lounges attract an upmarket clientele.

Youth hostels

Non-members can stay in youth hostels on payment of a supplement, and there is no age limit.

Stadsdoelen NJHC – *Kloveniersburgwal 97, 1011 KB Amsterdam*, ☎ *(020) 624 68 32. 184 beds*. Right by the red-light district.

Vondelpark NJHC – *Zandpad 5, 1054 GA Amsterdam*, ☎ *(020) 589 89 99. 475 beds*. The busiest and best-located youth hostel.

EATING OUT

The capital offers a huge variety of eating experiences. The following restaurants have been selected for their food, decor and/or distinctive setting. The **Michelin Red Guide Benelux** contains a larger selection of restaurants, with a gastronomical emphasis.

BUDGET RESTAURANTS

De Rode Leeuw (Hotel Amsterdam) – *Damrak 93*, ☎ *(020) 555 06 66*. Brasserie on the busy Damstraat, serving Dutch specialities such as kapucijners, kidney beans served with bacon and onion.

Haesje Claes – *Spuistraat 275*, ☎ *(020) 624 99 98*. Simple food, generous portions, and excellent value for money.

Indrapura – *Rembrandtsplein 42*, ☎ *(020) 623 73 29*. Indonesian.

Kantijl & De Tijger – *Spuistraat 291-293*, ☎ *(020) 620 30 74*. Indonesian.

Tom Yam – *Staalstraat 22*, ☎ *(020) 622 95 33*. Thai cuisine.

OUR SELECTION

Bordewijk – *Noordermarkt 7*, ☎ *(020) 624 38 99*. Open evenings only. Trendy restaurant in the Jordaan serving contemporary cuisine.

De Gouden Reaal – *Zandhoek 14*, ☎ *(020) 623 38 83*. Superbly located restaurant on the old harbour; a weekly changing menu of French local dishes.

De Vijff Vliegen – *Spuistraat 294-302*, ☎ *(020) 624 83 69*. Dutch cooking in an atmospheric, typically Amsterdam setting; a jumble of little rooms, beautifully decorated in 17C style.

Le Garage – *Ruysdaelstraat 54*, ☎ *(020) 679 71 76*. Modern brasserie with an arty atmosphere and international clientele. The owner has a cooking programme on Dutch television.

In de Waag – *Nieuwmarkt 4*, ☎ *(020) 557 98 44*. This restaurant is in the city's historic weigh house (*waag*). The menu emphasises fish from the IJsselmeer, and there is also a wine bar. You can eat out on the large terrace in summer.

Sea Palace – *Oosterdokskade 8*, ☎ *(020) 626 47 77*. Floating oriental restaurant with a great view of Amsterdam.

OUT AND ABOUT IN AMSTERDAM

Amsterdam is believed to have around 1 000 cafés, renowned for their friendly and cosy atmosphere. Some serve snacks and simple meals.
The area around **Leidseplein** and Rembrandtsplein is particularly busy in the evenings. The Stadsschouwburg, or municipal theatre, is located on the former; the area also has a wealth of small theatres, cafés, cinemas and discos, as well as the Holland Casino. **Rembrandtsplein** is mainly known for its restaurants, large terrace cafés and clubs.

Drinking

BROWN CAFÉS

Brown cafés are a typically Dutch phenomenon, so named because of their nicotine-stained ceilings and wooden interiors. They are often not very large, and so tend to get crowded quickly. The most authentic brown cafés are in the city centre and the Jordàan.

Café Hoppe – *Spui 18-20*. A meeting place for writers, journalists and other denizens of the literary world; in summer, customers also spill out onto the pavement.

De Admiraal – *Herengracht 563*. This café makes its own gin in one of Amsterdam's oldest distilleries.

't Papeneiland – *Prinsengracht 2*. This is one of the city's most romantic brown cafés, with Delft tile decoration, an old-fashioned stove and a delightful waterside location.

't Smalle – *Egelantiersgracht 12*. A tiny café with a terrace overlooking the canal.

PROEFLOKALEN

Proeflokalen are a relic of the 17C, when merchants came to sample drinks being sold by importers; *proeflokaal* simply means tasting place. Today, you can try and buy gin and other spirits here.

De Drie Fleschjes – *Gravenstraat 18*. This *proeflokaal* is always pleasantly busy, with a throng of people at the bar, and walls lined with carafes of exotically named drinks like *crème de roses*, *parfait amour* and *ratafia*.

The dining room, Hotel Canal House

Wynand Fockink – *Pijlsteeg 31 (near Dam); open daily from 3pm to 9pm.* Wynand Fockink offers a wide selection of gin and other local spirits, with the chance to try before you buy. There is also an attractive courtyard.

GRANDS CAFÉS

Café Américain – *Leidsekade 97 and Leidseplein 26*. An Amsterdam institution; despite its rather high prices, this wonderful brasserie is a must for lovers of Art Deco.

Café Dantzig – *Zwanenburgwal 15*. Large café with a terrace on the Amstel and a separate reading area. A good place to put your feet up after a visit to the Waterlooplein flea market.

Café Luxembourg – *Spui 22*. Actually somewhere part-way between a brown café and a grand café; at its best in the late morning, though it also serves a great breakfast.

De Jaren – *Nieuwe Doelenstraat 20-22*. This huge modern café is particularly popular with young locals; its delightful two-level terrace on the Amstel gets packed in fine weather.

De Kroon – *Rembrandtsplein 17*. This is an Amsterdam landmark, with a very varied clientèle. The room on the first floor is a sight in itself, and the terrace has an enjoyable view of the square.

BARS

Café de Sluijswacht – *Jodenbreestraat 1*. This cheerful little waterside café lies opposite the Rembrandthuis, and the terrace offers a view of the Oude Schans. Don't worry if you've had a glass or two and things look a little strange; it's the building that's leaning at an angle, not you.

De Prins – *Prinsengracht 124*. Pleasant café with terrace, right by the Anne Frankhuis.

Walem – *Keizersgracht 449*. Attractive designer interior with a garden at the back.

Morlang – *Keizersgracht 451*. Next door to Café Walem. An often busy place, with a youngish clientele and a scenic waterside terrace.

Oibibio – *Prins Hendrikkade 20-21*. This New Age café right by the Centraal Station is part of a whole complex, including a shop, a tea garden, a vegetarian restaurant, a beauty salon, a concert venue and even a sauna.

VOCafé in de Schreierstoren – *Prins Hendrikkade 94-95*. This café has two rooms, one furnished with antiques and the other used as a reading room. It also has two terraces, one beside the water.

COFFEE SHOPS

Although you can actually go into a coffee shop just for a drink, their main purpose is to sell legal soft drugs such as hashish and marijuana.

Night-life

What's on in Amsterdam is published every three weeks, and gives full listings of music, dance, theatre and other events. It is available in VVV tourist offices and some bookshops.

You can book tickets direct or through **VVV Theatre Ticket Service** (Centraal Station, Leidseplein or Stadionplein) or **Amsterdamse Uit Buro** (AUB), *Leidseplein 26, Amsterdam,* ☎ *(020) 621 12 11, Mondays to Saturdays 10am to 6pm.*

Clubs – **Escape**, *Rembrandtsplein 11*, is Amsterdam's biggest disco; **iT**, *Amstelstraat 24*, is an extravagant venue with go-go girls, drag queens, and special gay evenings.

Casino – **Holland Casino**, *Max Euweplein 64*, ☎ *(020) 620 10 06*.

Jazz, rock, pop concerts – **Arena Stadium**, *Arena Boulevard 3*, ☎ *(020) 679 04 35*, performances by big international names; **Bimhuis**, *Oude Schans 73*, ☎ *(020) 623 13 61*, a must for jazz lovers; **De Melkweg**, *Lijnbaansgracht 234*, ☎ *(020) 624 84 92*, concerts and dance nights in an old milk factory; **Paradiso**, *Weteringschans 6*, ☎ *(020) 626 45 21*, dancing and rock concerts in a former church.

Classical music and opera – **Koninklijk Theater Carré**, *Amstel 115-125*, ☎ *(020) 625 52 25*, circus, variety, musicals; **Muziektheater (Stopera)**, *Waterlooplein 22*, ☎ *(020) 625 54 55*, performances by the Nederlandse Opera, the Nationale Ballet and the Nederlands Dans Theater; **Stadsschouwburg**, *Leidseplein 26*, ☎ *(020) 624 23 11*; **Beurs van Berlage**, *Damrak 213*, ☎ *(020) 627 04 66*, concerts by the Netherlands Philharmonic Orchestra and others; **Concertgebouw**, *Concertgebouwplein 2-6*, ☎ *(020) 671 83 54*, home of the world-famous Royal Concertgebouw Orchestra; **Felix Meritis**, *Keizersgracht 324*, ☎ *(020) 623 13 11*, classical concerts in a magnificent 18C auditorium.

Shopping

Most shops are closed on Monday mornings. Many, particularly in the city centre, are open until 9pm on Thursdays.

Department stores and shopping centres – **De Bijenkorf**, *Damrak 1*, department store; **Magna Plaza Center**, *Nieuwezijds Voorburgwal 182*, an upmarket indoor shopping centre with some 40 shops; **Metz & Co**, *corner of Keizersgracht and Leidsestraat*, design, gifts etc; **Vroom and Dreesmann**, department store, *Kalverstraat 201*.

Fashion – There are plenty of exclusive and trendy fashion stores, luxury shoe shops and jewellers in the **Museum District**, and particularly in **PC Hooftstraat** and **Van Baerlesstraat**. The pedestrianised **Kalverstraat** and Nieuwendijk have many more down-to-earth clothes shops.

Diamond factories – Ten of these are open to the public. Information from the VVV, ☎ *(06) 340 340 66*.

Antiques – Most of the antique shops are located around the main canal area (Singel, Herengracht, Keizersgracht and Prinsengracht), and more especially in **Spiegelstraat**, **Nieuwe Spiegelstraat** and **Kerkstraat**.

Markets

Even if you don't buy anything, the markets are a great place for people-watching.

Albert Cuypmarkt – *Albert Cuypstraat; Mondays to Saturdays, 9.30am to 5pm; general goods.*

Flower market – *Singel, between Muntplein and Koningsplein; Mondays to Saturdays, 9.30am to 5pm.*

Book market – *Oudeman-huispoort, Mondays and Saturdays, 10am to 4pm; Spui, Fridays, 10am to 6pm.*

Flea market – *Water-looplein; Mondays to Saturdays, 9am to 5pm.*

Antiques market – *Nieuw-markt; May to September, Sundays, 9am to 5pm.*

Indoor flea market – *Looiersgracht 38, Saturdays and Sundays, 11am to 5pm.*

The dining room, Hotel Canal House

PRACTICAL INFORMATION

General information – The VVV tourist office has branches in and opposite the **Centraal Station**, on the corner of **Leidseplein** and **Leidsestraat**, on **Stadionplein**, next to **Amstel Station** and at **Schiphol**. These are all open daily, ☎ (0900) 400 40 40; their website is at www.noord-holland-tourist.nl.

Parking – Parking is very difficult and expensive in Amsterdam, and is free only after 11pm. If you break the rules, you risk getting ticketed or even clamped; in the latter case, call the **clamping assistance** line on ☎ (020) 620 37 50. You can avoid all these problems by buying a daily parking permit from your hotel or using one of the (equally expensive) **multi-storey car parks**.
There is free parking at the **park and ride centres** on the outskirts of the city, though their isolated location means that parking here at night is not recommended.

Public transport – Information and tickets, including one-day travel cards and strippenkaarten (strips of tickets), are available from the VVV tourist office. The **Circle-Amsterdam Ticket** is valid for one to nine days and allows unlimited use of trams (including express services), buses and the metro. The **Circle-tram** is particularly useful, as it serves most of the main sights and hotels.

Alternative transport – Renting a **bicycle** ⊘ is definitely the best way of getting around and avoiding parking problems.
Canal bikes ⊘ are available for hire in various places, and are an ideal means of transport if you're not in a hurry.
The **Museum Boat** ⊘ follows a circular route from the Centraal Station and stops near all the main museums.

Events – Amsterdam has a constant succession of festivals and similar events (*see Calendar of events, for dates and phone numbers, or contact the VVV*). They include the **Holland Festival**, the **open-air theatre** season in **Vondelpark**, the **Prinsengracht Concert**, the **Bloemencorso** or flower parade from **Aalsmeer to Amsterdam**, and the **official entry of Santa Claus** into the city.
A number of important annual trade fairs take place at the **RAI** exhibition and conference centre.

G. Sioen/CEDRI

If you've still got time, go to...

The following sites are marked on the town plans; details are given in the Michelin Green Guide Amsterdam.

NIEUWE ZIJDE

Sexmuseum Amsterdam Venustempel

OUDE ZIJDE

Hash Marihuana Museum – Tattoo Museum
Koffie- en Theemuseum – Prinsenhof

THE CANALS

Amstelkerk – De Duif

De Appel – De Krijtberg
Multatuli-Museum – Woonbootmuseum
Torensluis – West-Indisch Huis
Leidsegracht

MUSEUM DISTRICT

Vondelkerk

JORDAAN

Elandsgracht – Lauriergracht – Lindengracht
Theo Thijssen Museum

PLANTAGE

De Gooyer Windmill – Verzetsmuseum

THE PORT

Haarlemmerpoort – Java-Eiland
Open Haven Museum – Vereniging Museumhaven Amsterdam
Werf 't Kromhout

PIJP

Gemeentearchief Amsterdam

OUTSKIRTS

Amstelstation – Amsterdam Arena – Rembrandt Tower
Bezoekerscentrum het Bosmuseum – Elektrische Museumtramlijn
Amsterdam
Van Leers office building – Peter Stuyvesant Stichting

OUDERKERK AAN DE AMSTEL

Oudheidkamer
Portuguese-Israeli Cemetery – Sint-Urbanuskerk

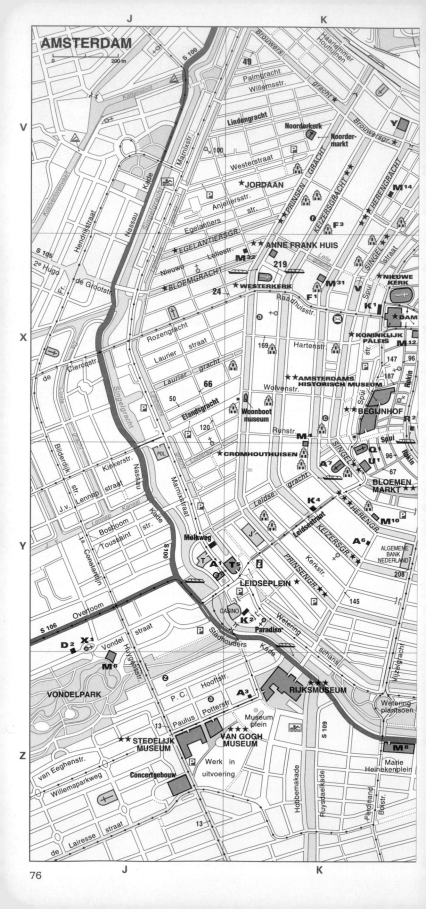

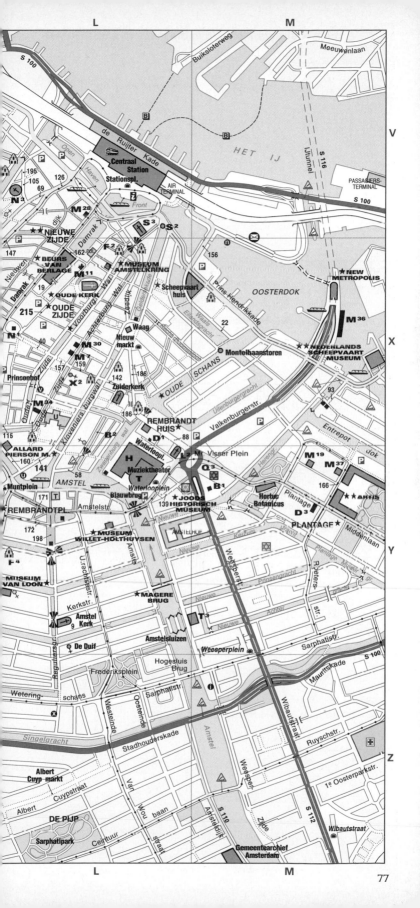

Index of streets included in the maps of AMSTERDAM

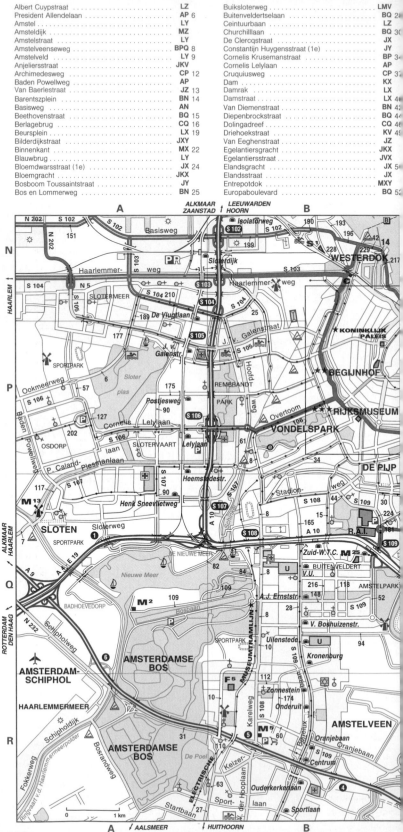

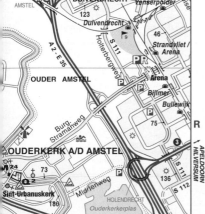

SIGHTSEEING WITH AMSTERDAM STREET MAPS

(M) = See **Museums**   (T) = See **Theatres**

★ OLD AMSTERDAM

★ Nieuwe Zijde

Centraal Station – The huge central station on three artificial islands in the River IJ aroused great controversy when it was built between 1881 and 1889, mainly because it blocked off the view of the port. Designed by the architects PJH Cuypers and AL van Gendt, it is now one of the city's best-known buildings.

★ **Beurs (Commodities Exchange)** – Built between 1897 and 1903, this is the principal work of **Berlage**, the ardent functionalist and pioneer of modern architecture in the Netherlands. It has a simple brick exterior, and inside, the open steel framework supports a glass roof.
Since 1987, it has been used as a cultural centre for exhibitions, conferences and concerts. The **Beurs van Berlage Museum** ⊙ contains a small permanent exhibition dealing mainly with the construction of this distinctive building.
The 1913 **Stock Exchange** is also on Beursplein.

★ **Dam** – The Dam, Amsterdam's main square, is at the junction of the two large central thoroughfares, Damrak and Rokin, on the site of the dam across the Amstel. Overlooking this very busy square are the Royal Palace and the Nieuwe Kerk.
The **Nationaal Monument**, built in 1956 by the sculptor Raedeker, symbolises humanity's suffering in times of war and has become a popular meeting place. The oldest building in the square is the **De Wildeman café** at no 11; this has a charming red-brick façade dating from 1632.

★ **Koninklijk Paleis** (Royal Palace) ⊙ – In 1648, Jacob van Campen began building a new town hall to replace the old Gothic one destroyed by fire in 1652 and depicted in a painting by Saenredam. The town hall became the Royal Palace in 1808 during the reign of Louis Bonaparte.
It is an imposing classical building, square in shape, and was built on 13 659 wooden piles. The east and west façades are topped by tympana carved by Artus I Quellin, of Antwerp, who also decorated the interior.
On the ground floor is the court of justice **(Vierschaar)** where the death sentence was pronounced. The judges sat on a marble bench, above which were marble reliefs depicting the qualities expected of them: charity, wisdom and justice. The public could watch the proceedings through grilles.

81

In the citizens' room **(Burgerzaal)** on the first floor, the floor decoration depicts th
eastern and western hemispheres and the northern night sky. There is also
famous sculpture by Artus I Quellin of Atlas holding the celestial globe on hi
shoulders. It was in the Council Room **(Schepenzaal)** that Queen Juliana abdicate
in 1980. The mantel painting of Moses descending from Mount Sinai is b
Ferdinand Bol, one of Rembrandt's pupils.

★ **Nieuwe Kerk** ⊘ – The Protestant New Church or Church of St Catherine is th
national church of the Netherlands. It is here that the country's sovereigns ar
crowned; Queen Wilhelmina's coronation was held here on 6 September 1898
that of her daughter Juliana 50 years later to the day, and Queen Beatrix o
30 April 1980.
This lovely Late Gothic building was pillaged and gutted by fire several times
After the fire in 1645 its tower, designed by Jacob van Campen, remaine
unfinished.
The church has a wooden vault, a mahogany **pulpit**★ carved by Vinckenbrink in th
17C, and a copper chancel screen which is one of the masterpieces of Johanne
Lutma, Amsterdam's famous gold and silversmith. The main organ case (c 1650
was designed by Van Campen.
The church contains the tombs of several Dutch admirals, including that of Michie
de Ruyter, the commander of the fleet in the Second and Third Anglo-Dutch Wars
by the Belgian sculptor Rombout Verhulst. The poet Vondel and the famou
bell-founders François and Pierre Hemony were also buried here, but their grave
have been removed.
The Nieuwe Kerk is also used for major **temporary exhibitions**.

Magna Plaza – *Nieuwezijds Voorburgwal 182*. Behind the Koninklijk Paleis is
former post office designed by CG Peters in 1899. This was converted in 199
into an upmarket shopping centre with some 40 stores.

Madame Tussaud Scenerama ⊘ – Here, modern technology including audic
animatronics has led to the creation of a fascinating museum of life during th
Golden Age, a time of great artistic activity and economic prosperity, a
demonstrated by the scenes depicting Rembrandt, Vermeer and Jan Steen. Ther
is also a fine **revolving cylindrical model** of 17C Amsterdam. The exhibition ends wit
many well-known figures from the Netherlands and abroad, including member
of the Dutch royal family, politicians, and sportsmen and women.

Kalverstraat – This very busy pedestrian precinct is the most important shoppin
street in Amsterdam.

★★ **Amsterdams Historisch Museum** ⊘ – *Access via Kalverstraat 62, Sint-Luciër
steeg 27 or Gedempte Begijnensloot. A useful brochure and map are included i
the price of entry.*
In this museum, housed in a 15C former orphanage, Amsterdam's history i
chronicled in paintings, sculptures, and documents.
Sint-Luciënsteeg is named after the Convent of St Lucy that preceded the orphanage
Access to the buildings is through a small gateway surmounted by the city's coa
of arms. On the left is the boys' playground; the cubby-holes where they used t
keep their belongings are in the east wing. Opposite, a building in the classica
style hosts temporary exhibitions. On one wall there is a large collection o
picturesque **façade-stones** from the city's old houses, and there is also a free **galler
of schutterstukken**★, group portraits of companies of the civic guard. The entranc
to the museum is through the second courtyard, formerly reserved for the gir
orphans.

Follow the rooms in numerical order; these are spread over several floors.

In the first room, an illuminated map shows the city's remarkable expansion. Th
city was built on sand, erected a town hall and began to trade with the rest of th
world. In 1345 a miracle made it a centre of pilgrimage, and then Amsterdam wa
subjected to Spanish rule. During this period it began to extend its influenc
around the world. At its peak, it built a new town hall, the present Royal Palace
The city began attracting many artists, and large numbers of buildings wer
constructed, including several churches.
Although the town had become wealthy, it did not forget those living in poverty
charitable institutions abounded, and their regents, or governors, liked havin
their portraits painted.
In the 18C, despite strong competition from foreign countries, Amsterdam sti
occupied a prominent position in the world of the arts.
In 1795 the French arrived; the towns lost their independence but the country wa
unified. During the 20C, Amsterdam has remained extremely dynamic. Th
last rooms house collections of prints and various archeological finds. As yo
leave, visit the **17C Regents' Room** on the left, where the directors of the orphanag
met and which has been beautifully restored.

Enter the Begijnhof via the passage in the courtyard.

★ **Begijnhof** – The Beguinage is a haven of peace in the heart of the city. Founded in the 14C, it is one of the few such institutions remaining in the Netherlands (see **BREDA**). Beguines are women belonging to a lay sisterhood; although they take no vows, they devote themselves to religious life and wear a habit.

The tall 17C and 18C houses with small front gardens are arranged around an area of grass where the former church of the Beguines stands. This has belonged to the English Presbyterian community since 1607.

Nos 11, 19, 23 and 24 have beautiful sculpted façade-stones, while the tall and elegant house at no 26 was that of the mother superior of the Beguinage. At nos 29-31 there is a hidden Catholic chapel, built by the Beguines in 1665. Not far away is the city's oldest house, no 34, dating from the 15C and with a wooden **façade**★; note the large number of façade-stones incorporated into the wall of the courtyard on the left.

The Bequinage

Rokin – This dock is situated at the far end of the Amstel, the continuation having been filled in. At the far end of the dock stands an **equestrian statue** of Queen Wilhelmina by Theresia van der Pant.

Langebrugsteeg leads into Amsterdam's oldest quarter, around which the city developed.

As you cross Oudezijds Voorburgwal, you will see the old houses and warehouses which line this canal.

★ Oude Zijde

Sint-Nicolaaskerk – This neo-Renaissance-style Catholic church very close to the Centraal Station was designed by AC Bleys.

Schreierstoren – This defensive tower, known as the "weeping tower", formed part of the city wall. Legend has it that sailors' wives came to say goodbye to their husbands; hence the name.

There is a bronze plaque commemorating the Englishman, **Henry Hudson**, who discovered the river which bears his name while working for the Dutch East India Company in 1609.

Huis Leeuwenburg – *14 Oudezijds Voorburgwal*. This picturesque 17C house has a stepped gable of rust-coloured brick and lattice windows with red shutters. A carved façade-stone depicts a fortified castle sheltering a lion.

From the bridge over the lock where the two canals meet, there is an attractive **view**★: on one side, the Oudezijds Kolk with its old houses rising from the water, and the dome of the Catholic church of St Nicholas (1887), and on the other side the Oudezijds Voorburgwal, with its lovely series of old façades and the Oude Kerk in the distance.

★ **Museum Amstelkring Ons' Lieve Heer op Solder** (Amstelkring Museum of Our Lord in the Attic) ⊘ – After the Union of Utrecht in 1579, when the Catholics were driven out of their churches by the Reformation, they were forced to celebrate mass in private houses. This secret chapel fitted out in the attics of three houses was used

The hall, Amstelkring Museum
of Our Lord in the Attic

for Catholic worship from 1663 until the construction of the new Sint-Nicolaaskerk in 1887, whereupon it was converted into a museum for the Amstelkring Foundation. Services and concerts are sometimes held here.

The staircase leading to the 2nd floor passes in front of the hall, which is in pure 17C Amsterdam style, and the abbot's room with a box bed. The **church**, whose two superimposed galleries occupy the third and fourth floors of the houses, has interesting 18C furnishings. In one room, on the same floor as the confessional, there is an interesting exhibition of church silver, most of it from this secret chapel.

Opposite the museum, the gable of no 19 has enormous sculptures of dolphins on either side.

★ **Oude Kerk** ⊘ – The present Old Church, dedicated to St Nicholas, was built in the 14C. It is the oldest in the city. In the 16C the bell tower was topped by an elegant spire whose carillon was in part cast by François Hemony; there is an excellent **view★★** from here.

The church's interior was seriously damaged by the Iconoclasts, but its 16C Lady Chapel still has three elegant 16C **stained-glass windows★**. The **organ★** above the entrance to the nave was made in 1724 by Jan Westerman. In 1642 Rembrandt's wife Saskia was buried here, and the church is the final resting place of many famous people, including the painter Pieter Aertsen, the writer Roemer Visscher, the architects Justus and Philips Vingboons and the composer JP Sweelinck. The church hosts various cultural events, such as organ recitals, exhibitions and theatre performances.

The Walletjes – *(Oudezijds Achterburgwal, Oudezijds Voorburgwal, Trompetter steeg etc)*. This area in the middle of the tourist centre is notorious as Amsterdam's **red-light district**. It has many beautiful old houses along the narrow streets.

Nieuwmarkt – Amsterdam's oldest market square is between the Chinese district *(Zeedijk and the surrounding area)* and the red-light district.

Waag or St.-Anthoniespoort – This imposing fortified gateway (1488), flanked by towers and turrets, was converted into a weigh-house *(waag)* in 1617 and restored in 1996. The top floor served as an anatomy theatre, where surgeons and their students could attend public dissections, often on the corpses of criminals who had been condemned to death. Rembrandt's famous painting, *The Anatomical Lesson of Dr Deigman* (now in the Amsterdams Historisch Museum), documents the lecture given by Dr Deigman in 1656. The building also has a café and restaurant.

Trippenhuis – *Kloveniersburgwal no 29*. This elegant Classical edifice was built between 1660 and 1664 by Justus Vingboons for the Trip brothers, who were cannon manufacturers; the chimneys are in the shape of mortars.

Oudemanhuispoort – A covered passage between Kloveniersburgwal and Oudez ijds Achterburgwal, once the site of a home for elderly men *(oudemanhuis)*, now a book market.

Universiteitsmuseum de Agnietenkapel – *Oudezijds Voorburgwal 231*. Near the Oudemanhuispoort, the **Agnietenpoort** leads to this chapel, once the home of the Athenaeum Illustre (illustrious college) of 1632, a predecessor of the university. The buildings are currently being used by the university, and temporary exhibitions are held here.

Grimburgwal – This canal was built in the early 14C and marked the southern boundary of the city. The beautiful **Huis op de Drie Grachten**★ (House on the Three Canals), dating from 1609, stands at the confluence of the Oudezijds Voorburgwal, the Oudezijds Achterburgwal and the Grimburgwal.

★ **Allard Pierson Museum** ⊘ – This is the archeological museum of Amsterdam University, and contains a remarkable collection of antiquities from Egypt, the Middle East, Cyprus, Greece, Etruria and the Roman world.

First floor – This section contains items from Egypt (such as **funerary masks**★, sculptures and Coptic textiles), the Middle East (Iranian pottery and jewellery) and archeological finds from Syria, Anatolia, Palestine and Mesopotamia (including cylinder-seals and cuneiform writings).

Second floor – This is devoted to Greece, Etruria and the Roman Empire. The collection includes the **Amsterdam Kouros**★ (c 590 BC), ceramics (including **red-figure jars**★), a Roman sarcophagus (c AD 300) and various items of Etruscan earthenware and sculpture.

Between the flower market★★ and Rembrandtsplein★

Muntplein – This busy square is dominated by the Mint Tower, **Munttoren**. The tower, the remains of a 17C gateway, has a spire which was added by Hendrick de Keyser and which has a **carillon** ⊘. In 1672, during the war against France, money was minted here.

★ **Bloemenmarkt (Flower Market)** – The stalls in this highly picturesque market beside the Singel are supplied by barges. Some of the stalls are on the barges themselves, transforming them into floating greenhouses.

Tuschinskitheater – *Reguliersbreestraat 26-8*. This beautiful cinema in genuine Art Deco style was built in 1921 by HL de Jong. Note particularly the expressive **front façade**, the very beautiful **carpet** in the foyer, and the overwhelming **interior**★ of the Tuschinski 1 auditorium.

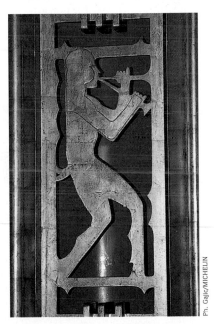

Tuschinskitheater – Art Deco detail

★ **Rembrandtsplein** – This square is a popular destination for local people out for an evening stroll. There are many large cafés around the square, with its statue of Rembrandt by Royer (1852).

Thorbeckeplein – With its many nightclubs, this square is very busy in the evenings.

Rondom and Waterlooplein

Waterlooplein – On this large square, which has a **violin market** and an **antiques market**, stands the **Mozes-en Aäronkerk**. This Catholic church is used for exhibitions, concerts and performances. The southern part of the square is occupied by the highly controversial Stopera (from *stadhuis* and *opera*). This modern complex includes the **Muziektheater** and the **Stadhuis**, or city hall, finished in 1986 and 1988 respectively. Both were designed by the Austrian architect Wilhelm Holzbauer and the Dutchman Cees Dam. The 1 689-seat theatre is home to the Nederlandse Opera and the Nationale Ballet, and the foyer provides a lovely view of the Amstel and its bridges.

The black marble **monument** standing in front of the city hall at the corner of the Amstel and the Zwanenburgwal commemorates the resistance by Jewish citizens who lost their lives during the Second World War.

★ **Museum Het Rembrandthuis** ⊘ – *Jodenbreestraat 4-6*. Rembrandt's house is situated at the heart of the old Jewish quarter. Rembrandt bought it in 1639 for 13 000 guilders, payable over six years, and lived here until he was evicted by his creditors in 1659. The interior is currently being restored to its original 17C condition.

Ph. Gajic/MICHELIN

The house has a collection of prints and other works by the artist *(illustration: s⟨ Admission times and charges)*. The new wing has a rotating exhibition of abo⟨ 250 etchings, giving a unique and almost complete overview of his work in th⟨ medium. Some of Rembrandt's drawings are also on display, and there are a fe⟨ canvases by one of his teachers, Pieter Lastman, as well as works by his pupi⟨ and predecessors.

★ **Oude Schans** – The **Montelbaanstoren** stands on this attractive canal. This towe⟨ along with the Sint-Anthoniespoort, was part of the city walls in the 16C.

Zuiderkerk ⊘ – The first church built in Amsterdam after the Reformation wa⟨ designed by Hendrick de Keyser and constructed between 1603 and 1611; it ⟨ flanked by a **tower**★ (1614). At present, the church is used to house urban plannir⟨ exhibitions.

Further along, at no 69 St-Antoniesbreestraat, is the beautiful **Huis de Pinto**, whic⟨ was built c 1600 and once belonged to a rich Jewish merchant. It is now a publ⟨ library.

★ **Joods Historisch Museum** ⊘ – The Museum of Jewish History is housed in ⟨ complex of four synagogues on Jonas Daniël Meijerplein. The first one on the si⟨ was the Grote Synagoge or Grote Sjoel, built in 1671, but as the congregatio⟨ expanded new ones were built on neighbouring plots: the upstairs or Obbene Sjo⟨ in 1685, the third or Dritt Sjoel in 1700 and the new or Nieuwe Synagoge in 175⟨ The latter is recognisable by the Ionic columns at the entrance and by the dome⟨ roof.

The **Nieuwe Synagoge** examines different aspects of Jewish identity: religio⟨ Zionism, persecution and survival.

The **Grote Synagoge**★, with its white marble Holy Ark (1671), describes the Jewis⟨ year, its religious celebrations and the steps to adulthood. The display als⟨ includes Torah scrolls, shields, mantles, nine-branched candelabra and othe⟨ ceremonial objects. The renovation work brought to light a **mikveh**★, a bath use⟨ for ritual purification.

Portugese Synagoge ⊘ – This massive building, lit by tall windows, was built ⟨ 1675 by Elias Bouman as a place of worship for three Portuguese congregatio⟨ which had just united.

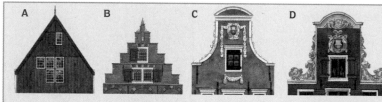

Gables

There are countless different forms of gables. Late medieval houses were made of wood, an had simple **pointed gables (A)**. Later on, they were built with pin- nacles or **crow steps (B)** *(see Huis Leeuwenburg above)*. A pitched roof was hidden behind the gable.

Later on, gables became taller, and **Dutch gables (C)** and **neck gables (D)** were used. These had triangular or cur- ved pediments, often elaborately sculpted on either side.

The finest houses had broader façades and a roof run- ning parallel with the street. The roof was hidden by a large pilaster gable ending in a triangular pediment or an **emblazoned balustrade crowned with statues and a coat of arms (E)**.

Finally, a large type of house developed with pilasters and a **triangular carved pediment (F)**. The façade was sometimes made of stone and decorated with gar- lands. The many warehouses mostly have a simple, undecorated **spout gable (G)**.

The interior remains as shown in Emmanuel de Witte's painting in the Rijksmuseum, with wide wooden barrel vaults supported by very high columns, galleries for the women, the Ark of the Covenant, and large **copper chandeliers** as the only decoration. There is no curtain (Parochet) in this synagogue, as this feature was unknown in the Jewish tradition of Spain and Portugal.

De dokwerker, the statue of a docker by Mari Andriessen in the square by the synagogue, commemorates the strike launched by the dockers on 25 February 1941 in protest against the deportation of Amsterdam's Jewish population.

Blauwbrug – The "blue bridge" is a copy of the Alexandre III Bridge in Paris; it has a view of the Muziektheater to the north, and the Magere Brug to the south.

★ **Magere Brug** – The "thin bridge" is a highly photogenic wooden drawbridge across the Amstel, dating from the 17C and still manually operated. It is attractively lit at night *(April to September)*. The wooden 17C **Amstelsluizen** or Amstel sluices refresh the water in the city's canals twice a week in winter and four times a week in summer. The large building to the east of the Magere Brug is the **Theater Carré**, dating from 1887, which offers a wide variety of entertainment. Several clock towers are visible from the approach ramps of the bridge, including that of the Zuiderkerk.

★ THE CANALS

The canals – Most of the houses which line the canals in the centre of the city were built in the 17C and 18C by wealthy merchants.
Although somewhat similar in appearance, with their narrow façades and front steps, they differ in the colours of their bricks – pink, blue, violet or grey – and in the way their gables are decorated. Beams with pulleys project over the pediments; the narrow staircases make it impossible to bring in furniture.

★ **Boat tours** ⊙ – A boat tour gives an excellent view of the most important canals as well as part of the port. The route varies according to which locks are open.

★ Singel

Nieuwe Kerk or Ronde Lutherse Kerk – The high-domed New Church, or Round Lutheran Church, was built on the Singel between 1668 and 1671. It is now a concert hall ⊙ and **conference centre**.
Nearby, at no 7, is Amsterdam's **narrowest house**.
The **flower market** *(see below)* is at the end of the Singel.

★ Herengracht

This is one of the main 17C canals where wealthy merchants came to live. The houses vie with one another in their rich decoration, and particularly that of their gables.

Number 168: Theatermuseum ⊙ – The theatre museum forms part of the Netherlands Theatre Institute, and is located in various houses along the Herengracht. No 168 was built in 1618 and converted by Philips Vingboons in 1638. It has a fine stone **neck gable**★, the oldest in Amsterdam, decorated with the coat of arms of the former owner, Michiel de Pauw.
The **interior**★, redesigned in the Louis XIV style in about 1730, is richly decorated with stucco, murals and ceiling paintings, many of them by **Jacob de Wit**. There is also an ornamental spiral **staircase** leading from the basement to the attic.

Ph. Gajic/MICHELIN

Staircase in the Theatermuseum

The museum's permanent display includes the famous miniature stage created by Hieronymus van Slingelandt, together with stage costumes, theatre posters and other items.

The **Huis Bartolotti**★ next door at no 170 was built by Hendrick de Keyser around 1617. Its wide brick façade, with a highly ornate gable, has a large number of ornamental white stone carvings.

★ **Starting at no 364: Cromhouthuizen** – Built by Philip Vingboons in 1662, this group forms a harmonious whole. The Classical-style façades are enhanced by more Baroque decoration (note the *oeil-de-boeuf* windows). One of them houses the **Bible Museum** ⊘.

Nos 386-394 – A lovely series of façades. At no 394, below a graceful gable, an attractive **façade-stone** depicts the four sons of Aymon, legendary figures from a heroic poem, mounted on their horse Bayard.

Gouden Bocht – The large, elegant houses on the second bend in the Herengracht are known collectively as the Golden Bend. In the 17C, this was the area favoured by wealthy Amsterdam citizens who could afford double-fronted houses; these are now mostly occupied by banks and consulates.

During the period when these houses were built, facades were becoming wider and although the new Classical style meant that pediments were flatter, they were still richly decorated. They had a coat of arms or allegorical scene in the middle with a balustrade on either side bearing flame ornaments or statues.

★ **No 475** *(on the opposite bank)* – This house with a stone façade was built by **Daniël Marot** and Jacob Husley and decorated by Jan van Logteren.

The ABN-AMRO Bank building on the corner of Vijzelstraat is by the architect **De Bazel**, a contemporary of Berlage.

No 497: Kattenkabinet ⊘ – The Cat Gallery, located in a beautiful 17C house, holds temporary exhibitions consisting mainly of works of art depicting cats.

★ **No 476** – This elegant mansion was built around 1740. It has a very fine façade with six Corinthian pillars and decorative festoons. The openwork attic above the main part of the building has a balustrade decorated with the owner's blazon and an eagle above.

No 502: Huis met de Kolommen – The House with the Columns was built in 1671 for a rich merchant of the Dutch East India Company, and altered in the 18C; the balcony supported by columns dates from this period. In 1927, it became the **mayor's official residence**, where distinguished guests are received.

★ **No 605: Museum Willet-Holthuysen** ⊘ – This mansion, built in approximately 1687, has a series of elegantly furnished rooms evoking the lifestyle of rich merchants of the time. There are also collections of pottery, glassware, gold and silver.

The **garden**★ has been restored to the original design of **Daniël Marot**.

★★ Keizersgracht

★ **No 123: Huis met de Hoofden** – This attractive restored brick house dates from 1624. Its façade is similar to that of the Huis Bartolotti *(see above)*, and is decorated with six sculpted heads of Roman gods; hence its name, House of the Heads.

★ **No 672: Museum Van Loon** ⊘ – This stately mansion was built between 1671 and 1672 by Adriaan Dortsman, and has been altered on various occasions since; it once belonged to the painter **Ferdinand Bol** (1616-80). It has a stairwell decorated in stucco with magnificent **banisters**★ from the second half of the 18C, and numerous portraits.

There is also a small Classical-style coach house in the lovely French-style **garden**★.

★★ Prinsengracht

★ **Westerkerk** ⊘ – *Illustration: see ABC of architecture.* This church was built between 1619 and 1631 by Pieter de Keyser, based on the plans of his father Hendrick. An important programme of restoration was carried out between 1985 and 1990, returning this brick and stone Renaissance-style building to its original colours.

The remarkable carillon in the 85m/280ft high **bell-tower**★★ dates from 1638 and is the work of the **Hemony brothers**. The tower is topped by the imperial crown commemorating Emperor **Maximilian of Austria**, who gave permission for it to be added to the city's coat of arms above the three crosses of St Andrew. The fine **view**★ from the top of the tower takes in the central canals and the Jordaan district.

The church **interior** is very plain; the nave has wooden barrel vaulting and the 12 chandeliers are copies of the original ones. The magnificent painted organ panels are the work of **Gerard de Lairesse** (1641-1711).

Rembrandt was buried here in 1669, one year after his son Titus, though the exact location of his tomb is not known.

Beside the church, at no 6 **Westermarkt**, stands the house where **Descartes** lived in 1634; this is commemorated by a stone on the front of the house.

The **Homomonument**, commemorating gay men and women who died in the Nazi concentration camps, is close to the apse of the Westerkerk.

** **Anne Frank Huis** ⊘ – This narrow building erected in 1635 extends back a considerable way, and has an extension behind it which was enlarged in 1740. It was here that **Anne Frank**'s father, a German Jew who emigrated in 1933, hid seven members of his family and friends in July 1942. They were betrayed, arrested and sent to Auschwitz in August 1944; only the father returned. The moving diary kept by his 13-year-old daughter was found in the house, and displays a rare sensitivity. The Anne Frank Foundation spreads her message of peace throughout the world.

A revolving bookcase reveals a secret passage which leads to the bare rooms where the family hid. As well as permanent exhibitions on Anne's life, and on war and anti-Semitism, there are temporary displays on current issues.

Reguliersgracht

From the bridge which crosses this canal, there is a lovely **view*** to the right of some of its seven bridges.

Continue onto Keizersgracht, where there is another attractive **view*** of a picturesque group of old houses.

Return to Herengracht.

From the bridge across the canal, there is another very scenic **view*** to the left and right.

* Leidseplein

This is possibly the liveliest square in Amsterdam. There are many theatres in the area, including the well known municipal theatre, the **Stadsschouwburg**, as well as restaurants and nightclubs. The **American Hotel**, dating from 1902, combines elements of Art Nouveau and the Amsterdam School, as well as a beautiful Art Deco café.

Max Euweplein is the home of the **Max Euwe Schaakcentrum** (chess centre) and the **Holland Casino**.

Further on, at no 6 Weteringschans, is the **Paradiso**, a church which the city has converted into a youth centre and experimental theatre.

Leidsestraat – This long and pleasant pedestrian street links Leidseplein to the city centre.

THE MUSEUM DISTRICT *allow one day minimum*

** Rijksmuseum ⊘

The famous national museum was founded by Louis Napoleon, the brother of Napoleon Bonaparte, in 1808. The present building was constructed between 1876 and 1885 by PJH Cuypers in a style combining neo-Gothic and neo-Renaissance features. It includes an exceptional collection of 15C to 17C paintings, including magnificent works by Rembrandt and Vermeer, and also has important departments of sculpture and applied arts, Dutch history, prints and Asiatic art.

15C to 17C paintings – *First floor, east wing; room numbers appear in brackets.* The collection of **Primitives** includes works by **Geertgen tot Sint-Jans** (201), whose *Adoration of the Magi* has a delightful landscape background; Jan Mostaert, whose painting of the same subject (202) is set amid an Italian Renaissance scene; the Master of Alkmaar, famous for his *Seven Works of Charity* (202); Jacob Cornelisz van Oostsanen, whose ornamental style is apparent in his triptych of the *Adoration of the Magi* (203), and Cornelis Engebrechtsz, an early Mannerist (204).

In the **Renaissance** section, **Lucas van Leyden**'s *Adoration of the Golden Calf* (204) shows great mastery of composition and an expressive and lively technique; **Jan van Scorel** depicts a *Mary Magdalene* (205) of very Italian elegance.

The art of Pieter Aertsen (206) is more realistic, while Antonio Moro's portraits show considerable restraint. Both Cornelis Cornelisz van Haarlem and Abraham Bloemaert are representatives of **Mannerism**. There is also a still-life with flowers by Velvet Brueghel as well as some lovely landscapes by the Antwerp painter, Joos de Momper.

In the **Golden Age**, painting styles varied a great deal. Hendrick Avercamp specialised in winter scenes, such as *Winter Landscape* (207). **Frans Hals** (209, 210) produced outstanding portraits such as that of *Isaac Massa and his Wife*, while the vivid and rapid brushwork of *The Merry Toper* is reminiscent of Impressionism.

RIJKSMUSEUM

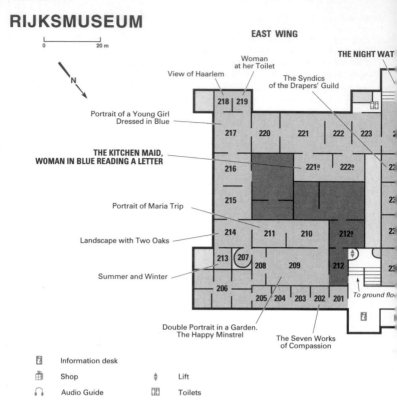

EAST WING

Information desk

Shop

Audio Guide

Lift

Toilets

Several rooms are devoted to the work of the great master **Rembrandt**. *The Stone Bridge* (211) is one of the few landscapes he painted, and dates from 1638.

It is interesting to compare the 1631 portrait of Rembrandt's mother meditatively reading the Bible (211) to the painting of a similar subject by his pupil Gerrit Dou, which is more austere in style.

Frans Hals' pupil Judith Leyster is represented by a genre piece, *The Serenade* (213).

Pieter Saenredam specialised in churches and other interiors, such as that of Amsterdam's old town hall.

There were numerous artists painting landscapes; these included Van Goyen, with his *Landscape with Two Oaks* (214), and Salomon van Ruysdael, who painted a *Landscape with Ferryboat* (214).

During this period, portraits were also very much in vogue; Rembrandt painted his portrait of the elegantly dressed *Maria Trip* (215) in around 1640, while his contemporary Ferdinand Bol produced the fine *Portrait of Elisabeth Bas* (215).

Paulus Potter chose to depict animals, while **Jan Steen** specialised in cheerful domestic scenes (*The Feast of St Nicholas*, 216).

Other leading landscape artists included **Jacob van Ruysdael** (*The Windmill at Wijk bij Duurstede*, 217, and *View of Haarlem*, 218) and Meindert Hobbema (*Watermill*, 217). Adriaen van Ostade was more interested in villagers and their daily lives (*Peasants in an Interior: The Skaters*, 218).

Philips Wouwerman (220) and Adam Pynacker (221) were two fine landscape painters. Also on display are some outstanding seascapes and naval battles by Willem van de Velde the Younger (220).

The four works (221a) by **Vermeer** are all masterpieces: *The Little Street* (c 1658), painted from the windows of his house; *The Milkmaid* (c 1658), pouring milk with a measured gesture, *Woman in Blue Reading a Letter* (c 1662), in luminous blue tones, and finally *The Love Letter* (c 1666).

Room 222a presents portraits by Terborch, a *Self-portrait with Pipe* by Gerrit Dou, and a sentimental scene by Metsu, *The Sick Child*.

Pieter de Hooch is famous for his geometric interiors (*The Pantry*, 222). Also in this room is *Girl at a Window: The Daydreamer* by Nicolaes Maes.

Room 224 contains Rembrandt's *The Militia Company of Captain Frans Banning Cocq and Lieutenant Willem van Ruytenburch*, known as **The Night Watch**. Commissioned by a company of the civic guard, this enormous group portrait was

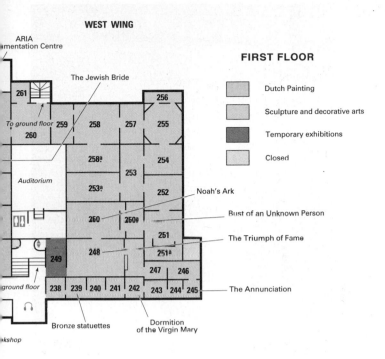

WEST WING

ARIA
mentation Centre

FIRST FLOOR

The Jewish Bride

- Dutch Painting
- Sculpture and decorative arts
- Temporary exhibitions
- Closed

261

To ground floor 259 258 257 255 256

260

258ª 254 253

Auditorium 253ª 252 — Noah's Ark

250 250ª — Bust of an Unknown Person

251 — The Triumph of Fame

248 251ª

249 247 246

ground floor 238 239 240 241 242 243 244 245 — The Annunciation

Bronze statuettes Dormition of the Virgin Mary

kshop

completed in 1642 and displayed in the company's headquarters in Kloveniers-burgwal, before being transferred to Amsterdam's town hall in 1715. At that time, it was made smaller by cutting large strips off the edges. During the Second World War, It was hidden in caves near Maastricht (see MAASTRICHT: Outskirts). It owes its name to the darkened varnish, which was cleaned in 1947, but the painting in fact depicts the company in broad daylight.

The guards are shown in great agitation, as though taken by surprise; the captain is giving the signal to depart, and some of the guards have their faces half hidden, resulting in a very original group portrait.

There are a number of details which add to the feeling of spontaneity: the little girl with a bird attached to her belt walking through the group, the barking dog, the dwarf running and the man with a helmet covered with leaves. Spots of bright colour offset the rather grey tones of the guards' uniforms: the bright yellow of the girl's and the lieutenant's costumes, the red outfit of the guard reloading his gun and the captain's red scarf.

The pictures from the **Italian School** include numerous Primitives, such as a remarkable Madonna of the Lily by Fra Angelico and a Mary Magdalene by Crivelli. There are some interesting portraits by the Florentine painter Piero di Cosimo and views of Venice by Guardi. Works from Spain include a lovely Virgin and Child by Murillo.

The Flemish paintings include two works by **Rubens**.

The Gallery of Honour (229-236) contains major paintings by Dutch masters from the second half of the 17C; the late works by Rembrandt are particularly noteworthy. The Portrait of Titus in a Monk's Habit dates from about 1600. The Self-Portrait as the Apostle Paul (1661) shows Rembrandt as a disillusioned old man (229), while the portrait of a couple known as The Jewish Bride (1668-69) is full of light and tenderness (229).

The Syndics, a masterpiece dating from 1662, shows the inspectors of the Drapers' Guild grouped behind a table with a warm red tablecloth. Although their expressions are serious, this portrait is full of life (230).

Room 231 has a work by Nicolaas Maes, a contemporary of Rembrandt: Old Woman at Prayer.

Another of his pupils who was greatly influenced by the master was Aert de Gelder (Portrait of Ernst van Beveren, 232).

Aelbert Cuyp was a very versatile landscape painter whose compositions featured shepherds, cattle and small human figures (234).

The Feast of St Nicholas by Jan Steen

Sculpture and Applied Arts – *First floor, ground floor and basement, west wing.* This important section takes up numerous rooms, and has a rich collection of furniture and works of art (sculpture, paintings, gold and silver, glassware and tapestries) from the 15C to the 20C.

Particularly worthy of note among the collection of Dutch sculpture are **The Meeting of St Joachim and St Anne**, a moving late-15C work in wood by an unknown artist (241), and the elegant and lively groups by **Adriaen van Wesel** from the same period, such as the *Angels Playing Music* (241) and the *Death of the Virgin* (242), as well as a rood screen made in about 1500 (248). The Anunciation of the Virgin Mary (245) by the German sculptor **Tilman Riemenschneider** is typically Late Gothic, while the 16C Brussels wall tapestry *The Triumph of Fame over Death* (248) shows the influence of the Italian renaissance.

Other notable 17C works include the tapestries made in Delft by the Flemish artist Sperint (250a and 253), a terracotta bust by **Hendrick de Keyser** (250a), a Renaissance oak cabinet of a style very common in the Netherlands (252, *illustration: see Introduction, Art*), a lovely bouquet painted by Velvet Brueghel (253), engraved glassware (253), a Ceylonese colonial bed (253a), silver by the Van Vianen brothers and Johannes Lutma (254), Delftware (255), polychrome porcelain (257) and a bombé chest (260; *illustration: see Introduction, Art*).

The ground floor and basement have displays of 18C to 20C furniture and very fine collections of porcelain, glassware, textiles, dolls' houses and other items.

Dutch history – *Ground floor, east wing.* The history of the country from the Middle Ages to the present day is documented mainly by works of art.

The large room is devoted to the Golden Age and its wars, sea battles and daily life. There is a portrait by Van Dyck of the young Prince William II and his wife Mary Stuart, daughter of Charles I; he was 15 and she was 9 when they were married in 1641. The stadtholders are evoked in a series of portraits, and other pictures document the Batavian Republic, the period of Napoleonic rule, the Battle of Waterloo (in a large painting by Pieneman) and the monarchy.

Print Room (Rijksprentenkabinet) – *Ground floor, west wing.* The museum possesses a very large number of drawings and engravings, from the 15C to the present, which are exhibited in rotation. There are also **temporary exhibitions** of drawings and prints from abroad.

18C paintings – *First floor, south wing; rooms 10, 11, 12 and 14. Can also be reached directly via the entrance at Hobbemastraat 19.* The 18C paintings are hung in rows one above the other, as was customary at the time when they were painted. Most of these are rather formal portraits of elegant women, and men in wigs. The works by **Cornelis Troost** deserve special attention; Troost was also an actor, and many of his paintings depict lively theatre scenes. The pastels room includes works by the Swiss artist Jean-Etienne Liotard and portrait miniatures.

Costume and textiles – *First floor, south wing; room 15.* A changing selection of items from the collection is on display, including 18C and 19C Dutch costumes, oriental carpets, lace and linen damask.

19C paintings – *First floor, south wing; rooms 16 to 21.* These rooms cover the Napoleonic Era, Dutch Romanticism (Barend C Koekkoek; WJJ Nuyen's *Shipwreck on a Rocky Coast*) and the Hague School (Weissenbruch, Mauve, Josef Israëls). George Breitner and Isaac Israëls are important representatives of Dutch Impressionism.
There are also a few works by foreign artists, including **Goya**'s extraordinary *Portrait of Ramón Satué*, and Monet.

Girl in Kimono (detail, 1894), by George Breitner

Asiatic art – *Ground floor, south wing; can also be reached directly via the entrance at Hobbemastraat 19.* The seven rooms of this particularly interesting department display a changing selection of more than 500 objects from the museum's rich collections of sculpture, painting and applied art. These come from many different cultures in China, Japan, Korea, Indonesia, India, Pakistan, Sri Lanka, Thailand and Vietnam. The Chinese sculpture includes an elegant, relaxed-looking seated figure of Bodhisattva Avalokiteshvara (Guanyin, 12C), and some magnificent porcelain. Highlights of the Japanese collection include ceramics for the tea ceremony, lacquer items and delicately painted screens (1630-60) by an artist from the Onkoku School. India is represented with a 12C bronze figure showing the cosmic dance of Shiva. One of the most striking of the small sculptures is a 7C or 8C bronze Buddha Shakyamuni, with its beautifully folded monk's habit; this probably comes either from southeast India or Sri Lanka.

Van Gogh Museum ⊘

This museum opened in 1973, and was designed by the architect **Gerrit Rietveld**. It has a collection of over 200 **paintings** and around 600 **drawings** by Vincent van Gogh (1853-90), as well as the **letters** he wrote to his brother Theo and **works by contemporaries** such as Toulouse-Lautrec, Gauguin and Odilon Redon. The painting collection traces the artist's development from the sombre canvases of his early career to the violent tonalities of his last years. Temporary exhibitions of late-19C art are also held.

Vincent van Gogh

Born in Zundert, near Breda, Van Gogh began sketching as a child, but only became conscious of his vocation at the age of 27. He then threw himself into drawing, before taking up oil painting the following year in The Hague. At first, Van Gogh was inspired by the dark landscapes and thatched cottages of the Drenthe region. Later on, he and his parents moved to a presbytery in the village of Nuenen *(see NUENEN)*. Here, he produced a series of portraits of peasants, with strikingly intense expressions, which served as studies for *The Potato Eaters* (1885).

Van Gogh, *Self-portrait with a straw hat* (1887)

After a stay in Antwerp, the artist moved to Paris in February 1886. During 1887 and 1888, under the influence of the Impressionists, he began using brighter colours in his paintings. Examples include *View of Paris* from Vincent's Room, *View of the Rue Lepic*, *The Pont de la Grande Jatte*, *Road beside the Seine at Asnières*, and numerous self-portraits, including *Self-Portrait at the Easel*. Van Gogh also painted landscape paintings influenced by Japanese art.

During the period from February 1888 to May 1889, he strove to reproduce the bright, contrasting colours he saw in Arles, with paintings of Provençal orchards, *The Zouave*, *Pont Langlois with Road beside the Canal* and *Sunflowers*.

Between May 1889 and May 1890, the first signs of mental illness began to be reflected in his paintings of windswept cornfields and twisted olive trees and cypresses, all in more muted colours. This illness resulted first in a stay in Arles hospital and then in his admission to the mental hospital at St-Remy-de-Provence from May 1889 to May 1890, where he painted his room in Arles as he remembered it. In 1890, after a quiet period in Auvers-sur-Oise, near Paris, Van Gogh painted the moving *Cornfield with Crows*. On 27 July of the same year, he shot himself in a fit of depression, and two days later the artist's stormy life came to a premature end.

★★ Stedelijk Museum ⊙

Built in 1895 and enlarged in 1954, this modern art museum has a very vari collection covering the period from 1850 to the present day. This includ paintings, sculpture, drawings and prints, applied art and industrial desig posters and other items. There are also paintings by artists such as Cézann Monet, Picasso, Léger, **Malevitch**, **Chagall**, **Mondrian** and Van Doesburg. Rece trends in European and American art are well represented, and the museum al holds major exhibitions and other events.

Vondelpark – This park, named after the famous 17C Dutch poet and dramati Joost van den Vondel, is 48ha/120 acres in area and is located betwe Singelgracht and Amstelveenseweg. It was designed by DJ Zocher in 1864 a extended and landscaped by his son LP Zocher in 1874. Since 1996, the park h been a listed national monument.

It is popular with walkers, cyclists and horse riders, and has a fine collection over 120 different kinds of tree, including chestnuts, oaks, poplars, swan cypresses and catalpas, as well as vast lawns, a rose garden and sparkling lak and fountains. In summer, performances are given in the open-air theatre, and t **Filmmuseum** ⊙ is also located in the park.

In Vondelpark

Concertgebouw – The famous concert hall, completed in 1888, is the home of the Royal Concertgebouw Orchestra; the title Royal was bestowed by Queen Beatrix to mark the orchestra's centenary in 1988.

Hollandse Manege – AL van Gendt, the architect of this riding school dating from 1882, was clearly influenced by the Spanish Riding School in Vienna. The neo-Classical building is decorated with stucco and cast iron and was beautifully restored in the 1980s; it is still in use.

★THE JORDAAN

This area dates from the 17C, and has been thoroughly restored over recent years. Its many warehouses with colourful shutters have been converted into apartments, and the area is full of attractive shops and cafés. The Jordaan's picturesque nature has made it very popular with students, artists, and the well-off middle classes. It was originally inhabited by French immigrants, and its name is believed to derive from the French word *jardin*, because so many of its canals and streets bear the names of flowers.

Noorderkerk – Built in 1623 by Hendrick de Keyser, this church is in the shape of a Greek cross. A **bird market** is held in Noorderplein on Saturday mornings. In the neighbouring Westerstraat, a large **second-hand market** takes place on Monday mornings, and in spring and summer there is a **farmers' market** specialising in organically grown products.

★ **Brouwersgracht** – The Brewers' Canal is lined with attractively restored warehouses. Nos 172 to 212 are particularly interesting. No 118, the De Kroon warehouse, has a carved stone on its façade depicting a crown, which is what its name means. There is a row of houses with crow-stepped gables dating from 1641 near the bridge where Brouwersgracht and **Prinsengracht** meet. The popular Papeneiland, a small brown café, is located here.

Karthuizerhofje – *Karthuizerstraat nos 69-171 (enter by no 173 or after no 85).* These delightful almshouses, the biggest in Amsterdam, were built in 1650 by the municipal architect, Daniël Stalpaert.

Claes Claeszoon Hofje – A 17C almshouse *(entrance at Eerste Egelantiersdwarsstraat 3)* with a picturesque inner courtyard.

★ **Egelantiersgracht** – This canal, with its beautiful 17C and 18C houses, has retained the typical charm of yesteryear.

★ **Bloemgracht** – This canal, sometimes ironically called the Herengracht of the Jordaan, used to be occupied by dyers and dye manufacturers. There are three magnificent houses with stepped gables, nos 87 to 91, and many others have façade stones, including nos 19 (a pelican), 23 (a unicorn), 34 (a trout) and 77 (a sower).

Façade stones

After the huge fire of 1452, all new houses were required to be built of stone with tiled roofs. In the absence of house numbers, a small sculpted façade stone was used, showing the emblem of the owner or the symbol of their trade. This practice ended when house numbering was introduced by the French. The **stones** that survive are often highly imaginative.

★THE PLANTAGE

This eastern residential area was developed in the 19C, and takes its name from the area's many parks.

Hortus Botanicus ⊙ – The botanical garden was created in the late 17C for the cultivation of medicinal plants. In addition to the outdoor part of the garden, there is also a greenhouse representing three different climatic zones, with plants from the Mediterranean, Africa and South America, and a palm house.

Nationaal Vakbondsmuseum ⊙ – The national trade union museum is located in the headquarters of the Dutch diamond workers' union, founded in 1894 by Henri Polak and Jan van Zutphen. The imposing building was designed in 1900 by **Hendrik Petrus Berlage**, and soon gained the nickname of Burcht van Berlage (Berlage's Castle). The magnificent **staircase★**, council chamber and boardroom are particularly worth seeing, and the museum itself is devoted to the history of the trade union movement.

★★ **Dierentuin Artis** ⊙ – This is one of Europe's oldest zoos, named after the society that founded it in 1838, Natura Artis Magistra (Nature, Mistress of Art). It has some 6 000 animals and approximately 750 species. The small mammals house has lemurs, desert foxes, otters and other animals, and there is also a reptile pavilion, an ape enclosure, and a newly restored **aquarium★** dating from 1882.

The domed **Planetarium** has a 630m²/6 780sq ft screen on which a Zeiss projector accurately recreates the movements of the stars and planets, and state of the art audio-visual equipment is used to create special effects. There is also a small **Geological Museum**.

Hollandse Schouwburg – This former theatre was used during the war as a transit camp for Jews, and has a memorial to those who died.

Muiderpoort – This 18C gate is the one through which Napoleon entered the city.

Artis

★ **Tropenmuseum** ⊙ – The Museum of the Tropics is part of the Royal Tropical Institute, and focuses on the third world. The displays include works of art, a wide variety of everyday objects, reconstructions of homes and shops, photographs and slide shows. They cover the tropical and subtropical regions of Africa, Asia, the Middle East, Oceania and Latin America. The Kindermuseum, or **children's museum**, holds two-year exhibitions for young people aged six to 12.

Temporary exhibitions and regular concerts of Indonesian gamelan music are also held.

THE PORT AREA

Oosterdok

★ **Nederlands Scheepvaart museum** ⊘ – The Netherlands Shipping Museum is located in the arsenal of the Dutch Navy, an impressive building in the Oosterdok dating from 1656. It has interesting collections of items relating to Dutch maritime history, including maps, globes and atlases, model ships, nautical instruments, paintings and prints.

Among the boats moored along the quays is the **Amsterdam**★★, a replica of an 18C merchant ship belonging to the Dutch East India Company, complete with cargo and (from April to October) a crew, as though it has just returned from a voyage to Asia.

★ **New Metropolis** ⊘ – This science and technology centre on the River IJ opened in 1997. Bright green and shaped like the bow of a ship, it was designed by the Italian architect **Renzo Piano**. It provides hands-on displays on subjects as varied as medicine and money, and is particularly ideal for children. There is a beautiful **view**★★ of the city from the roof.

Prins Hendrikkade – On the corner of this quay and the Binnenkant is the impressive **Scheepvaarthuis**★, or Shipping House. This was built in 1916 by the principal architects of the Amsterdam School, Van der Mey, Michel de Klerk and PL Kramer, and is the first example of their style. From the bridge to the east, there is a fine **view** of the Montelbaanstoren.

Entrepotdok – On this canal stand 84 warehouses dating from between 1708 and 1829 and rebuilt in the 1980s for use as offices, low-cost housing, and cafés. The development is a fine example of sensitive urban renewal.

Western port area

Realeneiland – This is one of the islands in the western part of the port, lined with warehouses. On **Zandhoek**, overlooking the Westerdok, is a row of restored 17C houses with attractive facing-stones.

Spaarndammerbuurt – Corner of Zaanstraat and Oostzaanstraat. This beautiful low-cost housing area was designed in the 1920s by **Michel de Klerk**. It is one of the finest creations of the Amsterdam School of architecture. The **Het Schip**★ apartment block in Hembrugstraat has an Expressionist-style tower.

THE PIJP

This area is actually an island linked to the rest of the city by 16 bridges. It was a working-class area in the 19C, and its long, narrow streets have given it its nickname of the Pipe, while its cosmopolitan population has also led it to be called the Latin Quarter of Amsterdam. The Pijp is a lively area full of cafés, restaurants and shops.

Heineken brewery ⊘ – The brewery on Stadhouderskade was built in 1864, and has been open to the public since 1988. There is a tour *(in English only)* describing the history of the company and the methods used to brew beer; a free sample is available at the end.

Albert Cuypmarkt – This market in the 3km/1.5mi long Albert Cuypstraat has been in existence since 1904, and sells just about anything under the sun.

★ **De Dageraad** – *Area around Pieter Lodewijk Takstraat.* This complex of 350 workers' apartments was built between 1919 and 1922 by **Michel de Klerk** and Piet L Kramer for the De Dageraad housing association. Its unusual forms, undulating orange-tiled roofs and rounded beige-brick façades make it one of the finest products of the Amsterdam School.

EXCURSIONS

Sloten – *10km/6mi to the west. Leave Amsterdam via S 107, Plesmanlaan and Nieuwemeerdijk.*
This village, which grew up in the 11C, still has a boundary post dating from 1794 laying down the outer limit beyond which the city of Amsterdam must not expand. The **Molen van Sloten** ⊘ is a polder-mill from 1847 placed on the site of the original mill in 1989. There is a tour explaining how it works; the screw is capable of raising 60 000l/13 000 gal of water per minute through a difference in level of 1.5m/5ft. A slide show and some wax figures describe the life of the miller's famous son, **Rembrandt**.

South of Amsterdam – *24km/15mi – about 1hr. Follow Amsteldijk and the west bank of the Amstel.*
Ouderkerk aan de Amstel – This picturesque village is a popular Sunday outing for people from Amsterdam. To the north is a **stage mill**.

Amsterdamse Bos – This is Amsterdam's main woodland area, an immense park strewn with lakes offering boating and fishing, with a permit.

Amstelveen – A modern commuter district which contains several **heemparken**, or parks devoted to native flora. The best-known is **Dr JP Thijssepark** *(between Amsterdamseweg and Amsterdamse Bos)*. This has been the home of the **Cobra Museum voor Moderne Kunst**★ ⊘ *(Sandbergplein 1)* since 1995. This surprisingly light building designed by Wim Quist houses a fine collection of modern art, including works by the **Cobra movement**. This international movement (its name derives from Copenhagen, Brussels, Amsterdam) was established in Paris in 1948 by a Dane, **Asger Jorn**, two Belgians, **Christian Dotremont** and **Joseph Noiret**, and the Dutch artists **Appel**, **Constant** and **Corneille**. They sought to break away from the dullness of neo-traditional post-war art, by taking their inspiration from folk and primitive art and most importantly from drawings by children and mentally ill people. This resulted in spontaneous, experimental, colourful and often cheerful works. The museum does not have a permanent exhibition; the pieces are shown in rotation. Related movements, such as the Dutch groups **Vrij Beelden** and **Creatie**, are also represented. Together, they give an excellent overview of abstract and semi-abstract art in the Netherlands between 1945 and 1955. The museum also holds exhibitions of contemporary art.

Schiphol – Amsterdam's international airport lies 4.5m/14ft below sea level in what used to be a bay of the Haarlemmermeer Lake. It is one of Europe's leading transit points for air travellers.

Not far from the runways is the **Aviodome** ⊘, a distinctive building with an aluminium domed roof, housing a collection of items from the National Aviation Museum. The history of air and space travel is traced using models, and there is also an exhibition on civil aviation. There is a cinema in the basement.

Round tour, 65km/40mi – *About 4hr. Leave Amsterdam by Mauritskade. After the second bridge (Schellingwouder Brug), turn off towards Schellingwoude, then pass under the road towards Durgerdam.*

Just before **Durgerdam** there is an excellent **view**★ of the village. The houses are painted in different colours; some have wooden gables. There is also an attractive square church with a pyramid-shaped roof and a clock tower.

Past Durgerdam, the narrow, winding road across the dike offers fine views of what used to be the Zuiderzee.

Durgerdam

★ **Marken** – *See MARKEN.*

Monnickendam – This small port was formerly renowned for its eels. The town is overlooked by the 16C brick tower, the **Speeltoren**. Opposite, the town hall or **stadhuis** is an 18C patrician house with a decorated pediment; note the snake-shaped balustrades. In the same street (Noordeinde) and in Kerkstraat, several houses have picturesque gables and façade-stones.

Nearby, in Middendam, stands the weigh-house or **Waag**, a small building dating from about 1600 with pilasters and an elaborately carved gable. To the south, the Gothic **Grote Kerk or Sint-Nicolaaskerk** is a triangular hall church with a fine 16C carved wooden choir screen.

Volendam – *See VOLENDAM.*

Edam – *See EDAM.*

Broek in Waterland – This village of brightly painted 17C and 18C houses is full of flowers in summer, and has a long-established reputation for being clean and tidy. Some of the 17C houses are U-shaped, and some have two doors, the front door being used only for weddings and funerals.

On the edge of the lake, the Havenrak, is the small white pagoda-shaped pavilion where Napoleon was received when he visited the village in 1811, the **Napoleon-huisje**.

The **church** by the canal was burned down by the Spaniards in 1573, and rebuilt between 1585 and 1639. In the north aisle, there is an interesting stained-glass window (c 1640) recalling these events.

Return to Amsterdam via S 116.

APELDOORN

Gelderland

Population 151 703
Michelin maps 908 I 5 and 211 U 9
Town plan in the current Michelin Red Guide Benelux

The town of Apeldoorn, with its broad, shady lanes and many parks, lies in the heart of the Veluwe *(see Introduction)*.

In the past, agriculture and the paper industry were the main sources of income here. From 1870 onwards, the paper mills were unprofitable and were converted into laundries. This industry continued to expand thanks to the pure spring water found locally, and by 1921 Apeldoorn had 66 laundering businesses.

Markets are held in the square outside the new town hall, with second-hand clothes being sold on Mondays, fruit and vegetables on Wednesdays, and general goods on Saturdays.

A tourist steam train, the **Veluwsche Stoomtrein** ⊙, runs southwest from Apeldoorn to Dieren *(23km/14mi)*.

Historisch Museum Apeldoorn ⊙ – The local museum is located on the first and second floors of the old town hall; it documents the history of the town and the surrounding area from prehistoric times to the 20C. Particularly interesting items include bell beakers found during excavations, and objects and documents relating to the paper industry.

Apenheul (Berg en Bos) ⊙ – *4km/2mi to the west.* Leave Apeldoorn via Kennedy-laan and JC Wilslaan. Apenheul means "apes' refuge", and most of the apes here, representing 27 different species, are able to roam free in the woodlands. They include rare woolly monkeys, over 120 squirrel monkeys, half-apes from Madagascar, and Barbary apes, which spend their time swinging through the trees or crowding round visitors. They are also accomplished pickpockets, and visitors are given special bags to put their belongings in. The larger animals, such as the **gorillas** (of which the Apenheul has the largest group in the world), and the bonobos or dwarf chimpanzees, live on separate islands. Feeding time is a particularly good occasion to see them. There is also a separate tropical animals section for children, **Dajak Farm**. The **Berg en Bos** (hill and forest) nature reserve is ideal for walks.

EXCURSION

Het Loo Palace and Museum – *See Nationaal Museum Paleis Het LOO.*

ARNHEM

Gelderland Ⓟ

Population 134 960
Michelin maps 908 I 6 and 211 U 11
Plan of the conurbation in the current Michelin Red Guide Benelux

Arnhem is the capital of Gelderland province, a former duchy. Situated on the Neder Rijn or Lower Rhine, one of the branches of the Rhine which separated from the IJssel, Arnhem is an important road junction.

Boat tours ⊙ – On the Gelderland rivers.

HISTORICAL NOTES

A coveted duchy – In the Middle Ages, Arnhem was the residence of the counts of Geldern, who fortified it in the early 13C and granted it city rights. It was a prosperous town trading in goods along the Rhine and the IJssel, and belonged to the Hanseatic League. Geldern became a duchy in 1339.

Arnhem was taken by Charles the Bold in 1473, and then by Emperor Maximilian (Charles the Bold's son-in-law) in 1505. Invaded by Emperor Charles V, the duchy was defended by **Charles of Egmont**, who was killed in battle in 1538. His successor ceded his rights to the duchy to Charles V in the Treaty of Venlo (1543). In 1585, under the reign of Philip (Charles V's son), the town was taken from the Spanish. It passed to the French during the 1672 to 1674 war, and then to the Austrians between 1795 and 1813.

Arnhem was the birthplace of Professor Hendrik Antoon Lorentz (1853-1928) who, with his former pupil Pieter Zeeman, received the Nobel Prize for Physics in 190 for his work on electromagnetic radiation.

A garden city – Arnhem is a very pleasant city, with many parks and gardens an an attractive setting in the foothills of the **Veluwe**. Prior to the last war, it was on of the favourite retirement places for colonials returning from Indonesia; the substantial residences are dispersed throughout the woods.

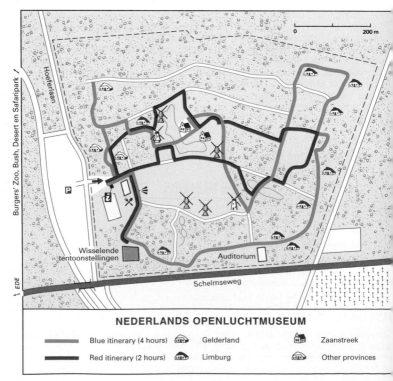

NEDERLANDS OPENLUCHTMUSEUM

Blue itinerary (4 hours)	Gelderland	Zaanstreek
Red itinerary (2 hours)	Limburg	Other provinces

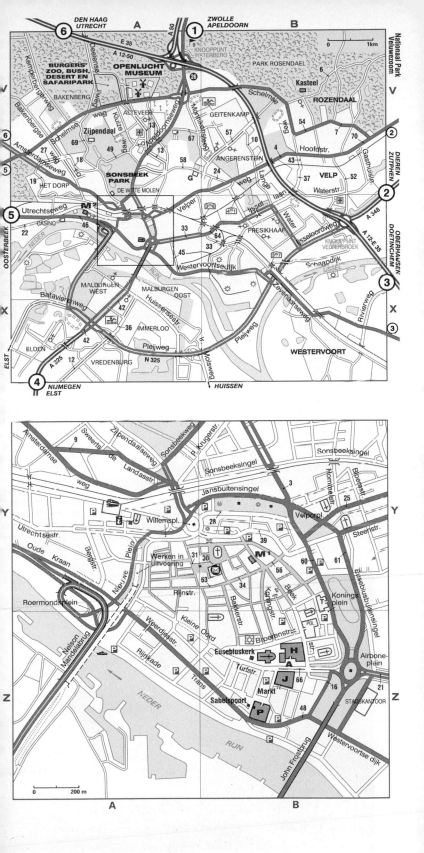

On all town plans north is at the top of the page.

The Battle of Arnhem (17-27 September 1944) – The name Arnhem is associated wit
one of the most tragic episodes in the liberation of the Netherlands. The aim o
Operation Market Garden was to gain access to the Ruhr, via a corridor north fro
the Belgian border across the three great rivers.

On 17 September 1944 more than 10 000 men of the 1st British Airborne Divisio
were parachuted into **Oosterbeek**, west of Arnhem. They were to march on Arnhem t
secure a bridgehead on the Neder Rijn and hold it until the 20 000 Americans (18t
101st and 82nd US Airborne Divisions) and the 3 000 Poles parachuted to the sout
could ensure the movement of troops over two important canals to the north o
Eindhoven, then the Maas at Grave and the Waal at Nijmegen. General Montgomer
who directed **Operation Market Garden**, counted on surprise to disorganise the enem
In this way he hoped to reach IJsselmeer, divide the country in two and isolate th
German troops located to the west, preventing them from retreating to German
then continue to the Ruhr. The operation was unfortunately a failure.

On the 18th thick fog enveloped Arnhem, making help impossible. Only a fe
battalions of parachutists from Oosterbeek had reached the town. After nine day
of desperately hard fighting the **Red Devils**, who had not managed to capture th
bridge, left 2 000 dead and more than 5 000 wounded or missing in the ruins of th
town. On the other hand 500 soldiers were given shelter by the townspeople an
2 300 were evacuated towards the south during the night of 25-26 September.

In the meantime the progress of armoured divisions effecting a junction had bee
held up by several German attacks. The crossing of the Maas at **Grave** (o
19 September) and the Waal at **Nijmegen** (the 20th) made it possible for the Allies t
come within sight of Arnhem, but it was too late. The bridge over the Neder Rijn wa
according to Browning, "a bridge too far". For more details read *A Bridge Too F*
by Cornelius Ryan.

Had the operation been a success, the terrible famine which occurred during th
winter of 1944 and 1945 in the country's western provinces could have been avoide
Arnhem was liberated by the Allies on 8 April 1945, shortly before the Germa
capitulation.

Arnhem today – The town rapidly rose from the ruins, and is now a thriving centr
of textile manufacturing, metals, retailing, technological research and othe
industries. It also plays an important administrative role within the eastern part o
the Netherlands.

Arnhemse meisjes, small puff-pastry biscuits, are the speciality of Arnhem.

★★ NEDERLANDS OPENLUCHTMUSEUM ⊘
(NETHERLANDS OPEN-AIR MUSEUM) *4hr*

The museum is set in 44ha/109 acres of undulating parkland. Around 100 authent
farmhouses, cottages, barns, windmills, workshops and a steam-operated dair
factory *(see Introduction: Industrial heritage)* from all the Dutch provinces hav
been assembled here to illustrate rural architecture and life in the past.

Netherlands Open-Air Museum – Interior of a Marken fisherman's house

The buildings, from all over the Netherlands, are decorated and furnished appropriately. Special exhibitions (such as pottery and ornamental folk art) and demonstrations (bread and paper making, as well as a variety of handicrafts) add interest to the visit.

From the road in front of the restaurant there is a delightful view of several windmills grouped around a clearing. The taller ones are grain mills while the smaller ones are typical examples of **polder mills** *(see Introduction: Traditions and folklore)*.

The buildings from some of the provinces are grouped together, as in the case of the handsome half-timbered farmsteads from Limburg (nos 100-104) or the farmhouses from Gelderland (nos 1-19).

However the most picturesque corner is without doubt the one representing **Zaanstreek** with its very characteristic houses. The green-painted buildings with variously-shaped gables are attractively decorated with white trims.

The calm waters of the nearby pool are reminiscent of the Zaan and are spanned by a wooden lever bridge.

In the building reserved for **temporary exhibitions** traditional costumes and other items are shown in rotation. Tableaux illustrate scenes from daily life set against a background of typical interiors peopled with models wearing traditional costumes, some of which are still worn.

ADDITIONAL SIGHTS

Markt – This long square is bordered by the Law Courts, the **Paleis van Justitie** and, at the end, by the Gelderland seat of government, the **Huis der Provincie**. This was destroyed during the war, and a simple new building with an inner courtyard was constructed by JJM Vegter in 1954. Adjoining it is the **Sabelspoort**, a 14C fortified gateway (altered in 1645), which is all that remains of the town's ramparts.

Grote Kerk or Eusebiuskerk ⊙ – Near Markt, this church was erected in the 15C on the site of a Romanesque church. It was destroyed during the Battle of Arnhem. Both the church and its tower (93m/305ft) were rebuilt in the neo-Gothic style; the upper part is in a more modern style.

The tower has a new 53-bell carillon, the largest in western Europe, and a small carillon of seven bells. A panoramic glass lift takes visitors up between the bells to a height of 73m/240ft, where there is a magnificent **view**★ of the town and the surrounding area.

The richly decorated **mausoleum** of Charles of Egmont, the last Duke of Geldern, dates from 1538. Look out for the "man in the box" against the pillar beside the tomb. Also of interest are the large Salvator Clock given by Charles to the church, and the tomb of Jodocus Sasbout (1546) to the right of the clock. The inscription *Homo Bulla* (man is a soap bubble), the young woman and the decaying body all symbolise the transience of life.

Duivelshuis – The Renaissance Devils' House was built in 1545 and greatly restored in 1829; it suffered no damage during the war. It takes its name from the strange statues and grotesque heads which decorate its walls. The building was the last dwelling place of the bloodthirsty general **Maarten van Rossum**, chief of the armies of the Duke of Gelderland, Charles of Egmont, and adversary of Emperor Charles V.

According to legend, Van Rossum had these demons carved to offend the magistrates of Arnhem, who refused to allow him to pave his front steps with gold.

Formerly the town hall, the house is still occupied by various municipal departments.

Behind is the new **stadhuis**, or town hall, built in 1964 and designed by JJ Konijnenburg. In the distance is the restored 14C **Sint-Walburgiskerk**, which has two different towers.

★ **Historisch Museum Het Burgerweeshuis** ⊙ – This beautifully restored 18C mansion was used as a public orphanage *(burgerweeshuis)* from 1844 to 1920. Today, it houses a rich collection of decorative arts: 15C Arnhem **guild silverware**★, oriental porcelain (in the marble wall-fountain in the dining room), glass, rare local pottery, 17C paintings and other items. The **Rococo-style regentenkamer** (boardroom) has oil-painted wall-hangings showing three episodes from the life of Alexander the Great; these are copies of designs for wall-coverings by Charles Le Brun for Louis XIV. The picture of Pallas Athene and Mercury (the god of trade) on the stucco ceiling reminds us that the mansion was built for a successful soap dealer.

A magnificent Rococo staircase leads to the first floor, which houses temporary exhibitions, a collection relating to local topography, and a collection of 19C paintings, silverware and tobacco boxes.

The top floor chronicles the story of Arnhem from prehistory to the present day, using archeological finds, paintings, photographs and videos.

* **Museum voor Moderne Kunst** ⊙ – A former 19C men's club, standing on a hill overlooking the Rhine, houses Arnhem's museum of modern art. The original mansion, with its striking hexagonal centre section, has been renovated and expanded. The museum has interesting collections of modern and contemporary art, with the emphasis on Dutch artists, and has a policy of ensuring that at least half its acquisitions are by women artists such as Ansuya Blom and Marlene Dumas.

The museum also holds around 20 exhibitions a year of contemporary and applied art.

The permanent collection includes work by **magic realists** (Carel Willink, Raoul Hynckes, Pyke Koch) and **contemporary artists** such as Dick Ket, Wim Schuhmacher and Charley Toorop. There are also a number of fine paintings by the young artist Jan Mankes (1889-1920) and by the **New Figuratives** (Roger Raveel, Reinier Lucassen and Alphons Freymuth).

The new garden room (which has a view of the Rhine) houses the post-war applied art and design section. This includes ceramics, glass and other design, as well as the country's largest collection of Dutch post-1960 **jewellery**.

The garden, which also has a beautiful view of the Rhine, has a collection of old and contemporary sculpture.

* **Sonsbeek Park** – This park of 75ha/185 acres, together with the adjoining Zijpendaal and Gulden Bloem parks, is one of the most beautiful in the Netherlands. Built in the English landscape style, it was declared a national monument in 1963. It is an undulating area with woodlands, large meadows, a string of streams, lakes, a castle and a 16C watermill, De Witte Molen. The barn beside this houses a visitors' centre, which offers suggested walking routes and also includes a herb garden. Elegant turn-of-the century houses are located around the park.

* **Burgers' Zoo, Bush, Desert en Safaripark** ⊙ – This exceptional zoo (burgers means people's) places a major emphasis on education and scientific research as well as recreation. Artificial ecosystems have been created so that visitors can see animals in their natural habitat.

Burgers' Desert recreates the North American desert, complete with rocks, sand dunes and cactuses. This is home to turkey vultures, lynxes, collared peccaries and colourful hummingbirds. A cave area containing nocturnal animals, and an abandoned mineshaft, lead from the desert to the tropics.

Burgers' Bush – This greenhouse (90m/96yd by 200m/218yd) recreates the ecosystem of a tropical forest, with trees and plants from Asia, Africa and South America. These include rice, sugar cane, pineapple, vanilla, banana and coffee plants as well as mahogany and rubber trees. Amid this colourful vegetation complete with a waterfall and suspension bridges, there are live birds, amphibians, reptiles and mammals. The more timid animals such as butterflies, exotic birds, manatees and caimans tend to show themselves when there are not too many visitors.

The next stage in this journey of discovery is the tropical beach and lagoon of **Burgers' Ocean**. A tunnel through the coral reef provides a first-hand view of an extraordinary undersea world: corals, sponges, sea anemones, starfish and a wealth of other creatures. Hundreds of colourful fish accompany the visitor onto an impressive panorama (20m/66ft by 6m/20ft) showing life in the dark depths of the ocean, where sharks, rays, jellyfish and other creatures lurk.

Burgers' Mangrove is still being developed, and shows the fish, crabs, snails and turtles that live amid the mangrove roots in this tidal environment.

Finally, **Burgers' Savanne** is a wide open space in which giraffes, zebras, ostriches, rhinoceroses and antelopes roam freely. The wild animal enclosure is home to lions and cheetahs. There is also a group of chimpanzees, which has been closely studied, large numbers of birds of prey and a nocturnal animal house.

EXCURSIONS

* **Nationaal Park Veluwezoom** – *Round tour of 20km/12mi. Leave Arnhem by Beekhuizenseweg.*

The Veluwezoom National Park is a vast area (4 600ha/11 362 acres) of pine and silver birch forest and undulating heathland situated to the north of Arnhem on the edge (zoom) of the Veluwe. The park has many footpaths and cycle routes, and there are several car parks.

Rozendaal – A small 18C castle, **Kasteel Rosendael** ⊙, flanked by a 14C tower, stands on the edge of a lake in the heart of its own **park** ⊙. Several furnished rooms are open to the public and in summer tea is served in the orangery.

The road climbs and descends as it crosses the forest and then goes through the hamlet of **Beekhuizen**. Beyond, roads run either side of a magnificent row of beech trees to reach the plateau and the national park.

Ch. Bastin – J. Evrard

Kasteel Rosendael

In the vicinity of the **Posbank** there are several viewing points, at an altitude of 100m/328ft, which offer good **panoramas★** of the rolling heathland stretching away to the horizon. There are many footpaths and the area makes good walking country.

The road then descends to Rheden.

The **visitors' centre** ⊘ *(bezoekerscentrum)* occupies an old farmhouse on Heuvenseweg. Ramblers will be able to find detailed maps here, as well as information concerning nature and the environment.

Turn left at the bottom of Schietbergseweg, towards Dieren.

De Steeg – To the east of the village, among the woods, the 17C **Kasteel Middachten** ⊘ is surrounded by a double moat. There is a fine view of the castle from the 5ha/12 acre **garden** ⊘. Inside, the original furnishings have been preserved, including portraits, miniatures, and a library.

Returning to Arnhem by the main road, there is another moated castle, **Kasteel Biljoen**, on the left just before Velp.

Enter Arnhem by Zutphensestraat.

The southern Veluwezoom – *25km/16mi to the west – about 2hr 30min. Leave by ⑤ on the town plan.*

Oosterbeek – To the north of this small town, on the road to Warnsborn, just after the railway, is the **Airborne Kerkhof** war cemetery. This is the last resting place of the Allied troops who fell during the Battle of Arnhem; there are more than 1 700 gravestones (1 667 British and 79 Polish).

The Huize Hartenstein (Utrechtseweg 232) was the headquarters of General Urquhart, the commander of the 1st British Airborne Division, in September 1944. It houses the **Airborne Museum** ⊘, which covers Operation Market Garden and the Battle of Arnhem, and has many photographs, weapons and other objects belonging to allied and German troops. General Urquhart's headquarters have been reconstructed in the cellar.

To the south, on the banks of the Rhine, the terraces of the **Westerbouwing** *(restaurant)* offer a fine view over the river and the Betuwe with its orchards.

Drive towards the north bank of the Rhine.

Doorwerth – The village of Doorwerth stands on the river's edge, not far from the wooded area known as Doorwerthse Bos; it was badly damaged in 1944 during the Battle of Arnhem.

Kasteel Doorwerth, in its riverside setting, dates originally from 1260 but was enlarged c 1600. This massive four-square castle and its outbuildings are still encircled by moats. Armorial bearings add a decorative touch to the main entrance. Several furnished rooms, in the north and east wings, are open to visitors. The south wing houses the **Museum voor Natuur- en Wildbeheer** ⊘, or museum of nature and game conservation, with exhibitions on the various aspects hunting and game. The fine collections of weapons, stuffed animals, pictures a photographs are attractively displayed.

Continue on towards Renkum and pass under the motorway to take the road Wageningen.

Wageningen – It is appropriate that this industrial town should be known for i **agricultural university** (Landbouwuniversiteit), as it lies in the heart of orchard a market gardening country. The De Wereld building (Gen. Foulkesweg 1) was th venue for the talks which led to the German army's capitulation on 5 May 194 in the presence of General Foulkes, commander of the Canadian troops.

On the Grebbeberg, 5km/3mi from Wageningen, there is a Dutch milita cemetery commemorating the battle that took place here in 1940. A pa opposite leads to the **Koningstafel** or king's table, which has a view over the Rhi and the Betuwe. It was one of King Frederick V of Bohemia's favourite walks; I took refuge in the Netherlands after having been defeated by the Austrians 1620.

Rhenen – Rhenen is known for its large zoo, the **Ouwehands Dierenpark** ⊘, with ov 1 600 animals in a wooded park. A large aviary of exotic birds, a primate hous a dolphinarium and an aquarium add to the interest of the visit. There is also bear forest in which 13 brown bears and eight wolves roam free and can I observed from a walkway, and a tiger forest, where Amur tigers are bred. Thes combined with the recreation centre, lake and children's zoo, make the Ouw hands Dierenpark a very popular attraction.

The beautiful clock tower of the **Cunerakerk** ⊘ has been restored since it wi bombed in 1945.

ASSEN

Drenthe P

Population 54 691
Michelin maps 908 K 2 and 210 Y 5
Town plan in the current Michelin Red Guide Benelux

Assen owes its existence to a nunnery, founded in the 13C, of which one can see th chapel, the old town hall, on the main square or Brink. Today, this modern ar spacious town is laid out beside **Asserbos**, a pleasant woodland area to the south. Th area is known for its many megalithic monuments *(see HUNEBEDDEN).*

Until 1602 members of the States, or Provincial Assembly of Drenthe met out doors, in the Germanic style, at the Balloërkuil *(see below)* where they dispense justice. Due to its central location Assen was chosen as capital of the Drenthe in 18C during the reign of Louis Bonaparte.

To the south of Assen, a motorcycle **racing circuit** (Tourist Trophy Circuit or TTC) used for the Dutch Grand Prix.

Drenthe – For a long time this province was ill-favoured. The Scandinavian glacier which spread over the north of the Netherlands, left a sandy and not very fertile so In places it is covered with **heathland** with a few clumps of oak or pine.

In the wetter areas, **peat** developed on the poor morainic soils left by the glacier Drenthe was at one time the largest peat-producing region and local peat working ha left a dense network of canals, built to transport the peat.

Today much of the area has been brought into cultivation, by clearing and th judicious use of fertilisers, and the region now has a very different aspect. Shee moors have given way to pastures or plantations of conifers. Well fertilised pe bogs, with sand and the upper layer of peat, can make good arable land for growir potatoes, cereals and market garden produce; many ex-colonials have taken ov farms in the area.

The farmhouses in Drenthe are very picturesque with their vast thatched roofs ar are for the most part hall farmhouses *(see Introduction: Farmhouses).*

★ **Drents Museum** ⊘ – *Brink 1.*

The Drents Museum is housed in a complex of historic buildings: the forme Provinciehuis or provincial government building (1885), the abbey, the Droste huis or sheriffs' building and the **Ontvangershuis★**, the former home of th receiver-general. The museum has a very wide-ranging collection which attractively presented with the help of audio, video and interactive media.

There is a particularly interesting historical and **archeological section★** with a outstanding display on prehistoric times. This includes a large number artefacts from the local burial mounds known as hunebedden *(se HUNEBEDDEN),* fields of funerary urns, and objects preserved by peat bog such as a canoe from 6300 BC (discovered in Pesse, south of Assen) and 3 and 5C bodies including that of a strangled girl from Yde. In the Discover Room, children can explore the daily lives of prehistoric people for themselv

The extensive collection of decorative arts (furniture, everyday objects, local silver and ceramics), as well as the period rooms and costume collection, provide a detailed picture of local life, while the paintings by the Hague masters show the Drenthe landscape at its best.

The GeoExplorer section shows how this landscape was created, taking visitors on a spectacular journey back to the beginning of the Earth's history.

Finally, the museum has an important collection of art from around 1900, in which Art Nouveau and Art Deco are particularly well represented. In addition, it holds regular temporary exhibitions.

Behind the garden of the Ontvangershuis, there is a charming statuette of the young **Bartje**, the famous character of the local novelist Anne de Vries (1904-64). The statue was the work of Suze Berkhout (the original is in the town hall).

OUTSKIRTS

Rolde - *6km/4mi to the east - local map see HUNEBEDDEN.* In a wood to the west of Rolde is a former place of assembly, **Balloërkuil**, an open clearing several metres below ground level. Beyond the church, turn left onto a paved path signposted *hunebedden*. In a wood there are two **of these burial mounds** (D 17/18); one of them is covered with seven slabs. Both have their entrances on the south side.

Hooghalen - *9km/5mi to the south.* In Hooghalen, turn left onto the Amen road. The **Herinneringscentrum Kamp Westerbork** ⊙ commemorates the war and the persecution of Jews in the Netherlands using photographs, films, drawings, objects and monuments. Anne Frank was deported from Westerbork to Auschwitz.

After photo A.van Iterson/MICHELIN

Bartje

EXCURSION

Norg, Leek and Midwolde - *27km/17mi via N 373; turn right after 3km/2mi.*

Norg - This charming Drenthe village with numerous thatched cottages is built around the Brink, a large shady square. It has a small Gothic church with a saddleback roof.

Leek - To the north of town the moated manor of **Kasteel Nienoord** stands in extensive parkland. It was rebuilt in 1886 and it now houses the National Carriage Museum, or **Nationaal Rijtuigmuseum** ⊙. This includes many unique carriages, some drawn by goats, royal children's carriages and 17C and 18C sledges. During the summer season the carriages in the outbuildings are occupied by costumed figures.

There is a further collection of stagecoaches in a modern building, which stands beside a delightful shell-covered pavilion dating from c 1700.

Midwolde - The small brick **church** ⊙ with a saddleback bell-tower contains a fine **marble tomb**★ made by Rombout Verhulst in 1669

Nationaal Rijtuigmuseum, Kasteel Nienoord

Nationaal Rijtuigmuseum, Kasteel Nienoord

for Anna van Ewsum. The young woman is shown leaning gracefully over the mortal remains of her husband. The cherubs in white marble represent the couple's children. In place of the seventh cherub there is now a statue of Anna van Ewsum's second husband; this statue by Bartholomeus Eggers was added in 1714.

Note the carved pulpit (1711), the tall choir stalls (c 1660-70) and the small organ (1630) with lead pipes.

BERGEN OP ZOOM

Noord-Brabant

Population 63 233

Michelin maps 908 D 7 and 211 K 14 – Local map see DELTA

Town plan in the current Michelin Red Guide Benelux

In the Middle Ages Bergen op Zoom was already the venue for two important annual fairs, and in 1287 it became the chief town of an independent fiefdom. The old port today partially filled in, was once linked to the Oosterschelde. The town was long regarded as invincible after withstanding two sieges by the Spanish; in 1588 by the Duke of Parma, Alessandro Farnese, then again in 1622 when it was besieged by Spinola's troops.

The town's fortifications were strengthened c 1700 by **Menno van Coehoorn** (1641 1704), an engineer who had already designed numerous strongholds throughout the country. However, Bergen was unable to withstand the French army in 1747, during the Austrian War of Succession. The ramparts were demolished in 1868 and the boulevards mark their former location.

Bergen op Zoom is renowned for its carnival *(see Practical information)*. The sandy soils of the forested countryside around the town are good for growing asparagus.

SIGHTS

Stadhuis ⊙ – The town hall stands on Grote Markt and comprises three buildings; the one in the middle and the one on the right have attractive limestone fronts and date from 1611. They have a perron bearing the **town's coat of arms**; two savages support the coat of arms crowned by a coronet, and the arms themselves show three St Andrew's crosses and three hills (Bergen means hills).

Near Grote Markt, there is a massive stone **bell-tower** (14C), which locals call De Peperbus (the Pepperpot), due to the shape of its 18C lantern turret. The tower belonged to **the Grote Kerk or Sint-Gertrudiskerk** which was destroyed in 1747 by the French *(see above)*; although the church was rebuilt it was destroyed by fire in 1972. Other remains include the nave walls, the 15C transept and chancel, as well as a second 16C transept.

★ **Markiezenhof** ⊙ – *Steenbergsestraat 8.*

Antonie and Rombout Keldermans, from the famous family of architects in Mechelen, built this 15C and 16C palace for the marquises of Bergen op Zoom. The palace remained in the family until 1795 and has been restored; it is one of the finest Late Gothic town palaces in western Europe. The main façade is quite attractive with stonework on the lower part, where decorative ironwork adorns the windows, and brickwork, patterned with string courses, on the rest of the façade right up to the crow-stepped gables and dormer windows. The palace is now a cultural centre, including a **museum**, an art gallery used for temporary exhibitions, a library and a restaurant. There is also a small, picturesque arcaded

Inside the Markiezenhof

courtyard. The great hall or **Hofzaal** is remarkable for the carved stone chimney-piece (depicting St Christopher) of 1522, and for its paintings, furniture and silverware, giving an idea of the elegant environment in which the marquises lived. In the wing, which was renovated in the 18C, there are lovely rooms in the styles of Louis XIV, Louis XV and Louis XVI. The second floor is devoted to the history of Bergen op Zoom, and includes a scale model of the town's fortifications and a collection of objects and banners used in processions, which is of particular interest to children.

Gevangenpoort or Lieve Vrouwepoort – *Accessible via Lieve Vrouwestraat, opposite the Markiezenhof.*
This 14C gateway is all that remains of the town's medieval ramparts. The brick façade facing inwards is flanked by two bartizans, or lookout turrets; two enormous stone towers stand outside the gateway.

Ravelijn "Op den Zoom" – *To the northeast of the town.*
This small moated outwork is one of the last remaining parts of the fortifications built by Van Coehoorn. Opposite it is an attractive park, A van Duinkerkenpark, laid out around a lake.

EXCURSION

Wouw and Roosendaal – *15km/9mi to the northeast via A 58 – local map see DELTA.*

Wouw – The Gothic **church** ⊙, restored after the Second World War, contains some fine 17C Baroque **statues**. These formed part of the choir stalls, which disappeared during the war. They are now on consoles in the chancel, and in the aisles on either side of the confessional boxes. The figures are shown in very lifelike poses.
The stained-glass window on the west side of the tower, depicting the Resurrection, is by Joep Nicolas (1937).

Roosendaal – This town is an important railway junction and industrial centre with a modern shopping district, De Rozelaar. There are several nature reserves nearby, notably **Landgoed Visdonk** and the **Rucphense Heide** (1 200ha/2 964 acres). The **streekmuseum De Ghulden Roos** ⊙ is a local museum in the 18C presbytery, **Tongerlohuys** *(Molenstraat 2)*. It contains an interesting collection of tableware, local hats, and works by the Belgian artist Alfred Ost. There is also a reconstruction of a village shop.

BOLSWARD★

Fryslân
Population 9 248
Michelin maps 908 H 2 and 210 S 4
Local map see SNEEK

Bolsward, or Boalsert in Frisian, is one of the 11 towns of Friesland. The date of its foundation is inscribed on a façade stone of the town hall, 713. Its name is believed to mean "the land of Bodel, surrounded by water"; the ending *ward* or *werd* refers to a small mound *(see LEEUWARDEN: Excursions)*.
In the past Bolsward was linked to the Zuiderzee and it grew rapidly to become a prosperous and powerful town. In the 11C it was granted the privilege of minting coins and became a Hanseatic town.
Today it is a peaceful place. Every three years, it awards a prize for Frisian literature named after **Gysbert Japicx** (1603-66) who was the first literary writer to use Frisian; written Frisian had been obsolete for many years.
Situated in the centre of a rich pastoral region, Bolsward is also the seat of a school specialising in nutrition technology.

SIGHTS

★ **Stadhuis** ⊙ – The town hall is an elegant Renaissance construction dating back to the years 1614 to 1617. The centre of the street front is marked by a projecting central block and a gable surmounting a fine 18C perron decorated with two lions bearing the town's coat of arms. At the top there is a tall octagonal clock tower with a **carillon**.
In the **council room**, there is a splendid carved door by the cabinetmaker Japick Gysberts, who also undertook the decoration of the lovely wooden chimney-piece framed by stone telamones.
One of the rooms on the first floor, with great timber beams supporting the weight of the tower, houses a collection of antiquities, including Frisian silverwork, traditional costumes, and artefacts from archeological excavations.

Martinikerk ⊘ - This large Gothic church, now Protestant, was built in the middle of the 15C. Like most Frisian churches, it has a saddleback roof.

Inside, great round piers support the vaulting of the three naves. The **choir stalls★** (late 15C) have interesting sculptures combining realism with a degree of naivety. The scenes which are shown on the lateral partitions are particularly noteworthy.

- Manna, a saint; on the other side: St Catherine and the philosophers, St Barbara;
- St Christopher; on the other side: St George and the dragon;
- Moses and the Jews, baptism of Christ, spies and the bunch of grapes.

Against the north wall, pew near the nave:
- Judgement of Salomon, St Martin, Abraham's sacrifice; above the lectern: an alchemist;
- St Peter and St Paul, heaven and hell; on the other side: God and angel musicians, the Last Judgement.

Choir stalls (detail), Martinikerk

Against the north wall, pew near the apse:
- the Virgin crushing the dragon; on the other side: Judith beheading Holofernes;
- dragon, Bolsward's coat of arms, Temptation of Christ.

Equally interesting are the figures on the high backs, the picturesque illustrations of parables shown on the misericords, the figures on the cheekpieces, and the grotesque figures of the lecterns.

The **pulpit★** (17C), with a tiered canopy, is decorated with elegant motifs in the Frisian style.

The central panel depicts a Bible and the signs of the Zodiac; the other panels depict the seasons. Above there is a frieze of fruit and vegetables; below a series of shells.

The floor is embedded with tombstones.

The organ was made in 1775 by Hinsz of Groningen. The church's remarkable acoustics make it a popular venue for recording concerts.

EXCURSION

Witmarsum - *10km/6mi to the northwest.*

Near the main road there is a statue of **Menno Simonszoon** (1496-1561). He was born in Witmarsum, and became vicar of Pingjum, then the parish priest of his native town and, finally, in 1536, turned his back on Catholicism to become an Anabaptist. He founded the *doopsgezinden* brotherhood or **Mennonites**. In 1539 he summarised his doctrine, which was more pacific than that of John of Leiden; belief in the Bible, rejection of the baptism of children, an emphasis on personal piety, and a refusal to obey all the established Church's dogma. The Mennonite religion spread to Germany, Switzerland and North America, where it still has its adherents.

The Mennonites of Witmarsum meet in a small church located on Menno-Simonsstraat, the **Menno-Simonskerkje** ⊘, which was rebuilt in 1961. The prayer area has a portrait of Menno Simonszoon, and the sacristy has various objects commemorating him. Further down the street is a monument to his memory, located on the site of his first church.

In the Netherlands, use Michelin map 907 *or* 908.

In Amsterdam, use Michelin Town Plan 36, *with a street name index, one-way streets, and an enlargement of the city centre.*

BOURTANGE

Groningen – Population 434
Michelin maps 908 M 2 and 210 X 4

Bourtange, close to the German border, is one of the best-preserved fortified villages in the Netherlands. There are also remains of the **fortifications** ⊙ outside it.

HISTORICAL NOTES

Bourtange was built during the Eighty Years War on a sandy ridge *(tange)* in the extensive marshes to the east of Groningen. The fortress overlooked a narrow pass on the road between Groningen, Lingen and Westphalia. It was built by **Adriaan Anthoniszoon** for Prince William of Orange, who hoped it would enable him to free Groningen from Spanish occupation, but was not completed until 1593 through lack of money. When Groningen surrendered a year later, Bourtange became part of the frontier fortifications.

Because of its strategic position close to the border of the German Empire, it was considerably expanded and reinforced. Outworks, crownworks and a moated outer wall were built during the first half of the 17C. The southeastern side was further reinforced between 1738 and 1742 with two outworks and a demilune, or half-moon-shaped fortification.

Until 1851, Bourtange was a military fort permanently occupied by some 300 soldiers and their families. Eight years later, it was transferred to civil use, the reinforcements were not maintained and the fort fell into disrepair.

Bourtange was made a listed monument in 1967, and extensive rebuilding has restored it to its appearance in 1742, when it was at its largest.

SIGHTS *Illustration: see Introduction, ABC of architecture*

Car park beside the information centre.

Bourtange is a classic example of a fortress in the **Old Netherlands style**. The core consists of a bastioned pentagon surrounded by two moats. The southeastern side, facing the enemy, has the strongest fortifications; originally, the whole of the outer area on this side was dug out so that it could be flooded.

The only access to the fort is via two narrow paths following a complicated route of bridges and outworks to the Marktplein, or market square. From here, 10 streets radiate outwards to the bastions and the main ramparts. This layout, similar to that used at Coevorden *(see EMMEN)* made it possible for troops to move around quickly and to be seen by their commanders.

The **Museum De Baracquen**, a reconstructed barracks, contains items found in the fortress.

The **Protestant church**, the former synagogue, an officer's apartment and the horse mills can also be visited, and the former powder magazine has an informative slide show about the fortress.

BREDA★

Noord-Brabant
Population 156 364
Michelin maps 908 F 7 and 211 N 13
Plan of conurbation in the current Michelin Red Guide Benelux

At the confluence of the Mark and the Aa, Breda was formerly one of the country's main fortified towns and the centre of an important barony. Today it is a dynamic city and a great commercial and industrial centre. Benefiting from its position on one of the main access routes into the country, it is a welcoming stopping place with large pedestrian precincts.

With numerous parks, Breda also has very attractive suburbs and large areas of woodland, such as the **Biesbos** to the west and the **Mastbos** to the south. To the east, **Surae** is a recreational park with a bathing area.

In February *(see Calendar of events)*, Breda holds its well-known **carnival★**. Around Easter there is the Netherlands Art and Antiques Fair and in May the International Jazz Festival. At the end of August there is the Taptoe, a military music festival *(see Calendar of events)*. The month of October brings the Breda Flower Show, held in the Grote Kerk.

HISTORICAL NOTES

The residence of the House of Nassau – Breda obtained its city rights in c 1252. It became part of the Breda barony, but in 1404, this passed to the Nassau family, who adopted Breda as their family seat. The 13C fortifications were rebuilt (c 1535) by Count Henry III of Nassau, and the ring canals mark the former alignment of the walls, which were destroyed shortly after 1870.

The Compromise of Breda – Although the treaty was actually concluded in th
month of September at Spa (now Belgium), the Compromise of the Nobility or o
Breda was signed in Breda Castle in 1566. Its aim was to abolish the Inquisition.
Following this reunion a delegation of about 300 nobles set out for Brussels t
petition the Governor, Margaret of Parma to convene the States General and chang
the edicts against heretics (ie the Protestants). She burst into tears; her counsellor
the Count of Berlaymont, responded in jest with the phrase: "What, Madam, afrai
of these *gueux* (beggars)?" This taunt did not displease the Calvinists, who from the
on took the name **beggars** for their movement and the beggar's bowl as the symbo
of their fight against Spanish rule. The Calvinists' actions then knew no bounds: i
August the **Iconoclasm** was unleashed, and churches were pillaged and statue
destroyed. In 1567 Philip II of Spain sent the tyrannical Duke of Alba, a
governor-general, to punish the rebels, root out heresy and re-establish roya
authority in the Spanish Netherlands.

An ardently disputed stronghold – In 1581 Breda was pillaged by the Spanish, wh
occupied the castle, the family seat of William the Silent. In 1590, Maurice of Nassa
took the town by surprise, 70 of his men having been able to enter by hiding unde
a load of peat in a barge belonging to Adriaan van Bergen. In 1625, after a long siege
Breda surrendered to the Spanish commanded by the Marquis of Spinola. Thi
episode was immortalised by Velázquez in *The Surrender of Breda-Las Lanza*
(1634-35). The town was recaptured in 1637 by the Prince-Stadtholder Frederick
Henry.
The Treaty of Breda of 1667 ended the Second Anglo-Dutch War (1665-67) an
confirmed English possession of Nieuw Amsterdam, which became New York. Th
Dutch retained Guiana (now Suriname). The negotiations and the signing of th
treaty took place in the castle.
During the French Revolutionary Wars, the town was taken by Dumouriez in 1793
He was forced to evacuate it after the defeat of Neerwinden (Belgium), and then ha
to withdraw from the Netherlands.
Breda was once again under siege in 1794, this time by Pichegru, but onl
surrendered when the whole country was occupied. It became part of the Deux
Nethes *département* (with Antwerp as its county town) until 1813: that year, at the
approach of the Russian vanguard, the French garrison sallied
out but the population of Breda prevented their return.
On 11 and 12 May 1940 Breda marked the most northerly
point of the Allied advance into the Netherlands; the Dyle
Manoeuvre, a Franco-British operation to force a
breakthrough to the north and provide protection to Amsterdam, was a failure. The soldiers had to hastily withdraw to
Belgium, and Breda was liberated by the Allies in October
1944.

★ GROTE OF ONZE-LIEVE-VROUWEKERK ⊙ *45min*

The church is an imposing 15C and 16C edifice in the
Brabant Gothic style. With three naves, it was
enlarged in the 16C by the addition of a number of
chapels and an ambulatory. Its tall **bell-tower**★ of
97m/318ft with a square base and octagonal top is
surmounted by an onion-shaped dome. The **carillon**
has 49 bells.
The interior, with its typical Brabant Gothic-style
columns – their capitals decorated with crockets
– and triforium, contains numerous tombs. The
most striking one is the **tomb**★ of Engelbracht II of
Nassau (1451-1504) and his wife in the Chapel of
Our Lady, to the north of the ambulatory. This
Renaissance alabaster monument was carved in
the manner of Michelangelo, and probably
designed by Thomas Vincidor of Bologna. The
recumbent statues lie under a slab held up by
four figures; they depict Julius Caesar
(representing military courage), Regulus
(magnanimity), Hannibal (perseverance) and
Philip of Macedonia (prudence). Engelbracht's
armour lies on top of the slab. The vault under
the tomb contains the mortal remains of **René de
Chalon**, Henry III of Nassau and Anna van Buren, William of Orange's first wife. In the
ambulatory is the 15C tomb of Engelbracht I
and his son Jan van Nassau.

Grote of Onze-Lieve-Vrouwekerk

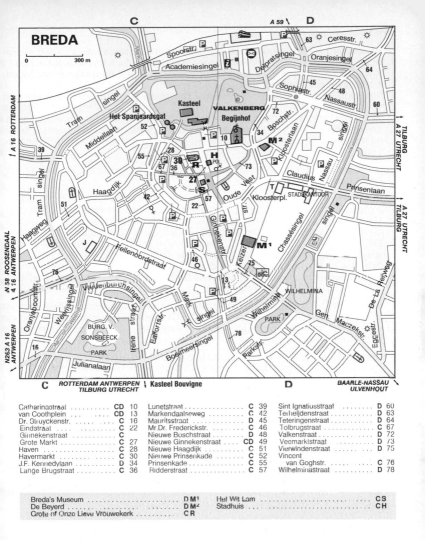

The 15C wooden chancel stalls are carved with satirical motifs illustrating vices, proverbs etc. Other unusual reliefs were added after 1945.

In the north transept there is a triptych by Jan van Scorel whose central panel illustrates the Finding of the True Cross. At the end of the south aisle there is a bronze baptismal font (1540) made in Mechelen, Belgium, of Gothic construction with Renaissance motifs. The organ case is decorated with a 17C painting depicting David and Goliath and the Ark of the Covenant. The organ, a fine instrument, with its oldest parts dating from the 16C, can be heard when **concerts** ⊙ are held.

ADDITIONAL SIGHTS

Leave from the point where Nieuwe Prinsenkade becomes Prinsenkade.

From here you have a lovely view of the Grote Kerk's bell-tower.

Het Spanjaardsgat – These remains of the fortifications, known as the Spanish Gap, consist of two large towers with small onion-shaped domes flanking a watergate, which was used to drain the moat.

Hidden behind the thick walls is the **castle** ⊙, an immense building with numerous windows, surrounded by a moat; the north façade (visible from the Academiesingel) is flanked by octagonal turrets. Since 1828 it has been occupied by the Royal Military Academy.

This old fortified castle was redesigned from 1536 onwards by **Thomas Vincidor da Bologna**, and was William the Silent's favourite retreat until his departure for the revolt which was declared in 1567. It was here that the Compromise of Breda *(see above)* was signed by the nobles.

The castle's present aspect dates from between 1686 and 1695, under Stadtholder William III of Orange, who continued Vincidor's original plan.

Havermarkt – This charming little square in front of Grote Kerk was at one time the hay market. There are several busy cafés around the square.

113

★ **Valkenberg** – This pleasant park with its magnificent trees was once part of the castle grounds. Nearby is the Beguinage, or **Begijnhof**, which was founded in 1267. It was transferred here in 1531 and comprises 29 simple houses arranged round a courtyard with a herb garden and a chapel.

The Beguines are a Catholic community, but unlike nuns, they do not make any vows.

At the entrance is the Béguinage's former chapel, which has become a Walloon Church, **Waalse Kerk**. The Frisian, **Peter Stuyvesant** (1592-1672) was married here; he was the last Dutch governor of Nieuw Amsterdam (New York) from 1647 to 1664.

Grote Markt – From the middle of this large square there is a fine view★ of the Grote Kerk.

Stadhuis ⊘ – Dating from the 17C, the town hall was rebuilt in 1767. It contains a copy of Velázquez's painting, The **Surrender of Breda**, the original of which is in the Prado Museum in Madrid. Opposite, on the corner of Reigerstraat, there is a lovely house with a crow-stepped gable. To the south of the square, at no 19, is **Het Wit Lam** (The White Lamb), the former meat hall and premises of the crossbowmen's guild. The pediment of the façade bears the date 1772 and a depiction of St George slaying the dragon.

Several pedestrian precincts converge on Grote Markt; a food market is held here on Tuesday and Friday mornings and a flea market on Wednesdays.

De Beyerd ⊘ – This former almshouse has been transformed into a centre for the visual arts (Centrum voor beeldende kunst). The centre also organises temporary exhibitions on international contemporary art, architecture, ceramics, photography and design.

Breda's Museum ⊘ – The rich history and archeology of the barony of Breda is chronicled in this former police barracks. The story of Breda as a bishopric is also traced in an important collection of religious art, including statues of saints, paintings, church silver and richly decorated textiles. There is a display of local arts and crafts, and temporary exhibitions are held.

OUTSKIRTS

Kasteel Bouvigne ⊘ – *4km/3mi. Leave to the south along Duivelsbruglaan before turning right.*

This castle stands on the edge of the **Mastbos**, a lovely wood of pines and beech crisscrossed with cycle paths and rides; the name is said to derive from the word *boeverije* meaning low meadow. The moated castle was built in 1612 and it is flanked by a high octagonal turret with an onion-shaped dome.

EXCURSIONS

Baarle-Nassau – *37km/23mi to the southeast via Gen. Maczekstraat.* This village is both Dutch and Belgian; the Belgian part, Baarle-Hertog, consists of some 30 enclaves on Dutch soil. In the 12C the village of Baerle was divided in two; the southern part was ceded to the Duke of Brabant (Baarle-Duc or Baarle-Hertog), and the northern part was united to the Breda barony and called Baarle-Nassau. At present each community has its own town hall, church, police station, school and post office. The border is so complicated that houses of different nationalities stand side by side: a small flag alongside the house number indicates the nationality of each household.

From Hoeven to Willemstad – *50km/31mi to the west. Leave by Haagweg, N 58, and turn right towards Etten-Leur.*

Hoeven – The Simon Stevin Observatory, **Volkssterrenwacht Simon Stevin** ⊘, and a **planetarium** are located here. They are named after the Flemish scientist, Simon Stevin (1548-1620).

Oudenbosch – This village, also known as Klein (Little) Rome, is overlooked by the enormous **Basiliek van de HH Agatha en Barbara**. It was built by PJH Cuypers between 1867 and 1880, as a smaller version of St Peter's in Rome. The dome, however, is 68m/224ft high. The façade (1892) is a copy of the west front of the Basilica of St John Lateran in Rome. The interior was decorated by an Antwerp sculptor. The **Nederlands Zouavenmuseum** ⊘, or Museum of Pontifical Zouaves, tells the story of the 3 000 Dutch people who, in the 19C, volunteered to defend the Papal States in Italy.

Beyond Standdaarbuiten take A 59 and then A 29 to reach Willemstad.

Willemstad – *Local map see DELTA.* This fortified town in the shape of a seven-pointed star dates from 1583. It is one of the finest example of a fortress in the Old Dutch style, and owes its name to its founder, William of Orange. Willemstad was designed by **Adriaan Anthoniszoon**.

Today it has a marina which is very popular with holidaymakers. The octagonal **church** and its tree-shaded cemetery are encircled by a small moat. The church was completed in 1607 and claims to be the first Protestant church in the Netherlands. The 17C former town hall, close to the harbour, is distinguished by its octagonal tower.

D'Orangemolen is a tall white walled mill dating from 1734.

The **Prinsenhof** ⊘ or Mauritshuis was built in the 17C for Prince Maurice of Orange. It stands in its own park, within the old town walls, and is now the home of the tourist office; there is also a small historical collection.

From Raamsdonksveer to Biesbosch – *50km/31mi to the north via St Ignatiusstraat.*

Raamsdonksveer – The **Nationaal Automobielmuseum**★ ⊘ is near the Geertruidenberg exit of the A 27 motorway. With over 200 vehicles on display, it traces the history of the car from its origins to the present day. A number of carriages, 18C sledges, racing trophies, posters and other car accessories add to the interest of the main collection.

The hall to the left of the entrance contains cars by the Dutch manufacturer Spijker. The company was operational from 1899 to 1925 and its vehicles were popular with the Dutch royal family in the early years of the 20C. The American-built Ahrens-Fox fire engine belonged to the Rotterdam city fire brigade, while Elvis Presley owned the bright red Cadillac Fleetwood Brougham (1976).

The area to the right of the entrance includes such pioneers of the road as the Peugeot Double Phaeton (1894), the Benz Victoria (1899) and the Panhard & Levassor (1895). There is also a 1907 Bikkers steam-operated street-sweeping machine which belonged to the city of Amsterdam.

Amid the serried ranks of the models and racing cars in the other halls, look for the magnificent **Auburns, Duesenbergs and Cords**★★★ of the 1920s and 1930s by the American manufacturer and advocate of front-wheel drive, Errett Lobban Cord. The superb 1932 Bugatti Type 50 is one of only two remaining models.

There is a comprehensive section on Japanese car manufacturers, especially Toyota.

Geertruidenberg – This small fortified town on the Amer is organised round a triangular **square** overlooked by the massive tower of Sint-Geertruidskerk. The town hall, or **stadhuis**, has a lovely 18C façade overlooking the square. Nearby, a Baroque fountain splashes.

Drimmelen – Drimmelen stands on the banks of the Amer, and since the completion of the Delta Plan (*see DELTA*) it has become an excellent water sports centre attracting increasing numbers of tourists; it is also popular with anglers. The **marina** can accommodate up to 1 400 boats.

★ **De Biesbosch** – The Biesbosch (or Biesbos) consists of four parts, three of which are crisscrossed by roads. The fourth (Zuidwaard) is entirely surrounded by water. The **boat tour**★ ⊘ gives a good overall view of the region.

This area of 40 000ha/98 000 acres suffered badly during the St Elisabeth Flood in 1421. The important diking work undertaken over the last five and a half centuries has reduced the submerged area to a mere 6 000ha/14 820 acres. Although very busy with pleasure boats, the Biesbosch is rich in wildlife. Coots, godwits and redshanks are common, and plovers, herons and pheasants are also sometimes glimpsed in the area. Reeds, rushes and grassland are the main vegetation on the many small islets, but numerous other plants are also to be found: willows, ash, loosestrife, willow (used in wickerwork), hogweed, arrowhead, valerian and cress.

When the Haringvliet estuary was closed off, the Biesbosch was no longer tidal and willow began to flourish in this new ecosystem. Recreational facilities in the Biesbosch include rowing, sailing and canoeing.

The Biesbosch was made a national park in 1994 and the new management policy included the designation of several recreation areas, a bird sanctuary and three reservoirs to supply the Rotterdam and Dordrecht regions with water.

BRIELLE

Zuid-Holland
Population 15 745
Michelin maps 908 D 6 and fold 23 (inset) and 211 J 11

Brielle, generally known as Den Briel (pronounced bril), stands on the island of Voorne. This fortified historic town was once a busy port at the mouth of the Maas. On 1 April 1572 the Sea Beggars (*Gueux de Mer* or *Watergeuzen*), with the support of William the Silent, left England and landed at Brielle. This was the signal for the uprising of Holland and Zeeland against the Spanish occupation. In July, 19 priests were executed in Brielle of which 16 had just been made prisoners by the Sea Beggars at Gorinchem. Known as the martyrs of Gorkum, they have been canonised.

Each year, on 1 April, Brielle commemorates the taking of the town by the Sea Beggars with a costumed parade and a series of plays.

Brielle was the birthplace of Admiral **Maarten Tromp** (1598-1653), famous for his victory against the Spanish at the Battle of the Downs in 1639. Today, it is a tourist centre benefiting from the proximity of **Brielse Meer**, to which it is linked by a ferry for pedestrians and cyclists.

Reminders of the past include fortifications, laid out as an esplanade, and peaceful quays bordered with old houses, like **Maarland** to the north of the town. At the far eastern end of Maarland, beyond a bridge, there is a fine **view** over the docks and the tower of the Gothic church, Sint-Catharijnekerk.

Historisch Museum Den Briel ⊘ – Behind the 18C *stadhuis*, on the **picturesque Wellerondom** square, this small museum, installed in a former prison and weigh-house, is devoted to the turbulent history of the town and the island of Voorne.

Grote Kerk or Sint-Catharijnekerk ⊘ – Although this church was started in the Brabant Gothic style in the 15C, it remains unfinished. It has a massive stone tower 57m/187ft high. The carillon, cast in 1660 by one of the Hemonys, has been enlarged and now has 48 bells.

DELFT★★

Zuid-Holland
Population 94 030
Michelin maps 908 E 5, fold 24 (inset) and 211 L 10
Plan of the conurbation in the current Michelin Red Guide Benelux

The town of Delft is known the world over for its blue and white ceramics, Delftware. With its tree-lined canals, famous monuments and museums, Delft is also one of the Netherlands' most charming towns.

It was the home town of the jurist **Grotius**, as well as the artist **Vermeer** and the naturalist **Antonie van Leeuwenhoek** (1632-1723) who, thanks to the microscopes which he perfected, made a multitude of discoveries in both botany and zoology.

HISTORICAL NOTES

A prosperous city – Delft, which means moat, was probably founded by Godefroy the Hunchback, Duke of Lower Lothringen in 1074. Count William II of Holland granted the city its charter in 1246 and Delft reached the peak of its prosperity in the 13C and 14C based on the cloth trade and its brewing industry. At the end of the 14C the town's authorities decided to build a canal linking the city to the Maas to facilitate the transportation of its products. Slowly the small town of Delfshaven grew up around the newly established port, which became part of Rotterdam in 1886.

In 1428 Jacoba or Jacqueline of Hainaut (*see GOES*) signed the **Treaty of Delft** by which she gave her territories of Holland, Zeeland and Hainaut to Philip the Good, while keeping the title of countess.

The 15C fortifications preserved the town's compact layout until well into the 19C. Delft was extensively damaged by the large fire of 1536 and it has few edifices dating from before the 16C. In 1654, the explosion of a powder magazine completed the destruction.

Today Delft is an intellectual centre, due to its schools of Natural Sciences, its hydraulic laboratories and its Technical University. A nuclear reactor was built in 1963 for research and development purposes. The modern university buildings are in the new suburbs to the southwest of the town.

Among its industries there is the manufacture of yeast.

The father of international law – Hugo de Groot or **Grotius** (1583-1645), one of the greatest intellectuals of his time, was born in Delft. He was a theologian, philosopher, politician, diplomat and poet, but is best known for his legal writings and notably his *De Iure Belli ac Pacis* (*On the Law of War and Peace* – 1625) which became the accepted authority on matters of civil rights and earned its author the sobriquet "father of international law".

Accommodation

This beautiful old town has many hotels in historic buildings; the following is a selection.

BUDGET HOTELS

Leeuwenburg – *Koornmarkt 16, 2611 EE Delft,* ☎ *(015) 214 77 41, Fax (015) 215 97 59. 38 rooms.* This hospitable and typically Dutch hotel is located in two mansions in the heart of the town, and has comfortable rooms of varying sizes.

OUR SELECTION

De Ark – *Koornmarkt 65, 2611 EC Delft,* ☎ *(015) 215 79 99, Fax (015) 214 49 97. 24 rooms.* Further along the same street is this smaller hotel, this time in three restored old buildings and again with comfortable rooms. The breakfast room has historic furnishings, and the hotel has its own parking.

Museumhotel en Residence – *Oude Delft 189, 2611 HD Delft,* ☎ *(015) 214 09 30, Fax (015) 214 09 35. 51 rooms.* This unusual hotel was once a row of smart 17C canalside houses with an attractive courtyard. It is full of antique and modern objets d'art, and the modern rooms, lounge and garden contain displays of contemporary ceramics. Almost a museum, and also a top-class hotel.

Restaurants

De Zwethheul – *Rotterdamseweg 480 (5km/3mi southeast of Delft),* ☎ *(010) 470 41 66.* Although this restaurant is outside the centre, it is worth a detour. Apart from its superb view of passing boats, and its pleasant terrace, the food is excellent. Treat yourself!

L'Orage – *Oude Delft 111b,* ☎ *(015) 212 36 29.* Arts restaurant with good food and a beautiful town-centre location.

Le Vieux Jean *Heilige Geestkerkhof 3,* ☎ *(015) 213 04 33.* Typically Dutch decor, but typically French cooking.

De Klikspaan – *Koornmarkt 85,* ☎ *(015) 214 15 62.* Excellent food served in an old canalside warehouse. The restaurant is called "the tell-tale" after the resident parrot, but don't worry; the bird is the very model of discretion.

Van der Dussen – *Begijnhof 118,* ☎ *(015) 214 72 12.* This trendy restaurant is housed in the superb 13C Begijnhofje, or almshouses, and offers tasty exotic cuisine in a historic setting.

Practical information

General information – VVV Delft *(Markt 83-85, 2611 GS Delft,* ☎ *(015) 212 61 00)* has information on sights, excursions, cultural events, restaurants, maps etc. It also publishes a brochure listing the town's hotels, pensions and camp sites.

Transport – All parking in the town centre is either metered or pay and display. Daily parking permits are available for 5, 10 or 15fl at the VVV. The main sights in the historic town centre are within walking distance of one another, and buses operate outside this area.

Tours and walks – A 1hr 30min walking tour of the town leaves the VVV on Tuesdays at 2pm from early April to late August. There is also a **tour by horse-drawn tram**, departing from outside the town hall in Markt; reservations are required on ☎ (015) 256 18 28.

Boat trips – These leave from outside Koornmarkt 113, ☎ (015) 212 63 85, daily between 9.30am and 6pm from mid March to the end of October. The tour follows the Nieuwe Delft, ie Hippolytusbuurt and Voorstraat, passing the Oude Kerk and returning via Oude Delft and Koornmarkt.

Shopping – The old town centre has numerous shops, and there is an indoor shopping centre, In de Hoven, on the edge of town.

Markets – A **general market** takes place on Markt on Thursdays, while the **Brabant Peat Market** takes place on Saturdays. Plant and flower sellers set out their wares on Hippolytusbuurt on Thursdays, and a **flea market** is held along the canals every Saturday from mid April to the end of September. An **art market** also takes place on Heilige Geestkerkhof from mid April to mid September.

Delft specialities – The town still has a few factories making Delftware using traditional methods. The following are open to the public: **De Koninklijke Porceleyne Fles Anno 1653 Royal Delft**, Rotterdamseweg 196, ☎ (015) 256 92 14; **De Delftse Pauw**, Delftweg 133, ☎ (015) 212 49 20; **Aardewerkatelier de Candelaer**, Kerkstraat 14, ☎ (015) 213 18 48.

Almshouses – Delft's beautiful old *hofjes* are worth a visit: the **Begijnhof** and the Old Catholic Church, Bagijnhof 21; Hofje van Gratie, Van der Mastenstraat 26-38; the **Pauwhofje**, Paardenmarkt 54-62; the **Klaeuwshofje**, Oranje Plantage 58-77.

Night-life – **Theatre, cabaret, dance, musicals:** Theater de Veste, Asvest 1, ☎ (015) 212 13 12. **A special night out:** Stadsherberg De Mol, one of Delft's oldest buildings (1563), is at Molslaan 104, ☎ (015) 212 13 43. It is now a restaurant serving medieval dishes in suitably old-fashioned surroundings.

De Koninklijke Porceleyne Fles Anno 1653 Royal Delft

Following the Synod of Dort, Grotius who was a Remonstrant and follower of Oldenbarnevelt, was imprisoned in Slot Loevestein. He managed to escape and went to live in Paris, where in 1634 he became the Swedish Ambassador to France.

Johannes Vermeer (1632-75) – Delft and its townspeople were the whole universe of Vermeer, one of the Netherlands' greatest Old Masters, who was born and died in Delft.

Early on he applied himself to painting scenes of daily life, and he is one of those who, without breaking with tradition and without giving up the realism current at the time, revolutionised pictorial art.

Vermeer avoided the anecdotal and his subject matter tended to be banal and everyday, however he displayed an extraordinary sense for composition, geometry, for the use of unctuous matter, vivid tones (lemon yellow, sky blue) remarkably blended, and above all, for the marvellous light effects for which Vermeer is the great virtuoso.

This play of light is particularly fine in the famous *View of Delft* or in the portraits of women suffused with light and grace like the *Girl with a Pearl Earring (illustration: see The HAGUE)* and *The Lacemaker*.

The Mauritshuis in The Hague and the Rijksmuseum in Amsterdam have the greatest number of works by Vermeer, who was not in fact a prolific artist.

His contemporary, **Pieter de Hoogh** or **Hooch** (1629-84) was born in Rotterdam and spent a long time in Delft before going to Amsterdam. He depicted the life of the well-to-do bourgeois seen in interiors with open doors and windows, creating clever perspectives and light effects on the floor.

Delftware – In the second half of the 17C Delft acquired a reputation for making ceramics which soon spread over all of Europe.

Heir to the Italian majolica techniques, Delftware is tin-glazed earthenware and characterised by its remarkable lightness and its particularly shiny aspect, due to the application of a translucent coating.

At first Delft was known for its monochrome painting of blues on a white background; this is still one of the characteristics of Delftware today.

At the end of the 17C, the production became more varied, polychromy appeared, and there was not a design or shape, coming from China or Japan, which the Delft artists did not try out in order to satisfy the tastes of European clients fascinated by the Orient.

In the 18C the influence of Sèvres and Meissen porcelain expressed itself in objects with mannered outlines and decoration, while some of the pieces remained faithful to traditional Dutch scenes where one sees small boats sailing on the canals spanned by humpback bridges.

In the beginning of the 18C, Delftware reached its peak. But a decline set in rapidly, caused mainly by English competition and porcelain, made first in Germany and later throughout Europe. However, production continues today in several local factories.

Decorating Delftware

Ch. Sappa/HOA QUI

★★ HISTORIC CENTRE AND THE CANALS *allow half a day*

Markt – This long, narrow square stretches from the Nieuwe Kerk to the Stadhuis. In the middle stands a statue of Grotius *(see above)*.

★ **Nieuwe Kerk** ⊙ – This Gothic church (1381) has a brick tower crowned with a stone spire whose top has weathered to black. The carillon has bells cast by one of the Hemonys. The church contains the crypt of the princes of the House of Orange. Only a few members of this family were not buried here: Stadtholder and King of England, William III lies in Westminster Abbey, John William Friso in Leeuwarden, Philip-William, eldest son of William the Silent, in Diest (Belgium). The interior with three naves is plain. The squat columns support pointed arches, which become even more acute in the chancel.

Under the vault of dark wood, the clerestory windows of the nave rise above a tier of blind lancet windows which is replaced by a triforium in the chancel.

The well-lit nave contrasts with the more sombre light reflected by the rich stained-glass windows of the transept and the wide ambulatory. The glazing dates from 1927 to 1936 and they depict figurative motifs in warm colours. The exception is the stained-glass window portraying Grotius, in the north transept, by the master **Joep Nicolas** (1897-1972) with its muted grey and blue tones.

The **mausoleum of William the Silent**★ stands in the chancel, above the royal crypt. This imposing Renaissance edifice in marble and black stone was made by Hendrick de Keyser from 1614 to 1621. In the middle of a peristyle quartered by great allegorical figures, the prince lies in full-dress uniform, under the eyes of a bronze Fame. At his feet lies his ever-faithful dog. At the head of the recumbent marble statue, a bronze statue depicts William the Silent in armour.

In the centre of the chancel, the entrance to the House of Orange's crypt is indicated by a large emblazoned slab.

In the ambulatory, paved with tombstones, there is the mausoleum of King William I by William Geefs (1847) and further on a simple monument to Grotius (1781) and another by the Italian sculptor Canova to Prince Willem George Frederik.

The tower ⊙ – From the penultimate platform there is a **panorama**★ over the new town which lies beyond the ring canal. Both the Technical University and the nuclear reactor are quite easy to pick out and away on the horizon are Rotterdam and The Hague.

The Stadhuis and statue of Hugo de Groot

Stadhuis – The old town hall burnt down in 1618, it was rebuilt two years later by Hendrick de Keyser. Since the 1960s restoration it has recovered its 17C aspect with its mullioned windows set in lead and its low shutters. The shell-decorated façade fronting the square is dwarfed from behind by the old 15C keep, all that remains of the original *stadhuis*.

There is a fine view of the Nieuwe Kerk and its tower at the far end of the square.

Waag – The weigh-house (1770) has been transformed into a café. Nearby is the meat market, **Vleeshal**, the façade of which is appropriately adorned with two ox heads (1650).

William the Silent

William was born in 1533, in Dillenburg Castle in Germany, to Count William of Nassau and Juliana of Stolberg. On the death of his cousin **René de Chalon** (1544) William the Silent *(illustration: see Introduction, History)* inherited his possessions in France and in the Low Countries, and took his title of **Prince of Orange** as well as his motto *Je maintiendrai* (I shall maintain). In 1559, Philip II of Spain made him **Stadtholder** of the provinces of Holland, Zeeland and Utrecht.

Philip II took measures to repress the Calvinists and in so doing encouraged the growth of an opposition movement, which was lead by William of Orange and the **counts of Egmont and Hornes**. In 1566 the Iconoclasm *(see BREDA)* began. William, convinced he was under threat, fled to Dillenburg (1567). The counts of Egmont and Hornes were less lucky, they were executed in Brussels in 1568. In 1570 William, who had been brought up as a Catholic, became a Calvinist and he then began to give open support to the Beggars campaigns, both on land and sea. The capture of Brielle by the Sea Beggars on 1 April 1572 was only the beginning of a long and bitter conflict. The States of Holland met in Dordrecht in July and approved the revolt and acknowledged William of Orange as Stadtholder *(see DOR-DRECHT)*.

From 1572 onwards the prince often resided in Delft. In 1579 by the Union of Utrecht the provinces of Holland, Zeeland, Utrecht, Gelderland and Zutphen decided to join the fight; the other provinces followed suit fairly soon afterwards.

In 1581 Philip II offered a reward for the assassination of the prince; William of Orange retaliated with the well-known *Apologie*. He sought support from François of Anjou, brother of King Henri II of France, but the latter died (1584) before he could help.

On 10 July 1584 William the Silent was assassinated in the Prinsenhof *(see below)* in Delft.

Koornmarkt – *Cross the canal.*
This is the landing-stage for the boat trips mentioned above. At no 81 there is a lovely Renaissance-style house with medallions, called De Handboog (the bow). At no 67 the 18C patrician house, where the painter **Paul Tetar van Elven** lived (1823-96), is now a **museum** ⊙ containing furniture, painting by Van Elven and his contemporaries, and ceramics.

★ **Legermuseum** ⊙ – *Enter through Korte Geer, the continuation of Koornmarkt.*
The two former arsenals housing the Army Museum date from 1602 and 1692; they used to belong to the States of Holland and Western Friesland. The third building was used as a warehouse by the Dutch East India Company. The historical exhibition in the Gebouw 1692 building retraces the evolution of the Dutch army through the ages. Impressive collections illustrate the different stages of development of national military history: weapons (pistols, rifles, cannons), armour, uniforms, headgear (helmets, shakos), banners and trappings, not to mention means of transport, paintings and scale models. These cover the Roman and medieval periods, the Eighty Years War, in which the army reformer Maurice of Orange and his half-brother Frederick Henry distinguished themselves, the French domination (1795-1813) and its upheavals, the Belgian Revolution (1830), and the two World Wars. The post-war events relative to Indonesia and the Cold War are also represented. The 1602 building focuses more specifically on V-weapons, and holds temporary exhibitions.

★ **Oude Delft** – The somber water of the canal shaded by lime trees, the humpbacked bridges and the elegant façades make an attractive picture.
At no 39 the lovely house of the Dutch East India Company, **Oostindisch Huis**, has been restored. The façade carries the company's coat of arms and its initials: VOC. The weathervane is shaped like a ship.
Turn back and follow the quay.
One soon sees the slightly leaning spire of the Oude Kerk. Built of a sombre-coloured brick, it is flanked by four pinnacles, and is crooked, earning it the nickname of Scheve Jan, Crooked Jan. On the opposite quay there is the charming Gothic chapel, Kapel van het H Geestzusterhuis. From Nieuwstraat Bridge there is a fine **view**★ over the canal. At no 167 the Delft Water Board, **Hoogheemraadschap van Delfland**, an old patrician house (c 1520), displays a sumptuous Renaissance stone façade decorated with sculptured tympana. The portal is topped with polychrome armorial bearings.
No 169, **Het Wapen van Savoyen**, has a fine façade emblazoned with the arms of the House of Savoy and contains the local archives.

★ **Prinsenhof** ⊙ – *No 183. Enter from St Agathaplein, reached through a gateway on Oude Delft.*
The relief above one of the former gates on Oude Delft is a reminder that in the 17C the Prinsenhof was converted into a cloth market. It originally included a convent (St Agatha) before becoming, in 1572, the residence of William the Silent, who was assassinated here in 1584 by Balthazar Gerard. The Moordhal, or Assassination Hall, still has two bullet holes at the bottom of the stairs to the first floor.
The palace (Prinsenhof: the Prince's Court) now houses a museum with important historical collections relating to the Eighty Years War and the House of Orange-Nassau. The Historical Room on the first floor has angel figures on the ceiling and numerous portraits on the walls. The museum also has many still-life paintings and schutterstukken (portraits of companies of the civic guard) and some fine tapestries. The buildings, in Late Gothic style, date from the 15C and 16C and are grouped around two courtyards. After the Reformation, the chapel of the old monastery was given to the Wallonian Reformed Church and services were held in French for Protestants who had fled from the Southern Netherlands.

Oude Kerk ⊙ – Dedicated to St Hippolytus, this 13C church, which is reflected in the waters of Oude Delft was enlarged four times. Since the 16C it has three chancels and the beginning of a transept. The tower, which leans, embedded in the main nave, is built on the foundations of a watchtower. It has the second biggest bell in the Netherlands (9t).
Numerous memorial slabs (16C-18C) are set in the pavement. The finely carved Renaissance pulpit resembles the one in the Grote Kerk in The Hague.
The stained-glass windows (1972) in the chancel, the transept and at the end of the side aisles, made by Joep Nicolas have lovely figurative compositions.
Several famous people are buried in this church. In the main chancel Admiral Piet Hein is shown lying in full armour: it is the work of Pieter de Keyser, the son of Hendrick.
In the chapel near the north chancel, is the Baroque mausoleum of Admiral Tromp by Rombout Verhulst. The low relief depicts the naval battle of Terheyde, where the admiral was killed in 1653.
To the north of the tower, near the stained-glass window depicting William the Silent, there is the monument to the naturalist Van Leeuwenhoek.

DELFT

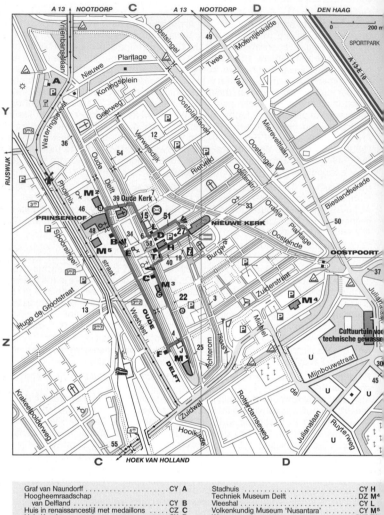

Hippolytusbuurt – This tree-lined canal is one of the oldest in Delft. On the corne of Hippolytusbuurt and Camaretten is the fish market (still in operation), next t which stands the former meat market. Opposite this is a 16C house (Kaaskop with crow-stepped gables.

Voldersgracht – This is a picturesque canal, lined on the south side by a fe corbelled houses.
From the second bridge, there is a fine view of the Nieuw Kerk's tower.

ADDITIONAL SIGHTS

★ **Oostpoort** – Formerly called St Catherine's Gate, it is the only one remainin from the town walls. It is a lovely dark brick construction, flanked wit two slender octagonal turrets dating from the 15C and 16C. There is a fine vie from the picturesque white lever bridge in front of it. A canal passes under th annexe.

Cultuurtuin voor technische gewassen ⊙ – This botanical garden has been used to grow a wide variety of plants for Delft Technical University since 1917. Its purpose is purely scientific and educational. It has glasshouses with tropical and subtropical plants, and there are also two short walking routes for visitors to the tree and herb garden.

Techniek Museum Delft ⊙ – This museum is located in the former mechanical engineering laboratory of the Technical College, and consists of three very large halls dating from about 1910. These provide an overview of technology past and present, including steam-operated machinery and engines. Hall 3 contains the Museum IJkwezen, or weights and measures museum, with a collection of measuring and weighing equipment.

★ **Museum Lambert van Meerten** ⊙ – This beautiful 19C canalside mansion has a magnificent collection of **Dutch and foreign tiles**★ from the 16C to the 19C. The attractive little passageway from the hall to the vestibule is decorated with Gothic and Renaissance-style motifs, while the monumental staircase depicts a naval battle between French, English and Dutch ships. Other tiles and tile pictures depict flowers, animals, and traditional crafts. The museum also has collections of Delftware, furniture and other items from the estate of the industrialist Lambert Van Meerten (1042-1904).

Volkenkundig Museum Nusantara ⊙ – Nusantara means island kingdom between two hemispheres, and the museum's collection is devoted to the history and cultures of Indonesia and its 13 000-plus islands. It includes such items as statues, masks, weapons, textiles, shadow puppets and jewellery. One of the rooms contains *Javanese gamelan instruments*, and the museum also hosts temporary exhibitions.

Graf van Naundorff – The tree-lined square at the far end of Noordeinde canal, the continuation of Oude Delft, is the last resting place of the pretender Naundorff. Until recently it was claimed that he was the son of Louis XVI, but this has now been disproved by DNA testing.

DELTA★

Zuid-Holland – Zeeland
Michelin maps 908 and 211

In the coastal provinces of Zuid-Holland and Zeeland the estuaries of the Rhine, Maas and Scheldt form a complicated network of islands, headlands and channels known as the Delta.

HISTORICAL AND GEOGRAPHICAL NOTES

At the mouth of three great rivers – The Rhine divides into two branches as it crosses the Netherlands, the Neder Rijn and the Waal. The **Neder Rijn** (Lower Rhine) becomes the Lek, then the Nieuwe Maas before entering the Nieuwe Waterweg. The **Waal**, the main arm of the Rhine, flows into the Lek and the Maas. The **Maas**, which also has several names (Bergse Maas, Amer) flows into the Hollands Diep. The Oosterschelde is a former estuary of the **Schelde** (Scheldt), which presently flows into the Westerschelde.
The rivers thread their way between the islands, some of which have become peninsulas.

A region under constant threat – The islands built up slowly towards the end of the Middle Ages as the rivers deposited sediments. They are generally very low-lying, many below Amsterdam Reference Level and most under 5m/16ft. The coastline is protected by high dunes while the banks of the rivers are strengthened by dikes. Several times throughout history these have proved vulnerable when the great surge tides swept inland.
On the feast day of **St Elisabeth** (19 November) 1421 the flood waters inundated the entire Delta and swept as far inland as Dordrecht and the Biesbosch area. Six villages were inundated and 10 000 lost their lives.
There was another great disaster on the night of 31 January 1953 when, under the combined effects of low atmospheric pressure and high tides, the water breached the dikes in several places. Once again the islands were inundated; 1 835 died and a further 500 000 were left homeless. The effects were felt as far inland as the Hollandse IJssel.

The Delta Plan – Three years after the tidal wave of 1953, two options were under discussion to prevent the recurrence of similar tragedies: heighten the existing dikes or dam the major estuaries and inlets of the Delta. In 1958 the Delta Plan was incorporated in an Act of Parliament.

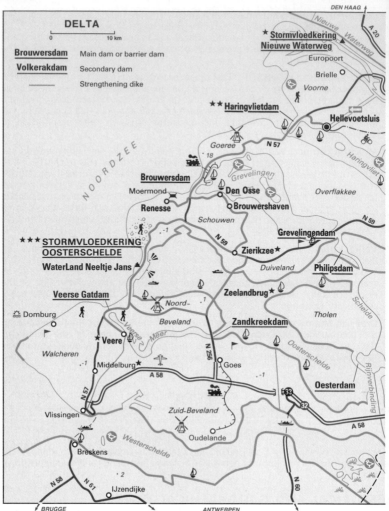

Four **main dams**, two with locks, closed off the inlets of the North Sea and several secondary dams closed off the estuaries further inland. The **secondary dams** afforded initial protection from high tides during the construction of the main dams. Once the main dams were finished the importance of the secondary ones diminished, although they proved a considerable asset to the road network.

The completion in May 1997 of the storm barrier in the Nieuwe Waterweg, which flows through Rotterdam, meant that the Delta Plan had been implemented in full after nearly 40 years. The Wester-schelde, which gives access to the port of Antwerp, is now the only inlet remaining open. The dams have many advantages: they shorten the coast-line by approximately 700km/435mi, and they form fresh-water lakes inland (ie Haringv-

> ### Boat trips
>
> Boat trips are available in the northern part of the Delta, leaving from Rotterdam *(see ROTTERDAM)* and Willemstad, or further along the Oosterschelde from Zierikzee *(see ZIERIKZEE)* or WaterLand Neeltje Jans *(see below).*

lietdam and further to the east two auxiliary dams, Philipsdam and Oesterdam). They reduce the seepage of salt water into the water table, limit the risk of floods, form ideal stretches of water for recreational purposes, improve the road network and encourage the development of the region.

The Delta Plan also included the raising and strengthening of existing dikes along navigable waterways and the development of the Biesbosch area.

The Scheldt-Rhine Canal, to the east of the Delta, was completed in 1975 and links Antwerp to the Volkerak, a distance of 37km/23mi.

Dams and bridges – Already by 1950 the Brielse Maas, downstream from Rotterdam, had been transformed into a lake called the Brielse Meer. Since it was necessary to leave the New Waterway open for navigation a storm surge barrier, **Stormvloedkering Hollandse IJssel**, was built between 1954 and 1958 on the Hollandse IJssel near Krimpen aan de IJssel in the eastern suburbs of Rotterdam. A mobile gate is raised to allow ships through. The reserve lock (120x24m/394x79ft) alongside is for larger vessels and ships in general when the gates are closed. Following the completion of the storm barrier in Nieuwe Waterweg in 1997, the Rotterdamse Waterweg can now also be fully closed (see ROTTERDAM: Excursions).

The Haringvliet estuary was closed off by the **Haringvlietdam** while further inland the secondary **Volkerakdam** linked Overflakkee to the province of Noord Brabant. Built between 1957 and 1969, the dam has three large sluice caissons and is itself linked to **Haringvlietbrug** which spans the waterway to the north towards Beijerland.

To the south, the Brouwershavense Gat Channel is closed by the **Brouwersdam** with inland the **Grevelingendam** on the waterway of the same name. The latter links Duiveland and Overflakkee and when it was built between 1958 and 1965, 170 000t of rubble were tipped as infill from the gondolas of a cableway. The **Philipsdam** is a prolongation to the southeast.

The year 1986 saw the completion of the Oosterschelde Storm Surge Barrier, **Stormvloedkering in de Oosterschelde**. In the event of a bad storm or when the water level reaches a critical point, it is now possible to close off this estuary, the widest (9km/6mi) and the deepest (40m/130ft) in the Delta. Two dams east of the estuary, **Oesterdam** (1986) and Philipsdam (see above) protect the Scheldt-Rhine Canal from tidal flow. The Oosterschelde is also spanned by the **Zeelandbrug**.

The saltwater channel, Veerse Meer to the south of Noord-Beveland is closed off by **Veerse Gatdam**, which is backed up by a secondary dam, **Zandkreekdam**, on the saltwater Zandkreek channel between Noord-and Zuid-Beveland. Built between 1956 and 1960, the 800m/2 625ft long dam has a lock (140x20m/459x65ft) spanned by a swing bridge for traffic.

Two companies provide regular boat services across the estuary. There is a project under discussion to bridge the crossing.

THE STORM SURGE BARRIER

Stormvloedkering in de Oosterschelde – Construction of the storm surge barrier began in 1976, and was completed 10 years later. The road running along the dam was opened in 1987.

This gigantic and unique structure is 3km/2mi long. It is built across three tidal channels of the Oosterschelde and two artificial islands which were originally used as construction bases.

The original project involved the river being completely closed off, but this was changed to keep the link with the sea open. The barrier consists of 65 prefabricated concrete piers and 62 sliding steel gates. Each pillar is 30-38m/99-125ft high, and weighs up to 18 000t. The gates are normally raised, but can be closed in less than an hour in the event of high water or a storm. This construction preserves 75% of the tidal flow in the Oosterschelde and thus the unique estuary habitat with its fish and its oyster and mussel beds.

Ir Topshuis on the former artificial island of Neeltje Jans houses the central control room and **Waterland Neeltje Jans** ⊙, which gives an idea of the importance of the Delta Project to the area as a whole and the history of land reclamation and hydraulic engineering in the Netherlands. A working model reproduces the 1953 floods and explains the safety measures implemented since then. The film *Delta Finale* recounts the successive stages of the development of the dam: the making of the different prefabricated elements, the preparation of foundations in the sandy channel bed, the floating and sinking into position of the concrete piers and finally the fitting of the computer controlled sluice gates.

The tour of one of the pillars of the dam is also worthwhile, particularly when a flood occurs; access to the pillar is through the control room, equipped with oil pumps and electrical controls. Note the powerful current: in the Oosterschelde each tide displaces 800 million cubic metres of water.

Another high point is the futuristic **Waterpaviljoen**, which uses light, sound and other effects to show the cycle of water. In summer, there are nature walks on the island, and it is also possible to climb one of the pillars of the barrier, go on a tour of the Oosterschelde or play in the water playground.

Oosterschelde storm surge barrier

HELLEVOETSLUIS TO VEERE

99km/62mi - allow a day

Hellevoetsluis – This small village on an inlet of the sea, Haringvliet, has a marina.

★★ **Haringvlietdam** – This major civil engineering project was undertaken from 1955 to 1971.

Initially an artificial construction site was built in the middle of the estuary and surrounded by an encircling dike. A cableway was used in the final stages, a method that had already been used on the Grevelingendam. Concrete blocks were tipped from the gondolas into the final channel to be dammed.

Some 5km/3mi long, the Haringvlietdam has 17 drainage sluices of 56.50m/185ft. Their gates take 20min to open using a hydraulic press system with 68 presses set within the 16 pillars and the abutment piers. Normally these sluice gates are closed and the water is forced back to the Nieuwe Waterweg. The drainage locks help to achieve a balance between fresh and saltwater. A shipping lock has been made near the small port to the south.

Brouwersdam – The dam was built from 1963 to 1972 between the islands of Goeree and Schouwen; there is no lock. To complete the north channel, Springerdiep, sluice caissons were made, the same system which had been used for the first time when building the Veerse Gatdam. The south channel, Brouwershavense Gat, was filled in using the cableway system whereby 15t loads of concrete blocks were dropped each time by the gondola.

Between the Brouwersdam and Grevelingendam is the saltwater but tideless lake, Grevelingenmeer.

Renesse – This small village on the north coast of the island of Schouwen has a lovely sandy beach. Just to the east is a fine 16C to 17C manor, **Slot Moermond** ⊘, with a 14C porch.

Den Osse – This recent marina is well hidden by the dikes.

Brouwershaven – This was originally a prosperous port trading in beer from Delft (*brouwer*: brewer); however life today revolves around its small pleasure boat harbour.

Brouwershaven suffered during the 1953 floods. This was the home town of the statesman, **Jacob Cats** (1577-1660), nicknamed Father Cats, who was Grand Pensionary of Holland and West Friesland from 1635 to 1651. He was also known for his poetry. Brouwershaven has a lovely 15C Gothic church, the **Sint-Nico-laaskerk** ⊘, with a transept and ambulatory. The pulpit and font screen are in the Rococo style. The town hall, **stadhuis**, of 1599 has a Renaissance façade in stone, highly decorated, and topped by a pinnacle.

* **Zierikzee** – *See ZIERIKZEE.*

* **Stormvloedkering in de Oosterschelde** – *See above.*

* **Zeelandbrug** – *Illustration: see Admission times and charges.* In 1955 this bridge was built to link Zierikzee to the former island of Noord-Beveland. The crossing was paralleled with the opening of the road along the Oosterschelde Barrier. This impressive feat of engineering bridges the 5 022m/16 476ft waterway in 50 arches at a height of 17m/56ft above water level. The swing bridge on the Schouwen-Duiveland side gives passage to boats with tall masts.

Veerse Gatdam – This dam was built (1958-61) from a point west of Veere on the island of Walcheren to the former island of Noord-Beveland. It is 2 700m/8 858ft long, and in spite of protection from a sandbank is very exposed to storms, due to its northwesterly orientation. It was the first dam to use sluice caissons; these were placed on the bed of the channel and the sluice gates were then closed at slack water and this prevented the formation of a destructive current. Another small saltwater and tideless lake, the Veerse Meer, lies between this dam and the Zandkreekdam to the east.

* **Veere** – *See VEERE.*

Michelin on the Net : www.michelin-travel.com

Our route planning service covers all of Europe – twenty-one countries and one million kilometres of highways and byways – enabling you to plot many different itineraries from wherever you are. The itinerary options allow you to choose a preferred route – for example, quickest, shortest, or Michelin recommended.

The network is updated three times weekly, integrating ongoing road works, detours, new motorways, and snowbound mountain passes.

The description of the itinerary includes the distances and travelling times between towns, selected hotels and restaurants.

DEVENTER*

Overijssel
Population 69 131
Michelin maps 908 J 5, 210 W 9 and 211 W 9
Plan of the conurbation in the current Michelin Red Guide Benelux

Deventer stands on the east bank of the IJssel in the south of the province of Overijssel. This former Hanseatic town has a historic centre full of character which is witness to a rich past.

HISTORICAL NOTES

As early as the 9C it was a prosperous port. At the end of the 9C, the city became the residence of the Utrecht bishops, who fled from their town threatened by the Vikings. The remains of an 11C episcopal palace have been found in Nieuwe Markt. The town soon played an important religious role. The theologian **Gerhard Groote** (1340-84), born in Deventer, was the innovator of a spiritual movement, the **Devotio Moderna** (modern devotion). One of his pupils, Florentius Radewyns, following the wishes of his master, founded in Deventer c 1384 the first monastery for the **Order of the Brethren of the Common Life**, a community devoted to the education and care of the poor, which had a great intellectual influence in Europe. Those who passed through his school included Thomas à Kempis (*see ZWOLLE*), Pope Adrian VI (*see UTRECHT*), Erasmus (1475-76) and Descartes (1632-33).

In the 16C the artist Hendrick Terbrugghen was born in Deventer. At the end of the 17C, the painter Gerard Terborch, born in Zwolle, came to work here, dying in 1681.

In the 16C and 17C printing was an important enterprise in the town: already in the 15C numerous incunabula were produced.

Today the metallurgical industry, as well as chemical, graphic and foodstuff industries are among the main activities of this town; a well-known gingerbread (**Deventer koek**) is made here.

Deventer is an Old Catholic Episcopal See.

Boat tours ⊙ – Tours on the IJssel offer fine views of the city.

TOWN CENTRE 2hr

Brink – It is the main square of the town, so named, as in all localities of Saxon origin. A market is held here (Friday mornings and Saturdays). At nos 11

Bussink's Deventer gingerbread shop

and 12, there is an early 17C façade decorated with shells. The richly decorated **Penninckhuis** dates from 1590.

Waag – This is a large, slightly leaning weigh house built in 1528 in the late Gothic style and complemented in 1643 by the addition of a tall perron resting on arcades. On the north façade hangs a huge cauldron in which, it is purported counterfeiters used to be boiled.

The building contains the **Historisch Museum De Waag** ⊙, displaying several collections related to the town's history: archeological findings, paintings, drawings and miscellaneous objects. Note the splendid 17C majolica oven and the bicycles believed to be the oldest in the Netherlands.

De Drie Haringen – This merchant's house (1575), known as the House of the Three Herrings, has a fine Renaissance façade decorated with a façade stone depicting three herrings.

On the other side of the street no 69 (public library) has an elegant façade.

Speelgoed- en Blikmuseum ⊙ – The biggest public collection of toys in the country has been set up in two medieval houses. Most of the exhibits were made after 1860: construction sets, train sets, dolls, games, mechanical toys and miniature tea sets. One section presents a range of packaging tins, manufactured in the Netherlands between 1800 and 1980.

Retrace your steps and turn right into Bergstraat.

Bergstraat – In this street of Bergkwartier or hill quarter, which has been restored, there are several fine old façades; lovely view over the two towers of the Bergkerk.

Sint-Nicolaas or Bergkerk – Building started c 1200 and the two great west front towers, with spires, date from that period. In the 15C the rest of the building was remodelled in the Gothic style.

Return to Brink via Kerksteeg and Menstraat. Polstraat then leads to Grote Kerkhof.

Grote Kerkhof – The Grote Kerk and Stadhuis are both on this square.

Stadhuis ⊙ – The town hall complex (greatly restored) is in three parts: the Raadhuis, the Wanthuis (also giving on to Polstraat), and the Landshuis. The joint façade of the Raadhuis and the Wanthuis dates from the 17C; its architect Jacob Roman also designed Het Loo Palace in Apeldoorn.

The **Landshuis** has a lovely brick façade (1632) punctuated by pilasters and topped by a pinnacled gable.

In the hall several 17C and 18C group portraits of guilds are exhibited. A room on the first floor of the Raadhuis has a lovely canvas by Terborch: the **Aldermen's Council**, painted in 1657.

Grote Kerk or Sint-Lebuïnuskerk – It bears the name of Lebuin, the Saxon Apostle, who built a church here in the 8C.

The Romanesque church founded c 1040 by Bernulphus, Bishop of Utrecht, was converted after 1235 and then again in the 15C in the Gothic style. It is a vast building flanked to the west by a tower topped with an octagonal lantern in wood designed by Hendrick de Keyser.

Its carillon, which was cast by one of the Hemonys, can be heard during **concerts** ⊙.

In the hall-type interior the remains of a double transept can still be seen. The stellar vaulting has paintings round the keystones (16C). Other paintings can be seen, notably under the porch near the tower; the *Bearing of the Cross* dates from the 16C. The 19C great **organ** ⊙ has 3 000 pipes.

The Romanesque crypt (1040), under the chancel, is remarkable with its six short pillars, cabled or decorated with geometric motifs.

Tower ⊙ – From the top (219 steps) there is a lovely view of the city.

Return to Brink via the pedestrian area.

ADDITIONAL SIGHT

Buyskensklooster – This early 15C building has recovered its brickwork walls. It is the former convent of St Agnes where the Sisters of the Common Life lived, following the rules set forth by Gerhard Groote. It contains the **town archives** (no 3) and a library, the Stadsbibliotheek or **Atheneumbibliotheek** ⊙, where there are interesting **exhibitions** of books and manuscripts.

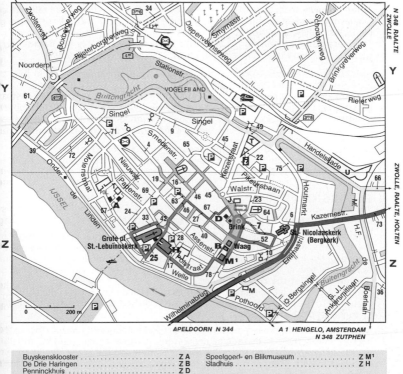

EXCURSION

Holten and Markelo – *26km/16mi to the east via Snipperlingsdijk.*

Holten – This town, situated in the Salland region, attracts many tourists, drawn by the wooded and sandy heights of the **Holterberg** (alt 60m/200ft), which mark the southern limit of the Scandinavian glaciers.
On the Holterberg, there is the **Natuurdiorama Holterberg**★ ⊘. About 10 large **dioramas**★ bring to life ecosystems and their fauna, which are to be found locally; some are shown with their winter coats. Note the diorama showing a group of Scandinavian elks being attacked by wolves.
In a nearby clearing is a beautifully landscaped **Canadian military cemetery**, with 1 496 graves of Canadians killed in the Second World War.

Markelo – At the beginning of the century an important field of funeral urns *(see Introduction: History)* was found north of Markelo.
Markelo has an **open-air theatre (Openluchttheater)**, **De Kösterskoele**.

DOESBURG

Gelderland
Population 10 908
Michelin maps 908 J 5 and 211 V 10

At the confluence of the IJssel and the Oude IJssel, Doesburg, an old stronghold of the Zutphen earldom, was a prosperous commercial town in the Middle Ages and a member of the Hanseatic League in 1447. This lovely town in the Achterhoek *(see ZUTPHEN: Excursion)* has kept some vestiges of its past, notably the remains of ramparts dating from 1630 *(to the south)* and several Gothic and Renaissance façades.

Boat trips ⊘ – On the IJssel.

SIGHTS

Grote Kerk or Martinikerk ⊘ – This Gothic church dedicated to St Martin (15C) is lit by tall Flamboyant windows. Its high tower was destroyed in 1945, but has been rebuilt and has a carillon. Organ concerts are given in summer.

Waag – Now a restaurant, this attractive weigh house (c 1500) has tall picture windows with painted shutters, topped by tympana and a gable decorated with pinnacles. Inside, in a typical setting, the weigh house scales can be seen.
There are other interesting houses in the same street, notably the **Baerkenhuizen** (nos 29-31), two Renaissance buildings of 1649 with voluted gables.

Stadhuis – It stands opposite the Waag. Dating from the 14C, it has an interesting façade on Roggestraat.
The **Streekmuseum De Roode Tooren** ⊘ is at nos 9-11 in the same street. Reconstructions include a clog-maker's workshop, a room where a cigar-maker chopped tobacco and an old grocer's shop. Note the scale model of a pontoon bridge: near Doesburg the banks of the IJssel were linked by this type of bridge until 1952.

Doesburgsch Mosterd- en Azijnmuseum ⊘ – *Boekholtstraat 22.*
In this factory, founded in 1457, vinegar and mustard are prepared according to traditional methods using small wooden barrels.

EXCURSION

Doetinchem and 's-Heerenberg – *22km/14mi to the southeast.*

Doetinchem – On the banks of the Oude IJssel, this town, situated in the heart of the Achterhoek, formerly belonged to the Zutphen earldom. It was badly damaged by a bombardment in 1945. Today, it is a modern industrial and commercial town. The traditional manufacturing of wooden clogs is still one of the specialities of the city and its vicinity.
Doetinchem has a large **wall mill** (1850) near the Oude IJssel (now the VVV).
6km/4mi to the east of the town stands the large **Kasteel Slangenburg**, surrounded by moats and a beautiful **park**; it belongs to the Benedictine Order.

's-Heerenberg – The imposing castle, **Huis Bergh** ⊘, dominates this village close to the border. Built in the 13C by the Van den Berghs, it was altered in the 17C. In 1946 its last owner bequeathed the castle and its contents to the State. The interior is embellished with antique furniture, paintings and carvings on wood and ivory. Nearby, the Gothic castle chapel has become the parish church.

DOKKUM

Fryslân

Michelin maps 908 J 2 and 210 V 3 – Local map see LEEUWARDEN

The small town of Dokkum, in the north of Friesland, was once a flourishing port. Today it hides behind the remains of its tree-covered ramparts, from which only a few bell-towers and tall mills emerge. As the town is built on a mound, it has several steeply sloping streets.

St Boniface and his 52 companions were murdered here in 754. This English-born missionary came to Friesland in 716 to convert the people to Christianity; he then attached himself to St Willibrord in Utrecht. He was killed during his second mission to Friesland, and is buried in Fulda, Germany, where he had founded a monastery.

SIGHTS

Zijl – From this wide bridge, there is a fine **view** over Klein Diep (meaning small canal) bordered by a mill, and the Groot Diep (large canal). The simple 17C **stadhuis**, or town hall, has a white clock tower and a 19C neo-Classical façade. On the other side of the canal are three lovely early-17C houses with crow-stepped gables which have been well restored.
Follow Diepswal to reach the museum.

Museum Het Admiraliteitshuis ⊘ – This regional museum is installed in the former Admiralty House (1618) and a neighbouring 18C house; note the Admiralty House's small Renaissance-style portal.
The collections are varied: Dokkum silverwork, a Frisian sledge of carved wood, paintings, antique chests, items excavated from ancient burial mounds, 19C toys, and Frisian folk art. There is a display of local costume on the top floor, including an interesting black cap from the Carolingian period found in a burial mound.

Waag – *Grote Breedstraat*. This small weigh-house (1754) has two decorated pediments, one of which bears the town's coat of arms (a cresent moon and three stars).

Grote Kerk or Sint-Martinuskerk ⊘ – A mound and a church were erected here to commemorate the murder of St Boniface. The present building in the Gothic style is now a Dutch Reformed church; the chancel dates from the 15C. Inside the elevation over the side aisles includes a very tall gallery.
A great number of tombstones are embedded in the floor; note the Frisian pulpit with elegant carved panels portraying a lion, a pelican and a falcon.

Bonifatiuskapel – *Leave Dokkum to the south in the direction of Leeuwarden and once beyond the lever bridge take the second road on the left.*
In the middle of the square stands the statue (1962) of the bearded monk, St Boniface, shielding his head with his Bible from his Frisian attackers.
The chapel dedicated to St Boniface (1934) in the small park is the centre for a popular annual pilgrimage *(see Calendar of events)*.

DOORN

Utrecht

Population 10 117

Michelin maps 908 H 5 and 211 R 10

Situated on the edge of a wooded region, the small town of Doorn has a castle of the same name on its southern outskirts.

Huis Doorn ⊘ – Surrounded by moats, set in the middle of a lovely park, this castle was the home of the ex-Kaiser of Germany **Wilhelm II**, from 1920 to his death in 1941. Forced into exile after he refused to abdicate in November 1918, he was first given refuge in Kasteel Amerongen. Then, in May 1920, he and the Empress Augusta Victoria moved into Doorn Castle which he had acquired. His wife died the following year. In 1922 he married Hermine, Princess of Reuss.
The original castle was built in the 14C by the Bishop of Utrecht to defend his territory (altered in 1780) and the tower on the southwest side is part of the medieval castle.
Now a **museum**, the castle contains souvenirs of Wilhelm II, who brought his **collections** ★ (paintings, tapestries) from the imperial palaces. These are displayed in a setting which has remained unchanged since the Kaiser's death.
One room is devoted to Frederick the Great (King Frederick II of Prussia, 1712-86), the most famous representative of the Hohenzollern family, who was a great art lover and collected paintings and pastels of the French School (Nicolas Lancret, Watteau's contemporary) as well as snuffboxes.
There is also a fine collection of family silver, consisting mainly of presents received by the Hohenzollerns in the 19C and 20C as well as a good collection of uniforms, helmets, boots and ceremonial sabres which belonged to Wilhelm II. Kaiser Wilhelm's mausoleum stands in the park.

DORDRECHT*

Zuid-Holland

Population 117 258
Michelin map 908 F 6 or 211 N 12
Plan of the conurbation in the current Michelin Red Guide Benelux

In the south of the province of Zuid-Holland, Dordrecht, which the Dutch familiar call Dordt, is an important river centre between the Beneden Merwede, branch of th Rhine, the Noord, which links it to Rotterdam and the Nieuwe Maas, the Dordtse K which links it to the Maas and the Oude Maas. It is also a great pleasure boat harbou and yachts are anchored at most of the town's quaysides, and more to the east, the Wantij. The old town has kept its colourful quays, its canals and its old façade while the southern quarters rival with their bolder constructions.
It inspired many painters including Van Goyen (1596-1656); a number of 17C an 18C artists were born here *(see below)*. **Ary Scheffer** (1795-1858), painter of biblic and religious scenes, was Louis-Philippe's court painter.

Boat trips ⊘ – Dordrecht is the departure point for boat trips through the Biesboscl

HISTORICAL NOTES

According to the chronicles, the town was destroyed by the Vikings in 837.
In 1220 it acquired city rights from the Count of Holland, William I, and because o this, it is considered the oldest town in the earldom. It was fortified at the end of th 13C. The 14C was a period of great prosperity for Dordrecht due to the privilege o applying stop-over tolls, which beginning in 1299, were levied on goods coming fror the Rhine. The 15C, on the contrary, was a time of disaster: there was th unsuccessful siege in 1418 by Count John of Brabant as part of the struggle betwee the Hooks and Cods; the St Elisabeth's Day Flood of 1421 which isolated the tow making it an island; the great fire of 1457 and then its capture in 1480 by John o Egmont. In the 16C the town recovered its splendour.

The cradle of independence – It was in the Dordrecht Court of Justice (Het Hof) tha the first free assembly of the Holland and Zeeland States was held in July 1572. Th capture of Brielle by the Sea Beggars in April of that same year had precipitated th event.
In Dordrecht the delegates of the 12 confederate states of Holland and the nobilit decided to deliver the country from the Duke of Alba's armies, and they proclaime William the Silent as stadtholder. In this way they laid the foundation for the futur United Provinces *(see Introduction: History)*.

Synod of Dort – Dordrecht was also the meeting place between 1618 and 1619 o the great synod of Protestant theologians who came to settle the controversy tha had arisen between the moderate **Remonstrants** or Arminians, supporters of Arminiu who upheld that the blessings of grace were open to all, and the **Gomarists**, supporter of **Gomarus**, a strict Calvinist who defended the principle of predestination. The latte group won, with the help of Maurice of Orange, and carried out bloody persecution on their opponents, such as Oldenbarnevelt *(see AMERSFOORT)* and Grotius *(se DELFT)*.

The De Witt brothers

Dordrecht was the birthplace of the De Witt brothers, distinguished 17C statesmen.
Johan de Witt (1625-72) became the Grand Pensionary of Holland in 1653. Although he was an excellent administrator, he had less success in foreign affairs. He was unable to avoid the defeat of the Dutch fleet by England in 1654, which marked the end of the First Anglo-Dutch War. In addition he was hostile to the predominance of the House of Orange and as a result, he was quite unpopular for being out of step with popular opinion.
After having won the Second Anglo-Dutch War (1665-67) and withstood the War of Devolution led by Louis XIV (1667-68), Johan de Witt managed to get approval for the **Perpetual Edict** of 1667, which abolished the Stadtholdership and thus the Orangist power in the province of Holland.
However, the same year (1672) that Louis XIV and Charles II united against the United Provinces in the Third Dutch War, the people, feeling threatened, repealed the Perpetual Edict; William of Orange, was elected Stadtholder as William III and army commander. Finally, **Cornelis**, the brother of Johan de Witt and burgomaster of Dordrecht in 1666, was wrongly accused of conspiring against William III and was imprisoned in the Prison Gate in The Hague. While visiting him, Johan de Witt was the victim of an uprising and was murdered with his brother near the prison *(see The HAGUE)*.

---

t this synod, the union of all Protestant churches in the country took place, except
or the Remonstrants, and a joint doctrine (canons of Dort) was established. The
neologian **Episcopius**, who had pleaded the cause of the Remonstrants, then founded
Remonstrant Church in Antwerp (1619).

Birthplace of 17C painters – A number of 17C painters were born in Dordrecht.
Some of them were Rembrandt's students.

Ferdinand Bol (1616-80) went to live in Amsterdam where he worked in Rembrandt's
studio. His works, notably the numerous portraits tinged with seriousness, are very
like those of his master, for their chiaroscuro, the abundance of impasting and the
harmony between warm colours.

He also did the famous guild painting, *The Governors of the Leper Hospital* (1649),
exhibited in the Amsterdams Historisch Museum.

Nicolaes Maes (1634-93) was also influenced by Rembrandt, whose pupil he was from
1648 to 1652, in Amsterdam. More realist than the latter, he chose common people,
modest subjects, scenes which he made somewhat touching and which he enriched
by his science of chiaroscuro and reddish tones. The best known of his works is *Girl
at a Window: the Daydreamer* in the Rijksmuseum in Amsterdam. At the end of his
life, on the contrary, he painted fashionable portraits.

Samuel van Hoogstraten (1627-78) studied with Rembrandt, then after having travelled
a great deal in Europe, returned to his birthplace. He painted mainly portraits and
interior scenes which, by their effects of light and perspective can be compared to
those of Pieter de Hooch. **Godfried Schalcken** (1643-1706) was his pupil.

Aert van Gelder (1645-1727) was first a pupil of Van Hoogstraten, then of the ageing
Rembrandt, in Amsterdam. His biblical scenes owe a lot to the technique of the great
master, notably the sumptuous clothes and the slightly theatrical composition.

Albert Cuyp (1620-91) was influenced by Jan van Goyen and painted landscapes of very
studied composition with luminous backgrounds, immense skies and in the
foreground horsemen or peaceful herds of cattle.

From the 17C to the present – In the early 17C Dordrecht was first supplanted by
Amsterdam, and then by Rotterdam. The town became French in 1795.

Today Dordrecht has a flourishing industrial sector as firms are particuarly attracted
by its good location. Industries include chemicals, shipbuilding, aeronautics, electronics and the building industry. The tertiary sector is highly developed.

★ OLD TOWN *half a day*

★ **Grote Kerk or Onze-Lieve-Vrouwekerk** ⊘ – Legend has it that the church was
started by a young girl, St Sura, who, wishing to build a chapel to the Virgin and

possessing only three *daal-
ders*, saw, each time she
prayed that three new coins
were miraculously added to
her treasure. In fact a
chapel existed in the Middle
Ages. It was enlarged in the
13C, then in the 14C, but a
fire destroyed the building
in 1457. The present
church, which is Protes-
tant, was built between
1460 and 1502 in Brabant
Gothic style.

The massive **tower** has
remained unfinished be-
cause it leans on the north
side: it ends in a terrace
with four clock faces
outlining its square shape.
The **carillon** ⊘ (1949)
consists of 49 bells.

Interior – It is very large
(108m/354ft long) and
imposing with its 56 pillars
topped in Brabant Gothic
style with crocket capitals.
The oak **choir stalls**★ are
finely carved by the Fleming Jan Terwen between
1538 and 1542 in the
Renaissance style, and are
among the most beautiful
in the country.

Grote Kerk, Dordrecht

The low reliefs above the backs of the last row, north side, depict secula
triumphs, notably those of Emperor Charles V; south side, religious triumph;
There are also lovely cheekpieces and misericords carved with fantastic subject;
The Baroque chancel screen (1744) is elegant. In a chapel of the ambulatory o
the east side, three stained-glass windows depict episodes in the town's history
the flood of 1421, the fire of 1457 and the capture of the town in 1480.
The pulpit (1756) with a marble base is in the Rococo style. The **organ** ⊘ was bu
in 1671 by Nicolaas van Hagen of Antwerp. 17C and 18C stone slabs pave th
church floor.

Tower ⊘ – *279 steps.*
On the way up take the chance to get a closer look at the 1626 clock.
From the top terrace, there is a superb **view★★** over the old town where the house
huddle together alongside the canals and docks. Note the length of the roofs: lan
bordering the canals was so expensive that houses were built backwards from th
canal with façades as narrow as possible. One can also see the rivers which circ
round the town, spanned by large bridges, and modern Dordrecht.
To the right of the tower, the Leuvebrug over the Voorstraathaven has four lo
reliefs sculptured in stone in 1937 by **Hildo Krop** (1884-1970); they depict
prisoner, a baker, a dairywoman and an apothecary-surgeon in a naive style.

Blauwpoort or Catharijnepoort – Near this very plain gateway, dating from
1652, there are warehouses and a beautiful patrician house with a perron, the 18
Beverschaep: its door is topped by a naiad and a triton embracing one another; o
the pediment a sheep *(schaap)* and a beaver *(bever)* support the coat of arms.

Nieuwehaven – Pleasure boats find shelter in this dock with tree-lined quayside;

★ **Museum Mr Simon van Gijn** ⊘ – This lovely residence (1729) and its content
were bequeathed to the town by the banker **Simon van Gijn** (1836-1922), a grea
art collector. It contains rooms decorated in the styles of the 18C and 19C
including elegant fireplaces, rich furnishings, tapestries, paintings, silver, glas
and porcelain. Flemish wall hangings dating from 1730 hang in the reception ha
The living areas on the lower floor (the red drawing room, the dining room an
the garden room) were built and furnished in 1886. The kitchen, at the end of th
corridor on the left, features copper utensils and a fine fireplace adorned wit
glazed earthenware tiling, all dating from around 1800.
On the first floor are an Old Dutch study and library, and a bedroom and bathroo
dating from 1883. The scale model in the passage is of the *Bleiswijk*, a ship whic
belonged to the Dutch East India Company. There is also a very fine gold leathe
room from c 1686, the only fully preserved one of its kind.
The second floor has temporary exhibitions and a selection of prints and drawing
from the Gijn Atlas. On the top floor is a collection of 19C toys, including doll;
dolls' shops and houses, and children's dinner services.

From the quay on the north side, there is a fine **view** of Nieuwehaven and part o
the Grote Kerk with its clerestory, transept and massive tower. There is also
lovely view in the other direction over Kuipershaven lined with warehouses.

Kuipershaven – Numerous barges are crammed into coopers' quay whic
specialised in the wine trade.
At nos 41-42, a barrel is shown on the grill forming a transom window above th
door. In the transom window of no 48 a basket is depicted.

Groothoofdspoort – It was the main gate (1618) to the town. Topped by a dome
it is covered on both sides with ornaments and low reliefs in sandstone. From th
quay, situated on the north side, there is a fine **view★** over the wide confluence o
the Merwede, the Noord and the Oude Maas rivers.
On the other side of the gate near the lever bridge, the **Wijnhaven** (wine port)
harbour for pleasure boats, and the chapel with its pinnacle make a colourf
picture.

Wijnstraat – This unevenly paved street lined with picturesque houses, a
lop-sided, is another association with the wine *(wijn)* trade. Some houses ar
Renaissance, still with crow-stepped gables (nos 73-75; with the emblem of
cock: no 85), others are in the Louis XIV style (no 87).
Cross the canal.
The city's oldest residences line this canal in the central area.

Voorstraat – This busy shopping street is the town's main thoroughfare. Ther
are some interesting façades: at no 178 the façade has a lovely Rococo decor; a
no 188 is the **Muntpoort** of 1555.
At the beginning of the pedestrian precinct, on the left, near the Augustijnenkerk
at no 214 a porch gives on to **Het Hof**, the former Court of Justice where the State
General met in 1572.
Opposite Het Hof, at the corner of an alley leading to a bridge, there is a fin
Renaissance façade with two-coloured tympana decorated with sculptured head;

DORDRECHT

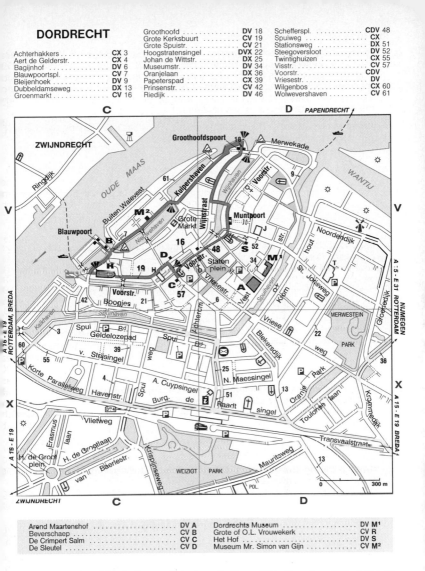

Schefftersplein – This is the market place; in the middle there is a 19C statue of the painter Ary Scheffer.

Visstraat – This street, whose name means Fish Street, leads to Dordrecht's very modern commercial quarter. At no 7 there is a lovely small Renaissance house, **De Crimpert Salm** (1608). Very elaborate, it has a façade stone depicting a salmon *(zalm)* and is topped by a lion. As is usual in Dordrecht, the windows are framed with mouldings ending in corbels.

Cross the bridge towards Groenmarkt.

Views over the canal, which is narrow here, and the old town hall, a white neo-Classical building. On the bridge there is a monument (1922) to the De Witt brothers.

Groenmarkt – Former vegetable market. On the right, at no 39, the **De Sleutel** house has a façade decorated with a key *(sleutel)* and tympana with recessed orders. Dating from 1540, it is reputedly the oldest in the town.
At no 53, there is a fine façade with ogee-shaped tympana.

Grote Kerksbuurt – The house at no 56 has a charming façade.

ADDITIONAL SIGHTS

Dordrechts Museum ⊙ – This museum contains an interesting collection of paintings. Many are by 17C artists who were born in the town, namely Aelbert Cuyp, Nicolaes Maes and Samuel van Hoogstraten. Dutch Romanticism is present, as well as pictures illustrating The Hague School and the Amsterdam School. In the section on 18C and 19C art, special attention should be given to the biblical

135

scenes and portraits of **Ary Scheffer**: *Self-portrait at the Age of 43* (1883) an
especially *Frédéric Chopin*, a remarkable picture of the great composer (1847)
Scheffer's illustrations for *Histoire de la Révolution française*, a book written b
the French politician Adolphe Thiers (1797-1877), are also on display.
Various 20C artistic movements, such as magic realism and Cobra, are als
represented in the museum's collections.

Arend Maartenshof – This old almshouse (1625) has kept its original characte
with small low houses surrounding a courtyard.

EDAM

Noord-Holland
Population (with Volendam) 26 505
Michelin maps 908 G 4 and 210 P 7

An important cheese centre, Edam is a small, quiet and charming town, crisscrosse
by canals still lined with a few fine 17C houses.
It is overlooked by the **Speeltoren**, a tall tower with a carillon, the remains of a churc
demolished in the 19C.
In fact, it was formerly a busy port on the Zuiderzee, known for its shipyards.

Edam cheese – Originally made in Edam, it is now made in several other regions
It is prepared with slightly skimmed milk, and is similar in texture to Gouda, but i
differs by its easily identifiable shape: a ball with a yellow crust, covered with a thi
red coating if it is for export.

SIGHTS

Dam – The main square on either side of the Damsluis is overlooked by the 18C
stadhuis, or town hall, with its clock tower.
A lovely house (c 1530) contains the small local museum, the **Edams Museum** ⊘

Kaasmarkt – This square is the site of the former cheese market. Th
Kaaswaag ⊘, where cheese was weighed, is decorated with painted panels and nov
houses an **exhibition** on cheesemaking.

Grote Kerk or Sint-Nicolaaskerk ⊘ – The 15C church has lovely early 17C
stained-glass windows and a fine organ.

EINDHOVEN

Noord-Brabant
Population 197 766
Michelin map 908 H 7 and 211 M 14
Town plan in the current Michelin Red Guide Benelux

This important industrial centre continues to grow. In 1900 Eindhoven had barely
5 000 inhabitants; now it is the fifth largest city in the Netherlands. Textile and ciga
factories began appearing here in the early 19C, but by the end of the century they
had been supplanted by Philips and, in 1928, by Van Doorne's Auto Fabrieken, bette
known as DAF. Because of its industrial importance, Eindhoven was bombed severa
times during the Second World War, and hardly any historic buildings survived.

The city of light – Eindhoven owes its spectacular expansion mainly to Philips *(se
below)*, which expanded from a simple lightbulb factory into an internationa
electronics giant. Apart from lighting, Philips also makes audio and video equipment
medical items, small household appliances, electronic components and other items
Philips Natlab, the world's second largest laboratory, is where the video recorder, the
CD and the CD-I were developed.
On the edge of the city, on Noord-Brabantlaan, stands the **Evoluon**, a huge building
(1966) supported by 12 V-shaped concrete pillars and resembling a large flying
saucer. It was designed for Philips' 75th anniversary by the two architects, Kalff and
De Bever, and is currently used for trade fairs.

A modern city – Although industrial and laid out to a modern urban plan, Eindhover
is a pleasant city. Bustling commercial activity prevails, notably in the pedestrian
precincts. The city is well provided with recreational activities, parks and greer
spaces, like the **De IJzeren Man**, to the east, and the forests of Kempen are ideal for
walking.
The Eindhoven carnival is always a lively and popular event *(see Calendar of events)*
The city also has one of Europe's leading technical universities.

★ STEDELIJK VAN ABBEMUSEUM ⊙ 1hr 30min

This building opposite the town hall was bequeathed to the city in 1936 by the industrialist HJ van Abbe. The museum has a rich collection of paintings and sculpture from 1900 to the present, concentrating especially on contemporary art since 1945.

The museum is currently being rebuilt and expanded, and the work is scheduled for completion in 2001. In the meantime, its collections are housed in the former shop for Philips employees on Vonderweg opposite the P.S.V. stadium. **Entr'acte**, as this short-term accommodation is called, holds temporary exhibitions of modern art.

The collection itself consists of an overview of modern art: the Cubism of Picasso, Braque, Juan Gris; Orphism or poetic interpretation of the real with Delaunay, Chagall, Fernand Léger; the De Stijl movement with Mondrian, Van Doesburg; Constructivism with a great number of works by El Lissitzky, Expressionism of Kokoschka, Kandinsky, Permeke; Surrealism with Miró, Ernst, Pieter Ouborg, Francis Bacon.

Postwar artists include the French abstract painters such as Bazaine, Sam Francis (born in California), and Serge Poliakoff (1906-69) of the Ecole de Paris.

The CoBrA movement is represented by Karel Appel, Asger Jorn, Corneille. Apart from subject-matter painters such as Dubuffet, Tàpies, there are also works by Vasarely, Lucio Fontana, Klein, the Zero group (Mack, Piene and Uecker), the Americans of Pop Art including Morris Louis, Robert Indiana, Frank Stella.

Conceptual Art (Kosuth, Barry, Brouwn, Kawara), Minimal Art (Judd, André, Sol LeWitt) and contemporary German painting (Kiefer, Baselitz, Penck) are also represented.

Horse and Flautist (1951) by Karel Appel

ADDITIONAL SIGHTS

The centre – The area between Vestdijk and Keizersgracht houses the modern **Muziekcentrum Frits Philips** and the **De Heuvel Galerie** shopping centre. The **town hall** (1949-55) was designed by J van der Laan and J Kirch; the **Liberation Monument** (1954) on the square in front of it is by Paul Grégoire.

Museum Kempenland ⊙ – *St-Antoniusstraat 5-7*. This museum, installed in the old Steentjeskerk, evokes the history and customs of the town and its hinterland, Kempenland. The collections concern archeology, beliefs, textile industry, handicrafts: note the clocks made in Eindhoven c 1800.
Temporary exhibitions concerning history and art are organised.

Prehistorisch Openluchtmuseum Eindhoven ⊙ – *Boutenslaan (southern ring road) 161b*. This open-air prehistoric museum recreates a settlement in Kempen-land during the Iron Age (750-50 BC). The houses have been reconstructed based on excavations in Noord-Brabant and Kempen, and using simple iron tools and natural materials. Volunteers re-enact the daily lives of Iron-Age peasants,

---

Philips and Eindhoven: a company town

In 1891, Gerard Philips set up a lightbulb assembly plant on Emmasingel. After five difficult years his brother Anton *(whose statue now stands at the railway station)* came to his help, and from then onwards the business took off in a big way. The factory began making radio valves, X-ray tubes and medical equipment, and exporting it across Europe. In 1914 Gerard set up the natural sciences laboratory Natlab, which has since been responsible for many important forms of new technology *(see above)*. Later, in collaboration with DAF, Philips established the Technical Collge (1955), now Eindhoven Technical University.

By 1929, Philips had 20 000 employees and provided jobs for 70% of the local workforce. It opened new factories and offices on Emmasingel and Mathildelaan with names like De Witte Dame (The White Lady), De Bruine Heer (The Brown Man) and De Lichttoren (The Lighthouse). The city council could not keep up with this dramatic expansion, and Philips began building its own facilities for employees and their families: a theatre, a library, schools, and most importantly housing, such as the Philipsdorp garden village on Frederiklaan *(see Introduction: Industrial heritage)*. The company also set up its own sports club, Philips Sportvereniging, whose football team (P.S.V.) is one of the country's best-known.

However, the close ties between Philips and Eindhoven ended in 1998, when the company moved its headquarters to Amsterdam. Now, new uses are being sought for its many buildings. De Witte Dame and De Bruine Heer will house offices, apartments, small businesses, the Academy of Industrial Design, the European Design Centre and the public library. The small lightbulb factory opposite, where it all began, will probably become a Philips Museum.

---

including a blacksmith making iron objects, a weaving-shed dyeing wool and flax, ovens being used to fire pots and bake bread, people working in the fields and the herb garden, chickens running around everywhere and pigs rooting in the cattle pen. Other aspects of this ancient society are also brought to life: pagan images, a sacred oak, and even prehistoric musical instruments. This museum project is an example of experimental archeology, which attempts to answer questions about people in earlier times by living in the same way as they did. The museum particularly comes to life at weekends and when special events are held.

Het Witte Dorp – *Geldropseweg and Sint-Jorislaan*. The White Village, a complex of 264 white homes with red roofs, was designed by WM Dudok, the architect of Hilversum's town hall. This fine example of functionalist residential building was financed by a private housing association and built between 1937 and 1974. It is a listed monument.

EXCURSION

Helmond, Asten and De Groote Peel★ – *38km/24mi. Leave to the northeast by A 270.*

Helmond – This is an active textile manuacturing centre. Standing in its own parkland, the medieval **castle**★ ⊙ is an imposing quadrilateral building with an inner courtyard, corner towers, an encircling moat and a park.

Asten – To the northwest of this village, a modern building houses the **Beiaard- en Natuurmuseum Asten** ⊙, a museum of carillons and natural history.

The **carillon section**★ has information on bell making, a collection of small bells from all over the world, and clocks, carillons and chiming mechanisms, some of which can be played.

The natural history section houses a series of stuffed animals, butterflies and insects, a reproduction of the ecosystem of the De Peel marshes and an aquarium with species found in the Peel lakes.

To the southeast of Asten stretches a large marshy zone called **De Peel** (*peel* means marsh). The lakes mark the site of former peat bogs.

★ **De Groote Peel** – *Access to the south by Moostdijk, near Meijelse Dijk.* This area of about 1 400ha/3 460 acres has been a **protected national park** ⊙ since 1984. The varied and tranquil landscape, with large stretches of water, makes an ideal nesting place for waterfowl, and it has one of the most varied bird populations in Western Europe. In the autumn, thousands of migratory birds use the Groote Peel as a resting or assembly place on their long trek south. In spring, around 90 bird species hatch here, including bluethroats, stonechats and **black-headed gulls**. This gull is about 40cm/16in long and is white but in summer, its head becomes completely black. It can be found on the coasts in winter, but it often comes to nest inland, notably near the lakes. In early spring, black-headed gulls come in thousands to make very neat nests between the clumps of reeds which cover the submerged roots. Males and females share the task of sitting on the eggs and jealously defending their nest.

Apart from birds, the Grote Peel is home to foxes, deer, toads, lizards and numerous insect species.

The visitor centre, **Bezoekerscentrum Mijl op Zeven** Ⓥ, is located in a typical Brabant farmhouse. It has documentation on the nature reserve itself, and the local flora and fauna.

Three signposted nature trails make it possible to discover this fascinating natural environment.

EMMEN

Drenthe
Population 94
Michelin maps 908 L 3 and 210 AA 6
Local map see HUNEBEDDEN

The prosperous market centre of Emmen is a pleasant town bordered to the north and the east by fine forests.

The southern end of the Hondsrug has numerous *hunebeds*, prehistoric funerary monuments.

SIGHTS

★ **Hunebed of Emmer Dennen (D45)** – *Access by Boslaan, direction Emmer Compascuum. It is situated near a large crossroads and is well signposted.*
This remarkable *hunebed*, an alleyway covered with six enormous slabs encircled by uprights, was erected on a mound right in the middle of the forest. Standing in an attractive setting it is popular with painters.

Hunebeds along the Odoorn road – There is a succession of megalliths as one drives northwards.
Coming from the centre of Emmen towards Odoorn, after the last farm, bear left on a path signposted "hunebed".
Between the trees there is a **long grave**★ (D 43); the shape of the burial mound has been reconstructed and two covered alleyways are hidden.
The whole is surrounded by uprights between which are piles of rocks which hold up the earth.
A few hundred yards further to the north, on the left side of the road, there is a small *hunehed* (D 41) covered with capstones.
On leaving Emmen, on the right, a lane marked *hunebedden* goes through the forest to a large clearing of heather. Three *hunebeds* (D 38/40) stand in this lovely setting: one is half buried, the second, also buried, was given the shape of a square, while the third is covered with fallen stones.

★ **Noorder Dierenpark** Ⓥ – This zoo is particularly interesting for its great variety of species. In an enormous aviary there are colourful birds from South American tropical forests. A tropical garden houses more than 1 000 fluttering butterflies. The seal pool and the "Africanium", which incorporates a series of greenhouses, a natural history museum, and an ethnographical museum, are other attractions. A 1.5ha/4-acre area of African savanna is home to giraffes, zebras, antelopes, rhinoceroses, cranes, and impalas, and there is also a new sewer full of rats.

EXCURSIONS

Noorsleen, Schoonoord and Orvelte★ – *40km/25mi to the west – local map see HUNEBEDDEN.*
Noordsleen – This charming village of the Drenthe, with a restored mill, has two *hunebeds*.
Access by the small road to Zweeloo and a lane on the right signposted "hunebedden" (D 51).
On the left, is a small covered alleyway still topped by three capstones (four have disappeared). Further on the right, the **hunebed**★ (D 50) shaded by a large oak which grows in its centre, is better preserved. Five slabs are still in place as well as the oval crown of upright stones. The entrance pillars are on the south side.
Schoonoord – 3.5km/2mi to the south of the locality, in the woods near a riding centre, a *hunebed* (D 49) has been partially reconstructed. Above, the heather-covered ground forms a mound and hides the large slabs which form the *hunebed's* roof. This *hunebed* is called **De Papeloze Kerk** (church without a priest); congregations met here at the beginning of the Reformation.

Orvelte, museum village

* **Orvelte** – This museum-village in the heart of the Drenthe comprises a collection of typical farmhouses and barns with thatched roofs. Cars are not permitted. Many of the villagers still go about the traditional agricultural activities of cattle and sheep rearing and cereal growing. Others keep alive traditional crafts and trades: miller, blacksmith, clog-maker, potter...

Coevorden – *21km/13mi to the southwest*. An old fortified town designed by **Menno van Coehoorn**, Coevorden has kept several interesting monuments. The **castle** is a fine building flanked by a corner turret, with walls of rose-coloured roughcast and pierced in the left part of the façade (15C) by tall narrow windows. Part of it is occupied by the town hall; in the basement there is a restaurant. Near Markt *(Friesestraat 9)*, there is a picturesque late Renaissance **house** with voluted gables and ornamentation: bright red shells, heads of women, cherubs, Moors and inscriptions.

On Marktplein, facing the docks are the three 17C roofs of the Arsenal (restored), which contains the local museum, **Gemeentemuseum "Drenthe's Veste"** ⊘.

To the east, beyond Weyerswold *(6km/4mi)* typical thatched cottages of the Drenthe stand beside innumerable small oil wells; the **Schoonebeek** region was once rich in petroleum.

ENKHUIZEN*

Noord-Holland
Population 16 263
Michelin maps 908 G 3 and 210 Q 6

Enkhuizen was the main Frisian settlement and seat of their chiefs until 1289 when West Friesland passed to the counts of Holland. The town had one of the largest herring fishing fleets which brought great prosperity; three herrings figure on the town's coat of arms. The port continued to flourish until it silted up in the 18C. Then the building of the Barrier Dam in 1932 put an end to its maritime activities.

Enkhuizen was fortified in the mid 16C and it was one of the first towns to revolt against the Spanish in 1672. Around 1600 the city walls were rebuilt. When its maritime activities ceased in the 20C the town then looked to its rich agricultural hinterland for a living and today it is an important market town and centre for bulb growing. The walls are now a pleasant promenade.

Enkhuizen is linked to Lelystad, the main town of Flevoland, by the dike road *(31km/19mi)*. This was originally to have enclosed the fifth and last polder around the edge of the IJsselmeer *(local map see IJSSELMEER)* but the Markerwaard project was abandoned in 1986.

Enkhuizen was the birthplace of **Paulus Potter** (1625-54), the famous animal painter, whose best-known painting, *The Bull Calf*, hangs in the Mauritshuis in The Hague.

Boat trips ⊘ – *Boats leave from Spoorhaven for Stavoren, Urk and Medemblik (in combination with the steam tram).*

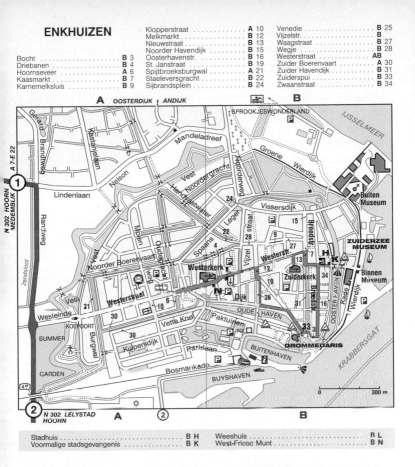

★ OLD TOWN 5hr

Enkhuizen has numerous 17C façades in Renaissance style, their fine decoration bearing witness to its former prosperity.

Westerstraat – This is the town's main street. There are lovely façades, notably that of no 158 to the north, dating from 1617 with the town emblem on a gable: a young girl bearing a coat of arms depicting three herrings.

Westerkerk or Sint-Gomaruskerk ⊙ – This church is a 15C and 16C building. Its free-standing wooden tower built in the 16C on a stone base was rebuilt in the 19C in the neo-Classical style. The hall-interior has three naves of equal height, covered with a wooden vault. There is also a fine wooden **rood screen**★ with six richly carved panels (16C), tympana, pulpit (both 16C), a replica of the one found in the Grote Kerk in The Hague, and a 1547 organ case.

Opposite the church is the former Mint of West Friesland, **Westfriese Munt**, with a lovely, finely decorated façade dating from 1617.

Further on at no 109 the façade of the Orphanage or **Weeshuis** has been rebuilt after the original façade (1616).

Turn right to take Melkmarkt and Venedie.

Dijk – At no 32, a house (1625) displays the motto: "Contentement passe rychesse" (happiness is worth more than riches).

★ **Drommedaris** ⊙ – This imposing and well-known building (now a café) which was part of the town's enclosure was, like the one in Hoorn, intended for keeping watch over the entrance to the port. It consists of a circular tower and an adjoining gatehouse. Note the decoration above the doorway. It has a carillon cast by Hemony, which is one of the best in the country.

From the top there is a **panorama**★ of Enkhuizen, its port, IJsselmeer and in the distance Friesland.

From the quay to the south of the tower, there is a fine **view**★ to the east over the docks (Zuiderspui) and the backs of houses with picturesque wooden conservatories overlooking flowered gardens.

Zuiderspui – This short street has some interesting façades: no 1 has five polychrome coats of arms, from left to right can be seen those of Hoorn (a horn), the House of Orange, West Friesland (two lions), Enkhuizen and Medemblik.

Breedstraat – Several houses have interesting façade stones notably: no 81, called Den Kuiser Maegt (the young girl from Enkhuizen), depicting the town's coat of arms; no 60, an old boat, and no 59, a young girl also holding the town's coat of arms.

Stadhuis – The town hall is an imposing building dating from the end of the 17C. Above the door there is an excerpt from a poem by Joost van den Vondel. The interior is decorated with paintings, painted ceilings, tapestries and murals. On the corner of Zwaanstraat stands the **old prison**, a small building, whose picturesque façade dates from 1612.

* **Zuiderzeemuseum** ⊙ – The Zuiderzee Museum is made up of two sections. One is the indoor museum, consisting of 12 linked buildings around three courtyards. Some are 17C houses and warehouses formerly belonging to the Dutch East India Company, while others are modern concrete and glass constructions.

* **Binnenmuseum** (Indoor Museum) ⊙ – The covered reception hall is reached via the first courtyard, which preserves much of the atmosphere of the Golden Age, and the second, where the ship collection is visible through a glass wall. The museum has a variety of permanent **exhibitions**. One uses maps, paintings (including the life-size *Catching a whale off the coast of Spitsbergen*, Storck, 1690), tools and various objects to evoke the whaling industry, highly active in the region from the 17C to the 19C. The ship collection has a number of old vessels including wooden sailing boats which used to cruise along the Zuiderzee, a flat-bottomed fishing boat and a vessel from Urk which was pulled along the ice.

Zuiderzeemuseum, Enkhuizen

The beautifully restored **pepper store** looks and smells just as it did when it was owned by the East India company in the 18C. Other exhibitions deal with fishing in the **North Sea and Zuiderzee**, the region's constant **battle against the water** (including a computer animation on the subject of the Afsluitdijk), and **water transport**. Together, they give a varied picture of seven centuries of Zuiderzee history.

** **Buitenmuseum** (Open-air Museum) ⊙ – *Entrance opposite the Binnenmuseum, or access by the ferry leaving the car park near the entrance to the dike linking Enkhuizen to Lelystad.*
This museum is a reminder of daily life in the old Zuiderzee fishing ports between 1880 and 1932, completion date of the Barrier Dam (Afsluitdijk). More than 130 shops, houses and workshops from around 30 localities have been reconstructed to make up the charming districts of this **village-museum**. Although

---

The gaper, a typically Dutch phenomenon

In the art-nouveau pharmacy De Grote Gaper, there is a colourful collection of heads with their tongues sticking out. These humorous images, known as *gapers*, were used as shop signs by Dutch pharmacists. They were a reminder that people had to open their mouths wide when taking the medicines they sold, and of course patients also had to show their tongues to the doctor.

---

one may find, concentrated in the same quarter, houses coming from different towns or villages, the plans of each district are based on reality and each structure is made to scale. Everything in the museum conspires to evoke life in bygone days: the furniture, the tools, the layout of the gardens, the church from old Wierengen Island and the reconstruction of Marken port in 1830, with the smell of tannin in the air. Visitors may buy old-fashioned candy, go for a ride on an old boat, or see the sailmaker, ropemaker and fish curer at work. Shops and manufacturing are also well represented: there is a spice shop, a butcher's, a pharmacy, a steam laundry, an agricultural credit bank and even three lime kilns.

Children can dress up in a traditional costume during their visit, and there is a **children's island** where they can investigate how children lived in Marken around 1930.

There is also a **nature reserve** attached to the museum, containing plants, birds, a duck cage and a Bronze-Age farmhouse.

Return to Westerstraat.

Here, too, there are lovely gables, shop signs and façade stones (a cooking pot, a bull's head etc).

Zuider Kerk or Sint-Pancraskerk ⊘ – This church is flanked by a fine Gothic tower, the wooden cap of which was added in the 16C. Its carillon was cast by the Hemony brothers.

ENSCHEDE

Overijssel

Population 147 912

Michelin maps 408 L 5 and 210 AA 9

Enschede, situated in the green countryside of the Twente region, is the largest town in Overijssel province. An important industrial centre, it specialises mainly in textiles. Its rapid expansion due to the development of industry only started at the beginning of the century. Severely damaged by fire in 1862 and bombarded in 1944, it is, today, a modern city. The vast campus of **Twente University**, founded in 1964, lies to the northwest of the town.

Twente and the textile industry – *See also Introduction: Industrial heritage.* The ready presence of water made it possible to wash the fibres and work the looms. Twente formerly specialised in the processing of linen, which was cultivated, retted, spun and woven on the spot. **Almelo** was the centre of this activity. Twente linen was exported to Norway and to Russia where the Vriezenveen *(7km/4mi to the north of Almelo)* merchants had founded a colony near St Petersburg.

In the 18C, linen was replaced by cotton which was less costly; at the same time they produced in large quantities a twill of linen and cotton called bombasine *(bombazijn)*. In the early 19C weaving and spinning production were industrialised with the development of looms driven by steam-power.

The metallurgical industry also developed greatly at this time; in 1960, together with the textile industry, it represented 86% of the town's industrial activity. Since then, the development of artificial fibres, foreign competition and economic recession have caused the decline of the textile industry.

Presently, alongside heavy metallurgy and that of processing, the building industry and the tertiary sector are developing.

★ RIJKSMUSEUM TWENTHE ⊘ *1hr 30min*

The building erected in 1930 to plans by Muller and Beudt was extended by Ben van Berkel between 1995 and 1996. The museum boasts a large collection of art and decorative arts from the 13C to the 20C.

★ **Old Masters and Applied arts** – *Right-hand wing.* The pre-20C and decorative arts section in the right-hand wing is an atmospheric display in differently-coloured rooms. It includes superb medieval **manuscripts**, incunabula, gold and silver, and **sculpture**. The collection of **late medieval painting** contains altarpieces and

Rijksmuseum Twenthe

Portrait of a six-year-old girl (1594),
attributed to Jan Claesz

portraits by such artists as Van Cleve, Cranach and Holbein the Younger; there are also **16C and 17C landscapes** (Brueghel the Younger, Van Goyen, Ruysdael and Avercamp), and still-life paintings by Bosschaert and others. There are works by Jan Steen, Teniers and Terborch, and etchings by Rembrandt.

The **18C**, in which the museum plans to specialise in the future, is represented with works by De Wit and Troost. There is also a collection of glass, silver and furniture from this period. The museum has paintings by the **Romantics** (Koekkoek, Schelfhout and Leickert) and there is a separate room devoted to the Barbizon School (Daubigny, Troyon) and to the **Hague and Amsterdam schools** (the Maris brothers, Mauve, Israëls, Breitner). This section ends with **Impressionism** (Jongkind, Monet, Sisley) and an early work by Mondriaan.

Return to the entrance via the passageway alongside the courtyard, where there is a collection of **Delftware and grandfather clocks**. *From here, the collection of modern and contemporary art can be viewed in chronological order in the left-hand wing.*

Modern and contemporary art – *Left-hand wing.* Here, the emphasis is on the development of Dutch art, with works by Toorop, Redon, pre-war **expressionists** (Sluiters, Gestel), the **Cobra group** (Appel, Constant, Corneille, Lucebert), the **Hague experimental** and **informal artists** such as Ouborg and Wagemaker. **Systematic, serial and fundamental art** from the 1960s and 70s is also represented.

Contemporary painters from the Netherlands include Sjoerd Buisman, Marlene Dumas, Cornelis Rogge and Henk Visch.

The museum also stages interesting **temporary exhibitions**.

ADDITIONAL SIGHTS

Museum Jannink ⊘ – This museum is located in a renovated textile mill dating from 1900. Until 1964 there were 30 000 spindles here, plus 567 looms in an adjoining single-storey building which has now disappeared.

The museum's collections illustrate the history of the Twente since 1600, with the emphasis on the textile industry over the past 150 years.

Workers' interiors, which have been recreated, show the effects of this evolution on living conditions (cottage industry and rural life; then the move to the city to be closer to the factory with all it entails, increased comfort...). Also displayed are the tools used through the different periods: spinning wheels, winding machines and looms. An exhibition of aerial photographs shows how Enschede has grown, and on the first floor there is a display about daily life here in olden times.

Natuurmuseum ⊘ – The ground floor of this natural history museum displays minerals and fossils, mostly discovered in the region; the invertebrate section features insects, shells and coral.

The first floor is devoted to fauna: **dioramas** show the main species of mammals and birds found in the Netherlands, aquariums and small ponds for reptiles; one room has an exhibition on whales. In the basement there are precious stones as well as radioactive and fluorescent minerals.

Volkspark – In the southeastern part of this park, one of the many green areas of Enschede, there is a monument erected to the memory of victims of the Second World War: a group of bronze statues (a hostage, people in the Resistance, soldiers etc) by the sculptor **Mari Andriessen**.

Stadhuis – The town hall was built in 1933 by G Friedhoff, who was influenced by Stockholm's town hall. This rather austere brick building is flanked by a tall square bell-tower with slightly bulging walls.

Hervormde Kerk – This sandstone Reformed Church stands on Markt, the town's main square. It was begun c 1200 and enlarged in the 15C but has kept its great Romanesque **tower** (13C), with its paired openings. The spire was added at the beginning of the 20C. There is a sundial dating from 1836 on the right-hand outer wall of the church, opposite the VVV.

ENSCHEDE

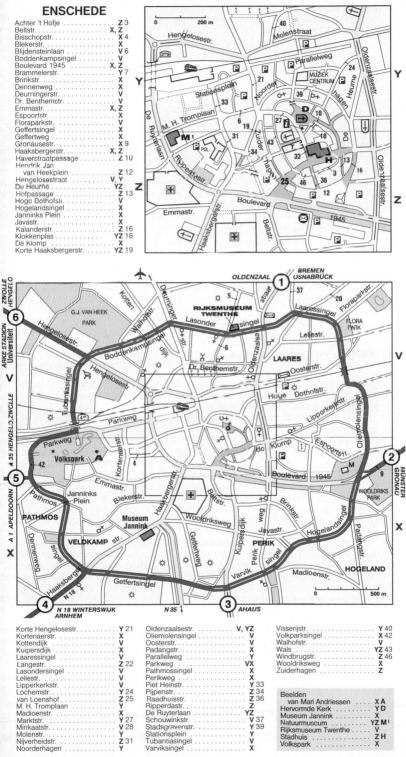

EXCURSION

Northern Twente – *80km/50mi. Leave by ① on the town plan and allow about 5hr.*

The route crosses the northern part of **Twente**. Known for its industrial activities, Twente is also a verdant region where the land, cut by waterways, is divided into pastures and magnificent forests.

Scattered throughout the area are large farms with wooden gables and sometimes half-timbered walls.

Oldenzaal – This small industrial town, near the German frontier, is an old, once fortified settlement, which has kept its concentric streets round a lovely Romanesque basilica, the **Sint-Plechelmusbasiliek** ⊙.

A church existed here in 770. The present edifice, with three naves and a transept and dedicated to the Irish saint, St Plecheln, dates from the early 12C.

The square bell-tower, its massive aspect characteristic of the region, was built in the 13C. In 1950 the church was given the title of basilica.

The interior is impressive, with the groined vaulting of the nave resting on great square piers. The chancel and the south aisle were rebuilt in the Gothic style in the 15C. The south arm of the transept has a triptych (Adoration of the Magi) attributed to the Fleming, Pieter Coecke van Aalst. The Baroque pulpit has vigorously carved figures.

Not far away is **Het Palthe Huis** ⊙ *(on Marktstraat)*, now a museum. This house with its charming Baroque façade was bequeathed to the Oldenzaal antiquities collection by the Palthe family and displays traditional objects in 17C period rooms. There is also a reconstructed apothecary's shop, and in the attic a 17C chair where a murderer was held for 110 days.

Denekamp – This small town, situated in one of the loveliest parts of Twente, has kept its strange tradition of *midwinterhorens*, which translated means horns of mid-winter. They are horns of carved wood which are blown at the approach of Christmas *(see Calendar of events)* in Twente villages; their origin remains mysterious. Near the town stands a castle, **Kasteel Singraven** ⊙. A lovely road runs alongside the Dinkel, a tree-lined calm waterway where there is a lovely 15C **watermill** ⊙; grain is still ground here and wood is sawn; the building on the left houses a restaurant. The 17C **castle** flanked by a square tower is reflected in the Dinkel, one of whose branches waters the magnificent park. The furniture, tapestries (Beauvais, Aubusson), porcelain collections, paintings (Salomon van Ruisdael, Van de Capelle) all add to the refined atmosphere of the 18C interior.

* **Ootmarsum** – Built on a mound, round a Gothic church, this charming village with concentric streets has been restored; lovely, elaborately decorated Renaissance façades and wooden gables can be admired.

On Kerkplein stands the **Church of St Simon and St Judas** ⊙. This church is in the Romanesque-Gothic transitional style, which is reminiscent of Westphalian churches by the use of stone and by its thick square tower to the west (partly demolished). The apse is Gothic as well as the fourth bay. Inside, the polychrome colours highlight the lines of the pointed arches, the small columns and ribs. At the end of the north side aisle, there is a lovely statue in wood of the Virgin (c 1500); in the aisles there are modern stained-glass windows. The organ in Westphalian style, has been restored. In the display cabinets are silver liturgical plate and a lovely chasuble (1749) embroidered with the effigy of the church's patron saints. On the south side aisle a tomb is used as a columbarium.

Ootmarsum also has two small museums: the **Onderwijsmuseum Educatorum**, which deals with the history of education, and the open-air **Openluchtmuseum Los Hoes** ⊙. This includes a barn, a carriage works and other buildings around an old farmhouse (1890-1910) of the "los hoes" type *(see Introduction: Traditions and folklore)*. This gives a fine picture of how local farmers lived and worked around 1900, and an interesting exhibition, "Ootmarsum in its historical perspective", describes the town's rich past.

Take the road to Almelo.

Kuiperberg – From the belvedere on top of the Kuiperberg (alt 65m/213ft) there is a **view** over Ootmarsum and the wooded countryside. Next to it stands an old Jewish cemetery.

Continue to Delden via Almelo and Borne.

Delden – Delden is an important agricultural market centre. **Kasteel Twickel** ⊙, the former residence of the counts of Wassenaar, stands to the north of the town. Founded in the 14C, it was altered in the 16C (main door) and the 17C. It is surrounded by moats and lovely **gardens**.

The **Grote Kerk or Sint-Blasiuskerk**, a Gothic style sandstone hall-church, has a heavy square tower.

The old town hall *(Langestraat 30)* houses both the VVV and a small salt museum, the **Zoutmuseum** ⊙. Located not far from the country's main rock salt deposits, it explains the origin, extraction and use of salt, as well as its importance to humans, animals and plants.

Hengelo – This commercial and industrial town (metallurgy, electricity, electronics, chemicals) has modern buildings, in particular the **town hall**, the work of Berghoef (1963). Since 1972, to the east of town, a new experimental residential quarter is being built by the architect Piet Blom.

Return to Enschede by ⑥ on the town plan.

FLEVOLAND ★

Flevoland

Michelin maps 908 G 4, H 4, 5, I 4, 5
and 210 P 8, Q 8, 9, R 7, 8, 9, S 7, 8, 9, T 7, 8, U 7,8 –
Local map see IJSSELMEER

Flevoland is in fact two polders (Oostelijk Flevoland and Zuidelijk Flevoland) which represent the most recent achievements in the Zuiderzee reclamation project *(see IJSSELMEER)*.

Oostelijk Flevoland – This was the third polder created on IJsselmeer, after Wieringermeer polder and the Noordoost polder. An area of 54 000ha/133 380 acres, it was diked and drained between 1950 and 1957. The largest part of this polder is destined for agriculture (75% of the area) while 10% of the land has been turned into meadows and woods, 8% for housing and the rest alloted to canals, roads and dikes. Before being exploited, the land was first sown with reeds. Farmhouses hidden behind screens of poplars and enormous barns are scattered over this flat countryside, crisscrossed by clusters of young trees. Tall trees indicate an already old dwelling place. In the fields, drained by ditches, sheep, cattle and ponies graze. There are numerous lapwings, golden pheasants and water birds such as the coot, a small dark wader whose black head has a white spot.

Since 1960 towns and villages have sprung up: Lelystad, Dronten, Swifterbant, Biddinghuizen; piles placed on a sand bed ensure the stability of the construction. Wide straight roads cut across the polder. Some have been built on the ring dikes. Lakes such as the **Veluwe**, separating the polder from the Zuiderzee's former coast, act as regulators and have become recreation lakes with bathing areas.

Zuidelijk Flevoland – It is separated from the Oostelijk Flevoland polder by a security dike, the Knardijk, parts of the road being forbidden to traffic. It is surrounded by a dike built between 1959 and 1967. In 1968 this polder of 43 000ha/106 210 acres had largely been drained. Half the area is devoted to agriculture, 25% to dwelling areas, 18% for meadows and woods. The rest is taken up by canals, dikes and roads.

To the north, near Oostvaarders dike, there is a nature reserve **De Oostvaardersplassen**. This marshland is a refuge for birds including some very rare species.

Since 1975, **Almere**, a town with a pleasure boat harbour, is being built to the south on Gooi Lake; it should accommodate 180 000 inhabitants by 2005.

Another residential area, Zeewolde, is being built level with Harderwijk; it already has a large pleasure boat harbour.

SIGHTS

The polders are at their best in May and June, when the oilseed rape fields are in flower.

Walibi-Flevo ⊙ – *Spijkweg 30, Biddinghuizen*. This new amusement park replaces a previous one with an agricultural theme, the Flevohof, and is located on the Veluwemeer lake in the district of **Biddinghuizen**. The many attractions offer plenty of choice for thrill-seekers, including water-based rides, the sensational El Condor which involves looping the loop five times, the rotating G-Force and the blood-curdling Space Shot which launches visitors 60m/200ft into the air. A tropical glasshouse and a large collection of cacti reflect the park's previous use. There is also a showground for special events, a camp site, an open-air theatre and a conference centre.

Lelystad – Lelystad, capital of Flevoland, bears the name of the engineer Lely. This new town was built to accommodate a population of 80 000 by the year 2000. Individual houses and bungalows are the rule. The **Agora**, a community building constructed in 1976, marks the centre of town.

Lelystad is linked to Enkhuizen by a dike, Markerwaarddijk *(31km/19mi)* with a road running along the top. The Oostvaardersdiep, a canal 300m/985ft wide, forms a waterway stretching between Amsterdam and the northern part of the country. The Houtribsluizen, two large locks spanning the Oostvaardersdiep separate the Markermeer from the IJsselmeer.

Nieuw Land Poldermuseum ⊙ stands near the locks, and houses a permanent exhibition on the reclamation work carried out on the Zuiderzee. The history of the region's relationship with water is chronicled using historic film and sound recordings, models, interactive computer programs etc and deals with subjects as varied as fishing, trade, geology and early cultures. The construction of dykes, the creation of polders and their first inhabitants are all covered.

★ **Batavia dock** ⊙ – Set up next to the information centre is the **Batavia**★, a replica of a merchant ship belonging to the Dutch East India Company. The original vessel

Morand-Graham/HOA QUI

The Batavia

was built in Amsterdam in 1628. During her maiden trip, she ran aground on some reefs off the west coast of Australia; some of the 341 crew managed to survive the shipwreck and the subsequent massacre which took place on the nearby islands. The wreck itself has since been salvaged, and is now on display in the West Australian Maritime Museum in Fremantle.

The reconstruction of the ship was the work of a group of young people undergoing specialised training, and began in 1985. Since the launch of the replica, the dock has expanded into a shipbuilding centre using traditional techniques.

Apart from the Batavia, two other vessels are on display: the half-completed Flevo-aak, a modern version of a traditional barge, and a replica of De Zeven Provinciën, begun in 1995. This was the famous flagship of Admiral Michiel de Ruyter, built in 1664 and one of the largest of its time. The guided tour begins with a film in the visitor centre, and then takes visitors to see the boat and the workshops where the pulleys, sails and carved wooden sculptures are made; these recreate the atmosphere of Holland's Golden Age. The tour ends with a visit to the Batavia itself, showing how a 17C merchant vessel was a combination of a warehouse, a fortress and a community of individuals.

The **Nederlands Instituut voor Scheeps- en Onderwaterarcheologie** (Dutch Institute for Maritime Archeology) and the **Nederlands Sportmuseum** are located near the dock.

Shipwreck – *To the south of Lelystad. Access by the Oostranddreef; at the roundabout (Rotonde) turn left, then the first road on the right, right again at the next crossroads. Nearby a narrow lane leads to the wreck.*
In the middle of cultivated land the skeleton of a ship has been left where it was found during drainage of the polder in 1967. Called *De Zeehond* (the seal), dating from 1878, it transported bricks, a pile of which can be seen nearby.

Dronten – This new town, standing right in the heart of the polder, was planned round a church with an openwork tower, and a community centre, **De Meerpaal**. This immense glass hall, built in 1967 by Frank van Klingeren, is effectively an extension of Marktplein.

The length of time given in this guide
  - for touring allows time to enjoy the views and the scenery ;
  - for sightseeing is the average time required for a visit.

Fryslân

Michelin maps 908 H 2 and 210 S 3

This small Frisian town (Frjentsjer) had a famous university which was founded in 1585, where Descartes became a student in 1629. It was closed in 1811 during the reign of Louis Bonaparte.

SIGHTS

* Stadhuis ⊙ – The town hall is a splendid building in the Dutch Mannerist style, dating from 1591, with a double gable; it is topped by an elegant octagonal tower. The Council Chamber *(Raadzaal; ground floor at the end of the corridor)* and the Registrar's Office *(Trouwzaal; first floor)* are hung with 18C painted leather, in rich colours.

* Planetarium ⊙ – At a time when a number of his contemporaries feared the end of the world due to the exceptional position of the stars, the Frisian **Eise Eisinga** decided to prove that the situation was not dangerous. This wool-comber, who had been interested in astronomy since childhood, built an ingenious system (1774-81) whereby the movement of the stars was depicted on his living room ceiling. Eisinga represented with surprising precision the celestial vault as known by 10C astronomers.

This planetarium, whose movement can be seen in the attic, is the oldest European one in working order.

The charming House of the Corn Porters, **Korendragershuisje**, can be seen at the end of Eisingstraat.

Eise Eisinga's planetarium

Museum 't Coopmanshûs ⊙ – *Voorstraat.*
This museum installed in the Waag and the large adjoining 17C and 18C houses, pays tribute to **Anna Maria van Schurman** (1606-78). A celebrated entomologist and draughtsman, who belonged to the Labadist community founded by the French émigré **Jean de Labadie** (1610-74), she advocated bringing Protestantism back to Primitive Christianity.

The history of the former university is illustrated by portraits of professors and a "xylotheque" – an outstanding collection of wood samples presented in the form of books, presented to Franeker University by Louis Bonaparte in about 1810. The museum also displays several splendid collections of Frisian silver, porcelain and glass. Note the miniature charity fête by J Kooistra. The building is also used to stage exhibitions on modern art.

In the same street, at no 35, the **Martenahuis** was built in 1498.

Martinikerk – This Gothic church has 15C paintings, and figures of saints on the pillars. The floor is strewn with finely sculptured tombstones in the Frisian style.

Weeshuis – The former orphanage's door is topped with 17C inscriptions. Nearby, the **Cammingha-Stins** is a lovely 15C and 16C residence, now used by a bank (on the first floor, exhibition of coins and medals).

GIETHOORN★★

Overijssel

Michelin maps 908 J 3 and 210 V 6

The small town of Giethoorn stands in a waterlogged fenland area. It owes its name to the great number of wild goats *(geitenhoorns)* found in the area by the peat-workers. In Giethoorn the houses border the canals, dug in the past by the peat workers to transport the peat. The many lakes found locally are the flooded hollows created by peat digging on a massive scale.

Visiting the village ⊘ – No cars are allowed into the village and it must be visited on foot (a path runs alongside the main canal) or by boat. Visitors can choose to hire a rowing boat, a punt, a motor boat or a yacht or take a boat trip.

A lakeside village – The pretty thatched cottages of Giethoorn face onto the canals spanned by hump-backed bridges or simple footbridges. Well-tended lawns and gaily planted flowerbeds slope down to the water's edge.

The bicycle is the most popular form of transport although many locals use flat-bottomed punts (punters). Even bridal processions can be seen punting along the canals.

Kameeldak roofs – The hall-type farmhouses *(see Introduction: Farmhouses)* are remarkable for their thatched hump-backed roofs. When more and more land was reclaimed the grain yields increased and the farmers had to extend their storage space. Since land was at a premium they extended upwards and as a consequence the farm buildings became taller than the farmhouse. Roofs with this change in level were called camel-backed *(kameeldak)*. Another characteristic of these farms is that they have no carriage entrance as everything was transported by water. Hay was stored in the barn above the boathouse.

The lakes – The broads which stretch to the east and south of the village are vast stretches of water scattered with small reed-covered islands. The entire area is a unique ecological habitat rich in birdlife.

Giethoorn

EXCURSION

Wanneperveen, Vollenhove and Blokzijl – *Round tour of 26km/16mi.*

Wanneperveen – In this small town which, like many peat-bog villages has a name which ends in *veen* (peat-bog or fen), thatched cottages run for several miles alongside a road planted with pear trees. Not far from the village's west entrance, one can see the **cemetery** with its free-standing bell-tower scantily built with a few beams, characteristic of Southern Friesland; note in the main street, at no 94, a lovely house with a crow-stepped gable, the **old town hall**.

Vollenhove – This was another of the historic ports on the Zuiderzee, before the Noordoostpolder was reclaimed. On **Kerkplein** stand a few fine monuments: **Sint-Nicolaaskerk**, a late Gothic church with two naves and its free-standing bell-tower, the **Klokketoren** which was used as a prison; adjoining the bell-tower is the **old raadhuis**, a 17C brick and sandstone porticoed building converted into a restaurant; finally the lovely façade with crow-stepped gables of the **Latin School** (1627) (now used by the VVV and a bank) has an entrance with two carved stelae in front. From the church's east end one can see the bastions of the old rampart where pleasure boats are moored. The new town hall is housed in **Oldruitenborgh** manor house, set in the park of the same name.

Blokzijl – This was also one of the prosperous old ports on the Zuiderzee and a member of the Hanseatic League. The Dutch East India Company used the port as a haven for its East Indiamen when storms arose. The lovely 17C houses along the now deserted waterfronts are witness to past prosperity. Kerkstraat, which leads to the 17C church, is also picturesque.

GOES

Zeeland

Population 34 328

Michelin map 908 C 7 and 211 I 13 – Local map see DELTA

Town plan in the current Michelin Red Guide Benelux

The former port of Goes, which owed its prosperity to the salt trade and the madder industry *(see Introduction: Industrial heritage)*, is today the main centre of Zuid Beveland. The town is surrounded by meadows and orchards.

A canal links it to the estuary of the Oosterschelde.

Goes has preserved, through the location of its canals, the layout of its 15C ramparts. A small **steam-operated tram** ⊙ runs between Goes and Oudelande.

Jacqueline of Hainaut or Jacoba – Goes was one of the ancestral seats of the counts of Zeeland and the town is closely associated with the turbulent Jacoba, daughter of William VI. On his death in 1417 she inherited the earldoms of Hainaut, Holland and Zeeland, and was envied by many. She was a fierce opponent of the **Cods** *(see GORINCHEM)*. In 1421 she had left her second husband John IV, Duke of Brabant, who dispossessed her of the Holland earldom by giving it to John of Bavaria, Jacoba's uncle and supporter of the Cods. The following year she married Humphrey, Duke of Gloucester, fourth son of King Henry IV, brother to King Henry V of England. Later, to escape from the intrigues of Philip the Good, who had invaded her territories, she took refuge in Goes. She was forced by Philip to sign an agreement in Delft in 1428, the Treaty of Delft, in which she recognised him as heir and promised never to remarry. The promise was soon broken (1432) and Jacoba lost her title of countess (1433); three years later she died in Slot Teilingen, near Sassenheim.

Market day – The weekly market on Goes's Grote Markt *(Tuesdays; see Introduction: Traditions and folklore)* gives the occasional opportunity of seeing the Zeeland costumes of Zuid-Beveland. The headdresses are very beautiful, square for Catholics and oval for Protestants.

SIGHTS

Grote Markt – The town's main square, is overlooked by the 15C **stadhuis** which was altered in the 18C and has a Rococo façade.

Grote Kerk or Maria Magdalenakerk ⊙ – Part of the church was built in the 15C, and rebuilt in 1621 after a fire. The main nave is very high. Similar to the two transept portals of the Hooglandsekerk in Leiden, the **north portal** is finely decorated in the Flamboyant style, and has a wide window topped by an openwork gable.

Inside, the church has a remarkable 17C **organ** ⊙, crowned with an 18C canopy.

Turfkade – *To the north of Grote Markt.* This peat quay is lined with lovely crow-stepped gabled façades.

EXCURSION

Kapelle and Yerseke – *15km/9mi east – local map see DELTA.*

Kapelle – The **Dutch Reformed Church** ⊙ with its imposing 14C bell-tower and corner pinnacles is visible from afar, across the low-lying polderland.

In the nave note the decorated balusters and heads of satyrs. The main chancel, decorated with Gothic blind arcading in red brick contains a 17C tomb.

Next to the village cemetery, to the west, there is a **French military cemetery**, the last resting place of the French soldiers who died in the Netherlands in 1940.

Yerseke (or Ierseke) – This small port on the Oosterschelde specialises in oyster and mussel beds and lobster catching. The Oosterschelde storm surge barrier has floodgates which make it possible for Yerseke to benefit from tides and continue its activities.

GORINCHEM

Zuid-Holland

Population 32 573

Michelin maps 908 F 6 and 211 O 11

On the borders of three provinces (Zuid-Holland, Noord Brabant and Gelderland) Gorinchem, often called **Gorkum** is an important waterway junction, at the confluence of two large rivers, the Waal (branch of the Rhine) and the Maas, as well as the Merwedekanaal and a small river, the Linge.

It has a large marina to the west.

Hooks and Cods – Gorkum dates from the 13C and because of its strategic position it has suffered numerous sieges.

In 1417 it was the site of a ferocious fight between the Hooks (Hoeken), supporters of **Jacoba** *(see GOES)* who had inherited the town, and **Willem van Arkel**, on the side of the Cods (Kabeljauwen). The latter wished to reconquer the town, which had belonged to his father. He lost his life during a skirmish in the city.

Gorkum was one of the first strongholds wrested from the Spanish by the Beggars in 1572. Among the prisoners taken by the Beggars, there were 16 priests who were executed at Brielle the same year; they are known as the martyrs of Gorkum.

Gorinchem was the birthplace of the 16C painter **Abraham Bloemaert**, who spent most of his life in Utrecht.

HISTORIC CENTRE *45min*

The historic core is girdled by the star-shaped outline of the bastions and ramparts which have been transformed into an esplanade. It is crossed by the River Linge, which forms a picturesque harbour, the **Lingehaven**.

Grote Markt – The old neo-Classical **town hall** (1860) houses the VVV tourist office and the **Gorcums Museum** ⊘, which has a collection of paintings, sculpture, models, toys and silver chronicling the town's history. The town's collection of visual art since 1945 consists mainly of works by local artists, including Ad Dekkers, which are displayed in temporary exhibitions.

At no 23 Grote Markt is the **Hugo de Grootportje**, a small Baroque structure which is all that remains of the house where the famous jurist and scholar Hugo Grotius fled after escaping from prison in Slot Loevestein *(see Excursions)*.

Groenmarkt – The 15C **Grote Kerk or Sint-Maartenskerk** is located in this square. The church's tall early-16C Gothic **tower** ⊘ (Sint-Janstoren) is particularly worth seeing, since it is crooked. The builders realised during its construction that it was leaning over to one side, but all they could do was adjust the top part of the tower accordingly.

Burgerkinderenweeshuis – On the 18C façade of the old orphanage, also called **Huize Matthijs-Marijke**, a carved stone depicts Christ and children, between the founders of the orphanage.

Huis "'t Coemtal van God" – A narrow-fronted house with a crow-stepped gable, decorated with Renaissance-style medallions (1563).

Slot Loevestein

GORINCHEM

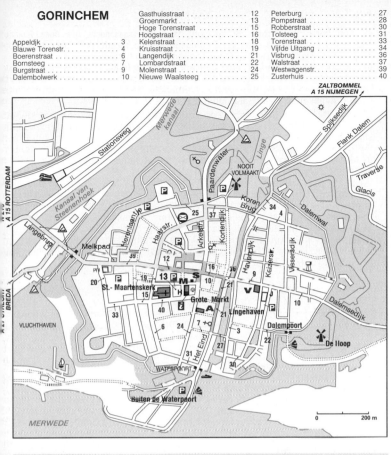

Dalempoort – This lovely, small rampart gateway, square with a high roof topped by a pinnacle, dates from 1597; it was enlarged in 1770. It is the only one of the town's four gateways to remain.

From here, one can see the tall wall mill called **De Hoop**, Hope (1764).

Buiten de Waterpoort – This tree-lined esplanade stretches from the south of the old watergate (Waterpoort), closed in 1894 to enlarge the road. Boat trips leave from this landing-stage.

There is a fine **view** over Dalem Gate, the mill and the river; to the southeast, on the opposite bank, one can see, among the greenery, the tall bell-tower of the church of Woudrichem and the pink brick Slot Loevestein.

EXCURSIONS

Leerdam – *17km/11mi to the northeast. Leave Gorinchem by Spijksedijk, take the motorway to Nijmegen and leave at the Leerdam exit.*

This town, situated on the Linge, has become the main glass-making centre in the Netherlands since the creation of its factory in 1878.

To the southwest, in a villa on the Oosterwijk road *(Lingedijk 28)*, is the **Nationaal Glasmuseum** ⊙. This displays interesting collections of glass and crystal from different countries, notably from Leerdam (19C and 20C) but also from Scandinavia and Italy (since the 18C).

Woudrichem and Slot Loevestein – *21km/13mi to the south. Leave Gorinchem by Westwagenstraat, turn left after the first bridge and take the motorway towards Breda, leaving at the Woudrichem exit.*

Woudrichem – At the confluence of the Rhine (Waal) and the Maas, this small town, commonly called **Workum**, is still enclosed in its encircling bastioned ramparts which have been turned into an esplanade. Formerly it belonged to the region of Heusden and Altena. It obtained its city charter in 1356. By the Peace of Woudrichem in 1419, John of Bavaria obtained important rights over his niece, Jacoba's *(see GOES)* territories. Workum has a small pleasure boat harbour with a ferry for pedestrians to Slot Loevestein.

To the south one enters the town by **Koepoort**. On the right is the squat **tower** of the Gothic church, the walls of which are decorated with medallions.

To the north near the 15C prison gate, **Gevangenpoort**, the **Oude Raadhui** *(Hoogstraat 47)* has a graceful Renaissance-style façade with a crow-steppe(gable and a flight of steps in front topped by two heraldic lions.

In the same street, at no 37, note a façade stone depicting an axe chopping wood(and opposite, two twin houses of 1593 and 1606, whose façade stones evoke b' their sculpture a golden angel and a salamander, and by their inscription: To th(Golden Angel and To the Salamander, their respective names.

Slot Loevestein ⊙ – All that can be seen through the screen of trees are the high slat(roofs of this solid fortress in pink brick, flanked with four square towers an(surrounded by moats and ramparts.

Slot Loevestein was built between 1357 and 1368 by Dirk Loef van Horne, Lor(of Altena. The Count of Holland, Albrecht van Beieren (of Bavaria), seized it i1 1385 and surrounded it with an enclosure.

In the 15C the castle was transformed into a prison by Jacoba who had just seize(Gorkum. In 1619 Grotius, who had been taken prisoner the previous year, wa imprisoned in Loevestein. There he devoted himself to the preparation of legal an(theological works. His escape remains famous. He managed to escape in Marcl 1621 by hiding in a chest which had been used to bring him books, and was the(given shelter in Gorkum temporarily, before reaching France. Inside the castle on(can visit large rooms with lovely chimney-pieces. In one of them is the chest use(by Grotius for his escape.

GOUDA*

Zuid-Holland

Population 71 486

Michelin maps 908 F 5 and N 10

Gouda (pronounced how-dah) owes its fame to the stained glass in the church, it cheese, its pipes and its pottery. Situated at the confluence of the Hollandse IJsse and the Gouwe, this peaceful town is crisscrossed by several canals.

In the Middle Ages, Gouda, then called Ter Gouwe, developed under the protectio1 of its castle, which was destroyed in 1577. It had received its city charter in 1272 In the 15C, brewing and trading brought great prosperity to Gouda, while the 16(marked a decline. The town picked up again in the 17C due to the cheese trade an(the manufacture of pipes introduced by English potters. Today there is also th(production of candles, Gouda having the biggest factory in the country, and pottery

---

Gouda cheese

Gouda, together with Edam, is one of the most famous cheeses in the Netherlands. Marketed in Gouda, it is a product either from a factory or from farms (its name then becomes *boerenkaas* meaning farm cheese).

Gouda is made with fresh or pasteurized (when it is factory-made) cow's milk. It is either young, medium or old. The indication *volvet 48+* means that its fat content is at least 48%.

Other specialities of the town are *stroopwafels*, or syrup waffles.

P. Duval/HOA QUI

Gouda is the home town of **Cornelis de Houtman** (c 1565-99), who was in charge of an expedition to the East (1595-97) and founded the first Dutch trading post in East India (Indonesia) on the island of Java. While on his second journey, he was murdered by the sultan of Sumatra.

Boat trips Ⓥ – Tours are organised to the Reeuwijk Lakes.

★ THE OLD TOWN CENTRE *3hr*

Markt – In the centre of the main square stands the *stadhuis* with its characteristic tall silhouette. Several markets take place in this square, particularly the **cheese market** and **craft market** Ⓥ.
No 27, the Arti Legi, houses the Tourist Information Centre.

★ **Stadhuis** Ⓥ – The lovely mid-15C Gothic town hall was restored in the 19C and 20C.

It has a very decorative sandstone façade on the south side with a gable, flanked by turrets and adorned with a small balcony. The staircase in front is in the Renaissance style (1603).

On the east side is a **carillon**, whose small figures come to life every half hour; it depicts the scene of Count Floris V of Holland granting the city charter to Gouda in 1272.

The interior of the Registrar's Office (Trouwzaal) is worth visiting; it is decorated with tapestries woven in Gouda in the 17C.

Waag – The Classical-style weigh-house was built in 1668 by Pieter Post. The façade is decorated with a low relief depicting the weighing of cheese which formerly took place here. It now houses the **Kaasexpo-seum** Ⓥ, a museum tracing the development of the cheese and dairy industry in the Netherlands as a whole, and Gouda in particular.

Behind the Waag the lovely **Agnietenkapel** has been restored.

Stadhuis, Gouda

Ch. Sappa/CEDRI

★ **Sint-Janskerk** Ⓥ – Founded in the 13C, the church of St John was rebuilt and expanded three times after the great fires of 1361, 1438 and 1552. Fronted by a small tower – the remains of the original church – it is surrounded by numerous pointed gables enhanced by large stained-glass windows.

The interior is very light, and sober in the extreme. Architecturally speaking, it is a late Gothic basilica with prominent side aisles, surmounted by wooden barrel vaulting.

★★ **Stained glass** (Goudse Glazen) – The church is renowned for its magnificent collection of 70 stained-glass windows. Forty were spared by the Iconoclasts, the others were made after the Reformation. The largest, of which there are 27, were donated by the king, princes, prelates or rich bourgeois.

The 13 most remarkable stained-glass windows, in both the eastern and the central parts of the church, are attributed to the **Crabeth brothers** (Dirck and Wouter) who made them between 1555 and 1571 when the church was Catholic. They illustrate biblical subjects. The works of the Crabeth brothers are numbered:

5: The Queen of Sheba pays a visit to Solomon
6: Judith beheading Holofernes
7: Dedication of Solomon's temple and the Last Supper (a present from Philip II, King of Spain, and Mary Tudor, Queen of England)
8: Heliodorus, temple thief, chastened by the angels

12: Nativity
14: Sermon of St John the Baptist (Gouda's patron saint; his colours, white representing purity and love, and red symbolising suffering, appear in the town's coat of arms)
15: Baptism of Jesus (the oldest window, 1555)
16: First sermon of Jesus
18: Jesus's message to St John in prison
22: The purification of the temple (window donated by William the Silent and symbolising the Church's fight for purification)
23: Elijah's sacrifice and the Ablutions, donated by Margaret of Parma, governor of the Low Countries at the time of the revolt
30: Jonah cast up by the whale (tall window above the ambulatory, to the left of the chancel).

More recent stained-glass windows which date from the Protestant period were added between 1594 and 1603 on the western side. Donated by the free towns of Holland, they depict armorial bearings, historical events, allegories and a few biblical scenes. They include:
25: the raising of the siege of Leiden (in 1547) in the middle of floods; portrait of William the Silent; silhouette of Delft (illustration: see Introduction, History)
27: the Pharisee in the temple
28: the adultress
28A (right aisle): Stained-glass window by Charles Eyck placed in 1947 and evoking the Liberation of the Netherlands.

The seven stained-glass windows in the **chapel** (door under window 14 in the chancel) depict the Arrest of Jesus, Christ Mocked, the Scourging, the *Ecce Homo* at Pontius Pilate's House, the Bearing of the Cross, the Resurrection, Ascension and the feast of Pentecost; they are attributed to Dirck Crabeth or his pupils and come from a nearby convent.

The organ at the end of the church (west side) dates from 1736. The new organ in the chancel dates from 1974. Interesting tombstones are strewn over the floor of the building.

Walk round the church to the right, to the north entrance of the Museum Het Catharina Gasthuis.

★ **Museum Het Catharina Gasthuis** ⊘ – Installed in the former St Catherine's Hospital (Gasthuis), this municipal museum has a varied collection of paintings, period rooms and items illustrating the history of the hospital and the town. It also holds temporary exhibitions.

To the north of the museum, there is a gateway dating from 1609, the **Lazaruspoortje**, leading to the garden and the museum entrance. It has a polychrome low relief depicting Lazarus the leper at the table of a rich man, and comes from the former lepers' home.

GOUDA

The old part of the hospital (1542), where the wards once were, is now used for temporary exhibitions. A 19C municipal pharmacy is on display in an adjoining room.

Behind the 17C to 19C period rooms is the **Great Hall** (Ruim) devoted to the Gouda civic guard; the schutterstukken, group portraits of companies of the civil guard, include one by Ferdinand Bol. Next door are the boardrooms, the kitchen and pantry and the chapel. The latter is devoted to **religious art**: 16C altarpieces, an *Anunciation* and *altar to St Hubert* by Pieter Pourbus, a collection of silver, and a chalice given to the town by Jacoba of Bavaria in the 15C.

A small cellar contains torture instruments of the 16C and 17C, and a "lunatics' cell", the only surviving one of its kind in the Netherlands.

On the upper floor there are collections of toys, the reconstitution of the surgeons' Guild Room, and paintings by the Barbizon School and The Hague School (Anton Mauve, Isaac Israëls, Jacob Maris) as well as Jan Toorop.

ADDITIONAL SIGHTS

Museum De Moriaan ⊙ – Under the sign of the Blackamoor *(moriaan)* evoking a tobacco shop, this Renaissance-style house built c 1625 has a lovely façade overlooking the picturesque Gouda canal. It has been converted into a **Museum of Pottery and Pipes**. The tobacco shop of 1680 has been reconstructed. Fine collections of clay pipes and decorated Gouda pottery are displayed in elegant settings, bearing witness to the town's rich tradition as a centre of the pottery industry, which began producing the famous Gouda clay pipes in the 17C. In about 1900, it began making ornamental ceramics instead *(see Introduction: Art)*.

Jeruzalemstraat – At the corner of Patersteeg is the **Jeruzalemkapel**, a 15C chapel. Opposite, on the other corner is the former orphanage, **Weeshuis** of 1642, now a library, with a lovely façade with a voluted gable, and beside it, a doorway topped by a low relief depicting two orphans.

On the opposite pavement, at no 2, an old people's home, **Oude Mannenhuis** opens by a door (1614), altered in the 18C.

At the far end of Spieringstraat is the **municipal park** with an 1832 windmill, **Walmolen 't Slot**, which was formerly used for milling grain. In the park there is a tree which was planted when Queen Wilhelmina came of age in 1898.

EXCURSIONS

★ **Reeuwijkse Plassen and Woerden** – *30km/19mi to the north. Leave Gouda by Karnemelksloot. After the canal, take the second road on the left in the direction of Platteweg.*

★ **Reeuwijkse Plassen** – Even though these vast stretches of water are much appreciated by water sports enthusiasts, the road winding between the lakes goes through a captivating landscape.

After Sluipwijk, go in the direction of Bodegraven then Woerden.

Woerden – Woerden was an important stronghold on the Oude Rijn and was for long considered the key to Holland: those who occupied Woerden had access to the rest of the country. In 1672 Louis XIV's armies, commanded by the Duke of Montmorency-Luxembourg, defeated William III's Dutch army. The town is still surrounded by a moat which edges its bastioned enclosure. The 15C **castle**, beside the town's southern gate, has served as a quartermaster's store since 1872. There are imitation machicolations running along the façade.

The old town hall is now occupied by the municipal museum, or **Stadsmuseum** ⊙. This delightful small building dating from 1501 is flanked by a turret and has a lovely tiled first storey with voluted gables above.

An old pillory takes up the right part of the façade. Woerden also has a stage mill (1755), De Windhond (The Greyhound).

Oudewater and Schoonhoven – *34km/21mi. Leave Gouda by Nieuwe Veerstal and follow the very narrow dike road; passing is difficult.*

This road, which follows the Hollandse IJssel, offers picturesque **views**★ of the river with its marshy banks and thatched farmhouses.

Oudewater – Oudewater is one of the Netherlands' oldest small towns and was the birthplace of **Jacob Arminius** (c 1560-1609) *(see DORDRECHT)*, and the Primitive painter **Gerard David** (c 1460-1523), who moved to Bruges in 1483.

Oudewater is famous for its witches' scales, which can be seen in the Waag, or weigh-house; the small Witches Museum in the attic retraces the history of witchcraft with engravings and documents.

This fine Renaissance building with crow-stepped gables and brick mosaic tympana is near Markt, which spans a canal.

In the 16C women accused of witchcraft came from afar to be weighed at Oudewater in the presence of the burgomaster of the town. If the woman's weight was not too light with respect to her size she was too heavy to ride a broomstick, so she was not a witch. They were then given a certificate of acquittal. All the people weighed in Oudewater were acquitted. The last certificate was issued in 1729.

Next to the weigh house, at no 14, note the Renaissance façade (1601) of Arminius's birthplace: the tympana are decorated with shells; a niche contains a statue of Fortune.

Other attractive façades, dating from the town's period of prosperity at the end of the 16C, are to be admired in the quiet streets of Oudewater (Wijdstraat). At no 3 Donkere Gaard, near Markt, there is a fine house. Near Markt, the Renaissance **stadhuis** has a side façade preceded by a flight of steps and topped with a crow-stepped gable.

Take the Gouda road to Haastrecht, then follow the valley of the Vlist towards Schoonhoven.

It is a picturesque **route**★. The road, shaded by willows, runs alongside the river

Collectie Nederlands Goud-, Zilver- en Klokkenmuseum

Bracket clock (c 1715) by A Witsen;
Nederlands Goud-, Zilver- en
Klokkenmuseum, Schoonhoven

banks with their abundant vegetation. Beautiful reed-covered roofed farmhouses with a conical haystack topped with a small roof, line the road.

Vlist – Lovely wooden windmill.

On leaving Vlist, cross the river.

Schoonhoven – This charming, small town at the confluence of the Vlist and the Lek, is known for its traditional gold and silverware; a few smiths continue the craft today. The town is traversed by an attractive canal and linked to Lek's south bank by a ferry.

The **Stadhuis**, dating from the 15C, overlooks the canal. Although it has been modernised it retains a tall roof topped by a pinnacle (carillon).

On Dam, in the centre of the canal, is the **Waag** or weigh-house, an original building of 1617 with a hipped roof. It is now a restaurant.

Nearby is the **Nederlands Goud-, Zilver- en Klokkenmuseum** ⊙, or Netherlands Gold, Silver and Clock Museum. This has a fine **collection** of **wall clocks**★ from Friesland and the Zaan, French dial cases, 18C timepieces, a large number of watches, a collection of 17C to 20C silverware from several countries and a silversmith's workshop.

The town's south gate, **Veerpoort**, which dates from 1601, opens onto the Lek. Some lovely houses can be seen in the town, notably no 37 Lopikerstraat: the 1642 façade is decorated with a double crow-stepped gable and red shutters.

's-GRAVENHAGE

See Den HAAG

GRONINGEN

Groningen ℗
Population; 168 688
Michelin maps 908 K 2 and 210 Y 3
Plan of the conurbation in the current Michelin Red Guide Benelux

Groningen is the dynamic provincial capital and the main town in the north of the Netherlands. The town is located at the northern extremity of the Hondsrug with polderlands to the north and peat bogs to the southwest.

The town's university and various other colleges mean that it has a young population, and it is dominated by students, who fill the many outdoor cafés in summer. Groningen also has a remarkably large number of cyclists; over half the population travels to school and work by bike.

HISTORICAL NOTES

A settlement already existed by the year AD 1000. The town was given its first set of city walls in the 12C and by the beginning of the 13C Groningen belonged to the Hanseatic League. A convention concluded in 1251 with the neighbouring cantons made Groningen the only grain market in the region, bringing it six centuries of prosperity. Under the Bishop of Utrecht's authority the town passed into the hands of the Duke of Geldern in 1515. Then, trying to escape from the Habsburg authority, it finally gave in to Charles V in 1536. It joined the Union of Utrecht in 1579 and was taken by the Spanish in 1580 and then by Maurice of Nassau in 1594.

An era of prosperity followed with the construction from 1608 to 1616, of a new enclosure *(7km/5mi)* defended by 17 bastions. The university was founded in 1614; it very quickly acquired a great reputation and students came from all over Europe. Descartes chose it in 1645 to arbitrate in his conflicts with Dutch theologians. Today, with its approximately 20 000 students, it still plays an important part in the life of the town. In 1672 the town resisted against the troops of the Bishop of Munster, ally of Louis XIV. The fortifications were strengthened in 1698 by Coehoorn and razed to the ground in 1874 to allow for the extension of the city. A few remains in **Noorderplantsoen** have been transformed into a garden.

The town of Groningen is the homeland of the painters **Jozef Israëls** (1827-1911), head of The Hague School and **Hendrik Willem Mesdag** (1831-1915), who was one of its members.

A dynamic town - Groningen is an important communications junction. It is linked to the sea by means of important canals and its port is centred on the Oosterhaven and the Zuiderhaven.

Groningen is a large industrial centre (metallurgy, hi-tech, printing, food, asphalt and steel). The town is Western Europe's number one sugar beet centre. Groningen has an important congress and exhibition centre, the **Martinihal**, near the racecourse, in the new districts, which are developing to the south. Other important examples of modern architecture include the Groninger Museum, the Waagstraat complex and the offices of Nederlandse Gasunie.

The surrounding lakes (Leekstermeer, Paterswoldse Meer, Zuidlaarder Meer) draw watersports enthusiasts.

Groningen gas - Groningen is the oil capital of the Netherlands and nerve centre of its power supply ever since oil was found in the Drenthe near Schoonebeek *(see EMMEN: Excursions)* in 1945. Between 1959 and 1960, large deposits of natural gas were also discovered in the province of Groningen. The reserves are estimated at more than 2 000 billion m³, which makes it one of the largest deposits in the world. The region features 29 extraction centres which all have several winding shafts. One of these centres is located in **Slochteren**, east of Groningen. Half the country's production of natural gas is channelled through pipelines towards Belgium, France, Germany and Italy.

Accommodation

Groningen is best-known for the futuristic Groninger Museum, but it also has a number of attractive hotels in historic buildings.

OUR SELECTION

Auberge Corps de Garde – *Oude Boteringestraat 74, 9712 GN Groningen,* ☎ *(050) 314 54 37, Fax (050) 313 63 20, 25 rooms.* A 17C guard-house and an adjoining building on the Boteringebrug are now a cosy hotel, with large, comfortable rooms and antique furniture.

Schimmelpennick Huys – *Oosterstraat 53, 9711 NR Groningen,* ☎ *(050) 318 95 02, Fax (050) 318 31 64, 38 rooms.* A pleasant hotel in an old mansion close to Grote Markt, with a choice of suites or rooms overlooking the courtyards. There are rooms of various sizes with modern decor; the main emphasis, as in the rest of the hotel, is on white. Breakfast is served in the Baroque Room, the conservatory or the garden.

Hotel de Ville – *Oude Boteringestraat 43, 9712 GD Groningen* ☏ *(050) 318 12 22, Fax (050) 318 17 77, 45 rooms*. Behind the simple exterior of these restored mansions is a chic but charming hotel. Quietly located in the old town centre, it has a classically styled interior and spacious modern rooms. The bar in the conservatory looks out onto an attractive courtyard garden.

Restaurants

De Pauw – *Gelkingestraat 52,* ☏ *(050) 318 13 32*. This centrally located restaurant has an unusual formula: the main course consists of a trolley buffet placed beside your table, with starters and desserts to order.

Restaurant Grand Café Schimmelpennick Huys – *Oosterstraat 53,* ☏ *(050) 311 18 72.* Enjoy a cup of coffee, a light meal or a full dinner, and rub shoulders with the great and good of Groningen. You can eat in the conservatory, the Jugendstil or Empire Rooms, or the pleasantly green courtyard. *See also Hotel Schimmelpennick Huys above.*

Bistro 't Gerecht – *Oude Boteringestraat 45,* ☏ *(050) 589 18 59.* French-inspired bistro next to (and part of) the Hotel de Ville. Long benches, wooden panelling and mirrored walls; traditional, mainly French, cuisine.

Muller – *Grote Kromme Elleboog 13,* ☏ *(050) 318 32 08.* This restaurant in one of Groningen's busiest areas for night-life serves excellent food to a smart clientele.

Martinitoren, Groningen

Ni Hao – *Hereweg 1,* ☏ *(050) 318 14 00*. Chinese restaurant near the station

Brasseries, cafés, bars, coffee shops...

De Apedans – *Verlengde Oosterstraat 1*. This trendy bodega restaurant has a tastefully designed interior and serves simple food.

Het Goudkantoor – *Waagplein 1*. An elegant building housing one of the town's busiest café-restaurants; a must if you're in the Waag area.

Newscafé – *Waagplein 5*. The architecture, the interior and the atmosphere are those of 1950s Miami. If the cocktail bar, reading table and jazz music aren't enough, you can also surf the internet. A 1950s menu is served in a relaxed atmosphere on the first floor.

't Feithhuis – *Martinikerkhof 10*. This trendy town-centre café provides day-long sustenance, from breakfast, brunch and lunch through to soups, salads and tea

Practical information

General information – The tourist office, **VVV Groningen** (Gedempte Kattendiep 6, ☏ (0900) 202 30 50 or www.vvvgroningen.nl), can help with information on sights, tours and accommodation. It also offers special accommodation packages and can book hotels and tickets for plays, concerts and other events

Transport – If yours is a short visit, there are many clearly **signposted car parks** in the centre of Groningen. If you are staying for longer, park at one of the **Park and Ride sites** on the outskirts of town and take the Citybus to the centre which is largely car-free and not accessible to through traffic. To drive from one part of town to another, you will have to go back to the ring road.

Public transport timetables and tickets are available from the VVV. Groningen is an ideal cycling town, with an extensive network of cycle paths. You can hire a **bicycle** in the Central Station or under the library.

Walks and tours – The VVV sells street maps and suggested **walking routes**, and **guided walks** depart from here on Monday afternoons in summer. ARRIVA (☎ (050) 368 81 05) offers **bus tours** of Groningen on Tuesdays, Fridays and Saturdays from late June to early September, departing from the Central Station and Grote Markt.

Boat trips – **Canal tours** leave from the Groninger Museum and Central Station between June and August (☎ (050) 312 83 79).

Shopping – Groningen's main shopping street is **Herestraat**, but there are other good areas for shopping. These include the historic **Korenbeurs** or corn exchange, at A-Kerkhof 1, and the modern Waagstraat complex on Grote Markt.

Markets – On Good Friday, Vismarkt becomes a blaze of colour as the annual **flower market** takes over. There are also **weekly markets**: one on Tuesdays, Fridays and Saturdays selling general items on Grote Markt and Vismarkt; an **organic food market** and small flea market on Vismarkt on Wednesdays, and a **non-food market** on Grote Markt on Thursdays. Various Sunday markets are also held.

Theatre and concerts – The VVV publishes a newspaper giving details of all the events, concerts and exhibitions taking place in Groningen, and also sells tickets. The main theatres are the **Stadsschouwburg** (municipal theatre) at Turfsingel 86, ☎ (050) 312 56 45, and **De Oosterpoort**, Trompsingel 27, ☎ (050) 313 10 44.

Night-life – Groningen's thriving night-life centres on the areas around Grote Markt and the Waag, Gedempte Zuiderdiep and Kromme Ellebogen. Most of the discos are in Poelestraat and Peperstraat. Unlike many other towns and cities there are no fixed closing times, and most cafés are open until 3am. Other attractions include **Holland Casino**, Gedempte Kattendiep 150 (☎ (050) 312 34 00), and cinemas; the VVV publishes a weekly film listing every Thursday.

Events – The **Groningen Liberation Festival** takes place on 5 May each year, and consists of music and theatre events. The **Chamber Music Festival** is also held in May. In June, **SwingIn' Groningen** sees live jazz and other music on stages in and around Grote Markt. The high point of the summer is **Noorderzon** (Northern Sun), a very lively theatre and music festival in August offering something for young and old alike. The **raising of the siege of Groningen** is celebrated on 28 August, and for a weekend in September Groningen is transformed into an African, American or Asian city in the **Landenfestival**, or Countries Festival.

AROUND GROTE MARKT *1hr 30min*

Grote Markt – Prolonged by Vismarkt, the fish market, this vast and busy square, lined by the town's main buildings, forms the city centre. Grote Markt gives onto the different pedestrian precincts; the main shopping street is Herestraat. Various markets take place here *(see Travellers' addresses)*.

Stadhuis – The neo-Classical town hall (1810) is linked by a glassed-in footbridge to a modern annexe, which by its sheer size dwarfs the Goudkantoor.

* **Goudkantoor** – This gracious Renaissance Gold Office, built in 1635, has elegant façades with finely worked gables; the windows are topped by shells.
Originally the provincial tax collector's office, it was used in the 19C as a place to hallmark precious metal (*goud*: gold – *kantoor*: office). It is now a café and restaurant *(see Travellers' addresses)*.

Martinikerk ⊙ – This church, the second on this site, was rebuilt in the 16C. It is known for its **tower**★, which is the pride of Groningen. Some 96m/315ft high with six storeys, this bell-tower is topped by a weathervane in the shape of a horse depicting St Martin's mount. It has a carillon cast by the Hemony brothers.
Inside the church, the chancel is decorated with 16C frescoes depicting scenes in the life of Christ.
From the top of **Martinitoren** ⊙ there is an interesting **view** over Groningen and its canals, Grote Markt, the roofs of Martinikerk, the Prinsenhof and its garden.

ADDITIONAL SIGHTS

* **Noordelijk Scheepvaartmuseum** ⊙ – The Northern Shipping Museum is located in two beautifully restored medieval merchants' houses: the Gotisch Huis *(on the left)* and the Canterhuis *(on the right)*. It is devoted to inland water transport and coastal shipping in the northern part of the Netherlands, since the 6C.

Groninger Museum

The scale models of ships, navigational instruments, charts, paintings and ceramics are particularly well displayed and retrace the stages which have marked the history of shipping: the brilliant period of the Hanseatic League to which Groningen belonged, the Dutch East and West India Companies, the activities relative to peat extraction and its transportation by boat, the coastal shipping of bricks and schooners which replaced the traditional galliots.

Niemeyer Tabaksmuseum ⊘ – This tobacco museum is located behind the Gothic House, which houses the Northern Shipping Museum *(see above)*.
A fine collection of pipes from all over Europe, snuffboxes and jars illustrate the use of tobacco over the centuries. A 19C tobacco merchant's shop has been reconstituted.

⭐ **Groninger Museum** ⊘ – The highly original, **polymorphous building**⭐⭐ (1992-94) housing the Groninger Museum lies opposite the station, on a small island in the Verbindingskanaal. Because the museum's collections were very diverse, different architects and designers were asked to work together on the design. Each of the three main buildings has its own distinctive character, and uses different materials, colours and forms.
The museum is entered through a golden tower designed by Alessandro Mendini (b 1931), which is used as a store. The lower part of the west pavilion is clad in red brick, and is the work of Michele De Lucchi (b 1951); this houses the archeological and historical collections, which are shown in rotation. The round room above it was designed by Philippe Starck (b 1949); in the display case that follows the sloping wall and in the maze of curtains, there is a particularly fine **Oriental porcelain collection**⭐, including pieces from the wreck of the East India

Company vessel *De Geldermalsen*. Mendini designed the first of the two pavilions one above the other, on the east side, in which temporary exhibitions of contemporary art are held. The upper one, a superb example of Deconstructivism, was designed by Coop Himmelblau. It houses the collection of visual art from 1500 to 1950, which includes works by the local artists' group, De Ploeg, or temporary exhibitions.

Martinikerkhof – This lovely square, laid out on the site of a 19C cemetery (*kerkhof*), is surrounded by houses, which have been attractively restored.

To the northeast is the **Provinciehuis**, rebuilt in 1916 in neo-Renaissance style and flanked by an onion-shaped turret.

On its left, the Cardinaal House has a small Renaissance façade (1559), whose gable is decorated with three heads: Alexander the Great, King David and Charlemagne. This façade is the reconstitution of a Groningen House, which was destroyed. To the north of the square, the Prinsenhof, originally built for the Brethren of the Common Life (*see DEVENTER*) became the Bishop of Groningen's residence in 1568. Preceded by a courtyard and a 17C portal, it is built onto the Gardepoort, a small gateway (1639).

Behind the **Prinsenhof** there is a small 18C garden, the **Prinsenhoftuin**, with hedges, roses and herbs. It opens onto the Turfsingel, a canal where peat (*turf*) was transported, via a gateway called the **Zonnewijzerpoort** which has an 18C sundial on the garden side.

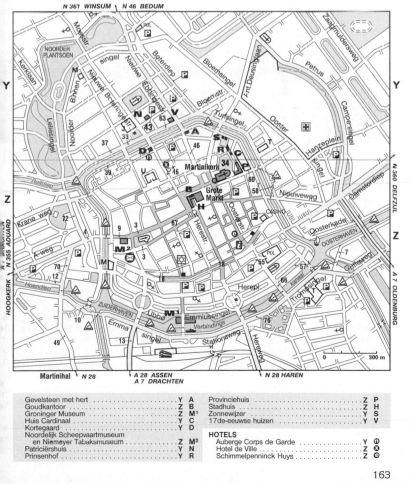

Ossenmarkt – At no 5 there is a fine 18C **patrician house**; it is a good example o the local architectural style, with its wide façade with rows of rather narrow windows topped by shells.

Not far away, at the corner of Spilsluizen and Nieuwe Ebbingestraat, stand two 17C houses. The one on the left is also characteristic of the Groningen style.

On the other side of the canal a sculptured stone depicting a stag juts out from the wall of a house.

At the corner of Spilsluizen and Oude Boteringestraat is the former guard-room **Kortegaard** with a covered gallery (1634) where cannons once stood *(see Travellers addresses)*.

OUTSKIRTS

Hortus Haren/Het Verborgen Rijk van Ming ⊘ – *6km/3mi south. Leave Groningen via Hereweg; Hortus Haren is to the south of Haren.* Hortus means botanical garden, and this 21ha/52-acre area contains various **themed gardens** such as sculpture and rose gardens, with others focusing on particular countries and regions such as Great Britain, France, or Bengal. Exotic trees and plants grow in the greenhouses, while the denizens of the vivarium include grisly bird-eating spiders.

Beside the Hortus is **Het Verborgen Rijk van Ming**, or The Hidden Empire of Ming. This recalls the time of the Ming Dynasty (1368-1644), and includes rocks, bridges pagodas, hundreds of red carp and many flowering plants, all brought to the Netherlands from China. There are also demonstrations of calligraphy, t'ai chi and silk painting, and tea ceremonies are held in the Roar of the Dragon teahouse.

EXCURSIONS

Aduard, Leens and Lauwersoog – *27km/17mi northwest by motorway.*

Aduard – Of the old Cistercian abbey founded in 1163 only the refectory remains Built in 1300, it has become a Dutch reformed church, or **Nederlandse Hervormd Kerk** ⊘. Although the façade is sober, the interior has interesting decorativ details: Gothic bays alternating with blind arches with a brick background depicting geometric motifs, bays on the ground floor surrounded by ceramic cabl moulding. The 18C furnishings are elegant: pulpit decorated with coats of arms pews with carved backs, the lords' pews topped by a canopy with heraldic motif and copper lecterns.

Leens – **Petruskerk** ⊘, a church built in the 12C and 13C, houses a lovely baroqu **organ**★ built by Hinsz in 1733.

Lauwersoog – *Local map see WADDENEILANDEN.* Departure point for ferries t Schiermonnikoog. Lauwersoog is situated near the **Lauwersmeer**, a former arm o the sea, which like the Zuiderzee, has been closed off by a dike completed in 1969 and around which polders are being reclaimed.

A small museum, **EXPOZEE** ⊘, is housed in a large building. Scale models photographs and illuminated maps give an interesting presentation on th Lauwersmeer polders and the protection of the Waddenzee. There is also a tanl containing animals from the Waddenzee.

★ **Rural Churches** – *Round tour of 118km/73mi to the northeast. Leave Groninge by Damsterdiep.*

Every village in the province of Groningen has its brick church which dates fron the 12C and 13C and is usually in the transitional Romanesque-Gothic style Architecturally they are quite simple but they are often adorned with attractiv decorative brickwork both inside and outside. Sometimes they are built o artificial mounds, and the saddleback roof of the bell-tower often emerges fron behind a screen of tall trees. Characteristic features of the interiors are th frescoes, lovely carved furnishings and hatchments. The farmhouses of the regio are also quite imposing *(see Introduction: Farmhouses)*.

Garmerwolde – The nave of this 13C village's church was demolished in the 19C so it has a free-standing **bell-tower**★ ⊘. The flat east end has bays outlined b recessed arches and a gable with blind arcading. The interior still has some 16 frescoes on the vaults and an 18C carved pulpit.

Ten Boer – On a mound, a 13C church, topped by a pinnacle, has some lovel decoration, especially on the north side: bays outlined by recessed arches medallions, multifoil blind arcading and gables both with reticulate brickwork

Stedum – Built on a mound surrounded by moats, this typical church with its ta saddleback roofed bell-tower is picturesque. A frieze runs above the modillion sculptured with characters or heads of animals.

Loppersum – This large Gothic **church** ⊘ has two transepts with blind arcading o the gables. The interior is interesting for its **frescoes**★, which decorate the uppe part of the chancel vaults and the Lady Chapel. In the chapel south of the chance there are numerous memorial slabs.

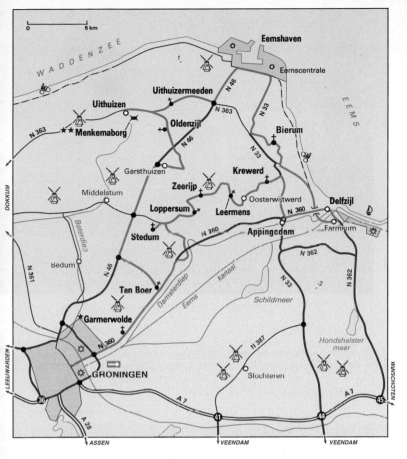

Zeerijp – Next to its free-standing bell-tower, the **church** ⊙ dating from the 14C, has a gable in two parts with blind arcading and a brick mosaic.
The interior is remarkable for its **domes**★ with brick decoration which varies in each bay: chevrons, interlacing... Blind arcading decorates the end of the nave. The organ, the Renaissance pulpit, and hatchments are also worth seeing.

Leermens – This 13C church has a flat east end decorated with blind arcading and a background decorated with brick motifs.
On arriving at Oosterwijtwerd, there is a large farmhouse with four roofs.

Krewerd – This **church** ⊙, built on a mound, has vaults decorated with brick motifs. The organ dates from 1531.

Appingedam – Renowned for its agricultural markets (April and October), it is a welcoming town with a long pedestrian precinct, Dijkstraat Promenade and crossed by a canal, the Damsterdiep.
From the footbridge (Vrouwenbrug) over the canal there is a fine **view**★ of the overhanging kitchens and the town hall's pinnacle. Appingedam's marina is nicely situated in the town centre.
The **old raadhuis**, flanked by a 19C bell-tower, dates from 1630. The façade, with bays topped by shells, is decorated with a pelican, a statue of Justice and a voluted pediment.
The 13C **Nikolaikerk** has some lovely frescoes, which were discovered when it was being restored.

Delfzijl – Delfzijl is an industrial city and a busy shipping port on Dollard Gulf; it is linked to Groningen by Eemskanaal. The town's main activities are petrochemicals and the manufacture of soda.
To the south of the town, at **Farmsun**, an aluminium smelting works, supplied with alumina from Suriname, was the first of its kind in the Netherlands, when it was built in 1956. Delfzijl also has a large pleasure boat harbour; **boat trips** ⊙ are organised.
From the dike on Dollard, there is a **view** over the harbour and the town, overlooked by a tall wall mill, called **Molen Adam** (1875).
On a square near the station, a monument topped by a swan, **Het Zwaantje**, commemorates the Resistance.

Oldenzijl – The Romanesque church

A small **statue of Maigret** on the lawns of the Damsterdiep *(600m/656yd from the pumping station to the west of Eemskanaal, opposite the RWR warehouses)*, is a reminder that **Georges Simenon** (1903-89) was a visitor in 1929. It is believed that he created his most famous character, police inspector Maigret, while in Delfzijl

Bierum – On a mound there is a small 13C **church** ⊙, whose bell-tower was reinforced by a flying buttress. The semicircular east end of the chancel dates from the 14C.

The interior is roofed with geometrically decorated ribbed domes on which a few traces of frescoes remain. The organ dates from 1792 to 1793, the baptismal font from the early Middle Ages.

Around the church the cemetery has remarkable 19C sculptured memorial slabs depicting symbols of life (trees) and time (hour glasses).

Eemshaven – This new port was built on reclaimed polderland of Emmapolder and Oostpolder. The port started trading in 1973 and has given rise to an important industrial zone. To the east the imposing **Eemscentrale** power station has been powered by natural gas since 1976.

Uithuizermeeden – The **church** ⊙ with a 13C nave and a transept (1705) has a white tower rebuilt between 1896 and 7. The pulpit was sculptured in the 18C.

Uithuizen – The small **Hervormde Kerk** ⊙ contains a remarkable organ built in 1700 by Arp Schnitger and a noble's pew from the same period.
To the east is **Menkemaborg★★** *(see MENKEMABORG)* and, opposite it, the **Stichting Museum 1939-1945** ⊙ where the Second World War is evoked by a collection of vehicles and arms.

Oldenzijl – The small Romanesque church and its churchyard stand on a mound encircled by a moat and a screen of trees. Inside the plainness of the brick walls is broken by several small round windows trimmed with mouldings and the decorative effect of the blind arcading in the chancel.

Return to Groningen by Garsthuizen, St-Annerhuisjes, Ten Boer and N41.

*On the cover of Michelin Green Guides,
the coloured band on top indicates the language :*
    blue for French
    pink for English
    yellow for German
    orange for Spanish
    green for Italian, etc.

Den HAAG★★

THE HAGUE or's-GRAVENHAGE – Zuid-Holland 🄿
Population 442 159
Michelin maps 908 D 5 and 211 K 10 and folds 1 and 2 (inset)
Plan of the conurbation in the current Michelin Red Guide Benelux

Although The Hague, whose official name is 's-Gravenhage (generally shortened to
Den Haag), is home to the Dutch government and Parliament, as well as many foreign
embassies, it is only the provincial capital. Dutch monarchs have been enthroned in
Amsterdam since 1813. This coastal town is a pleasant and quiet residential
community, with a multitude of squares, parks (more than 700 public gardens) and
several canals. The Hague sprawls over a large area and has a relatively small
population, earning itself the title of the biggest village in Europe. It is marked by
a certain aristocratic charm and is considered to be the most worldly and elegant
town in the Netherlands; in fact, some of its 19C colonial atmosphere still remains.
However, the city also has some important modern architecture, such as Rem
Koolhaas's Danstheater and H Hertzberger's transport and planning ministry
building. The De Resident development between the Binnenhof and the station has
involved a large number of international architects, including Richard Meier, who
designed the new city hall.
The Hague was the birthplace of William III (1650-1702). **Christiaen Huygens** the great
scientist *(see Excursions)* and the brothers **Jan** (1903-94) and **Nikolaas Tinbergen**
1907-88; one received the Nobel Prize for economics (1969) with the Norwegian R
Frisch, the other the Nobel Prize for medicine (1973) with the Austrians K Lorenz
and K von Frisch.

HISTORICAL NOTES

A meet – Up to the 13C, The Hague was just a hunting lodge built by Count Floris IV
of Holland in the middle of a forest which stretched northwards to Haarlem.
About 1250 his son, William II, who had been proclaimed King of the Romans (1247) by
the Pope in his fight against Emperor Frederick II, built a castle on the site of the present
Binnenhof. Floris V completed the work of his father by adding the Knight's Hall.
At the end of the 14C, abandoning Haarlem, the Count of Holland, Albert of Bavaria
and his retinue came to live in The Hague.

A village... – 's-Gravenhage, the Count's Hedge or Die Haghe, the hedge, rapidly
developed without being more than a place of residence and rest. The cloth trade,
which started in the 15C was not enough to make it a mercantile town.
The confederation of cities which constituted the Low Countries at the time refused
to admit The Hague to their governing council. However, it was in The Hague that
Philip the Good, in 1432 and 1456 held the chapters of the Order of the Golden
Fleece.
The absence of fortifications brought destruction upon the city: as in 1528 when it
was attacked by Maarten van Rossum, famous captain of a Gelderland troop of
mercenaries. In 1581, the act declaring Philip II of Spain's disavowal by the States
General of the United Provinces was posted on the door of the Knights' Hall.

..which develops – In the 17C, The Hague found peace and prosperity again. Seat
of the States General of the United Provinces, then the government, it became an
important centre of diplomatic negotiations. The main coalitions against Louis XIV
were sealed here.
From the middle of the 17C to the end of the 18C substantial mansions in Renaissance and Baroque styles were built round the medieval centre of the Binnenhof.
The French entered The Hague in 1795. Eleven years later the town had to cede its
rank of capital to Amsterdam where Louis Bonaparte had installed his government.
In 1814 the government and the Court returned to The Hague. But the title of capital
remained with Amsterdam, where the king was enthroned in 1815.
The 19C confirmed the residential character of the town which had become the
favourite residence of colonials returning from Indonesia. This period marked it so
profoundly that it is sometimes referred to as the widow of the Indies. Even today,
The Hague has a sizeable Indonesian community.

The Hague School – Between 1870 and 1890 a group of painters in The Hague tried
to renew painting and notably the art of landscapes in the manner of the Barbizon
School in France.
A group of artists gathered around the leader, **Jozef Israëls**, a painter of fishing scenes
and portraits: **JH Weissenbruch** (1824-1903); **Jacob Maris** (1837-99), painter of dunes and
beaches; **HW Mesdag**, painter of numerous seascapes and the famous *Mesdag Panorama*
(see below); **Anton Mauve** (1838-88), painter of the Gooi heathland; **Albert Neuhuys** (1844-
1914), painter of household interiors; **Johannes Bosboom** (1817-91), painter of church
interiors; and **Blommers** (1845-1914), painter of the life of fishermen. Neuhuys and
Mauve, having worked in Laren, are sometimes attached to the Laren School.
The Hague painters did not set out to achieve brilliant colours nor great draftman-
ship. Greys and browns were the dominant colours and their works nearly always
expressed a certain melancholy.

Benedictus de Spinoza

The great philosopher Spinoza spent the last seven years of his life in The Hague; he died here in 1677. Born in Amsterdam in 1632, this Jew of Portugese origin was a brilliant scholar. In 1656 Spinoza was excommunicated and banished from Amsterdam by the synagogue authorities for questioning the orthodox Jewish doctrines and interpretations of scripture. He took refuge for a time in Ouderkerk aan de Amstel, then went to live in Rijnsburg near Leiden in 1660. For three years he devoted himself to philosophy and polishing lenses to earn a living.

ROGER-VIOLLET

After a few years spent in Voorburg, a suburb of The Hague, in 1670 he moved into a modest residence in Paviljoensgracht.

It was only after his death that his *Posthumous Works* published in 1677 appeared in Latin; it included the **Ethics**, which became universally famous.

The diplomatic town – The Hague was chosen several times as a centre for international negotiations, including the peace conferences of 1899 and 1907. Finally the construction of the Peace Palace (1913) established its vocation as a diplomatic town.

It is the seat of the International Court of Justice, an organisation dependent on the UN, the Permanent Court of Arbitration and the Academy of International Law.

The modern city – The new suburbs of The Hague extend as far as the dunes on the coast, and include fine examples of many different 20C architectural styles. To the north, the Dutch Convention Centre (Nederlands Congresgebouw) has been open to

Morning ride along the beach (1876), Anton Mauve; Rijksmuseum, Amsterdam

he public since 1969. The city's orchestra, the Haagse Residentie-Orkest, has its wn modern concert hall on the Spui, the 1 900-seat Dr Anton Philipszaal, built in 987. The Danstheater, headquarters of the Nederlands Dans theater, was opened the same year and seats 1 000 people.

he Hague is also the headquarters of many major companies, including Shell, Amoco nd Esso.

Accommodation

s The Hague is the country's diplomatic, administrative and commercial entre, hotels are mostly modern business-oriented ones. However, it does ave two unusually good 19C hotels *(see Something special)*.

YOUTH HOSTEL

JHC City Hostel Den Haag – *Scheepmakerstraat 27, 2515 VA Den Haag,* ☏ *(070) 315 78 78, Fax (070) 315 78 77. 220 beds.* Close to the station, and as its own brasserie.

BUDGET HOTELS

Bali – *Badhuisweg 1, 2587 CA Scheveningen,* ☏ *(070) 350 24 34, Fax (070) 354 03 63. 29 rooms.* These rooms belong to the Bali restaurant *(see below)* and nearly all have their own shower or bath. The hotel is close to he Circustheater and only 400m from the beach.

El Park – *Belgischeplein 38, 2587 AT Scheveningen,* ☏ *(070) 350 50 00, Fax (070) 352 32 42. 12 rooms.* These villas converted into a hotel stand on a quiet square in Scheveningen. The rooms have every comfort, and there is garden and terrace.

OUR SELECTION

Petit – *Groot Hertoginnelaan 42, 2517 EH Den Haag,* ☏ *(070) 346 55 00, Fax (070) 346 32 57. 20 rooms.* This hotel is located in an elegant mansion near he Haags Gemeentemuseum. It has comfortable rooms and its own car park.

Corona – *Buitenhof 42, 2513 AH Den Haag,* ☏ *(070) 363 79 30, Fax (070) 361 57 85. 26 rooms.* Right in the heart of the city, close to the Binnenhof, and thus the ideal base for a visit to The Hague. The comfortable rooms are decorated in Louis XVI style or Art Deco.

SOMETHING SPECIAL

es Indes – *Lange Voorhout 54, 2514 EG Den Haag,* ☏ *(070) 363 29 32, Fax (070) 345 17 21. 70 rooms.* This stately hotel, formerly the residence of a wealthy baron, is a journey back in time to the 19C. It has red carpets, high eilings, grand staircases, marble and stucco, obviously in combination with very modern facility. For a taste of bygone days, there's none better, but be varned: it doesn't come cheap.

Kurhaus – *Gevers Deynootplein 30, 2586 CK Scheveningen,* ☏ *(070) 416 26 36, Fax (070) 416 26 46. 247 rooms.* This imposing 19C icheveningen beach hotel offers a choice of royal suites or luxury rooms. The hotel is full of character: the huge domed Kurzaal *(see below)*, the outside errace overlooking the sea and of course the thermal baths which gave this tylish hotel its name.

Restaurants

THE HAGUE

It Rains Fishes – *Noordeinde 123,* ☏ *(070) 365 25 98.* Trendy fish restaurant offering "fusion cuisine": western products prepared in eastern style, with sometimes surprising but always delicious results.

ulien – *Vos in Tuinstraat 2a,* ☏ *(070) 365 86 02.* Art Nouveau-style French restaurant opposite the Hotel des Indes *(see above)*.

Saur – *Lange Voorhout 47,* ☏ *(070) 346 25 65.* A French restaurant in a beautiful location opposite the Paleis. Food is served at the bar downstairs.

The Raffles – *Javastraat 63,* ☏ *(070) 345 85 87.* Indonesian cuisine.

Shirasagi – *Spui 170,* ☏ *(070) 346 47 00.* Japanese restaurant with food prepared at the table *(teppan-yaki)*.

Brasserie Buitenhof – *Buitenhof 39,* ☏ *(070) 363 79 30.* Atmospheric brasserie restaurant of the Corona hotel *(see above)*. A good place for a genteel cup of coffee; covered terrace.

SCHEVENINGEN

Bali – *Badhuisweg 1,* ☏ *(070) 350 24 34.* One of the country's oldest ndonesian restaurants.

Westbroekpark – *Kapelweg 35,* ☏ *(070) 354 60 72.* Once you've had enough of the sea, sample the delicious cuisine of this restaurant in the park, overlooking the famous rose garden.

Seinpost – *Zeekant 60,* ☎ *(070) 355 52 50.* A circular restaurant offerin[g] excellent fish dishes and a wonderful view of the North Sea.

Kurzaal – *Gevers Deynootplein 30,* ☎ *(070) 416 26 36.* Lunch or dine in sty[le] at this buffet restaurant in the imposing old concert hall of the Kurhaus.

Brasseries, cafés, bars, coffee shops...

't Goude Hooft – *Dag. Groenmarkt 13, Den Haag,* ☎ *(070) 346 96 1[3].* International cuisine in one of The Hague's best-known brasseries, with it[s] own sun terrace.

Le Mangerie – *Laan van Roos en Doorn 51a, Den Haag,* ☎ *(070) 364 37 5[0].* More international food, in a beautiful interior with a wooden mezzanine.

Deining Brasserie de la mer – *Stevinstraat 80 (at the corner of Badhuisweg[)] Scheveningen,* ☎ *(070) 358 92 92.* Quiet brasserie away from the buzz of th[e] boulevard; particularly ideal if you get peckish late at night, as the kitchen [is] open till midnight. Meals are served in the garden on warm summer's night[s].

Museumcafé Het Paleis – *Lange Voorhout 74, Den Haag,* ☎ *(070) 362 40 61.* Th[e] café in the basement of the Museum Het Paleis has the original Art De[co] interior of the Krul coffee house in The Hague, and is a good place for a drin[k] before or after a visit to the museum.

Slagerij P.G. Dungelman – *Hoogstraat 34, Den Haag,* ☎ *(070) 346 23 00.* Not [a] bar or café, but a butcher's serving wonderful hot croquettes!

Practical information

General information – The **VVV tourist offices** in **The Hague** *(Koningin Julianaple[in] 30, winkelcentrum Babylon, 2595 AA Den Haag)* and **Scheveningen** *(Geve[rs] Deynootweg 1134, 2586 BX Scheveningen)* both have the same telephon[e] number, ☎ *(0900) 340 35 05.* They can provide information on sights[,] events, cultural activities and accommodation packages, and publish an annua[l] information guide including a list of bars, restaurants, hotels, youth hostel[s,] apartments and camp sites. Hotel rooms can be booked by the reservation[s] department of the **Stichting Promotie Den Haag,** ☎ *(070) 363 56 76.*

Emergencies – The Hague's **Tourist Assistance Service (TAS)** offers help to foreig[n] tourists who are victims of crime or road or other accidents. It is open dail[y] from 9am to 9pm at Zoutmanstraat 44, ☎ *(070) 310 32 74.*

Transport – Parking in the centre of The Hague or Scheveningen is difficu[lt] and expensive. Most **parking is metered**, and if you don't put enough into th[e] meter or park illegally you are likely to be clamped. If this happens, go to th[e] payment office in the multi-storey car park behind the Central Statio[n.] Alternatively, use one of the many well-signposted **car parks**.

The main sights in the city centre are within walking distance [of] one another, but you can also take a **bus** or **tram**. You can buy individual ticket[s] from the driver, but it is cheaper to buy a **strippenkaart** or strip of ticket[s] beforehand. These are available from VVV offices, post offices, nearly a[ll] tobacconists and newsagents, and in many hotels. If you will be in The Hagu[e] for several days, a **meerdagenkaart** (multi-day travel card) is a good idea.

Tours and walks – In summer, the VVV organises two **guided bus tours** of th[e] town: a royal tour of the palaces of The Hague and Scheveningen, and a[n] architectural tour of the city's buildings, both ancient and modern. Fo[r] bookings, ☎ *(0900) 340 35 05.* The VVV also sells booklets giving details o[f] **self-guided walking tours** on various themes.

Boat trips – Depart daily from **Scheveningen harbour** between June an[d] September. **Fishing trips** are also possible. Information: Rederij Groen, D[r.] Lelykade 1d, ☎ *(070) 355 35 88;* Rederij Fortuna, opposite Dr. Lelykade 54[,] ☎ *(070) 355 54 61;* Sportvisserij Trip Noordzee, Dr. Lelykade 3[,] ☎ *(070) 354 11 22;* Rederij Vrolijk, Dr. Lelykade, ☎ *(070) 354 20 10.*

Shopping – The Hague is a great place to shop. In addition to the big **city-centr[e] department stores** and chains (eg Maison de Bonneterie, Bijenkorf, Meddens, Mark[s] & Spencer) there are lots of excellent small shops in the streets and square[s] around the palaces. Indoor shopping is available at the stylish Passage (Hofwe[g] 5-7/Buitenhof 4-5) and at the Babylon shopping centre next to the Central St[a-] tion. But The Hague is best-known for its countless **antique shops** and **commercial a[rt] galleries**; the VVV publishes brochures full of useful shopping suggestions. Lat[e-] night shopping is on Thursdays, when the shops are open until 9pm.

The best places to shop in **Scheveningen** are Palace Promenade, Gevers Deynoo[t-] plein and the boulevard. Late-night shopping day is Friday, except in Palac[e] Promenade, where the shops are open every day from 10am to 10pm.

Markets – The Hague has excellent markets several days a week. There ar[e] **general goods markets** in Herman Costerstraat (Mondays, Wednesdays, Friday[s] and Saturdays) and on Markthof (daily except Sundays). A **farmers' market** take[s] place by the Grote Kerk on Wednesdays. A lively **antique and book market** is hel[d] on Lange Voorhout on Thursdays and Sundays from May to September, an[d] on Thursdays on the Plein during the rest of the year.

Herring seller

Theatres and concerts – Classical music: Dr. Anton Philipszaal, Spuiplein 150, ☎ (070) 360 98 10; Sunday morning concerts in the Circustheater, Gevers Deynootplein 50, ☎ (070) 351 12 12. **Pop, rock, blues:** 't Paard, Prinsegracht 12, ☎ (070) 360 16 18. **Theatre and dance:** Koninklijke Schouwburg, Korte Voorhout 3, ☎ (070) 346 94 50; Lucent Danstheater, Spuiplein 152, ☎ (070) 360 49 30 (home of the world-famous Nederlands Dans theater); Nederlands Congresgebouw, Churchillplein 10, ☎ (070) 354 80 00; Theater aan het Spui, Spui 187, ☎ (070) 346 52 72; Diligentia, Lange Voorhout 5, ☎ (070) 365 18 51.

Night-life – **Scheveningen's Boulevard** is the place to be: crowded and boisterous with something for everyone, including shops, street cafés, restaurants, bars and discos. If the weather drives you indoors, you might opt for a musical at the **Circustheater**, a night at the movies, or a flutter at the **Holland Casino**.

Events – An annual Indonesian fair, **Pasar Malam Besar**, is held on the Malieveld in June, and includes theatre performances, lectures, stalls and music. The famous **North Sea Jazz Festival**, in July, is a magnet for jazz and blues fanatics from all over the world. Modern dance enthusiasts make a beeline for the annual **CaDance Festival** at the Theater aan het Spui, and the international **Holland Dance Festival** takes place on alternate years. Scheveningen has its own annual **Sand Sculpture Festival** in May and June, and the traditional **Herring Festival** is in late May, when the first batch of new Dutch herring is auctioned.

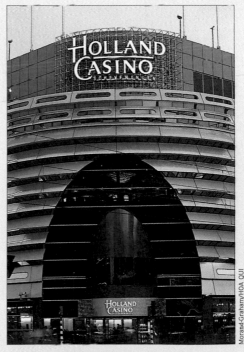

Scheveningen – Holland Casino

CENTRE *half a day*

Stately mansions line the wide avenues around the Binnenhof, the centre of the country's political life. Nearby, shops are grouped in pedestrian precincts o covered passages: the town has a great many antique dealers and luxury boutiques.

Buitenhof - This is the outer courtyard of the old castle which once belonged to the counts of Holland. A statue of King William II stands in the centre.

★ **Binnenhof** - Enter by the Stadtholder doorway to reach an inner courtyard (binnenhof) in the centre of which stands the Ridderzaal, or Knights' Hall. The buildings all around date from different periods in Dutch history. They now house the Upper House of Parliament and the Ministry of General Affairs (*north wing*) part of the State Council (*west wing*) and the Lower House (*south and east wing* as well as the new extensions).

Index of street names and sights for maps of DEN HAAG

Van Oldenbarnevelt *(see AMERSFOORT)* was executed in this courtyard on 13 May 1619.

Binnenhof visitors' centre ⊘ – This has a **model** of the Binnenhof and a historical timescale showing the political history of the Low Countries over the past 12 centuries. It is also the starting point of a tour, which begins with a video about the Binnenhof and continues through the Ridderzaal and the Upper and Lower Houses of Parliament.

★ **Ridderzaal** ⊘ – An **exhibition** ⊘ in the cellars of the Ridderzaal *(no 8a)* explains the origin and workings of the two chambers and the roles of the head of State and the monarch.

The Ridderzaal, built as a banqueting hall for Count William II of Holland, was completed c 1280 by his son Count Floris V. The building, which looks very much like a church, was located in the prolongation of the old castle. Its façade with a pointed and finely worked gable is flanked by two slender turrets. Inside, the great hall, restored, has recovered its Gothic vault with openwork beams.

DEN HAAG

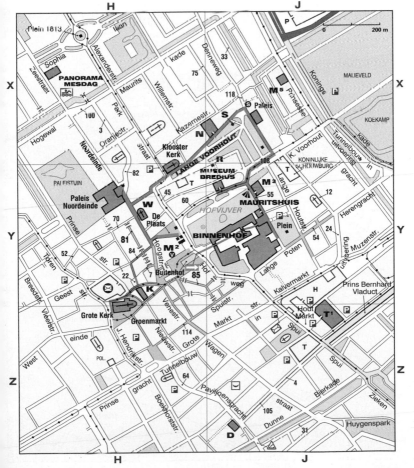

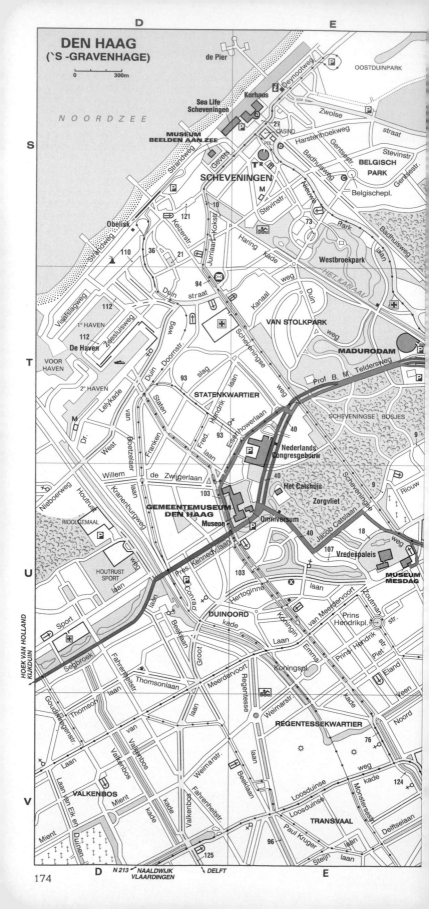

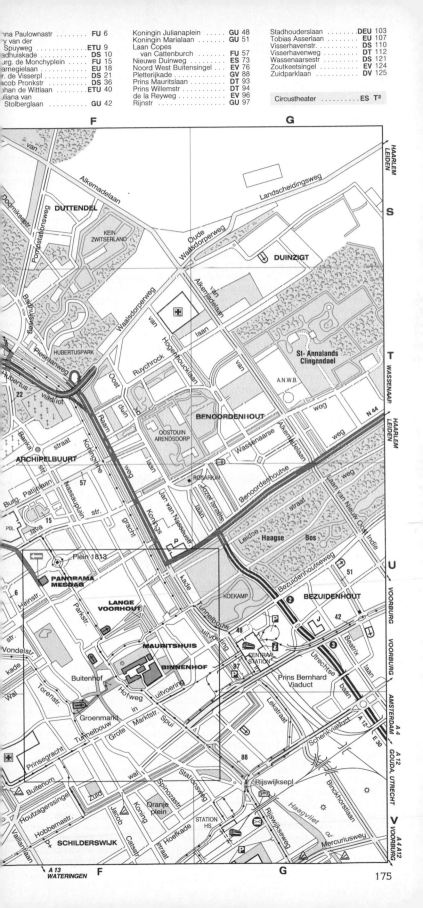

175

It is here Since 1904 the two chambers of the States General have gathered in the Ridder road for a ceremonial opening session and to listen to a speech made by the Queen. The back of the building, visible from the Binnenhof's second courtyard, consists of the old castle built c 1250 by Count William II. The main hall became, in 1511, the hall of sessions of the Holland and West Friesland Court and was called the Roll Court.

Eerste Kamer ⊘ – The Upper Chamber is situated in the 17C north wing, in the **Stadtholders' Quarters** (or residence), bordered by a covered gallery. It is the former assembly hall of the Holland and West Friesland States (17C).
Since 1848 it has been used as a place of assembly for the Upper House or Senate which consists of 75 members elected for four years by the 12 Provincial States. It has a wooden ceiling painted in the Baroque style by two of Rubens' pupils: A de Haan and N Wielingh.

Trêveszaal – Not open to the public.
The Truce Hall, where in 1608 a twelve-year truce with Spain was prepared, is now used by the Council of Ministers. It was rebuilt in 1697 by Marot in the Louis XIV style.

Tweede Kamer ⊘ – The Lower Chamber is composed of 150 representatives elected for four years by universal suffrage.
Between 1815 and 1992 the former **ballroom** (presently undergoing restoration) situated in the wing added by the Stadtholder William V in the late 18C, was used to accommodate the deputies; decorated in the Louis XIV style, the ballroom had a balcony and several boxes.
In 1992 the members of the Lower Chamber moved to **modern buildings** (Entrance Plein 2A) based on plans by the Dutch architect Pi de Bruijn and set up among the existing constructions to the south of the Binnenhof.
The central hall, whose glass roofing lets in the daylight, houses an original work of art by Lex Wegchelaar, made with marble elements taken from a low relief (1938) by RN Roland Holst.
The plenary sessions are held in the hemicycle; from the public gallery one can see going from left to right, the seats occupied by the Christian Democrats, the Liberals, D66, the small Christian groups, the Labour Party and the Green Left. Behind the speaker's chair are painted panels by R van de Wint.

Plein – The Ministry of Defence overlooks this square; in the centre stands the statue of William the Silent (1848). No 23 is a splendid 18C building designed by Daniel Marot. In winter a market selling antiques is held on the square.

★★★ **Mauritshuis** ⊘ – This museum is named after Prince Johan Maurits of Nassau-Siegen who in around 1640 commissioned Pieter Post to build this elegant residence to plans by Jacob van Campen. It was built in a strictly Classical style with its height, width and depth all approximately the same (c 25m/80ft (illustration: see Introduction, Art). Since 1822, it has been the home of the royal painting collection, one of the finest in the world; the relatively small number of paintings makes for a most agreeable visit.
The collection is still expanding, and is displayed in the form of temporary exhibitions, each highlighting a particular aspect of this rich assemblage of artworks. The permanent collection as described below is therefore rarely all on show at the same time.

Ground floor – This is devoted to foreign schools and the Flemish School.
The first room of the **Flemish School** is remarkable with the pathetic Lamentation of Christ (c 1450) by Rogier van der Weyden, the penetrating Portrait of a Man by Memling, and Christ Carrying the Cross by Quentin Metsys.
There are four lovely portraits by Holbein the Younger (16C), one of a young woman by the German Bartholomeus Bruyn, Holbein's contemporary; two portraits by Antonio Moro, including one of a goldsmith.
Two rooms are reserved for **Rubens** and his contemporaries. The Adoration of the Shepherds by Jordaens and canvases by David Teniers are near a rich collection of works by Rubens: Isabella Brant, his first wife, Hélène Fourment, his second, Michel Ophovius, bishop of 's-Hertogenbosch, and finally the famous Garden of Eden with the Fall of Man (c 1615) where the two personages painted by Rubens can be seen against a landscape painted with charming meticulousness by Jan Bruegel the Elder.

First floor – Among the Dutch painters of the **Golden Age**, **Rembrandt** is the reigning master here.
Between the portrait of the artist when he was 23 (1629; illustration, see LEIDEN), which holds one's attention by its meticulous precision of detail, its taste for scrupulous observation, and the portrait of 1669, one of his last works, with an overwhelming depth, one can see the whole evolution of the painter.
The Anatomy Lesson of Doctor Nicolaes Tulp (1632), his first group portrait painted when he was 26, brought him glory; the research in composition, the contrasts of light give the scene a dramatic intensity already characteristic.

The same emotion appears in the luminous *Susanna* of 1637, one of the rare nudes by Rembrandt, the *Simeon in the Temple* (1631) with its subdued muted light, or in the more fiery works like the pathetic *Saul and David* (1658); *The Two Negroes* (1661).

The museum also has two admirable paintings by **Johannes Vermeer**, the *View of Delft* (c 1660) which was so admired by Van Gogh, and the *Girl with a Pearl Earring* (also c 1660). To these two masterpieces one can compare the *Diana*, one of the first paintings already showing the limpid and serene poetry of the Delft master.

The museum has a number of genre paintings: some Jan Steens, where the verve, malice, and delicacy bring charming anecdotes (*Merry Company*, *Girl Eating Oysters*), some Van Ostades with scenes of country life (*The Violinist*), portraits by Frans Hals such as the brilliant *Head of a Child* (c 1625), some Ter Borchs of great sensitivity, and The *Young Mother* by Gerrit Dou.

Girl with a Pearl Earring, Johannes Vermeer

There are also landscape painters; painters of rivers like Van Goyen, Van de Velde, the countryside, like Salomon van Ruisdael and his nephew Jacob van Ruysdael, skaters, like Avercamp, domestic animals, like Paulus Potter (*The Bull*, 1647). There are also some small gems: the famous *Goldfinch* (1654) which Carel Fabritius, Rembrandt's pupil, painted the year of his death; he was only 32.

Hofvijver – Lit at night in summer. From Korte Vijverberg, there is a lovely **view**★ over the lake in which you can see the Mauritshuis reflected, the octagonal tower of the Prime Minister's quarters, the windows of the Truce Hall and the Upper Chamber. In the middle of the lake, which has a fountain, there is an island planted with trees. Storks have nested here for many years, and the stork appears in the city's coat of arms.

Hofvijver

Haags Historisch Museum ⊘ – The collections of the Hague Historical Museum, installed in the former premises of the Archers' Company of St Sebastian (1636), illustrate the history of the town and the life of its townspeople: archeological findings, eggshell porcelain, church silver, views of the city and other items.

Follow Lange Vijverberg.

★ **Museum Bredius** ⊘ – This museum has a privileged setting: a fine mansion built in 1757. The painting collection features many of the works left to the town by Abraham Bredius (1855-1946), an art historian and former director of the Mauritshuis.

In the remarkable section on 17C art, you can admire the famous *Satyr among the Peasants* by Jan Steen, a fine *Christ's Head* by Rembrandt, *Festivities on the Ice* by A van der Neer, along with canvases by Albert Cuyp, Adriaen van Ostade, Willem Pieter Buytewech and JJ van de Velde.

On the floor above, note the drawings by Rembrandt and Jacob van Ruysdael. At no 8 there is a façade attributed to Daniel Marot.

★ **Lange Voorhout** – Along the tree-lined avenues of Lange Voorhout with vast lawns there are some of the most beautiful patrician residences in The Hague. Most of them are occupied by embassies.

There is a large **antiques market** on Lange Voorhout in the summer.

Paleis ⊘ – The former palace of Queen Emma (1858-1934), wife of William III and mother to Wilhelmina, stands at the far end of the main avenue. Its elegant 18C façade was the work of Pieter de Swart.

In front of the **Hotel des Indes** *(nos 54-56; see Travellers' addresses)*, there is a lovely statuette, **The Stroller** dedicated to the chronicler Elias.

No 34 – This edifice was built between 1734 and 6 by Daniel Marot. Between 1813 and 1814 William I, first king of the Netherlands, lived here. The building now houses the Supreme Court of Appeal.

At no 15, on the opposite side, stands the building bought by the painter Mesdag to house the **Pulchri Studio** association, of which he was the president from 1889.

Kloosterkerk – This former convent chapel built in the 15C and 16C is used for organ concerts and choral services.

Noordeinde – This busy street lined with antique shops crosses the square where the **Paleis Noordeinde** stands. Also called Het Oude Hof, this 16C and 17C building with two wings at right angles was occupied by Louise de Coligny, widow of William the Silent, by the princes Maurice and Frederick Henry, sons of the latter, and by King William I. Queen Beatrix has installed her offices here.

Opposite there is an equestrian statue of William the Silent.

Return via Noordeinde, past Heulstraat.

Waals-Hervormde Kerk ⊘ – The Walloon Reformed Church was built in 1807 by Louis Napoleon to be used by the French-speaking Protestant community of The Hague which formerly met in the castle chapel.

After the mid 16C the Protestant refugees, fleeing persecution in the Southern Netherlands (Belgium), established French-speaking parish communities. These increased in the 17C with the arrival of the Huguenots from France. The cult is still practised today in **Walloon churches** which are part of the Dutch Reformed Church.

De Plaats – In the centre of this square is the statue (1887) of Johan de Witt who was put to death here at the same time as his brother Cornelis *(see DORDRECHT)*.

Museum de Gevangenpoort ⊘ – This 13C gatehouse was part of the ducal castle on the Binnenhof. In the 15C it became a prison, where a number of famous figures including Cornelis de Witt *(see DORDRECHT)* were incarcerated. It is now a museum, with a collection of medieval instruments of torture and punishment.

★ **Galerij Prins Willem V** ⊘ – In 1773 the Stadtholder of the United Provinces, William V, converted the second floor of the house, adjoining the Prison Gate, into a picture gallery. This gallery was open to the public; it may be seen as the very first public museum in the history of the Netherlands. The prince's collection featured mainly 17C landscapes, genre scenes and paintings of still life. In 1815 King William I donated the collection to the state and it was transferred to the Mauritshuis in 1821.

The gallery has been restored and decorated in the manner of the 18C: the paintings fully cover the walls, up to the vaulted ceiling embellished with Louis XVI stucco work.

Although it only features a few works belonging to the original collection, the present display of 17C paintings is extremely interesting. It includes landscapes by Philips Wouwerman, *Veere Church* by J van der Heyden, a number of works by Jan Steen, *The Bear Hunt* by Paulus Potter, *Portrait of Abraham Boom* by Thomas de Keyser (son of Hendrick de Keyser), *Girl with a lamp* by Gerard Dou, and a picture by Van de Velde the Younger: *The War Ship at Sunset*.

Groenmarkt – This is the central square of The Hague with both the town hall and the Grote Kerk. Numerous pedestrian precincts start from here, notably **Paleispromenade** to the north, and **De Passage**, the large covered passage built in 1880, to the south.

Grote Kerk or Sint-Jacobskerk ⊘ – Flanked by a tower with a carillon of 51 bells, this great brick hall-type (three naves of equal height) church (c 1450) is roofed with a wooden vault. In the chancel (c 1500), there is the tomb of Admiral Jacob van Wassenaar van Obdam and the coat of arms of the knights of the Order of the Golden Fleece who held their chapter in this church in 1456. Several stained-glass windows are worth seeing in the ambulatory: on one Charles V is shown kneeling at the Virgin's feet. The pulpit of 1550 is beautifully sculpted. The church is now used for cultural and commercial events.

Oude Raadhuis – The old town hall has a lovely 16C façade with crow-stepped gables. The 18C side façade is elegantly decorated. At the top of the richly ornamented front is the motto Ne Jupiter Quidem Omnibus (Even Jupiter cannot please everyone). The statues above the centre section depict Justice and Prudence with the coat of arms of The Hague and a Latin inscription which, loosely translated, means "Wise men learn by other men's mistakes, fools by their own".

BEYOND THE CITY CENTRE *half a day*

★ **Panorama Mesdag** ⊘ – Installed in a rotunda on piles, lit by hidden windows, this extraordinary landscape of 120m/394ft in circumference and 14m/46ft high shows Scheveningen as it was in 1881. The artist **Hendrik Willem Mesdag** was commissioned to paint this immense canvas in 1880. In 1879 from the top of the highest dune in Scheveningen, he had already reproduced the landscape on a glass cylinder, a replica of which is shown here.

This work, which is very much in the tradition of the Hague School, took only three months. Mesdag painted the sky, the sea, the beach with boats; his wife, Sientje Mesdag-van Houten, did the village; Théophile de Bock, the dunes; Breitner probably painted the figures and Blommers the woman in costume and her child. Despite the differences in technique it remains a unit; the perspective is marvellous, the sky above the sea has a soft luminosity, while behind the village the bell-towers of The Hague can be picked out.

Since the spectator is 14m/46ft away from this painting and standing on flotsam-strewn sand, the effect is that of looking down on the panorama from the top of a high dune. In the absence of a harbour, the flat-bottomed boats were dragged into and out of the water by horses.

In the entrance hall, added in 1910, paintings and watercolours by Mesdag and his wife are exhibited; note the lovely sombre tonalities.

★ **Museum Mesdag** ⊘ – Using the fortune he inherited from his father, Mesdag constructed this building beside his home in 1887 to house his growing collection of arts and crafts. He bequeathed everything to the State in 1903, and remained the director of the collection until 1911. The original house is now part of the museum. On the ground floor, in the studio where his wife Sientje formerly painted, authentic objects and a reconstruction of the original decoration recreate the atmosphere of Mesdag's former studio.

The museum allows an interesting comparison to be made between the Barbizon School (mid 19C) with Millet, Daubigny, Corot, Théodore Rousseau, Courbet, and The Hague School with Bosboom, Mauve, the Maris brothers, Jozef Israëls and obviously Mesdag, the painter of seascapes. In the paintings of the two schools one finds fairly sombre tones, often greys, and a distinct preference for nature and landscapes.

Vredespaleis ⊘ – The Peace Palace was inaugurated a year before the start of the First World War, on 28 August 1913. On the initiative of Czar Nicholas II the first **Peace Conference** took place in The Hague (at Huis Ten Bosch) in 1899.

It was decided at that time to create a Permanent Court of Arbitration which was defined in 1907 during the Second Peace Conference which took place in the Knights' Hall.

In the meantime the American industrialist and philanthropist, Andrew Carnegie, donated the funds to house this Court and equip it with a library, the Netherlands government donated the land and the French architect Cordonnier was put in charge of the construction.

In 1922 the palace became, in addition, the seat of the Permanent Court of International Justice which in 1946 became the **International Court of Justice** (the United Nation's main judicial organ). It also houses the Academy of International Law of The Hague, founded in 1923. Each nation has contributed to the furnishings and decoration of the palace. The Japanese room, hung with sumptuous tapestries, is where the Administrative Council meets, and where French is the official language; the members sit round an immense table with seats decorated with the various countries' coat of arms.

Walk alongside **Zorgvliet Park** to see **Het Catshuis**, the Dutch Prime Minister's house which belonged to **Jacob Cats**.

Follow Kennedylaan and Stadhouderslaan to reach the Gemeentemuseum.

★★ **Gemeentemuseum Den Haag** ⊙ – The Hague's municipal museum is a masterpiece of 20C museum architecture. Designed by **HP Berlage** and built in 1935, it consists of a reinforced concrete skeleton with a brick facing. A gallery leads to the different exhibition rooms, designed to take the maximum advantage of natural light. A major restoration completed in October 1998 has restored it, Berlage's last design, to its former glory; it also included the addition of a fashion gallery.

The rich and very varied collections consist of decorative arts, 19C and 20C visual arts, costumes, musical instruments, drawings and prints.

Decorative arts – This section includes ceramics from Italy and Spain, Venetian glassware (15C and 16C), blue and polychrome Delftware and glassware manufactured in the Netherlands (17C and 18C). The collections of local silverware (15C to 19C) and porcelain and ceramics (1776-90; 1885-1914) give a picture of the items made in The Hague. Other objects are on display in 17C and 18C period interiors.

Decorative arts from the turn of the 20C (including major examples of Dutch Art Nouveau) and modern design are well represented.

The 15 new rooms around the fashion gallery feature masterpieces of decorative art from the Islamic world and the Far East.

Modern art – The museum houses works by great masters of the 19C and 20C. The **French School** is well represented, with paintings by Courbet (*Bridge, House* and *Waterfall*), Sisley (*The Seine at Le-Point-du-Jour*), Monet (*The Louvre Quay, The Nets* and *Wisteria*), Signac (*Cassis, Cape Lombard*), and Van Gogh (*Garden at Arles* and *Poppy Field*). The museum also has three paintings by Picasso (*Woman With a Pot of Mustard, Harlequin, Sibyl*), and single works by Braque, Léger and Marquet.

Like Van Gogh and Van Dongen, Jongkind worked in France for much of his life. The work of this artist, regarded as a precursor of French Impressionism, is well represented.

The collection of German Expressionists includes works by Kirchner, Schmidt-Rottluff, Von Jawlensky and Kandinsky.

The museum offers an excellent overview of **Dutch painting** from the 19C to the present; the Romantics with W Nuyen, The Hague School (the Maris brothers, Jozef Israëls, Weissenbruch, Anton Mauve and Isaac Israëls), and Breitner, Verster and Toorop. However, the Gemeentemuseum is best-known for its large collection of paintings and drawings by **Piet Mondriaan**, including his last, uncompleted painting Victory Boogie-Woogie (1943-44). It also owns important works by other pioneers of abstract art, such as the **De Stijl** group *(see AMERSFOORT)*.

Among the post-war Dutch artists represented are Appel, Corneille, Constant, Schoonhoven, Van der Heyden and the sculptor Carel Visser. There is also work by foreign artists such as Vasarely, Arp, Ernst, Henry Moore and Francis Bacon.

Music – In addition to an extensive collection of musical instruments from all over the world, there is an exceptional display of European instruments from the 16C to the electronic age. Exhibitions are held in the music print section.

Fashion gallery – This new gallery has temporary exhibitions on historic and contemporary clothing and the work of specific designers.

Print collection – This has an impressive selection of works by 19C French artists including Daumier, Bresdin, Redon and Toulouse-Lautrec. Works by modern Dutch artists include watercolours and drawings by the Hague School, prints by Werkman and a significant proportion of the work of **MC Escher**. Temporary exhibitions are held.

Museon ⊙ – This modern museum presents collections referring to the history of the Earth, dealing with subjects such as geology, biology, ethnology and technology.

Omniversum ⊙ – The films and other presentations shown on this huge screen (840m²/9 042sq ft), which also serves as a

Evening dress (1997),
Yoshiki Hishinuma

planetarium, are aimed at familiarising the viewer with the world of science, astronomy and aeronautics. Two projection systems – Omnimax 70mm and the computerised planetary projector Digistar – around 40 loudspeakers and a great many projectors for special effects make for a breathtaking visual experience.

Nederlands Congresgebouw – The Netherlands Conference Centre was built to plans of the architect JJP Oud by his son between 1964 and 1968. The conference centre is a vast building with walls of sky-blue tiles and yellow bricks, overlooked by a triangular 17-storey tower. The entrance, on the north side, is indicated by a large composition by Karel Appel in red and blue mosaic.

Among the many meeting rooms, the large conference centre (seating capacity 2 000) is three storeys high. It can be used for entertainment: concerts, theatre, ballets. In the basement the festival hall, which can hold 4 000 people, is used for banquets and exhibitions.

Follow Prof BM Teldersweg, which crosses the Scheveningse Bosjes.

★★ **Madurodam** ⓥ – This miniature town is named after George Maduro, a reserve lieutenant in the Hussars during the Second World War, who was betrayed and who died in Dachau in 1945. Madurodam was built in 1952, and was originally intended for children, but adults will also enjoy the superb 1:25-scale models. It is essentially a microcosm of the Netherlands, with buildings, monuments and typical scenes from all around the country, including bulb fields, windmills and farmhouses from the different provinces. The miniature town was completely renovated during the 1990s. In addition to the old favourites such as the Sint-Janskathedraal in 's Hertogenbosch, the Domtoren in Utrecht, Anne Frank's house in Amsterdam, the Muiderslot, and the Waterpoort in Sneek, new buildings have been added, including the ING Bank in southeast Amsterdam, the De Maas office building and the Erasmus Bridge in Rotterdam, the environment ministry in The Hague and the new Groninger Museum.

Madurodam

Working trains, cars, buses and boats and night-time lighting add to the fascination of this living town.

The indoor Sand World uses five panoramas with 3.5m/10.5ft sand sculptures. These are made simply from sand and water, and tell the story of the Netherlands and its struggle against the sea.

ADDITIONAL SIGHTS

Haagse Bos – Crossed by Leidsestraatweg, these woods surround the royal palace, **Huis ten Bosch**, where the first Peace Conference was held in 1899. This edifice was built in the 17C by Pieter Post for Amalia van Solms, widow of Stadholder Frederick Henry. It is Queen Beatrix's official residence.

Westbroekpark – This park surrounded by lakes (rowing) is famous for its **rose garden** *(early July to late September)* where an international exhibition is held annually.

Sint-Annalands Clingendael – This extensive park, with its meadows shaded by majestic trees and strewn with lakes, was once private property; there is a Japanese garden.

Heilige Geesthofje – Built in 1616, this almshouse is a charming enclosure with small low houses with crow-stepped dormer windows. Opposite, near the house (no 74) where Spinoza ended his days, stands the statue of the illustrious philosopher.

Museum van Het Boek/Museum Meermanno-Westreenianum ⊘ – On Prinsessegracht, lined with 18C mansions, this museum houses the Baron van Westreenen's collections. The ground floor is usually devoted to exhibitions about books. On the first floor, in the library, there are **manuscripts and incunabula** from the medieval period; the oldest dated books printed in the Low Countries were published in 1473 in Aalst (Belgium) and in Utrecht. The museum also contains Greek, Roman and Egyptian antiquities.

⌂⌂⌂ SCHEVENINGEN

Belonging to The Hague administrative district, Scheveningen is an elegant seaside resort with a very large and busy beach. It has often been devastated by storms: the storm of 1570 submerged part of the village. The church, which, in the past, was located in the town centre, is now near the beach. Today Scheveningen is protected by many breakwaters and a high dike.

The **Circustheater**, dating from 1904, is the only theatre in the Netherlands capable of staging very large-scale productions such as operas and musicals. It was refurbished in 1993.

The beach – *Illustration, see Admission times and charges* – This long and wide stretch of fine sand is lined for 3km/2mi by a boulevard, Strandweg, which is the continuation to the east of a pedestrian path. In summer this is where holiday-makers can be seen but it is also popular in winter with the townspeople who come to enjoy the invigorating sea breezes or linger with a coffee on one of the café terraces. Some substantial transformations have recently occurred on this seafront. Overlooking the beach, the imposing restored **Kurhaus** (1885; *see Travellers' addresses*) is now home to a casino; special events are also held here.

Kurhaus, Scheveningen

The **Pier**, a long promenade jetty, leads to four constructions built on piles offering entertainment. An observation tower 45m/148ft high offers a panorama of Scheveningen, The Hague, the dunes towards Wassenaar and out to sea.

The port – Beyond the lighthouse, towards the west, the fishing port remains very busy. Two inner docks have coasting vessels, pleasure boats and a fleet of trawlers. The **obelisk** commemorates the place where William I landed from England to take possession of his throne in November 1813. First situated to the east of the port near the dunes, around Dr de Visserplein as it is shown on the Panorama Mesdag, the fishing village has grown with new quarters to the south and west of the port: they are large quadrilateral brick buildings arranged round a courtyard with wide porches.

Older women remain faithful to the traditional costume: black dress and apron with a black cape in winter (on Sundays it is a pastel colour) or a light-coloured shawl in summer. The headdress, placed on a metal headband fixed with two hairpins is distinctive: the end of the headband in the shape of an oval buckle of filigree gold stands up on the top of the head. On Sundays the bonnet is of lace.

★★ **Museum Beelden aan Zee** ⊘ – This seaside sculpture museum is located in a pavilion on the boulevard, built by King William I in 1826 to provide rest and sea air for his ailing wife, Queen Wilhelmina. The museum around the pavilion was designed by the Dutch architect Wim Quist and opened in 1994. It comprises 10 indoor and outdoor exhibition areas: three rooms, three patios, three terraces and a passage lined with niches. On display is the exceptionally varied collection of Mr and Mrs Scholten-Miltenburg. It consists of works from the second half of the 20C by artists from all over the world, such as Karel Appel, Fritz Koenig, Francisca Zijlstra, Shinkichi Tajiri, Waldermar Otto, Man Ray and Igor Mitoraj. The theme of the collection is the **universality of the human figure**, with all its different experiences, feelings and moods. There is a great variety of styles, and of materials too: traditional media such as bronze, stone, ceramics and wood, and more modern ones such as steel, tin plate, wire netting and plastic.
On the **south patio**, there is a magnificent bronze sculpture of the royal family by Arthur Spronken. There is a fine view of the North Sea from the **sea room**.

Sea Life Scheveningen ⊘ – This aquarium features life forms from the beach to the deepest depths of the sea, and includes sharks, rays, sea anemones, crabs, conger eels and jellyfish. There is also an underwater observatory, a tropical reef adventure and an underwater tunnel.

EXCURSIONS

Wassenaar – *12km/7mi to the north; leave The Hague via Benoordenhoutseweg*. Wassenaar is one of the most attractive residential suburbs of the Randstad conurbation, and large numbers of people commute from here to The Hague. It has many substantial villas hidden among trees.
The **Duinrell theme park** ⊘ is hidden amid the woods and dunes, and includes a large recreation area, roller coasters, numerous water attractions and a large tropical swimming-pool complex, the **Tikibad** ⊘.

Voorburg and Zoetermeer – *16km/10mi to the east; leave The Hague via Brinckhorstlaan*.

Voorburg – Hofwijck Manor stands quite near Voorburg station, and today it houses the **Huygensmuseum** ⊘. This small manor surrounded by water was designed by **Constantijn Huygens** (1596-1687) and built by the architect Pieter Post in the years 1641 to 1643. Part of the symmetrical garden still exists today. Constantijn Huygens, who acted as first secretary to the stadtholders Frederick Henry, William II and William III, was also a poet and a composer. He decided to have Hofwijck built as a refuge from his busy life in The Hague; *hof wijk* means refuge from the court. His son **Christiaan Huygens** (1629-1695) invented the pendulum clock. This great astronomer and physicist enjoyed a worldwide reputation. In 1663 he was made a member of the Royal Society in London, then of the Académie Royale des Sciences in France. After a long stay in Paris, Christiaan returned to the Netherlands. He settled into Hofwijck, where he lived until his death. The collections in the museum retrace the history of the family: portraits, original editions of works by Constantijn Huygens and a replica made in Leiden of Christiaan Huygens' world-famous pendulum clock.

Zoetermeer – This new town was designed to take pressure off The Hague and it was estimated that in its final phase the population would reach 110 000 to 115 000. The new town developments are centred on an existing village with an 18C **church** sporting a Gothic tower and wooden spire (1642). The historic core is now prolonged by a new shopping centre and business complex. The lake, the *meer* in the name Zoetermeer, was created as a result of peat extraction. It was drained in 1614.

Naaldwijk – *16km/10mi to the south via Oude Haagweg*. Cross the market-garden region of **Westland**, cut by canals, spread with thousands of greenhouses, orchards and gardens between The Hague, Hoek van Holland and the coastal dunes; flowers are cultivated as well as vegetables (tomatoes, lettuce and cucumbers). In the heart of Westland, Naaldwijk (sometimes called the Glass Town) is a large horticultural centre and has a major **auction** ⊘ of cut flowers and potted plants *(Dijkweg 66, Honselersdijk)*.
On Wilhelminaplein, the old 17C **town hall** has a Baroque voluted gable. Not far away, behind the Gothic church, the Holy Ghost Almshouse, **Heilige Geest Hofje**, groups picturesque, 17C low houses with tall dormer windows arranged round a chapel of the same period.

Noord-Holland ℗

Population 148 908
Michelin maps 908 E 4 and 211 M 8
Local map see KEUKENHOF
Plan of the conurbation in the current Michelin Red Guide Benelux

Historical capital of the Holland earldom and county town of Noord-Holland province, Haarlem, situated on the Spaarne, was the birthplace of Frans Hals. It is the centre of a large bulb-growing region. In spring, the Bloemencorso or flower parade starts in Noordwijk and ends in Haarlem (see Practical information).

HISTORICAL NOTES

Haarlem was founded in about the 10C on the edge of the offshore bar, near the inland seas, which have now disappeared, between Haarlem and Wijk (present Wijk aan Zee).
Haarlem was the residence of the counts of Holland and it was fortified in the 12C. It obtained its city charter in 1245. In the 13C some of the townspeople took part in the Fifth Crusade and the capture of Damietta in Egypt in 1219. The bells of the Grote Kerk are still called damiaatjes in memory of this great deed. In the 14C Haarlem expanded but all that remains of its fortifications is the late-15C gateway, Amsterdamse Poort, to the east.

A bloody siege – During the uprising against the Spanish, Haarlem was besieged for seven months (1572-73) by the troops of Dom Frederico of Toledo, son of the Duke of Alba. During the winter, William the Silent managed to provide the town with supplies by the Beggars, who came on skates over Haarlemmermeer, but despite the heroic defence by the whole population, the town capitulated in June 1573; the inhabitants were massacred. It was only in 1577 that Haarlem sided with the States General.
The 17C marks the peak of Haarlem; the town took advantage of the fall of Flemish cities by developing the linen industry and made a fabric sold all over Europe under the name of holland (a plain weave linen).

Haarlemmermeer – Formed by peat exploitation, this great lake of about 18 000ha/44 460 acres was a threat to Amsterdam and Leyden due to storms. As early as 1641, the famous hydraulic engineer **Jan Adriaenszoon Leeghwater** had suggested draining it by using windmills and making polders. The work was not undertaken until two centuries later when steam powered **pumps** gradually replaced windmills. Three pumping stations were installed (one of which was invented by Cruquius) and the work was completed in 1852.
The present territory of Haarlemmermeer, which has become a district borough, is an average 4m/13ft below sea level, and Schiphol Airport, which is located there is 4.5m/15ft below. The silty marine deposits found under the peat bogs are very fertile.

The meeting place of artists – Haarlem is the town of **Claus Sluter** (c 1345-1406), a sculptor who, working for the dukes of Burgundy in the Charter house of Champmol near Dijon produced works of great realism. The following artists were born in Haarlem in the 15C: the painter **Dirck Bouts** who went to live in Louvain (Belgium), **Jan Mostaert** (c 1475-1555/6) a religious painter influenced by Italian art, while Geertgen tot Sint Jans came to live here.
In the 16C **Maarten van Heemskerck** (1498-1574) was the pupil of **Jan van Scorel** during his stay in Haarlem, from 1527 to 1529. **Cornelis van Haarlem**, Mannerist painter (1562-1638) and **Willem Claesz Heda** (1594-1680), famous for his still-life paintings, were born in this town. The engraver **Hendrick Goltzius** (1558-1617), **Pieter Claesz** (1597-1661), another specialist of still-life paintings, and **Pieter Saenredam** (1597-1665), painter of luminous church interiors, all ended their days here. **Hercules Seghers** (1589/90-1638), a remarkable landscape painter, also lived here.
Born in Haarlem, **Lieven de Key** (c 1560-1627) was a great Renaissance architect.
Bartholomeus van der Helst (1613-70), **Philips Wouwerman** (1619-68) painter of horses, imitated by his brother Pieter, **Nicolaes Berchem** (1620-83) who, contrary to his father Pieter Claesz painted landscapes, were also born in Haarlem. **Salomon van Ruysdael**, born in Naarden (c 1600-70) settled in Haarlem. This serene painter, whose art is very near that of Van Goyen had a preference for wooded shores reflected in calm water, and monochromes.
His nephew and pupil **Jacob van Ruisdael** (1628/9-82) was born in Haarlem. He painted more tormented landscapes, already romantic with dark cliffs, waterfalls, trees menaced by storm and disquieting chiaroscuros. **Meindert Hobbema** (1638-1708) was his pupil.

Frans Hals

This painter was born in Antwerp c 1582, but his family went to live in Haarlem around 1595. Frans Hals became the portrait painter of the town's bourgeois at a time when the portrait and particularly group portraits (guilds, brotherhoods) were in fashion. Of the 240 works ascribed to Hals, no fewer than 195 are portraits.

Hals abandoned the tradition of rigid poses and stilted compositions and he introduced, especially to his commissioned works, a certain vitality and more natural attitudes for his subjects. In some cases he went so far as to catch them unawares. His bold and fluent brushwork was considered sloppy at the time. He enlivened his canvases with bright splashes of colour on scarves and flags. His rapid but expressive brush strokes, which foreshadowed modern art and especially Impressionism, gave his models a life, a mobility which made his portraits real snapshots.

For a long time a frank cheerfulness radiated from his paintings, but after 1640 there was no longer the verve and fantasy in his works. In the famous group of regents and regentesses the return to black and white, verticality, expressionless faces, even disenchantment, left a sinister impression, almost a forewarning of his death two years later (1666) at the age of 84. Frans Hals's pupils included **Judith Leyster** (1609-60), the Fleming **Adriaen Brouwer** and **Adriaen van Ostade** (1610-85), painter of village scenes. The latter's pupils were his brother Isaack as well as Jan Steen.

Banquet of the Officers of the Haarlem Militia Company of St Hadrian by Frans Hals

AROUND GROTE MARKT *1hr 30min*

★ **Grote Markt** – This great square is bordered by the Grote Kerk, the Stadhuis and the former meat market.

In the square there is a statue of **Laurens Coster** (1405-84) (his real name was Laurens Janszoon) considered in the Netherlands to be the inventor of printing in c 1430, that is to say about 10 years before Gutenberg.

★ **Grote Kerk or Sint-Bavokerk** ⊘ – *Entrance: Oude Groenmarkt 23*. This large 15C church, which should not be confused with the Catholic St Bavo's *(Leidsevaart)*, has an elegant wooden lantern tower covered with lead sheeting, 80m/262ft high over the **transept crossing**★.

Inside, admire the short nave and, in the long chancel *(illustration: see Introduction: ABC of architecture)*, a lovely cedar-wood vault. The gravestones on the floor include that of **Pieter Saenredam**, and **Frans Hals** is also buried here. Note, also, a 17C pulpit with a Gothic sounding board, choir stalls (1512) carved with amusing subjects, the copper lectern in the shape of a pelican (late 15C) and above all the lovely early 16C **chancel screen**★, backed by finely worked brass.

The great **organ**★ ⊘ *(illustration: see Introduction, Art)* built by Christiaen Müller in 1738 has been decorated according to the drawings of Daniel Marot. For a long time it was considered one of the best instruments in the world and it is said that Handel and Mozart (as a child) came to play this instrument. An international organ festival is organised every two years in Haarlem *(see Calendar of events)*.

Vishal ◷ – The fish market was built in 1769, up against the northern façade o St-Bavokerk; like the meat market, it is an annexe of the Frans Hals museum (temporary exhibitions).

★ **Vleeshal** ◷ – The Meat Hall is an ornamental building in the Mannerist style, buil by Lieven de Key between 1602 and 1604. It has richly decorated dormer window and a façade decorated with the heads of oxen and sheep. The building is part o the Frans Halsmuseum, and is used for temporary exhibitions. The basemen houses the **Archeologisch Museum Haarlem**.

Verweyhal ◷ – This hall, also part of the Frans Halsmuseum, is named after th Haarlem-born Impressionist painter Kees Verwey; some of his work is on displa in the museum.

★ **Stadhuis** ◷ – The town hall, with its slim tower, is a 14C Gothic building to which numerous alterations have been made; the protruding section on the right has a gallery on the ground floor and a 15C and 17C voluted façade, while on the lef there is a Renaissance-style loggia above the flight of steps. The **Gravenzaal**, o Counts' Hall on the first floor has kept its original appearance; the paintings which hang here are copies of old murals from the Carmelite convent and depict th counts of Holland.

★★★ FRANS HALSMUSEUM ◷ 1hr 30min

Since 1913, this museum has occupied a **former almshouse for old men** dating from 1608; it is said to have been designed by the architect Lieven de Key. prior to being used as a museum the building was an orphanage (1810-1908).
The façade is characteristic of this type of institution with, on either side of th entrance, a row of low houses topped with a crow-stepped gable and window. Th principal façade looks over the main courtyard around which the rooms ar arranged.

Works by Frans Hals – The eight paintings of civic guards (room 21) and regent by Frans Hals constitute a remarkable collection making it possible to follow th evolution of the master's style. The first painting which marks the alread brilliant beginnings of the painter dates only from 1616 when Hals was abou 34 years old. It is the **Banquet of the Officers of the Haarlem Militia Company of St George** The mobility of the characters and their personality are shown in an extraordinar way. The atmosphere is less restrained in the *Banquet of the Officers of th Haarlem Militia Company of St George* and the *Officers of the Haarlem Militi Company of St Hadrian*, both painted in 1627 and rich in spontaneity and colour In the **Officers of the Haarlem Militia Company of St Hadrian** of 1662, Frans Hals display the height of his virtuosity.
The **Officers of the Haarlem Militia Company of St George** of 1639, with a self-portrait o the artist (figure no 19 in the top left-hand corner) is the last of this genre.
In 1641 a tendency for restraint and solemnity appears in Frans Hals' work and predominates in the *Regents of St Elizabeth's Hospital* (room 25).
The sombre colour of the garments underlines the expression on the faces and th very studied attitude of the hands.
In 1664, Hals was over 80 when he produced *Regents of the Old Men's Hom* (room 28); in this daring, somewhat cynical study of six characters, Hals had th cheek to portray one of them as being quite tipsy with his hat perched on the bac of his head. Painted the same year, the painting of the **Regentesses of the Old Men' Home** (room 28) with furrowed hands, bony faces, unindulgent looks, com municates a sentiment of anguish and discomfort.

Other collections – Apart from Frans Hals' works, the museum contains ric collections of paintings, furniture and objets d'art.
In the series of **old masters**, first there are the works of Jan van Scorel including the famous *Baptism of Christ*, those of Maerten van Heemskerck and Cornelis va Haarlem *(Baptism of Christ)*.
The main 17C masters notably those of the Haarlem School are represented b landscapes of Esaias van de Velde, Van Goyen, Van Ostade, Salomon van Ruisdae and Jacob van Ruysdael, a scene by Ter Boch, animals by Wouwerman and Cuyp still-life paintings by Pieter Claesz, Willem Heda, Floris van Schooten an Abraham van Beyeren.
There are also some fine portraits by Verspronck (1597-1662). Note the fin collection of 17C and 18C silverware; a book of tulip drawings by **Judith Leyster** pupil of Hals, the reconstitution of an apothecary with Delftware jars and, in a room with Dutch gilded leather, an 18C **doll's house**.
In a modern wing there are **modern and contemporary Dutch paintings**, notably by Isaa Israëls, Jan Sluyters (1881-1957) and members of the Cobra Group.
Opposite the museum, the lovely small houses with crow-stepped gables belonge to St Elizabeth's Almshouse. Hals did a portrait of the regents of this charitabl institution.

HAARLEM

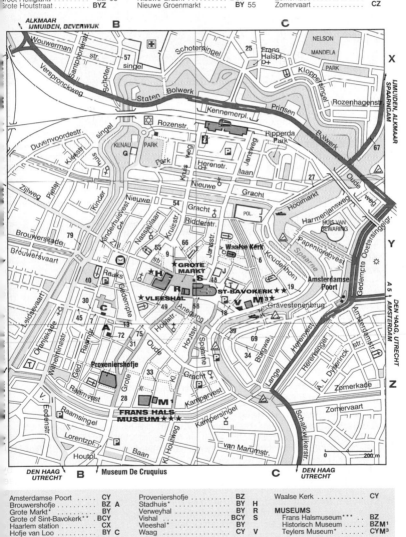

ADDITIONAL SIGHTS

★ Teylers Museum ⊙ – This is now the oldest public museum in the Netherlands, built after the Haarlem wool and silk manufacturer Pieter Teyler van der Hulst (1702-78) who wrote a will leaving all his money to the furtherance of the arts and sciences. Construction began in 1779.

187

The old rooms, and particularly the beautiful stucco-decorated **Ovale Zaal** (1784), have kept their attractively antiquated appearance. They contain displays of early fossil finds, mineral formations and scientific instruments, including the largest electrostatic generator ever built, dating from 1791.

The old Aquarellenzaal, or Watercolour Room, was converted in 1996 to house a changing selection from the superb **collection of drawings**★★. This consists of around 2 500 works by Dutch masters such as Goltzius, Rembrandt and Schelfhout, some 1 500 Italian works by artists including Michelangelo, Raphael, Pietro Testa and Annibale Carracci, many of which formerly belonged to Queen Christina of

Teylers Museum – the Ovale Zaal (1784)

Sweden, and drawings by Dürer, Watteau, Boucher and others.

The two painting rooms contain interesting examples from the Romantic Era, and works from the Hague School including *Summer Landscape* by Barend Cornelis Koekkoek, *The River Lek at Elshout* by J Weissenbruch, and *Evening at Sea* by Hendrik Willem Mesdag. The numismatic collection contains examples of Dutch medals from the 16C to the 20C, and coins from Gelderland and West Friesland. The new wing (1996) is used for temporary exhibitions.

At the corner of Damstraat stands the **Waag**, or weigh-house, built in 1598 in the Mannerist style and attributed to Lieven de Key.

Amsterdamse Poort – This late-15C gateway, preceded on the town side by two turrets was also a watergate commanding the Spaarne.

Historisch Museum ⊘ – This small museum tracing the town's history includes a model of Haarlem in 1822.

Hofjes (Almshouses) – Among the numerous charitable institutions, which the people of the wealthy town of Haarlem had from the 15C on, there is the **Proveniershof** of 1592 which opens by a large doorway on Grote Houtstraat, the **Brouwershofje** (1472) in Tuchthuisstraat and the **Hofje van Loo** of 1489, visible from Barrevoetestraat.

Haarlem Station – The Netherlands' first railway line, between Amsterdam and Haarlem, was built in 1839 *(see Introduction: Industrial heritage)*. The elegant Art Nouveau station, dating from 1908, is still in use.

Waalse Kerk – The Walloon Church is Haarlem's oldest place of worship, and was the chapel of the Béguinage until 1586.

Kathedrale Basiliek St.-Bavo ⊘ – *Via Leidsevaart*. The sacristy of this very large neo-Gothic basilica, built between 1895 and 1906 by JT Cuypers, son of PJH Cuypers *(see Introduction: Industrial heritage)*, contains the **treasury**: a large collection of liturgical objects, mainly gold and silverware (15C to 20C). Note the early 16C robes which come from an old Béguinage in the town.

OUTSKIRTS

Museum De Cruquius ⊘ – *7km/4mi to the southeast via the Dreef, northeast of a large bridge on the road to Vijfhuizen. Local map see KEUKENHOF. Illustration: see Introduction, Industrial heritage.*

This museum, on the edge of old Haarlemmermeer, is installed in one of the three pumping stations, which were used to drain it. The station bears the name of the hydraulic engineer Nicolaas de Kruik, alias **Nicolaas Cruquius** (1678-1754), instigator of a project (1750) to drain the lake.

The museum presents interesting material on the technical developments in the history of man's fight against the sea, and on the creation of polders: scale model illustrating the theory of a polder, animated scale model showing the part of the Netherlands which would be flooded by the sea in the absence of dikes and dams.

Visitors may also admire the station's original **steam engine**★, fitted with eight beam engines and eight pumps. Built in Cornwall, this unique machine was inaugurated in 1849: its importance was recognised by the American Society of Mechanical Engineers, who awarded it the prestigious title of International Historic Landmark in 1991.

Stoomgemaal Halfweg ⊘ – *8km/5mi east via A5 towards Amsterdam (Zwanenburg exit).* This is the world's oldest working steam-driven pumping station, built in 1852. It originally had a capacity of 25 000l of water a second. One of the two steam boilers has been dismantled to show the mechanism of the pumping station.

Spaarndam – *8km/5mi to the northeast via Spaarndamseweg, which becomes Vondelweg, then after a bend, take Vergierdeweg on the right.*
The houses of this picturesque village, where eels are smoked, huddle up along both sides of the dike. This is interspersed with several locks making it possible to link the Spaarne and the IJ.
On one of these locks there is a statue of **Hans Brinker**. According to legend the young boy plugged a hole he had discovered in a protection dike with his finger for a whole night and thus saved the town from being flooded. The origin of this anecdote is a children's book written in 1873 by the American novelist Mary Mapes Dodge, *Hans Brinker or the Silver Skates.* Beyond this small monument is the marina; a path makes it possible to walk alongside the water to reach the Oost and Westkolk docks to see some beautifully restored houses.

Zandvoort – *11km/7mi. Leave Haarlem via Leidsevaart. Town plan in the current Michelin Red Guide Benelux.*
This is one of the busiest seaside resorts in the Netherlands. A large avenue runs along the dunes which overlook the beach. Since 1976 Zandvoort has had a **casino**. The **Circus Zandvoort** *(Gasthuisplein 5)* is a fine example of modern architecture by Sjoerd Soeters, built in 1991 and including a cinema and a theatre.
The famous Zandvoort **racing circuit** lies to the north of the town. The Dutch Formula 1 Grand Prix was held here until 1985.

EXCURSIONS

★ **Bulb fields** – *See KEUKENHOF, Bulb fields.*

From Bloemendaal aan Zee to Beverwijk   *35km/22mi to the north via Verspronckweg.*

Bloemendaal aan Zee – This is Haarlem's family beach.

Bloemendaal – Behind the chain of dunes, this is an elegant residential centre where the villas stretch over wooded hills.
In the open-air theatre or Openluchttheater *(Hoge Duin en Daalseweg 2)* theatrical performances are given in summer. Nearby is the highest dune in the country, **Het Kopje** (50m/164ft). Further to the north are the ruins of **Kasteel Brederode**, destroyed by the Spanish in 1573.

Nationaal Park Zuid-Kennemerland – *Visitor centre at the southeast entrance to the park.* This national park, 1 250ha/3 088 acres in area, is situated on the long line of dunes edging the North Sea, and crisscrossed by footpaths and cycling tracks. Large numbers of migratory birds pass through here.

IJmuiden – IJmuiden, at the far end of the North Sea canal, is famous for its locks but it is also a seaside resort and ranks as the country's biggest fishing port and the seventh largest in Western Europe. It has a fleet of around 40 herring trawlers, and the catch is sold by auction in the busy fish market.
Three **locks**★ make it possible for seagoing ships of up to 80 000t to sail up to Amsterdam. The north lock, the most recent, begun in 1919, was inaugurated on 29 April 1930. It is 400m/1 312ft long, 40m/131ft wide and 15m/49ft deep.

Beverwijk – Together with Heemskerk, this community forms the residential area of the IJmond, one of the country's leading industrial zones. It has lovely dunes covered with forests which separate it from the seaside resort of **Wijk aan Zee**.

The chapter on Practical Information at the end of the guide lists :
local or national organisations providing additional information,
recreational sports,
thematic tours,
suggested reading,
events of interest to the tourist,
admission times and charges.

189

HARDERWIJK

Gelderland
Population 37 975
Michelin maps 908 H 4 and 210 S 8

Harderwijk was another of the Hanseatic League ports on the old Zuiderzee, and i
has retained a few picturesque lanes, the remains of its brick ramparts and its port
where one can eat excellent smoked eel.

On the edge of **Veluwemeer** *(see FLEVOLAND)*, Harderwijk, which has two pleasur
boat harbours and a beach, attracts many tourists. The hinterland, which is part o
the Veluwe with great stretches of dunes, forests and heathland, is very attractive
and includes several nature reserves.

The famous Swedish botanist **Carolus Linnaeus** (Carl von Linné, 1707-78) and pionee
of scientific classification is closely associated with Harderwijk as he attende
the university. Founded in 1647, this institution was abolished by Napoleon in
1811.

White ducks are bred in the vicinity.

Boat tours ⊘ of the Flevoland polders depart from Harderwijk.

SIGHTS

* **Dolfinarium** ⊘ – This very popular attraction stands next door to the
Veluwestrand leisure centre with its beach, not far from one of the marinas. I
is the largest marine mammal park in Europe and boasts numerous species
dolphins, sea lions, walruses, seals, black killer whales and tame rays in a
touch-tank.

Old Town – A number of well-restored Renaissance houses and 18C patrician
residences with ornamental Rococo doorways are the heritage of a more
prosperous era. Enter the old town through the charming 14C to 16C **Vispoor**
(near Strandboulevard) which leads to the old fish market. The Kleine Marktstraa
on the right leads into the main square, **Markt**, where the **stadhuis** (1837) i
recognisable by its portico crowned with a pinnacle.

Donkerstraat is a pedestrian street with numerous grand 18C mansions which riva
one another for the elaborateness of their Rococo doorways. Looking u
Academiestraat on the left one can see the 16C tower, **Linnaeustorentje**, whicl
marks the site of the university's botanical gardens.

At the far end of Donkerstraat an 18C mansion at no 4 is now home to the **Veluw**
Museum ⊘. On the ground floor a room is devoted to Veluwe's past. The old colleg
rostrum illustrates the importance of education in Harderwijk's past; the low sea
was occupied by examination candidates, while the upper seat was reserved fo
the rector. The history of the college is evoked on the first floor where, notabl
there are portraits of professors. Apart from Carolus Linnaeus, both Hermar
Boerhaave *(see LEIDEN)* and Constantijn Huygens received doctorates in Hard
erwijk. Coins from the Gelderland Mint, installed in Harderwijk from 1584 to
1806, Veluwe costumes and old Zuiderzee scale models of boats complete the
museum's collections.

Taking Smeepoortstraat, a shopping street on the right, pass in front of the **Grot**
Kerk ⊘, a tall 14C church.

At the far end of the street, Bruggestraat (lovely 18C portals) returns to Markt

EXCURSION

Elburg – *20km/12mi to the northeast.*
In the 14C Elburg was a busy mainland port looking out on the Zuiderzee and
even belonged to the Hanseatic League. Today this small town encircled by its
walls and protective canal retains its medieval character but now looks out across
the polders of Flevoland. The streets are laid out in a regular grid pattern and
often fronted by attractive houses as in the row alongside the Beekstraat Canal
The black and white cobblestones of the narrow pavements make attractive
patterns.

The only town gate to remain is the one that faced northwards onto the sea
the **Vischpoort** ⊘. This 14C tower is flanked by watch turrets. At the other end
of the street the **stadhuis** now occupies part of a former convent (Agnietenk
looster) dating from 1418. The collections of the **Gemeentemuseum** ⊘, or
Municipal Museum, are displayed in the Gothic chapel and other conventua
buildings.

The 14C **Sint-Nicolaaskerk** ⊘, now a Protestant church, has a massive square tower
In the neighbouring street, Van Kinsbergenstraat, there is a series of interesting
houses, one of which looks like a keep.

Boat trips ⊘ are organised on the lakes of Veluwemeer and Drontermeer.

HARLINGEN

Fryslân

Population 15 274

Michelin maps 908 H 2 and 210 R 3

Local map see WADDENEILANDEN

Harlingen, Harns in Frisian, which already existed in the 9C under the name of
Almenum, received its city charter in 1234. The dike, which protected it, having been
submerged, was consolidated by Caspar (or Gaspar) de Robles, governor of the
northern regions of the Low Countries in 1573.

The only seaport in Friesland – Harlingen was formerly a great whaling port, with
its boats sailing as far as Greenland until c 1850.

Today, this town at the mouth of Harinxma Canal is a centre of shrimp and prawn
fishing, and exports dairy products to Britain. It is also the departure point for boats
to the islands of Terschelling and Vlieland (see WADDENEILANDEN).

Harlingen now also has two pleasure boat harbours.

Industries have been set up to the north and the east of town; the larger tankers can
berth at one of the docks.

Harlingen has a school of fluvial navigation and a educational institute for shipbuilding.

Each year there are Fishing Days (**Visserijdagen** – see Calendar of events) and ring
tournaments (ringrijderij) as well as a naval review.

SIGHTS

The charm of its old streets makes Harlingen an attractive town. It is pleasant to
stroll along the main street, Voorstraat and along the quays of the two old ports,
the Noorderhaven and the Zuiderhaven. There are some interesting 16C to 18C
façades.

* **Noorderhaven** – This dock, which has become a marina, is lined with picturesque
houses and warehouses.

On the north quay, there are some lovely façade stones.

On the south side stands the 18C **stadhuis**, topped by a low relief depicting the
archangel St Michael; the rear of the building giving onto Voorstraat is flanked
by a tower with a carillon.

Gemeentemuseum Het Hannemahuis ⊙ – Voorstraat 56.

Installed in the Hannemahuis, an 18C residence, this museum is devoted to the
history of Harlingen and its maritime past.

The regional furniture, the seascapes by Nicolaas Baur, a painter born in Harlingen
(1767-1820), engravings, collections of Chinese porcelain, Frisian silverware and
scale models of ships, are all beautiful. A room, looking onto the garden, has a
lovely collection of earthenware tiles.

At the far end of the street, near the canal, there is the statue of a schoolboy,
Anton Wachter, hero of a series of novels by **Simon Vestdijk** (1898-1971), a famous
writer born in Harlingen; his works describe middle-class provincial life.

De Stenen Man (Stone Man) – At the top of a dike to the south of the port there
is a monument crowned with two bronze heads, erected in 1774 in memory of
the Governor Caspar de Robles (see above).

Michelin travel publications :
more than 220 maps, atlases and town plans ;
12 Red Guides to hotels and restaurants in European countries ;
more than 160 Green Guides in 8 languages to destinations around the world.

HAVELTE

Drenthe

Population 6 409

Michelin maps 908 J 3 and 210 W 6

This village in the Drenthe, with some handsome farmhouses covered in thatch, has
two hunebeds.

* **Hunebeds (D 53 and D 54)** – *Take the road to Frederiksoord to the north and
opposite a café, there is a road on the right signposted "hunebedden".*

These two prehistoric graves stand in a lovely clearing carpeted with heather.
One is still topped by seven enormous slabs in front of which, on the southeast,
is a very conspicuous entrance. The other, smaller one, has a slightly curved
shape.

HEERENVEEN

Fryslân
Population 39 491
Michelin maps 408 I 3 and 210 U 5

Heerenveen was founded in the 16C by Frisian lords, hence its name which means the Lords' Peat or Fen.

4km/2mi to the south, the flowered houses of **Oranjewoud** are hidden among the 100-year-old trees of a 17C Nassau Frisian property, crossed by small canals. Two manor houses, **Oranjewoud** and **Oranjestein** ⊙, adorn this magnificent landscape *(access by Prins Bernhardlaan)*.

The lovely municipal park, De Overtuin, and paths in the woods make it a pleasant place for walks.

HEERLEN

Limburg
Population 96 143
Michelin map 908 I 9 and 211 U 17

This town was the main centre of the Netherlands' coalfields which cross Limburg, continue into Belgium, in the Maaseik region, and the Aachen basin in Germany. Mining started in 1896 *(see Introduction: Industrial heritage)* and was abandoned in 1975. Nevertheless, a number of industries have been established in the region and Heerlen is becoming an important commercial centre.

The city possesses a modern quarter built round a vast pedestrian precinct, **Promenade**, and a theatre (Schouwburg), built in 1961.

The Romanesque Sint-Pancratiuskerk has for a tower the old castle keep built in 1389 by the Duke of Burgundy, Philip the Bold.

Coriovallum – Heerlen, ancient Coriovallum, was a Roman camp on the great route going from Boulogne-sur-Mer to Cologne via Maastricht. In 1C AD, another route crossed this Roman camp (Xanthus-Trier). Important Roman baths (2C-4C) were found in Heerlen.

> **Thermenmuseum** ⊙ – This museum houses the remains of the Roman baths which can be seen from an elevated walkway. It also contains objects found during excavations: coins, bronze statuettes and pottery. Models, reconstructions and a light show give an impression of the building as it once was.

EXCURSION

Kerkrade – *10km/6mi east of Heerlen.*
This border town has been a centre of mining activity since the Middle Ages. Since mining ceased Kerkrade has diversified its industrial sector.

Every four years *(see Calendar of events)* an International Music Competition **(Wereld Muziek Concours)** is held here; it draws groups of amateur musicians.

Industrion ⊙ – This new museum traces the development of industry and the way in which it has influenced society. In the past, Limburg was particularly important for its minerals: marl for making cement, clay as a raw material for the ceramic industry (particularly in Maastricht) and of course gravel and coal. Life was tough for workers in these industries, as the reconstruction of a street and a single-room home shows, and a miner describes his work underground. This interactive hands-on display gives a vivid picture of life in the past, and there is also a working metal factory.

★ **Abdij Rolduc** ⊙ – *Go towards Herzogenrath and turn left before the railway.*
This former abbey stands to the east of the town high on the valley slope overlooking the River Wurm, which marks the frontier. The abbey buildings have been transformed to serve as a cultural centre, a gymnasium, and a seminary.

The **abbey church** (abdijkerk) is surrounded by 17C and 18C buildings. Started in the early 12C, it has been restored several times, in particular in the 19C by Cuypers who replaced the Gothic chancel by a Romanesque one. On the west side, it has a façade with a massive porch tower flanked by two square towers.

Inside, level with the first and third bays of the nave, pseudo-transepts have been built in the side aisles. The **capitals**★ in the nave are very varied. Note also the bases of certain engaged columns in the side aisles. The heightened apse is trefoil in shape and built above a Romanesque crypt (remarkable capitals).

Den HELDER

Noord-Holland

Population 60 387

Michelin maps 908 F 3 and 210 N 5 – Local map see WADDENEILANDEN

en Helder owes its importance to its position on the Marsdiep Channel, which
eparates it from Texel Island.

riginally **Huisduinen**, a simple fishing village, expanded eastwards. In 1500 the new
own took the name of Den Helder.

 was the scene of a heroic exploit of Commander Lahure who, crossing the frozen
larsdiep at the head of 400 hussars belonging to Pichegru's army, captured the
utch fleet blocked in the ice, in January 1795. In 1811 Napoleon made Den Helder
 stronghold. He called it the Gibraltar of the North, and visited it in October of that
ear.

oday it is the **Netherlands' chief naval base**, and also the departure point for boats to
exel. Navy Days are held here in July of each year.

Marinemuseum ⊙ – This museum evokes the history of the Dutch Royal Navy
with a selection of scale models, instruments, photos, uniforms, emblems, maps,
paintings, engravings and videos. The collection includes a submarine, a Second
World War minesweeper and a 19C vessel, the *Schorpioen*.

Nationaal Roddingmuseum Dorus Rijkers ⊙ – The national maritime rescue
museum includes lifeboats, equipment, prints and models, as well as a ship's
bridge and numerous hands-on exhibits which are ideal for children.

Fort Kijkduin ⊙ – This is one of Den Helder's six forts. It has been extensively
restored, and now contains an exhibition, a marine aquarium and two restaurants.
The tour of the underground passageways and vaults brings the fort's history to
life, and the aquarium in the former bunkers has a particularly interesting glass
tunnel.

In clear weather, the fort has a fine **view** of the De Razende Bol sand flats, the
North Sea and the island of Texel.

EXCURSION

Callantsoog and Schagen – *27km/17mi to the south.*
The road runs along a dike behind which there are several beaches.

Callantsoog – To the south there is a nature reserve, **Het Zwanewater**. The reserve
stretches over 580ha/1 432 acres among coastal dunes and the moors round two
lakes which attract many birds. The best time to visit is around mid May during
nesting time. From afar one can see the breeding grounds, generally among the
reeds. Spoonbills *(illustration: see WADDENEILANDEN)* arrive from Egypt and
Spain at the end of February and leave again in July and August.

Schagen – On Thursdays in summer *(see Calendar of events)* a colourful **market**
(Westfriese markt) is held in this town where the costumes of West Friesland are
worn.

's-HERTOGENBOSCH

DEN BOSCH – Noord-Brabant ℗

Population 126 516

Michelin maps 908 H 6 and 211 Q 12

Plan of the conurbation in the current Michelin Red Guide Benelux

apital of the Noord-Brabant province, 's-Hertogenbosch is also the seat of a Catholic
ishopric. It differs from other towns in the country by its Mediterranean character
 hich can be seen in its noisy carnival *(see Calendar of events)*.

HISTORICAL NOTES

 he great forests of the area were the hunting ground of Duke Godefroy of Brabant,
 ence the name 's-Hertogen Bosch, the Duke's Wood. Today the town is usually called
 en Bosch, the Woods. But marshland has replaced the forests.

 he castle, built at the end of the 12C, was the centre around which the town grew.
 s-Hertogenbosch received its city charter in c 1185 from Henry I, Duke of Brabant.
 he town owes its prosperity to the wool and cloth trades.

 1 1561 Philip II of Spain, who reigned over the Low Countries, made 's-Hertogen-
 osch a bishopric, dependent on the Archbishop of Mechelen.

 aken by the Spanish in 1579, the town only surrendered to the Prince of Orange
 rederick-Henry, son of William the Silent, in 1629, after a long siege. Its 17C
 ortified wall is still clearly marked by a line of bastions and canals in the old moats.

 he modern town – 's Hertogenbosch, an important road and rail junction, is well
 ituated on the Zuid-Willemsvaart Canal near the Maas. Numerous commercial and
 ndustrial establishments have developed here.

A magician's art

's-Hertogenbosch was the birthplace of **Hieronymus Bosch** (c 1450-1516) whose real name was Jeroen van Aeken. The life of this painter is not well known, except that he lived a comfortable life in this town.

Solitary genius, Hieronymus Bosch did not belong to any school. At the most one can see Flemish influence in his landscapes with distant perspectives, and the naturalistic tone given in scenes he painted (precision of plants, study of animals) and in the somewhat archaic outline drawings of his characters. But with this visionary painter, reality is put to the use of a prodigious imagination.

The Prodigal Son, Hieronymus Bosch

Museum Boymans-van Beuningen

Objects and animals take strange shapes, men and beasts fill fantastic scenes of a dream-like universe, even nightmarish, where it is often difficult to distinguish hell from paradise.

Condemning evil, denouncing the ravages of sin was probably the intention of this mysterious artist who was as passionately interested in alchemy as ethics judging by the presence of numerous symbols in his works.

His early works were mostly simple and sober, then later the compositions became more complex and the subjects more and more strange, such as in the most extraordinary of his works, the *Garden of Earthly Delights*, where the painter would have had no cause to envy the Surrealists. This last painting is in the Prado Museum in Madrid, but one can see several fascinating works by Hieronymus Bosch in the Museum Boijmans-Van Beuningen in Rotterdam.

The weekly cattle market, which takes place on Wednesdays in the **Brabanthallen**, is a particularly important one.

The town has several recreation areas: the **Zuiderplas** (64ha/158 acres) where one can bathe, go sailing, row, fish etc; **Oosterplas** (65ha/160 acres) a large lake (bathing) and the **Prins Hendrik Park** where there is a deer park and another large lake, **De IJzeren Vrouw**. A new **Provincial House** (Provinciehuis) was built between 1968 and 71 to the southeast of the town.

★★ SINT-JANSKATHEDRAAL ⓧ 45min

St John's Cathedral is one of the most beautiful churches in the Netherlands. It was assigned to the Protestant faith from 1629 to 1810, after which Napoleon returned it to the Catholic faith. In 1929 it was given the status of basilica.

Built between 1380 and 1530 in the Brabant Gothic style, it has been much restored since the 19C.

It has a 13C belfry porch whose **carillon**, placed in 1925, has become famous.

The cathedral *(plan: see Introduction: ABC of architecture)* seen from **Parade**, the square to the south, has impressive proportions and a wealth of ornamentation. The fantastic world of grotesque personages astride the flying buttresses may have inspired Hieronymus Bosch. Other amusing figures decorate the side chapels' gable spandrels.

The apse is superb with its numerous radiating chapels round the ambulatory. A squat tower with five lantern turrets rises above the transept crossing.

Interior – The very luminous interior has a grandiose appearance with its five naves, 150 columns which, according to the characteristics of the Late Brabant Gothic, are a cluster of slender columns without capitals.

The last restoration, completed in 1985, has brought to light the vault frescoes which are very varied. The oldest, in the chancel, date from the first half of the 15C.

Note the canopy, slightly turned and finely worked, above a statue leaning against a pillar of the transept crossing.

The pulpit with its 16C Renaissance low reliefs, the 15C restored stalls and the 17C Renaissance-style organ case by Florens Hocque are worth seeing.

Sint-Janskathedraal, 's-Hertogenbosch

The copper baptismal font (1492), in the chapel on the left of the great organ, is a masterpiece by a Maastricht coppersmith. In 1629, when Frederick-Henry, Prince of Orange seized 's-Hertogenbosch, the canons left the town for Brussels, taking with them the altarpieces which Hieronymus Bosch had painted for the cathedral.

The rood screen, which from 1610 to 1866, was at the transept crossing was replaced in 1985 by a black stone podium decorated with biblical scenes; the original is now in the Victoria and Albert Museum in London.

Among the stained-glass windows, all made after 1850, note the window in the north arm of the transept made by Marius de Leeuw (1965).

St Anthony's Chapel in the south arm of the transept has a fine **15C altarpiece**[A] by the Antwerp School which came from a local village. The six small scenes of the lower part, in rather naive fashion depict the birth and childhood of Jesus, but the main theme of the altarpiece is the Passion of Christ, with the Calvary in the centre.

The figures carved in wood, notably the Virgin on the right panel (the Lamentation) are particularly remarkable for their expressions.

The Chapel of Our Lady, on the right of the great organ, has a miraculous 14C statue of the Virgin.

There are numerous memorial slabs on the cathedral floor.

ADDITIONAL SIGHTS

Markt – This very busy square is in the heart of the city, where one of the main shopping pedestrian precincts starts, **Hinthamerstraat**.
In front of the Stadhuis stands a statue (1929) of Hieronymus Bosch.

Stadhuis ⊘ – Dating from the 15C it was given a Classical façade in 1670. Part of its **carillon** was cast by the Hemony brothers. On the ground floor, the Trouwkamer has lovely Cordoba leather hangings. The 16C vaulted cellar has been transformed into a café-restaurant.

De Moriaan – This building, which houses the Tourist Information Centre (VVV), has, to the north of Markt, a brick façade with a 13C crow-stepped gable.

★ **Noordbrabants Museum** ⊘ – The North Brabant Museum is set up in the old governor's mansion, built by Pieter de Swart in the years 1768 to 1769. The ornamental features of the forepart and the pediment serve to counter the severity of the freestone façade.

's-HERTOGENBOSCH

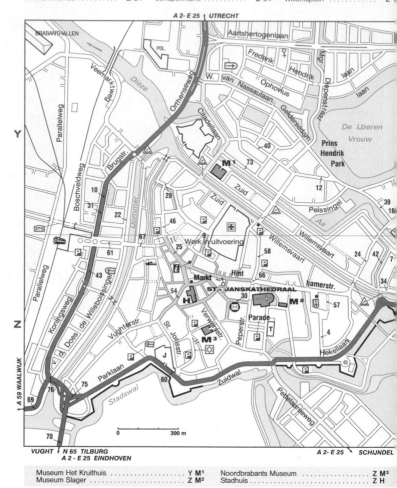

The museum retraces the history of the North Brabant province, focusing on several themes: the medieval town, the guilds, the Eighty Years War, the church, popular art and archeology. The highly interesting collection features objects excavated from various sites, including an **amber statue of Bacchus** (c AD 200) found in a woman's tomb in Esch. The painting collection presents the admirable *Study of a Brabant Peasant* by Van Gogh and *The Four Seasons* by David Teniers the Younger. One can also see sculptures, costumes and ornamental objets d'art (guild silverware, rustic jewellery from the 18C and 19C).

The temporary exhibitions held in the museum concern present-day topics and the Brabant.

Museum Slager ⊙ – This houses works by a family of painters, from Petrus Marinus Slager (1841-1912) to Tom Slager, born in 1918.

Museum Het Kruithuis ⊙ – This hexagonal brick edifice, dating from 1617 to 1621, is located in the northern part of town. It is built around a courtyard and was once circled by a moat. Until 1742 it was used as a powder magazine.

Today the restored rooms on the ground floor are the setting for exhibitions of design and contemporary art. The first floor presents collections of modern jewellery and ceramics, from 1950 up to the present day.

Boat trip on the Binnendieze ⊙ – A trip along this river, which in places flows under the houses and streets, is a pleasant introduction to the different facets of the city.

EXCURSIONS

Heeswijk-Dinther – *14km/8mi to the southeast via Maastrichtseweg.*
Northwest of this village stands the 14C **Kasteel Heeswijk** ⊘, set in the woods and surrounded by moats. It contains interesting furnishings and art objects.
At Heeswijk, a farmhouse museum, **Meierijsche Museumboerderij** ⊘ *(at Meerstraat 28)* retraces the life of Brabant peasants in 1900.

Drunen, Waalwijk and De Efteling – *25km/16mi to the west. Leave 's-Hertogenbosch by Vlijmenseweg.*

Drunen – To the south of the locality stretch the **Drunen dunes**, part of a large area of drifting sand.
The **Land van Ooit** ⊘ (Land of Yesteryear) amusement park has been designed with children in mind. It features giants, knights and maidens who speak their own language and have their own currency. Storytelling sessions, tournaments, a puppet theatre and a fountain garden make for an exciting visit.

Waalwijk – Main centre of the Netherlands' leather and shoe industry, Waalwijk has an interesting leather and shoe museum, the **Nederlands Leder- en Schoenenmuseum** ⊘, *Elzenweg 25.* An important collection of shoes from different countries (Japan, India, North America and Africa); reconstruction of a c 1030 shoe factory and a 1870 tannery. Other display cases show the evolution of the European shoe.

▲ **De Efteling** ⊘ – *South of Kaatsheuvel.* One of the main attractions of this 72ha/178-acre theme park is the **Fairy Tale Wood** (Sprookjesbos). Here the seven dwarfs weep around Snow White's glass coffin, the animals sing and the giant mushrooms play a harpsichord tune. Further along, in front of an Oriental palace, a fakir flies through the air on his flying carpet. Droomvlucht (Dream Flight) takes visitors through the magic land of fairy tales. This theme park also features a large haunted castle, a pond with rowing boats, spine-chilling rides, several restaurants and a hotel. A small steam-driven train takes visitors round the park.

Zaltbommel – *15km/9mi to the north. Leave 's-Hertogenbosch via Orthenseweg.*
This old stronghold, beside the Waal, received its city charter in 1229; its walls have largely been preserved.
On Markt, the **stadhuis**, restored, dates from 1763. At no 18 Boschstraat, next to a chemist's shop, there is a Renaissance house with caryatids. This, the main street, leads to the 14C watergate, **Waterpoort.**
In Nonnenstraat, to the west of the main street, the **Huis van Maarten van Rossum** has been converted into a regional museum, the **Maarten van Rossummuseum** ⊘.
It has a picturesque façade (c 1535) with tympana decorated with medallions, corner turrets and crenellations. Inside, the display includes objects from Roman times, discovered during excavations.
At the far end of Nieuwstraat is the 14C **Grote- of Sint-Maartenskerk**, restored and abundantly decorated, where the imposing 15C belfry porch is 63m/207ft high. The dikes edging the Waal offer lovely views of the river.

Heusden – *19km/12mi to the northwest via Vlijmenseweg.*
On the banks of the Maas, which here becomes the Bergse Maas, Heusden is an old stronghold fortified in 1581. The town has been restored. Inside its ramparts, which have been transformed into an esplanade, it has some fine façades.
Worth seeing is no 4 Hoogstraat (main street), a 17C house with very elaborate scrolls.
The **stadhuis**, rebuilt in 1956, has an automatic **carillon** ⊘ and a jack-o'the-clock.
The **Vismarkt**, fish market, near the dock, is surrounded by 17C houses. A covered market (Visbank) of 1796 still stands.
Heusden has three **post mills.**

Rosmalen – *6km/4mi northeast by N 50.*
The **Autotron Rosmalen** ⊘ automobile theme park has a wide variety of attractions for young and old. The **collection of vehicles**★ is displayed in the outbuildings of a Brabant farm. Each period in the development of the motor car is well represented: replica of the petrol-powered car invented by Benz in Germany, several De Dion Boutons and Panhard-Levassors, a Ford Model T (1909), Mercedes (1933) belonging to the ex-Kaiser of Germany Wilhelm II, American-built limousines (1940s), a Tatra 600 (1947) and a 1958 Daf. The racing cars include the 1978 Jameson Concorde, which was the most powerful car in the world with a top speed of 350kph/217mph. In the lakeside pavilion admire the magnificent models of the Dutch manufacturer Spijker (1899-1925); the prestige and refinement of the Spijker C4 was such that it was nicknamed the continental Rolls-Royce.
In the theme park itself, children can obtain their own driving licences and drive a Ferrari or a 4x4 jeep; there are also various rides.

HILVERSUM

Population 82 607

Michelin maps 908 G 5 and 211 Q 9

Town plan in the current Michelin Red Guide Benelux

Hilversum in the picturesque moors and woods of the Gooi is, in a way, a larg
residential suburb of Amsterdam: it is an extensive residential area with villa
scattered among the trees.

Because Hilversum is relatively high, it has long been the country's main centre o
broadcasting.

WM Dudok (1884-1974), the Netherlands' main exponent of cubic Expressionis
architecture, worked for Hilversum council from 1915 onwards. His creation
included the town hall, the municipal sports ground, various residential areas an
some 20 schools.

* **Raadhuis** – *To the north of town via Hoge Naarderweg. Illustration: se
  Introduction, ABC of architecture.*
  Built between 1927 and 1931, the town hall is the work of **Dudok**. For the mos
  part it is a harmonious juxtaposition of cubic masses where the differen
  volumes fall nicely into place offering a play of horizontal and vertical line
  overlooked by a tall clock tower. On the south side the clock tower is reflecte
  in a lake. The bare walls are of a fairly discreet yellow tinted brick. Inside a
  is functional and rational.

  Goois Museum ⓥ – *Kerkbrink 6.* This museum in the former town ha
  uses archeological finds, objects and photographs to chronicle the histor
  of Hilversum and the Gooi region. It also has a collection of Loosdrech
  porcelain.

*★THE GOOI

Round tour of 62km/39mi – allow a day

Leave Hilversum via Soestdijkerstraatweg.

Soestdijk – To the north of town is the Royal Palace, **Koninklijk Paleis**, residenc
of the Queen Mother (Princess Juliana). This former hunting lodge was used in th
summer by the Dutch sovereigns.

Baarn – A pleasant, leafy residential area. The artist **MC Escher** spent a large pai
of his life at Kasteel Groeneveld.

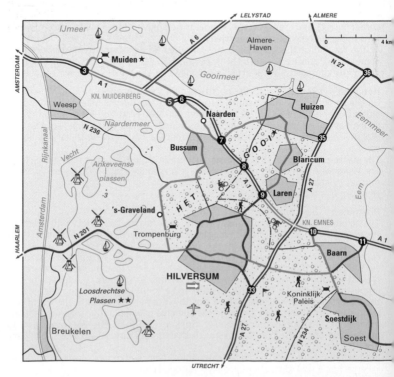

Near Laren one enters the **Gooi**. This densely wooded region of Noord-Holland is in fact an immense residential suburb with many substantial houses tucked away in lovely parks where Amsterdammers have chosen to live. There are still several tracts of heathland in the vicinity.

Laren – A residential town in a very pleasant site, Laren is a painter's haven. At the end of the 19C the **Laren School** gathered together several painters under the guidance of Neuhuys and Anton Mauve; several of the artists were also members of the Hague School.

In the town's centre, around the villa (1911) of the American painter William Henry Singer (1868-1943), a cultural centre **(Singer Museum)** ⊘ was built in 1956 by the painter's widow. It includes a theatre and a museum.

The interesting collections of the museum are shown by rotation: works by Singer with Impressionist tendencies; 19C and 20C French paintings (Corot, Boudin, Le Sidaner); the Laren (Hart Nibbrig), Amsterdam and Hague schools (Maris, Bosboom and Isaac Israëls). Sculpture is dispersed throughout the museum and garden.

Blaricum – Lovely residential town in the heart of the Gooi.

Hulzen – Since the closing of the Zuiderzee, this town has become industrialised and has a large marina.

Naarden – *See NAARDEN.*

The Muiderslot

P. van Riel/EXPLORER

Muiden – Near this small harbour used frequently by pleasure boats is a castle, the **Muiderslot**★ ⊘, standing on the banks of the IJmeer and at the mouth of the Vecht. It is an old brick fortress with stout corner towers, surrounded by a moat; its massive silhouette is visible from afar.

Built c 1204 to defend the mouth of the Vecht, it was rebuilt by Floris V, Count of Holland. He was assassinated here in 1296 by the nobles, who felt he granted too many privileges to the common people.

As of 1621 the castle became the meeting place for the **Muiderkring** (Muiden Circle), an intellectual and literary circle which gathered around the then owner of the premises, the historian and poet **PCHooft** (1581-1647). The distinguished participants included the jurist Hugo Grotius, the poets Joost van den Vondel and Constantijn Huygens and the writer Maria Tesselschae.

When Hooft died the castle fell into neglect but today the rooms have been refurbished and display their former 17C glory.

Bussum – An important residential town on the edge of the Gooi.

On leaving Bussum, turn right towards 's-Graveland.

's-Graveland – In the vicinity of this town, there are a number of fine manor-houses. **Trompenburg** *(not open to the public)* is probably the most elegant with its gracious silhouette reflected in the waters of the lake. Built by Admiral Cornelis Tromp, it consists of a rectangular house and a domed pavilion.

Return to Hilversum via ④ on the town plan.

HINDELOOPEN
Fryslân
Michelin maps 908 H 3 and 210 R 5 – Local map see SNEEK

This small town (Frisian name: Hynljippen), on the banks of the IJsselmeer, is one of the 11 towns of Friesland. It was once very prosperous due to its trade with Norway and was a member of the Hanseatic League.

The main road by-passes Hindeloopen which is a quiet and peaceful town with lanes winding between houses and gardens, its footbridges spanning small canals; the presence of many pleasure boats in summer tends to disturb the calm.

Hindeloopen – Dike and clock tower

Furniture and costumes – Since the 18C Hindeloopen has specialised in hand painted furniture, where red and dark green prevail. The colours as well as the motifs and shapes are inspired by Scandinavian styles seen by sailors during their long journeys. Hindeloopen was a close-knit community and each drawing was symbolic. The costumes also owed much to the Far East: made of cotton with large foliage in reds, greens or blues on a white background *(see Introduction: Traditions and folklore)*.

★ **Museum Hidde Nijland Stichting** ⊘ – Located near the church, this museum captivates by its reconstituted interiors, collections of fine traditional costumes, the series of tiles or earthenware pictures and its images of the great sailing ships of the past.

Het Eerste Friese Schaatsmuseum ⊘ – *Kleine Weide 1-3*. The First Frisian Skating Museum is a treasure trove for lovers of this sport; it includes skates, sledges, medals, photos, trophies and a detailed display on the famous Elfstedentocht, or Eleven Towns Race *(see LEEUWARDEN)*.

Nationaal Park De HOGE VELUWE★★★

Gelderland

Michelin maps 408 I 5 and 211 U10

The De Hoge Veluwe National Park, which covers 5 500ha/13 585 acres, is the Netherlands' largest nature reserve. It contains the famous Kröller-Müller Museum, the Sint-Hubertus hunting lodge, the Museonder underground museum, and countless sculptures and monuments. The park is a unique combination of nature and culture.

★ THE PARK ⓥ *Half a day*

History – This site was purchased in 1914 by an industrialist couple, Mr and Mrs Kröller-Müller, as a country residence. Mr Kröller wanted a place to hunt, and his wife wanted a culture park. The Sint-Hubertus hunting lodge was designed by HP Berlage, who had already designed office buildings for the couple, and was built between 1914 and 1920. Under Mrs Kröller-Müller's influence, sculptures and monuments were added to the northern part of the park. In 1938, the couple decided to give the site and their valuable art collection to the State, on condition that it built a museum, the Kröller-Müller Museum. These two great patrons of the arts lived in the park until they died, and were buried on the Franse Berg, the area of high dunes behind the museum.

Landscapes – A desolate landscape of heathlands, grass, sand dunes and lakes is interspersed with clusters of tall oak and beech trees, pine and birch woods. These are the many faces of the Hoge Veluwe, and it is worth a visit at any time of year. The rhododendrons flower in May and June, while in August there are great expanses of purple heather. In autumn, the deciduous trees are brilliantly coloured, and the park looks magical under a coating of snow.

A day in the Hoge Veluwe

● The park is served by **public transport** from Arnhem, Ede and Apeldoorn. Bus route no 12 runs through the park from late March to late October; the driver provides a commentary.

● The park has three **entrances**, at Otterlo, Hoenderloo and Schaarsbergen.

● There are large car parks at the three entrances, the Kröller-Müller Museum, the Sint-Hubertus hunting lodge and the visitor centre. The maximum speed in the park is 50kph/30mph. Only the surfaced roads (marked in white on the plan) may be used by cars.

● The **white bicycles** at the entrances to the park, the Kröller-Müller Museum and the visitor centre may be used free of charge and ridden anywhere on the paths. They should be returned to the place where they were issued at the end of the day.

● There are 42km/26mi of **signposted cycle paths**, including three routes (10km/6mi, 18km/11mi and 26km/16mi). Brochures detailing routes past most of the park's monuments and works of art are on sale in the visitor centre.

● Apart from certain areas reserved for game, visitors are free to walk anywhere in the park, and walking tours of various lengths are marked by **wooden poles** with coloured tops. Information and maps are available in the visitor centre.

● The park also has **five game observatories**. The most accessible of these are De Klep and the Vogelvijvers (bird lakes). The visitor centre has information on where and when to see specific animals.

● **Restaurants and toilets** are available at the visitor centre, the Kröller-Müller Museum and at the Schaarsbergen entrance. **Picnicking** is allowed anywhere, and there is a picnic area at the visitor centre. Cooking and fires are not allowed.

● **Dogs** and other animals are not allowed inside the buildings, and must be kept on a leash in the park.

● **Camping** in the park is permitted only on the camp site at the Hoenderloo entrance. There are also various sites outside the park.

● Tickets on sale at the entrances to the park provide entry to all sights except the Kröller-Müller Museum, entrance to which costs an extra 7fl.

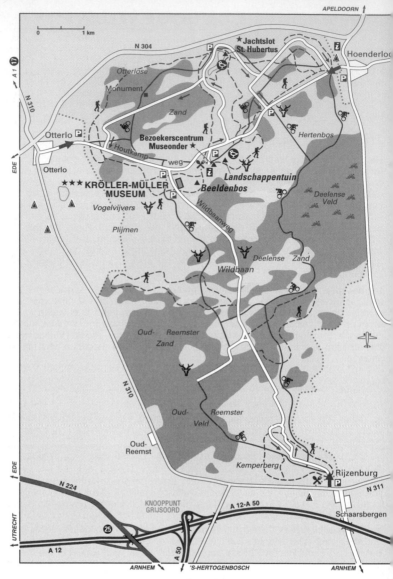

APELDOORN

N 304

★ Jachtslot St. Hubertus

Hoenderlo

Otterlose Monument

Zand

Hertenbos

Bezoekerscentrum Museonder ★

Otterlo

Houtkamp

weg

Landschappentuin

Deelense Veld

★★★ KRÖLLER-MÜLLER MUSEUM

Beeldenbos

Vogelvijvers

Plijmen

Wildbaanweg

Deelense Zand

Wildbaan

Oud-Reemster Zand

Oud-Reemster Veld

Oud-Reemst

Kemperberg

Rijzenburg

N 311

Schaarsbergen

N 224

KNOOPPUNT GRIJSOORD

A 12-A 50

UTRECHT

A 12

A 50

ARNHEM

'S-HERTOGENBOSCH

ARNHEM

EDE

A 1

N 310

EDE

N 310

NATIONAAL PARK DE HOGE VELUWE

🛈	Information
🐦	Birds
🦌	Game observation hide
🚲	Cycling track
🚶	Waymarked trail
▲	Campsite
✕	Restaurant
🅿	Car park
→	One way
	Quicksand
	Heathland
	Woodland

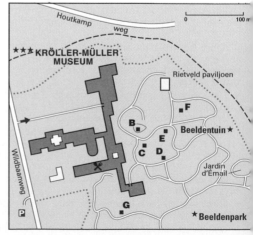

Houtkamp weg

0   100 m

★★★ KRÖLLER-MÜLLER MUSEUM

Rietveld paviljoen

F

B

Beeldentuin ★

E

C   D

Jardin d'Émail

G

★ Beeldenpark

Wildbaanweg

Fauna – The park has a rich wildlife ranging from red deer, moufflons, wild boar and roe deer to a wide variety of birdlife. Mid September to mid October, during the rutting season of the red deer, is a particularly interesting time to visit. The best time to observe the animals is in the late afternoon when they are searching for food, in winter and spring (ie till the end of May).

Visitor centre ⊘ – This snail-shaped building is linked to the Museonder, and offers detailed information about the park and its sights and recreation facilities. It also sells details of cycling and walking paths, and has an excellent display, including films, on the history, landscapes, flora and fauna of the park. The centre makes an ideal starting point for a visit to the park.

► KRÖLLER-MÜLLER MUSEUM ⊘ 3hr

The Kröller-Müller Museum was built to the designs of Henry van de Velde and is named after its founder, Mrs Kröller-Müller. The museum was inaugurated in 1938 and then in 1960 a Sculpture Garden was created. Some 17 years later W Quist was commissioned to build a new wing. The museum houses an important collection of paintings, sculptures and drawings, including works by Van Gogh.

To the right of the main entrance is the **sculpture room** (Deeldenzaal): The Rider and Horse by Marini (1952) is near works by Zadkine. Early 20C paintings are hung in the six rooms that follow.

There are a number of canvases by **Mondriaan** showing his diversity of style. The paintings by Van der Leck are followed by works of the **constructivists** (Strzeminski, Schlemmer) and **futurists** (Ballà, Severini and Boccioni). **Cubism** is represented by Picasso, Braque, Gris and Léger (Soldiers Playing Cards, 1917). One room is dedicated to the work of **Charley Toorop**. One of the most important works is The Beginning of the World, a bronze sculpture (1924) by Brancusi, regarded as marking the beginning of modern sculpture.

Further along, there are works by James Ensor and pointillist canvases by Seurat (Le Chahut), Van Rijsselberghe and Signac.

A selection of works by **Van Gogh** is arranged in chronological order from right to left around a patio. Looking at them in this order brings out the contrast between the sombre early works (The Potato Eaters, Weavers), and the later, more brightly coloured and dynamic paintings. The latter include The Olive Grove, Road with Cypress and Star, Evening Café, The Bridge at Arles, Old Man in Sorrow, The Good Samaritan (after Delacroix), and superb portraits such as Postman Roulin, L'Arlésienne (after a drawing by his friend Gauguin), and the Self-Portrait. There are also works of 1887 like the Faded Sunflowers, which was Mrs Kröller-Müller's first acquisition, and Still-life with Plaster Statue.

In the rooms behind the patio, along with **French Impressionists** (Cézanne, Renoir and Monet), there are landscapes by Jongkind, Millet and Corot. **Symbolism** is represented by the work of artists such as Jan Toorop and Johannes Thorn Prikker. Other 19C paintings include works by Israëls and Breitner.

Then come the Dutch painters of the Golden Age (Avercamp, Van Goyen and Van de Velde the Younger) and masters of the 16C such as Bruyn the Elder (Portrait of a Woman with a Carnation, with a vanitas on the reverse side), a Venus and Cupid (1525) by Hans Baldung Grien and a Venus and Cupid as a Honey Thief by Cranach. There are also works from 15C Italy and France.

Also on display are Greek ceramics, Chinese and Japanese porcelain, Mexican and African sculpture and 20C ceramics (Csàsky).

The **new wing** is used for displaying the collection of **contemporary sculpture** (Minimal Art, Zero Group and Arte Povera) in the form of temporary exhibitions. Giacometti's Striding Man (1960) is in the passage leading to one of the rooms.

► Sculpture garden and sculpture park ⊘ – Go through the museum to reach the sculpture garden.

This pleasant tree-shaded garden is the setting for some 20 sculptures by contemporary artists. On leaving the museum note the floating polyester sculpture by Marta Pan (1961) (B), Reclining Niobe by Permeke (1951) (C), The Great Penelope by Bourdelle (1912) (D) and The Air by Maillol (1939) (E). Further on is a **pavilion** designed by Rietveld in 1953.

The park contains many other works, including Dubuffet's **Jardin d'email** (1975), a white construction so large that it is possible to walk around inside it; Concetto Spaziale Nature, five spheres by Lucio Fontana (1965) (F); the Gigantic Trowel (1971) by Claes Oldenburg, Igloo by Mario Mertz and Construction of 56 Barrels by Christo. Finally, there is a very fine example of land art: Spin Out by Richard Serra (G), consisting of three steel discs in the hollow of a dune.

The **sculpture park**, on the steep slope of the Franse Berg, has another 10 sculptures.

K-Piece, by Mark di Suvero

Sculpture wood – *Enter via the road to the visitor centre.* This small site is dotted with contemporary sculptures: *Herbaceous Border* (1987) by F Morellet, the surprising *Otterlo Beech Tree* (1988) by Penone, André Volten quadruple composition *1:4 = 1 × 4* (1986) and *One* (1988), a bronze by Serra.

ADDITIONAL SIGHTS

★ **Museonder** ⊘ – The Museum Underneath is underground next to the visitor centre, and is a very original display of the world beneath the surface of the soil. It includes the underground lives of plants and animals, the role of ground water, the effects of climatic change on the soil and the history of the Veluwe landscape in a fascinating presentation using a wide variety of media.

Landschappentuin – This garden is actually a miniature version of the whole park, with a short walk showing its many different landscapes, and is ideal for anyone short of time. There is a hut made of turf at the beginning of the route.

★ **Jachtslot Sint-Hubertus** ⊘ – This hunting lodge is actually a large castle whose plan is the shape of a pair of antlers. It was built by Berlage between 1914 and 1920, and is regarded as one of his masterpieces. Both the building, with its 31m/102ft tower, and the two lakes and surrounding gardens are highly geometric. The interior and furnishings were also designed by Berlage. As in the rest of the building, every shape, colour and detail has symbolic significance, referring to the legend of St Hubert, the patron saint of hunters. This ingenious aspect of the building is described in detail on the tour *(free; booking at visitor centre compulsory)*. Mrs Kröller died here in 1939, and her husband two years later. Today, the hunting lodge is used as a residence for guests of the government.

EXCURSIONS

Otterlo – *1km or 0.5mi from the west entrance to De Hoge Veluwe National Park.* Otterloo is the home of the **Nederlands Tegelmuseum** ⊘, or Dutch Tile Museum. This has a large collection of over 10 000 Dutch wall and floor tiles dating from 1510 to the present day.

Tile production was introduced to the Northern Netherlands from Italy and Antwerp in the early 16C, and was initially influenced by Italian earthenware and Chinese porcelain. Around 1620, multicoloured patterns were replaced by the typical blue, followed in the 18C by Rotterdam purple. Dutch tiles were highly popular at this time, and were exported all over the world. Popular subjects included landscapes, children playing, artisans, flowers, animals, shepherds and Bible scenes. The latter were often found on fireplaces, where they were used as illustrations when telling stories. After a steep decline in tile production in the 19C, there was a revival around 1900 with the advent of Art Nouveau and Art Deco; the museum has some fine examples of these.

HOORN*

Noord-Holland

Population 62 313

Michelin maps 908 G 4 and 210 P 7

Plan of the conurbation in the current Michelin Red Guide Benelux

oorn is one of the most typical of the old Zuiderzee ports. With the creation of the reshwater lake, the IJsselmeer, it now enjoys the status of lakeside town and sailing entre. Despite the loss of its maritime activities Hoorn has remained a busy ommercial centre.

n old-fashioned **steam tram** ⊘ runs from Hoorn to Medemblik where the journey can e continued by boat to Enkhuizen. The original steam locomotives and carriages ake travellers back in time to the glorious days of steam.

HISTORICAL NOTES

town was founded c 1300 on the shores of the natural haven and it grew rapidly become the main settlement of Western Friesland. Overseas trade and fishing rought great prosperity to Hoorn.

was in Hoorn that the first large herring-net was made in 1416, marking the eginning of what was to become a flourishing industry.

the north of the town centre, gardens mark the course of the moats of the early 6C fortifications.

October 1573 the famous naval engagement, the Battle of the Zuiderzee, took lace just outside the harbour; the combined fleets of the towns of Hoorn, nkhuizen, Edam and Monnickendam – all towns already in the hands of the Sea eggars – defeated the Spanish under Admiral **Bossu**. However Hoorn's hour of glory ame in the 17C when it served as the administrative and commercial centre of all olland north of Amsterdam.

he town had one of the six chambers which comprised the federal organisation of e Dutch East India Company *(see Introduction: History)*.

1616 **Willem Schouten** (1580-1625) was the first to round the southernmost tip of outh America, 96 years after Magellan had discovered the Magellan Strait. chouten named the ultimate rocky headland of Tierra del Fuego Cape Horn, after is native town.

an **Pieterszoon Coen** (1587-1629), also a native of Hoorn, was the enterprising overnor General of the Dutch East Indies from 1617 to 1623 and again from 1627 his death in 1629. He founded Batavia, today Jakarta, and is generally considered be the founder of the Dutch commercial empire in the Dutch East Indies ndonesia).

ike the rest of the country Hoorn declined in the 18C and it was two centuries later efore it was to experience a recovery.

*OLD TOWN *3hr*

This was the original site of Hoorn and today a succession of old façades, many with lovely sculptured stones with a seafaring theme, can still be seen.

Achterstraat – The **Doelengebouw** (target building) at no 2 was formerly used for practice by the town's company of archers. The centre of the façade dates from 1615. The scene above the doorway shows the martyrdom of St Sebastian, the patron saint of archers.

Onder de Boompjes – On the corner of this canal and Pakhuisstraat an old storehouse of 1606 is decorated with a sculptured **facade stone** depicting two sailing ships of the United East India Company. To protect spices and other costly goods from enemy attack, these storehouses were usually located on the far side of town from the harbour.

Korte Achterstraat – At no 4 in this street is the old orphanage, **Weeshuis** (1620). A commemorative plaque recalls that Admiral Bossu was imprisoned in Hoorn after his naval defeat *(see above)*.
Not far away at no 4 Muntstraat, the house with the voluted gable adorned with the letters VOC (Verenigde Oostindische Compagnie) once belonged to the East India Company.

Nieuwstraat – In this shopping street stands the old **stadhuis** with its double crow-stepped gabled façade (1613).
The house at **no 17** presents a façade with Poseidon and his wife Amphitrite accompanied by dolphins; along with Poseidon's trident, these animals symbolised free trade and sea power.

West Friesland Museum

Kerkplein – At no 39 opposite a church (secularized), the **De Boterhal** or butter market, formerly St John's almshouse (St-Jans Gasthuis), is a fine 156 residence with a gable decorated with sculptures.

Kerkstraat – At no 1 there is an attractive 1660 façade.

★ **Rode Steen** – This picturesque square is overlooked by the Westfries Museum an by the Waag, or weigh-house. The name Rode Steen, red stone, refers to the bloc that was shed here during public executions. In the centre stands a 19C statue (Jan Pieterszoon Coen *(see above)*.

The house at no 2 has a façade stone depicting a blacksmith, hence its name: *Dyser Man* (The Iron Man).

Westfries Museum ⊘ – The West Friesland Museum is an elegant Baroque edifice dating from 1632. Its tall **façade**★ is imposing with its large windows, very colourful coats of arms (House of Orange and West Friesland) and cornices topped by lion supporters bearing the coats of arms of seven local towns: Alkmaar, Edam, Enkhuizen,

> When visiting Hoorn, don't forget to sample its wonderful smoked eel. Drop in on D Wormsbecher en Zoon's shop in Wildebrugsteeg and sample this delicacy at the counter or on the terrace.

Hoorn, Medemblik, Monnickendam and Purmerend. It was the seat of the State College: consisting of delegates from seven important towns, it governed We Friesland and the Noorderkwartier (Northern Quarter).

In the entrance note a lovely gate (1729).

In the basement there is an exhibition of finds from local excavation sites (Bronz Age tombs...).

On the ground floor there is a fine hall (Grote Voorzaal) decorated with a love chimney and guild paintings; the beams are supported by corbels sculptured wit coats of arms of the region's towns. On the first floor, the rooms decorated wit lovely furniture and objets d'art reproduce the refined interiors of the 17C an 18C including a great number of items brought back from the Far East by th Dutch East India Company.

The second floor is dedicated to Hoorn's maritime activities. There is a **portrait** **Admiral De Ruyter** by Ferdinand Bol (1667). Among the scale-models of ships, ther is a *flute* (a fly-boat) built in Hoorn in 1595.

HOORN

Stadhuis ⊠ POL. ⚓ S 9

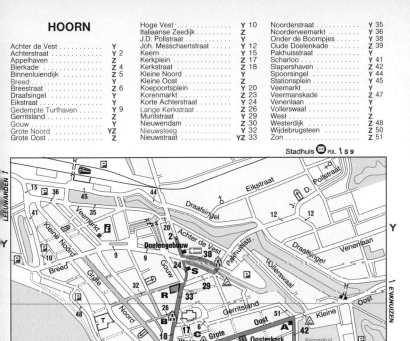

In the attic there are shop signs, scale-models of mills and ships, pottery. Temporary exhibitions are also held.

Waag – Probably the work of Hendrick de Keyser, the weigh-house is a fine 1609 building in blue stone, which today houses a restaurant. In a niche, a unicorn (the symbol of the town) holds a shield depicting a cornucopia.

Grote Oost – In this street the houses near the square are very steeply inclined and topped with imposing sculptured balustrades in the Rococo style.
No 43, the imposing **Foreestenhuis**, is named after Nanning van Foreest, one of the town's best-known governors. The elegant Louis XIV-style façade dates from 1724, and the balcony is supported by Atlas figures.

Oosterkerk – This recently restored church dates from the 15C and 16C; a façade, added in the early 17C, was topped with a charming wooden pinnacle. The church is now used mainly as a venue for cultural events.

Bossuhuizen – The frontage of these houses has a frieze in relief depicting the sea battle of 1573, in which Admiral Bossu was defeated. The left façade is very typical of old shops in Hoorn, with a ground floor topped by tall narrow windows separated by carved wood pilasters.

Oude Doelenkade – On the picturesque **Binnenhaven★** quay, or inside harbour, there is a row of old warehouses, note nos 21 and 17-19 with their façade stones depicting navigational scenes. In fine weather, the harbour is often busy with elegant sailing ships and crowds of onlookers.

★ **Veermanskade** – This quay is lined with a lovely series of restored houses. Most of the old merchants' residences have the typical façade of Hoorn, with carved wood pilasters. Some have lovely façade stones and are topped by crow-stepped or bell gables.
Note the birthplace of the navigator **Willem Bontekoe** (1587-1630); the façade displays a spotted cow (*koe*: cow – *bonte*: spotted).

207

Willem Ysbrantsz. Bontekoe – the hero of Hoorn

Willem Bontekoe (1587-1657) published his *Journael* in 1646. It was a great success, and was translated into a number of other languages. The book describes his adventures as the master of a United East India Company vessel from 1618 to 1625. The first part, describing his journey from Hoorn to Batavia (now Jakarta), became particularly famous. The voyage was a nightmare for the crew of 206; the mainmast broke not long after they set sail, there was an epidemic of scurvy on board, and the ship finally blew up not far from Batavia. Bontekoe describes how he and 54 other crew members survived this disaster and finally reached their destination.

The second part of Bontekoe's book is devoted to his years of sailing in Asian waters and fighting the Portuguese and Chinese, and the third section recounts his stay in Madagascar.

Bontekoe remains a source of inspiration even in the 20C: he was the subject of Johan Fabricius' 1924 bestseller, *De scheepsjongens van Bontekoe* (Bontekoe's Cabin Boys) though his role is not the heroic one portrayed in his own journal.

Hoofdtoren – Built in 1532 to keep watch over the port's main *(hoofd)* entrance in 1651 it was topped by a wooden pinnacle. On the other side of the tower sculpture depicts a unicorn, the symbol of the town. Since 1968 a trio of ship boys – bronze sculpture by Jan van Druten – contemplate the port from the foot of the tower. They are the heroes of a children's novel by Johan Fabricius dedicated to Bontekoe.

Bierkade – This is the quay where beer brought by ship from Hamburg and Bremen was unloaded. Nos 10 and 13 have interesting façades.
At no 4, two cheese warehouses from 1903 now house the **Museum van de Twintigs** **Eeuw** ⊘, or Museum of the Twentieth Century. This gives an overview of the rapi pace of technological change and the many discoveries made during the past 10 years.

Michelin Green Guides to European destinations :

Austria – Belgium and Luxembourg – Berlin – Brussels – Europe – France Germany – Great Britain – Greece – Ireland - Italy - London – Netherland – Portugal – Rome – Scandinavia and Finland – Scotland – Sicily – Spa – Switzerland – Tuscany – Venice – Vienna – Wales – The West Country England... and the collection of regional guides to France

HULST

Zeeland
Population 19 341
Michelin maps 908 B D 8 and 211 J 15

At the frontier with Belgium, Hulst is a small town with cheerful, colourful houses and streets paved with pink brick. It is an old fortified town which was located on an important defence line, and was built in accordance with the Old Dutch system *(se Introduction: Art)* with nine bastions and five ravelins, or triangular outworks.
In the past it was the capital of the Vier Ambachten, or Four Shires, comprising Hulst Axel, Assenede and Boechout (these last two cities became Belgian in 1830). Hulst 17C ramparts and numerous bastions, still encircled by moats, have been transformed into a grassy esplanade shaded by fine trees.

Reynart's city – The surroundings of Hulst are evoked in the Dutch tale written in the mid 13C and inspired by the medieval epic *Reynart the Fox*.
Near Gentsepoort is a monument (Reinaertmonument) in honour of Reynart.

SIGHTS

Grote Markt – The **stadhuis** with a perron flanked by a square tower, dates from the 16C.
The **St-Willibrordusbasiliek** is a fine Gothic edifice. Its tower (restored) has an excellent carillon. For more than a century (1807-1931), the church was used by both Catholics and Protestants: the chancel and ambulatory being reserved for the former, the nave for the latter.

Dubbele Poort – Near one of the town's gateways, important excavations have uncovered the remains of this early 16C gateway. A watergate as well, it stood over a navigable tunnel giving access to a military port.

From the top of the nearby ramparts, one can see the crow-stepped gable and octagonal turret of the **hostel** which belonged to Dunes Abbey, near Koksijde in Belgium. This hostel houses the **Streekmuseum De Vier Ambachten** Ⓥ, or Four Shires Local History Museum.

Stadsmolen – This windmill on the ramparts was built in 1792.

EXCURSION

Terneuzen – *24km/15mi to the northwest.* This port at the mouth of the Scheldt commands the entrance to Ghent Canal in Terneuzen.

Accommodating ships of up to 70 000t, it has three **locks**, the largest being 290m/951ft long and 40m/131ft wide.

In this complex of locks one can examine their workings closely.

HUNEBEDDEN★

Drenthe and Groningen

Michelin maps 908 K 2, 3, L 2, 3 and 210 Y 4, Z 4, 5, 6, AA 5, 6

A *hunebed* is a prehistoric funerary monument, with a side entrance usually orientated to the south. Megaliths of this type, which exist in the Netherlands, are grouped in the Drenthe where 53 have been registered and numbered. Only one is not included, that of Noordlaren which is in the province of Groningen.

Imposing dimensions – The smallest *hunebeds* are not less than 7m/23ft long whereas a length of 25m/82ft is not unusual. The biggest is near Borger: the slabs which form it weigh more than 20t. The megaliths used to build *hunebeds* are erratic boulders from the **Hondsrug** (Dog's back), an end moraine deposited by a Scandinavian glacier, which extended from Groningen to Emmen. At present *hunebeds* have lost their original aspect. In early days, in fact, the *hunebed* was hidden under a small burial mound, the earth being held up by a ring of upright stones; the space between these uprights was filled in with rubble. In Emmen and especially south of Schoonoord one can see reconstructed *hunebeds*.

A funerary monument – Hunebeds prove that prehistoric man lived in the Drenthe from 3 000 or 2 000 BC. They were used as collective burial chambers. Dishes, plates, tools and even jewellery were placed next to the bodies. Consequently excavations in the vicinity of the hunebeds have been very fruitful. The objects discovered, notably pottery, have made it possible to connect hunebeds with the civilization known as the Bell-Beaker folk.

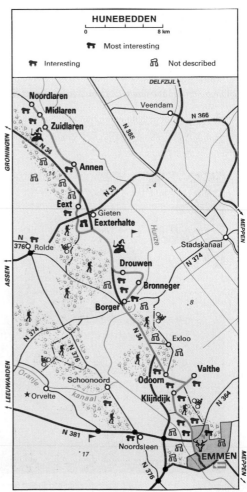

*HUNEBED TRAIL

From Emmen to Noordlaren

52km/32mi – allow 1 day

Emmen – *See EMMEN.*

Klijndijk – *Go towards Valthe on the right.* On leaving the village turn right ont
a sandy path, then left. Skirting the woods one reaches a long *hunebed* where tw
capstones remain.

Valthe – On leaving the village towards the northeast, on the right before a petro
station, a lane marked *hunebed (about 400m/0.25mi)* leads to *hunebed* D 37
surrounded by oaks. It is in fact two covered alleyways, one of which has bee
knocked down by three large oaks.
*Going towards Odoorn, on the left after a wood, there is a small lane marke
hunebed which leads to hunebed D 34.*
Set among heather, it is a small covered alleyway with two leaning slabs.

Odoorn – The town of Odoorn, at the heart of sheep-rearing country, organise
an important annual sheep market.
At **Exloo** *(4km/2.5mi north of Odoorn)* a sheep-shearing festival and a traditiona
handicraft festival are held each year *(for these two events see Calendar o
events).*
On leaving Odoorn, *hunebed* D 32 reached by a small path marked *hunebed*, i
hidden behind a curtain of trees. It is topped by four capstones.

Borger – *In the main street, take the road to Bronneger.* The **Nationa
Hunebedden Infocentrum** ⊙ is devoted to *hunebeds* and life during prehistori
times.
A little further on, surrounded by trees, is the Borger **hunebed★** (D 27), the bigges
of all. It is still topped by nine enormous capstones. Its entry on the south sid
is clearly visible.

Bronneger – *In this hamlet, a path marked hunebed leads to an oak wood.* Ther
are five small *hunebeds* (D 23/25 and D 21/22).

Drouwen – The *hunebeds* (D 19/20) are on a rather bare mound, near th
main road (they are visible from the road). One is surrounded by a circle o
stones.
*6km/4mi to the north of Drouwen, go left towards Assen, then turn right toward
Eext.*

Eexterhalte – Shortly after the fork, on the right there is a **hunebed★** (D 14) toppe
by six capstones. One can still see some of the stones encircling it.

Hunebed in Eexterhalte

Eext – In this village, in line with a bend, a path on the left leads to a *hunebed* (D 13), which has kept its original appearance; set in a cavity at the top of a mound, it consists of a square of uprights pressed closely together, and still has one of the capstones which served as the roof.
Two stones set further apart mark the entrance, located, exceptionally, on the east side.

Annen – Small *hunebed* (D 9) on the left of the road.

Zuidlaren – This small town is an important tourist centre.

Midlaren – The village has two *hunebeds. Turn left, between two houses, on to a dirt track called* Hunebedpad.
200m/656ft away, after having crossed a road, and behind two houses shaded by large trees there are two covered alleyways (D 3/D 4) each one made of several enormous slabs.

Noordlaren – *Before reaching the mill, take a lane on the left marked* hunebed *which leads to a grove.*
This *hunebed* (G 1), where there still remain two capstones resting on five uprights, is the only one in the Groningen province.

IJSSELMEER

Flevoland - Fryslân - Gelderland - Noord - Holland - Overijssel
Michelin maps 908 G 2, 3, 4, 5, H 2, 3, 4, 5 and 210

IJsselmeer is the name that has been given to the Zuiderzee since it was cut off from the sea by the construction of a barrier dam in 1932.

HISTORICAL AND GEOGRAPHICAL NOTES

The old Zuiderzee – The River IJssel formerly flowed into a series of small lakes. Enlarged progressively they developed into a large lake called **Lake Flevo** by the Romans and in the Middle Ages, known as **Almere** or Almari. In 1287 a tidal wave destroyed part of the north coast, enlarged the mouth of the Vlie, the lake's outlet and invaded the low-lying regions which surrounded it, turning it into a large gulf open to the North Sea.

It owes its name of Zuiderzee or South Sea to the Danes.

From the 13C to the 16C commercial ports developed such as Staveren, Kampen and Harderwijk, affiliated to the **Hanseatic League**, an association of towns in Northern Europe which had the monopoly of traffic in the Scandinavian countries. In the 17C and 18C, trade turned towards the Far East and brought prosperity to such towns as Amsterdam, Hoorn, Medemblik, Enkhuizen etc.

Creation of the IJsselmeer – The idea of closing the Zuiderzee by a dike goes back to 1667 when **Hendrick Stevin** published a work in which he proposed this means of fighting against the devastation created by the North Sea. In 1825 a violent storm ravaged the coasts of the Zuiderzee. In 1891 a project was presented by

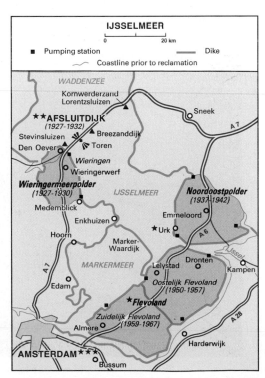

IJSSELMEER

the engineer **Dr C Lely** (1854-1929). It was only adopted by Parliament in 1918, following the terrible floods of 1916 and when Lely had become Minister of Public Works for the third time.

The aim envisaged was triple: by the construction of a dike to put an end to the floods which menaced the banks of the Zuiderzee, make a reserve of fresh water to stop the increasing salinity of the soil, and with the creation of polderland to gain 225 000ha/555 750 acres of fertile land.

The work on the IJsselmeer started in 1919; in 1924 the small Amsteldiep dike linking **Wieringen Island** to the mainland was completed.

Wieringermeer polder – From 1927 to 1930 this polder was reclaimed. It stretches over 20 000ha/49 400 acres in a former gulf of the Zuiderzee between Medemblik and Wieringen Island.

Immediately after the drainage, the polder presented a surface of muddy clay, so in order to continue the work it was necessary, even before the end of pumping (700 million m³/24 720 million cu ft of water) to drain the future collection ditches. In 1945, two weeks before their surrender, the Germans blew up the Wieringermeer polder dike and flooding ensued. The surging water created two gaps of more than 30m/98ft deep, engulfing a farm. These gaps could not be repaired and the dike had to be rerouted: it is the place called **De Gaper** (the Yawner). Again drained and returned to its former state, the polder is now a flourishing agricultural region.

Construction of the dike – The barrier dam, Afsluitdijk *(see below)*, was undertaken in 1927 between the Frisian coast and the former Wieringen Island by means of an artificial island (Breezand) built between the two points.

With clay dredged from the bottom of the Zuiderzee, a dike was built, against which sand was deposited; the sand doubled by a layer of clay was collected on the spot by pumping. As the work advanced the current grew stronger and the remaining channel was sealed off with great difficulty.

The barrier dam was completed on 28 May 1932. 30km/19mi long and 90m/295ft wide at sea level, it overlooks the sea by more than 7m/23ft and forms a new lake, the IJsselmeer.

Three large polders – Once the barrier dam was completed, the creation of the second IJsselmeer polder was undertaken, the **Noordoostpolder** and then the two **Flevoland★** polders.

The project concerning the development of the very last IJsselmeer polder **(Markerwaard)** has been abandoned. Only the northern part of the surrounding dike has been completed: a road, the N 302, now links Enkhuizen to Lelystad.

★★ AFSLUITDIJK (BARRIER DAM) *30km/20mi*

On the **Den Oever** side, at the dam's entrance, stands a **statue** of the engineer Lely on the left. On the seaward side the barrier dam has a breakwater which protects a bicycle path and a dual carriageway. Below the barrier dam on the IJsselmeer side, fishermen come to place their nets on the bottom of the lake, mainly to catch eels.

The barrier dam

The **Stevin Lock** which bears the name of the engineer Stevin (*see above*), forms the first group of locks for ships to pass through. They are also used to evacuate water.

At the point where the two sections of the barrier dam joined in 1932, there is now a **tower** with the inscription "A living nation builds for its future". From the top of this monument there is a **panorama** over Waddenzee and IJsselmeer. Near this edifice a footbridge spans the road.

Further on, a viaduct built in 1979 makes cross traffic possible between the two ports of **Breezanddijk** and gives drivers the possibility of turning back.

The **Kazemattenmuseum Kornwerderzand** ⊘, or Kornwerderzand Bunkers Museum, is by the Lorentzsluizen (*access via Kornwerderzand turnoff*). Seven of the 17 wartime bunkers have been restored to their original condition in May 1940 and opened to the public. You can now see the jute sacks on which the 225 soldiers slept, their mess tins in the kitchen, the working telephone switchboard, and cannons and machine guns ready for action. The museum also has displays on the period from 1932 to 1965, including the building of the Afsluitdijk, the German invasion in 1940, resistance and liberation, and the Cold War.

About 4km/2mi past Kornwerderzand, the Afsluitdijk reaches the east coast of the IJsselmeer and the province of Fryslân.

Place names in Fryslân

You may encounter both Dutch and Frisian placenames on maps and roadsigns. The following are the names of some of the places described in this book:

Dutch	Frisian	Dutch	Frisian
Grou	Grouw	Rinsumageest	Rinsumageast
Harlingen	Harns	Sloten	Sleat
Hinderloopen	Hylpen	Sneek	Snits
Hoorn	Hoarne	Twijzel	Twizel
Leeuwarden	Ljouwert	West-Terschelling	West-Skylge
Oudkerk	Aldtsjerk	Workum	Warkum

KAMPEN★

Overijssel
Population 32 398
Michelin maps 908 I 4 and 210 U 7
Town plan in the current Michelin Red Guide Benelux

Kampen extends along the IJssel's west bank, near the mouth of the river. In the Middle Ages it was a very prosperous port due to the herring trade. It was a Hanseatic League city with commercial ties extending over the whole Baltic area.

In the 16C there was a very rapid decline in the town brought about by the wars, which ruined the hinterland, and by the silting up of the IJssel. In the 19C a channel was made leading to the Zuiderzee but the closing of this sea reduced Kampen to the state of a river port. This barrier to its development resulted in many of the town's old buildings being preserved, and the town centre is surprisingly attractive, with nearly 500 historic monuments.

Hendrick Avercamp (1585-1634) – This artist called the Mute of Kampen (due to his disability) came to work in the town in the early 17C. From his Flemish master Gilles van Coninxloo, he learnt Bruegel's style. But by the delicacy of the tones used, the presence of innumerable people and the serene atmosphere, his winter scenes have a surprising originality.

His nephew **Barent Avercamp** (1612-79) was his pupil and faithful imitator.

Viewpoint – From the east bank of the IJssel, there is an overall view of the town, which is particularly beautiful at sunset. In the centre, the onion-shaped turret of the Oude Raadhuis and the Nieuwe Toren stand out, to the right the 14C Buitenkerk (1), to the left Sint-Nicolaas and the large towers of the Koornmarktspoort. This is arguably the most attractive riverbank in the Netherlands.

Boat trips ⊘ are organised to Ketelhaven.

Kampen harbour

SIGHTS

Oude Raadhuis ⊘ (2) – A little dwarfed by the new 18C town hall, the old town hall is a small edifice of 1543 crowned with galleries and flanked at the back by a slightly leaning octagonal tower with an openwork onion-shaped dome. Its pinnacle gable is surrounded by bartizans. On the façade the statues were replaced at the beginning of the century.
The **Magistrates' Hall**★ (Schepenzaal), with somber 16C oak wainscotting forming the seats, has an oak **bench** richly decorated with Renaissance style reliefs, next to a monumental **chimney-piece**★ by Colijn de Nole (1545). Dominated by the head and coat of arms of Charles V, the chimney-piece has a gracious statue of Charity in its centre.

Oude Vleeshuys – *Oudestraat 119.* The town's coat of arms is engraved on the stone façade (1596) of the old butcher's shop; it portrays two lions framing a fortified gateway.

Nieuwe Toren ⊘ – This tall square tower, erected in the 17C, has an octagonal bell-tower with a carillon cast by the famous Hemony brothers.

Gotische Huis – *On the right of the Nieuwe Toren.* This elegant residence with a very tall façade, crowned with pinnacles and pierced with numerous windows, contains the municipal museum, the **Stedelijk Museum** ⊘.
There is, notably, a collection of silverware of the boatmen's guild with a fine 1369 **goblet**★ of horn and silver and costumes of the region (Kampereiland) which included former Schokland Island.

Pass under the Nieuwe Toren and follow Nieuwe Markt to Burgwal, a quay running alongside Burgel Canal, which crosses the town; turn left.

Broederkerk (3) – This is the 15C former church of the Minorites (Franciscans).

Broederweg – On the right side of this street, there is a Gothic chapel, a former Walloon church which in 1823 became a **Mennonite church** (4).

Broederpoort (5) – It is a lovely gateway with a voluted gable (1465) flanked by graceful turrets.

After the gateway, turn left.

Plantsoen – This is the name of the pleasant park which follows the old ramparts: the moats form the Singelgracht.

Cellebroederspoort (6) – This elegant gateway, part of the 15C walls and flanked by steeply pitched roofed towers, was altered in the 17C in the Renaissance style.

Go through the gateway and follow Cellebroedersweg then Geerstraat. By Boven Nieuwstraat, on the right, one reaches Muntplein.

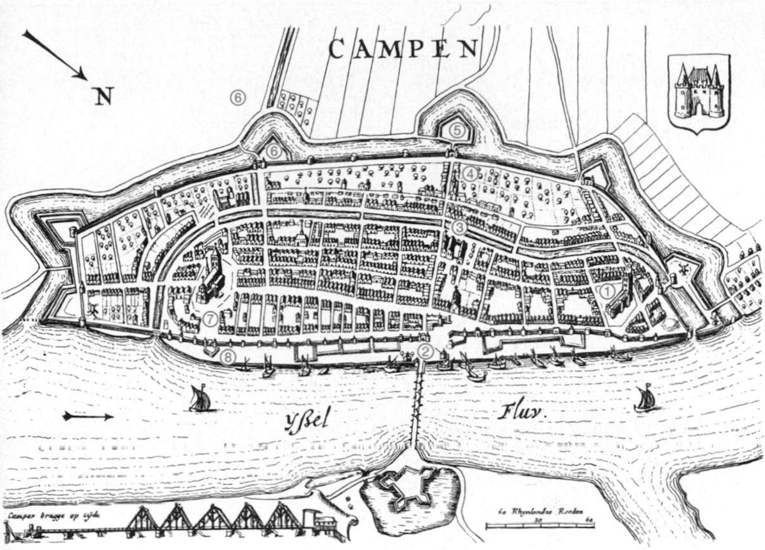

Sint-Nicolaaskerk or Bovenkerk ⊘ (7) – It is a vast Gothic edifice of the mid 14C, overlooked by a tower 70m/230ft high.
The interior is vast: nave and four aisles, a wide transept and a large ambulatory with radiating chapels. Note the 16C chancel screen and a Late Gothic stone pulpit.
The **organ** ⊘, dating from 1676, was altered in 1741 by Hinsz.

Koornmarktspoort (8) – It is the oldest gateway to the town. Dating from the 14C and situated on the old corn market, Koornmarkt, near St-Nicolaas, the gateway has kept its defensive character with a massive central keep flanked, since the 15C, by two squat towers.

KEUKENHOF★★ and BULB FIELDS★★★

Zuid-Holland and Noord-Holland

Michelin maps 908 E 5 and 211 L 9, M 9

Bulbs have been grown in the region around the Keukenhof for hundreds of years. In spring, the fields between Leiden and Haarlem resemble a vividly coloured chessboard (illustration: see Admission times and charges).

An original speculation – The tulip is said to have been brought from Turkey by Ogier Ghislain de Busbecq (1522-92), the Austrian ambassador, who gave bulbs to Charles de l'Ecluse (1526-1609), better known under the name of **Carolus Clusius**, a scientist, who at the time was in charge of the Emperor's garden of medicinal plants in Vienna. Professor at the University of Leiden in 1593, Clusius started to cultivate tulips on the sandy and humid soil which stretched along the North Sea between Leiden and Haarlem. This experiment was a great success.

The tulip vase

The tulip vase was a 17C Dutch invention. It was usually spherical or fan-shaped, and sometimes took the form of a pagoda. There were holes or tubes around the outside, each holding a single flower. Despite their name, the vases were not just used for tulips. Whole vases full of one type of flower were not fashionable in the 17C, particularly as tulips were so expensive; instead, people preferred to show off a selection of different flowers. The vases were often made as pairs, so that they could be placed at either end of a table or shelf in a similar way to candlesticks.

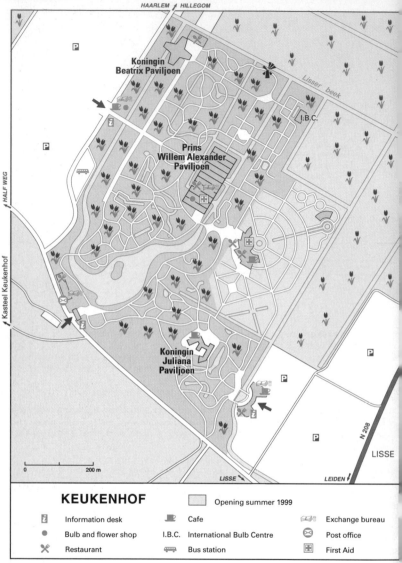

HAARLEM HILLEGOM

Koningin Beatrix Paviljoen

Lisser beek

I.B.C.

Prins Willem Alexander Paviljoen

HALF WEG

Kasteel Keukenhof

Koningin Juliana Paviljoen

N 208

LISSE

0   200 m

LISSE   LEIDEN

KEUKENHOF

☐ Opening summer 1999

🚹	Information desk	🍴	Cafe	💱	Exchange bureau
●	Bulb and flower shop	I.B.C.	International Bulb Centre	✉	Post office
✖	Restaurant	🚌	Bus station	⊞	First Aid

Meanwhile other flowers such as hyacinths and gladioli had been introduced but it was the tulip which attained the highest prices. Between 1634 and 1636 speculation was rife and "tulipmania" reached insane proportions. A rare tulip bulb was sold for 6 000fl. Buyers even went so far as to exchange one bulb for a coach and two horses, or acres of land or for a house. The Dutch States put an end to this speculation in 1636 and the flower industry was regulated. At the end of the 17C the tulip craze was taken over by that of the hyacinth.

★★THE KEUKENHOF

The **Keukenhof National Flower Exhibition** ⊘ has been held every spring since 1950. When a group of bulb growers was looking for an exhibition site, Keukenhof was chosen as the ideal location and has ever since served as the showcase for Dutch growers. Each year this extraordinary garden attracts nearly a million visitors.

The site was originally Jacoba van Beieren's *(see GOES)* kitchen garden *(keuken:* kitchen and *hof:* garden); the countess used the castle, which still stands nearby, as her hunting seat. The castle grounds are landscaped in the English style, contrasting with the geometric shapes of the surrounding bulb fields, and include fountains, water features, lakes with swans, themed gardens and works

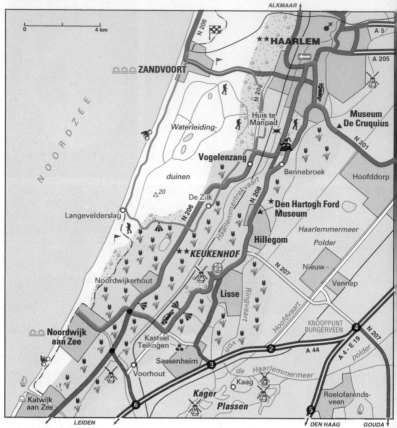

of art. The layout is changed each year, so there is always something new to see, and the brilliant colours of the tulips, hyacinths and narcissi form a striking contrast with the cool greens of the grass and trees. The less hardy plants are displayed in large greenhouses, and changing flower shows are held in the various pavilions. There is also a permanent orchid display. The Groningen windmill (1892, rebuilt 1957) on the north side of the park has a splendid view★ of the surrounding bulb fields.

★★★ BULB FIELDS

A few figures – Today bulbs cover an area of 16 500ha/41 230 acres in the country. The main production areas are in the south of Haarlem and to the north of the line formed between Alkmaar and Hoorn. Around a billion guilders' worth of bulbs are exported all over the world each year.

Bulb growing – The most widespread species in the Netherlands are the tulip, gladiolus, narcissus, lily and hyacinth but numerous other flowers are cultivated such as the iris, dahlia, crocus, anemone and freesia. Towards mid March the bulb fields take on their first colour with the blossoming of orange and violet **crocuses**, which are followed by white and yellow **narcissi** *(end March)*. Mid April the **hyacinths** flower as well as the early **tulips**. A few days later the most beautiful tulips open out. It is, therefore, at the end of April that the plain is usually at its most beautiful. Divided into multicoloured strips separated by small irrigation canals, it looks like an immense patchwork. It is the time of the Bloemencorso, the flower parade from Haarlem to Noordwijk *(see Calendar of events)*. The fields are then covered by irises, then **gladioli** *(August)*. Another floral float procession takes place in September *(see Calendar of events)* between Aalsmeer and Amsterdam.
Shortly after blossoming the stems are cut off by mechanical means, in order to strengthen the bulb. Once harvested, the large bulbs are sold. The bulbules are replanted in autumn.
Crossing the bulb fields by railway from Leiden to Haarlem offers lovely views; flying over them in an **aeroplane** ⊙ is even better.

EXCURSION THROUGH THE BULB FIELDS
Circular tour from Haarlem – allow a day

★ **Haarlem** – *See HAARLEM.*
Leave Haarlem to the south via Van Eedenstraat.
Going through the outskirts of Haarlem there is a succession of fine houses in spacious grounds before the first bulb fields appear. On the right is a 17C and 18C mansion, **Huis de Manpad**.
Take the first road on the right and once over the level crossing turn left.

Vogelenzang – The village is pleasantly set amid woods not far from the coastal dunes. Once again there are some prestigious villas in well-tended grounds.
To the south of De Zilk the pale tints of the sand dunes contrast with the brightly coloured carpet of flowers.
Beyond Noordwijkerhout the road starts climbing to the junction with the road to Sassenheim, which offers splendid **views**★ of the bulb fields.

⌂ **Noordwijk aan Zee** – *See LEIDEN, Excursions.*
Continue towards Lisse/Sassenheim. Just past the Voorhout sign on the right, turn left into Loosterweg.

★ **Keukenhof** – *See KEUKENHOF AND BULB FIELDS.*

Lisse – One of the main villages in the bulb-growing area. The **Museum de Zwarte Tulp** ⊘ (Black Tulip Museum), located in an old house in the centre, offers information about the bulb-growing industry and has a collection of preserved tulips.
Tours of the **Kagerplassen** lakes and the picturesque island village of **Kaagdorp** depart from Lisse.
Nearby, close to the important bulb-growing centre of **Sassenheim**, are the ruins of **Kasteel Teilingen**, where Jacoba or Jacqueline of Hainaut spent the last years of her life.

Hillegom – The **Den Hartogh Ford Museum**★ ⊘ *(Haarlemmerstraat 36)* has a display of 160 cars made by the Detroit manufacturer. They date from the period 1905 to 1948, and form the world's largest private collection of Fords. They include the popular Model T, of which over 15 million were made between 1908 and 1927, a Lincoln 160 from 1929, a Ford 181 phaeton from 1930 and a 1936 Ford 720 coupé. The last room contains lorries, buses, a crane and some fire engines, all made by Ford.
Continue towards Haarlem and follow the signs to Cruquius.

Museum De Cruquius – *See HAARLEM, Outskirts.*

Michelin Green Guides cover the world's great cities :

New York, London, Paris, Rome, Brussels, Barcelona, Berlin, Vienna, Washington DC, San Francisco, Chicago, Venice

LEEUWARDEN★

Fryslân P
Population 88 525
Michelin maps 908 I 2 and 210 T 3
Plan of the conurbation in the current Michelin Red Guide Benelux

Leeuwarden – Ljouwert in Frisian, is an attractive town of scenic canals and historic buildings. The former residence of the Frisian stadholders is now the dynamic capital and cultural centre of Fryslân.
The town is the centre of a thriving dairy farming industry and herds of the famous black and white cattle are a regular feature of the surrounding countryside. The famous Frisian cow has been immortalised by a larger than life bronze statue on the Harlingersingel-Harlingerstraatweg roundabout. The locals affectionately refer to it as **Us Mem**, Our Mother. The Friday cattle markets in the huge Frisian Expo Centre at the end of Tesselschadestraat, and the annual cattle inspection *(see Practical Information)*, reflect the importance of this industry. Fryslân is also well known for its beautiful black horses.
Famous figures who have lived in Leeuwarden include **Mata Hari**, **JJ Slauerhoff** and **MC Escher**. The writer **Simon Vestdijk** also spent his youth here.

HISTORICAL NOTES

Founded from the linking of three mounds located on the edge of the old **Middelzee** a sort of gulf, drained between the 14C and 18C, Leeuwarden gained some importance in the 12C when it was fortified.

Capital of Friesland – Friesland was a bone of contention between the counts of Holland and the dukes of Saxony whose feudal lord was the German emperor. In 1499 Emperor Maxilian gave the fief to **Duke Albert of Saxony** who elected to reside in Leeuwarden which had become the provincial capital. In 1516 Emperor Charles V gave the town a new set of fortifications.

After the independence of the United Provinces, Leeuwarden became the residence of the **stadtholders** of Friesland and Groningen in 1584. The first was **William Louis of Nassau** (1560-1620) son of John of Nassau (brother of William the Silent). In 1675 under Henry Casimir II (1657-96), the Frisian stadtholdership became hereditary. **John William Friso** (1648-1711) received the title of Prince of Orange as a legacy from the Holland stadtholder (and king of England) William III. Friso's son **William IV** (1711-51), stadtholder of Friesland, was chosen as the first hereditary stadtholder of the whole country in 1747.

The present dynasty in the Netherlands stems from him, the first king being his grandson William I.

In 1580 Leeuwarden received its new curtain wall and, in the beginning of the 17C, a few bastions to the north and west, which were razed in the 18C and today have been converted into the Prinsentuin, or Princes' Garden, are bordered by the Stadsgracht.

The Elfstedentocht

In winters when it is cold enough for the Frisian canals to freeze over, the whole country is gripped by Elfstedentocht fever. Once the ice reaches an average thickness of 15cm/6in, the green light is given for the preparations to begin. The organisers then have only 48hr to get the course ready and make arrangements for thousands of participants and tens of thousands of spectators from the Netherlands and abroad. At 5.30am on the third day, the starting signal is given and this 200km/125mi tour of 11 towns begins. It starts and finishes in Leeuwarden, and passes through Sneek, IJlst, Sloten, Stavoren, Hindeloopen, Workum, Bolsward, Harlingen, Franeker and Dokkum. All entrants completing the course within the regulation time receive a small silver cross. The current record, set in 1985, is 6hr 47min.

The last Elfstedentocht took place on 4 January 1997, for only the 15th time since the first official race on 2 January 1909, though the tradition is believed to date from the 18C.

A visit to Het Eerste Friese Schaatsmuseum (First Frisian Skating Museum) in Hindeloopen *(see HINDELOOPEN)* is a must for anyone interested in the history of the Elfstedentocht.

The 15th Elfstedentocht, 4 January 1997

Accommodation

Although Leeuwarden has only a few hotels, some of them are particularly characteristic.

BUDGET HOTELs

Wyswert – *Rengerslaan 8, 8917 DD Leeuwarden,* ☎ *(058) 215 77 15, Fax (058) 212 32 11. 28 rooms.* This hotel school to the north of the centre also offers inexpensive rooms. Service is provided by students under professional supervision.

OUR SELECTION

Van den Berg State – *Verlengde Schrans 87, 8932 NL Leeuwarden,* ☎ *(058) 280 05 84, Fax (058) 288 34 22. 6 rooms.* This small hotel and restaurant *(see below)* is located in a 19C country house in a quiet residential area south of the centre. The rooms are very spacious, with their own lobbies and luxurious bathrooms. The suite has a waterbed and jacuzzi.

Het Stadhouderlijk Hof – *Hofplein 29, 8911 HJ Leeuwarden,* ☎ *(058) 216 21 80, Fax (058) 216 38 90. 22 rooms.* This town-centre hotel is the former residence of the Frisian stadholders. The only room where there are still traces of this aristocratic past is the Nassau-zaal, where portraits of princes and counts from the Van Nassau-Dietz dynasty hang on the walls; it is now used for weddings. The rest of the hotel, including the large bedrooms, is decorated in a tasteful and very modern style.

Restaurants

Van den Berg State – *Verlengde Schrans 87,* ☎ *(058) 280 05 84.* This hotel and restaurant outside the centre of town *(see above)* offers excellent food, classic decor and a view of the garden; meals are served outdoors in clement weather.

Kota Radja – *Groot Schavernek 5,* ☎ *(058) 213 35 64.* Asian cuisine served in agreeable surroundings.

Brasseries, cafés, bars, coffee shops...

Het Haersma Huis – *Tweebaksmarkt 49.* This grand café lies a stone's throw from the Fries Museum and is an ideal venue for a snack before or after a visit to the museum. It has classic modern decor in a historic building, and there is also a terrace.

De Koperen Tuin – *Prinsentuin 1.* Watch the world go by from the terrace of this garden café as you enjoy lunch or just a drink or ice cream. There are free concerts on Sundays, and much of Simon Vestdijk's book *De Koperen Tuin* was set in the garden. However, the café is open only from early April to late September.

't Pannekoekschip – *Willemskade 69.* This delightful ship moored on Willemskade, between the station and the old town, offers a choice of 90 kinds of pancake.

Practical information

General information – The **VVV tourist office** at Stationsplein 1, ☎ (0900) 202 40 60, is the place to go if you need information about sights, tours, excursions or accommodation. It also offers special packages, and publishes an annual tourist guide to Leeuwarden.

Transport – There are two indoor **car parks**, De Klanderij and Zaailand, and a park and ride point next to the station. **Bicycles** are available for hire from the Zaailand car park.

Tours and walks – For information, contact the VVV.

Shopping – Leeuwarden is a pleasant place to shop, and has an extensive **pedestrian area**. Late-night opening is on Thursdays, and shops also open on the first Sunday of the month. The VVV sells a booklet on interesting places to shop in Leeuwarden.
Apart from all these modern shops, Nieuwesteeg, in the heart of town between Nieuwestad and Begijnestraat, has authentic old shops practising traditional crafts. These include a 19C corn chandler's, a barber's, a coppersmith's, a wine cellar and a coffee room; we defy you to leave empty-handed.

Night-life – There are two theatres, the modern glass **Stadsschouwburg De Harmonie**, Ruiterskwartier 4, ☎ (058) 233 02 33, and **Theater Romein**, Begijnestraat 59, ☎ (058) 215 82 15. There are also cinemas, and lots of lively bars in the town centre.

Events – There are numerous variations on the famous Elfstedentocht in summer, using such modes of transport as bicycles, cars (veteran and otherwise) and Shanks's pony. The annual **cattle stud inspections** at the Frisian Expo Centre are also well worth seeing.

In 1876 Margarethe Geertruida Zelle was born here. Having learnt to dance in the Dutch Indies (Indonesia), she went to Paris in 1903 and became famous as a dance under the name of **Mata Hari** (In Malayan: Eye of the Day). She was shot in 1917 for spying for the Germans.

Since 1909, Leeuwarden is the departure point of the famous **Eleven Towns Race** (Elfstedentocht).

SIGHTS

★★ **Fries Museum/Verzetsmuseum** ⊙ – The Frisian Museum and Resistance Museum is housed in two historic buildings on Turfmarkt: the 18C Eysingahuis and the monumental Kanselarij, or chancellery, linked by an underground tunnel. The museum has a very varied collection of items relating to Frisian culture.

Kanselarij – This former courthouse in the Renaissance style (1566), on Turfmarkt, has a wide, heavily decorated façade with a flight of steps, and a statue of Charles V at the top of the façade.

On the second floor there is a collection of the **top items** from each collection, including archeological finds, Frisian silver, Indian chintz, a chest from Hindeloopen and portraits. Objects from 16C Friesland are displayed in the adjoining rooms.

The first floor is mainly devoted to **17C painting**: still-life paintings, history paintings, landscapes and, most importantly, portraits. This genre was particularly popular during the Golden Age; the wealthy middle classes liked to immortalise themselves and their families for posterity. The best-known Frisian portrait painter of this period was Wijbrand de Geest. There is also a portrait from the studio of Rembrandt depicting Saskia van Uilenberg, the daughter of Leeuwarden's mayor and later Rembrandt's wife.

The **silverware**★★★ department in the vaulted cellars is one of the biggest and finest in the country. It includes a superb collection of 16C drinking horns and goblets, and the 17C and 18C Frisian ornamental silver is also particularly fine: the baroque Popta treasure, the finely engraved boxes with knots symbolising the marriage vows, and the oval brandy bowls with ornamental handles.

The top floor houses the **Frisian Resistance Museum**, with photographs and other objects evoking the atmosphere of the Second World War. It follows four families illustrating the different attitudes to occupation: collaboration, adaptation, resistance and persecution.

The tunnel and the modern section of the museum are used for temporary exhibitions of **modern Frisian art**.

Eysingahuis – This late 18C house is the former residence of the aristocratic Eysinga family. Its **period rooms** give a fascinating picture of life at the time, and include Louis XVI- and Empire-style furniture and Chinese porcelain. On the lower floor, there is a room devoted to the life of **Mata Hari**.

The paintings room on the first floor contains portraits, landscapes, seascapes and still-life paintings giving an overview of 19C **Frisian painting**. Well-known artists from that time include Laurens Alma Tadema and Christoffel Bisschop, who was also a collector of silver, porcelain, furniture, costumes and paintings. His collection is on display in the **Bisschop rooms**.

There are also two **Hindeloopen rooms** with furniture decorated with the typically colourful motifs of the region *(see Introduction: Art)*. Samplers and 18C and 19C Frisian clothing are exhibited in the **costume and textile room**.

The **archeology department** on the second floor focuses on three periods: the Stone Age, the Terp period and the late Middle Ages.

Over de Kelders – One of the quays on this canal is dug out of cellars *(kelders)*. From the bridge to the north there is a fine view over the quays of Voorstreek and the bell-tower of St Boniface.

The small **statue of Mata Hari** was erected in 1976 for the 100th anniversary of her birth.

Waag – The first floor of this 1598 building of red brick on Waagplein, in the centre of the town, is cantoned with heraldic lions. Above them is a frieze sculptured with various motifs. The weighing of butter and cheese took place here up to 1880. The large awning was to protect the goods from sunlight.

Weerd – This narrow street plunges into Leeuwarden's old quarter.

Hofplein – The **stadhuis** is on this square, a sober, classical building (1715) topped by a 17C carillon. At no 34 note a fine façade stone (1666) depicting Fortune. In the stadhuis annexe, added in 1760, the Council Room (Raadzaal) has a side façade with Rococo decoration topped by the lion which appears on the town's coat of arms.

Opposite this is the **Stadhouderlijk Hof** *(see Travellers' addresses)* or former residence of the Frisian stadtholders. The building itself dates from 1881, and has medieval remains underneath.

LEEUWARDEN

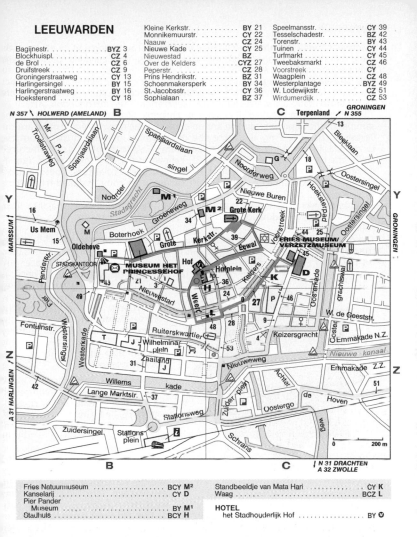

In the centre of the square there is a statue of William Louis, first hereditary stadtholder, called by the Frisians **Us heit** (Our Father).
At no 35 a façade stone depicts a stork.

Eewal – This wide main road is lined with elegant 18C residences. Some still have lovely façade stones (no 52: sailing ship, no 58: St James as a pilgrim).

Grote Kerk or Jacobijnerkerk ⓥ – Dating from the 13C, the Jacobin Church was reconstructed in the 15C and 16C and devastated by the revolutionaries in 1795. Since 1588 it has been the Nassau Frisian mausoleum. The great **organ** ⓥ was built between 1724 and 1727 by Christian Müller. The Oranjepoortje (1663) on the south side of the church was the entrance for the stadholder's family, and the copper orange tree above it refers to this fact.

Fries Natuurmuseum ⓥ – The former 17C municipal orphanage is now the home of the Frisian Natural History Museum, which has displays on the soil and the various landscapes of the region (mudflats, woodland, fens and cultivated land) and the plants and animals that live there. The basement has an excellent permanent exhibition, **Friesland onder Water**, in which visitors can explore the bottom of a drainage ditch. The whales and dolphins exhibition on the first floor includes the skeleton of a 15m/50ft **sperm whale** beached near Ameland in 1994.

Grote Kerkstraat – The tall house where Mata Hari is believed to have lived has been converted into the **Frysk Letterkundich Museum en Dokumintaasjesintrum**, or Frisian literary museum and documentation centre.
Further on at no 43 there is a fine façade stone depicting a lion and a fortified castle, then near the corner of Doelestraat, at no 17, a lovely Baroque portal is decorated with garlands in the Frisian style.

★★ **Museum Het Princessehof, Nederlands Keramickmuseum** ⓥ – During the 18C, this 17C palace (hof) was the official residence of Princess Marie-Louise of Hessen-Kassel (known familiarly as Maaike-Meu), widow of the Frisian stadtholder John William Friso, Prince of Orange. Her dining and music room or the ground floor is richly decorated: stucco ceiling, gold curtains, portraits and Chinese porcelain.

This palace and adjoining buildings are now the home of the Netherlands Ceramics Museum. Over 20 rooms contain collections of porcelain, pottery and stoneware pieces from many different countries (*illustrations: see Introduction, Art*).

The exhibits from **Asia** are displayed in chronological order (5 rooms). Some samples of the **Japanese production** are on show but the most splendid of all are the **Chinese porcelain**★★. They illustrate the development of the industry from the terracotta pieces made in the third millennium BC up to the objects manufactured under the Ching dynasty (1644-1912), renowned for its *famille verte, famille noire and famille rose*, much sought-after by European collectors. There is also a room devoted to "chine de commande", earthenware commissioned from China by Europeans.

European ceramics (5 rooms) are the subject of a beautiful display: majolica from Italy, Delftware, Wedgwood, porcelain, Art Nouveau and Art Deco ceramics (1900-30).

The museum also presents an extensive collection of **earthenware tiles**★★ mainly from Spain, France, Portugal and the Netherlands. The colourful tile pictures used on floors, walls and fireplaces are particularly interesting. There is also an Islamic collection with tiles from Turkey, Iran and elsewhere. Two rooms are devoted to the JWN van Achterbergh collection, giving an overview of Dutch ceramics between 1950 and 1985, and the museum also covers contemporary **European ceramics**.

Museum Het Princessehof – Nationaal Keramiek Museum Leeuwarden

Iranian tile (Lagwardina, c 1300)

Oldehove ⊙ – This massive Gothic tower in brick was never completed due to the instability of the ground, which explains why it leans sharply. The plan of the adjacent church, which was destroyed in 1595, is indicated on the square by coloured paving. From the top of the tower, there is an overall **view** of the town and the surrounding area; the Waddeneilanden are visible in fine weather. Nearby, a walking path through the **Prinsentuin** garden leads across the old, tree-covered quays of **Stadsgracht**, a wide canal which follows the outline of the fortifications. The garden also contains the **Pier Pander Museum** ⊙, mainly devoted to the work of this Frisian sculptor (1864-1919).

ADDITIONAL SIGHTS

Marssum – *5km/3mi to the west via Harlingerstraatweg.*
The **Poptaslot** ⊙, or Heringastate, preceded by a 17C gatehouse with voluted gables, houses 17C and 18C furnishings.
Nearby the old almshouse, **Popta-Gasthuis**, founded in 1711 is a picturesque group of low buildings with a monumental portal.

Otterpark Aqualutra ⊙ – *7km/4mi northeast via N 355 towards Groningen.* In 1988, when the last otter in the Netherlands died after being run over, the Netherlands Otter Station Foundation decided to set up a breeding centre (*not open to the public*) and a nature park. This now provides an opportunity to encounter a wealth of freshwater fauna, centring on the otter which, because it is at the top of the food chain, is a good way of gauging water quality. Otters are mainly active at night, so the best time to see them is at **feeding time**. The park also contains mink, polecats, beavers, storks and waterfowl, while the central exhibition building has aquariums, vivariums, exhibitions and films.

EXCURSIONS

Drachten – *27km/17mi to the southeast via Oostergoweg.*
In the Frisian countryside with rich meadows bordered by poplar trees, Drachten spreads with its great apartment complexes and brick houses. This town is a commercial and industrial centre with busy streets and pedestrian precincts adorned with statues.

Terpenland (Terp Region) – *Round tour of 118km/73mi. Leave by Groningerstraatweg. Turn left after 9km/6mi.*

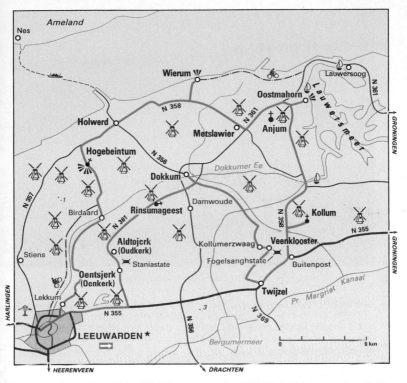

From the beginning of the 5C BC and up to the 12C AD in the low regions liable to sea or river flooding, the Frisians established their farmhouses and later their churches on man-made mounds called *terpen* (*terp* in the singular).

There are still about 1 000 of which two thirds are in the province of Friesland, and the rest in the province of Groningen where they are called *wierden* (*illustration: see GRONINGEN, Excursions*). Their average height is between 2m/6.5ft and 6m/19.5ft, and their area between 1ha/2.5acres and 12ha/29.5 acres. The excavations have been very successful.

The tour covers a region where most of the villages have a *terp* with a church of tufa and brick with rustic charm, and a tower with a saddleback roof rising from a curtain of trees indicating its presence. The typical Frisian countryside is scattered with lovely farmhouses with gables decorated with an *uilebord* (*see Introduction: Traditions and folklore; illustration, see Admission times and charges*). Windmills and beautiful black Frisian horses are also a common sight.

Oentsjerk/Oenkerk – This lovely forest-like castle park, **Stania-State**, is open to the public.

Aldtsjerk – This village, known as **Oudkerk** in Dutch, has a castle and a church on a *terp*.

Rinsumageest – The **church** ⊘, built on a *terp*, has a Romanesque crypt with two elegantly sculptured capitals. The interior is typical of Frisian churches.

Dokkum – *See DOKKUM.*

Follow the canal to the southeast.

The road soon climbs.

Turn right towards Kollumerzwaag.

Veenklooster – Charming village with thatched cottages round a *brink*. A fine alley leads to **Fogelsangh State** ⊘ built in 1725; museum on the site of an abbey and surrounded by a park.

Twijzel – All along the main road, which crosses this town for a couple of miles, stand a row of magnificent **farmhouses***. Behind the pleasant façade stands an enormous barn, often with a thatched roof (*illustration: see Introduction, Traditions and folklore*).

At Buitenpost, turn left.

Kollum – This town has a 15C Gothic **church** ⊘ with a 13C tower. The nave is separated from the side aisles by stocky columns. The vaults with painted ribs are decorated with naive frescoes, as is the north wall where one can see a St Christopher.

Farmhouse and Frisian horses

Oostmahorn – From the top of the dike, there is an overall view of **Lauwersmeer** *(see GRONINGEN: Excursions)*. Like the Zuiderzee, this low-lying region was flooded by the sea in the 13C. To avoid floods and create new polders a barrier dam has been built, creating the lake, a popular centre for watersports.

Anjum – This village has kept an 1889 windmill. On a small *terp* there is a Romanesque church, enlarged in the Gothic style.

Take the road to Dokkum, then turn right towards Metslawier.

Metslawier – Grouped round the old Gothic church, the old, remarkably restored houses form a harmonious whole.

Wierum – This is a small harbour with modest homes; its church is built on an oval *terp* and surrounded by a cemetery.

A staircase leads to the top of the dike: **view** over the Waddenzee, which at low tide appears, here, like an immense beach. The islands of Ameland and Schiermonnikoog are visible on the horizon.

Holwerd – It is the departure point for boats going to Ameland Island.

After Blija, turn left to Hogebeintum.

Hogebeintum – This village on the highest *terp* in Friesland (nearly 9m/30ft above sea level) has a **church** ⊘ typical of the northern Netherlands bearing a bell-tower with a saddleback roof and surrounded by a cemetery. It offers a fine view over the neighbouring countryside. The interior is interesting for the series of 16 **hatchments★** (from the 17C to the early 20C) which decorate the walls. On each carved wood panel, there is a coat of arms adorned with Baroque motifs, symbols of death (scythe, hour-glass, skulls and bones) and heads of cherubs in naive and rustic styles. There are also some lovely seignorial pews in wood, and on the ground numerous memorial slabs.

Reach Birdaard to the south and follow the Dokkumer Ee Canal towards the south. Via the village of Lekkum, Prof Mr PS Gerbrandyweg and Groninger straatweg, one returns to Leeuwarden.

LEIDEN**

LEYDEN – Zuid-Holland
Population 117 041
Michelin maps 908 E 5 and 211 L 10 –
Local map see KEUKENHOF AND BULB FIELDS
Plan of the conurbation in the current Michelin Red Guide Benelux

Built on the Oude Rijn, Leiden is an agreeable, lively town crisscrossed by canals. It is famous for its university, the oldest in the country, and has a number of exceptional museums and many idyllic *hofjes*, or almshouses. It is also a prosperous town where graphic arts and the manufacture of building materials are important.
To the southeast of the town stretches the Vlietland, a large recreational area.

HISTORICAL NOTES

In Roman times Leiden was called Lugdunum Batavorum. The medieval town grew at the foot of a fortified castle, the Burcht, erected in the 9C on an artificial mound. It owed its prosperity to its location on the Oude Rijn, which was then the main branch of the river, but the displacement of the mouth of the estuary towards Rotterdam reduced the town's role to that of an inland market.
In the 14C Leiden regained a certain prosperity with the linen industry introduced by weavers from Ypres (Belgium) taking refuge from the Black Death.
John of Leiden was born here in 1509. He was the leader of the Anabaptists, members of a religious sect, who took refuge in Münster, Germany in 1534, where they formed a theocratic community. Beseiged, the Anabaptists had to surrender in 1535 and John of Leiden died the following year.

A heroic siege – In the 16C the town was besieged twice by the Spanish. The first siege (end of 1573 to March 1574) failed. The second, started a month later was terrible. The population reduced to half due to plague and starvation revolted against the burgomaster Van der Werff, who offered his body to the famished. Revived by the courage of their leader, the inhabitants continued their resistance.
Finally, William the Silent had the idea of breaching the dikes to flood the surrounding countryside.
On 3 October, the Spanish were attacked by the Sea Beggars, who had sailed in over the flooded land on flat-bottomed boats; the Spaniards raised the siege, abandoning, at the foot of the ramparts, a big pot of beef stew *(Hutspot)*.
The inhabitants of Leiden were then supplied with bread and herring.
From then on a commemorative feast, **Leidens Ontzet**, takes place annually *(see Calendar of events)* with a historical procession, distribution of herring and white bread and eating of beef stew *(hutspot)* in memory of the pot left by the Spanish.
To reward the town, William the Silent founded a university here in 1575.

Leiden University – It was the first in the Low Countries liberated from Spain and for a long time rivalled that of Louvain, which had remained Catholic; it very quickly acquired a European reputation due to its relatively tolerant spirit and the great minds it drew there: the Flemish humanist Justus Lipsius (1547-1606); the philologist Daniël Heinsius (1580-1655); the famous theologians Gomarus, Arminius and Episcopius *(see DORDRECHT)*; the Frenchmen Saumaise (1588-1653), philologist, and Joseph Scaliger (1540-1609) philosopher; the physician and botanist **Boerhaave**, master of clinical education (1668-1738); and **Van Musschenbroek** (1692-1761), inventor in 1746 of the Leiden jar, the first electrical condenser.
In 1637 **René Descartes** (1596-1650), published anonymously in Leiden his *Discourse on Method* written in Utrecht, where he had formerly lived.
The influence of the university was increased by the fact that Leiden had become a great centre of printing in the 17C due to the illustrious **Elsevier** family; the family's first member, Louis who came from Louvain (Belgium) settled in Leiden in 1580.

The Protestant refuge – In the 16C and 17C Leiden welcomed numerous Flemish and French Protestants (who fled in 1685 because of the Revocation of the Edict of Nantes) as well as English.
In 1609 a hundred or so English Puritans arrived via Amsterdam, led by their spiritual leader **John Robinson** (c 1575-1625). They had left their country under the threat of persecution. Former farmers, they had to adapt themselves to their new urban condition and applied themselves to various handicraft trades. A printing press published religious works which were exported to England and Scotland. Their stay became difficult and the Puritans decided to leave Leiden and go to America. Sailing from Delfshaven on the *Speedwell* they reached England and embarked on the *Mayflower* in Plymouth.
The 102 emigrants among which there were 41 Puritans or **Pilgrim Fathers** landed in December 1620 on the southeast coast of Boston and founded Plymouth Colony, the first permanent settlement established in New England.

Accommodation

As a student town, Leiden has few really special hotels, but here are some suggestions.

YOUTH HOSTEL

Jeugdherberg Lits Jumeaux – *Lange Scheistraat 9, 2312 CR Leiden* ☎ *(071) 512 84 57, Fax (071) 512 87 63. 40 beds.* Located behind the Lakenhal, halfway between the station and the centre.

BUDGET HOTELS

Het Haagse Schouw – *Haagse Schouwweg 14, 2332 KG Leiden* ☎ *(071) 531 57 44, Fax (071) 576 24 22. 62 rooms.* This comfortable modern hotel, part of the Van der Valk chain, is outside the centre near the A 44 motorway. It is linked by a covered footbridge to a 17C inn, Het Haagsche Schouw, where the restaurant and dining rooms are located. Good value for money.

OUR SELECTION

De Doelen – *Rapenburg 2, 2311 EV Leiden,* ☎ *(071) 512 05 27 Fax (071) 512 84 53. 15 rooms.* This small hotel is located in a historic building a stone's throw from many of the main sights, and thus an ideal base for a visit to the town. Start your day in style in the beautiful breakfast room.

Restaurants

Oudt Leyden – *Steenstraat 51-53,* ☎ *(071) 513 31 44.* Atmospheric speciality restaurant. In 't Pannekoekenhuysje next door, delicious pancakes are served on Delft plates. Closed Mondays.

Anak Bandung – *Garenmarkt 24a,* ☎ *(071) 512 53 03.* Indonesian cuisine including rijsttafel. Meals served on the terrace in summer. Open evenings only.

Stadscafé/Restaurant Van der Werff – *Steenstraat 2,* ☎ *(071) 513 03 35.* A stylish place for a drink or snack when visiting the Rijksmuseum voor Volkenkunde

De Knip – *In Voorschoten, 5km/3mi from the centre of Leiden, Kniplaan 22 (4km/2mi via Veurseweg).* ☎ *(071) 561 25 73.* Wonderful meals served on a shaded waterside terrace. Closed Mondays.

Practical information

General information – The **VVV** tourist office (Stationsplein 210, 2312 AF Leiden, ☎ (0900) 22 22 333 or www.leiden.nl) has information on sights, tours, cultural events, excursions etc. The staff can also help with finding accommodation. The VVV publishes an annual brochure listing hotels, pensions and camp sites in and around Leiden.

Transport – **Car**: a 24hr parking permit (dagkaart) for the centre of Leiden costs 15fl and can be purchased from meters or the VVV. The Haagweg car park on the edge of town costs 5fl a day, including the shuttle-bus fare to the town centre. **Bicycles** can be hired at the Rijwielshop (bicycle shop) behind the station, ☎ (071) 512 00 68.

Tours and walks – The VVV sells leaflets detailing two walking tours: one of Leiden's almshouses and the other following in the footsteps of Rembrandt. It also organises tours.

Boat trips – **Canal tours** of the town centre depart from Beestenmarkt (operated by Rederij Rembrandt, ☎ (071) 513 49 38). Trips along the **Oude Rijn** to Avifauna leave from Oude Singel *(see Excursions)*; there are also **tours to Braassem** and the **polders** and **windmills** leaving from the harbour (Rederij Slingerland, ☎ (071) 541 31 83).

Shopping – The historic town centre is a pleasant place to shop. Late-night shopping is on Thursdays.

Markets – A large **general market** is held on the waterside in the town centre every Wednesday and Saturday from 9am to 5pm. This tradition dates back 900 years.

Night-life – Being a university town, Leiden has a very lively night-life, and the bars and cafés are particularly crowded on Thursday evenings.
Theatre and concert halls: information and bookings from the VVV.

Events – The **Leidse Jazzweek** is held in January in the town centre. The **Leidse Lakenfeesten** is a 10-day cloth festival held in July, featuring a cloth market, a parade, a street musicians' competition and other events. The raising of the **siege of Leiden** is commemorated on 2 and 3 October.

LEIDEN PAINTERS

Leiden School – From the 15C to the 17C a great number of painters were born in Leiden.

Geertgen tot Sint Jans (c 1465-c 1495), who died in Haarlem, is the most gifted painter of the late 15C. Still turned towards the Middle Ages, he showed, however, virtuosity in the treatment of fabrics (*illustration: see Introduction, Art*) and gave great importance to landscape.

Cornelis Engebrechtsz. (1468-1533) remained Gothic as well, with crowded compositions and rather tormented linear painting (Museum De Lakenhal). His pupil **Lucas van Leyden** (1489/94-1533) is the great Renaissance painter. Influenced by Italian art, his *Last Judgment*, which can be seen in the Lakenhal is a very fine work, for the balance of composition, sense of depth, elegant draughtsmanship and fine colours. Lucas van Leiden also originated the genre scene, using it for numerous engravings. In the beginning of the 17C a few painters of the Leiden School painted *vanitas*, still-life paintings where certain specific objects, representing the arts and sciences (books, maps...), wealth (jewellery...), earthly pleasures (goblets, playing cards), death (skulls)... are depicted with great precision often with a moralistic message. These subjects were appreciated by Jan Davidsz de Heem (*see UTRECHT*) when he stayed here before going to Antwerp.

Jan van Goyen, born in Leiden in 1596 went to live in Haarlem in 1631 where he died (1656). He was a great painter of pale, monochromatic landscapes: immense skies covered with clouds, shimmering water and skilful use of light and shadow.

Son of **Willem van de Velde the Elder** (c 1611-93), **Willem van de Velde the Younger** (1633-1707), specialised, like his father, in naval battles: the sun piercing through the clouds flooding light onto the sails and golden sterns of large warships and shimmering on a calm sea. The Van de Veldes ended their lives in London where they became court painters to Charles II.

Gerrit Dou (1613-75) is perhaps the most conscientious of all the intimist masters of Leiden. He took to chiaroscuro when in touch with his master, Rembrandt, but he mainly tried to render with the patience of a miniaturist and a stylistic touch, recalling his first trade as a glazier, scenes of bourgeois life (*Young Woman Dressing*, Museum Boijmans-Van Beuningen in Rotterdam).

His pupil **Frans van Mieris the Elder** (1635-81) depicted smiling people in refined interiors. **Gabriel Metsu** (1629-67) was a genre painter and a master in his manner of treating fabrics and the substance of objects; he treated with great sensitivity slightly sentimental subjects (*The Sick Child*, Rijksmuseum, Amsterdam).

Contrary to his contemporaries, **Jan Steen** (1626-79) depicts very busy scenes with humour. His paintings are the theatre of the whole human comedy where somewhat dishevelled people indulge in various pleasures; they play music, drink, eat and play in a very unruly atmosphere (*illustration: see AMSTERDAM*).

★ THE OLD TOWN AND ITS MUSEUMS 5hr

★ **Rijksmuseum voor Volkenkunde** ⊙ – This ethnology museum, famous for its collections of non-Western civilizations, is presently undergoing restoration work. Until its official reopening, it will be used as a venue for temporary exhibitions.

Molen de Valk ⊙ – This wall mill, the last in Leiden, built in 1743, bears the name of a bird of prey (*valk*: falcon). It has seven floors and the first ones were the living quarters where 10 generations of millers succeeded each other until 1964. Restored, it has become a museum.
The tour includes the repair workshop, the forge, the drawing room (zondagkamer) and a retrospective of Dutch windmills. In season its sails turn, but it no longer mills grain.

★ **Stédélijk Museum De Lakenhal** ⊙ – Installed in the old cloth merchants' hall (lakenhal), this is a museum of decorative arts (furniture, silverware, pewterware), which also contains a fine section of paintings. The whole history of the town unravels within these rooms.
The first floor focuses on the **textile industry** that has been so important to Leiden. The various stages of wool production are shown in a 16C series of paintings by Isaac van Swanenburg.
On the second floor the town's history is evoked, including the raising of the **siege of Leiden** on 3 October 1574. Its religious past is also chronicled; there is a chapel from the old Catholic church (*see UTRECHT*) and a display on the persecution and execution of the Remonstrants (*see DORDRECHT*) in 1623.
On the ground floor there is a fine collection of glassware, silver and tiles, as well as **painting and decorative arts** from the 16C to the 20C, including numerous Leiden masters.
By Cornelis Engebrechtsz. (room 16) there are two admirably detailed triptychs: Crucifixion and Descent from the Cross, as well as a small Carrying of the Cross. But the works of **Lucas van Leyden** dominate. In his luminous triptych of the **Last**

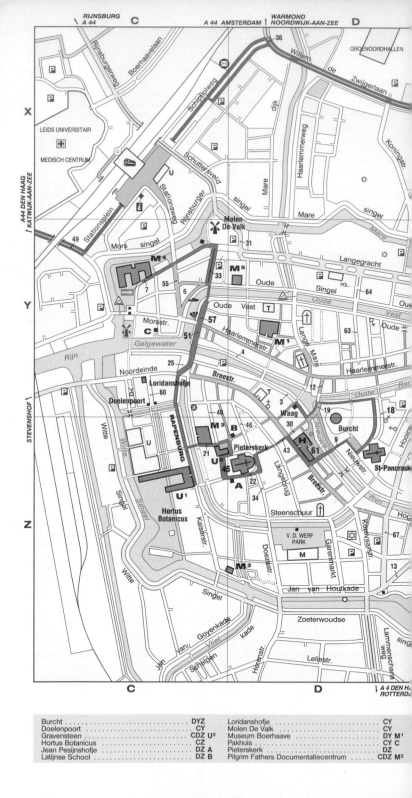

Judgement painted with assurance of draughtsmanship, the painter knew how to free the figures from constraint and rigidity. The central panel shows the Son of Man enthroned in thick clouds for the Supreme Judgment. On the panels heaven and hell are painted; on the back, St Peter and St Paul.

Among the 17C Leiden painters exhibited are Gerrit Dou, Jan Steen (animated scenes) and refined works by Mieris the Elder.

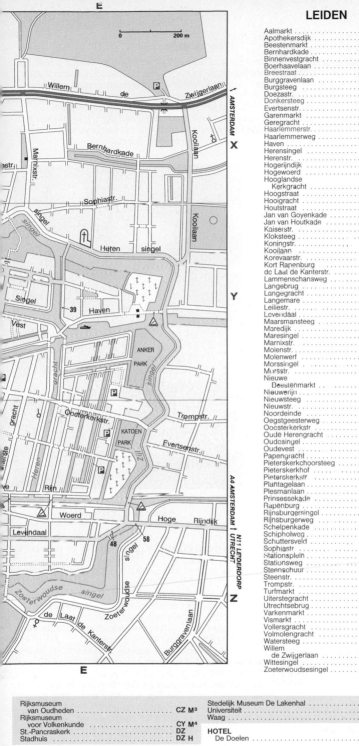

LEIDEN

Aalmarkt . . . . DY 3
Apothekersdijk . . . . DY 4
Beestenmarkt . . . . CY 6
Bernhardkade . . . . EX
Binnenvestgracht . . . . CY 7
Boerhaavelaan CX
Breestraat . . . . DYZ
Burggravenlaan . . . . EZ
Burgsteeg . . . . DZ 9
Doezastr. . . . . DZ
Donkersteeg . . . . DY 12
Evertsenstr. . . . . EZ
Garenmarkt . . . . DZ
Geregracht . . . . DZ 13
Haarlemmerstr. . . . . DEY
Haarlemmerweg . . . . DX
Haven . . . . EY
Herensingel . . . . EY
Herenstr. . . . . DZ
Hogerijndijk . . . . EZ
Hogewoerd . . . . DEZ
Hooglandse
  Kerkgracht . . . . DYZ 18
Hoogstraat . . . . DY 19
Hooigracht . . . . DZ
Houtstraat . . . . CZ 21
Jan van Goyenkade . . . . CZ
Jan van Houtkade . . . . DZ
Kaiserstr. . . . . CZ
Kloksteeg . . . . DZ 22
Koningstr. . . . . DX
Kooilaan . . . . EXY
Korevaarstr. . . . . DZ
Kort Rapenburg . . . . CY 25
de Laat de Kanterstr. . . . . EZ
Lammenschansweg . . . . DZ
Langebrug . . . . DZ
Langegracht . . . . DY
Langemare . . . . DY
Leiliestr. . . . . DZ
Levendaal . . . . EZ
Maarsmansteeg . . . . CYZ 30
Maredijk . . . . DX
Maresingel . . . . DFX
Marnixstr. . . . . EX
Molenstr. . . . . EX
Molenwerf . . . . CDY 31
Morssingel . . . . CY
Morsstr. . . . . CY
Nieuwe
  Beestenmarkt . . . . CY 33
Nieuwerijn . . . . EZ
Nieuwsteeg . . . . DZ 34
Nieuwstr. . . . . DZ
Noordeinde . . . . CY
Oegstgeesterweg . . . . DX 36
Oosterkerkstr . . . . EZ
Oude Herengracht . . . . EY 39
Oudsingel . . . . DEY
Oudevest . . . . DEY
Papengracht . . . . CYZ 40
Pieterskerkchoorsteeg . . . . . . DZ 43
Pieterskerkhof CD7 45
Pieterskerkstr . . . . DYZ 46
Plantagelaan . . . . EZ 48
Plesmanlaan . . . . CY 49
Prinsessekade . . . . CY 51
Rapenburg . . . . CZ
Rijnsburgersingel . . . . CDX
Rijnsburgerweg CX
Schelpenkade . . . . CZ
Schipholweg CX
Schuttersveld CX
Sophiastr. . . . . EX
Stationsplein CX
Stationsweg CX
Steenschuur . . . . DZ
Steenstr. . . . . CY 55
Trompstr. . . . . EZ
Turfmarkt . . . . CY 57
Uiterstegracht . . . . EZ
Utrechtsebrug . . . . EZ 58
Varkenmarkt . . . . CY 60
Vismarkt . . . . DZ 61
Vollersgracht . . . . DY 63
Volmolengracht . . . . DY 64
Watersteeg . . . . DZ 67
Willem
  de Zwijgerlaan . . . . DEX
Wittesingel . . . . CZ
Zoeterwoudsesingel . . . . DEZ

Rijksmuseum
  van Oudheden . . . . CZ M³
Rijksmuseum
  voor Volkenkunde . . . . CY M⁴
St.-Pancraskerk . . . . DZ
Stadhuis . . . . DZ H

Stedelijk Museum De Lakenhal . . . . DY M⁵
Universiteit . . . . CZ U¹
Waag . . . . CY

HOTEL
De Doelen . . . . CY ☺

The museum also possesses some fine 17C paintings: a still-life by J Davidsz. de Heem, *Horse Market* at Valkenburg by Salomon van Ruysdael, *View of Leiden* by Van Goyen and an early work by Rembrandt.

To the south of **Turfmarkt** there is a lovely **view** over the harbour and the mill. Further on, from **Prinsessekade** there is an old warehouse restored, giving onto Galgewater harbour.

Rembrandt

Rembrandt Harmensz van Rijn was born in Leiden in 1606. Son of a miller he lived near the Rhine, hence his name Van Rijn. His childhood remains mysterious. In 1620 he enrolled at Leiden University, but attracted by painting, he soon became an apprentice to Jacob van Swanenburgh, then, in 1623 in Amsterdam, to **Pieter Lastman** (1583-1633), a great admirer of Italy and Caravaggio.

Although he painted numerous portraits and even self-portraits, Rembrandt right from the start showed a leaning towards biblical history, which he first painted with minute detail typical of the Leiden School.

The artist, who never studied in Italy, contrary to the great painters of his time, adopted a very personal style. His chiaroscuro was not that of Caravaggio, where strong contrasts between light and shade existed, but an imperceptible change from shadow to people suffused with a warm light which occupied the centre of the painting. His works are steeped in a mysterious atmosphere from which an intense emotion and profound spirituality emanate.

Beginning in 1628 he took up etching and drawing, sometimes seeking inspiration from ordinary people (beggars etc). At the end of 1631, he settled in Amsterdam; it was then that he painted the famous **The Anatomy Lesson of Doctor Tulp** (1632). This group portrait brought glory to the young painter of 26. Orders started flowing in.

Rembrandt. Self portrait aged 23,
Mauritshuis, The Hague

Foto ° Mauritshuis

Rembrandt met Saskia whom he married in 1634. Several children were born, one of whom, Titus, was born in 1641.

In 1639 he moved to a house in the Jewish quarter, the present Rembrandthuis.

In 1642 he painted his greatest work, the **Night Watch**, a group portrait of members of the civic guard. This genre, which had already been revived by Frans Hals, is treated by Rembrandt with daring and complexity of technique up to then unequalled. However, not much interest was shown in this painting at the time, which became his most famous.

In addition, 1642 marked the beginning of the painter's misfortune: he lost his wife Saskia; he had already seen his parents die in 1630 and 1640.

He painted numerous portraits including that of the young Titus (1655), a solemn *Self-Portrait* (1652) but the wealthy art patrons began to abandon him with the exception of the burgomaster Jan Six. In 1657 and 1658 he was unable to pay his debts and had to sell his house and goods.

In 1661 his *Conspiracy of Julius Civilis*, ordered for the town hall, was refused (National Museum in Stockholm). In 1662 he lost his mistress Hendrickje Stoffels.

The Sampling Officials of the Drapers Guild (1662) was his last group painting, but he still did some marvellous paintings like the *Jewish Bride* before passing away, a year after his son Titus, in 1669. He had just completed his last self-portrait.

The Rijksmuseum in Amsterdam has an exceptional collection of the master's works.

Among Rembrandt's numerous pupils in Amsterdam, there was the landscape painter **Philips Koninck** (1619-88) and several painters originating from Dordrecht *(see DORDRECHT)* or Leiden like Gerrit Dou.

Rapenburg – It is the most beautiful canal in Leiden, spanned by triple-arched bridges and lined with trees. On the west side there are some fine houses: nos 19, 21, 25, 29, 31, 61 and 65.

Rijksmuseum van Oudheden – The national museum of antiquities has important collections of items from Egypt, the Middle East, Greece and Rome, as well as a Dutch archeology section. The **Egyptian collection**★★ ⊘ is particularly interesting.

The museum is currently undergoing major rebuilding and expansion, scheduled for completion in 2000. In the meantime, part of it is being used for temporary exhibitions of the various collections. The **Dutch archeology section** is also still open to the public, providing detailed coverage of the Netherlands' early history from 250 000 years ago to the Middle Ages.

In the entrance hall is the **Temple of Isis from Taffeh** in Nubia, dating from the Augustan age (27 BC to AD 14). It was given to the Netherlands by the Egyptian government as a gesture of thanks for its contribution to UNESCO's international campaign in connection with the Aswan dam. The building of the dam involved flooding a large part of Nubia, and various monuments had to be dug up and moved.

Stele (detail), c 1300 BC from Hoey

University – Since the 16C the administrative offices of the university have been housed in the chapel of a former convent. Upstairs on the first floor there is a "sweating room" where the nervous students waited to take their exams.

Hortus Botanicus ⊘ – The botanical garden was founded by the university in 1587 in a lovely riverside setting. In 1593, Clusius brought the first Dutch tulips into flower here. The garden contains centuries-old trees and rare plants (including a giant water lily, Victoria Amazonica). In spring and summer, the flowers create a riot of colour. The orangery and greenhouses are open to the public.

Latijnse School – The Latin School was founded in 1324 and in 1599 it was given a Renaissance frontage.

Continue to Breestraat via Pieterskerkkoorsteeg.

Gravensteen – This former prison is now home to the Law Faculty and has a lovely Classical front on the church side.

Pieterskerkhof – This square was originally the churchyard (kerkhof).

Pieterskerk ⊘ – St Peter's is a large and heavily built Gothic church with a nave and four aisles, whose construction began in the late 14C.
There are memorial slabs to the painter Jan Steen and Professor Boerhaave as well as the Puritan leader, John Robinson *(see above)*.

Jean Pesijnhofje – Built in 1683 on the site of John Robinson's house and intended for the members of the Walloon church, this almshouse took the name of its founder, Jean Pesijn, a French merchant of Huguenot origin. There is a memorial slab to John Robinson.

Breestraat – This, the town's main shopping street, is very busy. At the point where the itinerary crosses it, there is a **blue stone** where executions took place.

Stadhuis – Built c 1600 and damaged in a fire in 1929, it was rebuilt in its original style. Preceded by a perron, it is topped with a very decorative gable.

Vismarkt – It is the old fish market.
At the beginning of Nieuwstraat one can see the 17C entrance doorway of the **Burcht** topped by a lion with the town's coat of arms (two keys). This fortress was

built on an artificial mound at the confluence of the Oude Rijn and the Nieuwe Rij
There remains a stout curtain wall with crenellations and loopholes. Its watchpat
offers a panorama over the town.

Sint-Pancraskerk or Hooglandsekerk – This 15C church has interestin
Flamboyant sculptured portals at the transepts.

Hooglandse Kerkgracht – Alongside this filled-in canal is the old orphanag
Weeshuis, with a decorative panel above the doorway depicting foundlings.

Waag – The weigh-house was built between 1657 and 1659 by Pieter Post.

Leiden's "hofjes"

Hofjes are almshouses built round a central courtyard or garden; Leiden has
35 of them, and they are primarily a Dutch phenomenon. They were
originally intended as homes for the elderly poor, and were mostly set up
by wealthy church elders hoping to gain a place in heaven through the
prayers of the inhabitants, who received free accommodation and
sometimes food, drink and clothing. In return, they had to comply with a
strict set of rules laid down by the regents, or governors, who were usually
descendants of the dead founder. Sometimes the regents had a separate
meeting room, or *regentenkamer*, in the almshouses.

Most *hofjes* have only one entrance from the street, consisting of a
passageway (sometimes with a gatehouse) or entrance hall. In the past, the
gate would be opened and closed by a porter at fixed times of day.

Today, the *hofjes* are oases of tranquillity amid the hubbub of the city, and
are therefore very popular places to live. When you visit, please respect the
peace and privacy of the people who live there.

ADDITIONAL SIGHTS

* **Museum Boerhaave** ⓥ (Rijksmuseum voor de Geschiedenis van de Natuurwetenschapp
en van de Geneeskunde) – The national museum of the history of the natural science
and medicine is located in the former hospital where the famous scientist an
doctor Herman Boerhaave *(see above)* taught his medical students from h
sickbed.

Its very varied collection of instruments and documents is one of th
most important in the world, giving an overview of five centuries of natur
sciences and medicine. It includes the collection of astronomical and surgic
instruments formerly owned by Christiaan Huygens, inventor of the pendulu
clock, and the microscopes of the naturalist, Antonie van Leeuwenhoek. Th
reconstructed Anatomy Theatre contains a collection of human and anim
skeletons.

Pilgrim Fathers Documentatiecentrum ⓥ – In a small house behind th
municipal archives is a collection of objects and documents associated with th
Pilgrim Fathers. The varied collection includes a printing press, theological book
and a model of the *Mayflower*.

Loridanshofje – The 1656 **almshouse** at no 1 Oude Varkensmarkt has a simp
inner courtyard.
Further along the street is the 1645 gateway, **Doelenpoort**, crowned with a
equestrian statue of St George, the patron saint of the archers guild (*doele
means targets, and was the place where the archers practised).

★★ **Nationaal Natuurhistorisch Museum Naturalis** ⓥ – *Follow Plesmanlaa
towards The Hague; turn right into Darwinweg after the Academisch Ziekenhu
(hospital).*
The entrance to this Natural History Museum is located in the 17C pest-hous
which was built outside the centre because of its function. The buildings arour
the attractive courtyard include a **Nature Information Centre**.
The glass **zebra bridge** leads to the modern part of the museum, which contai
seven permanent exhibitions. These bring the complexity and richness of th
natural world to life in an exciting and interactive way.
The **Oerparade** (prehistoric parade) exhibition includes hundreds of fossils, dinosau
skeletons and a mosasaur, an extinct aquatic lizard. Don't miss the million-yea
old remains of Java Man, discovered in 1891 by the Dutch anthropologist Eugèr
Dubois. The lights in the central tree trunk trace the 3.8-billion-year evolutic
from the first life forms to the animals of today. The top of the tree is in the floo
of the **Natuurtheater**, where hundreds of animals run, fly, swim and crawl. The ric
variety of plants, fungi, algae and bacteria are displayed in an original wa
followed by stones and minerals.

Natuurtheater

Aarde, or Earth, shows how earthquakes and volcanoes occur, why the Earth's crust and the weather and the atmosphere are in a constant state of change, and what happens at the centre of the planet.

Leven (life) explores how humans and animals obtain food, protect themselves and reproduce.

On the walls of the **Ecosystemen** room, videos show the different types of ecosystems, such as the polar seas, deserts, tundra and tropical rainforests, and the relationships between animals, plants and the environment. You can also use a computer to create your own ecosystem.

The history of how different periods and cultures have viewed life and nature is explored in **Visies op natuur**. This uses quotations, art and everyday objects to examine the outlooks of Islam, the 18C Enlightenment, the Tao culture, ancient Egypt and other cultures.

Another unmissable attraction is the **Schatkamer** (treasury), which includes King William I's collection of precious stones, as well as unusual minerals and extinct animals such as the Cape lion and the Tasmanian wolf. In view of the fragility of the objects, the Treasury is open only from 1.30pm to 4.30pm.

Kijkje Aarde, a look at the Earth, is ideal for children, with stones, trees and animals talking about the various cycles that exist in nature.

The museum also holds **temporary exhibitions**, showing selections from the huge collection of 10 million mammals, insects, birds, butterflies, fossils and minerals normally held in the tower.

EXCURSIONS

Keukenhof – See KEUKENHOF, Bulb fields.

Alphen aan den Rijn – 17km/11mi to the east via the Hoge Rijndijk. Can be reached by boat.

Alphen aan den Rijn is a small industrial town on the banks of the Oude Rijn. **Avifauna** ⊘ is a substantial bird park, with large cages for rare birds, a tropical aviary, a lake complete with ducks, and ponds with pink flamingoes. It also has a large playground and is the departure point for **boat trips** to the Braassemermeer, the lake to the north of Alphen.

On the south side of Alphen is the archeological theme park, the **Archeon**★ ⊘ (signposted). This is divided into three areas showing what life in the Netherlands was like during the prehistoric, Roman and medieval periods, with people dressed in authentic costumes bringing the past to life.

In the park, where the planting is designed to be appropriate to each particular historical era, there are excellent reconstructions of settlements, camps and homes. The prehistory section, for example, includes the settlements of the early agriculturalists, the Vlaardingen culture and the builders of the prehistoric funerary monuments known as *hunebedden*. The Roman section includes a bathhouse, where visitors can obtain a massage, while gladiator fights are held in the amphitheatre (see daily programme for times).

The medieval section is bustling with people: the civic guard keeps an eye c
visitors as they enter, and the basket-maker, baker and shoemaker giv
demonstrations of their work. The monastery of Gravendam has bee
reconstructed based on excavations in Dordrecht, and here you can obtain
medieval meal prepared by the Friars Minor.

Katwijk aan Zee and Noordwijk aan Zee – *18km/11mi to the northwest; leav
Leiden by Oegstgeesterweg. Local map see KEUKENHOF: Bulb fields.*

⌂ **Katwijk aan Zee** – This is a popular resort not far from the bulb fields. The long sanc
beach is backed by lines of dunes.

⌂⌂ **Noordwijk aan Zee** – This fashionable seaside resort has excellent amenities for th
visitor. Again a wide sandy beach stretches seawards from the chain of hig
dunes. The annual flower parade, the Bloemencorso, *(see Calendar of event
leaves Leiden in the morning and arrives at Noordwijk in the evening.
Behind the dunes of Noordwijk is ESTEC, the technical branch of the Europea
Space Agency, where satellites are tested and European space projects ar
managed.
300m further on is **Noordwijk Space Expo** ⊘ *(Keplerlaan 3)*, where model rocket
real satellites, space suits, photographs, a slide show and other items tell the stor
of international space flight, with the accent on Europe. There is also a discover
trail for children, the reward for which is an astronaut's diploma signed by Wubb
Ockels, the first Dutchman into space.

Nationaal Museum Paleis Het LOO★★★

Gelderland

Michelin maps 908 15 and 211 U 9

Het Loo Palace and its gardens were opened to the public in 1984 following a
extensive restoration programme. The palace and gardens are surrounded by
650ha/1 626-acre **park** ⊘.

HISTORICAL NOTES

When **William III** (1650-1702), Prince of Orange and Stadtholder of the Unite
Provinces bought the 14C-15C castle, Het Oude Loo in 1684, this ardent huntsma
was fulfilling a lifetime's dream. In 1685 the first stone of Het Loo Palace was lai
about 300yd from the site of the old castle, by William's wife Princess **Mary**
daughter to James II. The palace was intended for the princely couple with their cou
and guests, as well as their large hunt. The presence of spring water made it possib
to provide water for horses and dogs and decorate the gardens with fountain
Situated in the heart of the Veluwe and abounding in game, it had a privilege
location.
The Royal Academy of Architecture in Paris supplied the plans for the palace whi
Jacob Roman (1640-1716), pupil of Pieter Post, was probably the main architect. Th
interior decoration and the design of the gardens were commissioned from **Dan
Marot** (1661-1752), a Parisian Huguenot, who probably arrived in Holland short
after the Revocation of the Edict of Nantes (1685).
In 1689 William III was proclaimed King of England after his father-in-law and uncl
James II, had fled the country. Het Loo Palace was to become a royal palace, and ha
to be enlarged: the colonnades which linked the main part of the building to the wing
were replaced by four pavilions and the gardens were further embellished.

1684	**William III**, Prince of Orange and Stadtholder of the United Province buys Het Oude Loo.
1685	Building starts at Het Loo. Revocation of the Edict of Nantes.
1688-97	War of the League of Augsburg.
1689	William and Princess Mary crowned King and Queen of England.
1692	An extension is made to the palace.
1694	Queen Mary dies in England.
1702	The Stadtholder-King William III dies without a successor.
1747-1751	**William IV**, son of John William Friso, hereditary Stadtholder of th United Provinces.
1751-95	**William V**, son of the precedent stadtholder.
1795	Conquest of the country by the French army; William V flees to Englan Het Loo siezed by the French, suffers from the destructive rage of th soldiers.
1795-1806	The Batavian Republic.

1806-10	Louis Bonaparte, King of Holland, puts rough-cast on the palace façade and commissions an English-style park.
1810	The Kingdom of Holland becomes part of the French Empire.
Oct. 1811	Emperor Napoleon stays briefly in Het Loo Palace.
1815	Het Loo, now State property, is offered to **King William I** as a summer residence.
1840	In Het Loo Palace, William I abdicates in favour of his son **William II**.
1849-90	Reign of **William III**.
1890-8	Regency of **Queen Emma**.
1898	Reign of **Wilhelmina**, only daughter of William III and Emma.
1901	Marriage of Queen Wilhelmina to Duke Henry of Mecklenburg-Schwerin.
1904-14	The State decides to extend and refurbish the palace.
1948	Abdication of Queen Wilhelmina, who retires to Het Loo Palace.
1962	Death of Queen Wilhelmina.
1967-75	Princess Margriet, daughter of Queen Juliana, and her family were the last members of the royal family to live in Het Loo.
1969	Queen Juliana donates the palace to the nation and it is decided to create a museum.
1977-84	Restoration of the palace and gardens.
June 1984	Opening of the **National Museum**.

TOUR ⏱ *about 3hr*

It is advisable to choose a sunny day to visit the palace in order to appreciate certain poorly lit rooms.

After having walked alongside the **royal stables** (fine series of vintage cars and sleighs, late 19C to early 20C) one reaches a wide avenue, where the beech trees form a magnificent vault; then one reaches the vast brick building flanked with long wings which surrounds the main courtyard.

A grille, painted blue and gold, closes the main courtyard, where a fountain decorated with dolphins was used to water the horses.

The finely proportioned building, built on a north-south axis, is impressive for its severe sobriety, characteristic of the Dutch Baroque style. The only decorative elements are the tympana in sandstone of hunting scenes, and the window sills. The east pavilions were intended for Queen Mary while those situated to the west included those of the King Stadtholder William III. The sash windows of the main part of the building and the pavilions were a novelty often believed to be a Dutch invention and characteristic of English Georgian style.

East Wing – It contains a collection of historic documents, ceramics, paintings and prints as well as objets d'art regarding the most illustrious members of the House of Orange. Many of the documents were written in French, the language used by the Dutch court until the regency of Queen Emma (1890).

West Wing – On the ground floor there is a video film show on the history of the palace and its restoration.

On the first floor the **Museum of the Chancery of the Netherlands Orders of Knighthood** (Museum van de Kanselarij der Nederlandse Orden) exhibits insignia, uniforms, Dutch and foreign Orders.

★ **Apartments** – *Access by a staircase on the side of the steps leading to the main building.*

From the vaulted cellars a staircase leads up to the **great hall** (**1**) where two 17C garden vases, after drawings by Daniel Marot, are exhibited.

The **old dining room** (**2**) is hung with 17C Antwerp tapestries. Note the cabinet (Antwerp, 1630), with biblical scenes painted by Frans Francken the Younger.

The remarkable **new dining room**★★★ (**3**) (c 1692) is a very good example of Marot's contribution to the palace's interior decoration. The white columns and pilasters, decorated with gold bands and the coffered ceiling give this room, hardly bigger than the old dining room, a majestic character. On the walls, the Brussels tapestries (c 1690) depict the armorial bearings and monograms of William III and his Queen, as well as a mirror (1689), in finely carved gilded wood, which came from Honselersdijk Kasteel (south of The Hague; the castle has since been demolished).

Here, as in other rooms, there are some admirable Dutch chairs (late 17C) with their high backs of finely worked wood.

At the end of the **white hall** (**4**) which has portraits of members of the Nassau famil who lived in Friesland, a staircase leads up to the **chapel** (**5**) where **organ concerts** (are held. The coffered stucco ceiling is by Marot. The Bible exhibited is a gift fro the Dutch people to their King, William III, who had shown generosity during th 1861 floods. It was in this chapel that many Dutch filed past to bid farewell Queen Wilhelmina (her funeral took place in Delft).

Go back down the stairs and take the left corridor.

At the end of the corridor and on the left **Prince William IV's Chamber** (**6**), a luminou room due to the yellow silk damask, has, apart from portraits of the stadtholde and his wife Anne of Hanover, Princess of England, daughter of George II, a cryst chandelier (c 1747) decorated with the coat of arms of the United Provinces ar those of William and Anne.

The walls of the **Frisian Cabinet** (**7**), opposite, are covered with gilded leather (18C portraits of the Frisian Nassaus.

On the first floor one passes through the **library** (**9**), laid out after Marot's drawing and decorated with a stucco ceiling inlaid with mirrors, to reach the **gallery** (**10** In its lovely decor of panelling and green damask, this gallery, with magnificer chandeliers, contains a lovely collection of paintings. Next to the window givir onto the main courtyard, there are portraits of René de Chalon and his wife Ann of Lotharingia (1542); William the Silent (two first portraits on the left) inherite the Principality of Orange from René de Chalon. Adriaen van de Venne (158 1662) has depicted the sons and nephews of William the Silent on horseback. C either side of the chimney there are William III and Mary, King and Queen England, Ireland and Scotland, by G Kneller, a German artist working at th English court. The portrait above the chimney showing the king stadtholder c horseback, is a study for a large painting exhibited in Hampton Court in Londo After having crossed the **drawing room** of the **Stadtholder William V** (**11**) where porcelain chandelier from Berlin hangs from the stucco ceiling, and portrai

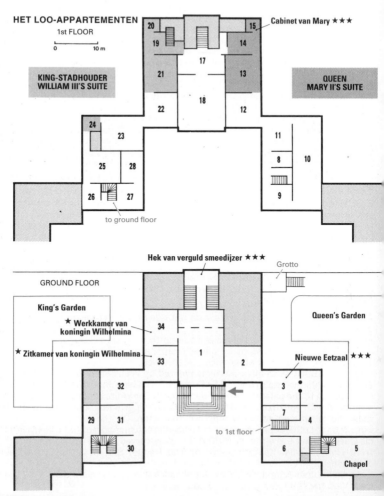

(1795) of William V and his wife, Princess Wilhelmina by John Hoppner, one enters the drawing room of the first Dutch King, **William I (12)**. The Empire chairs, covered in blue and gold cloth, were made in the Dutch workshop of A Eeltjes (1751-1836) for Het Loo Palace at the request of Louis Napoleon. On the walls there are portraits of the king and his daughter Marianne.

Move on to visit the apartments of Queen Mary and the King Stadtholder William III, reconstructed in their 17C layout.

In **Mary Stuart's Bedroom (13)** the sumptuous canopied four-poster bed (c 1685) is covered in Genova velvet; it comes from Kensington Palace in London, where Mary lived. The table, the two pedestal tables and the mirrors in silver and gilt silver (c 1700) are the work of an Augsburg gold and silversmith, J Bartermann. The decoration on the ceiling, where the four elements and the four cardinal virtues are depicted, is by the painter Gerard de Lairesse (1641-1721).

Mary Stuart's Dressing-room (14), where the walls are covered with 17C Dutch tapestries, adjoins the **Queen's Antechamber★★★ (15)**, which is decorated mainly in red and green. This lovely little room, where Mary had a splendid view over the gardens, has a lacquer cabinet (1690) made in England as well as Delft and Chinese porcelain.

The **great staircase (17)**, designed by Marot, has been reconstructed by W Fabri at the request of Queen Wilhelmina. The landscapes on the walls of the **great hall (18)** were painted by J Glauber (1646-1726); this room with lovely grisailles on a golden background is where King William I abdicated in 1840.

A passage with gilt leather hangings (**19**) leads to the **King Stadtholder William III's Closet (20)**. There is a fine Dutch writing desk (late 17C). In **William III's Bedroom (21)** the colours of the wall hangings are again blue and gold, the colours of the House of Orange-Nassau.

The next room (**22**) was laid out according to the taste of **King William II**, with neo-Gothic rosewood furniture (c 1845). On the right of the king's portrait, there is a portrait of his wife, Grand Duchess Anna Pavlovna, by JB van der Hulst.

When reconstituting **Sophia's Drawing Room (23)**, Princess of Württemberg and first wife of William III (1817-90), the watercolours painted at the queen's request, which depict the rooms she occupied, were an excellent reference. The 19C German artist Franz Xaver Winterhalter painted the portrait of Queen Sophia in a dark green dress.

The small room (**24**) which gives on to the King's Garden was the **King Stadtholder William III's Closet**. At the request of the sovereign, Melchior d'Hondecoeter (1639-c 1695) painter of still-life and animals, decorated the mantelpiece. The furnishings in **King William III's Bedroom** (1817-90) (**25**) are in walnut and ebony, inlaid with ivory, brass, mother-of-pearl and semi-precious stones.

The following three small rooms contain, respectively, objects relating to **Prince Henry** (1820-79) (**26**), brother of William III, a **collection of watercolours (27)** (note the painting on the left showing the palace's rear façade with the English garden) and toys and furniture which had belonged to **Queen Wilhelmina** as a child (**28**).

On the ground floor **Queen Sophia's Closet (29)** has been fitted out in Moorish style. There is also the **trophy room (30)** of Prince Henry, husband of Queen Wilhelmina. On the left of the windows there is the prince in hunting costume (1917) by J Kleintjes.

Queen Emma's Drawing Room (31), second wife of William III, and that of **Prince Henry (32)** are furnished according to the tastes of the time. The palace visit ends with **Queen Wilhelmina's Drawing Room and Office★ (33 and 34)** arranged as they were when she was alive. The statuette on the chimney in the second room is of Gaspard de Coligny (father to William the Silent's fourth wife, Louise) who led the Huguenot army in the 16C.

Go down to the vaulted cellars, then pass between the two staircases and turn right, then left to reach the gardens.

On your way, do not miss seeing the small **kitchen** covered in Delft tiles. Queen Mary used this room, when she prepared jam with fruit from her garden. The small **grotto**, restored, has shells, fine stones and marble decoration.

★ Gardens - *Go up to the terrace.*
The superb **garden gate (hek van verguld vmeedijzer)★★★** in gilded wrought iron used to provide access to the terrace. It took one year for a Dutch craftsman to recreate this masterpiece designed by D Marot by resorting to the techniques used in those days. Under the crown can be seen the initials of William and Mary (W and M), and in the lower part, orange trees and acanthus leaves.

The terrace, flanked by two statues in sandstone, symbolising the rivers which edge the Veluwe, affords a fine view over the gardens (6.5ha/16 acres).

Documents of the time as well as traces discovered under the layers of sand in the 19C English garden have made it possible to reconstitute the 17C gardens. In addition the choice of plants decorating the flower beds has been limited to species known at the time.

Statue of Venus, central fountain

There are four gardens:

The **lower garden**, surrounded on three sides by terraces, consists of four *parterre de broderie* (embroidery-like pattern) and four English-style parterres decorated with statues representing Flora and Bacchus *(east side)*, Apollo and Venus receiving a golden apple from Paris *(west side)*. The Venus adorning the central fountain is the replica of a statue by Gaspar Marsy (1625-81) which is in Versailles. Note the terrestrial and celestial globes; the first reflects the world as it was known in Europe at the end of the 17C, whereas the positioning of the second corresponds to that of the sky above Het Loo at the birth of Princess Mary Stuart. The waterfall in the middle of the east slope is decorated with a very graceful statue of Narcissus gazing at himself in the water, the copy of a work by the Belgian sculptor Gabriel de Grupello (1644-1730).

Beyond the path lined with a double row of oak trees which led to Het Oude Loo (a few turrets can be seen) extends the **upper garden**. This is delimited by colonnades – go up the staircase to see the view – and among the large trees in the English-style garden, there is a tulip tree, recognisable by its leaves ending not in a point but in a V-shaped notch. The king's fountain symbolises the power of the sovereign William III who wished it to shoot water higher into the air than those of his rival Louis XIV.

Distinguished people have witnessed to the qualities of the water: contrary to the water of Versailles, that of Het Loo was limpid and odourless.

The **King's Garden** *(to the west of the palace)* where blue and orange are the dominant colours, has a lawn, once a bowling green. The lovely Canadian maple tree in the corner of the lawn was a present from Queen Juliana to her mother Wilhelmina.

For the **Queen's Garden** *(to the east of the palace)* of more intimate character with its arbour of greenery, flowers in pastel shades have been chosen, as well as fruit trees (orange, apricot, cherry-plum and morello cherry trees).

MAASTRICHT★★

Limburg
Population 118 933
Michelin map 908 and 211 T 17
Plan of the conurbation in the current Michelin Red Guide Benelux

Once prized for its strategic location at the confines of Belgium and Germany, Maastricht is now the bustling cosmopolitan provincial capital of Limburg. The city was developed on the banks of the great River Maas from which it takes its name. The town is quite distinct from the rest of the country with its bustling pedestrian precincts, its squares with sprawling café terraces and an almost Mediterranean atmosphere, its Mosan-type stone houses and its very un-Dutch hilly hinterland.

A university town since 1976, Maastricht has five faculties, attended by a student population of around 7 000 (in 1991).

HISTORICAL NOTES

The original settlement grew around a fortified bridge built by the Romans on the Roman road from Bavay (in northern France) to Cologne, hence its name which means the Maas crossing (Mosae Trajectum).

St Servatius finding it safer than Tongeren (Belgium) transferred his bishopric here in 382. In 722 Sint-Hubert moved it to Liège. The town already belonged to the Frank kings. In 1204 it passed into the trusteeship of the Duke of Brabant who, in 1283, shared his power with the Prince-Bishop of Liège.

It was given its first defensive walls in 1229.

The sieges of Maastricht – Maastricht having rallied to the Revolt of the Netherlands, the Spanish led by the Duke of Parma, besieged the town in 1579, took it by surprise, devastated it and left only 4 000 people alive.

The United Provinces annexed the town in 1632.

In 1673, 40 000 French, commanded by Louis XVI appeared in front of Maastricht. The siege was terrible, the Dutch defense fierce. England contributed some 6 000 troops under the command of the Duke of Monmouth. But Vauban, who was directing the operations, won a victory for the French who lost 8 000 men on the battlefield, among them **D'Artagnan**, officer of the musketeers.

The French captured Maastricht again in 1748, due to a clever move by Maurice de Saxe, Marshal of Saxony.

Taken by Kleber in 1794, Maastricht was annexed to France, as was Breda.

In 1814 the town became part of the Netherlands kingdom.

In 1830 the garrison resisted against the Belgians, thus obtaining the right to remain part of the Netherlands, but this was only confirmed by the Treaty of London in 1839. The fortifications were partly demolished in 1867.

During the occupation, Maastricht was an important German army communications centre in the west. One of the first towns liberated, in September 1944, only its bridges were damaged.

The Maastricht Treaty – On 10 December 1991, the governments of the 12 EC members reached agreement in Maastricht on political, monetary and economic union. The Treaty on European Union was signed by the heads of government involved in February 1992, again in Maastricht.

Maastricht today – Continuing its tradition of a busy medieval centre on an important trading route, Maastricht is an active industrial centre specialising in ceramics, paper making and cement.

The annual **carnival**★ *(see Calendar of events)* is a highly popular event which draws large crowds of townspeople and visitors to the general merrymaking. The town is also known for its male voice choir, the **Mastreechter Staar**, founded in 1883.

Accommodation

Maastricht has an excellent choice of distinctive hotels and restaurants.

YOUTH HOSTEL

City Hostel De Dousberg – *Dousbergweg 4, 6216 GC Maastricht,* ☎ *(043) 346 67 77, Fax (043) 346 67 55. 250 beds*. On bus routes 55 and 56. It has its own café.

OUR SELECTION

Botticelli – *Papenstraat 11, 6211 LG Maastricht,* ☎ *(043) 352 63 00, Fax (043) 352 63 36. 18 rooms*. As its name suggests, the atmosphere in this quiet hotel a stone's throw from the Vrijthof is very much an Italian one. The panelled walls of this 18C house are decorated with trompe-l'œil paintings, and some of the rooms have fresco-style wall decorations. The furnishings are modern, and the spacious rooms are tastefully decorated. There is a beautiful courtyard garden between the front and back of the building.

d'Orangerie – *Kleine Gracht 4, 6211 CB Maastricht,* ☎ *(043) 326 11 11 Fax (043) 326 12 87. 32 rooms.* This charming hotel is located in two histori buildings near the Maas. The rooms of various sizes still bear traces of th original interior, such as stucco ceilings, marble fireplaces and thick beams The rest of the decor is in classic English and French style, and there is a enclosed garden at the back.

SOMETHING SPECIAL

Derlon – *O.L.-Vrouweplein 6, 6211 HD Maastricht,* ☎ *(043) 321 67 70 Fax (043) 325 19 33. 43 rooms.* This modern hotel near the Onz Lieve Vrouwebasiliek has a unique feature: Roman remains in th cellar. Important relics of a town square, a well and a road from ancien Maastricht were found here during rebuilding. This hotel is literally full o history.

Restaurants

TOWN CENTRE

Petit Bonheur – *Achter de Molens 2,* ☎ *(043) 321 51 09.* This restaurant lie hidden in the heart of the town, and has a rural French feel to it. In summer you can dine at the little tables in the courtyard.

Sukhotai – *Tongersestraat 54,* ☎ *(043) 321 79 46.* Excellent Thai dishe served in suitably oriental surroundings. The patio terrace is used i summer.

Au Coin des Bons Enfants – *Ezelmarkt 4,* ☎ *(043) 321 23 59.* This 16C buildin with its attractive interior offers authentic French cuisine. Meals are served o the terrace in fine weather.

Beluga – *Havenstraat 19,* ☎ *(043) 321 33 64.* This small restaurant in th Stokstraat quarter serves fine French-Tuscan cuisine and specialises in fish The quiet terrace overlooks a small square, Op de Thermen.

Toine Hermsen – *St.-Bernardusstraat 2,* ☎ *(043) 325 84 00.* The culinary hig point of this Burgundian town; a truly excellent restaurant near the Onze Liev Vrouwebasiliek.

RIGHT BANK (Wyck)

Gadjah Mas – *Rechtstraat 42,* ☎ *(043) 321 15 68.* Affordable, high-qualit Indonesian cuisine.

Mediterraneo – *Rechtstraat 73,* ☎ *(043) 325 50 37.* An Italian restauran further along this busy street.

Les Marolles – *Rechtstraat 88a,* ☎ *(043) 325 04 47.* Regional French cuisin in bistro-like surroundings, with long benches, wooden panels and mirrors o the wall.

't Pakhoes – *Waterpoort 4-6,* ☎ *(043) 325 70 00.* This likeable restaurant wa once a warehouse (pakhuis), and has its own terrace.

Brasseries, cafés, bars, coffee shops...

Eetcafé Rilette – *St.-Pietersstraat 54.* A welcoming café with art on the walls an a French and Italian menu.

Café Sjiek – *St.-Pietersstraat 13.* Despite its trendy-sounding name, a relaxe kind of place serving food like grandmother used to make. The terrace in th municipal park is a great place to sit in summer.

Café Bistro 't Liewke – *Grote Gracht 62.* This attractive old house near th Vrijthoftheater makes an excellent venue for an evening out, with its intimat decor and Italian-inspired food.

Practical information

General information – The VVV, or tourist office, is at Het Dinghuis, Klein Staat 1, 6211 ED Maastricht, ☎ (043) 325 21 21. It offers details of loca sights, events, cultural activities, and bargain accommodation packages. Th **reservations department** on ☎ (043) 321 78 78 will book you a hotel room, an the **VVV Ticket Point**, ☎ (043) 328 08 78, sells tickets for plays, concerts an cultural events.

Transport – Parking is not allowed in the centre of town except wher expressly stated. All **parking spaces** are either metered or **pay-and-display**, and i you do not pay the right amount you risk being clamped. Alternatively, use on of the many well-signposted **multi-storey car parks**.
The main town-centre sights are within walking distance of one another alternatively, you can hire a **bicycle** from Rijwielhandel Courtens, Calvariestraa 16, or the Aon de Stasie cycle shop on Stationsplein.

Tours and walks – The VVV organises walks in the historic town centre during the summer months. Leaflets with details of **self-guided walks** covering particular themes and areas are also available.

Boat trips – From late March to early December, **Rederij Stiphout**, ☎ (043) 325 41 51, organises various trips on the Maas, including day trips to Louvain and candlelight cruises.

Shopping – The best area is between Vrijthof and the station, where late-night shopping is on Thursdays. The best-known (and most expensive) shopping street is the picturesque **Stokstraat**. There are also a large number of art galleries and antique shops.

Terraces in the old town

Markets – There is a **small market** in Marktplein on Wednesdays, and a larger one on Fridays. On Thursdays, the small square with the clock in Stationstraat is the venue for a **farmers' market** selling organic fruit and vegetables, and a **flea market** is held in this street every Saturday.

Theatre and concerts – **Uit in Maastricht** includes detailed listings of all plays, concerts and other events, and is available from the VVV, which also sells tickets (telephone number: *see above*).

Theater aan het Vrijthof, Vrijthof 47, ☎ (043) 350 55 55, is the home of the Limburg Symphony Orchestra; **La Bonbonnière**, Achter de Comedie 1, ☎ (043) 350 09 35, offers performances with dinner included.

Organ concerts are held in various churches in summer, normally on Tuesday and Friday evenings. The town hall **carillon** is played every Friday morning, and on alternate Thursday evenings in summer. The **Mastreechter Staar**, the town's well-known male-voice choir, usually rehearses in the Staargebouw (the former Augustinian church) on Monday and Thursday evenings.

Night-life – Maastricht has various districts, each with its own distinct atmosphere, and all with plenty of bars and restaurants. **Rechtstraat**, on the right bank, is Maastricht's answer to the Rue des Bouchers in Brussels; the **Jekerkwartier** (around the stream called the Jeker) is the town's "Latin Quarter", full of students, artists, theatres, art galleries and bars; while the **historic old town** between Markt, Vrijthof and O.L.-Vrouweplein has numerous bars and places to eat.

Events – There is always something going on in Maastricht. It all starts with the **Grand Carnival**, followed by **Easter in Maastricht**, featuring international big bands, brass bands and choirs. May is the time of the **St Servaasfeest**, or festival of St Servatius, which includes processions and a fair. The **programme of summer events** includes organ and carillon concerts, a pop festival, and street theatre and in late August a Burgundian culinary festival, the **Preuvenmint**, takes place on the Vrijthof. The year ends with the **Festival Musica Sacra** and the town-centre **Christmas market**.

For sports lovers, there is the **Amstel Gold Race**, a cycling event that takes place in spring and begins and ends in Maastricht, and a showjumping event in autumn, **Jumping Indoor Maastricht**.

A number of trade fairs are held at the **MECC** exhibition centre, including the internationally renowned art and antiques fair, **TEFAF**. This specialises in 16C and 17C Dutch and Flemish painting, and also covers textiles, antiquarian books, manuscripts and maps, objects from classical antiquity, 20C art, and jewellery.

★ OLD TOWN *half a day*

Vrijthof – This square is the heart of the town, with a large number of pedestrianised shopping streets radiating out from it. It has many outdoor cafés and restaurants, and is overlooked by two churches, Sint-Servaasbasiliek and Sint-Janskerk.

To the south there is the Gothic façade of the 16C Spanish Government House, **Spaans Gouvernement** ⊘, where William the Silent was declared an outlaw by Philip II of Spain. This former chapter-house has a number of period rooms around an attractive courtyard, with furniture, paintings and collections of silver, porcelain, glass and ceramics dating mainly from the 18C.

★★ Sint-Servaasbasiliek ⊘

– This imposing monument, one of the oldest in the Netherlands, although often altered, was begun c 1000 on the site of a 6C sanctuary. It then had one nave and side aisles, a transept and a flat east end. In the 12C it was enlarged on the one hand by the present chancel, flanked by two square towers and an apse, and, on the other hand, by a monumental **westwork**. The westwork is characteristic of the Rhenish-Mosan style; the basilica is one of the first examples of this style. Topped by two towers, it is decorated with Lombard arcading. There is a carillon in the south tower of the westwork.

I. Hendrikx/GLOBAL PICTURES

Sint-Servaas with a model of the basilica

In the 13C the lovely south portal or **royal portal**★ (Bergportaal) was built and is now painted with vivid colours; the tympanum illustrates the death, ascension and crowning of the Virgin. In the 15C the side chapels and the north portal were added. The north portal gives on to cloisters also built in the 15C.

The whole building underwent extensive restoration on two occasions; in the late 19C and in the years 1981 to 1991.

Interior – On the basilica's entrance portal there is a 15C statue of St Peter.

The **chancel**★ vaults (restored) have recovered their 16C paintings. It is harmonious with its tall pillars and the gallery above the ambulatory.

Inside the westwork, on the first floor, is the Emperor's Room (Keizerszaal), topped by a dome. The **capitals**★ of the westwork are interesting for their rich decoration.

The last chapel on the north aisle, towards the transept, has a Sedes Sapientiae (Seat of Wisdom) and a seated Virgin and Child, of 13C Mosan type. Nearby is a doorway formerly the main access to the church, opening onto cloisters. Outside it is topped by a lovely tympanum depicting Christ in Majesty.

The **crypt**, which is under the nave, contains the tomb of St Servatius behind a grille, the sarcophagus of Charles the Simple (died c 993) who was the son of the Carolingian King, Louis IV d'Outremer, and on the old altar of St Peter, the sarcophagus of the bishops Monulfus and Gondulfus, founders of the primitive church in the 6C, as well as two other bishops, Candidus and Valentinus. The neighbouring crypt with square pillars, under the chancel, belonged to the 6C primitive church.

★★ **Treasury** (Kerkschat) – The collegiate chapel (12C) houses the treasury: a rich collection of liturgical objects, mainly gold and silversmiths' work, ivory, sacerdotal ornaments, paintings, altarpieces and statues.

There is notably a bust of St Servatius, a symbolic silver key decorated with foliated scrolls which would have been given to him by St Peter, the pectoral cross said to have belonged to St Servatius (late 10C), pieces of oriental cloth (c AD 600), as well as a great number of reliquaries and shrines of the late 12C.

The most remarkable object is **St Servatius's shrine** called Noodkist *(illustration: see Introduction: Art)*. In oak, covered with gilded copper, enamelled, chased and decorated with precious stones, it is an important work of the Mosan School (c 1160); at each end Christ and St Servatius are depicted, on the sides, the apostles.

St Janskerk – This Gothic church, Protestant since 1632, was built by the canons of St Servatius to be used as a parish church. Since 1987, it has been used by the Reformist community. Dating from the 12C, it was enlarged in the 15C with a chancel and a tower 70m/230ft high, decorated in the Utrecht style.

Take a few steps along Bonnefantenstraat.

From this street there is a fine viewpoint over a 17C house with crow-stepped gables and the botanical garden of the Natural History Museum, located on the other side of the canal.

Turn back and take Looiersgracht.

Grote Looiersstraat – On this charming shaded square surrounded by old houses, a sculptured group depicts children listening to the popular Maastricht storyteller, Fons Olterdissen.

★ **Walmuur** – The defensive walls still preserved to the south of town and dominated by numerous towers, shaded by beautiful trees and surrounded by pleasant gardens, are one of Maastricht's charms. On the two sections which exist one can go round the watchpath from where there are fine views.

Follow the watchpath, then leave it to take a footbridge crossing the ring canal.

Monseigneur Nolenspark – A lovely park laid out at the foot of the ramparts. Animals (deer etc) are kept in enclosures.

Take the watchpath again.

From the top of the first tower one overlooks the lakes where swans and ducks swim. On the north side of the ramparts one can see the **Bejaardencentrum Molenhof** building. Beside it, near the Jeker, hides an old watermill.

Continuing, one reaches the semicircular tower, **De Vijf Koppen**, where one overlooks a vast lake.

Helpoort – This gate, flanked by two round towers, belonged to the 13C curtain wall. It is the oldest town gate in the country.

Ph. Calic/MICHELIN

Westwork of Onze Lieve Vrouwebasiliek, Maastricht

★ **Onze Lieve Vrouwebasiliek** ⊙ – This is the oldest monument in town. It is thought that it is on the site of an old Roman temple where a cathedral was built at the time when Maastricht was the episcopal see.

The edifice already existed in the year 1000. The very tall **westwork** which precedes the church, as it does at Sint-Servaasbasiliek, dates from this period. It is flanked by two round turrets; its upper part, added c 1200 is decorated with Romanesque blind arcading. The nave and the beautiful apse date from the 12C.

Among interesting sculptures grouped under the left porch of the westwork, note the effigy of a bishop (c 1200).

Inside, the **chancel**★★ with an ambulatory topped by a gallery, thus forming two rows of superimposed columns, like the one at Sint-Servaasbasiliek, is remarkable. Furthermore, the richly decorated capitals are very varied.

The nave, like that of Rolduc Abbey near Kerkrade, has alternating thick and thin pillars supporting the vault, redone in the 18C. The transept was given pointed vaulting in the 15C. The organ case dates from 1652.

Maastricht – the picturesque Stokstraat

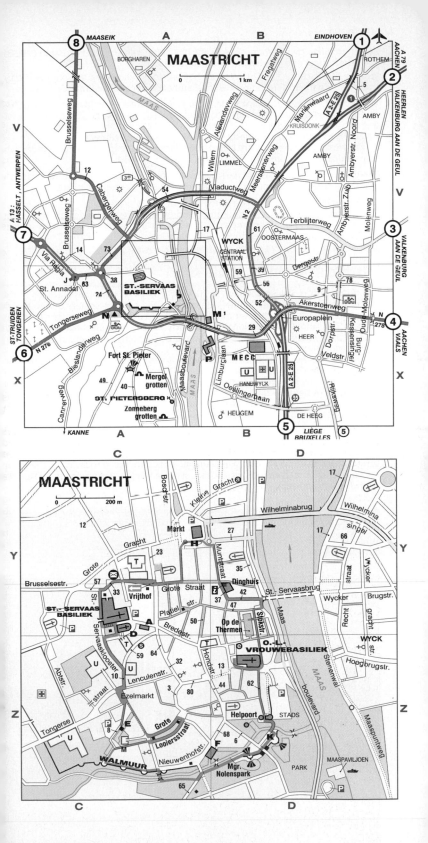

Pedestrian streets are nice for a stroll.
They are indicated on town plans.

The church has two Romanesque **crypts**, one under the transept crossing (1018) the other under the westwork, and 16C cloisters.

Treasury (Kerkschat) ⊘ – The treasury has precious reliquaries and shrines, ivory liturgical ornaments including Bishop Lambert's early 8C dalmatic.

Stokstraat – It is a pleasant pedestrian precinct where the lovely 17C and 18C restored houses, decorated with pediments, façade stones and signs, are now art antique and print shops.

At no 28 there is a façade decorated with sculptured friezes.

To the west, on a small square called **Op de Thermen**, paving stones indicate the site of remains of old Roman baths discovered here in 1840.

Dinghuis – This picturesque narrow-fronted building in the Mosan Renaissance style was formerly the courthouse. It now houses the tourist office.

Markt – On this busy main square a market takes place.

The **Stadhuis**, built between 1659 and 1665 by **Pieter Post**, who designed Huis ten Bosch in The Hague, is an imposing quadrilateral building preceded by a large perron and topped by a bell-tower with a **carillon**.

Return to Vrijthof by the pedestrian precinct crossing the shopping quarter.

THE RIGHT BANK (Wyck and MECC)

The monumental **Sint-Servaasbrug** (1280-1298) is one of the oldest bridges in the country. It crosses to the "other" Maastricht: the narrow streets of the **historic Wyck district** were once the commercial centre of the town. There are still many elegant 17C and 18C mansions, particularly on the long Rechtstraat; most of these are now bars and restaurants. There are also many commercial art galleries and antique shops here.

Further on is a new commercial and residential area, still partly under construction, which shows no traces of the area's rich past. It is home to the Bonnefantenmuseum, the **Maastricht Exhibition and Congress Centre** or MECC, and the **Gouvernment** or government building, built partly on an island, where the European Council met in December 1991. This meeting led to the signing of the Maastricht Treaty on 7 February 1992 in the Statenzaal of the building.

★★ Bonnefantenmuseum ⊘ – This museum re-opened in a new building on the site of a former ceramics factory beside the Meuse in 1995. The simple, E-shaped stone and brick building was designed by Aldo Rossi (1931-77). It has a prominent tower, 28m/90ft high; the Wiebengahal opposite the entrance to the main building is all that remains of an industrial complex dating from 1912 (see Introduction: Industrial heritage).

Bonnefantemuseum, Maastricht

The museum has very varied collections of art and **archeology**. The archeology collection *(first floor, left)* offers an overview of the prehistoric period, including findings from flint mines and human burials from the Bandkeramik period. It also includes items from Roman times (grave goods, wall paintings, funerary monuments and sculptures of deities), and from the early Middle Ages in Limburg.

The **pre-20C art department** *(first floor, right)* includes Southern Netherlandish works by studios and masters including Pieter Brueghel the Younger *(Census at Bethlehem)* and Harry Met de Bles *(Landscape with the Repudiation of Hagar)*, and early Italian panel paintings from Florence, Siena and Venice. There is an important collection of medieval sculpture from the Meuse region (c 1400-1550), dominated by the works of the early 16C Maastricht sculptor Jan van Steffeswert. Also worthy of particular attention are the superb **late medieval art objects***** from the Neutelings collection, which was given to the museum on long-term loan in 1996. The collection amassed by Willem Neutelings (1916-86) is of exceptionally high quality, consisting of complete domestic altars, wood and alabaster altar fragments, delicate ivory diptychs, parts of triptychs, sculpture groups and free-standing copper and bronze figurines. There are some beautifully expressive late-15C alabaster "St John's charger" from Nottingham (the name refers to the beheading of St John the Baptist) and a statue of the Assumption and Coronation of the Virgin Mary, which still bears traces of red and blue paint. There is a bishop's crozier (c 1240) from Limoges, ornamented with enamel, and a 16C Antwerp domestic altar with a centre panel showing Mary and Joseph with the infant Christ in a setting of Gothic architecture, and wings painted by Jan van Dornicke. The collection also includes a movingly simple 12C bronze of Christ Crucified, probably from near Mechelen in Belgium.

Selections from the museum's **modern art collection** are displayed in rotation on the second floor. This includes works by artists who made a name for themselves in the 1960s and 70s, such as Joseph Beuys, Marcel Broodthaers, Robert Mangold, Mario Merz and Sol Le Witt, as well as contemporary artists such as Imi Knoebel, Jan Dibbets, René Daniëls, Didier Vermeiren and Marien Schouten. Every four months, a different artist is commissioned to decorate the domed room in the tower.

A collection of large sculptures is displayed in the Wiebengahal, including a 12-part work in steel by Richard Serra, The Hours of the Day.

ADDITIONAL SIGHTS

Kazematten ⊙ – The casemates are to be found in Waldeckpark. They belonged to a system of fortifications which was built between 1575 and 1825. Most of the fortifications above ground were razed in 1867 but the network *(10km/6mi)* of underground galleries remains. Some of these galleries are open to the public and visitors who are able to tackle the labyrinth of corridors and stairs can visit the **Waldeck Bastion** with its domed vaults, gunpowder stores and lookout posts.

Not far away, near the fortified walls there is a bronze statue of D'Artagnan.

* **Sint-Pietersberg** – *2km/1mi to the south via Sint-Hubertuslaan and Luikerweg.* Between the valleys of the Maas and the Jeker, St Peter's Mount rises to more than 100m/328ft high. It is above all famous for its **caves**, old quarries which have been worked since Roman times. The stone, a sort of marl that hardens on exposure to the air, had been used for building numerous edifices in Maastricht. Today the galleries extend for more than 200km/124mi and are up to 12m/39ft high, and are decorated with charcoal drawings. They were excavated by lowering the floor level so that now the oldest drawings covering the walls are near the roof. The sedimentary rock contains a large number of fossils. In 1780 the head of a Prehistoric animal was found; it was called Mosasaurus *(Mosa:* the Maas). This was confiscated by the French in 1795 and is now on display in the Musée d'Histoire Naturelle in Paris.

During all the troubled periods the caves have been used to shelter the people of Maastricht; they have kept traces of these periods of refuge. This was not always a pleasant experience, since the temperature is about 10°C/50°F and it is very damp.

Fort Sint-Pieter ⊙ – From the fort's (1701) terrace, there is an overall view of the town. The innermost part of the fort is linked to the system of tunnels inside the hill.

Marl caves – northern tunnel system ⊙ – During the Second World War these caves sheltered Rembrandt's painting *The Night Watch*. There are graffiti here and a bas-relief of the Mosasaurus.

Continue along the road then take the second on the left, to reach other caves.

Zonnenberg tunnel system ⊙ – These caves are very similar to the preceding ones, steeped in history and a maze of corridors covered with graffiti.

OUTSKIRTS

Cadier and Keer – *5km/3mi to the east via ④ on the town plan.*
The **Afrika-Centrum** ⊘ exhibits interesting artistic and ethnographic collections concerning western Africa. The **Nederlands Wijnmuseum** ⊘ gives a detailed overview of everything to do with wine-growing and winemaking.

EXCURSIONS

From Meerssen to Susteren – *35km/22mi. Leave via ① on the town plan.*

Meerssen – Former residence of the Frankish kings. In 870 a treaty was signed sharing Lotharingia, the domain of King Lothair II (855-869) between the two brothers Louis the German and Charles the Bald, the King of France (in 879 the whole of Lotharingia came into the hands of the German Emperor).
In the 13C Meerssen attracted the monks from the Abbey of St-Remi in Reims. They built the fine **basilica** of the Blessed Sacrament (13C-14C). The chancel has a richly decorated stone tabernacle in the Flamboyant Gothic style (early 16C).

Stein – Stein is the home of the small **Archeologiemuseum** ⊘, *Hoppenkampstraat 14a*. Built to house a megalithic communal grave, the museum also has collections associated with Prehistoric, Roman and Merovingian sites in the region.

Sittard – Sittard which obtained its charter in 1243, was a very disputed stronghold. A large part of the town is still surrounded by ramparts. It is a busy commercial and industrial town (chemistry, electrical engineering, Volvo automobile factory).
Among the numerous festivities in the town, note in particular the carnival *(see Practical information)*.
On the **Markt**, the main square, there stands Sint-Michielskerk, in the 17C Baroque style, and a picturesque half-timbered house with a corbelled gable built c 1500.
In Rosmolenstraat, **Kritzraedthuis** is a lovely bourgeois house of 1620 where temporary exhibitions are held.
The 14C Grote Kerk or **Sint-Petruskerk** ⊘ has carved wood Gothic stalls, which are probably the oldest in the country.

Susteren – **Sint-Amelbergakerk** ⊘, an old abbey church, was built in the Romanesque style probably during the first half of the 11C.
The nave, very simple, covered with a flat ceiling, leans on square pillars alternating with squat columns. The crypt, outside the apse was probably inspired by that of Essen Cathedral in Germany. It contains an 8C sarcophagus and a 13C calvary.

Every year,
the **Michelin Red Guides** *are updated for those who appreciate fine dining, selected restaurants, local wines and specialities.*
The guide lists a range of establishments from the simplest to the most elegant, those with local flavour and the best value for the cost.
Plan better and save money by investing in this year's guide.

MARKEN★

Noord-Holland

Michelin maps 908 G 4 and 210 P 8

Separated from the continent in the 13C during the formation of the Zuiderzee, Marken was an island 2.5km/1.5mi from the shore until 1957. Now connected to the mainland, it is on the edge of the Gouwzee, a sort of inland sea. Marken, whose population is Protestant, has from the beginning, formed a close community. It has kept its atmosphere of days past with its wooden houses and townspeople who, in season, wear the traditional costume.
Before the IJsselmeer was created, the population earned its living from fishing; today it lives partly from tourism.

★ **The village** – The village consists of two quarters: Havenbuurt, near the port and Kerkbuurt, around the church. In the past, it was subject to regular flooding, so the houses were grouped on small mounds and built on piles. When there was a threat of flood, the openings under the houses were closed. Most of the houses are painted dark green, with slightly corbelled side gables. The **interiors** ⊘, painted and polished, are richly decorated with ceramics and ornaments. The box beds have a drawer which was used as a cradle.

Ph. Gajic/MICHELIN

Traditional costume, Marken

Costumes – The women wear a wide skirt and a black apron over a striped petticoat. The striped blouse, worn in summer, is covered with a corselet and a printed front. The headdress is just a gaily coloured lace and cotton skullcap from which a fringe of starched hair sometimes sticks out like a peak. The men wear a short vest, baggy trousers tightened at the knees and black socks. The children more rarely wear a costume; boys and girls wear a skirt and bonnet, only the shapes and colours differ. The costume worn on feast days, and particularly at Whitsun, is more elaborate.

Marker Museum ⓥ – *Kerkbuurt 44.* This small exhibition on the history of Marken is located in four fishermen's houses, once used for smoking herrings and eels.

MEDEMBLIK

Noord-Holland

Population 7 317

Michelin maps 908 G 3 and 210 P 6

Medemblik received its charter in 1289, when it became the capital of West Friesland. It was then part of the Hanseatic League. Today it is one of the ghost towns of the former Zuiderzee region.

The dike that limits the Wieringermeer polder to the east starts at Medemblik. To the north of the town, the Ir Lely pumping station is the most important one used to dry out the polder.

An old **steam tram** links the town to Hoorn and a boat service operates between Medemblik and Enkhuizen.

SIGHTS

Nieuwstraat – One of the most charming features of Medemblik is its main street, Nieuwstraat, which still has several old houses with pretty stone façades. At no 26 stands an unusual house: its 1613 façade presents a lintel decorated with four coats of arms.

The **Waag**, or weigh-house, at the end of the street boasts a façade with crow-stepped gables, embellished with a carved façade stone depicting a pair of scales.

Westerhaven – This quay, stretching along one of the port's two main basins (Westerhaven means western basin) retains several fine houses: nos 9-14, with crow-stepped gables, and nos 16-20.

In Torenstraat, which begins at Westerhaven, the old orphanage, **Weeshuis**, has a gateway surmounted by a low relief depicting four orphans (18C).

* Oosterhaven – Along the quay skirting this basin – Oosterhaven means eastern basin – stand a great many old façades: nos 22, 43 and 44 have carved stones. The far end of the quay affords a pleasant view of IJsselmeer.

Kasteel Radboud – The castle stands on the opposite side of Oosterhaven. It was built in the 8C by Radboud, King of Friesland. Around 1288 the Count of Holland Floris V fortified and altered the castle to keep the newly subjugated Frisians in check. Only one restored part exists today, surrounded by moats, the rest having been destroyed in the 17C and 18C.
The castle houses a small museum of archeological finds.

Nederlands Stoommachinemuseum – *Oosterdijk 4.* The imposing steam pumping station that houses this museum was used to drain the polder behind it until 1976. Today, it has an interesting collection of steam-operated machinery *(see Introduction: Industrial heritage).* The machines operate one weekend a month from April to October.

A new concept in travel planning.

When you want to calculate a trip distance or visualise a detailed itinerary ; when you need information on hotels, restaurants or campsites, consult Michelin on the Internet

Visit our Web site to discover our full range of services for travellers :
www.michelin-travel.com

MENKEMABORG★★
Groningen
Michelin maps 408 L 1 and 210 Z 2

This **castle** stands to the east of Uithuizen *(see GRONINGEN: Excursions)* and is screened by tall trees with a heronry, where herons nest from February to June. There are over 100 nests. The castle, originally a small defensive tower, expanded into a castle over the centuries. It is surrounded by a moat and a typically Dutch garden laid out in Renaissance and Baroque tradition; the grounds also feature a maze, an orchard and a vegetable garden.
The oldest part (14C) of the building, with only a few small windows, was extended by the addition of two wings in the 17C and 18C.
The interior is pleasantly furnished and decorated and gives some idea of how the local nobility lived during the 17C and 18C. The kitchen in the basement occupies the oldest part of the castle. In the other rooms note the 1700 oak chimney-pieces sumptuously carved with acanthus leaves, cherubs and female figures, portraits of past owners, a four-poster bed by Daniel Marot *(see Het LOO)* and lovely pieces of 17C Chinese porcelain.

The Menkemaborg

MIDDELBURG★

Zeeland ℙ

Population 44 668
Michelin map 908 B 7 or 211 G 14
Local map see DELTA

Middelburg is an old fortified town, with canals marking what used to be its outer limits. Two 18C wall mills still stand.

HISTORICAL NOTES

Formerly Middelburg was a prosperous commercial city, with its cloth trade and its imports of French wine from Argenteuil and Suresnes, shipped from the port of Rouen to Rouaansekaai.

The Sea Beggars captured it in 1574. In 1595 and 1692 the town was given its first line of fortifications with bastions. These have remained more or less intact up to the present, but the only old gate which remains is **Koepoort** to the north.

It is said that a spectacle manufacturer of Middelburg, Zacharias Jansen invented the microscope in 1590 and the telescope in 1604. However, some people prefer to attribute the invention of the microscope to Van Leeuwenhoek.

Middelburg continued to prosper in the 17C and 18C due to the Dutch East India Company which had a trading post here.

In 1940 heavy German bombing destroyed the historic centre of the town. Its monuments have been rebuilt and it remains the great Walcheren market.

In July and August, on the Molenwater, one can watch a **ringrijderij**, a sort of tournament where the aim is to unhook a ring. On Vismarkt, in summer *(Thursdays)*, there is an antiques market.

THE HEART OF TOWN

★ **Stadhuis** ⊘ – Overlooking **Markt** or main square, where the market takes place *(Thursdays)*, this imposing building, begun in 1452 by two members of the Kelder-mans family from Mechelen (Belgium), is inspired by the Brussels town hall. Almost wholly destroyed by fire in May 1940, it has been rebuilt in the same style.

The main façade is remarkable with its 10 first-floor, Gothic windows with finely worked tympana. Between each window double niches have statues, remade in the 19C, depicting the counts and countesses of Zeeland back to back. The roof is decorated with three tiers of dormer windows and, on the left, an elaborately pinnacled gable. The central perron was added in the 18C.

An octagonal turret, finely decorated and flanked by an openwork balustrade in the 17C, stands on the right.

A highly distinctive belfry 55m/180ft high is quartered by four pinnacles and dominates the whole.

The interior contains antique furnishings, in particular the immense **Burgerzaal**, the former cloth hall.

Behind the town hall there is a lovely restored chapel called the English Church, **Engelse Kerk**.

★ **Abbey** – Today the seat of the provincial government of Zeeland, this vast monastic building was, in the 12C a Premonstrant abbey (order founded by St Norbert in 1120), a dependance of St Michael in Antwerp. It was secularised after the capture of the town by the Sea Beggars.

To the east, the defensive gate, the **Gistpoort** on Damplein, has a lovely 16C façade showing a strong Gothic influence.

Historama Middelburg ⊘ – The history of the abbey and the monks, knights and princes who lived there is

Stadhuis

J. P. Lescourret/PIX

MIDDELBURG

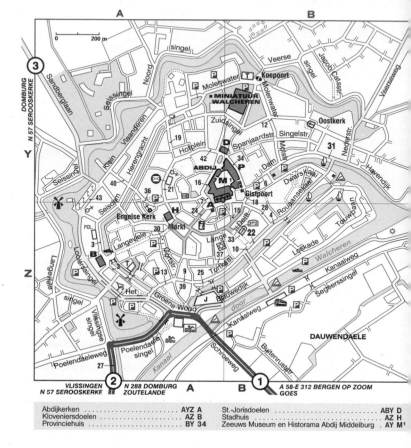

chronicled in a fascinating display in the medieval passageways and rooms of the monastery. The crypts show the daily lives of the monks, and a 20min video tells how the island of Walcheren, the town of Middelburg and the abbey itself came into being. There is a herb garden in the courtyard, and you can also see the bones of a mammoth that lived in Zeeland 10 000 years ago.

Abbey churches ⊘ – To the south of the abbey standing side by side are two churches. The **Koorkerk** with a 14C nave and apse has a 15C organ, whose case was renovated in the 16C. The 16C **Nieuwe Kerk** holds organ concerts in summer.

Against the former leans the tower known as **Lange Jan** ⊘ (Tall Jan). This 14C octagonal construction in stone, crowned with a small 18C onion-shaped dome, is 85m/279ft high. From the top there is a fine view over the abbey, the town and its canals.

★ **Zeeuws Museum** ⊘ – The Zeeland Museum has been laid out in the old hostelry of the abbey which is flanked by fine turrets. It has very varied regional collections. The archeological section focuses on the Celtic goddess **Mehallenia**; several votive steles dating from Roman times were found in 1647 in Domburg and in 1970 at Colijnsplaat (island of Noord-Beveland). The goddess is usually shown sitting, wearing a long dress and a wide-brimmed hat, accompanied by a dog and carrying a basket of fruit.

There is also a collection of fossils and animal bones discovered at the mouth of the Scheldt, and an 18C roomful of rarities where notably a planetarium can be seen.

Several of the fine series of local late-16C and early-17C **tapestries** illustrate Zeeland naval victories over the Spanish.

There are also collections of 17C and 18C decorative art, including furniture, Zeeland silverware, Chinese porcelain and Delftware, and of local costumes (*illustration: see Introduction: Traditions and folklore*). There is a painting collection, comprising work by old masters and by artists who found inspiration in Zeeland, including Jan and Charley Toorop and Jacoba van Heemskerck. Contemporary art from Zeeland is also represented.

ADDITIONAL SIGHTS

Kloveniersdoelen – It is the former arquebusiers' mansion, built in 1607 and 1611 in the Flemish Renaissance style. Since 1795 it has been used as a military hospital. It has a very wide façade in brick streaked with white stone and brightened by painted shutters. The central voluted gable bears a sculptured low relief of arquebuses, cannon-balls and topped by an eagle. Behind is an octagonal turret with an onion-shaped dome.

* **Miniatuur Walcheren** ⊘ – It is an open-air scale model of Walcheren Peninsula with its roads, dikes, ports and main buildings, made to a scale of 1: 20. Opposite stands the austere Koepoort (1735).

The quays – The **Rotterdamsekaai, Rouaansekaai** and **Londensekaai** are lined with fine rows of 18C houses, witness to the prosperity of that time.

Oostkerk – This octagonal church with an onion-shaped dome is of a fairly usual type among 17C Protestant buildings. **Pieter Post** was one of the architects who built it between 1646 and 1667.

Sint-Jorisdoelen – These old premises of the civic guard dating from 1582 were rebuilt in the original style in 1970. Its central voluted gable is topped by a statue of St George (Sint Joris).

EXCURSION

Round tour of the Walcheren Peninsula – *49km/30mi – allow 2hr – local map see DELTA. Leave by ③ on the town plan.*

Domburg – This seaside resort with a large beach situated at the foot of high dunes is very popular. To the west, the top of the highest dune offers an interesting **view** over Domburg and the coast.
The route follows the dunes which isolate Walcheren Peninsula from the sea. A few farmhouses surrounded by a curtain of trees line the route.

Westkapelle – This town is on the western point of Walcheren, where the dunes are not strong enough to hold out against currents and are reinforced by a **dike**. This extends over 4km/2.5mi and its highest crest is 7m/23ft above sea level. In 1944 it was bombarded by the Allies, which caused flooding of the island and made it possible to evict the Germans. In 1945 the breaches were repaired. Westkapelle, a family seaside resort, has a beach facing south. The **lighthouse** is on the top of the bell-tower of an old Gothic church which was destroyed by fire.

Zoutelande – Small seaside resort.

Vlissingen – *See VLISSINGEN.*

Return to Middelburg by ② on the town plan.

The Strand, Zoutelande

255

NAARDEN★

Noord-Holland
Population 16 797
Michelin maps 908 G 5 and 210 P 9
Local map see HILVERSUM

Naarden used to be the capital of the Gooi *(see HILVERSUM)*. It was formerly about 3km/2mi to the northeast of its present position, but was burned down in the civil war between the Cods and the Hooks in 1350. As it had been prone to flooding, it was rebuilt further inland. Naarden became an important stronghold, taken by the Spanish in 1572, then by the French in 1673.

Today it is a small, peaceful town, still circled by its extensive 17C **fortifications**★ shaped as a 12-pointed star with six bastions surrounded by a double ring of walls and canals.

Jan Amos Komensky, better known as **Comenius** (1592-1670), the educational reformer, was buried in Naarden. The town was also the birthplace of **Salomon van Ruisdael**, the famous 17C landscape painter.

SIGHTS

★ **Stadhuis** ⊙ – The fine Renaissance-style town hall with crow-stepped gables dates from 1601. The interior is embellished with old furniture; it contains 17C paintings and a scale model of the 17C fortifications.

Grote Kerk ⊙ – This Gothic church is dedicated to St Vitus. Inside, the wooden barrel vaulting is decorated with beautiful 16C **paintings**★ of scenes from the Old and New Testaments. From the top of the 45m/150ft tower (235 steps) there is an impressive **view**★ of the fortifications and, in fine weather, of Amersfoort, Amsterdam and Hilversum in the distance.

Exclusive shopping in a military arsenal

If you're interested in art, design and/or fine food, don't miss Het Arsenaal (Kooltjesbuurt 1). This 17C complex, formerly used to store weapons and ammunition, was converted into a design centre by the furniture designer Jan des Bouvrie in 1993. An elegant courtyard garden is surrounded by exclusive shops, a restaurant and a gallery of modern art. Elsewhere, there are many interesting small shops in Marktstraat and Cattenhagestraat.

Comenius Museum ⊙ – *Kloosterstraat 33.*
The collections displayed here illustrate the life and work of the Czech humanist. Born in Moravia, Comenius became bishop of the Bohemian or Moravian Brothers in 1648. Persecuted, he fled to Poland, then in 1656 went to Amsterdam, where he died. He devoted himself primarily to educational research.
Founder of the pedagogic methods concerning the development of a child's individual observation, a strong advocate of more stimulating teaching methods, he was one of the first to recommend education for all. His tomb can be seen in the **Comenius Mausoleum** ⊙ in the former Wallonian chapel.

Het Spaanse Huis – *Turfpoortstraat 27.*
The façade stone of this building (1615) depicts the massacre of the townspeople by the Spanish in 1572; hence its name, The Spanish House.

★ **Nederlands Vestigingmuseum** ⊙ – *Westwalstraat 6.*
The five pillboxes of one of the bastions *(Turfpoort)* have been transformed into a fortress museum. Cannons and other weapons, uniforms, engravings and an audio-visual presentation retrace the eventful history of Naarden. Highlights of the museum include the 61m/206ft long passageway intended to be used to listen to the enemy at night, and demonstrations of cannon firing *(information at entrance)*.

MICHELIN GREEN TOURIST GUIDES
Landscapes
Monuments
Scenic routes, touring programmes
Geography
History, Art
Places to stay
Town and site plans
Practical information

NIJMEGEN*

Gelderland
Population 147 206
Michelin maps 908 I 6 and 211 T 11
Plan of the conurbation in the current Michelin Red Guide Benelux

The only town in the Netherlands built on several hills, Nijmegen is the gateway to the delta region, due to its location on the Waal, main branch of the Rhine, and near the canal, the Maas-Waalkanaal.

HISTORICAL NOTES

An old Batavian oppidum, Nijmegen was conquered by the Romans under Emperor Augustus then burnt down in AD 70 by the Roman, Cerialis, General of Emperor Vespasian who was trying to quell the **Batavian revolt** stirred up the year before by **Gaius Julius Civilis**. It subsequently became a prosperous Roman city called Ulpia Novioma-gus. Nijmegen was one of Charlemagne's favourite places to stay and he built himself a castle on the present Valkhof. In the Middles Ages the town expanded west of this castle.

In the 14C it became a member of the Hanseatic League. In 1585 it was taken by Alessandro Farnese, Duke of Parma, but recaptured in 1591 by Maurice of Nassau.

The peace of Nijmegen – After the French, under the leadership of Turenne, captured it without difficulty in 1672, Nijmegen gave its name to three treaties which were signed there between France, the United Provinces, Spain (1678) and the German Empire (1679). They mark the peak of Louis XIV's reign who, at the outcome of the war against the United Provinces, which had started in June 1672, annexed to France the Franche-Comté and a part of Flanders. The United Provinces remained intact. It was during the preliminary conferences for these treaties that the French language began to impose itself as the diplomatic language (despite this the treaties were written in Latin as was customary).

In February 1944 the town was bombarded by the Americans. At the time of the Battle of Arnhem in September, Nijmegen was in the midst of heavy fighting. The bridge over the Waal, Waalbrug, built in 1936, which the Germans were threatening to destroy, was saved by a young inhabitant of the town, Jan van Hoof. A tablet to his memory has been put up in the centre of the bridge, on the east side. A **monument** at the southern end of the bridge commemorates the liberation of the town.

The Netherlands Catholic University founded in 1923 has been, since 1949, installed in a campus to the south of the town on the road to Venlo.

Nijmegen is the birthplace of **St Peter Canisius** (1521-97); he was named doctor of the church, when he was canonised in 1925.

Boat trips ⊘ – They are organised on the Waal.

SIGHTS

Grote Markt – In the centre of the square the **Waag**★, built in 1612 in the Renaissance style, has a lovely façade with a perron where the red and black colouring of the shutters and the somber red brick make an attractive combination. The ground floor is now a restaurant.

There is also a bronze statue of **Mariken van Nieumeghen**, heroine of a late 15C religious drama in which, seduced by the devil, she followed him for seven years before repenting. The hands of the statue have three iron rings with which the Pope had ordered Mariken to chain her neck and arms. They loosened themselves, when she had atoned for her sin.

Near the weigh-house there is a group of four 17C houses. One, the **Kerkboog** is identifiable by its decorated gable (1605) above a vaulted passage; the passage leads to Sint-Stevenskerk.

Near the chevet of the church, the old **Latijnse School** is a fine building of 1554.

Sint-Stevenskerk ⊘ – This large 13C Gothic church, enlarged in the 15C, is flanked by a massive square tower with an octagonal onion-shape domed pinnacle (1604) which has an 18C **carillon** ⊘.

The interior contains some lovely **furnishings**: the back of the door of the south arm of the transept (1632), the local gentry's pews in the Renaissance style by Cornelis Hermansz Schaeff of Nijmegen and the Renaissance pulpit by Joost Jacobs.

Note also the 18C princes' pew decorated with the armorial bearings of the town (eagles) and the province (lions), the **organ** ⊘ built in the 18C by König and the copper chandeliers.

Tower Access by the west façade. From the top (183 steps) there is a panorama over the town and the Waal. Note an old 15C curtain wall tower in Kronenburger Park.

The church's precinct has been restored; a flea market takes place here on Monday mornings.

To the north there are some lovely houses with gables, **Kannunikenhuizen** or the canons' houses.

Commanderie van Sint-Jan – This 15C and 16C brick building (restored) overlooking the Waal, is an old hospital. Founded in the 12C to shelter pilgrims going to the Holy Land, it came into the possession of the Order of the Hospital of St John of Jerusalem in the following century.

Stadhuis ⓥ – This fine 16C and 17C building, partly destroyed by the bombardments, was restored in 1953. It is flanked by an onion-shaped turret. The exterior is decorated with statues carved by Albert Termote depicting the emperors who were Nijmegen's benefactors or who had played a part in its history. On the corner is a statue of the Virgin.

Inside there are lovely rooms decorated in the old style, the Aldermen's Room (Schepenhal), the Registrar's Office (Trouwzaal). In the Truce Hall, **Trêveszaal**, where the walls are covered with verdure tapestries, the treaties of 1678 and 1679 were signed. In the Council Room (Raadzaal) and the Great Hall (Burgerzaal) hang other tapestries.

Valkhof – This park has been laid out on the site of a castle built by Charlemagne. It took the name of falcon's tower because Louis the Pious, son of Charlemagne and heir to his father's empire, bred falcons here for hunting. The castle rebuilt by Frederick Barbarossa in the 12C was destroyed in the 18C.

Sint-Maartenskapel – In the centre of the park are the remains of the Romanesque chapel of Frederick Barbarossa's castle. There remains a finely decorated oven-vaulted apse at the chancel's entrance, two columns with foliated capitals and blind arcades outside.

★ **Sint-Nicolaaskapel** – Near a terrace from where there is an interesting **view** over the Waal, this old chapel of the Carolingian castle stands hidden behind trees. It was probably modified in the 11C.

It has 16 sides and is topped by an octagonal turret. Inside one can see the pillars which encircle a central octagonal-shaped space. Upstairs there is a gallery with twin bays.

After photo Museum Het Valkhof

Emblem of the bargemen's guild,
Museum Het Valkhof

Belvedere – It is the name of an old watchtower (1640) of the old curtain wall, now converted into a restaurant, the terrace offers a fine **view** over the Waal.

Museum Het Valkhof ⓥ – This new museum designed by Ben van Berkel, deals with the history, art and culture of Nijmegen and Gelderland. In addition to one of the country's largest collections of Roman artefacts and works of art, it also has a fine collection of prehistoric and early medieval antiquities, mostly found during excavations in Nijmegen and the surrounding area. They include a bronze head of Emperor Trajan, silverware, jewellery, coins, glassware, bronze and all kinds of everyday objects. Prints, drawings and paintings help to bring the history of the town to life. There is an interesting triptych by an unknown master showing Christ on the cross with the parents of St Peter Canisius, Jan van Goyen's View of the Valkhof at Nijmegen, and The peace of Nijmegen, painted in 1678 for Louis XIV.

The museum also has a collection of modern and contemporary art, and holds temporary exhibitions.

★ **Nationaal Fietsmuseum Velorama** ⓥ – The national bicycle museum has more than 300 examples from Britain, France, Germany and the United States, illustrating the progress made from the first hobby-horse or Draisine to today's mountain bikes. Velocipedes with wooden wheels, penny-farthings and the American Star with its small front wheel were followed by the British Rover, an ordinary-sized bike with two wheels the same size. Bicycles became much more comfortable to ride after air-filled tyres were introduced in the late 19C, and shortly afterwards the bicycle began to enjoy unprecedented and growing popularity.

On the second floor, there is a small room devoted to old and new Dutch bicycles.

NIJMEGEN

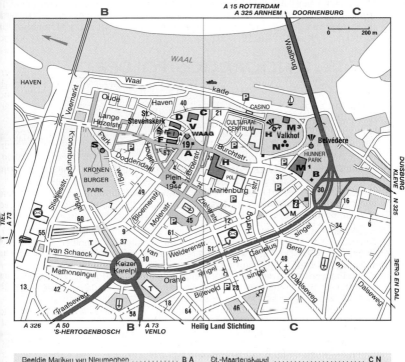

ADDITIONAL SIGHTS

Heilig Land Stichting (Holy Land Foundation) – *4km/2mi to the southeast via Groesbeekseweg*. The open-air Bible Museum, the **Bijbels Openluchtmuseum Heilig Land Stichting** ⏱, is to the north of Groesbeek. It takes you back to the Palestine of biblical times with displays illustrating a variety of aspects – religious, cultural, historical and archeological – of life at the time.

The history of the different peoples of the Bible is recounted in the main building while the open-air section (48ha/120 acres) evokes the country during Jesus' lifetime through a series of reconstructions: the Palestinian village with its synagogue, an inn, a fishing village and the Via Orientalis, a depiction of Jerusalem with its Jewish, Roman, Greek and Egyptian houses.

Bevrijdingsmuseum 1944 Rijk van Nijmegen ⏱ – *Wijlerbaan 4, Groesbeek*. The Liberation Museum is located in the place where Major-General James M Gavin landed with the 82nd Airborne Division on 17 September 1944. Original films, dioramas, photographs and models show events before, during and after the war; they focus on Operation **Market Garden** *(see ARNHEM)*, which is brought to life using a relief model with sound and light effects. In the **Dome of Honour**, shaped like a stylised parachute, is a roll of honour bearing the names of the 1 800 American soldiers who died at Nijmegen.

Berg en Dal – *6km/4mi to the east via Berg en Dalseweg*.
This village (whose name means Hill and Valley) is located in a region appreciated for its woodlands and undulating countryside.
The **Afrika Museum** ⏱ is installed to the south. *Postweg 6*. It contains a collection of sculpture including masks and objects used daily, laid out in a modern building and reconstitutions in the open air (Ghana and Mali dwellings, houses on pil

The **Duivelsberg**, a wooded hill 76m/249ft high, is crisscrossed with paths. By fol
lowing the signs "Pannenkoeken" (restaurant) one reaches a car park. From there
a signposted path leads to a belvedere: **view** over the German plain and Wijlermeer

EXCURSIONS

Doornenburg – *18km/11mi to the northeast. Leave by Waalbrug and turn
towards Bemmel and Gendt.*
This village has a 14C **castle** ⊘ which was rebuilt after the Second World War. It
is a tall square fortress surrounded by water, topped by turrets and linked by a
footbridge to a fortified courtyard where there is a chapel and a farmhouse.

NOORDOOSTPOLDER

Flevoland
Population 41 095
Michelin maps 908 H 3, 4, I 3, 4 and 210 S 6, 7, T 6, 7, R6, 7
Local map see IJSSELMEER

The Noordoostpolder was the second area to be reclaimed in the process of draining
the Zuiderzee, but only once the sea had become a freshwater lake.

Drainage – The polder covers more than 48 000ha/118 560 acres. The 55km/34m
long enclosing dike was built between 1937 and 1940. As of 1941 three pumping
stations at Vollenhove, Urk and Lemmer evacuated 1.5 billion m³/52 971 billion cu ft
of water. Collection and drainage ditches completed the draining process.
The polder includes the former island of Schokland, the highest point at 3.5m/11ft

Development – Once the land had been drained 500km/310mi of roads were built
and the future capital **Emmeloord** was built in the middle of the polder.
After years (1942-62) of improving and fertilising the soil the Noordoostpolder is
now mainly devoted to agriculture and over 1 650 farmhouses were built. The
smaller units were clustered round the villages while the larger farms were dispersed
in the outlying areas. The main crops are wheat, potatoes and sugar beet with an
occasional field of flowers; cattle and sheep graze the meadows.

SIGHTS

Emmeloord – The capital of the polder was laid out according to town planning
concepts of the time. Right in the centre of the town the **water tower** ⊘ built in
1957 provides water for the whole polder and true to Dutch traditions has a
carillon of 48 bells.
The **view** from the summit stretches north to the Frisian coast, southwest to Urk
and the power station on the Oostelijk Flevoland polder.

Schokland – This former island in the Zuiderzee was low-lying and difficult to
protect from the sea. Its three villages were abandoned in 1859. The former
church and a modern building have been converted into the **Museum Schokland** ⊘
(between Ens and Nagele) which relates the island's past: geology, prehistory and
more recent times. Items on display include archeological finds made during
reclamation work on the polder.

Schokland and UNESCO

Since the end of 1995, the former island of Schokland has been a UNESCO
world heritage site. It was chosen as an international symbol of the
centuries of struggle between man and the sea.
Schokland, now part of an artificial polder and previously surrounded by
the Zuiderzee, has not always been an island. In prehistory it was an area
of dry land, and the small lake did not appear until Roman times. This
gradually expanded into a sea, and ensured that the subsoil remained
untouched for centuries until the polderisation process began in 1941 and
archeologists examined the ground. They found the remains of ancient
houses built on piles and artificial mounds, and dozens of shipwrecks.
Ceramics, stone tools, furrows and even a burial site containing 20
skeletons, all dating from the period between 4500 and 1800 BC, were
unearthed. But the really important feature of this area is the large
quantity of prehistoric remains such as fossils and bones of mammoth,
aurochs and woolly rhinoceros, as well as large quantities of geological
material. The huge and rare erratic boulders deposited here by glaciers
during the Ice Ages are internationally renowned.

Urk

Behind the presbytery there are remains of the stockade which protected the island from the onslaught of the sea. Stelae set into the walls of the church and the presbytery indicate the levels of past floods.

★ **Urk** – The former island of Urk has been joined to the mainland since the creation of the polder, though it still forms a distinctive community with an island feel. Its traditions have been retained, including strict Calvinism and keeping Sunday as a day of rest. The older people still wear the traditional costume: for the men a black suit with a striped shirt; for the women a black skirt with a floral or embroidered panel on the front of the blouse, a lace headdress worn over a metal hairband ending in animal head motifs.

Urk once specialised in eel fishing, and today its fish auction is the most important in the Netherlands, dealing in fish from the IJsselmeer and the North Sea. The busy **harbour** makes an attractive picture with the gaily painted eel fishing boats. From beside the church on its mound there is a **view** of the enclosing dike and IJsselmeer beyond. The names of local fishermen who have drowned since 1815 are written around the edges of the terrace.

NUENEN

Noord-Brabant

Population 23 215

Michelin maps 408 H 7 and 211 S 14 (8km/5mi to the northeast of Eindhoven)

This town preserves the memory of **Vincent van Gogh** (*see AMSTERDAM: Museum district*) who, after having spent several months in the Drenthe, came to live, in the presbytery where his parents lived from December 1883 to November 1885. It was then that he really started to experiment with oils before leaving for Antwerp. He painted several portraits of country people, which he used as studies for his great canvas The Potato Eaters in the Kröller-Müller Museum.

SIGHTS

Monument to Van Gogh – *On a small triangular square at the junction of the road to Mierlo, near a large lime tree surrounded by lime shoots.*
This work by Hildo Krop in 1932 is a sober black stone stele, engraved with a sun and lying on a round pedestal with an inscription concerning Van Gogh's stay here.

Het domineeshuis – Just south of the monument, on the main street, at no 26 Berg is the presbytery where Vincent van Gogh's father died in March 1885. It looks exactly as the artist portrayed it.

Van Gogh Documentatiecentrum ⊙ – A custom-built building beside the new town hall (Gemeentehuis) houses an exhibition of photos and documents concerning the painter's stay in Nuenen.

Molen – *To the north, take a right off the main road towards 't Weefhuis (weaver's house).*
Near a pond there is a mill perched on a mound.

261

ROERMOND

Population 43 936
Michelin maps 908 J 8 and 211 V 15
Town plan in the current Michelin Red Guide Benelux

At the confluence of the Maas and the Roer, near the German and Dutch frontier, Roermond, the most important city of central Limburg, is an industrial town (Philips, insulators, paper, chemicals, dairy products). Due to its bisphoric founded in 1559 it is also the religious capital of this very Catholic province. Roermond was formerly the county town of Upper Gelderland.

It was granted its city rights in 1232 and was soon given a fortified wall of which the 14C **Rattentoren** on the Buitenop, remains.

Roermond was one of the first towns captured in 1572 by William the Silent coming from Dillenburg, but was recaptured by the Spanish in October.

Roermond then passed to Austria, France, and was only returned to the Netherlands Kingdom in 1815.

The town which suffered greatly in the last war has been partly rebuilt. It includes two marinas and vast stretches of water between the Maas and a side canal.

SIGHTS

Onze Lieve Vrouwe Munsterkerk ⊘ – *Munsterplein, in the town centre.* It is the old church of a Cistercian abbey. In Rhenish style, it was started in 1218 in the transitional Romanesque-Gothic style and restored at the end of the 19C by Cuypers (who was born here in 1827). On the west it is flanked by a massive porch framed by two towers with spires and topped by a dome flanked by two turrets at the transept crossing. The trefoil plan of the western part, with the transept arms ending in apsidals, the apse's outside gallery, the roofs of the towers and turrets in the shape of bishops' mitres, and the decoration of Lombard arcading are characteristics typical of Rhenish edifices.

The church has a Brabant altarpiece (c 1530) in carved and painted wood and at the transept crossing there is the tomb of the abbey's founders, the Count of Gelderland Gerald IV and his wife Margaret of Brabant.

Near the church, at the corner of Pollartstraat, the Prinsenhof, built between 1660 and 1670 is the old palace of the stadtholders of Upper Gelderland, during Spanish rule.

Take Steenweg, the main shopping street and a pedestrian precinct.

Kathedrale Kerk ⊘ – Dedicated to St Christopher, it stands near Markt. Built in 1410 in the local Gothic style, it was damaged during the last war, but since restored.

Opposite the cathedral there is a 1764 **Baroque house** (now a restaurant).

EXCURSION

★ **Thorn** – *14km/9mi southwest of Roermond. Leave Roermond via A 68.* Not far from the Belgian frontier, this large village built of pink brick, often painted white, has a certain charm. Near Plein de Wijngaard, its paving decorated with geometric motifs, stands the **abbey church** ⊘ preceded by a high brick tower striped with

Thorn

white stone. This is the old church of a women's abbey founded at the end of the 10C by Ansfried (who became Bishop of Utrecht in 995) and his wife Hilsondis. Rebuilt at the end of the 13C in the Gothic style, it has preserved from Romanesque times two staircase turrets and a crypt on the west side.

It was enlarged in the 15C, and remodelled in the Baroque style at the end of the 18C. It was restored by Cuypers at the end of the 19C. The interior is surprisingly white. The eastern chancel, raised and decorated by a Baroque altarpiece overlooks a Gothic crypt. The chapels in the aisles have interesting low reliefs. In the south aisle there are charming 17C and 18C statues of saints in the folk art tradition. At the end of the nave, a double flight of stairs leads to the canonesses' chancel. From here one reaches a small **museum** installed in the old chapter-house and the archives both of the 14C and 15C: treasury (reliquaries, crowns), engravings, documents. In the western crypt, which is Romanesque, there is a sculptured stone baptismal font (15C).

Take the main street (Akkerwal, Akker, Boekenderweg). At the second chapel (Sint-Antoniuskapel) turn left.

On a small shady square, the 1673 **Chapel Under the Lime Trees** (Kapel onder de Linden), was enlarged in 1811. Inside, the oldest part on the east side has fine Baroque decoration (stucco work, paintings) while the 19C part was decorated in the Empire style.

ROTTERDAM★★

Zuid-Holland

Population 589 987

Michelin maps 908 E 6, folds 25 and 26 (inset) and 211 L 11 and folds 37 to 40 (inset)

Local maps see DELTA and ROTTERDAM

Plan of the conurbation in the current Michelin Red Guide Benelux

The second most populated city in the kingdom, Rotterdam, one of the world's largest ports, is located on the **Nieuwe Maas** 30km/19mi from the North Sea. Rotterdam, at the mouth of two important waterways – Rhine, Maas and their tributaries – leading into the industrial heartland, is the meeting point of maritime and fluvial traffic. The city of Rotterdam sprawls over both banks of the river and is linked by tunnels, bridges and the underground. It is part of the **Rijnmond** a group of 23 municipalities part of **Randstad Holland**.

The university, named after Erasmus, was founded in 1973 by amalgamating the School of Advanced Economic Studies and Social Sciences with the Faculty of Medicine.

Almost destroyed during the last war, Rotterdam has been entirely rebuilt.

During the 1980s and 90s, radical changes have been made to the city's skyline, and Rotterdam's many new buildings have earned it the nickname of Manhattan on the Maas; it also has a great deal of important modern architecture. The latest challenge is the development of the **Kop van Zuid** on the other side of the Maas, where the city council intends to create a second centre for Rotterdam by around 2005. The Erasmus Bridge, completed in 1996, will link the two halves.

HISTORICAL NOTES

Rotterdam was originally a small village built on the dike *(dam)* on the small River Rotte. The town was still of little importance when Erasmus was born here.

Expansion – In 1572 the Spaniards pursued by the Sea Beggars, who had just captured Brielle, pleaded with the inhabitants of Rotterdam to be allowed to enter. Once inside, Admiral Bossu allowed his troops to pillage the town. After his betrayal, Rotterdam joined the revolt. From 1576 to 1602 ports were constructed which were used by the Sea Beggars' fleet; the town rapidly surpassed its rival, Dordrecht, and became the second largest in Holland. Nevertheless, when Rotterdam was captured by the French in 1794, its trade severely suffered.

Major dock work – It was only after Belgium and the Netherlands separated in 1830 that Rotterdam once again became a transit port for the Rhine. As the depth of the river in the estuary (Brielse Maas) had become inadequate for the increasingly large ships, an access canal had to be built across the island of Voorne in 1830, the Voornsekanaal.

The Voornsekanaal, also, became insufficient and in 1863 the Minister Jan R Thorbecke approved the plans drawn up by the young hydraulic engineer **Pieter Caland** (1826-1902) for the construction of a waterway crossing the sandy plains separating Rotterdam from the North Sea. The **Nieuwe Waterweg**, a waterway

Erasmus Roterodamus

This was the way the great humanist Geert Geertsz signed his name throughout his life. He was born here in 1469 but spent little time. As a child, Erasmus lived in Gouda, studied in Utrecht, then in the school of the Brethren of Common Life at Deventer and later at 's-Hertogenbosch.

An orphan with nowhere to turn, Erasmus became a monk in 1488 at the convent of Steyn, near Gouda, and studied the Ancient world.

In 1493 having left the convent, he became secretary to the Bishop of Cambrai, whom he accompanied on his travels. He was, however, attracted by learning, and succeeded in getting a scholarship to study theology at the Sorbonne, while continuing to write many works.

During a stay in England, in 1499, he met Thomas More, the author of *Utopia*, who was to become a close friend. In 1502, fleeing the plague, which had spread through France, he arrived at the University of Louvain and soon became a professor there.

A tireless traveller, Erasmus was in Italy in 1506, where he published his **Adagia**, a commentary on quotations and proverbs from Antiquity; then in London in 1509 where he wrote and published two years later his *In Praise of Folly*. In Basle in 1514, Erasmus met Holbein who in 1515 illustrated an edition of *In Praise of Folly* and made several portraits of the humanist.

When, in 1517, Luther put up the 95 theses which triggered the Reformation, Erasmus was in Louvain. He at first refused to take part in religious quarrels but, when the Faculty of Theology condemned Luther's Theses, his neutrality created problems. After spending some months at Anderlecht, near Brussels in 1521, he left for Switzerland where he calmly continued with his literary endeavours and published, in 1526, an enlarged edition of his **Colloquia Familiaria**, satirical dialogues, which was very successful.

The Prince of Humanists died in Basle in 1536.

18km/11mi long and 11m/36ft deep at low tide, was dug between 1866 and 1872, and is comparable to Amsterdam's Noordzeekanaal, without locks. The port of **Hoek van Holland** was built at the sea-end for passenger traffic. In 1997, the final project of the Delta Plan was completed: the gigantic storm surge barrier near Europoort *(see DELTA, and below)*.

New docks started to be built on the south bank of the river towards 1870 (Binnen Dock, Entrepot Dock, Spoorweg Dock) which were bigger than the old ones and linked to the railway.

Between 1876 and 1878 two bridges were built across the Maas (Willemsbrug and Koninginnebrug) as well as a railway viaduct 1 400m/4 598ft wide spanning the river.

Three man-made harbours were built, the Rijn Dock (1887-94), the Maas Dock (1898-1905) and the Waal Dock (1907-31), which became the largest artificial harbour in the world. Subsequently the port was extended along the north bank of the Maas, to the west (Merwe Dock, 1923-32).

Delfshaven, the small outer harbour that had been part of Delft since 1400, was incorporated within Rotterdam in 1886.

A martyred city – On 14 May 1940 Rotterdam suffered German bombings that destroyed almost all of the old town. Only the town hall, the central post office, the stock exchange and Erasmus' statue were spared.

In March 1943, Allied bombing completed the destruction. 280ha/692 acres were razed, 30 000 houses and buildings set on fire.

The port was also very badly bombed during the last war and, moreover, was sabotaged in 1944 by the Germans who destroyed 7km/4mi of docks and 20% of the warehouses.

Accommodation

otterdam is a city of modern architecture, and this is not the place to go
)oking for quaint old hotels.

OUTH HOSTEL

JHC City Hostel Rotterdam – *Rochussenstraat 107-109, 3015 EH Rotter-
am, ☎ (010) 436 57 63, Fax (010) 436 55 69. 14 rooms*. Near the
Museumpark.

UDGET HOTELS

reitner – *Breitnerstraat 23, 3015 XA Rotterdam, ☎ (010) 436 02 62,
ax (010) 436 40 91. 32 rooms*. Small, central hotel in a quiet street. The
imple rooms of varying sizes all have shower/bath and toilet.

UR SELECTION

ew York – *Koninginnehoofd 1, 3072 AD Rotterdam, ☎ (010) 439 05 00,
ax (010) 484 27 01. 72 rooms*. Once the former headquarters of the
Iolland-Amerika shipping line, this is one of the few Rotterdam hotels to be
)cated in a historic building. It is on the other side of the Maas, and therefore
ot particularly central, but highly recommended nevertheless.

ntel – *Leuvehaven 80, 3011 EA Rotterdam, ☎ (010) 413 41 39,
ax (010) 413 32 22. 150 rooms*. This modern business hotel is next to the
MAX theatre and has a view over the Nieuwe Maas, the Erasmusbrug and
euvehaven. It has a pool, sauna and gymnasium, and a free guarded
nderground car park.

arkhotel – *Westersingel 70, 3015 LB Rotterdam, ☎ (010) 436 36 11,
ax (010) 436 42 12. 187 rooms*. The rooms in the modern, silver-coloured
ower of this hotel have a magnificent view of the city. It is within walking
istance of the shopping and entertainment areas, and has its own garden,
auna, solarium, fitness and massage room, and parking.

Restaurants

afé Rotterdam – *Wilhelminakade, ☎ (010) 290 84 42*. This café-restaurant is
ight by the Hotel New York and located in the magnificent departure lounge
f the Holland-Amerika Line. The glass wall on the Nieuwe Maas side provides
wonderful view of the city and the Erasmusbrug, which is lit at night.

ip - *Van Vollenhovenstraat
5, ☎ (010) 436 99 23*. A
leasant brasserie near Mu-
eumpark. Its name means
hicken, but it serves lots of
ther things too. There is a
mall garden at the back.

rasserie De Tijdsgeest – *Oost-
Vijnstraat 14-16, ☎ (010)
'33 13 11*. Trendy bras-
erie in a number of old
ouses and warehouses
ear the Oude Haven. Good
alue for money. Terrace.

e Engel – *Eendrachtsweg
9, ☎ (010) 413 82 56*.
ne of the places to be in
otterdam, serving good
)od in an informal setting.

oompjes – *Boompjes 701,
☎ (010) 413 60 70*. The
avilion in which this
estaurant is located is one
f Rotterdam's architec-
ural highlights, with big
lass walls allowing diners
） watch the busy shipping
raffic on the Nieuwe Maas;
he terrace is open in sum-
ner.

Night-life in the Oude Haven

Morand-Graham/HOA QUI

Vorld Trade Center – *Beur-
plein 37, ☎ (010) 405 44 65*. Excellent cuisine served on the 23rd floor of
he World Trade Center, with yet another impressive view of Rotterdam
icluding the cube apartments, Euromast, the Kralingse Bos and the Lauren-
kerk: don't let your food get cold!

Brasserie La Vilette – *Westblaak 160*, ☎ *(010) 414 86 92*. Chic but lively brasserie offering good food that won't break the bank.

Parkheuvel – *Heuvellaan 21*, ☎ *(010) 436 07 66*. This top-class restaurant one of the city's finest, with a view of the ships on the Nieuwe Maas throw in for good measure.

Practical information

General information – The tourist office, **VVV Rotterdam** (Coolsingel 67, 300 AN Rotterdam, ☎ (0900) 40 340 65) can help with just about anything yo need to know, including sights, tours, cultural events, excursions, an bookings for hotels, theatres and concerts. It also publishes a handy guide t Rotterdam.

Transport – Park in one of the seven **multi-storey car parks** in the centre (charg payable) or the free **Park & Ride** sites on the edge of the city. **RET**, the city's publ transport company, has an extensive network of metro, bus and train line. Most of the main sights are easy to reach from the Central Station. In summe the tourist tram, **route no 10**, crosses the whole of the city. RET's service poir at Coolsingel 141, ☎ (0900) 92 92 sells tickets valid for one, two or thre days. **Bicycles** are available for rent in the cycle shop in the Central Statior ☎ (010) 412 62 20.

Blaak metro and train station

Walks and tours – The **VVV** organises a wide variety of guided and unguide bus tours, walks and cycle tours, as well as special business visits and taxi tour of the city or port. If you have a specific interest in architecture, conta **ArchiCenter Rotterdam** on ☎ (010) 402 32 34. The **Gilde van Rotterdam** offe walking tours of specific parts of the city and on particular themes such a architecture; ☎ (010) 436 28 44.

Boat trips – **Flying Dutchman**: harbour tours by hydrofoil, departing fro Parkkade opposite the Euromast, ☎ (010) 436 12 22. **Spido Havenrondvaarte** tours of the port and the Delta project, departing from Leuvehoof ☎ (010) 275 99 88. **Stichting De Crossboot**: trips to the Rottemeren lake and Delfshaven leaving from Zaagmolenbrug, ☎ (010) 414 97 51. **Wate bus**: a flat-bottomed open boat operating two routes, with a number c stops, departing from the Maritiem Buitenmuseum and Leuvekolk ☎ (010) 404 80 72. *For more details, see Admission times and charges.*

Rotterdam from the air – Get a bird's-eye view of the city from the **Euroma** *(see description below)* or the **World Trade Center**; alternatively, do it in style wit an air tour operated by **Kroonduif Air**, ☎ (010) 415 78 55.

Shopping – Rotterdam has many shopping centres, including the **Lijnbaar** Europe's first pedestrian area; the **Beurstraverse**, one of the city's architectur highlights; the Plaza, opposite the Central Station; and the 2km/1mi lon **Zuiderboulevard**. The **Vrij Entrepot** is a new shopping area in the Kop van Zui district. The area in and around the former warehouse De Vijf Werelddelen ha all kinds of shops, a World Market and numerous international restaurants an bars.

he many commercial art galleries are centred around **Witte de Withstraat**, the ultural hub of Rotterdam. The VVV sells a guide to some of the more nteresting places in which to be parted from your money. Most shops are open till 9pm on Fridays.

Markets – The **Centrummarkt**, one of the biggest markets in the country, takes place on the Binnenrotteterrein on Tuesdays and Saturdays. There is also a Sunday market here from April to October. An antiques market is held on Sundays during the summer on Schiedamsedijk. Other large markets include Markt Zuid on Wednesdays and Saturdays on the Afrikaanderplein, and Markt West, with a wide variety of exotic foreign products, on Grote Visserijplein on Thursdays and Saturdays.

Theatres and concerts – **R'Uit Magazine** gives a full monthly summary of all exhibitions, dance and theatre performances, concerts and other events. It is available free from the VVV and elsewhere. The easiest way to book tickets is at the **VVV's art and culture counter**. Leading venues include the Doelen concert and conference building, Schouwburgplein 50, ☎ (010) 217 17 00, the home of the Rotterdam Philharmonic Orchestra; **Rotterdamse Schouwburg**, ☎ (010) 404 41 11; **Theater Zuidplein**, Zuidplein 60, ☎ (010) 481 65 00; **antaren/Venster**, Gouvernestraat 133, ☎ (010) 436 13 11; and **Luxor Theater**, Kruiskade 10, ☎ (010) 413 83 26.

Night-life – For an evening with a difference, try the **Holland Casino** in the Plaza complex opposite the Central Station. Cinemas include the huge **IMAX** screen at Leuvehaven, the Pathé mega-cinema on Schouwburgplein, and **antaren/Venster** (Gouvernestraat) for cinephiles.

Events – There always seems to be some kind of festival going on. Annual events include the **International Film Festival** (January/February), the multicultural **Dunya Festival** (early June), **Poetry International** (June), the tropical-style summer **Carnival Street Parade** (July), the **Wereldhavendagen**, or World Port Days, in early September, and the arts and cultural event the **R Festival** in September.
The **World Tennis Tournament** and the **Rotterdam Marathon** take place in March and April; for more information, contact the tourist office.

A NEW CITY

Reconstruction of the city – Immediately after the war Rotterdam began rebuilding. Rational urban planning was adopted, which allowed for more open spaces and a cultural and commercial city centre.
Large numbers of people moved to the suburbs which led to the spectacular development of the built-up area. Many communities were set up almost overnight, such as **Hoogvliet** in the south and **Alexanderpolder** in the east, and Prins Alexanderpolder (1871).
The quarter south of the Maas was given a shopping centre, the **Zuidplein**; a theatre and a vast sports complex, the **Ahoy** (concerts, exhibitions).
Numerous recreational areas were created on the city outskirts to meet the recreational needs of the ever-growing suburban population. The most important are located to the west on the island of Voorne, not far from Brielle, and to the northeast along the Rotte.

The new port – *See the insets on Michelin maps 908 and 211.* In 1945 the reconstruction of the port began. It was decided that national industry should be developed. A new port, **Botlek**, was built in 1954 on the island of Rozenburg, where refineries and petrochemical plants were subsequently set up. When these facilities became inadequate, the new **Europoort** was added.
Finally, to accommodate the giant tankers, open-sea docks were built to the south of the Nieuwe Waterweg, in the Maasvlakte region, where an industrial zone was created around the port and its installations.

Port activity – With a total goods traffic of 315 million tonnes in 1997, Rotterdam is one of the world's largest ports. This gigantic concern employs altogether 315 000 people.
Petroleum and its by-products account for 120 million tonnes, or around 38% of the total activity.
Four important refineries (Shell, Esso, Kuwait Petroleum and Nerefco) have been set up between Rotterdam and the sea. They have led to the creation of a powerful chemical industry (ICI, AZCO, DSM, ARCO, Shell etc).
The port of Rotterdam enjoys a privileged situation at the mouth of two big European rivers and within easy reach of major road and railway networks, not to mention the presence of two nearby airports: Schiphol and Zestienhoven (a mile or so north of the town).

The port of Rotterdam

Both a home port and a port of transit, Rotterdam counts over 300 regula international shipping lines; in 1990 it received around 32 150 deep-se ships.

The port facilities have had to adapt to the remarkable increase in **container traff** (6 032 000 containers in 1998, as against only 242 325 in 1970). Transhipmer centres *(distriparken)* have been set up, offering storage, distribution an reassembling services; they are located near the huge shipping terminals designe to receive the container vessels.

Bridges and tunnels – There are a number of tunnels and bridges spanning th Maas.

Maastunnel – Opened in 1942, the Maas Tunnel is 1 070m/3 510ft long of whic 550m/1 804ft are under the river. Covered with yellow tiles, it has four separat galleries: two one-way roads for cars (6 000 an hour) placed side by side, and tw upper levels for cyclists (8 000 an hour) and pedestrians (40 000 an hour) wit eight escalators.

Beneluxtunnel – This was built in 1967 to relieve some of the traffic from th Maastunnel, which had become inadequate, and to allow a crossing between th two banks while avoiding the city centre. It is 1 300m/4 265ft long and the rive bed was dredged 22.5m/74ft deep.

★★ **Willemsbrug** – This cable-stayed bridge, recognisable by its red gateway-shape pylons, was designed by C Veerling and opened in 1981. The dual carriagewa across this bridge forms an important traffic artery.

Van Brienenoordbrug – This bridge to the east was inaugurated in 1965. It has single span 297m/974ft long, rising 25m/82ft above the water. It ends in bascule bridge on the north side. Since 1992 the 12-lane Tweede Brienenoordbru (Second Bridge) has regulated traffic flow in the area.

★★ **Erasmusbrug** – *Illustration: see Introduction: ABC of architecture.* Ben van Berk designed this bracket-constructed single-pylon bridge, which is 800m/2 600 long. It was officially opened in 1996, and has become known among local peop as The Swan. The bridge consists of two approach ramps with a fixed steel cab bridge and a movable steel bascule bridge between them. The bridge links the cit centre with the Kop van Zuid, where 125ha/300 acres of former port area ha been redeveloped for residential and business use. There are also plans fo recreational and other facilities.

Transportation – Rotterdam has a huge ring motorway for motorists who wish t avoid the city centre.

Index of street names and sights for maps of ROTTERDAM

Rotterdam is also an important railway junction and a new railway tunnel (3km/2mi long) has been built to replace the railway viaduct and bridges over the Maas.

The city was the first in the Netherlands to build an underground, which was inaugurated in 1968.

① THE CENTRE *about 3hr*

The centre of Rotterdam is a mass of high-rise office blocks, shops and banks, with decorative detailing provided by a large number of sculptures.

Stationsplein – If you turn your back to the **Central Station** (1957), the **Delftse Poort**★ office building is on your left. This was designed by A Bonnema, and houses the Nationale Nederlanden insurance company. The two mirror-glazed towers are 93m/300ft and 150m/487ft high.

Kruisplein – To the right is the **Bouwcentrum** or **Building Centre** whose façade has an enormous reproduction of Picasso's **Sylvette**. Inside the building there are architectural exhibitions. On the side façade overlooking the Weena, note Henry Moore's brick **relief** (1955).

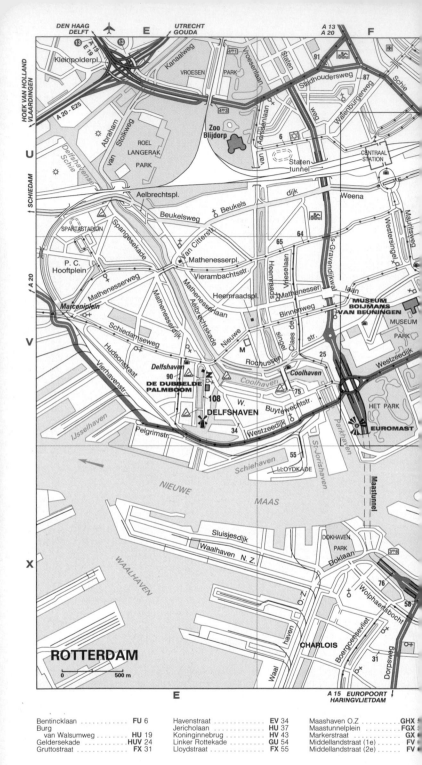

De Doelen – It is an immense concert hall and congress centre built in 1966; the main auditorium seats 2 222 people.

To the north of Westersingel stands a statue symbolising the Rotterdam Resistance.

Schouwburgplein – This square has been completely redesigned by Adriaan Geuze. The esplanade, which has an underground car park beneath it, has been clad in metal plates, some of which can be raised to serve as a podium. The three huge desk lamps that light the area can be controlled by members of the public.

270

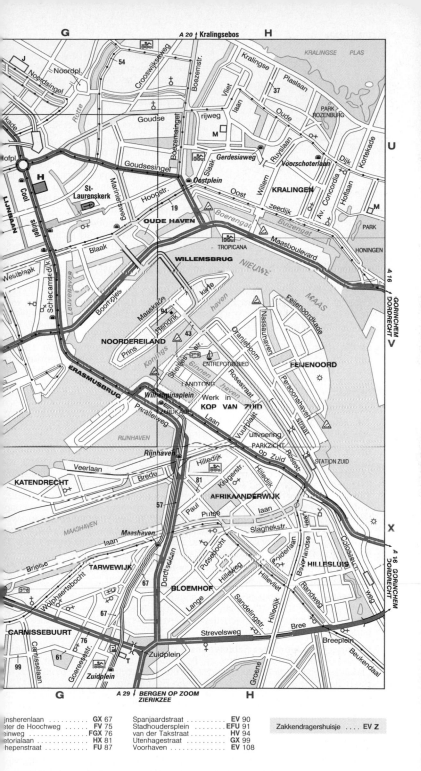

The Pathé mega-cinema on the western side, clad in corrugated metal, was designed by K van Velsen. The Schouwburg, or theatre, was designed by W Quist and opened in 1988.

Lijnbaan – This shopping promenade (1951-53 and 1962-66) may not look particularly modern now, but it was ahead of its time in the 1950s. The architects. Van den Broek and Bakema, designed adjoining low-rise shops with tall flats behind them. The idea of a traffic-free shopping centre provided inspiration for cities all over the world.

After photo VVV Rotterdam

The Bear Cubs by Anne Grimdalen

Cross Lijnbaan to reach the town hall.

Note the charming little sculpture by Ann Grimdalen, **The Bear Cubs** *(De Beertje 1956).*

Opposite the town hall is the **War Memorial**. was made by Mari Andriessen in 1957 three generations are depicted.

Coolsingel – This is the city's mar thoroughfare and the town hall, the po: office and the stock exchange are situate here. There are many modern compositior on the sidewalks and building façades, a well as several statues. Shaded lawns mak it a pleasant place to walk.

Stadhuis ⊙ – Built between 1914 and 1920 a good example of period architecture, it one of the few edifices which was spared. has an excellent **carillon** ⊙. Among oth statues, in front of the building, is one of the great jurist, Grotius, by Hetterr (1970). On the façade of the building opposite there is a mosaic (1954) by Va Roode depicting Erasmus on his way to Basle.

The **post office**, dating from the same period as the town tall, features, in i interior, a remarkable concrete framework. Facing the stock exchange, in fror of the department store De Bijenkorf (The Beehive), stands a gigantic met **Construction**; it is the work of Naum Gabo (1957) and illustrates the reconstructic of the town. The stock exchange, **Beurs**, built between 1936 and 1940, surmounted by a bell-tower. The **World Trade Center★** (1983-86), a 23-storey bloc erected above the stock exchange hall, is a distinctive landmark. Designed by th architect RB van Erk, it has the shape of a flattened ellipse with green glas façades.

Go between the post office and Beurs to cross Rotte Canal.

The **Statue of Erasmus** on Sint-Laurensplein is the work of Hendrick de Keyser ar was finished in 1622, after his death (1536).

Grote Kerk or Sint-Laurenskerk ⊙ – Completed in 1646, with its truncate tower built into the transept, this Gothic church was destroyed in 1940, the restored. It now has, once more, a fine façade with a new bronze door (1968) b Giacomo Manzù *(War and Peace)* and a chevet with Gothic tracery.

The **interior★** is spaciously conceived in the Gothic Brabant style, the severity c which is attenuated by the warm colours of the panelled vaults, the copp chandeliers, the great red and gold organ (1973), and the 18C gilded ironwor of the sanctuary. The slightly protruding transept contains 17C admirals' tomt and a fine 16C organ case. The organ case in the chancel dates from 1725. Th bronze baptismal font (1959) is by Han Petri.

Cross the pedestrian bridge spanning the Rotte. When you reach the back of th stock exchange (Beurs), turn left into Korte Hoogstraat.

Beursplein – The rebuilding of this square to the designs of Pi de Bruyn wa carried out in 1994. The plan includes the Beurstraverse (an undergrour shopping mall below Coolsingel), department stores, an apartment block and a c< park.

★ **Historisch Museum Het Schielandhuis** ⊙ – Built between 1662 and 1665 house the administrative centre of the Schieland dikes. The carefully balanc< Classical façade is richly decorated with Baroque sculpture. The building is no the main home of the Historisch Museum Rotterdam.

The three 18C period rooms on the first floor contain paintings by local artis' and other items made in Rotterdam, including silver, glass and furniture. Tr Regency room is devoted to the works of **Adriaen van der Werff** (1659-1722); his fir technique and the quality of his works – such as *Self-Portrait with Medallion* brought this painter international recognition. The large central room has wor by 17C Rotterdam painters.

The first floor is also used for temporary exhibitions of prints and drawin< from the **Atlas Van Stolk collection**, covering the history of the Netherlands. addition, there is a section on the history of Rotterdam showing its grow from a small 13C settlement to a major international port. It includes item such as the oldest surviving Dutch clog, dating from about 1280; more tha 40 portraits of directors of the Dutch East India Company (see Introductio History); statues from merchants' houses, and the white flag with whi Rotterdam capitulated in 1940. The remains of the city's churches have particular importance: Rotterdam lost all its old churches during th 1940 bombardment.

ROTTERDAM

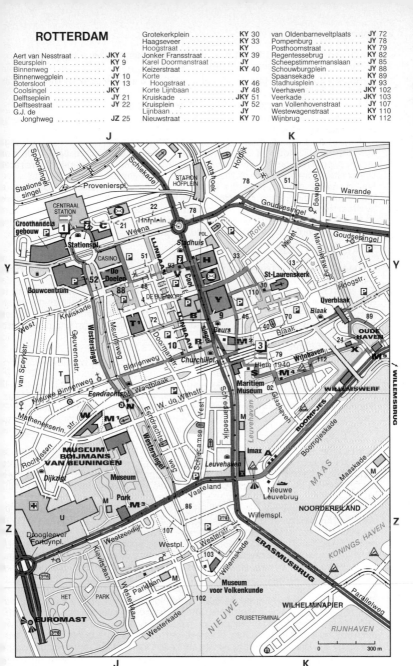

The top floor deals with everyday life in times gone by, and includes a toy kitchen from 1853, a reconstitution of a dairy (1910-68), a doll's house and a collection of clothes and accessories dating from 1760 to the present day. Opposite the Schielandshuis is the 31-storey Schielandtoren (Schieland Tower). At 104m/338ft, it is one of Europe's tallest residential buildings.

Cross Coolsingel and turn left into Binnenweg.

On Binnenweg, an amusing statue portrays **Monsieur Jacques**, a typical citizen o' Rotterdam, by Wenckebach (1959).

Binnenwegplein – **Het Ding** *(The Thing; 1969)* is a giant mobile by the American artist George Rickey.

At the end of Binnenweg, turn left into Eendrachtsplein.

Westersingel – This street has a public garden containing a headless statue by Rodin, **Man Walking**.

There are also a number of art galleries in the Westersingel. If you cross the bridge opposite no 22, you will see the facade of the reconstructed **Café de Unie** or Mauritsweg. This was designed by JJP Oud in 1925, and its lines and colours recall compositions by members of the abstract movement, De Stijl.

Finally, on the other side of the Weena, you will pass the **Groothandelsgebouw** o Wholesale Building. This office block dates from 1949 to 1951, and was designed by the architects Maaskant en Van Tijen. It is a symbol of the city's reconstruction, an impressive building covering an area of 2ha/5 acres, with the companies located there providing work for 5 000 people.

★★ ② AROUND THE MUSEUMPARK

In the space of only a few years, the area around the **Museumpark** has become the cultural heart of Rotterdam.

The park (1988-93) was designed by the architect **Rem Koolhaas**, who was born in Rotterdam in 1944. He created three areas, each with its own distinct character one paved with white shell grit and small apple trees, one consisting of a black asphalt podium, and one with a lake and a winding path, creating a romantic effect.

A number of important museums adjoin the park.

★★★ **Museum Boijmans-Van Beuningen** ⊘ – *Because of building work scheduled fo completion in late 2000, only part of this museum is open. The pre-20C ar collection is permanently on display, and temporary exhibitions are being held in conjunction with the nearby Kunsthal.* Located on the edge of a park, this fine ar museum is in a building inaugurated in 1935, to which a wing was added in 1972 Besides an excellent collection of Old Masters, the museum contains a large number of modern and contemporary works of art, engravings and drawings and a decorative arts section.

In 1958 the museum was enriched by the DG Van Beuningen donation, while in 1972 the Willem Van der Vorm Collection was given on loan. The Vitale Bloch bequest, a collection of paintings and drawings from the 15C to 1950, wa acquired in 1978. The museum also organises temporary international exhibi tions.

Old Masters – *Old building, first floor.* There is a remarkable collection of primitiv art. The *Three Marys at the Open Sepulchre* is a major work by the **Van Eycks**. There are admirable paintings by **Hieronymus Bosch**, *The Marriage at Cana, St Christopher* and in particular *The Prodigal Son* where one can appreciate the painter's poeti humour, his flights of imagination, and his mastery of colour. Note a Virgin and Child surrounded by angel musicians, *The Glorification of the Virgin,* masterpiece by **Geerten tot Sint Jans**. The Prophet Isaiah is shown on the left pane of the famous altarpiece by the **Master of the Annunciation of Aix** (Aix-en-Provence) *The Tower of Babel* by **Bruegel the Elder**, the delightful *Portrait of a Young Schola in a red beret* (1531) by **Jan van Scorel**, and works by **Pieter Aertsen** etc represent the 16C. The 17C painting collection is particularly interesting. There are two portraits by **Frans Hals**; church interiors with masterful use of light by **Piete Saenredam** and **Emmanuel de Witte**; a portrait by **Rembrandt** of his young son Titus; the distant horizons of **Hercules Seghers** and **Van Goyen**; and nature's atmosphere rendered by **Hobbema** and **Jacob van Ruysdael**. There are also interior scenes by **Ja Steen** and **Gerrit Dou**.

The **Rubens** collection has, among other sketches, a remarkable series on the theme of Achilles' life.

In the fine group of Italian paintings from the 15C to 17C, there are works by the Venetians: Titian, Tintoretto and Veronese.

Willem van der Vorm Collection – It includes, notably, an interesting series of 17C paintings with Rubens, Van Dyck, Rembrandt *(Tobias and his Wife)* and many Dutch masters such as Gerrit Dou, Ter Borch *(Woman Spinning)* and Van de Velde with two seascapes.

19C French painting is represented by the Barbizon School. There are works by Daubigny, Théodore Rousseau and Corot *(Ville d'Avray)*. For the 18C, Huber Robert, Chardin and Watteau should be mentioned for France, and the Venetian Francesco Guardi, for Italy.

Prints and Drawings – *Print room, new wing.*

This important collection, a part of which is exhibited during temporary exhibi tions, covers the 15C to the present day. It includes works by Albrecht Dürer Leonardo da Vinci, Rembrandt, Watteau, Cézanne and Picasso.

Modern and Contemporary Art – *Old building, first floor and new wing*.
It covers the period from 1850 to the present. The Impressionist artists Monet, Sisley and Pissaro are represented as well as Signac, Van Gogh, Mondrian and Kandinsky (*Lyrisches*). Note the small 14-year old ballet dancer, a graceful statuette by Degas.

Among the Surrealist works there are paintings by Salvador Dali (*Sundial, Impressions of Africa*) and René Magritte (*The Red Model, Reproduction Forbidden*). The collection also includes works by Kees van Dongen, who was born in Delfshaven.

The contemporary art collection is exhibited by rotation; it includes sculptures by Richard Serra, Oldenburg, Joseph Beuys, Bruce Nauman and Walter De Maria, and Donald Judd and paintings by the Germans Kiefer and Penck, and the Italians Cucchi, Clemente and Chia.

Dutch contemporary art is represented by Van Elk, Carel Visser, Rob van Koningsbruggen and René Daniels.

Among the contemporary trends are works by Milan Kunc and Salvo as well as sculptures by Thomas Schütte, Bazilebustamente and Niek Kamp.

Finger on cheek, Kees van Dongen

Decorative Arts – *Old building, ground floor*.
The museum also has a very rich collection of objets d'art; glassware (17C), silverware, majolica and Persian, Turkish (13C), Spanish, Dutch, Italian (15C-16C) and Delftware.

* Nederlands Architectuurinstituut ⊘ – The Dutch architect Jo Coenen designed this complex, known as NAi, which opened in 1993. Born in 1949, Coenen has gained an international reputation, and is a senior lecturer at the Technische Universität in Karlsruhe. A number of other architects, including the Czech, Borek Sipek, were involved in designing the interior of the complex, which consists of four buildings, each serving a different function and with its own style.

As you enter from the Museumpark side, you will see a sculpture by Auke de Vries in the pond on the left. The tall, transparent section of the institute houses the offices and a library of some 35 000 books and journals on Dutch and foreign architecture and related subjects, which is open to museum visitors. Underneath the transparent section, level with the pond, are an auditorium and the foyer.

After the reception desk, a ramp leads to the different levels of the exhibition wing, recognisable from the outside by its purplish-brown brick walls. This wing is used to stage temporary exhibitions on various aspects of architecture, urban planning, landscape architecture and related disciplines.

The curved wing on concrete pillars on Rochussenstraat is known as the collection wing (*accessible only on group tours*). This houses archives of items relating to Dutch architecture from 1800 to the present day, including working drawings and models by leading architects such as Cuypers, Berlage, Rietveld, Coenen, Koolhaas and Weeber. The outer walls have no windows, and are clad in red-painted corrugated steel. At night, the colonnade is lit in changing colour combinations in a light installation designed by Peter Struycken.

Chabotmuseum ⊘ – The Chabotmuseum building dates from 1938; the architects GW Baas and L Stokla created a functional-looking villa of glass, steel frames, a flat roof and whitewashed walls in the spartan Nieuwe Bouwen style of the 1920s, 30s and 40s. Since 1991, the villa has been an appropriate home for the drawings and paintings of the local Expressionist artist Hendrik Chabot (1894-1949). Chabot was also a graphic artist and sculptor, and created often moving portrayals of war refugees and other subjects.

Nederlands Architectuurinstituut, Jo Coenen

Kunsthal ⊘ – This building beside the Westzeedijk holds important temporar
exhibitions of the visual arts, architecture, design and non-Western cultures.
The architect, Rem Koolhaas, has made ingenious use of the difference in leve
between the Museumpark and the dyke. A series of exhibition spaces are groupe
around a slope linking the two areas. The facade on the park side is made o
travertine and glass; on the dyke side, a service road runs underneath the buildinç
The figures of the camel driver and his camel on the roof, by the artist Henk Visch
are a reminder of the temporary, nomadic nature of the exhibitions.
To the left of the Kunsthal when seen from the dyke is the new glass pavilion o
the Natuurmuseum, which has a 15m/50ft whale skeleton inside.

★ ③ **CITY OF WATER** *about 3hr*

A walk through this part of the city gives a good overview of the city's links wit
the sea.

Maritiem Museum Prins Hendrik ⊘ – This museum is located on Leuvehaver
Rotterdam's first artificial sea-harbour. It has permanent displays and temporar
exhibitions; the former include *I name you...*, *Shipbuilding in the Netherlands*
covering the rich history of this industry in the Netherlands since the 17C an
allowing visitors to design a ship using a computer. Another display chronicles th
hard lives of seafarers: what they wore, what they ate, and how they obtaine
medical treatment. *Professor Plons* is an interactive exhibition for children
providing an enjoyable introduction to the world of ships and shipping.
Leuvehaven is also the home of an old armoured vessel, the **Buffel** (1868). Cabin
belonging to the different crew members are on view, as well as the prison cell
and the well-appointed captain's cabin.

IMAX – Enter from the quayside. From the comfort of your seat, enjoy the 70mm images (including feature films) projected by the IMAX system onto a slightly curved screen (23m/75ft high and 17m/56ft across). Combined with six-channel sound, the effect is sensational.

At the end of Schiedamsedijk, turn left across the Nieuwe Leuvebrug.

The Nieuwe Leuvebrug offers an excellent view of the **Erasmusbrug**★★ *(see above).*

★ **Boompjes** – In the 17C, this was an elegant promenade with a double row of lime trees; hence its name, which means little trees. Now, it is a modern boulevard with a variety of places to eat and drink, and residential and office buildings. The three towers, the **Boompjestorens**, were designed by the architect Henk Klunder and are lit in red, blue and yellow at night.

Continue along Boompje-skade until it widens out; turn left into Scheepmak-ershaven and follow the quay to the right.

The 92m/300ft-high white office block, **Willemswerf**★, is the headquarters of the shipping company Nedlloyd. The architect, Wim Quist, built it in two sections; the other, beside the Nieuwe Maas, is wedge-shaped.

Follow the Boompjes under the Willemsbrug approach road.

★ **Oude Haven** – The old port was Rotterdam's first harbour, built in 1325. It is now a pleasant place for a stroll, and visitors can sit out on one of the busy terraces in fine weather.

The **Witte Huis**, or White House, on the southwest side, is the only remnant of the pre-war period. This 11-storey office block dates from 1897 to 1898, and was the Netherlands' first skyscraper.

The three Boompjestorens, Henk Klunder

J.L. Bohin/EXPLORER

The old Dutch commercial sailing ships of the Inland Waterways Museum, **Openlucht Binnenvaart Museum**, can be seen moored in Oude Haven.

Nearby the impressive form of the cable-stayed **Willemsbrug**★★ *(see above)* spans the Nieuwe Maas.

Overblaak – The architect Piet Blom built his cube-shaped apartments **(kubus-woningen)** over a pedestrian bridge between 1978 and 1984. One corner of each cube is precariously perched on a concrete column. One **apartment** ⊘, no 70, is open to the public. The so-called Pencil or Het Potlood apartment block towers above the area.

Behind the cube apartments is the entrance to the **Blaak metro** and railway station (1983-93; *illustration, see Travellers' addresses*). The architect, H Reijnders, placed a huge canopy of coloured neon tubes over the street-level part of the station.

Go back to the Oude Haven, follow Geldersekade to the Wijnhaven and cross the Wijnbrug.

In the **Wijnhaven** (Wine Port), you will see five polyester storage containers and a pontoon. This is the **Museum Schepen uit Verre Landen** ⊘, or Museum of Ships from Distant Lands, which has a collection of traditional ships and a display giving details of their technical and cultural background.

Turn right across the Regentessebrug; turn left and then right to reach Plein 1940.

A sculpture by the Franco-Russian artist Zadkine, **Monument to a Devastated City** (1953) is located to the north of the Leuvehaven; the man's heart has been torn out, and he gestures in despair, symbolising Rotterdam's suffering during the war.

277

④ DELFSHAVEN

From Delfshaven, Delft's old port, the Pilgrim Fathers embarked in 1620 fo England from where they sailed for the New World.

Piet Hein was born here in 1577, the Admiral who distinguished himself in Mexico in 1628, against the Spanish. The painter **Kees Van Dongen** was born here in 187′ (d 1968). He portrayed violently coloured female figures.

Voorhaven – It is a picturesque quay and has a chapel with a pinnacle known a the Pilgrim Fathers' Church, and a charming lever bridge.

★ **Museum De Dubbelde Palmboom** ⊘ – The Double Palm Tree Museum i attractively installed in two converted warehouses dating from 1825. chronicles the long history of Rotterdam as a trading city. On the first floor archeological finds show that goods were being imported here as early a 2400 BC. The polychrome tile picture, A Thousand Fears, dates from c 1610 an is one of the oldest such scenes to have been produced in the Netherlands. Th following rooms contain luxury items imported by the United East Indi Company.

Industrialisation and the history of the port from 1870 to 1970 is the theme o the second floor, which focuses on the manufacture and storage of goods.

The third floor contains reconstructions of Rotterdam shops and other interior from the 1930s to the 1960s.

Finally, the top floor is devoted to the history of Delfshaven, including the Pilgrim Fathers and the sea hero Piet Hein, of whom there is a statue (1870) not far from the museum, opposite Coolhaven.

Zakkendragershuisje ⊘ – To the north of Voorhaven, beside the lock, thi renovated 17C building is where porters used to gather when ships had to b loaded or unloaded. It contains a tin smelting workshop where traditiona methods are still used.

Nos 34 and 36 have interesting façade stones depicting animals.

ADDITIONAL SIGHTS

★ **Euromast** ⊘ – This boldly designed tower was built in 1960 to celebrate th opening of Floriade, the World Horticultural Show; it is situated in Rotterdam Park, close to Parkhaven.

From the viewing platform, which is 100m/328ft up, there is a remarkable **view**★ of the city and the port. There is also a restaurant at this level.

The Space Tower was added in 1970 and it brings the total height of Euromast to 185m/607ft. The spectacular glass lift revolving around it holds 32 people who may admire a **panorama**★★ stretching 30km/ 19mi in all directions, including the immense Delta formed by the Maas and the Rhine, hemming in the Europoort. At night the sight is truly breathtaking.

Museum voor Volkenkunde ⊘ – *Closed until September 2000 for repairs.* On the quays of the Nieuwe Maas, this Ethnography Museum which is in the old Royal Yacht Club building, is devoted to the cultures of non-Western peoples.

Diergaarde Blijdorp ⊘ – In a floral park, this zoo contains an interesting collection of over 2 000 animals, including some rare species (okapis etc). Taman Indah is a reconstructed rainforest, with its own hot, wet climate, and is home to

Euromast

elephants, rhinoceroses and tapirs. There are also monkeys' islands, a bat cave and a nocturnal animals house. The large Riviera Hall includes aquariums, terrariums containing reptiles and amphibians, a tropical hothouse and aviaries.

Kralingsebos – This wood surrounds a big lake (Kralingseplas) and has two windmills on the north side.
In one of them, the **Ster** ⊙ (Star) an old spice mill dating from 1740 and rebuilt in 1969, snuff manufacture can be seen.

★★ THE PORT

See "A new city" p. 267 and the insets on Michelin maps 908 and 211

Nieuwe Maas

Short harbour tour ⊙ – The boat sails down the Maas to Eemhaven, and departs from Leuvenhoofd *(see Travellers' addresses and map of Rotterdam)*.
The boat heads west, following the north bank. It passes on the right Het Park and Euromast. The air vents of the Maastunnel can be seen.

Lloyd Kade – This was the dock for ships trading with Indonesia.

Delfshaven – This was once the port for Delft.

Merwehaven – This is the biggest dock for miscellaneous goods, on the north bank.

Schiedam – *See SCHIEDAM.*

Wilhelminahaven – Naval repairs on a floating dock.
To the west the gulf, then **Wiltonhaven** can be seen; it is used for naval construction and repair workshops.

Here the boat turns round and crosses the river to sail back up the opposite bank towards Rotterdam.

Pernis – Chemical industries, including petrochemicals and artificial fertilisers.

Eemhaven – The boat enters this vast series of docks specialised in container traffic and transhipment of goods.

Waalhaven – Originally built for iron and copper ore tankers, at present this dock also handles containers and miscellaneous goods.

Maashaven – Beyond the Maastunnel, this grain dock, now supplanted by Botlek and Benelux Dock, also handles miscellaneous goods.

Rijnhaven – This dock is lined by quays, where in the past, the great transatlantic liners of the **Holland-Amerika** Line moored. Elegant cruise ships still moor here.

Longer tour of the port ⊙ – This tour goes all the way to Botlek. *See Travellers' addresses p. 266.*

Europoort and Maasvlakte

The vast installations of Europoort, built between 1958 and 1975, cover 3 600ha/8 892 acres on the south bank of Nieuwe Waterweg. Europoort continues to the west by Maasvlakte whose development dates from 1965 to 1971. Some docks can take cargo boats drawing 21.9m/72ft of water.

Car tour – *79km/49mi to Maasvlakte. Leave Rotterdam via ① on the map and take the Beneluxtunnel on the left.*
At the south exit there is a fine view of the Pernis oil terminal.

Take the motorway on the right, running alongside a railway line.

Botlektunnel – Opened in 1980 under the Oude Maas which comes from Dordrecht, this tunnel has a single carriageway 500m/1 640ft long and 21m/69ft below sea level. It was built to relieve the traffic congestion on the old bridge.

Botlek – It is a grain port and oil terminal. Moreover, it has installations for chemical products, bulk transport and naval repairs.

Leave the Europoort road opposite, and continue right to rejoin the river.

Rozenburg – On the Het Scheur, the river's opposite bank, is the Maassluis *(see below)* industrial sector. Near the Rozenburg church there is a windmill, De Hoop (Hope).

Shortly afterwards leave the Europoort road on the left to take Noordzeeweg which runs between the Nieuwe Waterweg and the Calandkanaal.

On the left unloading facilities for oil tankers of different companies can be seen. The end of the road goes around an old radar station: there is a **view** of the Hoek van Holland, Europoort and the estuary which is divided by a dike; towards the north, there is the entrance to the Nieuwe Waterweg leading to Rotterdam, and to the south, the entrance to Europoort – 30 000 ships pass through the estuary every year.

Return by the same route and take the Calandbrug, then go under Brielsebrug to reach Europoort.

To the right one goes alongside the oil terminals which have already been seen and to the left **Hartelkanaal**, which has recreational areas on either side of it; and on the edge of **Brielse Meer** an artificial lake for pleasure boats and once a branch of the Maas, the Brielse Maas.

Dintelhavenbrug – A bridge over an access canal to Dintelhaven, the mineral port. From this bridge one can occasionally see a ferry in **Beneluxhaven**, which like Hoek van Holland, is a port for ferries between England (Kingston upon Hull) and the Netherlands.

Once over the Suurhoffbrug, turn right towards Maasvlakte.

Oostvoornse Meer – This lake was created by the closing of the Brielse Gat in 1965; swimming, surfing and sailing facilities have been provided.

Maasvlakte (Maas Plain) – A stretch of sandy land reclaimed from the North Sea to accommodate the inevitable extension (around 1 200ha/3 000 acres) of Rotterdam's port. At present, the **8th Petroleumhaven** houses an oil terminal (Maasvlakte Olie Terminal). A container terminal (Europe Container Terminus B.V.), an electric power station (E.Z.F.) and a security firm (RISC) have been set up on **Europahaven**. A company specialised in the handling of goods lies near **Amazonehaven**. Facilities for the storage and transhipment of minerals (E.M.O.) along with a branch of Holland's national gas board (Nederlandse Gasunie) are in the **Mississippihaven**.

A new lighthouse has replaced that of Hoek van Holland as the Maasvlakte development had left it stranded inland. To the west stretches a beach.

Europoort tour ⊘ – The tour allows one to grasp the extent of the port installations. The boats leave from Leuvehoofd *(see Travellers' addresses and map of Rotterdam)*.

EXCURSIONS

From Schiedam to Hoek van Holland – *31km/19mi by the A 20 motorway going west.*

Schiedam – *See SCHIEDAM.*

Vlaardingen – This major river and sea port used to specialise in herring fishing. Today it is also an important industrial and commercial centre. From the banks of the Nieuwe Maas one can look at the unending traffic of ocean-going ships toing and froing from Rotterdam. Downstream along the south bank is the Botlek oil terminal.

Maassluis – This port is on the Scheur, between the Nieuwe Maas and the Nieuwe Waterweg. To protect Rotterdam from flooding, a **storm surge barrier★** has been built in the Nieuwe Waterweg between Maassluis and Hoek van Holland. This opened in May 1997, and consists of two immense white gates that are able to close off the 360m/1200ft Nieuwe Waterweg completely. Both gates have steel trusses resembling horizontal versions of the Eiffel Tower, capable of withstanding up to 35 000t. The whole complex is largely controlled automatically, and is the only one of its kind in the world. The Keringhuis information centre has a permanent exhibition about the barrier.

Hoek van Holland – At the mouth of the Nieuwe Waterweg, this is the passenger port for Rotterdam and for ferries going to England (Harwich). It is an impressive sight to see the ships heading for Rotterdam or the North Sea. Opposite are the Europoort installations.

An artificial beach was created north of Hoek van Holland in 1971.

Brielle and Oostvoorne – *41km/26mi to the southwest. Leave Rotterdam via Dorpsweg.*

Brielle – *See BRIELLE.*

Oostvoorne – This is a seaside resort situated near a chain of dunes. A 311ha/768-acre nature reserve, the **Duinen van Voorne**, has been laid out in the dunes; the reserve is crisscrossed by paths. A visitor centre provides information about the reserve's flora and fauna.

Windmills and polders – *Round tour of 81km/50mi – about 3hr.*

Leave Rotterdam via Maasboulevard, go towards Gorinchem and turn off towards Alblasserdam.

The narrow dike road follows the Noord, a stretch of water frequently used. Between the Noord and the Lek lies the **Alblasserwaard**. This old **waard** (low land surrounded by rivers) has a ring of dikes around it and has been made into a polder.

Alblasserdam – This town on the Noord has shipyards for naval construction.

Kinderdijk – Kinderdijk means children's dike, for it is said that during the great floods which occured on St Elisabeth's feast day in 1421, the sea washed up on the dike a crib with a crying baby and a cat.

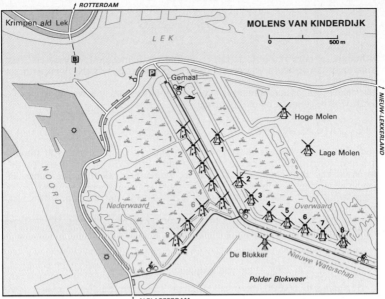

MOLENS VAN KINDERDIJK

Towards the end of the village an opening between houses on the right gives a pretty view of the windmills which dot the plain.

★★ **Kinderdijk windmills** ⊘ – *Illustration: see Introduction.* Near the Nederwaard pumping station, along the boezems, or drainage pools for the polderland, stand 19 windmills. Their exceptional number, their size and the beauty of the marshy plain have made them famous, and they were designated as a UNESCO world heritage site in 1997. Up to 1950 they helped drain the Alblasserwaard, which is below sea level; today, their sails turn for tourists only on Windmill Days *(see Practical information)*.

One can walk along the dikes or take a **boat tour** ⊘.

The eight windmills of the Nederwaard are round stone polder mills *(see Introduction: Windmills)* dating from 1738 (1 to 8). The interior of the second **mill** ⊘ can be visited.

A little further on there is a smaller hollow post mill *(see Introduction: windmills)* called De Blokker.

There are also eight windmills with rotating caps along the other canal, but octagonal in shape and thatched (1 to 8) dating from 1740. Hidden behind them are two other windmills built in 1740 and 1761.

Continue by car along the dike road which follows the Lek.

From Nieuw-Lekkerland on, just down to the right of the dike, large T-shaped farmhouses can be seen; they are thatched and have haystacks beside them protected by a little roof *(illustration: see Introduction, Farmhouses)*. Orchards surround these farmhouses. Other windmills can soon be seen.

At Groot-Ammers take the Molenaarsgraaf road.

Soon four **windmills** appear in single file along the canal. Three are hollow post mills, the fourth is an octagonal polder mill.

Further on rejoin the large canal which crosses the Alblasserwaard and follow the south bank until you come to Alblasserdam.

The **road**★ which is almost at water-level is picturesque. There are large hall-farmhouses *(see Introduction: Farmhouses)* and windmills along the way. Some of these farmhouses have a safety exit a little above ground level, which led into the living room and which was used during floods.

Return to Rotterdam via Maasboulevard.

SCHIEDAM

Zuid-Holland

Population 74 889

Michelin maps 908 E 6, fold 24 (inset) and 211 L 11

Although it is part of the Rotterdam conurbation, Schiedam (pronounced Sreedam) is a typical small town whose centre is surrounded by canals, lined with several windmills.

Shipbuilding yards and numerous industries make it a busy town but its main claim to fame is its jenever, or gin, industry.

HISTORICAL NOTES

About 1260 a castle was built in Schiedam and one of its towers still stands near the new town hall. It received its city rights in 1275. In 1574 the castle was destroyed by the inhabitants so that it would not fall into the hands of the Spanish.

Schiedam is the homeland of **St Lydwine** (1380-1433), patron saint of the sick and missions to the sick.

The town has a large park, **Beatrixpark** to the north with lakes, and nearby the **Groenoord** open-air swimming pool.

The home of Jenever

Beginning in c 1600 the inhabitants of Schiedam started to make spirits from grain, and finally specialised in the distillation of juniper berries (*jenever*) making gin. At one time Schiedam had 400 distilleries, and the monumental 18C and 19C mansions, warehouses, windmills and former distilleries along the canals bear witness to the industry's importance. Today, only about five remain, some use young juniper berries (*jonge genever*) and others old juniper berries (*oude jenever*) which make a more full-bodied gin. Each distillery has its own recipe, which is carefully kept secret.

There are a number of picturesquely named varieties, such as hassebassie, neut, pikketanissie and schiedammertje, but they all taste equally good.

SIGHTS

Stedelijk Museum ⊘ – *Hoogstraat 112.*

Located in the centre of Hoogstraat, the town's main pedestrian street, the museum is installed in an old 1787 hospital, Sint-Jacobs Gasthuis; it is a large building with a portico. Its collections concern archeology, the history of the town, and (mainly Dutch) contemporary art such as the CoBrA group, systematic painting, Pop Art and New Figurative Art.

In the basement, there is the National Distillery Museum, **Nederlands Gedistilleerd Museum De Gekroonde Brandersketel** ⊘. Old labels, advertisements, miniatures and stills illustrate the making of gin in the 19C, and a wide variety of gins, liqueurs and bitters can be sampled.

Windmills – The town was formerly surrounded by 19 huge mills, mainly used for milling grain intended for the distilleries.

Five stage mills stand along Noordvest, the canal marking the course of the old ramparts; these are among the tallest in Europe.

De Walvisch (The Whale) – This is the southernmost of the five mills, and dates from 1794.

Continuing along the quay towards the north, one can see the four other mills.

De Drie Koornbloemen (The Three Cornflowers) – This mill of 1770 was used to grind cattle food.

De Vrijheid (Freedom) – Started in 1785, it still mills grain.

De Noord (The North) – This mill of 1803 is 33.33m/109ft tall including the cap; maximum height of sails 44.56m/146ft. Its premises are used for tasting sessions by an important distillery, whose buildings are opposite.

De Nieuwe Palmboom (The New Palm Tree) – This is the home of the **Nederlands Malend Korenmolenmuseum** ⊘, or Netherlands Corn-Milling Museum. The windmill is still in operation and used for milling rye and malt for the De Gekroonde Brandersketel distillery. The museum shows what it was like to live and work in a windmill.

Zakkendragerhuisje (Porters' House) – *Take the road opposite the Stedelijk Museum and cross the Lange Haven, the town's central canal; fine view over the picturesque quays. Then follow the quay (Oude Sluis) on the right.* Behind the old Grain Exchange or Korenbeurs, there is a gracious 1725 building with a curving gable topped by a turret.

Maasboulevard – From this boulevard near the pleasure boat harbour, there is an interesting **view** of the heavy maritime traffic between Rotterdam and the sea. The port of Pernis, on the opposite bank, is linked to Schiedam by the Beneluxtunnel.

Help us in our constant task of keeping up-to-date.
Send your comments and suggestions to

Michelin Tyre PLC
Travel Publications
38 Clarendon Road
WATFORD
Herts
WD1 1SX
Tel : (01923) 415000/ANG

Web site: www.michelin-travel.com

SLUIS

Zeeland

Population 6 455 (Sluis-Aardenburg)
Michelin maps 908 B 8 and 211 F 15

This small tourist town, pleasant and busy, is situated near the Belgian frontier. With Damme it was an outer harbour of Bruges in the 14C when it was at the mouth of the Zwin, today silted up. The grassy mounds which one sees on entering the town are remains of the old ramparts, turned into an esplanade.

SIGHTS

Stadhuis ⊘ – It is overlooked by a tall 14C **belfry**, the only one existing in the Netherlands. It is decorated with four turrets and a jack-o'the clock. From the top of the bell-tower there is a fine **view** stretching over the plain. The Council Room has a lovely 18C grille.

Molen de Brak ⊘ – This wall mill, destroyed in 1944, was rebuilt in 1951. Its three floors reached by steep ladders make it possible to understand how it works. From the handrail the **view** extends over the surrounding countryside and the Zwin.

EXCURSIONS

Sint-Anna ter Muiden – *2km/1mi to the northwest, near the frontier.*
At the foot of the church's imposing 14C brick tower, the small triangular square, the rustic houses and the water pump form a charming picture. Note a thatched wooden barn at the far end of the square.

Aardenburg – *8km/5mi to the southeast.*
Its fine Gothic church, with characteristics of the Scheldt Gothic style (which developed in Belgium), contains 14C and 15C sarcophagi, with interesting paintings on their inside panels.

IJzendijke – *22km/14mi to the east.*
This old stronghold only has a small halfmoon-shaped bastion or ravelin remaining from its ramparts, covered with earth and surrounded by water. Nearby, there is a lovely windmill.
The spire topped with a golden cock, which one sees in the middle of this small town, belongs to the oldest Protestant church (1612) in Zeeland.
At no 28 Grote Markt is the Regional Museum, **Streekmuseum West-Zeeuws-Vlaanderen** ⊘. Apart from a rustic interior of 1850 from Cadzand with its fine stove, there are implements used in the cultivation of flax and madder and a section devoted to the Zeeland plough horses.

Breskens – *29km/18mi to the north.*
A fishing port at the mouth of the Westerschelde, Breskens, is the departure point for the **ferry** ⊘ to Vlissingen. It also has a pleasure boat harbour.
From the promenade laid out on top of the dune, between the fishing port and the ferry terminal, there are fine views over the beaches and the Scheldt.

SNEEK

Fryslân

Population 30 052

Michelin maps 908 I2 and 210 T4

Town plan in the current Michelin Red Guide Benelux

Sneek (Snits in Frisian) is a small, active and very popular tourist centre. In the Middle Ages it was a port on the Middelzee, an inland sea, which has since disappeared.

Gateway to the Frisian Lakes – Sneek is situated in the centre of a region much appreciated for its lakes, in particular Sneekermeer which is used for different water sports. Sneek has a marina and several sailing schools. One can hire motorboats, sail boats, or participate in boating excursions in season (apply to the VVV).

Every year regattas are organised during the great Sneekweek. In addition, every summer for a fortnight, the skûtsjesilen, regattas with skûtsjes are held on the Frisian lakes and IJsselmeer. Several Frisian towns have one of these old trading boats (skûtsjes) with dark brown sails and a wide and flat hull flanked by two leeboards. *For information about both events and an illustration, see Practical information.*

Waterpoort

SIGHTS

★ **Waterpoort** – This elegant 1613 gateway in brick decorated with sandstone protected the entrance to the port. Its central part pierced with arcades and forming a bridge over the Geeuw is flanked by two turrets.

Stadhuis ⊙ – Dating from the 16C, modified in the 18C, the town hall has a lovely Rococo façade, with tall windows and green shutters, and a richly carved perron guarded by heraldic lions.

Fries Scheepvaartmuseum en Oudheidkamer ⊙ – *Kleinzand 14.* This museum is devoted to Frisian navigation, both fluvial and maritime, with a large collection of boat models used in the 18C and 19C, reconstituted pleasure boat interiors, 17C to 19C paintings, sail and mast workshops and navigational instruments.

In the house, beside the canal, admire the lovely collection of Frisian silverware, especially from Sneek. Several interiors have been recreated including the delightful room, from a neighbouring farm, decorated with naive 18C Frisian landscape paintings.

★ FRIESE MEREN (FRISIAN LAKES)

Round tour of 134km/83mi – about 1 day

Leave Sneek in the direction of Bolsward.

The most attractive part of Friesland is without doubt this area of broads and canals with picturesque and historic villages. Here and there one can catch a glimpse of a church standing high on an artificial mound (terp) behind a screen of trees. In summer the waterways are alive with pleasure boats.

★ **Bolsward** – *See BOLSWARD.*

Near the Workum crossroads, take a minor road towards Exmorra.

Exmorra, Allingawier and Ferwoude are situated on the tourist route (Aldfaers Erf).

Exmorra – In the small **museum** ⊘, a country grocer's shop, a rural house and a classroom of 1885 have been reconstructed. Further on, the charming 13C church on a terp, surrounded by a cemetery, has been restored.

Allingawier – Near the church with a saddleback roofed bell-tower is a typical old Friesland **farmhouse** ⊘ named Yzeren Kou: a large building contains the huge barn and the stable; the annexe, the living quarters, on the first floor leave room underneath for the dairy.

Makkum – It is a picturesque fishing port on the edge of IJsselmeer and crossed by a canal. It has naval shipyards.

Since the 17C tin-glazed earthenware has been made here and above all tiles similar in style to those of Delft, but more rustic (*see Introduction: Art*). On the main square, the **Waag** is a fine construction of 1698. It houses the Tourist Information Centre (VVV) on the ground floor and the Museum of Frisian Ceramics, **Fries Aardewerkmuseum De Waag** ⊘, in the two attics and in the adjacent house. The museum displays objects used daily or for decorative purposes (plates, platters, hot plates) from 1600 to 1880. Note especially the objects (blue paintings on white backgrounds) from Makkum and Harlingen dating from the 18C, the period when Frisian earthenware was at its peak.

Among the painted tile scenes note the one on the chimney-piece from a wealthy Makkum farmhouse and the scene depicting a Frisian earthenware factory in 1737 (a copy; the original is in the Rijksmuseum in Amsterdam).

In Tichelaar's Royal Pottery and Tile Factory, **Tichelaars Aardewerk- en Tegelfabriek** ⊘, founded in 1594, one can see an exhibition of earthenware and visit the workshops to see the different stages in pottery making.

Take the narrow road in the direction of Workum. The road runs parallel to the dike on one side and the canal on the other. Keep your eyes open for herons.

In Gaast, turn left to reach Ferwoude.

Ferwoude – In this locality an old farmhouse and its carpentry **workshop** ⊘ (1845) is open to the public. Opposite is the village church, topped by a pointed spire.

Workum – *See WORKUM.*

Hindeloopen – *See HINDELOOPEN.*

Stavoren – *8.5km/5mi from Koudum.* A fishing village, Stavoren (Starum in Frisian) has two pleasure boat harbours. It is linked to Enkhuizen by a boat service (*see ENKHUIZEN*). In the past, Stavoren was the capital of the Frisian kings, and a member of the Hanseatic League. Evangelised in the 9C by St Odulphus, it

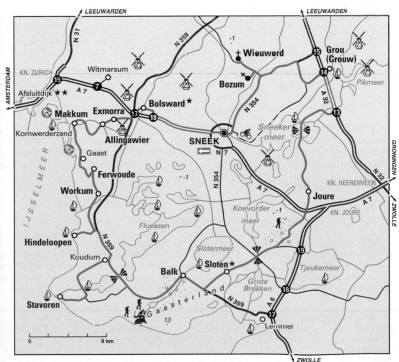

flourished in the 11C. Its port was excellent in the 14C. Then it silted up, as legend has it, because of a rich widow of Stavoren who ordered one of her ships' captains to bring her a precious cargo. The latter returned to Stavoren with wheat: furious the widow had all the wheat thrown into the port.

After Koudum there is a fine **view**, from the lever bridge, over the two lakes on either side of the road. One soon crosses the wooded region of **Gaasterland**, which stretches southwest of Balk.

Balk – Near Slotermeer, this locality is crossed by a canal bordered with several lovely 18C houses, witness to a former prosperity due to its butter trade, for which Balk was the centre.

* **Sloten** – Near Slotermeer and on the fringe of the wooded Gaasterland region, Sloten (Sleat in Frisian) an old fortified town, seems as though it was built on a reduced scale, which accentuates its charm; narrow streets, and tiny 17C and 18C houses run alongside the small canal lined with lime trees.

Following the quays, where ducks waddle, one reaches **Lemsterpoort**, an old watergate and its **mill** of 1755; lovely view over the canal and the lakes where yachts sail in season.

From the lever bridge near Spannenburg, there are lovely views over a wide canal.

Joure – Since the 17C this town has specialised in clockmaking. It also has a large firm dealing in tobacco, tea and coffee. The **Museum Joure** ⊘ deals with all these activities, and also includes the small house where Egbert Douwes was born and an early 20C shop.

A few miles north of Joure, the road runs along a narrow strip of land between two lakes; there are some fine **views**. On the left **Sneekermeer** is one of the most frequented Frisian lakes.

Grou – Near a lake, it is a very popular water sports centre.

Wieuwerd – The village has a **crypt** ⊘ with strange powers. Built in the 14C on a small terp surrounded by a cemetery, this small church, altered in the 19C was used as a tomb in the 17C and 18C for 11 people. The corpses were protected from decomposition by an antimonious gas which rose from the ground: four of the mummies are exhibited under a sheet of glass. To illustrate this phenomenon several birds, one of which was a parrot (1879), were suspended from the vault.

Bozum – This charming village has a 12C and 13C **Romanesque church** ⊘, restored, built of tufa and brick in front of a tower with a saddleback roof, and lined on the west by a semicircle of lovely low houses. The interior is rustic and the paintings in the chancel (c 1300) are very faded.

Return to Sneek via ① on the town plan.

STADSKANAAL

Groningen
Population 33 016
Michelin maps 908 L 2 and 210 AA 5

In this former fenland area, which has been reclaimed as agricultural land, the villages are linear settlements strung out along the main canals and they give the impression of being one long village. Stadskanaal (canal town) is one of them and well merits its name.

EXCURSIONS

Ter Apel – *20km/12mi to the southeast.*
Ter Apel's former convent, **Museum-Klooster Ter Apel** ⊘, is pleasantly situated in a park which boasts some splendid oak trees. The church and two ranges of the cloisters are all that remain and the visitor can visit the cloisters, the refectory and the cellar, where the sarcophagi that were found during excavations in the cloister garth are now on show. The church has a Gothic rood screen of carved wood (1501) and stalls of the same period which are quite plain but have misericords carved with quaint figures. Note the attractive gallery in the chancel.

Nieuweschans – *35km/22mi to the northeast.*
This small quiet village lies in the eastern part of the province of Groningen quite near to the German border. The low houses have been tastefully restored.

STAPHORST★

Overijssel
Population 15 022
Michelin maps 908 J 4 and 210 W 7

The neighbouring villages of Staphorst and **Rouveen** form a world of their own. The townspeople belong to a strict form of Protestantism, a bastion against the innovations of modern life: even now cars are not allowed to run during Sunday services. Women, young and old alike, wear the traditional costume but quite rightly refuse to be photographed.

Farmhouses – The two villages stretch out along the road for over 8km/5mi. The thatched hall-type farmhouses are all identical with trimly painted green doors and blue window frames.
Another characteristic of these farmhouses is the line of doors along one of the side walls. On the right side of the farmhouse the blue shelf for the empty milk cans is often finely carved.

Costumes – The attractive woman's costume is worn quite often. Although rather dark (black shoes, stockings and pleated skirt with a blue or black apron) it is brightened up by a floral bodice-front (kraplap) and with a matching bonnet.
A red (blue if in mourning) tartan fichu is sometimes worn over the shoulders. In winter a blue cardigan is worn over the costume.
The older women still wear the head band with spiral antennae *(see Introduction: Traditions and folklore)*. The bonnet is reserved for small girls. When the children come out of school (around noon and 4pm) one can see young girls prettily attired in their local costumes pedalling past on their bicycles.

Ph. Gajic/MICHELIN

Staphorst local costume

TIEL

Gelderland
Population 35 690
Michelin maps 908 H 6 and 211 R 11

Tiel is nicely situated on the banks of the Waal in the centre of a fruit-growing region the **Betuwe**; the orchards make a magnificent sight when the trees are in blossom Tiel was another of the Dutch towns which belonged to the Hanseatic League.
A harvest thanksgiving procession celebrates the end of the **fruit-picking season** (see Calendar of events).

EXCURSION

Buren and Culemborg – 19km/12mi to the northwest.

Buren – This small town hemmed in by its walls has been the object of some quite extensive restoration work. In 1492 it became the seat of a countship which passed to the House of Orange when Anne van Buren married William the Silent. The **old orphanage** dating from 1613 is a fine building with green and red shutters and a porch with heavy ornamentation. It contains the **Museum der Koninklijke Marechaussee**, retracing the history of the gendarmerie and police force in the Netherlands. Not far away, part of the curtain wall bordering the river has been turned into a promenade and affords lovely **views** over the river and the Betuwe orchards.
In the main street, Voorstraat, is a **church** with a 15C bell-tower crowned by an octagonal Renaissance upper part, itself topped out with a pinnacle turret. The **stadhuis**, recognisable by its Rococo doorway, was rebuilt in the 18C. Nearby, in a building against the wall, is a small cart museum, the **Boerenwagenmuseum** (Achter Boonenburg 1).
At the end of Voorstraat is a brick town gateway and a 1716 **wall mill** named after the Prince of Orange.

Culemborg – This historic village received its charter in 1318 and became the seat of an earldom in 1555. Some sections of its old walls still stand. It was the birthplace of **Jan van Riebeeck** (1619-77), who in 1652 founded the Cape Colony (now Cape Town) for the Dutch East India Company as a stopping place on the way to the East Indies.
In **Marktplein** the Flamboyant Gothic stadhuis sports heraldic lions above the perron. The **Binnenpoort** is the only gateway to remain.

TILBURG

Noord-Brabant
Population 183 002
Michelin maps 908 G 7 and 211 P 13

Tilburg, located on the Wilhelminakanaal, is one of the Netherlands' largest towns in terms of population. It is a bustling place, with several shopping centres, including the Heuvelpoort, the Schouwburgpromenade and the modern Emma-passage Tilburg is proud of its annual nine-day July **fair**, the largest in Benelux and one of its major attractions in the summer. It is also the venue for the **Festival Mundial**, focusing on the third world, which is held in Leijpark in June.
The economy of the town was long dominated by the **textile industry** (see Introduction Industrial heritage), and in 1871 there were 125 woollen mills employing 4 600 people. These were mainly family businesses with a low degree of speciali sation, but they failed to modernise and keep pace with increasing competition from the rest of Europe in the 1960s. The main industries now are chemicals photographic products, paper and printing.
Tilburg has a student population of over 25 000, with educational institutions including the Catholic University of Brabant and the Tilburg Theological Faculty. The country's first and only rock academy opened here in September 1998.
The town was also the birthplace of the artist **Cornelis van Spaendonck** (1756-1840) and his brother Gerardus (1746-1822), both of whom specialised in flower paintings and worked in Paris.
King William II regularly stayed in Tilburg, and the distinctive English Romantic-style palace he had built on Willemsplein now houses the tourist office. The king died in Tilburg in 1849.

SIGHTS

Stadhuisplein – There are quite a number of recent buildings in Tilburg's main square. The shopping streets leading off to the north are now pedestrian zones.

Stadsschouwburg – The 1961 municipal theatre was the work of the architect Bijvoet and Holt. Glass curtain walls adjoin incurved surfaces of bare brick.

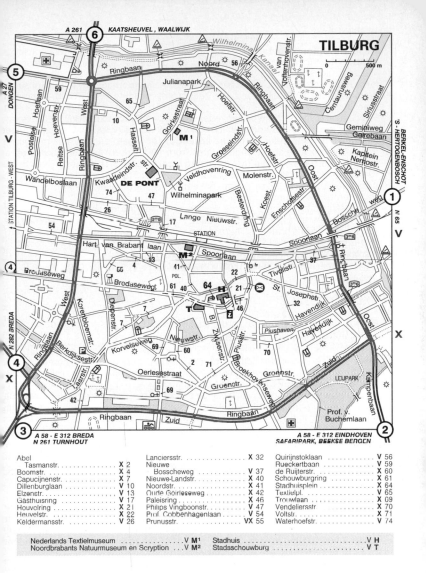

TILBURG

Stadhuis – The sober lines of the black granite-clad town hall were the work of Kraayvanger. It was built in 1971, and adjoins the neo-Gothic palace of King William II.

Noordbrabants Natuurmuseum and Scryption ⊙ – The Natural History Museum, dealing with the flora and fauna of Noord-Brabant, is located diagonally opposite the station. Beside it is the Scryption, a museum of the many different aspects of written communication. Its collection includes several thousand typewriters, calculators and office machines, a large number of inkstands, pens and other writing equipment, and documentation on such subjects as stenography, Braille and secret writing.

★★ **De Pont (Stichting voor Hedendaagse Kunst)** ⊙ – Jan de Pont (1915-87) was a local businessman who, shortly before he died, asked that part of his estate should be used to promote modern art. A foundation was therefore set up, and at the beginning of the 1990s the Amsterdam architects Benthem Crouwel converted a former woollen mill into an exhibition space. This magnificent exhibition space, with an area of over 4 200m²/45 000sq ft, is flooded with natural light, and is used to display a selection of the foundation's very varied art collection. This includes works by Richard Serra, Marlene Dumas, Thierry De Cordier, Gerhard Merz, Anish Kapoor, James Turrell, Jan Dibbets, Marien Schouten, Rob Birza, Guido Geelen and Richard Long. Alongside the large central hall are the former woolsheds, which are ideally suited to works requiring a more intimate display area.

The museum also holds temporary exhibitions, and makes its garden available to an artist in the summer.

289

* **Nederlands Textielmuseum** ⊙ – This museum is very appropriately housed in a former textile factory in Goirkestraat, one of the last such factories to survive. The four oldest buildings have been restored; these are the main halls, built for large, heavy machinery, which has a distinctive sawtoothed roof to maximise the amount of natural light, and the four-storey building used for the spinning machines.

The central focus of this working museum is a permanent exhibition on the textile industry in the Netherlands, which shows the technological and social changes wrought upon the industry by the advent of the steam engine. The museum's impressive working steam engine dates from 1906. There are a number of other machines of the kind used by the Tilburg wool industry. The wool arrived in the factory in large sacks, and first had to be washed. The fibres were mechanically untangled, blended, and carded to make the fibres lie parallel. The wool could then be taken to the spinning machine.

Demonstrations of some of the textile machines are given, and the museum describes various aspects of the industry: knitting, dyeing, linen manufacture, fabric-printing and braiding. There is also a visual arts and design department with works by Dutch artists in which textiles play an important part, and an interesting display of Dutch household textiles since 1890.

There is also a shop selling items such as scarves and linen goods made in the museum.

EXCURSIONS

* **Beekse Bergen** – *4km/3mi to the southeast via ② on the town plan.*
This country park lies to the north of Hilvarenbeek and covers a total area of 425ha/1 050 acres. It incorporates a beach park, a safari park and a small zoo.

Safari park ⊙ – This spacious park (110ha/272 acres) is now home to over 1 000 animals free to roam at liberty within their enclosures. Lions, rhinoceroses, hyenas, cheetahs, antelopes, zebras and baboons are only some of the residents of the drive-through area, which can be toured by bus or boat, or in your own car. The section with the penguins, flamingos, squirrel monkeys and other rare species can be visited on foot. For the children there is a small zoo with a collection of young animals.

Speelland ⊙ – This amusement park centres on a lake, and offers a variety of pursuits including waterbiking, rowing, sailing and swimming. Land-based activities include minigolf, trampolining, and pony rides. A cable-car gives visitors a bird's-eye view of the whole park.

* **Oisterwijk** – *10km/6mi to the east via ① the town plan.*
This pleasant holiday centre offers a choice of excursions in its immediate vicinity, where wooded dunes, heather-clad moors and numerous lakes are to be found. In the town itself the **house** at nos 88-90 Kerkstraat dating from 1633 has an elegant gable. The charming square, **De Lind**, in front of the town hall is planted with lime trees to form a marriage way traditionally followed by wedding processions.

UTRECHT★★

Utrecht ℙ
Population 233 951
Michelin maps 908 G 5 and 211 P 10
Plan of the conurbation (showing motorway network with access roads)
in the current Michelin Red Guide Benelux

Utrecht is a lively but intimate town with a maze of streets and numerous old buildings testifying to its long and rich history. Its picturesque canals, wharves and terraces give it a unique character; it is also a university town and a commercial centre well-known for its trade fair, which was first held in 1917. The Catholic church also plays an important role.

Every year a **Festival of Ancient Music**★ is held here. The Dutch Film Week organises screenings of all the films made in Holland during the previous year *(see Calendar of events)*.

HISTORICAL NOTES

Utrecht was founded at the beginning of our era on the Rhine (now called Oude Rijn), which passed through the town at that time. Under the Roman Empire the town was called Trajectum (ford) from which it gets its present name.

In the 7C it was chosen as the seat of Friesland missions. **St Willibrord** (658-739), a Northumbrian, was made Bishop of the Frisians in 695, settled in Utrecht, Friesland then being considered a dangerous place.

Accommodation

Utrecht is primarily a university and business town, and there are few hotels with much in the way of old-world charm.

YOUTH HOSTEL

NJHC Ridderhofstad – *Rhijnauwenselaan 14, 3981 HH Bunnik,* ☎ *(030) 656 12 77, Fax (030) 657 10 65. 22 rooms.* 6km/4mi east of the centre by no 40/41 bus towards Rhijnauwen.

BUDGET HOTELS

Ouwi – *F.C. Dondersstraat 12, 3572 JH Utrecht,* ☎ *(030) 271 63 03, Fax (030) 271 46 19. 28 rooms.* This small hotel consists of a row of mansions in a quiet street on the edge of town. The rooms are small but clean, with en-suite bathrooms. Good value for money.

OUR SELECTION

Mitland – *Ariënslaan 1, 3573 PT Utrecht,* ☎ *(030) 271 58 24, Fax (030) 271 90 03. 92 rooms.* Modern hotel in a leafy location on the outskirts, with a waterside restaurant and leisure facilities including a pool, sauna, tennis and bowling.

Malie – *Maliestraat 2, 3581 SL Utrecht,* ☎ *(030) 231 64 24, Fax (030) 234 06 61. 29 rooms.* This hotel is located in a 19C building near the centre. The rooms are comfortable, with modern furnishings, and there is a terrace in the large garden.

Restaurants

Wilhelminapark - *Wilhelminapark 65,* ☎ *(030) 251 06 93.* This pavilion in the park is an ideal way of escaping the hustle and bustle of Utrecht. The food is excellent, there is a view of the lake, and you can eat outside in summer.

Bistro Chez Jacqueline - *Korte Koestraat 3-5,* ☎ *(030) 231 10 89.* Friendly bistro near the tourist office.

Brasseries, cafés, bars, coffee shops...

Toque toque – *Oudegracht 138.* Pleasant corner café serving delicious international cuisine.

Stadskasteel Oudaen – *Oudegracht 99.* This medieval castle is now home to a brewery, complete with copper brew-kettles, a tasting room, a waterside terrace, a restaurant, and theatre performances too.

De oude muntkelder – *Oudegracht 112.* A canalside cellar serving excellent pancakes and omelettes.

Canalside terraces, Oudegracht

Café restaurant Winkel van Sinkel – *Oudegracht 158*. A meal or drink in this ol‹ warehouse provides an opportunity to admire the attractive central atriun with its glass roof and balustraded gallery.

Film-theatercafé 't Hoogt – *Slachtstraat 5*. Busy arts café where you can watch play or film and then have a drink afterwards.

Stairway to Heaven – *Mariaplaats 11-12*. A rock café with a restaurant. Liv‹ concerts on Wednesdays, and dancing on Thursdays, Fridays and Saturdays‹

Practical information

General information – The **VVV tourist office** is in the same complex as th‹ Muziekcentrum Vredenburg (Vredenburg 90, 3501 DC Utrecht ☏ (0900) 414 14 14 or www.tref.nl/utrecht/VVV). It offers information o‹ sights, cultural and other events, accommodation packages, and tickets fo‹ theatre and other performances. For hotel bookings, contact **Utrecht Hot‹ Service** on ☏ (030) 231 75 76.

Transport – Parking in the streets of Utrecht is difficult and expensive; it i‹ free only after 11pm. If you want to avoid getting ticketed or clamped, us‹ one of the many **multi-storey car parks**, which are signposted. It is actually no‹ possible to drive across the centre of town; instead, use the ring road. Ther‹ is a park and ride site at the Galgenward stadium east of the centre. All the main sights are within walking distance of one another. Contact the **VV‹** for information on travel by **bus**, **tram** or **bicycle**.

Tours and walks – The VVV sells brochures giving details of **walking routes** o‹ various themes. It also offers a **guided walk around town** on Sundays from mi‹ May to mid September. Tours by **horse-drawn carriage** leave from Domplein.

Boat trips – Tours of the canals, and further afield on the **Vecht**, the **Kromm‹ Rijn** and to the **Loosdrechtse Plassen**, depart from the quay on Oudegracht. Reder‹ Schuttevaer, ☏ (030) 272 01 11; Rederij Lovers, ☏ (030) 231 64 68.

Shopping – **Hoog Catharijne** is the Netherlands' largest indoor shoppin‹ precinct; another is **Shoppingcenter La Vie**, though shopping is much mor‹ interesting in the large pedestrian area in the old town. Late-night shoppin‹ is on Thursdays. For a truly authentic shopping experience, try the **Museum voor het Kruideniers‹ bedrijf** (Grocer's Shop Museum) in a small street behind the Statenkamer. Thi‹ attractive shop dating from 1873 sells all kinds of old-fashioned delicacies‹ such as sweets, liquorice and peppermint, all measured out using coppe‹ weights.

Markets – There is a **general market** on Vredenburg every Wednesday an‹ Saturday, and a **farmers' market** on Fridays. On Saturdays, a flower marke‹ takes place on the Bakkerbrug and part of the Oudegracht, and another o‹ Janskerkhof. Finally, a flea market is held in Breedstraat on Saturda‹ mornings.

Specialities – **Boterspritsjes**, delicious butter shortbread biscuits, are a loca‹ delicacy.

Theatres and concert halls – **Uitloper**, a free weekly publication available i‹ many cafés, restaurants and theatres, lists all the films, theatres an‹ exhibitions on offer. **Muziekcentrum Vredenburg**, Vredenburgpassage 77, ☏ (030) 231 45 44; **Stads‹ chouwburg** (municipal theatre), Lucas Bolwerk 24, ☏ (030) 230 20 23; **Werftheater**, Oudegracht aan de werf 60, ☏ (030) 231 54 40; **Huis aan de Wer‹** Boorstraat 107, ☏ (030) 231 53 55.

Night-life – Utrecht is a university town, and has countless bars and cafés‹ There are large numbers on Janskerkhof, Neude and of course the canalsid‹ cellars where you can eat and drink outdoors in summer.

Events – **Bluesroute**, held on the third weekend in April, offers free concert‹ throughout the town centre. The international **Spring dance** festival also take‹ place in April. The **Festival aan de Werf** is an international theatre and visual art‹ event, while at Whitsun, the Maliebaan is the venue for **Stoom** (Steam), ‹ nostalgic event featuring a wide variety of steam-driven vehicles and a‹ old-fashioned fair. The prestigious **Holland Festival Oude Muziek** (late August t‹ early September) includes a large number of concerts of music from the 11‹ to the 19C. The **Netherlands Film Festival** in late September is when the country'‹ top film prize, the Golden Calf, is awarded.

t the time of Charlemagne, who extended his empire northwards, the area ecame part of the Carolingian Empire. After the Treaty of Meerssen, Utrecht ecame a fief of the German emperors. Under their domination, Bishop Balderik 918-976) succeeded in enlarging the bishopric's jurisdiction. Having become very owerful, the bishops extended their sovereignty over the present-day provinces f Utrecht, Overijssel, Drenthe and Groningen: their territory was called the **Sticht**. he town received its charter in 1122 and was surrounded by ramparts (rebuilt 4C).

orn in Utrecht in 1459, **Adrian VI**, tutor to Charles V and then a professor in Louvain Belgium), was the only Dutch Pope (1522-23).

harles V took possession of the Sticht in 1528. Made an archbishopric by Philip II f Spain in 1559, the bishopric of Utrecht, from that time, covered all the main towns f the area, except 's-Hertogenbosch. However, the town's prosperity was coming o an end as the commercial centre had moved towards the coast.

n 1577 the inhabitants expelled the Spanish garrison.

he Union of Utrecht – In January 1579 the representatives of the states of Holland nd Zeeland, and the territories of Groningen and Utrecht, and the stadtholder of ielderland united to sign the **Union of Utrecht**; they decided that no separate agreement vould be made with Philip II and that the Protestant religion would be the only one uthorised in Holland and Zeeland; in the other regions, practice of the Catholic eligion would not lead to prosecution. In the same year signatures were added by epresentatives from Overijssel, Friesland and Drenthe and some southern towns uch as Antwerp.

his treaty, following the Union of Arras by which the Duke of Parma had forced the outhern states to submit to Spain, was the cause of the split between south and orth Low Countries (which later became the United Provinces).

n 1635, **René Descartes** stayed in Utrecht (Maliebaan 36–38) and wrote the *Discourse* n *Method* which was published in Leiden.

he year 1636 was marked by the founding of Utrecht University, the second in the ountry after the one in Leiden.

he schism of the Old Catholics – In the 15C a first schism shook the bishopric of Jtrecht, where the chapter had retained the privilege of electing its bishops. In 1423, pposition to a pontifical candidate caused a bitter conflict between the partisans of he two opposing bishops.

n 1702 the Archbishop of Utrecht, Petrus Codde, accused of Jansenism, was lismissed from his duties by the Pope. In 1723 the Chapter of Utrecht elected a uccessor, Cornelis Steenoven, without pontifical agreement. Thus, in 1724, the Old atholics Church was formed in Utrecht. A large number of French Jansenists, leeing to the Netherlands after the condemnation of their religion by the papal bull *Jnigenitus* in 1717, became members of this independent church with Jansenist endencies.

n 1870 a group of Germans, refusing the dogma of pontifical infallibility, joined the hurch of Old Catholics in Utrecht. In 1889 a great meeting of members of this hurch, coming from several countries, took place in Utrecht. This religion is still ractised in the Netherlands where it has about 10 000 followers.

he Utrecht School of painting – In the 16C a school of painting with a strong Italian nfluence developed in Utrecht.

an van Scorel (1495-1562) born near Alkmaar, lived in Utrecht, apart from a visit to taly and a stay in Haarlem. He helped spread the Italian influence in the Netherlands; *he Baptism of Christ* (in the Frans Halsmuseum in Haarlem) is one of his best works. Iaarten van Heemskerck his pupil, was also a Romanist painter (16C Northern European rtists who were greatly influenced by the Italian Renaissance). An excellent portrait ainter (*Portrait of a Young Scholar* in the Museum Boijmans-Van Beuningen in Rotterdam), Jan van Scorel also had as a pupil **Antoon Mor** (1517-76) who made his areer particularly in Spain, under the name of **Antonio Moro**, where he painted with alent the court of Philip II.

n the beginning of the 17C, **Abraham Bloemaert** (1564-1651), born in Gorinchem, assed on his admiration for Italian painting to many of his pupils: Hendrick Ter Irugghen or **Terbrugghen** (1588-1629) who, born in Deventer, worked mostly in Jtrecht; on his return from Italy he was one of the first to take his inspiration from :aravaggism (those artists greatly influenced by Caravaggio's chiaroscuro), **Gerard an Honthorst** (1590-1656) born in Utrecht, also became, after a visit to Italy, a faithful mitator of Caravaggio; **Cornelis van Poelenburgh** (c 1586-1667), who painted with recision luminous landscapes scattered with Roman ruins.

)ne who remained uninfluenced by the problems of chiaroscuro was **Jan Davidsz de leem** (1606-1683/4). He was born in Utrecht and lived in Leiden and then in Antwerp, nd specialised in the *vanitas* still-life paintings, especially paintings depicting a table)aded with plates, glasses and dishes of food. His son, Cornelis de Heem, imitated is subjects as well as his sophisticated style.

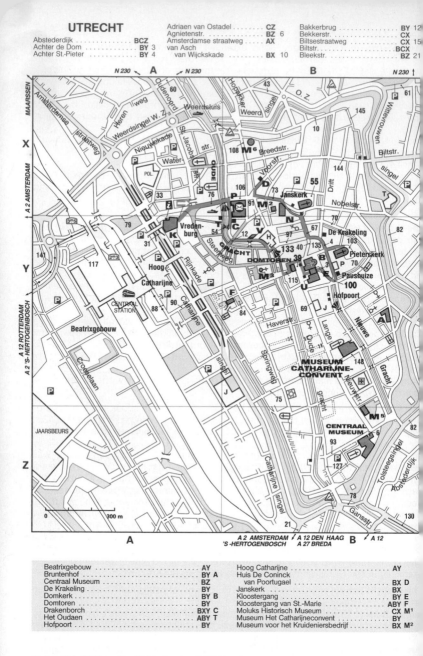

UTRECHT

From the 17C to the 19C – In the 17C Utrecht was a very important fortified town; a ring of canals, today, marks the course of the fortifications. The town was occupied by the armies of Louis XIV from 1672 to 1674 and in 1712. Prepared in Utrecht's town hall in January 1712, the **Peace of Utrecht** was signed in 1713 in Het Slot van Zeist *(see Excursions)* and brought an end to the Spanish War of Succession which had broken out in 1701, caused by the accession to the throne of Philip V, Louis XIV's grandson.

In 1806 the King of Holland, Louis Bonaparte, stayed with his court in a private mansion in Utrecht *(at no 31 Drift)*.

The famous **Utrecht velvet** with its long strand and embossed ornamentation, used for covering walls and furniture, is no longer made in the area. It was a velvet woven with linen, goats' hair (which replaced silk) and cotton.

Modern Utrecht – Utrecht has been expanding since the middle of the century and has many new quarters and buildings. Among many achievements there is a very large indoor shopping mall, the **Hoog Catharijne**, a municipal theatre (1941) by Dudok, the **Rietveld-Schröderhuis** (1924) by Rietveld and the **Kanaleneiland** (or island of canals) quarter (1962) to the west near the Amsterdam-Rijnkanaal and the **Muziekcentrum** (1979) on the Vredenburg, designed by the architect Hertzberger.

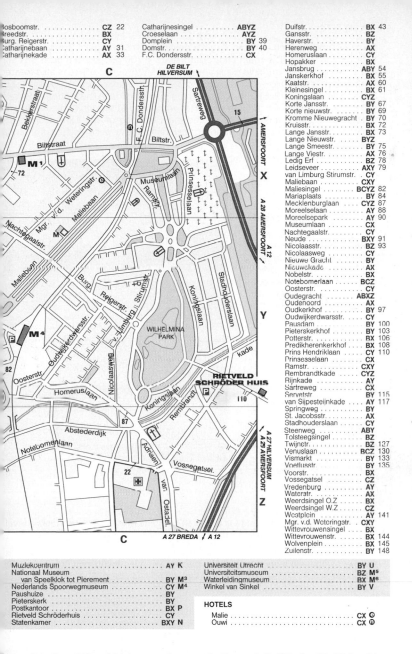

The university of Utrecht has a new campus to the east, **De Uithof**, with 17 faculties. Its **Educatorium**, or educational centre, was designed by the leading Dutch architect Rem Koolhaas.

There are many statues in the town. Among them are the *Fountain of the Muses' Feast* (1959) by JC Hekman in front of the theatre, and *Queen Wilhelmina* by Mari Andriessen in Wilhelmina Park (1968). Others are cited in the text on the tour of the town.

★ OLD TOWN *half a day*

The tree-lined canals ★★ (Oudegracht and Nieuwe Gracht) of Utrecht's city centre are edged by canalside quays which are much lower down and onto which open vaulted cellars.

Vredenburg - Most of Utrecht's animation is concentrated on this large square which links the old town with the new quarters. The old fortress of Charles V stood here, the foundations were discovered during the laying out of the square. A Music

Centre (**Muziekcentrum**) with an original design by the architect Herzberger was built here in 1979. The main auditorium seats 1 700 people, and both this and the smaller auditorium have glass domes. The VVV tourist office is also located in this complex.

To the west, the new **Hoog Catharijne** shopping mall extends to the station. This vast urban complex includes shopping galleries with air-conditioning in the basement, a large hotel and the **Beatrixgebouw**, the main building of the Exhibition Palace (Jaarbeurs) where there are international fairs and a permanent commercial exhibition.

From Oudegracht bridge, there is a fine **view** over the canal (reach via Lange Viestraat). On the left is the open dome of the neo-Classical **Augustinuskerk** (1839).

The Oudegracht

* **Oudegracht** – Narrow, spanned by numerous bridges, this old canal which crosses the town from one end to the other, originally linked the Rhine to the Vecht. It is one of the city's animated centres, both on the upper quays and the lower quays, which are lined with shops and restaurants.

At the point where it forms a bend one can see the **Drakenborch**, a house rebuilt in 1968 in the old style.

Opposite at no 99, the 14C Het **Oudaen** house (see Travellers' addresses) has a tall façade topped by crenellations.

Cross the first bridge (Jansbrug).

The quay on the opposite side is reserved for pedestrians. One soon has a lovely **view*** of the cathedral's tall Domtoren.

Return to the other quay.

On this bridge and along Oudegracht there is a flower market on Saturdays. The **Winkel van Sinkel** (1839) at the end of Oudegracht is one of the country's oldest warehouses. Both the large caryatids in the portico and the four white sculptures at the top are made of cast iron.

Pass in front of the **stadhuis** with its neo-Classical façade (1826) which conceals ruins dating from the Middle Ages. From here, there is a fine **view*** of the continuation of the Oudegracht and of the Domtoren.

Vismarkt – This is the old fish market, which operated from the 12C until well into the 20C. Fish were kept in large baskets in the canal to keep them fresh.

Nationaal Museum van Speelklok tot Pierement – *see The museum district p 298.*

** **Domtoren** ⊘ – This bell-tower was formerly linked by an arch to the nave of the cathedral, which was destroyed shortly after a church service in 1674 by a hurricane which also devastated the town. Built between 1321 and 1382 in the Gothic style, restored at the beginning of the 20C, it influenced many other bell-towers in the country, of which it is the highest. Its three recessed floors, the first two are square and of brick, the last, octagonal and of stone, soar up to 112m/367ft in height. It has a fine carillon, most of the bells having been cast by the Hemony brothers.

From the topmost gallery (465 steps), there is an immense and magnificent **panorama**** over the town and the surrounding area.

Domplein – This square extends between the Domtoren and the Domkerk. A line of paving stones indicate the nave's old layout.

★ Domkerk ⊘ – The tall silhouette of its transept stands miraculously preserved from a hurricane in 1674, hidden behind it is the chancel. Both are Gothic, built between 1254 and 1517 on the site of Sint-Maartenskathedraal, destroyed by fire. The chancel with five chapels radiating round the ambulatory was inspired by that of Tournai Cathedral.

The bronze **doors** (1996) are by Theo van de Vathorst. The outsides are decorated with newspaper cuttings (evangelical texts) in seven languages: Dutch, Frisian, English, Japanese, Greek, Latin and Syrian. The relief at the top shows St Martin dividing his cloak. The insides depict the works of charity, in contemporary form on the left, and in historic form on the right.

Inside there are **funerary monuments**, in particular, in the second chapel, south side of the ambulatory, the black marble tomb of Bishop Guy of Avesnes, who died in 1379.

The neo-Gothic organ, built in 1831, is used for concerts. The stained-glass windows (1926 and 1936) are by Roland Holst.

The Domkerk was formerly a cathedral, but this title is now held by the church, Catharijnekerk, next to the Museum Catharijne Convent.

Utrecht University – Built at the end of the 19C in the neo Renaissance style, it incorporates the cathedral's old **chapter house** (1409), the present great lecture hall or **Aula**. The Union of Utrecht was signed in this room on 15 January 1579. The seven coats of arms on the stained-glass windows evoke the provinces and the signatory regions. On the wall seven tapestries woven in 1936 bear the emblems of the various faculties.

The statue (1887) on the square outside the university depicts **Jan van Nassau**, the brother of William the Silent, who instigated for the Union of Utrecht.

Kloostergang – A replica of a 10C runic stone from Jelling (Denmark), evoking the conversion of the Danes to Christianity, stands at the entrance to the 15C cathedral cloisters. Around the cloisters, the gables have low reliefs illustrating the life of St Martin, patron saint of the old cathedral and of the city. The **view** of the transept and the apse of the cathedral from this intimate cloister garden is very pretty.

Go past a fountain with a statue of a canon writing to reach the south side of the cloisters. In the street called Achter de Dom (meaning behind the cathedral) is the back of the old chapter-house. The medieval building beside it is a cloister house where canons lived.

Pausdam – At the junction of two canals, this is a beautiful square where the **Paushuize** stands. This elegant house, intended for Pope (*paus*) Adrian VI was only completed in 1523, the year of his death. The stepped gable on the canal has a statue of the Saviour.

Nieuwegracht – This canal is similar to the Oudegracht, but is lined with elegant residences. One can see Hofpoort, a 17C Baroque doorway of the Law Courts, and no 37, a lovely old house.

Further on, at no 63, is the Museum Catharijneconvent (see below).

From the bridge, a fine **view** over the canal and Domtoren can be had.

Walk back to Pausdam and turn into the picturesque Kromme Nieuwegracht. The houses on the left side all have their own little bridges.

Pieterskerk – Assigned since 1656 to the Walloon Protestant community, this interesting early Romanesque church was built in 1048. Pieterskerk is one of the four churches in the shape of a cross which Bishop **Bernulphus** wished to build round Sint-Maartenskerk, which was then the cathedral. Two of these churches have disappeared: abbey church of Sint-Paulusabdij and Sint-Mariakerk, where only the cloisters remain. The two others, Pieterskerk and Janskerk are all that remain of the famous **Bernulphus' Cross** of churches.

The vaults in the transept are Gothic, but the nave in pure Romanesque style is roofed by a wooden barrel vault held up by 10 red-sandstone columns with typical cube-shaped capitals. Some of the columns have been moved to the end of the church and replaced by copies. The raised chancel is built over the crypt. Four **low Mosan reliefs★** (c 1170), found during the church's restoration, are embedded in the wall in front of the chancel. They show the Judgment of Christ by Pilate, the Crucifixion, the angel outside the empty tomb and the three Marys with the herbs. The Romanesque baptismal font has corners decorated with heads. In the chapel towards the left, which has oven vaulting, one can see the remains of Romanesque frescoes: the Virgin on the moon's crescent.

Concerts are given on the new organ at the far end of the church.

* **Crypt** – The groined vaulting is supported by stout fluted columns. In the apse ther is a red-sandstone sarcophagus which contains the remains of Bishop Bernulphus founder of the church.

At no 8, on the corner of Achter Sint-Pieter and Keistraat, there is a lovely 17(house, **De Krakeling**; the front is decorated with festoons and the door with a palm tree.

Janskerkhof – On Saturdays, the beautiful 17C and 18C houses aroun this square provide a picturesque backdrop to the colourful flowe market.

In the middle of the square is the Romanesque Gothic **Janskerk**, founded by Bisho Bernulphus as the northern end of the cross of churches. The building ha undergone major restoration and houses, among other things, an early musi performance centre.

The small building (1683) with a coat of arms opposite the church is the **mai guard-house** of the States of Utrecht, whose members met in the Statenkame opposite. In front of it is a **statue of Anne Frank**, and to the right an equestrian statu of **St Willibrord**.

To the south of the square is the old restored **Statenkamer**, where the State General of the province met. This building, which originally belonged to monastery of Friars Minor, is now the law faculty of Utrecht University.

Post Office – Despite what its exterior might suggest, this building on Neud is pleasantly well lit inside. It was designed in the style of the Amsterdam Schoc by J Crouwel and built between 1918 and 1924. The extraordinary **parabol vaulting*** is made up of lines of glazed yellow brick and glass, and the imposin black statues symbolise the five continents, trade and prosperity. The statu in the vestibule represents mail sent by land (horses), sea (fish) and ai (birds).

Huis De Coninck van Poortugael – Dating from 1619, the House of the King o Portugal has a charming Mannerist façade with a crow-stepped gable; above th ground-floor windows are the coats of arms of Nijmegen and Portugal. The ma in the centre with a sceptre is King Philip III of Portugal and Spain.

The heads of an ox and two rams on the façade on the other side of the stree belong to the former **Grote Vleeshuis**, or meat market (1637).

THE MUSEUM DISTRICT

The Utrecht Museum District was established a few years ago in the old town. Th project is still in progress, and comprises the following museums.

Nationaal Museum van Speelklok tot Pierement ⊘ – Located in an ol five-aisled Gothic church, the Buurkerk, this museum has a magnificent collectio of 18C to 20C **mechanical musical instruments****. The guide operates a number c these during the tour.

Exhibited are old clocks and music boxes, pianolas and orchestrions made fo cafés and dance halls, a Steinway player piano (1926) and a Hupfeld automati violin (1910).

The museum also houses a superb collection of barrel organs, small street organ and enormous fair or dance organs *(see Introduction: Art)*.

** **Museum Catharijneconvent** ⊘ – This large museum of religious art is house in the Late Gothic convent of St Catherine (originally a monastery belonging t the Knights of St John) and an 18C canalside house. It is devoted to the histor of Christianity in the Netherlands, and has the country's largest collection o **medieval art*****.

The very varied collections are beautifully displayed. They include magnificer liturgical robes (such as the 15C cope of David of Burgundy), manuscripts an miniatures (including the finely worked evangeliarum of Lebuinus, made fron ivory and semi-precious stones), gold and silver objects, sculptures, altarpiece and paintings by such artists as Geertgen tot Sint Jans, Jan van Score Rembrandt, Frans Hals and Pieter Saenredam.

The history of the Catholic and Protestant churches, and events such as th Iconoclasm and the Reformation, are inextricably tied up with that of the countr as a whole. The differences between the two churches are explored in the canalsid house, focusing on such themes as church interiors, religious art, services, the rol of religion in everyday life (going to church, praying and reading the Bible), an the relationship between church and State.

The **Sint-Catherinakerk** can also be visited from the museum (subject to certai conditions).

★ Universiteitmuseum ⓥ – This museum is the home of the collections built up by Utrecht University since it was established in 1636. The visit begins with the **Bleulandkast★**, dating from 1816, which is divided into four sections and contains an impressive collection of medical preparations and wax models. The embryology section, in particular, is not suitable for those of a sensitive nature!

A permanent exhibition, **Geleerd in Utrecht** (Learned in Utrecht), gives a picture of university education in the late 19C and early 20C; visitors can sit on old benches and listen to some of Utrecht's most famous lecturers. The display cases around this contain scientific instruments, botanical and zoological preparations, and the famous Van Swinden collection. This includes the standard metre and kilogram given to Van Swinden, the Dutch member of France's Metre Committee in 1799, to bring an end to the differences between weights and measures in different countries. Temporary exhibitions are held on the first floor. On the second floor are two **unique collections★** relating to dentistry and ophthalmology, with often bizarre instruments and models displayed in rotation. The **Rarities collection** between the two includes stuffed animals, skeletons and fossils, and a camel's intestine, nearly 5m/16ft long, hangs from the ceiling.

Behind the museum is the **Old Botanical Garden** (1724), with greenhouses, orangeries, a seed-house and gingko trees, and the Regius Garden, used to grow medicinal plants.

The **Beyerskameren**, a late 16C almshouse with a courtyard, is located at the end of Lange Nieuwstraat on the left. The impressive baroque building in Agnietenstraat is the **Fundatie van Renswoude**, built in 1756 as a school for orphans. Around the corner to the left is a row of beautiful small brick almshouses, the **Kameren Maria van Pallaes**, founded in 1651. On the right, on the corner of Lange Nieuwstraat and Agnietenstraat, is the **Willem Arntzstichting**, formerly the country's oldest psychiatric institution and now part of the Central Museum.

★ Centraal Museum ⓥ – *The museum is currently undergoing large-scale renovation and expansion, and is closed until late 1999.* This museum is housed in the former monastery of St Agnes, and contains rich collections relating mainly to Utrecht and the surrounding area.

It includes a number of **period rooms** combining visual and decorative arts from 1625, 1750 and 1975. The highlights of the collection are on permanent display: **silverware**, including 17C work by the Vianen brothers; a 17C **doll's house**; the important **Rietveld collection★★★** (the world's largest) and an overview of **contemporary design**. The **pre-20C painting collection** includes work by Jan van Scorel, Abraham Bloemaert and the Utrecht School, Pieter Saenredam, and the Utrecht Caravaggists Hendrick Terbrugghen and Gerard Honthorst. The modern painting collection is dominated by the Utrecht Surrealist **Moesman** and the magic Realist **Pyke Koch**. The **Van Baaren collection** contains work by late 19C and early 20C Dutch and French artists (Jongkind, Breitner, Van Gogh, Isaac Israëls, Fantin Latour, Daubigny, Maris, and Charley Toorop). The most important exhibit in the archeology department is the **Utrecht Ship**, dating from c 1100 and weighing some 13t, which was excavated in Utrecht in 1930. The museum also holds important temporary exhibitions.

Christ entering Jerusalem, Jan van Scorel (central panel of the Lochorst Triptych)
Centraal Museum, Utrecht

★ **Nederlands Spoorwegmuseum** ⓥ – The former Maliebaan Station is the setting for the Dutch Railway Museum.

Inside, films, paintings, documents and scale models illustrate the history of the Dutch railways, beginning with the evolution from horse-drawn carriages to the first steam train. The Netherlands' first railway was built between Amsterdam and Haarlem in 1839. Excellent scale models and films in the auditorium give an idea of the subsequent history of railways, from the steam locomotive to the high-speed train.

Outside on the tracks, no longer used, there are more than 60 magnificent locomotives, wagons, carriages and tramcars. One of the museum's high lights is a reconstruction of the engine *De Arend* (the eagle) which in 1839 with another engine *(De Snelheid)* drew the first train to run in the Netherlands.

There is also a signal box, an atmospheric reconstruction of a station, a children's railway, and an exciting multimedia display called **Holland Rail Show**.

OTHER SIGHTS

Bruntenhof – This picturesque line of low houses forms part of a 1621 **almshouse**. The main entrance has a Baroque portal. The Leeuwenberchkerk (1567) on the left was once part of a pest-house.

Kloostergang van Sint-Marie – Only the Romanesque cloisters in brick remain of this church built in the 11C, one of the four churches of Bernulphus' Cross *(se Pieterskerk)* which was demolished in the 19C.

Waterleidingmuseum ⓥ – The town's oldest water tower, dating from 189? and still in use, chronicles the history of the mains water supply and of washing and ironing. It also has a fine view of the town.

Moluks Historisch Museum ⓥ – This museum deals with the history and culture of the Moluccan people of Indonesia, from their war with Japan to the arrival of the first immigrants in the Netherlands in 1951. There is a reconstruction of one of the rooms where Moluccan families were first housed when they arrived, and temporary exhibitions are also held.

★★ **Rietveld Schröderhuis** ⓥ – Restored after the owner's death (Mrs Schröder, i 1985), this world-famous house, built in 1924, illustrates perfectly the architectural theories of the **De Stijl** movement to which **Gerrit Rietveld** (1888-1964) belonged.

In response to Mrs Schröder's demands (she attached a great deal of importance to communicating with nature; every room has a door to the outside) Rietveld created an open plan where the different elements placed at right angles determined the space. Breaking away from the traditional house, Rietveld limited himself to neutral tones – white and grey – for the large surfaces and primary colours for the linear details.

Visiting the interior enables one to appreciate the originality of the layout both simple and clever. On the ground floor the rooms are clearly divided, while the first floor is a large open space with sliding partitions to close off the living room and bedrooms.

Rietveld Schröderhuis, Utrecht

EXCURSIONS

Zeist – *10km/6mi. Leave Utrecht by Biltsestraatweg.*
Zeist is a charming and elegant holiday resort nestling among lush woods. In the centre of the town, a path leads to the **stately home of Slot Zeist**, built between 1677 and 1686 by Willem van Nassau-Odijk with interiors designed by Daniël Marot. **The Peace of Utrecht** *(see above)* was signed here in 1713. The building was originally surrounded by magnificent grounds. It underwent major restoration between 1960 and 1969, and is now used as a cultural, conference and exhibition centre. On either side of the drive stand the buildings which house the **Moravian Brotherhood** community.

The sect was reinstated in the early 18C by the Count of Zinzerdorf. On his land in Germany he had sheltered the Moravian Brotherhood (or Bohemian Brotherhood) refugees from Moravia and Bohemia and disciples of Jean Hus, burned at the stake in 1415. The members of this sect are dedicated to the mystical adoration of God and Christ, preach fraternity among all men and live in a community. There exist around 430 000 representatives of this sect throughout the world.

★ **Loosdrechtse Plassen (lakes)** – *Round tour of 70km/44mi – allow 1 day. Leave Utrecht via Sartreweg.*

Westbroek – The picturesque route is edged by canals spanned by small bridges, each one leading to a house surrounded by a charming garden.
Set between verdant strips of land bathed in soft sunlight, the **Loosdrechtse Plassen**★★ covers more than 2 500ha/6 175 acres producing a rather silent and desolate landscape. These lakes are flooded peat workings. Particularly favourable for water sports, they are served by numerous pleasure boat harbours. The road is lined with villas.
After **Breukeleveen** the road follows the lake; there is a fine **view**.

Kasteel Sypesteyn ⊘ – This castle is located just outside **Nieuw-Loosdrecht**; it was rebuilt based on old illustrations between 1912 and 1927, and was later turned into a museum. Displayed inside are furniture, family portraits painted by N Maes and C Troost, old objets d'art and, in particular, Loosdrecht porcelain.
The castle is surrounded by a charming park (rose garden, orchard and maze).

Oud-Loosdrecht – This is the main tourist centre in the region. It has a large pleasure boat harbour.

Turn right then left towards Vreeland.

The road soon returns to the lake; it has lovely **views**.

Vreeland – An attractive **lever bridge** makes it possible to cross the Vecht, which one subsequently rejoins at Loenen aan de Vecht. The **Vecht**, formerly a great navigation way, since 1952, is doubled by the canal (Amsterdam-Rijnkanaal) from the Rhine to Amsterdam.
The road runs along this peaceful and winding river, on whose banks are charming villas and small manorhouses surrounded by magnificent parks.

Loenen – This small town with trim and flowered houses has a tall stage mill, with a handrail, called De Hoop (hope).

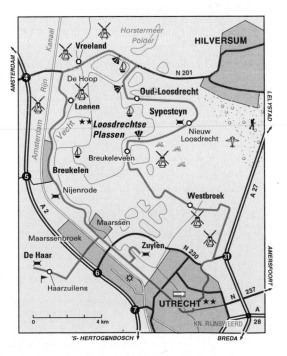

Breukelen – In the 17C this locality gave its name to a quarter in New York founded by Dutch settlers: Breukelen, pronounced in English as Brooklyn.
To the south of Breukelen, there is a pleasant **route**★ which offers views of lovely estates on the banks of the Vecht.

Haarzuilens – Kasteel De Haar

To the right of the road the 17C **Kasteel Nijenrode** was restored at the beginning of the 20C. The castle and its estate are now the seat of Nijenrode University.

Kasteel De Haar ⊘ – It stands to the west of **Haarzuilens** in the middle of a large park. This moated castle, the largest in the Netherlands, is an enormous 14C and 15C brick construction. It was burnt by Louis XIV's troops between 1672 and 1673, then rebuilt in 1892 by PJH Cuypers, the architect of the Rijksmuseum in Amsterdam, in the neo-Gothic style. The main building, with pepper-pot roof towers, is surrounded by wide moats and linked to a large entrance fort by a covered bridge.

The interior, which is still inhabited in summer, contains the exceptional **collections★** of Baron van Zuylen van Nyevelt, notably lovely old furnishings, 16C and 17C Flemish tapestries, Persian carpets, paintings and ceramics.

In the main hall there is a 14C Virgin and Child from an Augustinian priory in northern France.

Return to Haarzuilens, cross over the motorway and the canal, then turn right, then left to reach Oud-Zuilen.

Belle, the rebel of the Vecht

Isabella Agneta Elisabeth van Tuyll van Serooskerken, known for short as Madame de Charrière or Belle van Zuylen, still appeals to the modern imagination. This feminist before her time was born at Slot Zuylen on 20 October 1740, and spent her summers there and winters at the family's canalside house in Utrecht. She caused a great stir in the salons of Utrecht and The Hague with her interest in literature, science, philosophy and music, her unconventional attitudes and above all her satirical view of the aristocracy. When her first novel *Le Noble* was published in Paris and Amsterdam in 1763, her enraged father bought up all the copies and had them destroyed.

Belle van Zuylen's independent attitude was perhaps best illustrated when the famous Scottish writer James Boswell asked for her hand in marriage. Her reply was short and to the point: "I have no talent for subservience." At the age of 31, however, she escaped the stifling atmosphere of her parents' home by marrying a Swiss man, Charles-Emmanuel de Charrière de Penthaz. She moved to Neuchâtel in Switzerland, where she died in 1805. Belle wrote of her marriage: "I still feel that my thoughts, words and deeds are unhindered. I have a different name and do not always sleep alone, but that is all that has changed."

Slot Zuylen ⊙ – Situated near the Vecht at **Oud-Zuilen**, this castle is a solid medieval construction; it was rebuilt c 1751 and four octagonal towers were added. **Belle van Zuylen** was born here in 1740. The castle houses ancient objects illustrating the daily life of the past, lovely furniture, a richly endowed library and a Chinese porcelain collection.

One room is decorated with a large tapestry (1643) woven in Delft and depicting a landscape with a multitude of birds.

In the rooms where Belle van Zuylen lived, a portrait of her by a Danish artist, a few books and engravings evoke the life of the writer.

The **garden wall**, dating from 1740, is also interesting; sheltered bays are used to grow grapes, peaches, figs and other Mediterranean fruit.

Belle's sophistication is reflected in her many letters, including her 11 years of passionate correspondence with the Baron d'Hermenches, and in her novels and plays. She was a friend of Benjamin Constant and Madame de Staël, and wrote in French, the language of 18C culture.

Return to Utrecht by Amsterdamsestraatweg.

VALKENBURG AAN DE GEUL★

Limburg   Population 10 170

Michelin maps 908 I 9 and 211 U 7

Valkenburg is situated in the charming Geul Valley, between two branches of the river, a very old, little town, it belongs to the district borough of Valkenburg-Houthem.

It is much frequented in the summer by holidaymakers attracted by the gentle hills surrounding its fine parks and its other attractions.

The town has preserved two fortified gateways: 14C **Grendelpoort** and 15C **Berkelpoort** with its footbridge.

The caves – Marl stone, a sort of limestone, predominates in the surrounding hilly countryside as at Sint-Pietersberg not far from Maastricht. Marl stone has been quarried locally for centuries as a building stone. A certain number of these caves and galleries *(70km/44mi)* can now be visited and quite a number have been transformed into museums or other tourist attractions.

SIGHTS

Ruined castle ⊙ – The ruins of the castle of the lords of Valkenburg dominate the city. Only parts of walls and broken arches still remain. It was built in c 1087 and was altered during the Gothic period and was subjected to a great number of sieges; notably by the Count of Louvain (1122).

Louis XIV captured it in May 1672. It was taken back in December and razed to the ground the following year by order of the King Statdholder William III.

Many legends are attached to the ruins, such as that of Walram and Reginald of Valkenburg, who were both in love with Alix, the daughter of the Count of Juliers. Walram married Alix but the young couple was assassinated by Reginald.

From the top of the ruins there is a view over the town and the Geul Valley.

★ **Steenkolenmijn Valkenburg** ⊙ – *Access via Daalhemerweg.*

A coal mine has been reconstituted in the galleries of an old quarry *(see Introduction: Industrial heritage)*. The visit provides information on the methods of coal extraction as practised in Limburg before the last workings were closed. A film provides a realistic picture of a coal mine. Then walk along the galleries to see the trains for the transportation of miners or coal, the water pumps, the tunnel with the working coal face, with portable shaft supports, the evacuation of the coal and the different security systems.

Gemeentegrot ⊙ – These are ancient marl quarries which were already known to the Romans. They sheltered the population in time of war, notably in September 1944 on the town's liberation.

The sedimentary marl stone contains many fossils. The caves remain at a constant temperature of 14°C/57°F. The walls are covered with charcoal drawings and low reliefs, some representing the animals whose fossils have been found, such as the Mosasaurus *(see MAASTRICHT: Excursions)*; others represent artistic (Mona Lisa) or religious subjects.

The stone was gradually quarried downwards, leaving some drawings placed very high up.

Fluweelengrot ⊙ – This system of caves is connected to the castle by secret passages. They are named after their former owner, Fluwijn. Like the municipal caves, they are old quarries which housed refugees, who have left many drawings and low reliefs. Their temperature remains at 10°C/50°F.

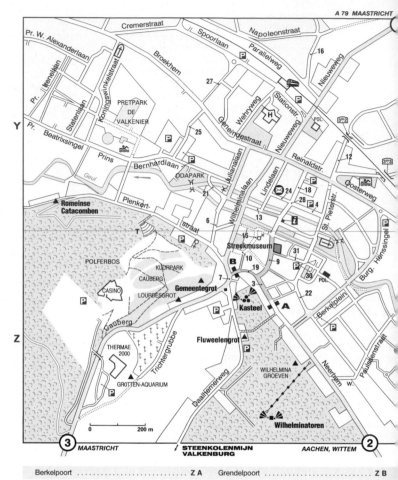

Wilhelminatoren ⊙ – *Access either by car from Daalhemerweg, then turn left or by chair-lift .*
From the departure point of the chair-lift, **caves** (Panorama-Grot) can be visited A film on prehistoric times is shown.
From the top of the tower (160 steps), 30m/98ft high, there is a good view of the town's wooded surroundings.

Roman Catacombs ⊙ – In the old quarries 10 Roman catacombs have been reconstructed. They were designed by the famous architect PJH Cuypers, based on drawings by archeologists.

Streekmuseum ⊙ – Objects found during excavations of the castle and paintings of the town, reconstructed workshops, mementoes of shooting companies are exhibited here. The museum also holds temporary exhibitions of contemporary art.

★ ZUID-LIMBURG

Round tour of 58km/36mi – about half a day
Southern Limburg is a transitional region between the Dutch plains and the Ardennes hills jutting out between Belgium and Germany.
It is a rural area whose appearance is not marred by the region's coal mines. Its fertile plateaux, lush valleys, its fields shaded by apple trees, its hilltops from which can be seen vast stretches of countryside, form a pleasant landscape dotted with fine manor-houses and white half-timbered farms *(see Introduction: Traditions and folklore)*.

Ph. Roy/EXPLORER

An orchard in Southern Limburg

Leave Valkenburg by ② on the town plan, going eastwards in the direction of Gulpen.

The road follows the verdant Geul Valley.

Oud-Valkenburg – On the left is the fine 17C **Kasteel Schaloen**, restored in the 19C by Cuypers. The park is watered by a branch of the Geul.
A little farther on, behind a chapel, is **Kasteel Genhoes**, built in the 16C and 18C and surrounded by moats.
After Wijlre, notice on the left **Cartils Kasteel**, in the middle of a fine park.

Wittem – On the right, the **Kasteel Wittem** is a 15C building, restored in the 19C in the neo-Gothic style. It is now a hotel-restaurant.
A road over the plateau leads to Vaals.

Vaals – A resort which owes its animation to the proximity of the German frontier and Drielandenpunt.
A winding road climbs through the woods to Drielandenpunt. 500m/0.5mi before the end of the road, on the left, there is a fine **view**★ of Aachen.

★ **Drielandenpunt** – It is the meeting point *(punt)* of three *(drie)* countries' *(landen)* frontiers: Germany, Belgium and the Netherlands. It is also the highest point in the Netherlands being at 321m/1 053ft.
From the top of the **Boudewijntoren** ⊘ there is a **panorama**★ over the region, Aachen close by, Germany's Eifel Forests, and in the distance, towards the west, Maastricht. There is also a maze.
Return towards Vaals and go to Vijlen.

Vijlen – This village still has a few half-timbered houses.
By a road through the woods one reaches the road from Vaals to Epen: pretty **view** over the hills to the south.

Epen – Resort where several houses still have half-timbered walls.
Before reaching the church, turn left.
A fine half-timbered farmhouse can be seen on leaving the village.
The climb gives fine **views**★ over the frontier hills to the south.
After Heijenrath there is a fine **view** on the right over Gulp Valley which one crosses at **Slenaken**, a small frontier village.
Then follow the river towards Gulpen. This is a pleasant drive through a landscape of lush fields.

Euverem – In pools near the Gulp nearly 500 000 trout are raised every year. Some of them are sent to neighbouring fish ponds.
At the junction of the road from Gulpen to Maastricht, there is a **view** on the right of Kasteel Neubourg. It lies at the bottom of a valley and is a vast building flanked by a square tower with an onion-shaped dome; it is now a hotel.

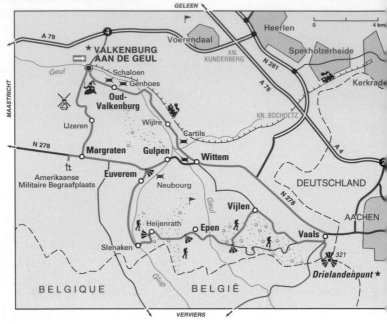

Gulpen – A resort at the confluence of the Gulp and the Geul.

Margraten – At the west of town lies the **Netherlands American Military Cemeter** which was laid out in 1944 by the American Army. On the left of the entrance small museum retraces the episodes of the war. On the walls the names of th 1 722 missing are engraved.
In the cemetery, dominated by a tall tower (chapel inside) lie the graves c 8 301 soldiers marked out by crosses placed in a semicircle; these soldiers fe during the breakthrough of the Siegfried Line.

Return to Valkenburg through IJzeren and Sibbe over the plain, enterir Valkenburg via Daalhemerweg.

VEERE★

Zeeland
Population 5 089
Michelin maps 908 B 7 and 211 G 13
Local map see DELTA – Town plan in the current Michelin Red Guide Benelux

Veere is situated on **Veerse Meer**, a former branch of the sea closed by a dam *(se DELTA)* which links Walcheren to Noord-Beveland.
Veere was under the protection of the Lord of Borsele and was a flourishing po because of its wool trade with Scotland – it was in the early 16C that Veere becam the port on the continent through which staple goods (exports of linen, salt and woo passed. The port was gradually ruined by the War of Independence. Veere is twinne with Culross in Scotland.
With no outlet to the North Sea for its fishing boats, Veere has become a sailin centre and a holiday resort. With its paved alleyways, its monuments and its bric houses, Veere is a charming town full of character.

SIGHTS

Campveerse Toren – This 15C tower is part of the town's old fortifications. is built of brick and decorated with bands of white stone and has a crow-steppe gable. It is now a restaurant.

★ **Schotse Huizen (Scottish houses)** ⊘ – *Kade 25 and 27*. Built in the 16C in the Goth Flamboyant style, these two buildings were used as offices and warehouses by th Scottish wool merchants who lived in Veere. The tympana of the windows ar doors are richly decorated. At no 25 the façade stone represents a lamb, symb of the wool trade; at no 27 it shows an ostrich.
Inside there are Zeeland costumes, porcelain and furniture, including a *sterre kabinet (see Introduction: Art)*. In a fine Gothic room there are the original statue of the lords and ladies of Veere, which once decorated the stadhuis.

* **Oude Stadhuis (Old Town Hall)** ⊘ – This is a charming little two storey Gothic building made of sandstone. It was started in 1474. The openings on the first floor are separated by recesses surmounted by canopies, under which are statues, remade in 1934.

The roof is flanked with octagonal turrets and dominated by a 1591 onion-shaped belfry, crowned with a balustrade with pinnacles and small columns. Inside there is a **carillon** ⊘ of 48 bells.

In the audience chamber on the **ground floor**, one of the oldest in the Netherlands, there is the silver gilt goblet which **Emperor Charles V** gave to Count Maximilian of Buren in 1546. The portraits displayed in the Council Chamber depict marquis and marchionesses from Veere, members of the House of Orange-Nassau.

Grote Kerk or Onze Lieve Vrouwekerk ⊘ – A massive 14C structure, with a large tower which was never completed.

Next to the church is the **municipal fountain**, a lovely Gothic monument of 1551, composed of an octagonal rotunda with diagonal arches and small columns.

Van der Leeden/BENELUX PRESS B.V.

Veere

VENLO

Limburg
Population 64 417
Michelin maps 908 J 7 and 211 W 14
Plan of the conurbation in the current Michelin Red Guide Benelux

In the northern part of the province of Limburg, near the German-Dutch frontier, Venlo is a small industrial town on the banks of the Maas.

HISTORICAL NOTES

A legend of the Middle Ages gives AD 90 as the date of Venlo's foundation by Valuas, chief of a Germanic tribe, the Bructeri. The name of the town's founder is commemorated at all the celebrations, parades and processions; the effigies of two giants representing Valuas and his wife are carried through the town.

Venlo was prosperous in the Middle Ages and was given city rights in 1343. In 1364 it became a member of the Hanseatic League.

Today it is the centre of a large market gardening area (asparagus, mushrooms, flowers, tomatoes and gherkins), which stretches north to the outskirts of Grubbenvorst. The town's immediate surroundings are covered with hothouses.

The carnival *(see Calendar of events)* is a very lively one.

Boat trips ⊘ – Boat trips are organised on the Maas. Landing-stage: Maaskade.

VENLO

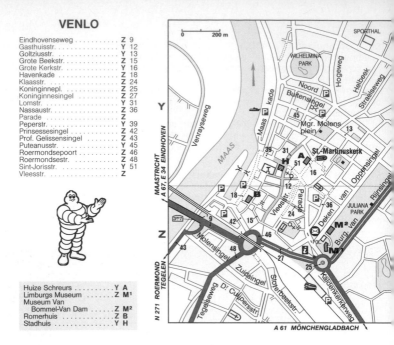

SIGHTS

Stadhuis – In the middle of Markt, the town hall is a fine quadrilateral Renaissance building (c 1600).

Sint-Martinuskerk ⊘ – Dating from the beginning of the 15C, it was damaged during the last war but has been restored and its tower, which has a carillon of 48 bells, rebuilt. The interior has interesting **furnishings★** and objets d'art.

The 15C Gothic **stalls** are carved to represent about 20 scenes of the Old and New Testaments; the misericords are decorated with various subjects (heads, evangelist symbols, foliage, proverbs, fables etc). On the left of the triumphal arch note a 16C Virgin and Child; on the right a 17C Christ; in the chancel of Sacraments north of the high altar, a carved 16C oak bench; in the chancel of Our Lady on the right of the high altar, a 15C limestone Pietà and an Ecce Homo painted by Jan van Cleef, a painter born in Venlo (1646-1716). The pulpit is Baroque. A beautiful brass **baptismal font**, dating from 1621, stands at the back of the south side aisle.

In the same street (Grote Kerkstraat), at nos 19-21, there is the interesting façade of the **Huize Schreurs** built in the Renaissance style (1588), topped by a volute gable; on the first floor, blind arcades lean on two corbels carved with the head of a lion; note also the carved coat of arms and the medallions.

Limburgs Museum ⊘ – *Closed for rebuilding until autumn 2000.* This regional museum deals with archeology, history and art.

One section is devoted to prehistory, the Roman occupation and the town's history. Another deals with decorative arts, including silverware, pewter, coins and weapons. The museum also organises temporary exhibitions.

Museum Van Bommel-Van Dam ⊘ – On the edge of Juliana Park, it is a pleasant modern and contemporary Dutch Art Museum which mainly holds temporary exhibitions.

Romerhuis – A 16C house with crow-stepped gable and pinnacles.

EXCURSION

Tegelen – *4km/3mi to the southwest via Prof Gelissensingel.*
This is a small industrial town well-known for its **Passion Plays** (Passiespelen) enacted every five years with all the population taking part *(see Calendar of events).*
Tegelen is also the home of the **Missiemuseum Steyl** ⊘, *St.-Michaëlstraat 7.* Housed in the buildings of a missionary community, it contains artefacts from Indonesia, New Guinea, the Far East, Africa, Chinese objets d'art, butterflies and stuffed animals from all over the world.
Not far from the museum *(Maashoek 2 b, Steyl)*, there is a **botanical garden Jochum-Hof** ⊘. It is an open-air garden with plants from the north of Limburg and a tropical hothouse (cacti, orchids and banana trees).

Arcen Castle gardens ⊘ – *9km/5mi north of Venlo via N 271.* The 32ha/80-acre gardens of this castle dating from 1653 include a Rosarium, lakes, a wood containing deer, oriental gardens and the Casa Verde, a large subtropical glasshouse. There is also a children's playground and a minigolf course.

VENRAY

Limburg
Population 36 690
Michelin maps 908 I 7 and 211 U 13

On Grote Markt, **Sint-Petrus Bandenkerk** ⊙, a large Gothic church, contains some interesting furnishings. Apart from the Baroque pulpit note a fine late-15C brass lectern and a remarkable series of wooden **statues** and the one in stone of St Paul; the oldest is of St James (15C). The Apostles, with their attributes, stand against the pillars of the nave. In the aisles there is a series of saints (a beautiful St Lucy) which come from old altars no longer in existence. At the entrance there is a Baroque statue of St Peter, shown as Pope.

EXCURSION

Overloon – *7km/4mi to the north.* For three weeks in the autumn of 1944 the British and Americans fought a battle round this village to support Operation Market Garden *(see ARNHEM)*, one of the biggest tank battles of the war, often compared to the one at Caen because of the terrible artillery bombardment and the number of tanks involved.

The **Nederlands Nationaal Oorlogs- en Verzetmuseum** ⊙, or National War and Resistance Museum, is to the east of Overloon in the woods where the fighting occured.

A signposted route is marked out in this 14ha/34-acre enclosure to display the large collection of German and Allied material which remains from the battle: tanks, planes, one-man submarine, a complete V1, a pocket submarine, guns, landmines, bombs, torpedoes etc.

In a building devoted to concentration camps (Kampengebouw), a standing exhibition illustrates the tragic plight of the victims through photographs, films, documents and various other objects.

Michelin Red Guides *(hotels and restaurants)*
Benelux – Deutschland – España-Portugal – Europe – France – Great Britain and Ireland – Ireland – Italia – London – Paris et environs   Portugal – Switzerland.

VLISSINGEN

FLUSHING – Zeeland
Population 44 568
Michelin maps 908 B 7 and 211 G 14 – Local map see DELTA

The only large maritime port at the mouth of the Scheldt, Flushing became important in the 14C on account of its commercial activities and herring fishing industry. Philip II embarked here in 1559 when he finally left the Low Countries for Spain. From 1585 to 1616 the town was pledged to the English as a guarantee of the costs incurred by the Earl of Leicester's army to uphold the United Provinces after the assassination of William the Silent.

Admiral de Ruyter (1607-76), born in Flushing, distinguished himself during the third war against England (1672-74) and was fatally wounded during a battle near Syracuse. The French draughtsman **Constantin Guys** (1802-92), nicknamed the painter of modern life by the poet Charles Baudelaire, was also a native of Flushing.

The town today – Flushing, which commands the entry to the Walcheren canal, is both a fishing port and an industrial centre with large naval shipyards. Warships are moored here. A maritime terminal runs a car ferry service towards England (Sheerness) and Flemish Zeeland (Breskens). Flushing also has a Naval College.

Boat trips ⊙ – Flushing is the starting-point for boat trips along the coast of Walcheren Peninsula.

The Boulevard – The town's seafront is a long avenue flanked by an esplanade known as the Boulevard.

The 15C **Gevangentoren** or Prison Tower stands here. Down below stretches a wide beach sheltered from northern winds. At the far end of the boulevard, on an old bastion built by Charles V, note the little lighthouse and the statue of Admiral de Ruyter. From there one has a nice **view** of the port below and the **Old Exchange** of 1635, a fine building with green shutters surmounted by a pinnacle.

Maritiem Attractiecentrum Het Arsenaal ⊙ – *Arsenaalplein 1.* This former arsenal, dating from 1823, now provides an exciting introduction to the seafaring world for young and old alike. It includes a parade of old and famous ships, a pirates' cave, and a chance to experience the sinking of the Titanic and be washed up on Treasure Island. The 64m/210ft crow's-nest gives a view across Zeeland, Belgium and the Westerschelde. The tour ends with a visit to the world beneath the sea, including aquariums and a whale skeleton.

Stedelijk Museum ⊙ – *Bellamypark 19*. This museum uses paintings, model and other objects to give an idea of the town's rich past. It focuses particularly on the local shipping industry and pilotage service, the famous admiral Michiel d Ruyter, and the East India Company. The display also includes items of cargo from ships that have run aground on the sandbanks.

Reptielenzoo Iguana ⊙ – *Bellamypark 33*. Over 500 living reptiles, amph bians and insects are on view here, including scorpions, pythons, frog and toads, iguanas, crocodiles, lizards, bird-eating spiders and stick insects There is also a baby room in which eggs are hatched and young animals ar kept.

VOLENDAM*

Noord-Holland
Population 26 505 (with Edam)
Michelin maps 908 G 4 and 210 P 8

Volendam, like Marken, stands on a small land-locked sea, Gouwzee. It is one o the best-known ports of the old Zuiderzee. Its townspeople wear the traditiona costume in summer and it has become a symbol of the Netherlands for foreigners though any sense of authenticity has long since been lost. Tourism is an importan activity.

Village – The long street, which runs along the top of the high dike, is just a lin of shops, but behind and below the dike there are picturesque narrow alleyway winding between small brick houses with wooden gables.

The Cartographers of 17C Europe

The daring and enterprise of Dutch merchant-seamen and navigators led to the rise of the United Netherlands as a maritime power. Amsterdam became not only the centre of international commerce but also of commercial cartography. The map-makers of the period were often indifferently engravers, publishers or cartographers.

Great names of Dutch cartography included Petrus Plancius; Mercator (of the projection and Atlas 1606); Hondius who revised Mercator's Atlas and mapped Sir Francis Drake's round the world voyage; Blaeu (Willem Jansz) publisher of the poet and dramatist Vondel and cartographer to the East India Company from 1634; his arch rival Johannes Jansonius, son-in-law to Hondius and successor to the family firm; and Van Keulen founder of a publishing house famous for its nautical charts.

*****Traditional costume** – The men wear black trousers with silver buttons, shor jackets over striped shirts, and round caps. The women's costume consists o a black skirt with a striped apron or a striped skirt with a black apron, a shir with a flowered front under a black short sleeved overblouse, and a necklac of large coral beads with a gold clasp, hidden in winter by a blue and whit shawl. When they are not wearing a pointed black bonnet they wear a lac cap for feast days, very tall with turned-up wings, whose shape is famous. Me and women wear clogs or buckled shoes. Visitors should watch the congregatio leaving church when the couples cross the little wooden bridge in front of th Catholic church.

Volendams Museum ⊙ – *Zeestraat 37*. This museum is located in a small sho and classroom. The exhibits include traditional costumes and jewellery, fishin equipment, and other everyday objects.

De WADDENEILANDEN★★

Wadden Islands

Michelin maps 908 F 2, 3, G 2, H 1, I 1,
J 1 and 210 N 4, 5, O4,5, P3, Q2, R2, S2, T2, U2, V2, W1,2.

The Wadden Islands are a unique nature reserve in the north of the country. There
are five inhabited islands, extending between the North Sea and the Waddenzee. The
largest, **Texel**, is part of the province of Noord-Holland; the others, **Vlieland**, **Terschelling**,
Ameland and **Schiermonnikoog**, are part of Fryslân. There are also smaller islands and
sandbanks, such as the bird island of **Griend**, **Rottumeroog** and **Rottumerplaat**, both in
Groningen province. The belt of islands continues northwards along the coasts of
Germany and Denmark.

The formation of the islands and the Waddenzee – Along with the German and
Danish islands, the islands are the remains of an ancient chain of dunes which
stretched as far as Jutland in Denmark.
As far back as the Roman period the sea had breached the chain of dunes
and invaded the flat hinterland forming the **Waddenzee**. In the 13C this was
connected to a vast gulf which had just been formed, the Zuiderzee *(see
IJSSELMEER)*

Tides and currents – The islands are still subject to the action of strong currents and
the North Sea continues its insidious undermining process to the west of the islands.
Kilometer posts are planted in lines along the beaches to record the movement of the
sand, and the breakwaters are built to reduce this movement.
To the east, the strong currents displace the sand which then silts up the Waddenzee.
At low tide, the sea leaves huge stretches of mudflats or sand called *wadden* (because
they can be waded across). These are popular with birds, but cause ships to make
large detours to follow the marked channels.
The Waddenzee can be walked with a guide, at certain times of year and when
weather permits *(see below)*.

The power of the wind – The constant strong west wind has always been the
greatest enemy of the Wadden region. Over the course of time, it has gradually
turned the islands round to the east; villages on the islands' west sides, such as
Westerburen on Schiermonnikoog and Westervlieland on Vlieland, have been swal-
lowed up by the sea.
Even today, huge areas of sand are forming on the southwest sides of the islands.
Since 1900, large-scale conifer planting has been carried out in an attempt to prevent
the spread of these areas, and this, combined with breakwaters, dikes and careful
maintenance of the dunes, has kept the large islands more or less in place. Some of
the sandbars, such as Noorderhaaks (better known as De Razende Bol, the
fast-moving ball) are constantly on the move.
The strong wind does have one advantage: because it makes the clouds move faster,
the Wadden Islands have less rain than other parts of the country.

Morand-Graham/HOA QUI

Dunes on Ameland

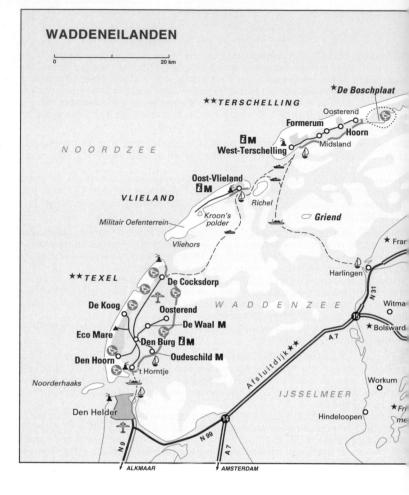

Battling against the sea – Time and time again, the low-lying islands have been flooded by big storms as the dunes and dikes prove unable to resist the power of the sea. For example, the small island of **Griend**, between Vlieland and Harlingen, was a prosperous place in the 13C; little by little it was eroded by the high tides, and had to be abandoned in the 18C; what remains of it now is an important breeding ground for birds. Likewise, the dike built between Ameland and the Frisian coast in 1871 was destroyed by storms 11 years later, and Rottumerplaat was regularly under water until 1950.

Landscape – The northern and western sides of the islands have wonderful beaches of very white sand bordered by **dunes**. The dunes have been planted with marram grass to prevent them from being carried along by the wind. They are particularly high and wide on Texel, but the highest dunes are on Ameland and Terschelling, where they reach a height of over 30m/100ft. The coniferous forests planted inland in the early 20C radically changed the appearance of the islands, which had hitherto been largely treeless.

The very flat south coasts of the islands are protected by dikes. The countryside is generally subdivided into several **polders** separated by small dikes, where numerous herds of cows and a few horses graze. Texel specialises mainly in sheep raising.

There are also several small harbours on the Waddenzee. They were once the departure point for fishing and whaling; today they are mostly marinas.

Fauna – All these islands form a vast sanctuary for **seabirds**. Some come to lay their eggs, including gulls of all kinds, spoonbills, and pintail ducks.

In the autumn a great number of **migratory birds** from Northern Europe (Scandinavia and Iceland) and from Siberia stop for a time on the Waddenzee, which is rich in food.

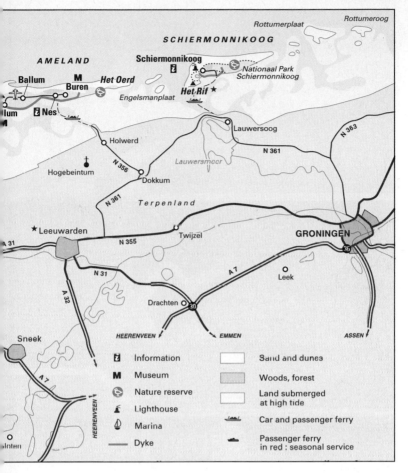

Information

M Museum

Nature reserve

Lighthouse

Marina

Dyke

Sand and dunes

Woods, forest

Land submerged
at high tide

Car and passenger ferry

Passenger ferry
in red : seasonal service

(fish and shellfish), then continue on their way to warmer climates (France, Spain and North Africa). This is so with the avocet. Others spend winter on the Waddenzee: they include among the waders a large number of different types of dunlins and oyster catchers.

Nature reserves have been designated on each island and in some cases visitors can only visit when accompanied by a guide. The largest reserves are usually on Forestry Commission (Staatsbosbeheer) land. Many areas are closed to the public during the nesting season, from mid March to mid August.

Seals used to come in great numbers to the sand banks on the north side of the islands, but their numbers were seriously depleted in the 1980s by a virus. Fortunately, there are now signs that the numbers are on the increase again, and you may be lucky enough to see them basking in the sun on one of the many sandbanks as you cross to the islands.

Flora – The **plant life** on the dunes, which are interspersed with small pools, is exceptionally varied. The most common species include the sea buckthorn with its edible orange berries, the Burnet rose, and grasses such as scurvy grass, Parnassus grass with white flowers and succulent plants such as milkwort. Terschelling is also the only place in Europe where cranberries are cultivated.

Tourism on the islands – Even if you are not interested in ornithology or botany, you will enjoy the natural beauty of the islands, an unpolluted environment (clear seas, the wild open expanses of dunes and a healthy climate), and the peace and quiet, though they do get very busy in summer. The islands also have a great deal to offer in autumn and winter.

Spoonbill

Silver seagull

Stork

P. Bourguignon/B. Coster/M. Danegger/F. Dupont/Ph. Prigent/F. Roux/JACANA

314

The drawbacks – Tourism has taken its toll, and the Wadden Islands are also used by the army; aircraft noise from the military bases on Texel and Vlieland has scared away some of the birdlife.
In addition rich reserves of natural gas have been found under the Waddenzee: a drilling platform has already been built between Den Helder and Texel.

The Wadden islands: practical advice

Getting there by boat – The ferry situation varies from one island to another; some are high-speed and others are not; some allow cars and others do not. Ferries are quite frequent in the high season, but in the low season they may be limited to one a day, or even none in bad weather. It is therefore a good idea to check the appropriate ferry company's 24hr information line a few days before you go; alternatively, consult teletext page 723. Cars can be left in the large harbour car parks on the mainland. *(For more information on each island, see below and Admission times and charges).*

Exploring the islands – The best way to get about is by **bicycle**, and on Vlieland and Schiermonnikoog, where cars are forbidden, it is the only way. Cycling or walking are also the best ways of seeing the nature reserves and dunes. Bikes can be hired on each island and in most villages. However, in the summer they can be hard to come by and it is highly advisable to bring a bicycle with you from the mainland. **Cycling and walking maps** are available from the VVV tourist office.
Most islands have **bus** services; another alternative is to travel by **taxi**, which is not only comfortable, but has the added bonus that the driver may tell you all about the area. Having your own car might be useful on Texel.

Accommodation – In season, it is best to reserve rooms through the island's Tourist Information Centre. There are a few hotels, but many islanders take in visitors. The VVV publishes an annual guide listing these, along with camp sites and holiday cottages.

Tours – The VVV can provide information on tours of the nature reserves or the mudflats, and birdwatching, seal-watching and beachcombing trips.

Walking across the mudflats ⊘ – These exciting trips, for which a guide is compulsory, take place from early April to late October. Most leave from Wierum (Fryslân) or Pieterburen (Groningen); *for addresses, see Admission times and charges.* VVVs also organise shorter trips of this kind.

Sports – Sailing, surfing, fishing, parachuting, horse riding, golf, skating, cross-country skiing: the islands have them all, and the VVV can provide you with further information. **De Ronde om Texel**, the world's biggest catamaran race, is held in June.

The Wadden islands on the internet – www.VVV-wadden.nl

AMELAND
Fryslân – Population 3 422

Ferry ⊘ – From Holwerd. Operated by Wagenborg Passagiersdiensten; information line ☎ (0519) 54 20 01.

VVV (tourist office) – In Nes, ☎ (0519) 546 546 or www.ameland.nl

---

This long island covering about 5 800ha/14 326 acres with its large stretches of dunes, fine sandy beaches on the North Sea, and woods, is very popular with tourists, including a large number of Germans who come here in the summer. Nearly 100km/60mi of bicycle tracks cross the island passing through woods and over dunes.

Like the other Wadden Islands, Ameland has its **nature reserves** for birds, including **Het Oerd** at the far eastern end of the island.

The inhabitants of Ameland specialised in **whaling** in the 17C and 18C. This activity was discontinued in the mid 19C but the captains' houses can still be seen here and there on the island, and in some places whale bones are still used as fences. The four picturesque villages are all conservation areas.

Nes – This is the island's chief village, overlooked by an isolated **bell-tower** with a saddleback roof, dating from 1664. In Rixt van Doniastraat, there are several old captains' houses, **Commandeurshuizen**, one-storey houses with a small lean-to on the side, and where the entrance door is slightly off-centre. A cordon of bricks or a geometric frieze outlines each floor, and there is often an iron anchor on the façade bearing the date when the house was built.

To the east, on the road to Buren, past the new Catholic cemetery, the old **cemetery** is accessible by a small road on the left. It still has ancient tombstones, some decorated with a weeping willow, others very narrow and nearly 2m/6ft high. Several graves of British airmen whose planes crashed here during the war are to be found in this cemetery.

A visit to **Natuurcentrum Ameland** ⊘ will give you a much greater appreciation of the island's natural environment. Slides, photographs, sound recordings and models are used to give an impression of the different landscapes: mudflats, salt marshes, polders, woodland, dunes and beaches. There is an aquarium of North Sea fish, and the skeleton of one of four whales which were stranded here in November 1997.

Buren – This is the island's easternmost village; further east is the Het Oerd Nature Reserve. The village square has a bronze statuette of a hook-nosed woman with a storm lantern, **Rixt van het Oerd** *(see below)*.

The **Landbouw en Juttersmuseum Swartwoude** ⊘ (Swartwoude Agriculture and Beachcombing Museum) uses photographs and other items to bring to life the harsh existence led by people on Ameland as recently as 1900. They eked out an existence from farming, fishing, poaching and beachcombing; the latter was made illegal in 1529, but was practised by poor coast-dwellers until late in the 18C. It was sometimes very lucrative when the cargoes of stranded ships were washed ashore, yielding such items as firewood, tins of food, alcohol and suitcases.

How Het Oerd got its name

Long ago, a widow called Rixt and her son Sjoerd lived at the eastern end of Ameland. They had virtually no contact with the other islanders, and lived off the land; the only thing of any worth that they possessed was a cow. Every day, Sjoerd would go poaching and Rixt would walk along the beach looking for useful objects that had been washed ashore. Everything went well until Sjoerd grew up and left home to become a seaman. At first Rixt managed on her own, but after a long period of finding nothing on the beach, she hatched a cunning plan. One dark and stormy night, she tied a storm lantern to the cow's head and led it up to the top of the highest dune. A ship in distress just off the coast of Ameland thought it had found a safe haven, and set a course towards the light. But it broke up on the rocks and all the crew drowned. Rixt hurried to the beach, full of expectation, but when she saw one of the bodies lying on the shore she screamed: it was her son Sjoerd. Ever since then, if you listen carefully as the stormy winds blow across the island, you can still hear her heart-rending cry: Sjoooerd, Sjoooe rd...

Ballum – The old tower amid the trees in the centre of this little village was used to tell the time, and also to sound the alarm when danger threatened. Take Smitteweg, next to the new town hall, to the southeast to reach the **cemetery** where some of the beautiful old tombstones depict sailing ships or weeping willows.

Hollum – To the south of the village stands a typically attractive church with a saddle-back roofed bell-tower. In the surrounding **cemetery** there are more 18C tombstones showing sailing ships.

Hollum was home to many of the captains of the whaling ships which operated out of Ameland, and one of their houses has been converted into a museum, the **Cultuur-His-torisch Museum Sorgdrager** ⊙. Pieces of local furniture and tiled walls grace the interiors, which make an ideal setting for the collections of earthenware, pottery, costumes and other objects related to whaling, fishing and the dairy industry.

A lifeboat museum, **Reddingsmuseum Abraham Fock** ⊙, is located in Oranjeweg. This is the home of the famous **Ameland lifeboat** ⊙, which is drawn down to the water by a team of horses. The museum traces the evolution from beachcomber to lifeboatman, and a video describes how the latter have operated now and in the past.

Ameland's red and white lighthouse is further to the northwest *(illustration: see the front of the guide)*.

Hollum – tombstone in the churchyard

SCHIERMONNIKOOG
Fryslân – Population 1 005

Ferry ⊙ – From Lauwersoog. Operated by Wagenborg Passagiersdiensten; information line ☎ (0519) 34 90 79.

VVV (tourist office) – ☎ (0519) 53 12 33 or 53 19 00.

This is the smallest of Waddenzee's inhabited islands: covering an area of 4 000ha/9 880 acres, it is 16km/10mi long and 4km/2mi wide, and has recently been designated a **national park**.

The only village, Schiermonnikoog, has two large beaches and a small lake (pleasure boats), the Westerplas.

To the east are the **Kobbeduinen** (dunes) and a nature reserve of 2 400ha/5 928 acres: **De Oosterkwelder**.

With its wild scenery, its dunes, woods, beaches and its tranquillity, Schiermonnikoog is one of the most pleasant islands in the group.

The island became Frisian in 1580 before passing into the hands of several land-owning families from 1639 to 1858 and finally becoming State property in 1945.

Schiermonnikoog – The houses of this village are built among the trees. It developed after Cistercian monks from Friesland settled here c 1400. The name of the island derives from *schier* meaning grey, *monnik* monk and *oog* island. A statue of a monk on the green in the town centre is a reminder of its past. Nearby, an arch made of two huge whale bones recalls the whaling of earlier times. The **visitor centre** ⊙ is housed in an old power station and contains an exhibition about the island's different landscapes. It also has the bones of one of four whales which were stranded on the island in 1997, and a small cultural and historical section. In Middenstreek, a street which runs towards the west, and in the parallel Langestreek, there are interesting **old houses** with asymmetrical roofs.

★ **The Rif** – Past the Westerplas, at the southwestern point of the island, lies a vast stretch of immaculate white sand reaching 1.5km/1mi in width. From Westerburenweg, a path which ends in the dunes, there is an excellent **view**★ of the Rif.

317

TERSCHELLING★★
Fryslân – Population 4 801

> **Ferry** ⊘ – From Harlingen. Operated by Rederij Doeksen; information line
> ☎ (0562) 44 27 70 or 44 32 20 (express service)
>
> **VVV tourist office** – In West-Terschelling, ☎ (0562) 44 30 00.

This very long island (28km/17.5mi) covers 11 000ha/27 180 acres and is the second largest of the Wadden islands, after Texel.

Terschelling is an island with many faces: wide sandy beaches, tall dunes, salt marshes and mudflats with hundreds of birds, dense coniferous forests, broad polders and a few small villages. The ideal way to explore it is by the many cycle paths that crisscross the island.

It welcomes many holidaymakers in summer, who enjoy its huge sandy beaches. Terschelling (pronounced Ter-srelling) still has a wild aspect. It is covered with vast areas of dunes where an abundant vegetation of grasses, flowers and moss grow. It also has several **nature reserves**, of which the largest is De Boschplaat.

Terschelling is the homeland of **Willem Barents** or Barentsz (c 1555-97), the navigator who, while trying to seek a northeast passage to India, discovered Novaya Zemlya in 1594 and Spitsbergen in 1596 *(see Introduction: History)*. The portion of the Arctic Ocean which lies between these two archipelagos bears his name, the Barents Sea. On his third expedition (1596-97), his boat was caught in the ice. He spent the winter in Novaya Zemlya in a hut made from boat planks, and he died in an attempt to return to civilization. In 1876 the ship's log was found.

The 10-day **Oerol festival** takes place every June, with events and performances being held all over the island, on beaches, in the dunes and in barns.

West-Terschelling – The capital of the island (known in Frisian as West-Skylge) is a small but lively port well situated in a large bay. It is overlooked by a square tower 54m/174ft high, the **Brandaris**, a lighthouse built in 1594 to replace the bell-tower of St Brandarius Chapel which had till then done sterling service as a lighthouse. The bell-tower was engulfed by the waves.

West-Terschelling – The marina at the foot of the Brandaris

At the foot of the tower lies a large **cemetery**. The 19C and early 20C tombstones, engraved with naively depicted boats, recall the maritime past of its inhabitants. One of the stones, in the middle of the cemetery, recalls the episode during which five of the island's lifesavers tried to rescue the survivors from the wreck of the *Queen of Mistley*, on 3 January 1880.

Terschelling Museum 't Behouden Huys ⊘ – *Commandeurstraat 30*. This regional museum is housed in two dwellings belonging to captains (commandeurshuizen) (1668). It bears the name of the hut in which Willem Barents was forced to spend a winter on Novaya Zemlya. At the entrance, note the fine sculptured paving stones.

The top floor of the left-hand house tells the story of Terschelling; the rooms on the ground floor are furnished in 19C style.
A new section of the museum contains a reconstruction of part of Willem Barentsz's ship, with a wide variety of objects and a panorama show recounting his voyages to the far north. The first floor is dedicated to pilotage and whaling. The other house contains model ships and related objects, together with a collection of flotsam and jetsam.

Centrum voor natuur en landschap ○ – *Burg. Reedekkerstraat 11*
This centre is devoted to the island's rich plant and animal life, with films and other media being used to show how dunes form, how dikes are built, how water is managed, and the role of forestry. It places particular emphasis on the bird island of Griend, and the De Boschplaat Nature Reserve. The centre also has large aquariums of fish, crabs and shellfish.

Formerum – A small windmill, **De Koffiemolen** (the coffee mill) is worth seeing. It has a thatched roof and dates from 1876; and is now used to mill grain.

Terschelling and its cranberries

Cranberry wine is a speciality of Terschelling, and the damp valleys between the dunes are almost the only place in Europe where cranberries grow. According to tradition it all started in about 1840, when a beachcomber, Pieter-Sipkes Cupido, found a barrel full of cranberries that had washed ashore from a ship. He took it into the dunes, opened it, and then left it there, disappointed that the barrel did not contain anything more valuable. But Terschelling had gained a new crop as a result.
The centre of the industry is in Formerum, but all over the island you can taste tarts, ice creams, jam, liqueur, wine and meat dishes prepared using local cranberries.

Hoorn – The Frisian name of this village is Hoarne. The 13C church built of brick in the Frisian style is surrounded by gravestones. The oldest date from the 19C and are topped by a low relief depicting a ship.

★ **De Boschplaat** ○   *No cars allowed; cycling paths in the western part.* Hay cart tours and guided walks are organised.
This nature reserve is the only **European natural monument** in the Netherlands, and a paradise for nature lovers. It covers 4 440ha/10 868 acres of the island's eastern point, which is uninhabited. Large numbers of birds come to nest on the dunes and estuaries. What makes it special is the large number of transitional zones between different ecosystems, for example between salt and fresh water, dry and wet, wind and shelter, and acid and alkaline soils. The vegetation is quite remarkable, as orchids and unique types of halophyte plants can be found (those growing on salty soil). A large part of the Boschplaat is closed to visitors during the nesting season.

TEXEL★★
Noord-Holland – Population 13 345

Ferry ○ – From Den Helder. Operated by Teso; information line ☎ (0222) 36 96 91.
VVV (tourist office) Emmalaan 66, Den Burg, ☎ (0222) 31 47 41 or www.texel.net.

Texel (pronounced Tessel) is 24km/15mi long and 9km/6mi wide, and is the largest of the Wadden islands. If therefore has less of an island feel than its neighbours, but this Netherlands in miniature still has much to offer.

The capital, **Den Burg**, is roughly in the centre. **De Koog**, to the west, gives access to the main beach. **Oudeschild** is a small fishing and pleasure port. **Oosterend**, **De Waal** and **Den Hoorn** are small, picturesque villages; **De Cocksdorp** is the most northerly, and its lighthouse has a view of Vlieland on a good day.

Bird Island – Birds are one of the most interesting features of Texel. Some 300 species nest and breed on the dunes or on the banks of the freshwater lakes. Texel has several State-owned **nature reserves**★ ○.
The waymarked nature trails are for walkers only.

Texel

De Eijerlandse duinen – These dunes belonged to an island, Eyerlandt, which has been joined to Texel since 1629 by a sand bar. Numerous birds nest here from the end of March to the end of July, especially eiders which provide the down to make eiderdowns.

De Slufter – This is a large area surrounded by dunes, linked to the sea by a gap. The vegetation growing here is impregnated with salt. About 40 different species of birds nest here.

From the top of the dunes, at the end of the Slufterweg, which can be reached by a stairway, there is a **view**★ over this amazing wild landscape which in July and August is covered with a mauve flower called sea lavender.

De Muy – This is a partly marshy area in the hollow of the dunes, where nearly 50 species of birds nest, especially white spoonbills with their characteristic beak, and the grey heron. There are interesting plants (orchids, pyrola and Parnassus grass).

De Westerduinen – Herring gulls nest on these dunes near the beach.

De Geul – This lake was formed in the dunes at the end of the last century. Several other small lakes have formed since. In the reeds one can see the spoonbill, the grey heron and the pintail duck.

Nearby a wealth of interesting plants grow on the dunes and marshes.

A fine viewpoint can be had over the reserve from the belvedere built on the **Mokweg**.

Eco Mare ⊙ – *Ruyslaan 92. Access by De Koog road and road 13.*

A building, set in the dunes to the northwest of Den Burg, houses this centre devoted to the Wadden islands and the North Sea, as well as a small Natural History Museum, **Natuurhistorisch Museum**, with collections on Texel, the Waddenzee region and the North Sea.

Texel and its sheep

The island's main activity, after agriculture and tourism, is sheep breeding (there are about 16 000 sheep on the island, and some 20 000 lambs are born each spring). There are a particularly large number of sheep sheds around the ironically named Hoge Berg or high hill (15m/50ft) in the middle of the island. These are like small half-barns with thatched roofs, used to store hay and feed as well as to protect the sheep against the bitter west wind and the snow. They also take shelter behind the garden walls of the farmhouses, but Texel sheep always spend the winter outdoors.

Apart from their extremely fine meat, which has a natural salty taste from the grass they eat, the sheep also provide excellent wool and milk; it is said that the wool has a healing effect on muscle pain and rheumatism. The milk is also used to make cheese and even soap.

The first section is about the island's evolution, from its geological formation during the Ice Age, up to its transformation into polders, and from its prehistoric inhabitants to the present-day tourist invasion.

In another section, the nature reserves' flora and fauna can be studied with the help of dioramas, show cases with stuffed birds and photographs of plants.

The underground **Waterzaal** (Water Hall) contains may aquariums, providing an interactive discovery tour of the world above and below the surface of the sea. It covers such subjects as seals, the beach, the effects of tides, the fishing industry, and the Waddenzee. There is also a tank in which visitors can touch tame rays. Young seals, and others recovering from illness and injury, cavort in the **salt water ponds** ⓥ outside; birds contaminated by pollution are also looked after here. The **Duinpark** (dune park) contains three waymarked walks.

Oudheidkamer ⓥ – *In Den Burg, in Kogerstraat, on a small shady square called Stenenplaats.* The Chamber of Antiquities is a former poorhouse, built in 1599; it is now a museum of paintings, costumes and everyday objects recalling local life. There is a tiny herb garden at the back.

Maritiem en Jutters Museum ⓥ – *In Oudeschild, southeast of Den Burg.*
The Maritime and Beachcombing Museum is located in the seaweed sheds around the De Traanroeier windmill. It contains lifeboats, a shipyard and a smithy. One of the sheds is fitted out as a beachcombers' storeroom, full of hundreds of often bizarre finds from the beach.

The various floors of the 19C grain warehouses deal with the pilotage and rescue services, and the history of the roadsteads where East India Company ships had to await fair winds so that they could sail into the Zuiderzee; these brought great prosperity to the island in the 17C and 18C. Finally, a room on the ground floor explores the subject of underwater archeology and the many shipwrecks in the Waddenzee.

Agrarisch en Wagen Museum ⓥ – *At De Waal, north of Den Burg.* The Agricultural and Cart Museum contains items formerly used on the island. On the top floor is a display showing the development of agriculture on Texel, and regular demonstrations are given in the smithy.

Oosterend – This picturesque village of green and white houses has four small churches, including one dating from the 11C which is the oldest on the island. The village is a conservation area.

VLIELAND
Fryslân – Population 1 160

Ferry ⓥ – *From Harlingen or Terschelling. Operated by Rederij Doeksen; information line* ☎ *(0562) 44 29 69 or 44 32 20 (express service).*

VVV (Vlieland) – ☎ (0562) 45 11 11.

This island, composed of dunes and woods, covering 5 100ha/12 597 acres is 20km/12.5mi long with a maximum width of 2.5km/1.5mi. There is only one small village, Oost-Vlieland. A single surfaced road crosses it from east to west. Only the army, at the western end, and tourists in season come and spoil the peace of this wild countryside. The island is also beautifully quiet, because only the islanders are allowed to use cars.

Oost-Vlieland – In Dorpsstraat, the main street, there are a few old houses. On the south side of the street a house has been converted to create the **Museum Tromp's Huys** ⓥ. This is a typical island home, with fine furniture and collections of antiques and paintings, including works by the Norwegian artist Betzy Berg who lived here at the beginning of the 20C.

A small visitor centre, **De Noordwester** ⓥ, has been fitted out near the church. Photographs provide documentation on the island's flora and fauna; there are also some aquaria and a beachcombers' storeroom.

The 17C **church** ⓥ on the other side of the square contains some whale jawbones from the adjoining **churchyard**. This has some interesting tombstones carved with hourglasses, anchors and ships, as well as the graves of soldiers from the Second World War.

To the left of the church is the beautiful 17C poorhouse or deacons' house, used to accommodate orphans, old people, and widows. There were a relatively large number of these, despite the island's relatively small population, since the sea claimed many men's lives.

From the top of the lighthouse to the west of the village, there is a **view**★ over Oost-Vlieland, the dark green woods forming a contrast to the pale colour of the dunes, and the Waddenzee, where at each low tide vast stretches of mud flats appear, covered with flocks of birds.

WORKUM

Fryslân
Michelin maps 908 H 3 and 210 R 5
Local map see Sneek

This small town (Warkum in Frisian) was once a prosperous seaport where the ee⸱ trade flourished. Now it is a large holiday and water sports centre.
It is well-known for its glazed pottery which is brown in colour and often decorate⸱ with a frieze of notched white scrolls.
Workum still has several interesting houses with crow-stepped or bell-shaped gable⸱ (kolkgevel).

Self-portrait, Jopie Huisman

Stichting Jopie Huisman Museum

Merk – It has a picturesqu⸱ collection of old buildings⸱

Stadhuis – The town hall ha⸱ a tall 18C façade.
On the left is the old tow⸱ hall, a small Renaissance⸱ style building decorate⸱ with a carved stone.

Sint-Gertrudiskerk ⊙ – Thi⸱ large Gothic church wa⸱ built in the 16C and 17⸱ and has an imposin⸱ separate **bell-tower** crowne⸱ with a tiny onion-shape⸱ dome.
Inside the church there is⸱ fine 18C pulpit and nin⸱ painted **biers** (gildebarer⸱ illustrating the activities c⸱ the guilds. They were use⸱ during funerals to carr⸱ the corpses of guil⸱ members to the cemetery⸱ The organ dates fror⸱ 1697.

Waag – The former weigl⸱ house is a fine 17C buildin⸱ with crow-stepped dorme⸱ windows. Inside is **Workum⸱ Erfskip** ⊙ (Workum's Her⸱ tage), a museum of local history with the accent on the shipping and ceramic⸱ industries, including the town's distinctive domestic ceramics (see above).

★ **Jopie Huisman Museum** ⊙ – Opposite the VVV (tourist office). This sma⸱ but attractive museum has a collection of paintings and drawings by th⸱ self-taught Frisian artist Jopie Huisman, born in Workum in 1922. Huisma⸱ also worked as a dealer in rags and scrap metal. His often moving canvase⸱ show a warm interest in ordinary people and everyday objects; the impressiv⸱ precision with which he painted shoes, dolls, household objects and clothe⸱ often makes them more tangible than the real objects in the display cases besid⸱ the pictures. Apart from oil paintings, the museum also includes fine in⸱ drawings, luminous watercolours, Frisian landscapes and caricature villag⸱ scenes.

ZAANSTREEK ★

Noord-Holland
Michelin maps 908 F 4 and fold 27 (inset) and 210 N 8

The Zaanstreek or Zaan Region is an area bordering the River Zaan to the north c⸱ Amsterdam.
The succession of riverside towns were regrouped in 1974 to form the district c⸱ **Zaanstad** (pop 134 397). This is now an important dormitory town for people workin⸱ in Amsterdam.
Originally the inhabitants gained a living from fishing. Then in 1592 Corneliu⸱ Corneliszoon built the first wind-powered saw mill. Many other windmills were bu⸱ for industrial purposes and there were soon more than 500 (see Introductio⸱ Industrial heritage). The timber in particular was used to build the warships for th⸱ navy and the great sailing vessels for Dutch merchants. The shipyard's reputatic⸱ was such that in 1697 the **Czar Peter the Great** paid a visit incognito to undergo a peric⸱ of training with a local shipbuilder.

Many of the windmills still exist. These industrial mills are usually very tall as they were built over the workshop; their sails were driven from a platform.

The local houses also had a very characteristic style and quite a number have been reassembled in the museum-village of Zaan.

*ZAANSE SCHANS

The museum-village takes its name from fortifications which were built in the late 16C against possible attacks from the Spanish. There is no longer any trace of the redoubt.

This living museum was established in 1950 when structures from all parts of Zaanstreek and especially from the town of Zaandam were re-erected here. The buildings have been restored and arranged to form a museum-village, where people live and work. The aim of the villagers is to preserve the traditional Dutch way of life.

Industrial windmills, Zaanse Schans

The village is laid out along a dike, **Kalverringdijk**, alongside which runs a narrow canal spanned by several little humpbacked bridges. Some of the houses line secondary canals which are themselves followed by paths, such as Zeilenmaker-spad *(see below)*.

Most of the houses are timber built and they display an amazing variety of gables. The houses are generally green in colour, or are tarred black, while the gables, window and doors are outlined in white. Each gable is topped out with a small wooden ornament *(makelaar)*.

Several of the houses, shops and windmills are open to the public.

Zaans Museum – The museum under construction to the east of the car park will be devoted to various aspects of the Zaanstreek.

Boat tours ⊙ are organised on the Zaan. See plan for departure point.

Klompenmakerij ⊙ – The clog-making workshop, located in the De Vrede visitor centre (a warehouse dating from 1721), organises demonstrations of this traditional craft.

Zeilenmakerspad – The sailmakers' path takes visitors past a small hollow **post mill**, De Hadel. The 17C house at no 4 has been given the odd name of the crowned bread roll (In de Gecroonde Duijvekater) and it houses a bakery museum, or **Bakkerijmuseum** ⊙.

Kaasmakerij Catharina Hoeve ⊙ – The Netherlands' two best-known cheeses, Gouda and Edam, are made in the traditional manner in this dairy, a 1988 replica of a farmhouse from the east of the Zaanstreek.

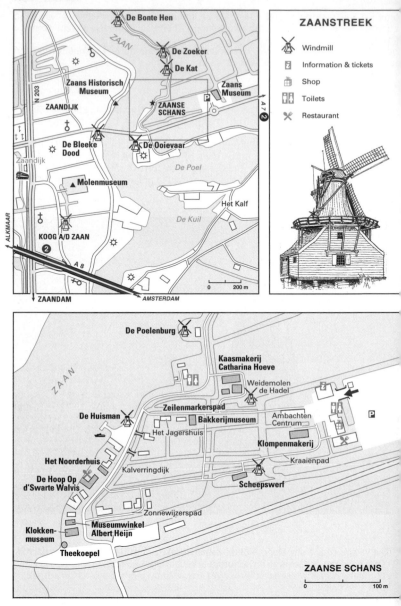

De Huisman – This 18C smock mill is used for making mustard.

Het Noorderhuis ⊙ – The reception room of this neck-gabled merchant's hous (1670) is open to the public, along with another room containing costume figures and old dolls.

De Hoop op d'Swarte Walvis – This reconstructed orphanage (1966) fror Westzaan now houses a famous restaurant.

Museumwinkel Albert Heijn ⊙ – This delightful old shop in a 19C house sel old-fashioned items such as sugar candy.

Klokkenmuseum ⊙ – The clock museum has a varied collection of timepiece made in the Netherlands.

Theekoepel – The Tea Dome, a small pavilion at the bottom of a garden, was onc a teahouse. Today it houses a **pewter workshop** ⊙.

De Poelenburg ⊙ – This postmill used for sawing wood dates from 1869; it built above the big workshop which turns with the mill when the sails are oriente to face the wind.

Verfmolen De Kat ⊙ – This mill, called The Cat, was used for extracting dye from tropical woods. In the 17C, there were 55 of these mills in the Zaanstreek.

Oliemolen De Zoeker ⊙ – In this oil mill, salad oil is made by grinding many types of seeds.

De Ooievaar – Industrial windmill, Zaanse Schans

ADDITIONAL SIGHTS

Zaandijk – The town of Zaandijk, on the opposite bank of the Zaan and forming part of the Zaanstad conurbation, has a local museum of antiquities, the **Zaans Historisch Museum** ⊙. The museum is housed in the brick-built home of a wealthy 18C merchant. Both the drawing room with its 19C furniture and the "good year room" with its tiled chimney-piece have been retained intact. It was the custom locally to add a room to the house when business prospered.
To the south is a 17C flour mill called **De Bleeke Dood** (Pale Death).

Koog aan de Zaan – In this small town there is an interesting Windmill Museum, the **Molenmuseum** ⊙. It is located in an attractive park, and shows different types of scale models★, ladders, tools, millers' garments, documents and engravings of the 17C to the 19C. There is also a large map showing the locations of the remaining 1 000 windmills in the Netherlands. In 1850, there were still 9 000.

Zaandam – This industrial town on the Zaan has, since 1876, been served by the North Sea Canal (Noordzeekanaal).
The **Czaar-Peterhuisje** ⊙, where Czar Peter the Great lived in 1697, can be seen at Krimp 23. The Czar spent some time here incognito in 1697, learning the craft of shipbuilding. It is built of wood but in 1895 it was enclosed by a brick construction, a gift of Czar Nicholas II.

ZIERIKZEE★

Zeeland
Michelin maps 908 C 7 and 211 I 13

Zierikzee is the main town on the island of **Schouwen-Duiveland** (population 32 493) and in the past it was a prosperous port on the Gouwe, a strait which separated Schouwen from Duiveland. The town maintained good relations with the Hanseatic League and later it became the residence of the counts of Holland and Zeeland.
The town is particularly remembered for an episode in its history when in 1576 the Spanish waded across the Zijpe, separating Schouwen-Duiveland from the mainland, in water up to their shoulders before taking the town.
Decline set in from the 16C; however the town has been able to preserve its heritage of 16C to 18C houses.
Schouwen-Duiveland is linked to Goeree Overflakkee in the north by the Brouwers-dam and the Grevelingendam and to Noord-Beveland in the south by the Ooster-schelde storm barrier and the Zeelandbrug (see DELTA).

Boat trips ⊙ – Zierikzee Harbour is the departure point for boat trips on the Oosterschelde.

SIGHTS

★ **Noordhavenpoort** – This double gateway presents two 16C Renaissance gables on the town side and an older crow-stepped gable on the outside.
The **Zuidhavenpoort** takes the form of a square tower quartered by four 14C corner turrets and is linked to the previous gateway by a lever bridge.

Oude Haven – Rows of elegant 17C and 18C houses line the quaysides of the old harbour. There are still some old ships to be seen.

Havenpark – On the north side of this square the house, **De Witte Swaen** dating from 1658 has a lovely Baroque gable. The house itself was rebuilt after the 1953 floods.
Adjoining the Gasthuiskerk is a former market, the **Beurs**, consisting of a Renaissance-style arcaded gallery with Tuscan columns.

's-Gravensteen – This one-time prison has a 1524 crow-stepped gable with ornamental wrought-iron grilles on the first floor windows. It is now home to the **Maritiem Museum** ⊙.

Stadhuis – The town hall was formerly the meat market. The outstanding feature of the building which has been altered several times is the usual wooden **tower** topped with an ornamental onion-shaped dome (1550) surmounted by a statue of Neptune. The tower has a **carillon** ⊙. Two decorative gables provide further ornamentation to the façade. The decorative pieces of wrought iron were for

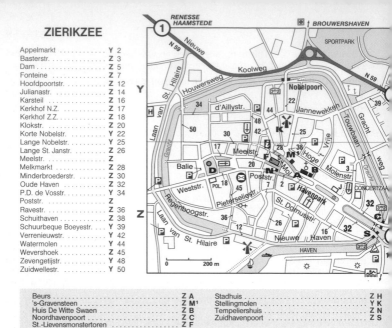

ZIERIKZEE

holding lighted torches. The **Stadhuismuseum** ⊙ inside is a local history museum
Most of the exhibits are displayed in the Harquebusiers' Hall with its fine timbe
ceiling.
Across from the stadhuis the 14C Huis De Haene, often called the **Tempeliershui**
is the oldest in town. The influence of Bruges (Belgium) architecture can be see
in the ogee-shaped mouldings of the windows.

Sint-Lievensmonstertoren ⊙ – This is the clock tower of the old Gothi
cathedral, which was destroyed by fire in 1832. Building work on the towe
started in 1454 and was supervised by a member of the Keldermans family, wh
were also responsible for Middelburg town hall. The tower rises to a height c
56m/184ft but it remains unfinished.
Next door is a great neo-Classical church (1848) preceded by a portico.

Nobelpoort – The outside of this 14C square town gate is flanked by two ta
towers, both later additions, topped by tall tapering pepper-pot roofs.
Further on is a tall 19C **tower mill** called De Hoop (Hope).

ZUTPHEN ★

Gelderland
Population 33 323
Michelin maps 908 J 5 and 211 W 10

Zutphen lies at the confluence of the IJssel, Berkel and Twentekanaal not far fror
the heathlands of Veluwe.
This pleasant historic city is the capital of the beautiful wooded region **Achterhoek**.
is an important commercial centre and its pedestrian precincts come alive on marke
days.

HISTORICAL NOTES

The county town of Zutphen became part of Geldern in 1127. In 1190 the tow
received its burgh charter but 10 years later (1200) it was transferred to the see c
Utrecht. In the 14C the town belonged to the Hanseatic League and built an enclosin
wall which was extended the following century.
Zutphen was then recognised as an important strategic point due to its easil
defendable position in the surrounding marshland (the name Zutphen, sometime
spelt Zutfen, comes from Zuidveen, the southern peat bog). Zutphen became one c
the richest towns in Gelderland and in the 16C it was given a second town wall c
which several sections still remain. The town was captured by the Spanish in 157
and only retaken by Maurice of Nassau in 1591. In 1586 the English poet Sir Phili
Sidney died of wounds received in an action to prevent the Spaniards from sendir
supplies into the town. The French occupied Zutphen from 1672 to 1674 ar
recaptured it again in 1795.

★ OLD TOWN 3hr

's-Gravenhof – Both the Sint-Walburgskerk and the stadhuis are to be found in this square. During excavations on the site in 1946 remains of the counts of Zutphen's castle were uncovered and today the outline of the castle can be traced on the pavement.

Sint-Walburgskerk ⊘ – This early 13C Romanesque church dedicated to St Walburga, was given successive extensions in Gothic style up to the 16C. The church was damaged in 1945 and lost the upper storey of its tower three years later. The original tufa facing of the tower has been repaired with limestone.

The exterior of the church is particularly attractive for the decorative roofscape above the trimming of balustrade and pinnacles and for the variety of building materials used.

On the north side the 15C Mariaportaal, **Doorway to the Virgin**, was rebuilt between 1890 and 1925.

Inside the vaulting is covered with 14C and 15C frescoes. The chancel has an extremely elaborate 15C ironwork **chandelier**. The plainer pulpit is 17C, like the organ case with its rich ornamentation. The **baptismal font** is a triumphant piece of copperwork cast in Mechelen, Belgium in 1527. It is decorated with the figures of the evangelists and saints with a pelican at the summit. The **library**★ dates from 1564 when it was built onto the ambulatory. The original aspect of the interior remains unchanged with low pointed vaulting and the supporting columns. The ribs descend to sculpted consoles and below in the place of capitals are numerous small figures. The library houses around 750 titles, including eight manuscripts and 80 incunabula; about 100 books are displayed on wooden stands: illuminated missals, anthologies of texts written by St Thomas Aquinas and Luther. It is one of the few libraries in Europe which has retained its original appearance and furnishings.

Stadhuis – This 15C building was considerably altered in 1716 and again in 1729. It adjoins the former **Vleeshal**, or meat market and its 15C frontage is best admired from Lange Hofstraat. Inside the great hall, **Burgerzaal**, has a lovely wooden ceiling.

Walk southwards along Lange Hofstraat.

Martinetsingel – From here there is an attractive **view**★ of the town wall with gardens sloping down to the green waters of the canal; of the pointed towers of the Drogenapstoren away to the right and Sint-Walburgskerk with its truncated tower in the background.

★ **Drogenapstoren** – This splendid gateway dates from 1444 to 1446. The change from square to octagonal is marked by crenellations and four octagonal turrets with pointed roofs. The tower itself is crowned by an even taller pointed roof.

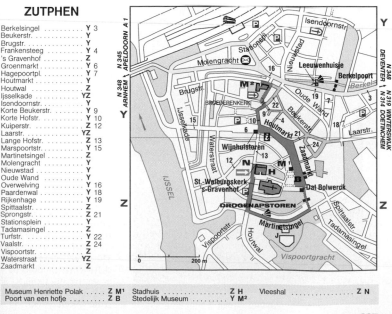

Dat Bolwerck – This attractive Gothic house (1549) is surmounted by pinnacles Next door are the 1639 cavalry barracks, **Ruiter Kortegaard**, with an attractiv scrolled gable.

Zaadmarkt – This was the site of the grain market, and is now a genera market. On the right at no 101 is the doorway of an **almshouse** dating from 1723.

Museum Henriette Polak ⊙ – The impressive **De Wildeman** mansion was altere in the 19C and today houses an interesting collection of paintings, sculpture and graphic arts by contemporary Dutch artists. Of particular interest are the bronz statuettes of *Queen Wilhelmina Aged 10* by **Mari Andriessen** and *A Child* by T Sondaar-Dobbelmann.

The secret chapel (1628) on the second floor was a refuge for Catholics. *Th Adoration of the Magi* is by the studio of Jan van Scorel (16C).

Houtmarkt – The lovely 17C Renaissance tower, the **Wijndragerstoren** ⊙, stand on the site of the former timber market. It was made by the Hemony brothers A market is held here every Thursday.

Stedelijk Museum ⊙ – The former Dominican convent is now the home o the municipal museum. The convent church stands to the south of a lovel garden.

The exhibits on the ground floor include sections on clocks and watches glasswork, gold and silverwork as well as some paintings. Look for the *View o Zutphen and the IJssel*, ascribed to Barent Avercamp. Barent worked in the sam style as his more famous uncle, Hendrick Avercamp.

The first floor is reserved for temporary exhibitions. The local collections on th second floor cover Zutphen and its immediate region.

Archeological finds and pottery are exhibited in the basement.

ADDITIONAL SIGHT

Berkelpoort – This 15C brick-built watergate spans the Berkel with three arches The entrances are flanked by watch turrets.

There is a good **view** ot the gateway from the footbridge to the west. Overlookin the footbridge is the **Leeuwenhuisje** with an overhang supported by lion-hea brackets.

EXCURSIONS

Achterhoek – *44km/27mi to the southeast by the Winterswijk road.*
Now known as Achterhoek, the area from Zutphen to the German border wa originally the county of Zutphen. It is an area of woodland (conifers, oaks an beeches) and pastures crisscrossed by quiet country roads and forest rides.

Vorden – This town has two 19C **windmills** with hand-rails. Vorden lies at the heart o a region where **eight castles** nestle in the surrounding woodlands: Vorden, Hackfor

Kiefskamp, Wildenborcl Bramel, Onstein, Medle and Wiersse. There are i actual fact 12 castles c small brick-built mano houses in all. Many wer rebuilt in the 18C in a quit plain style. The nobility attracted by the good hun ing provided by the local fo rests, elected to build sui able residences locally.

Some can only be reache on foot or by bicycle *(patł are signposted "openges eld")*.

Kasteel Vorden has a L-shape, with a slende octagonal tower in tł angle. Today the cast serves as the town ha Note the shell ornamen tion above the windows. The most impressive cast is **Hackfort**, flanked by tv great round towers. Ne: to it is a **water mill** datin from about 1700.

Kasteel Vorden

Groenlo – The historic city of Groenlo stands on the banks of the Slinge and is still encircled by sections of its town walls. The town is famous for its beer, Grolsch, meaning of Groenlo. In 1627 Groenlo capitulated to Prince Frederick Henry following a month-long siege.

The small **Grolsch Museum** ⊘ occupies a 17C farmhouse and presents displays of regional costumes, funerary urns, coins and other items.

Winterswijk – This town is also on the Slinge and in the surrounding forested areas the solitary but impressive farmhouses resemble quite closely those of the Twente (*see Introduction: Farmhouses*).

ZWOLLE

Overijssel Ⓟ
Population 101 902
Michelin maps 908 J 4 and 210 V 7
Plan of the conurbation in the current Michelin Red Guide Benelux

Zwolle has kept its special character in the historic centre within the ring of canals.

HISTORICAL NOTES

It was a member of the Hanseatic League in the 13C, linked to the Zuiderzee by the Zwarte Water, and for a long time it remained the depot for traffic between the Netherlands and northern Germany.

After the Spaniards left in 1572, its 15C curtain wall was considerably strengthened due to its strategic position. The wall was destroyed in 1674 during the Third Dutch War and little remains apart from the Sassenpoort in the south and, in the north, Rode Toren, which was partly demolished in 1845.

Today the ditches still surround the town and the pleasant gardens on the south and east sides mark the course of the ramparts and bastions.

Thomas a Kempis (1379/80-1471), who was a pupil at the School of the Brethren of the Common Life in Deventer, and to whom is attributed the *Imitatio Christi* (Imitation of Christ), lived in a convent to the north of the town (in Agnietenberg).

Gerard Terborch or Ter Borch (1617-81) was born in Zwolle. This painter, like his contemporary Gerrit Dou, is above all the dignified and meticulous painter of refined and peaceful interior scenes where young women wear shiny satin dresses; he also made excellent portraits and miniatures of the local notables.

Zwolle's main commercial activities are wholesale trade and transport, as well as graphics and metallurgy.

The town's specialities are Zwolse *balletjes*, sweets shaped like a small cushion with different flavours, and *blauwvingers*, shortbread in the form of fingers with chocolate tips.

Stedelijk Museum Zwolle – the Drostenhuis

ZWOLLE

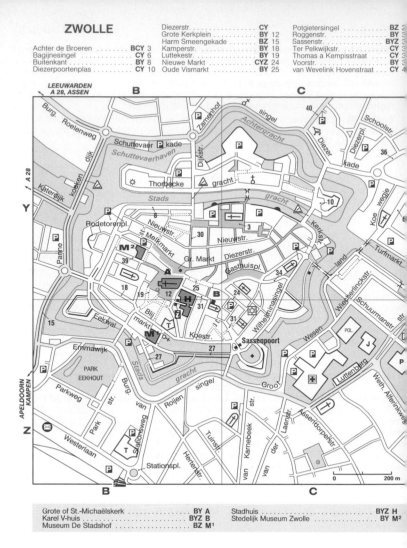

SIGHTS

★ **Stedelijk Museum Zwolle** ⊘ – The municipal museum is located in an elegan 16C mansion, the Drostenhuis, and a new wing.
The Drostenhuis contains a display of items relating to the town's rich past including a number of period rooms and fine collections of silverware from th Overijssel province. The new wing is devoted to contemporary art and cultura history, and around 10 temporary exhibitions are held here each year.

Grote Kerk or Sint-Michaëlskerk ⊘ – St Michael's is a hall-church with thre naves, dating from the 14C and 15C, of Protestant worship. Unlike th neighbouring church of Our Lady, it no longer has the traditional bell-tower, whic was a victim of successive disasters.
Inside note a remarkable early 17C carved pulpit and an organ loft of 1721. Th organ is excellent. It was made by the **Schnitger** brothers, sons of a well-know German organ builder, who lived in Groningen; it has 4 000 pipes. There is als a small 17C clock with a statue of St Michael which comes to life every half hou Attached to the left side of the fine 16C north portal there is a picturesque littl building with a decorated pediment: the **Hoofdwacht** or guard-room.

Stadhuis ⊘ – Beside the old town hall (15C and 19C) which had become too smal a new one has been built by the architect JJ Konijnenburg.
The façades are punctuated by types of concrete buttresses on top of whic appear a series of pointed red roofs. Inside the play of volumes and materials, an the arrangement of furniture make for a functional as well as aesthetic use c space.
The old part on the left, covered with mustard-yellow roughcast contain the **Aldermen's Hall** (Schepenzaal) dating from 1448. This old court room, no used for marriages, has a ceiling whose beams are held by 14 corbels wit

sculptures[★] depicting grotesque figures. Legend has it that the artists of Zwolle, rival town of Kampen, carved these heads to hold the governors of Kampen up to ridicule.

Note the brass chandeliers, and the small cupboards with locks set into the wall. Above the 16C fireplace there is a picture of the *Last Judgment*, which is a reminder of the room's original use.

On the terrace in front of the town hall there is a statue of Adam by Rodin.

Karel V-huis - A medallion of Charles V's head can be seen on the gable, giving his name to this house built in 1571, which has a fine Renaissance façade decorated with pilasters, carved friezes and a voluted gable above which are recumbent gods.

Sassenpoort - Built c 1409, the Saxon Gateway is the only one which still exists from the fortified town wall. It is flanked by four octagonal pointed turrets and topped by a spire. The building was for a long time used as a prison, and now houses models and photographs of the town.

Museum De Stadshof ⊙ - This museum of naive and outsider art is an international collection of paintings, drawings and sculptures by people from outside traditional artistic circles. The pieces have strong personal and expressive significance, and are often highly imaginative. In addition to the permanent collection, temporary exhibitions are also held.

Ecodrome ⊙ - *Willemsvaart 19*, on the southern edge of Zwolle. The Ecodrome combines enjoyable displays on natural history, geology and the environment. The Natural History Museum contains skeletons of animals from the Ice Age and a colourful collection of birds, while the Ecodrome pavilion takes visitors through the story of the Earth's evolution. There are also plenty of attractions for children in the grounds, such as a lake with swans and a Speleodrome.

Practical information

Travelling to the Netherlands

Formalities – Although the Netherlands signed the Schengen Agreement endin
internal border controls between member countries, which came into effect in 1995
travellers should nonetheless be equipped with proof of identity. This may take th
form of a European Identity Card (for nationals of EU member states) or a **passpor**
Holders of British, Irish and US passports require no visa to enter the Netherlands
although visas may be necessary for visitors from some Commonwealth countries
and for those planning to stay for longer than three months. We recommend yo
check visa requirements with your travel agent or with your local Dutch Embassy (U
address: Royal Netherlands Embassy United Kingdom, 38 Hyde Park Gate, Londo
SW7 5DP, ☎ 0171 590 3200). US citizens should obtain the booklet *Your Tri*
Abroad (US$1.50) which provides useful information on visa requirements, custom
regulations, medical care etc for international travellers. Apply to the Superintenden
of Documents, PO Box 371954, Pittsburgh, PA 15250-795, ☎ (202) 512-1800.

Customs Regulations – Since the implementation of the single European market i
1993, there are effectively no longer any restrictions on the quantities of good
which can be purchased within the EU by private travellers from its member states
A leaflet entitled *A Guide for Travellers* is available from HM Customs, UK (telephon
their Advice Centre: ☎ 0171 928 3344). Non-residents of EU member states shoul
enquire about customs regulations at their local customs service. For US citizen
Know Before You Go is available from the US Customs Service, PO Box 7407
Washington, DC 20044, ☎ (202) 927-6724.

By air – Various airline companies operate regular services to the internationa
airports in the Netherlands (Amsterdam-Schiphol, Rotterdam, Eindhoven an
Maastricht). Contact airlines and travel agents for information and timetables.

Those travelling from the UK can ring ☎ 0891 717 777 to listen to a list of selecte
tour operators to Holland. Calls cost 50p/min.

By sea – There are numerous cross-Channel services (passenger and car ferries
hovercraft, SeaCat, Le Shuttle) from the United Kingdom and Eire. For details appl
to travel agencies or to:

Hoverspeed, International Hoverport, Marine Parade, Dover, Kent CT17 9TC
☎ (01304) 240 241. **Dover to Ostend** 2hr.

Le Shuttle, ☎ (0990) 353 535. **Folkestone to Calais**, transports cars and passenger
through the Channel Tunnel in about 35min.

P&O European Ferries, Channel House, Channel View Road, Dover, Kent CT17 9T.
☎ (0990) 980 980. **Felixstowe to Zeebrugge**: crossing 5hr 15min; **Dover to Ostend an
Zeebrugge** 2hr-2hr 30min; **Dover to Calais** 15min.

The Channel Tunnel

This undersea tunnel is the realisation of dreams of linking Britain to mainland Europe which date back over 200 years. The Channel link consists of two single-track rail tunnels for passenger and freight transport, and one service tunnel for safety and ventilation. The tunnels are 50.5km/31mi long, 37km/23mi of which are under the Channel. Most of the tunnel is 40m/131ft beneath the seabed, in a layer of blue chalk. The trains have two levels for passenger cars (capacity 118 cars per shuttle) and one level for coaches and caravans. Special services operate for heavy goods vehicles. British, French and Belgian trains, including French TGVs, also use the tunnel. Journey time through the tunnel is ideally 35min, 28min of which are in the tunnel at a maximum speed of 130kph/80mph.

&0 North Sea Ferries: King George Dock, Hedon Road, Hull, Humberside HU9 5QA, ☎ (01482) 377 177. **Hull to Rotterdam**: night crossing 14hr; **Hull to Zeebrugge**: night crossing 14hr.

candinavian Seaways, Scandinavia House, Parkeston Quay, Harwich, Essex CO12 4QG, ☎ (01255) 240 240. **Newcastle to IJmuiden (Amsterdam)**: day crossing 19hr.

tena Line, Charter House, Park Street, Ashford, Kent TN24 8EX, ☎ (01233) 647 047. **Harwich to Hoek van Holland**: Fastcraft service 3hr 40min; **Dover to Calais** 15min.

By rail – Two rail services use the Channel Tunnel: the **Eurostar** service with direct high-speed passenger trains from London to Brussels and Paris, and **Le Shuttle** passenger and freight service from Folkestone to Calais (see above). The Eurostar service takes only 3hr 30min to travel from London-Waterloo to Brussels-Midi, from where you can take one of the frequent InterCity trains to Amsterdam. Eurostar timetable details and ticket reservations: ☎ 0990 186 186.

By road – When driving to the continent the ideal ports of entry for the Netherlands are Vlissingen, Rotterdam and Hoek van Holland. Depending on the point of departure it may be more convenient to land at Hamburg (seasonal service from Harwich), Zeebrugge (from Felixstowe and Kingston-upon-Hull), Ostend or Calais (both from Dover) and then drive on to the Netherlands.

Calais to Rotterdam via Antwerp: 305km/190mi – 3hr 30min.
Calais to Amsterdam via Antwerp and Rotterdam: 379km/235mi – 4hr 30min.
Hamburg to Amsterdam via Bremen: 472km/290mi – 4hr 50min.

To choose the most suitable route between one of the above ports and your destination, use the Michelin Road Atlas of Europe, or consult the Michelin route-planning service on the Internet (**www.michelin-travel.com**).

By coach – Eurolines operates coach services to Amsterdam, Breda, The Hague, Rotterdam and Utrecht. For details and reservations:
Eurolines, 4 Cardiff Road, Luto, Beds LU1 1PP, ☎ (01582) 404 511.

S. Dornelounkseb/EUREKA SLIDE

Touring in the Netherlands

By car

Documents – A valid **driving licence** is essential. Nationals of non-EU countries require an international driving licence (obtainable in the US from the American Automobile Association for $10, two passport-sized photos needed, ☎ 800-222-4357). Third party insurance is the minimum cover required by insurance legislation in the Netherlands, but it is advisable to take out additional insurance for fully comprehensive cover (the Green Card). Special breakdown and get-you-home packages are a good idea (AA, Five Star RAC, National Breakdown, Europ Assistance...).

Driving regulations – Traffic in the Netherlands drives **on the right**. The minimum age for driving is 18 for cars and motorcycles and 16 for mopeds. Children under 12 are not allowed to travel in the front seat as long as there is room for them in the back. Seatbelts are compulsory in the back as well as the front of the car.
Maximum **speed limits** for cars, caravans and small trailers are 50kph/31mph in built-up areas, 80kph/50mph on the open road, and 120kph/75mph on motorway (minimum speed on motorways is 70kph/45mph). Motorways *(autosnelweg)* are toll-free and all motorway junctions are numbered *(see the Michelin map series)*. There are however tolls for certain bridges and tunnels (Kiltunnel and Prins Willem Alexander Brug).
Priority must be given to cars coming from the right at junctions and on roundabouts unless shown otherwise. Give way also to trams, pedestrians boarding or alighting from trams, and pedestrians crossing the road into which you are just turning. Only pass trams on the right unless there is insufficient room. Trams generally have priority. Cyclists will pass on the right and have priority over motorists when the latter want to turn off the road.
The regulation **red warning triangle** must be carried, and displayed in the event of a breakdown.

Accidents – In the event of an accident the emergency number for ambulance and police is ☎ 112. Emergency telephones are to be found alongside the main roads.

Breakdown service – The main organisation is the ANWB (Koninklijke Nederlandsche Toeristenbond), the Royal Dutch Touring Club which operates road patrols *(Wegenwacht)* on main roads. If no patrol happens to pass then phone for assistance from one of the roadside telephones to the nearest ANWB office *(alarmcentrale* ☎ 0800 08 88. This breakdown service operates 24h/24h. The receptionist usually speaks several foreign languages. Foreign visitors who are not in the possession of a valid membership card of a club affiliated to the AIT (Alliance Internationale de Tourisme) must pay the cost of membership. Members of the Automobile Association (AA) with a valid International Circular Letter of Credit (IRK) obtain free assistance.
ANWB, PO Box 93200, 2509 BA The Hague, ☎ (070) 314 71 47.

Petrol – The following kinds of petrol are on sale in the Netherlands

Super	Super gelood
Super (unleaded, only 95 octane)	Super (loodvrij)
Diesel	Diesel
Euro (Unleaded, only 95 octane)	Euroloodvrij
LPG	Gas

Credit cards are sometimes accepted at petrol stations, but visitors are still strongly advised to have other means of payment with them.

Car hire – Cars can be hired in most major towns and resorts. The minimum age limit is 21 although some companies maintain a minimum age of 23 and possession of a valid licence for a minimum of one year. A current driving licence is required. It is cheaper to reserve in advance rather than to pay on the spot. All the major companies (Avis, Hertz, Budget and Europcar) are to be found in the main Dutch cities as well as local companies.

Signposting – In the Netherlands the names of certain foreign towns are often signposted in Dutch:
Belgium: Luik for Liège;
France: Parijs for Paris, Rijsel for Lille;
Germany: Aken for Aachen.
For useful motoring terms see the Phrase book.

Road maps – The Michelin map 407 covers all the Benelux countries at a scale of 1:400 000. Map 408 covers the Netherlands at a scale of 1:400 000 and has a comprehensive index as well as enlarged inset maps of the conurbations of Amsterdam and Rotterdam. The Netherlands is also covered at a scale of 1:200 000 with maps 210 and 211 which give both road and tourist information.

Tourist routes – The ANWB has organised and signposted about 40 itineraries ranging in distance from 80-150km/50-100mi. These routes have hexagonal signposts and take in the most picturesque regions and interesting towns. Leaflets showing the routes and main points of interest are available from the ANWB offices. Other tourist and heritage trails are organised by local authorities.

By train

Tickets and fares – The Dutch railway system is run by the Netherlands Railways (NS). Further information and reservations are available from Holland Rail, contact the NBT (☎ 0891 717 777, *address given on p 340*).

The Netherlands has an extensive and efficient railway network. There is an InterCity network of express trains linking major cities. It is not possible to reserve seats on national train services. There are two classes (first and second). A day return is cheaper than two singles. There are numerous organised day trips and group tickets (multi, family and teenager) at reduced rates.

If you arrive in a city or town by train, you can use the **Train Taxi** service to travel into the centre. These are operated in 111 towns and cities, and charge a set fare of 7fl regardless of the distance travelled. The taxi driver will wait (normally not for more than 10min) until he has enough passengers before setting off.

By bus, tram or metro

Tickets – A strip card *(strippenkaart)*, valid for buses, trams and metros throughout the Netherlands, can be bought from newsagents, tobacconists, stations, VVV offices and supermarkets. It works out cheaper than buying a single ticket each time you travel by bus, tram or metro. You should either feed it into a punching machine on board the vehicle, or get the driver to stamp it, cancelling one strip per journey and one strip per zone being travelled through. Once stamped the strip is valid for one hour, during which you can change vehicle without having to get it restamped. City centres are one zone, and the surrounding zones are shown on maps at bus, tram and metro stops.

General information

Currency – The unit of currency in the Netherlands is the guilder (abbreviated to fl, from its old name florin) comprising 100 cents. Approximate exchange rate: £1 is worth 3fl (US$1 = 1.9fl). Coins in circulation: 5 cents *(stuiver)*, 10 cents *(dubbeltje)*, 25 cents *(kwartje)*, 100 cents/1fl *(gulden)*, 2.50fl *(rijksdaalder)* and 5fl. Bank notes: 10, 25, 50, 100, 250 and 1 000fl. Prices are rounded up or down to the nearest 5 cents as there are no 1 cent coins.

Money can be changed at post offices, banks and GWK offices (exchange) and in some coastal VVV offices. Rates of commission can vary considerably between exchange bureaux so check before changing your money.

GWK – This international organisation specialises in currency exchange, handling all types of foreign currency, also cashing travellers cheques and paying cash on eurocheques as well as American Express, Access, Diners Card, Eurocard, JCB and Visa. GWK offices are found throughout the country, at major border crossing points and Amsterdam-Schiphol airport. They are usually open Mondays to Sundays early morning to late at night.

The following GWK offices are open 24hr: Amsterdam Central Station, Schiphol Plaza (NS-station), Antwerp-Breda border (E19), Cologne/Oberhausen-Arnhem border (E35), Osnabrück-Oldenzaal border (E30).

Most GWK offices also offer a hotel booking service, tickets to major attractions, maps, tourist guides and telephone cards.

Banks – These are open at least from 1pm to 4pm on Mondays, and from 10am t
4pm on Tuesdays to Fridays. However opening times vary a great deal from one plac
to another, and from one branch to another.
Some banks are open during late-night shopping.

Credit cards and Eurocheques – All major credit cards (American Express, Diner
Club, Eurocard, Visacard, Access and MasterCard) are accepted but always check i
advance.
Lost or stolen credit cards or Eurocheques should be reported to the followin
numbers as soon as possible:
     Visa: ☏ (020) 660 06 11
     Mastercard/Eurocard: ☏ (030) 283 55 55/283 60 00
     American Express: ☏ (020) 504 85 04/504 86 66
     Diners Card: ☏ (020) 557 34 07.
You should also report the loss or theft to the local police and your bank.

Tips – The bill is usually inclusive of service charge and VAT. An extra tip can be lef
for special service. The price shown on the taxi meter includes service charge althoug
it is customary to give an extra tip.

Post offices and postal rates – Post offices open from 9am to 5pm or 6pm o
Mondays to Fridays. In some larger towns they are open on Saturday mornings.
The postage for letters and postcards:
     letters to the UK = 1fl
     letters to the USA = 1.60fl (0-20g) and 2.80fl (20-50g)
     postcards to the UK and USA = 1fl.
     Some post offices house telephone facilities.

Telecenters – Amsterdam has two telecenters (Raadhuisstraat 48 close to the Dar
and a second at Schiphol airport). These centres provide facilities for making phon
calls, sending telegrams, sending and receiving fax or telex messages and makin
photocopies. They stock stamps and telephone cards. They are open Mondays t
Sundays 8am to 2am.

Telephones – To phone abroad from the Netherlands dial
     GB: 00 44;   **Australia:** 00 61;
     USA: 00 1;   **Eire:** 00 353;
     Canada: 00 1;
followed by the trunk code and subscriber's number.
Dutch dialling codes are given in the **Michelin Red Guide Benelux**. Amsterdam (020); Th
Hague (070); Rotterdam (010); Utrecht (030) and Maastricht (043). Telephon
numbers beginning with 0800 are toll-free; those beginning with 0900 are charge
at a special rate.
In the Netherlands the phone boxes are green. The grey telephones take coin
(25 cent, 1fl and 2.50fl pieces) while the blue phones accept pre-paid phonecards
Phonecards, in units of 10, 25 or 50fl, are available from Primafoon (Dutch Teleco
outlet), VVV offices, railway stations and post offices.

Some useful telephone numbers:

Ambulance, Police, Fire Brigade ☏ 112
Traffic reports ☏ (0900) 96 22
Lost baggage (train) ☏ (020) 557 85 44
Lost baggage (tram, bus or metro) ☏ (020) 551 49 11

Shops – Shops are usually open Tuesdays to Saturdays from 9am to 6pm (they ten
to close earlier on Saturdays 4pm or 5pm). Closed on Sundays and Monday:
sometimes only Monday mornings.
In many towns there is late-night shopping on Thursday or Friday evening. A larg
number of shops in the centre of Amsterdam are open on Sundays on a trial basi:
GWK offices are open Mondays to Saturdays from 8am to 8pm, Sundays 10am t
4pm.
Supermarkets are open from 8am to 8pm Mondays to Fridays and Saturdays 8a
to 6pm. Late-night shopping is usually to 9pm.

Restaurants – The usual opening times for lunch are from 11am to 2.30pm or 3pm
and for dinner from 5.30pm to 10pm or 11pm. There are some late-openin
restaurants in the larger cities.

Pharmacies – These are open Mondays to Fridays 9.30am to 5.30pm; lists o
chemists on call in the evening, at night or at the weekend are shown on the doo

Public Holidays – 1 January, Good Friday, Easter Sunday and Monday, 30 Apr
(Queen's Day or National Day), Ascension Day, Whit Sunday, Whit Monday, 5 Ma
(Liberation Day), 25 and 26 December.

Remembrance Day, 4 May, is not a public holiday.
Local festivals *(see Calendar of events)* can also mean that various public facilities will be closed.

Medical care – Visitors with medical insurance through a national health scheme with an agreement with the Netherlands must submit their international insurance document E111 to the doctor, dispensing chemist or hospital.
Visitors from countries which have not concluded internal agreements are advised to take out travel insurance in their home country.

Embassies

Australia:	Carnegielaan 4, 2517 KH Den Haag, ☏ (070) 310 8200.
Canada:	Sophialaan 7, 2514 JP Den Haag, ☏ (070) 361 4111.
Eire:	Dr. Kuyperstraat 9, 2514 BA Den Haag, ☏ (070) 363 0993.
UK:	Lange Voorhout 10, 2514 ED Den Haag, ☏ (070) 364 5800.
USA:	Lange Voorhout 102, 2514 EJ Den Haag, ☏ (070) 310 9209.

Eating out

The Dutch have a hearty breakfast and eat a light lunch around 12.30pm. The evening meal is usually eaten between 6pm and 7pm. *For restaurant opening times, see General information.*
The restaurants listed under **Travellers' addresses** in this guide have been selected for their setting, and the typical character of their fare. The **Michelin Red Guide Benelux** lists a wide selection of restaurants for varying budgets. There are also suggestions for those in search of local specialities. Visitors may also like to consult the **Michelin web site** (www.michelin-travel.com).

Neerlands Dis – The 140 restaurants of this nationwide chain are easily recognisable by their red, white and blue soup tureen emblem. They offer a selection of traditional Dutch dishes.

Tourist Menu – The restaurants displaying a blue wall plaque with a white fork serve a three course meal (starter, main course and dessert) at a reasonable price (40fl in 1997). A booklet is available from VVV offices.

Brown Cafés (Bruin café) – These traditional dark panelled bars are famous for their atmosphere, conviviality and comfort, more typical of a cosy sitting room. They are a sharp contrast to the chrome and glass designer bars popular with trendy clientele. The **cafés** of Amsterdam and other large towns are known for the friendly atmosphere during their cocktail hour when drinks are accompanied by small cubes of cheese and the famous small hot meatballs *(bitterballen)*.
Many so-called **coffee shops** specialise in the sale and consumption of soft drugs. Those in search of tea or coffee should look instead for tearooms.

Accommodation

Hotels and restaurants – The hotels listed under **Travellers' addresses** in this guide have been selected for their handy location, originality of character or value for money. They are listed in three categories: "budget hotels" with room rates of less than 150fl are small establishments offering a good standard of comfort at a relatively low cost; "we recommend" particularly charming hotels with rates between 195fl and 325fl per night; and "treat yourself" to one to two excellent more luxurious options.
For choosing a stopover for a few hours or a few days, the current **Michelin Red Guide Benelux** is an indispensable complement to this guide. It is updated every year and offers a range of hotels and restaurants with an indication of their standard of service and comfort, their location and their prices. Visitors may also like to consult the **Michelin web site** (www.michelin-travel.com).

Netherlands Reservation Centre (NRC) – This national reservation centre not only books a hotel room but also bungalows and apartments and is generally geared to those booking from outside the country. Nationaal Reserveringscentrum (NRC), Postbus 404, 2260 AK Leidschendam, Netherlands, ☏ (070) 419 55 00, fax (070) 419 55 19, or www.bookings.nl. Once in the Netherlands call into a VVV office which also offers an accommodation service.

Bed and Breakfast – The VVV offices have listings of families offering bed and breakfast style accommodation (although there is not so much of this type of accommodation available).

Reservations are also possible through Bed & Breakfast Holland, Theophile d
Bockstraat 3, 1058 TV Amsterdam, ☎ (020) 615 75 27, Fax (020) 669 15 73.

Youth hostels – These are open to young and old alike, who are members of thei
own national youth organisation or have an international card, and offer facilities fo
individuals, families and groups. Details from Stichting Nederlandse Jeugdherberg
Centrale (NJHC), Prof. Tulpplein 4, 1018 GX Amsterdam ☎ (020) 551 31 55.

Rented accommodation – A wide range of accommodation (bungalows, log cabins
holiday cottages, flats and apartments) from the luxurious to the rustic is available
for visitors. Details from the ANWB. Book through the Netherlands Reservation
Centre (see above).

Camping and caravanning – Camp sites are indicated by the symbol ö on Micheli
maps 210, 211 and 408. Campers must provide proof of identity before being
allowed onto a site. A list of camp sites in the Netherlands is available from VV
tourist offices. The ANWB publishes an annual guide Camping Nederland containing
a large number of camp sites which it has inspected. The ANWB guide Klein
Campings has details of sites on farms and elsewhere. Information about camping
in the grounds of country houses and castles is available from Administratie LKC
Nevenlandsehof 14, 7312 EX Apeldoorn, ☎ (055) 355 88 44.

Dutch camp sites are classified under the auspices of the Stichting Classificati
Kampeer- en Bungalowbedrijven, Postbus 93008, 2509 AA Den Haag
☎ (070) 324 54 83. The number of stars allocated (1 to 5) refers to sanitar
facilities, and the number of flags (1 to 5) concerns general and recreational facilities
Camping in places other than official camp sites is not allowed in the Netherlands
However landowners may obtain exemptions from this law from their local councils
Many camp sites in the Netherlands have hikers' cabins (trekkershut). These ca
normally accommodate four people and offer rudimentary facilities (beds, table an
chairs, cooking facilities and electricity), ideal for those on the move on cycling
hiking or canoeing holidays. A maximum of three nights can be spent in any on
cabin. It is necessary to book ahead through the NRC. Both the VVV and ANW
offices have lists of camp sites which have hikers' cabins.

Down on the farm – If you are interested in staying on a farm or pitching your ten
on one, contact the SVR (Stichting Vrije Recreatie) which has a list of 1 20
mini-camp sites. Dutch law limits the number of tents per farm to five.
Stichting Vrije Recreatie, ☎ (0183) 35 27 41.

Holiday villages – The Netherlands has a wide choice of holiday parks where you ca
rent accommodation (bungalows or apartments) on a weekly basis. The accent i
usually on sports and leisure facilities and the villages have the same classificatio
criteria as the camp sites (see above). The Netherlands Reservation Centre can hel
you with the choice of park and then make the reservation.

Tourist information

Netherlands Board of Tourism (NBT)

London: NBT, PO Box 523, London SW1E 6NT, ☎ (0891) 717 777 (premium rat
recorded message). Web site address is www.visitholland.com/

USA: NBT, 225 North Michigan Avenue, Suite 326, Chicago, IL 60601
☎ 1-800-953-8824 (free phone number).

Canada: NBT, 25 Adelaide Street East, Suite 710, Toronto, Ont M5C 1Y2
☎ (416) 363 1577.

Australia: NBT, 5 Elizabeth Street, 6th floor, Sydney, NSW 2000, ☎ 2 247 6921

VVV (Vereniging voor Vreemdelingenverkeer) – In the Netherlands the **Tourist Informatic
Centres** are indicated by ⓥ or VVV, three blue V's on a white triangle. These office
supply information on a wide range of subjects: hotels, restaurants, camp sites
rented accommodation, youth hostels, local events, cycling, sailing, sightseeing
opening hours and entertainment. They also sell tourist, cycling and walking map
and provide exchange facilities as well as a nationwide hotel reservation service. Th
addresses and phone numbers of the VVV offices in the main towns are given in th
listing of times and charges at the end of this guide (many are also listed in th
Michelin Red Guide Benelux) and they are located on all town plans by the symbol ⓔ
Most VVV's are open Mondays to Fridays 9am to 5pm and Saturdays 10am to noo
In summer the offices in major towns are usually open for a few hours on Sunday

ANWB – The **ANWB** (Koninklijke Nederlandse Toeristenbond) Royal Dutch Tourin
Club has offices throughout the country. ANWB, Wassenaarseweg 220, 2596 EC De
Haag, ☎ (070) 314 14 20, or www.anwb.nl.

GWK offices – These offer banking (exchange facilities, cash cheques or credit card
and tourist services and are to be found at airports, railway stations, border crossin
points, on motorways and in tourist resorts.

Museum Card – The holder of this card is entitled to free entry or reduced rates to 400 museums. Extra charges are made for special exhibitions. The card can be bought at most affiliated museums, VVV offices and all Netherlands Boards of Tourism.

Under 26 – This European cultural pass gives reduced rates for museums, theatres, concerts... For further information apply to Under 26, 52 Grosvenor Gardens, London, ☎ (0171) 823 53 63.

Tourism for the disabled – The Netherlands provides good facilities for the handicapped and all hotels, motels, guest houses, youth hostels, holiday bungalows and cottages, and camp sites accessible to the handicapped carry the international symbol ♿. Information is available from Stichting Informatievoorziening Gehandicapten Nederland, ☎ (030) 231 64 16 and the information department for the disabled of the ANWB, ☎ (070) 314 64 30. These two organisations publish *Travel Guide for the Disabled* which is aimed at Dutch tourists with a handicap but can be useful for foreign tourists. The **Michelin Red Guide Benelux** indicates rooms and facilities suitable for physically handicapped people.

The Netherlands Railways offer a comprehensive service for the disabled traveller which includes a free escort service. The train timetables are available in braille. *Access to the Channel Ports* is a guide for the disabled which gives information on the following Dutch ports: Hoek van Holland, Rotterdam and Vlissingen. This guide is available from Access Project (PHSP), 39 Bradley Gardens, London W13 8HE.

Entertainment

Theatre, Dance and Music – The title of cultural capital goes to **Amsterdam** with its 32 museums, 60 art galleries, 32 theatres and 12 concert halls. The 1986 Muziektheater, part of the modern Stopera development in its attractive riverside setting, provides state-of-the-art facilities for the **Nederlandse Opera** and the **Nationale Ballet**. The vitality of the ballet company owes much to its founder, the Russian choreographer Sonia Gaskall, and the choreographer Hans van Manen and its repertoire consists of traditional, classical and romantic ballets. In summer musicians from the two orchestras give free lunchtime concerts. Since its resplendent refurbishment the 100-year old Concertgebouw is the perfect setting for the performances of the famous **Koninklijk Concertgebouworkest** under the baton of Riccardo Chailly. Berlage's famous Beurs building has been refurbished to serve as a cultural centre and provides a home to the **Netherlands Philharmonic and Chamber Orchestras**. In summer, the open-air theatre in Vondelpark is the venue for free concerts.

The Hague is home to the more contemporary culture of the **Nederlands Dans theater** acclaimed for its adventurous performances in modern dance under the Czech-born artistic director, Jiri Kylian. The Anton Philipszaal is home to the city's **Residentie Orkest**.

The refurbished Circustheater (1904) in Scheveningen now serves as a venue for musical extravaganzas while the redecorated Schouwburg Theatre concentrates on drama. The North Sea Jazz Festival is a well known international event and welcomes as many as 1 000 musicians.

Rotterdam boasts the **Scapino Ballet** with its narrative ballet repertoire while the **Rotterdam Philharmonic** plays at the Doelen.

Tickets for major events (concerts, theatre, sports etc) can be obtained through most VVV offices. There is also a ticket hotline: ☎ (0900) 300 12 50.

Casinos – The eight official gambling palaces (Holland Casinos) offer an afternoon or evening of gambling where you can try your hand at Blackjack, Punto Banco, American or French Roulette or the jackpot machines in pleasant surroundings. There are casinos at Breda, Groningen, Nijmegen, Rotterdam, Scheveningen, Valkenburg and Zandvoort. They are open from 1.30pm to 2am and guests have to be at least 18 years of age and have valid identity with them and be appropriately dressed.

Cinemas – Most films are shown in the original version with Dutch subtitles. In larger towns there are usually two performances (6.45pm and 9.30pm).

The chapter on art and architecture in this guide gives an outline of artistic creation in the region, providing the context of the buildings and works of art described in the Sights section.

This chapter may also provide ideas for touring.

It is advisable to read it at leisure/before setting out.

Discovering the Netherlands

Which is the best time of year to visit?

The Netherlands is a land for all seasons and although the country is uniformly flat it is never dull, as there is a constantly changing play of light between sea and sky.

Spring – Without doubt the outstanding attractions are the bulb fields, a kaleidoscope of dazzling colours in season *(from mid April to end of May)*. The main bulb-growing areas are between Haarlem and Leiden and in the vicinity of Alkmaar. In spring the foliage of the countryside is a fresh green and the canalside trees add a splash of colour to townscapes.
The Betuwe region is a delight when the cherry orchards are in blossom *(from mid April to end of May)* and the bright yellow of the fields of oil seed rape makes a vivid picture in the provinces of Friesland, Groningen, Overijssel and Flevoland *(from mid May to early June)*.

Summer – The great stretches of sandy beach along the North Sea coast are popular with holidaymakers and locals alike. Here as in other popular resorts and holiday areas (Drenthe and Southern Limburg) it is always wise to book in advance as accommodation is scarce during the summer season. The many lakes, reservoirs, canals and waterways make this ideal sailing country and good for water sports. Throughout spring and summer flowers are everywhere: towns and villages are bright with well-tended public gardens and parks and cheerful flower boxes and window displays enhance even the plainest façades.

Autumn – By late August and early September the dunes and heathlands are bright with the purple of heather in bloom. The forests like those of the Veluwe start to sport their autumnal hues.

Winter – The winter landscapes have a charm of their own, as captured by past generations of Dutch artists, and even the towns take on an uncanny stillness as they lie muffled under their first mantle of snow. In the Netherlands, frozen lakes and canals are an irresistible invitation to skate and children are not the only ones to take it up.

Cycling

The Netherlands is traditionally the land of the bicycle and there is no better way of discovering the country at your leisure. There are approximately 16 million bicycles in the country, outnumbering the population. Bicycles are omnipresent and create their own rush hour.

Cycle lanes and cycle paths – The Netherlands has many special lanes and paths for cyclists (about 15 000km/9 320mi). Follow the special lanes – marked by a white bicycle on a blue sign – to be found in both towns and the countryside and you won't be bothered by other traffic. Normally cyclists are not allowed on footpaths.

Special signs – The paths are well signposted and is it important for cyclists to be able to recognise the main ones.
– blue circular sign with a white bicycle: bicycles *(fietsen)* and mopeds *(bromfietsen)* must use this lane which usually runs parallel to the road.
– rectangular black sign with the mention **Fietspad**: an optional cycle lane for cyclists but mopeds are prohibited.
– sign with **Fietsers oversteken**: give way crossing point for bicycles and mopeds. Care is required as motorists may be surprised to suddenly see cyclists emerging onto a road which had no cycle lane.

Cycling rules – Keep to the right and overtake other bicycles on the left. Never overtake cars on the left even when turning left. Only proceed two abreast if this does not hinder others. Bicylces and mopeds are not allowed on motorways. All bicycles must have lights that work. Children under 10 must use a special safety seat. Use clear hand signals to indicate a change of direction.

Hiring a bicycle – It is possible to hire a bicycle almost anywhere in the Netherlands. Over 100 railway stations have bicycles for hire, look for the blue and white square sign (NS-Rijwielshop). Rate: 7.50fl per day or 30fl per week. In towns there are numerous bicycle hire firms but cycle dealers and repair shops also have bicycles for hire *(fietsverhuur)*. A deposit and proof of identity are required.
Gears are not necessary in a flat country like the Netherlands so do not be surprised if your bike has none! Many bicycles have the traditional Dutch braking system where you have to back-pedal: you push backwards on the pedals to stop the back wheel. Practice is necessary for foreigners used to doing this to change gear.

Parking – It is advisable to lock your bike, especially in towns, and it is preferable to leave it in a guarded cycle park.

Cycle routes – The ANWB has marked out about 250 tours with an average length of 40km/25mi for bicycles and mopeds. These routes are waymarked by blue rectangular road signs which have a white hexagonal sign with a bicycle or by hexagonal white signs with indications in red. Descriptive leaflets are available for the different routes.

The Stichting Landelijk Fietsplatform has waymarked over 6 000km/3 730mi of national cycle routes **(LF-routes)**. These numbered routes follow cycle paths or quieter local roads. The association also publishes several guides for these routes. The VVV's provide information on local cycle routes. Mountain bike enthusiasts can explore the special network of ATB-routes.

Stichting Landelijk Fietsplatform, PO Box 846, Berkenweg 30, 3800 AV Amersfoort, ☎ (033) 465 36 60, Fax (033) 465 43 77.

A good map is a must. The small mushroom-shaped signposts waymarking the cycle paths are numbered and indicated on the maps.

For cycling events, contact the Nederlandse Toer Fiets Unie (NTFU), Postbus 326, 3900 AH Veenendaal, ☎ (0318) 52 14 21.

Water sports

Sailing – The Netherlands, with its rivers, canals, waterways, broads, lakes, reservoirs and the sea, provides ample opportunities for water sports, and with their tradition of being a seafaring nation the Dutch are enthusiastic sailors. There are over 300 000 boat owners, ie one boat per 47 inhabitants and there are at least 950 marinas or pleasure boat harbours throughout the country. Being so geared to sailing there is no shortage of good facilities (marinas, moorings, repair yards, fuel and water points, shops, restaurants and café's) for the visiting sailor.

Few places are far from a navigable waterway and one of the unexpected charms of sailing in Holland is that it is possible to sail into or through many of the town centres with their networks of canals.

The most popular sailing areas are the IJsselmeer (high seas possible), the lakes bordering the IJsselmeer polders (calmer waters), the lakes of South Holland, the Utrecht lake district (Loosdrechtse and Vinkeveense) and the Frisian lakes.

One of the Frisian lakes

Diot/CEDRI

Further information can be obtained from:

Koninklijk Nederlands Watersport Verbond (Watersports Federation), Runnenburg 2, Postbus 87, 3980 CB Bunnik, ☎ (030) 656 65 50, Fax (030) 656 47 83; ANWB Vakgroep Watersport (Watersports Section), Wassenaarseweg 220, 2596 EC Den Haag, ☎ (070) 314 77 20 (water sports information line).

Customs formalities – On arrival and departure visiting sailors with boats over 5.4m/18ft must report to the nearest customs harbour office which will issue the necessary sailing certificate. Boats capable of travelling at more than 16km/h should be registered at a post office and the licence costs 47.50fl. Insurance cover is compulsory with a legal liability of a minimum of 250 000fl. To use a sea-scooter you must be over 18 and have a Dutch licence to navigate.

Restrictions – There are **speed limits** on certain canals especially urban ones, but also on some of the busier waterways. For other regulations consult the *Almanac for Water Tourism* (I for general shipping rules and regulations and II for tide timetables,

opening times of bridges and locks and facilities offered by the various marinas).
These almanacs have introductions in English and are available from the ANWB an
some specialised bookshops.
Yachts with high fixed masts must look out for bridges with a limited headroom an
remember that some bridges only open at certain hours. At movable bridges ther
is often a fee to pay, usually well indicated, and the bridgeward will lower a clo
(klomp) for you to put the fee into.

Hiring a sailing or motor boat – In the high season it is best to book in advance
For lists of companies chartering boats apply to the Netherlands Tourist Board
ANWB, VVV offices or Friesland Holland Yachtcharter, Postbus 163, 8470 AI
Wolvega, ☎ (0561) 61 53 64, Fax (0561) 61 78 18.
Both the ANWB and the Netherlands Hydrographic Services (Hydrografische Dienst
Badhuisweg 169-171, 2597 JN Den Haag, ☎ (070) 316 28 01) publish **hydrographi
charts** which can be purchased from ANWB offices, water sports shops or goo
bookshops.

Canoeing – The calm waterways of the Netherlands provide ideal conditions for thi
sport. The VVV offices can provide more information on request.

Surfing – Again the opportunities are varied. Experienced surfers will enjoy th
rougher waters of the IJsselmeer or the North Sea waves. The inland waters of th
Utrecht lakes and the lakes bordering the polders are also suitable for surfing.

Historic ships – Some companies offer for charter historic canal and sea goin
vessels: flat-bottomed boats *(tjalken)*, fishing smacks *(botters)* and clippers. Skippe
and crew are provided in most cases.

Boat trips – For those who prefer to take it easy there are numerous boat trips t
choose from. For towns with a good canal network this is a relaxing way to sightse
and ideal for admiring all those canal houses. The following towns offer boat trip
on the canals: Alkmaar, Amsterdam, Delft, Groningen, Leiden and Utrecht. Other
such as Enkhuizen, Harderwijk, Kampen and Urk organise trips on the IJssel Lak
while Leiden (Rhine), Maastricht (Meuse to the Belgian border), Nijmegen (Waal)
Rotterdam (Rhine), Venlo (Meuse) and Zierikzee (Eastern Scheldt) propose rive
excursions.

Water-skiing – This sport is subject to quite strict regulations and it can only b
practised in authorised areas. In some cases it is necessary to obtain authorisatio
from the local authorities.

Fishing – Two documents are necessary: a fishing licence *(sportvisakte)* and a permi
(vergunning). The first is on sale in post offices while the second can be obtained from
the local Angling Associations (Hengelsportverenigingen) – addresses of these ar
available from the Nederlandse Vereniging van Sportvissersfederaties, Postbus 288
3800 AG Amersfoort, ☎ (033) 463 49 24, Fax (033) 461 19 28.

Rambling

The Staatsbosbeheer *(SBB symbol right)* and the
ANWB edit a series of eight rambling maps (Welkom
bij de boswachter) indicating footpaths and their
characteristics. These can be obtained from the
ANWB.

Rambling is popular in the Netherlands and there are
numerous annual meetings. The Four Day Walk takes
place in Apeldoorn and Nijmegen and the Tour of the
Eleven Towns of Friesland leaves from Leeuwarden.
Most of the forests and woods are State owned and
are administered by the Staatsbosbeheer. The
recreational facilities provided usually include, cycle paths, picnic areas an
footpaths. Many trails are waymarked and differentiated by colour. Signs give th
time required for each tour.
The Netherlands offers a network of about 30 long-distance footpaths (lange
afstand-wandelpaden or LAW) of 100km/60mi or longer, waymarked in white an
red. Details are available from the Stichting Lange-Afstand-Wandelpaden, Postbu
846, 3800 AV Amersfoort, ☎ (033) 465 36 60, Fax (033) 465 43 77, or Nivon
Nieuwe Herengracht 119, 1011 SB Amsterdam, ☎ (020) 626 96 61.

Other activities

Steam trains – Tourist trains are operated between Apeldoorn and Dieren, Hoor
and Medemblik as well as Goes and Oudeland.

Skating – When snow lies thick on the ground and frost has set in, the man
waterways and lakes are ideal for skating.

Bird watching – The wetlands (Biesbosch National Park, the Frisian lakes), th
Wadden Islands, the many low-tide mudflats and the polderlands provide a variet
of ecological habitats rich in birdlife, ideal for the amateur birdwatcher. For thos
interested in birdwatching the address to contact locally is Vogelbeschermin
Nederland, Driebergseweg 16c, 3708 JB Zeist, ☎ (030) 693 77 00.

Golf – The Michelin maps 210, 211 and 408 locate the country's golf courses, many of which welcome visitors. The Dutch Golf Federation's headquarters are at: Nederlandse Golf Federatie, Rijnzathe 8, 3454 PV De Meern, ☎ (030) 662 18 88.

Theme parks – Over recent years theme and leisure parks have attracted a surge of interest throughout Europe. The Netherlands has its fair share of amusement parks. Not all of the parks listed below are described in the guide:

Park	Theme	Where to find the fun
Apenheul	Monkeys	Apeldoorn
Aqualutra	Otters	Leeuwarden
Archeon	Archeological theme park	Alphen aan den Rijn
Artis	Zoo	Amsterdam
Autotron	Cars	Rosmalen
Avifauna	Birds	Alphen aan den Rijn
Beekse Bergen	Safari park	Hilvarenbeek
Blijdorp	Zoo	Rotterdam
Burgers' Zoo, Bush, Desert en Safari	Zoo and safari park	Arnhem
Dolfinarium	Sealife park	Harderwijk
Duinrell	Indoor aquadrome	Wassenaar
De Efteling	Amusement park	Kaatsheuvel
Hellendoorn	Adventure park	Hellendoorn
Land van Ooit	Amusement park	Drunen
Madurodam	Netherlands in miniature	Den Haag
Sealife	Sealife park	Scheveningen
Walibi Flevo	Amusement park	Biddinghuizen

Further reading

General background

Of Dutch Ways H Colijn *(Harper & Row)*

Holland A Hopkins *(Faber & Faber)*

The British and the Dutch KHD Haley *(George Philip)*

Art and architecture

The Embarrassment of Riches: An Interpretation of Dutch Culture in the Golden Age Simon Schama *(Fontana Press)*

Mondrian John Milner *(Phaidon Press)*

Vincent van Gogh: Paintings, Drawings (two volumes) Louis van Tiborg and Evert van Uitert *(Thames and Hudson)*

Vincent: A Complete Portrait Bernard Denvir *(Pavilion Books)*

Rembrandt: The Master and his Workshop Paintings, Drawings and Etchings (two volumes) *(Yale University Press)*

Rembrandt Ludwig Mune and Bob Haak *(Thames and Hudson)*

Rembrandt Annemarie Vels Heijn *(Sotheby's Publications)*

Rembrandt M Kitson *(Phaidon)*

The Paintings of the Willem van de Veldes MS Robinson

Jacob van Ruisdael: The Perception of Landscape EJ Walford *(Yale University Press)*

From Van Eyck to Bruegel Max J Frielander

Dutch and Flemish Painting: Art in the Netherlands in the 17C C Brown *(Phaidon)*

Dutch Painting RH Fuchs *(Thames and Hudson)*

Dawn of the Golden Age, North Netherlandish Art, 1580-1620 Kloek et al *(Yale University Press)*

Dutch Art and Architecture: 1600-1800 J Rosenberg, S Slive and EH ter Kuile *(Pelican History of Art)*

Dutch Houses and Castles J Guillermo *(Tauris Parke Books)*

Dutch Arts *(Ministry of Cultural Affairs)*

Guide to Dutch Art *(Ministry of Education, Arts and Sciences)*

The Gardens of William and Mary D Jacques and AJ van der Horst *(Christopher Helm)*

History

The Dutch Seaborne Empire 1600-1800 CR Boxer

The Dutch Revolt Geoffrey Parker *(Penguin)*

The Revolt of the Netherlands 1555-1609 Pieter Geyl *(Cassell)*

The Netherlands in the 17th Century 1609-1648 Pieter Geyl *(Cassell)*

Arnhem 1944: The Airborne Battle Martin Middlebrook *(Viking)*

The Diary of a Young Girl Anne Frank *(Pan)*

Fiction

The Glass Bridge (fiction) Marga Minco

The Black Tulip (fiction) Alexandre Dumas, edited by David Covard *(Oxford University Press)*

A Bridge Too Far (fiction) Cornelius Ryan

The Sorrow of Belgium (fiction) Hugo Claus

Max Havelaar (fiction) Multatuli *(Penguin)*

The Assault (fiction) H Mulisch *(Penguin)*

Mystic Body (fiction) F Kellendonk

In a Dark Wood Wandering: A Novel of the Middle Ages (fiction) Hella S Haasse

Miscellaneous

Through the Dutch and Belgian Canals P Bristow *(A & C Black)*

The Dutch Table Gillian Riley

Phrase book

Common words

NB for restaurant terminology, consult the current Michelin Red Guide Benelux.

U	you	goedemorgen	good morning
mijnheer	Mr	goedemiddag	good afternoon
mevrouw	Mrs, Ms	goedenavond	good evening
juffrouw	Miss	tot ziens	goodbye
rechts	right	alstublieft	please
links	left	dank u (wel)	thank you (very much)
ja	yes	nee	no
postkantoor	post office	postzegel	postage stamp
hoeveel/wat kost dit?	how much?	wat? waar?	what? where?
inclusief bediening	service included	en BTW	and VAT
apotheek	pharmacy	ziekenhuis	hospital

Numbers

een	one	zes	six
twee	two	zeven	seven
drie	three	acht	eight
vier	four	negen	nine
vijf	five	tien	ten

Towns and provinces

's-Gravenhage, Den Haag	The Hague	Leiden	Leyden
Noord-Brabant	North Brabant	Vlissingen	Flushing
Noord-Holland	North Holland	Zuid-Holland	South Holland

Road vocabulary

autosnelweg	motorway	parkeerschijf	parking disk
		verplicht	obligatory
doorgaand verkeer	through traffic	richting	direction
eenrichtings-verkeer	one-way street	uitrit	exit
inhaalverbod	no overtaking	verboden	prohibited
knooppunt	junction	verboden toegang	no entry
let op! gevaar!	caution! danger!	voorrang geven	give way
niet parkeren	no parking	werk in uitvoering	roadworks
omleiding	diversion	zachte berm	soft verge
overstekende wielrijders	cycle path crossing		

Tourist vocabulary

abdij	abbey	Onze Lieve Vrouwe	Our Lady
begraafplaats	cemetery	oost	east
berg	mountain, hill	opengesteld	open, accessible
Beurs	stock exchange	orgel	organ
bezienswaardigheid	sight	oud	old
bezoek	visit	oudheidkamer	antiquities (museum)
boerderij	farm	paleis	palace
boot	boat	plas	lake
brug	bridge	plein	square
dam	dam	poort	gate (to town)
dierenpark	zoo	raadhuis	town hall
dijk	dike	rederij	shipping company
duin	dune	Rijks	of the State
eiland	island	rondvaart	boat trip
gasthuis	hospice, old hospital	scheepvaart	navigation
gemeentehuis	town hall	schilderij	painting, picture
gracht	canal (in town)	schouwburg	theatre
groot, grote	great	singel	ring canal
grot	grotto, cave	slot	castle, fortress
gulden	florin	sluis	lock
haven	harbour, port	stad	town
heilige	saint	stadhuis	town hall
heuvel	hill	state	castle (in Friesland)
hof	court, palace	stedelijk	municipal
hotje	almshouse	straat	street
ingang	entrance	tegel	earthenware tile
jachthaven	pleasure boat harbour	tentoonstelling	exhibition
kaai, kade	quay	toegang	entrance
kasteel	castle	tuin	garden
kerk	church	uitgang	exit
kerkhof	churchyard	veer	ferry boat
kerkschat	treasury	vest	rampart
klooster	convent	vogel	bird
koninklijk	royal	vuurtoren	lighthouse
markt	market, main square	waag	weigh house
meer	lake	wal	rampart
molen	(wind) mill	wandeling	walking tour
museum	museum	weg	path, road
natuurreservaat	nature reserve	west	west
noord	north	zee	sea
		zuid	south

Michelin travel publications :
    more than 220 maps, atlases and town plans ;
    12 Red Guides to hotels and restaurants in European countries ;
    more than 160 Green Guides in 8 languages to destinations around the world.

347

Calendar of events

Listed below are the most important of the many festivals held in the Netherlands; others are mentioned in the descriptions of towns and cities in the alphabetical section of the guide.
A detailed calendar of festivals appears in leaflets produced annually by the VVV (Tourist Information Centre).

January-February

Rotterdam .... International Film Festival

In February or March during Lent

Breda .... Carnival★

Bergen op Zoom .... Carnival

Eindhoven .... Carnival

Venlo .... Carnival

's-Hertogenbosch .... Carnival

Maastricht .... Carnival★

Sittard .... Carnival

March (one week)

Maastricht .... The European Fine Art Fair★★ ☎ (073) 614 51 65

Late March to mid or late May

Keukenhof .... National Floral Exhibition★★★

1 April (Saturday before if the 1st is a Sunday)

Brielle .... Historical Festival

Last Saturday in April

Haarlem-Noordwijk .... Procession of floral floats

A floral float in the procession

Mid April to mid September, Fridays 10am-noon

Alkmaar .... Cheese Market★★

May to late September, Sundays

Tegelen .... Passion Plays (2000; every five years)

Late May

Breda .... Jazz Festival

1st Saturday in September	
Aalsmeer-Amsterdam	Procession of floral floats *(from about 9am-4pm)*
1st Sunday in September	
Zundert	Procession of floral floats
Early September	
Rotterdam	*Wereldhavendagen*
2nd Saturday in September	
Tiel	Harvest Fruit Parade *(2pm)*
3rd Tuesday in September	
The Hague	State Opening of Parliament: the Queen arrives in a golden coach
4th Wednesday in September	
Odoorn	Sheep market
Late September	
Utrecht	Netherlands Film Festival *(Golden Calf award)*
3 October (following Monday if the 3rd is a Sunday)	
Leiden	Leidens Ontzet: historical procession
1st Wednesday in October	
Leeuwarden	Show of prize Frisian bulls
3rd Saturday before 5 December	
Amsterdam	St Nicholas' official arrival *(Prins Hendrikkade)*
From 1st Sunday of Advent to 1 January	
Denekamp	Blowing of midwinter horns

Celebrations for the Queen's birthday

Nationwide events

National Museum Weekend . 3rd weekend in April

**Queen's Birthday
Celebrations** .... 30 April

National Mill and Cycle Day . 2nd Sunday in May

Open Monument Day .... 2nd weekend in September

Sports Competitions

Automobile and motorcycle races – The Dutch Grand Prix takes place in Assen on the last weekend in June.
Cross-country motorcycling is very popular and races on ice are held in ice skating rinks.

Cycling events – The Regional Cycle Day is held every year on the second Saturday in May. The tour of 11 Friesland towns (depart from Bolsward) is held on Whit Monday; Drenthe's 4-Day Cycling Event (Fietsvierdaagse) is held in mid July and Nijmegen's 4-Day Event in early August.

Water sports competition – Across the country different water sports activities are held throughout the summer. The most spectacular are the **skûtsiesilen**, *skûtsjes* regattas on the Frisian lakes. Among the other activities are Delta Week (Zierikzee) in early July and Sneekweek in early August.

Skûtsjes regattas

Walking – A 4-Day Walking Event takes place in Apeldoorn (mid July) and in Nijmegen (3rd or 4th week in July). The Frisian 11-Town Walking Event lasts five days (depart from Leeuwarden) between mid May and early June.

Traditional sports – Archers Processions *(boogschieten)* are held from mid May to late August in the Limburg.
Those who like ball games can watch **kaatswedstrijden** held in Frisian villages (early May to mid September; important meets in August).
The annual pole vaulting competition *(polsstokspringen)* is held in Winsum *(10km/6mi southwest of Leeuwarden)* in August.
The **Amstel Gold Race**, an international cycle race leaving from and returning to Maastricht, is held in March and April. The **Rotterdam Marathon** follows a course through the city centre in March and April.

Admission times and charges

As admission times and charges are liable to alteration, the information below is for guidance only.

⊙: Every sight for which times and charges are listed below is indicated by the symbol ⊙ after the title in the Sights section of the guide.

Order: The information is listed in the same order as in the Sights section of the guide.

Dates: Dates given are inclusive.

Last admission: Ticket offices usually shut 30min before closing time. Some places issue timed tickets owing to limited space and facilities.

Charge: The charge given is for an individual adult. Concessionary rates may be available for families, children, old-age pensioners and the unemployed. Prices are given in guilders (abbreviated to fl). Many places offer special rates for group bookings and some have special days for group visits. Large parties should apply in advance.

Churches: Churches cannot be visited during services and are usually closed between noon and 2pm. They are included in the following list if the interior is of particular interest.

Tourist offices (VVV): The addresses and telephone numbers of the local tourist offices, indicated by the symbol 🖪, are given below. The tourist offices provide information on local market days, early or late closing days as well as local events. Guided tours are organised on a regular basis during the tourist season in Amsterdam, Breda, Groningen, The Hague, Leeuwarden, Leiden, Maastricht, Rotterdam, Utrecht and elsewhere. Apply to the Tourist office.

Guided tours: Most tours are conducted by Dutch-speaking guides but in some cases the term "guided tours" may cover groups visiting with recorded commentaries. Some of the larger and more popular sights may offer guided tours in other languages. Enquire at the ticket desk or bookstall.

A

AALSMEER 🖪 Drie Kolommenplein 1 – 1431 LA – ☎ (0297) 32 53 74 fax (0297) 35 42 55

Flower auction (Bloemenveiling) – Open Mondays to Fridays from 7.30am to 11am. Closed weekends and public holidays. f7.50. ☎ (0297) 392185.

ALKMAAR 🖪 Waagplein 2-3 – 1811 JP – ☎ (072) 511 42 84 – fax (072) 511 75 13

Boat trips – ᷏ Early April to late October. Information from Rederij Woltheus, Kanaalkade, opposite no 60, ☎ (072) 5114840.

Cheese market (Kaasmarkt) – Mid-April to mid-September, Fridays from 10am to noon. ☎ (072) 5114284.

Hollands Kaasmuseum – Open April to October, daily from 10am to 4pm (Fridays from 9am). Closed Sundays and public holidays, and from November to March. f2. ☎ (072) 5114284.

Nederlands Biermuseum De Boom – ᷏ Open October to March, Tuesdays to Fridays from 10am to 4pm, weekends 1pm to 4pm. Closed Mondays, Easter Day, Whit Sunday, 25 and 26 December. f4. ☎ (072) 5113801.

Stadhuis – Guided tour only (20min), by appointment: Mondays to Fridays from 10am to 12noon and 2pm to 4pm. Closed weekends and public holidays. ☎ (072) 5114284.

Grote Kerk or St.-Laurenskerk – Open June to mid-September, daily (except Mondays) from 10am to 5pm. Closed Mondays. ☎ (072) 5140707 (tourist office).

Stedelijk Museum – Open Tuesdays to Fridays from 10am to 5pm, weekends and public holidays 1pm to 5pm. Closed Mondays, 1 January, 30 April and 25 December. f3. ☎ (072) 5110737.

Excursions

Museum Kranenburgh – Open Tuesdays to Sundays from 1pm to 5pm. Closed Mondays, 1 January and 25 December. f6. ☎ (072) 5898927.

Noord-Hollands Duinreservaat – Open daily from sunrise to sunset. f2. ☎ (0251) 662266.

Zee Aquarium Bergen aan Zee – ᷏ Open April to October, daily from 10am to 6pm; November to March, daily from 11am to 5pm. f9. ☎ (072) 5812928.

Broeker Veiling – ᷏ Open April to October, Mondays to Fridays from 10am to 5pm, weekends noon to 5pm. Closed November to March. f9.25. ☎ (0226) 313807.

🚻 Stationsplein 9 – 3818 LE – ☎ (0900) 112 23 64 fax (033) 465 01 08

O.L.-Vrouwe Toren – Open July and August, Tuesdays to Fridays from 10am to 5pm and Saturdays noon to 5pm. Closed September to June. f5. ☎ (0900) 1122364 (tourist office).

St.-Joriskerk – Open mid-June to mid-September, daily (except Sundays) from 2pm to 4.30pm. Closed Sundays and public holidays. f1. ☎ (033) 4610441.

Koppelpoort – ♿ Open July and August, Tuesdays to Fridays from 10am to 5pm, weekends and public holidays noon to 5pm. f2.50. Information from the tourist office, ☎ (0900) 1122364.

Puppet theatre – Performances on Wednesdays and Saturdays at 2.30pm. f8. ☎ (033) 4700153.

Museum Flehite – Open Tuesdays to Fridays from 10am to 5pm, weekends 1pm to 5pm. Closed Mondays and public holidays. f6. ☎ (033) 4619987.

Mannenzaal – Same opening times as Museum Flehite. ☎ (033) 4619987.

Culinair Museum – Open Tuesdays to Fridays from 10am to 5pm, weekends 2pm to 5pm. Closed Mondays and public holidays. f5. ☎ (033) 4631025.

Mondriaanhuis – Open Tuesdays to Fridays from 10am to 5pm, weekends 2pm to 5pm. Closed Mondays and public holidays. f5. ☎ (033) 4620180.

Excursions

Museum Dorestad – Open daily (except Mondays) from 1.30pm to 5pm. Closed Mondays, 1 January and 25 December. f3. ☎ (0343) 571448.

Amerongs Historisch Museum – April: open Tuesdays to Saturdays from 1.30pm to 5pm, Sundays 1pm to 5pm. May to October: Tuesdays to Fridays from 10am to 5pm, weekends and public holidays 1pm to 5pm. Closed November to March. f2.50. ☎ (0343) 456500.

Kasteel Amerongen – Open April to October, Tuesdays to Fridays from 10am to 5pm; weekends and public holidays from 1pm to 5pm. Closed Mondays and from November to March. f7. ☎ (0343) 454212.

Leersumse Plassen – Open mid-July to mid-March, from sunrise to sunset. Closed mid-March to mid-July. ☎ (0343) 431360.

🚻 Stationsplein 10-15 – 1012 AB – ☎ (0900) 400 40 40 fax (020) 625 28 69
🚻 Leidseplein 1 – 1017 PR – www.noord-holland-tourist.nl

Cycle hire – Amstel Rijwielshop, Julianaplein 1, ☎ (020) 6923584; Bike City, Bloemgracht 70, ☎ (020) 6263721; Damstraat Rent-a-Bike, P.Jacobszdwarsstraat 1, ☎ (020) 6255029; Holland Rent-a-Bike, Damrak 247, ☎ (020) 6223207; Koenders Take-a-Bike, Stationsplein 12, ☎ (020) 6248391; Macbike, 's-Graven-andestraat 49, ☎ (020) 6932104 and Mr.Visserplein2, ☎ (020) 6200985; Macbike Too, Marnixstraat 220, ☎ (020) 6266964; Moped Rental Service Amster-dam, Marnixstraat 208, ☎ (020) 4220266; Zijwind, Van Ostadestraat 108-110, ☎ (020) 6737026.

Canal bikes – Near Anne Frank Huis, the Rijksmuseum, Leidseplein and Keizersgracht/Leidsestraat: information from Canalbike, ☎ (020) 6265574. Mau-itskade and Prinsengracht/Leidsestraat: information from Aan de Wind, ☎ (020) 6929124.

Museum boat – Leaves from Centraal Station. Five stops near the main museums. Daily from 10am to 6.30pm. ☎ (020) 6256464.

Beurs van Berlage Museum – Open daily (except Mondays) from 10am to 4pm. Closed Mondays, 1 January. f6. ☎ (020) 5304113.

Koninklijk Paleis – Open daily from 12.30pm to 5pm. Closed 30 April, May, December to mid-February and during official events. f7. ☎ (020) 6204060.

Nieuwe Kerk – Open daily from 11am to 5pm. ☎ (020) 6386909.

Madame Tussaud Scenerama – Open daily from 10am to 5.30pm; July and August 9.30am to 7.30pm. Closed 30 April. f19.50. ☎ (020) 6229949.

Amsterdams Historisch Museum – Open Mondays to Fridays from 10am to 5pm, weekends 11am to 5pm. Closed 1 January, 30 April and 25 December. f11. ☎ (020) 5231822.

Museum Amstelkring Ons' Lieve Heer op Solder – Open Mondays to Saturdays from 10am to 5pm, Sundays and public holidays 1pm to 5pm. Closed 30 April. f7.50. ☎ (020) 6246604.

Oude Kerk – Open daily from 11am to 5pm (Sundays from 1pm). ☎ (020) 6258284.

Allard Pierson Museum – ♿ Open Tuesdays to Fridays from 10am to 5pm, weekends and public holidays 1pm to 5pm. Closed Mondays, 1 January, Easter Day, 30 April, Whit Sunday, 25 December. f9.50. ☎ (020) 5252556.

Munttoren: carillon concerts – Fridays 12noon to 1pm. ☎ (020) 6263947.

Museum Het Rembrandthuis – Open Mondays to Saturdays from 10am to 5pm, Sundays and public holidays 1pm to 5pm. Closed 1 January. f7.50. ☎ (020) 5200400.

Zuiderkerk – ☐ Open Mondays to Fridays from 12noon to 5pm (Thursdays to 8pm). Closed weekends and public holidays. ☎ (020) 6222962.

Joods Historisch Museum – ☐ Open daily from 11am to 5pm. Closed Yom Kippur. f8. ☎ (020) 6269945.

Portugese Synagoge – Open Mondays to Fridays from 10am to 12.30pm and 1pm to 4pm, Sundays from 10am to 12.30pm. Closed Saturdays and Jewish festivals. f5. ☎ (020) 6245351.

Self-portrait (1630) by Rembrandt, Museum Het Rembrandthuis

Boat tours – Information from the various operators: Noord Zuid, Stadhouderskade 25, ☎ (020) 6791370; Lovers BV, Prins Hendrikkade, ☎ (020) 6222181; Holland International, Prins Hendrikkade 33a, ☎ (020) 6227788; Plas C.V., Damrak Steiger 1-3, ☎ (020) 6226096; Kooij, Rokin 125, ☎ (020) 6233810; Meyers Rondvaarten, Damrak Steiger 4-5, ☎ (020) 6234208; Hof van Holland, Amstel 30, ☎ (020) 6237122; Boekel, Nassaukade 380, ☎ (020) 6233810; Canal Bus BV, Weteringschans 24, ☎ (020) 6239886.

Nieuwe Kerk or Ronde Lutherse Kerk: concerts – Sundays from 11am to noon. ☎ (020) 6212223.

Number 168: Theatermuseum – Open Tuesdays to Fridays from 11am to 5pm, weekends 1pm to 5pm. Closed Mondays, 1 January, 30 April, 25 December. f7.50. ☎ (020) 5513300.

Bible Museum – Open Mondays to Saturdays from 10am to 5pm, Sundays and public holidays 1pm to 5pm. Closed 1 January and 30 April. f5. ☎ (020) 6242436.

No 497: Kattenkabinet – Open Mondays to Fridays from 10am to 2pm, weekends and public holidays 1pm to 5pm. Opening times may vary in winter. Closed 1 January, 25 and 26 December. f10. ☎ (020) 6265378.

No 605: Museum Willet-Holthuysen – Open Mondays to Fridays from 10am to 5pm, weekends and public holidays 11am to 5pm. Closed 1 January, 30 April, 25 December. f7.50. ☎ (020) 5231822.

No 672: Museum Van Loon – Open Mondays, Fridays, Saturdays and Sundays from 11am to 5pm. Closed Tuesdays to Thursdays. f7.50. ☎ (020) 6245255.

Westerkerk – Open daily (except Sundays) from 10am to 4pm. Closed Sundays. ☎ (020) 6245378.

Anne Frank Huis – Open daily from 9am to 5pm (to 9pm from early April to late August); 1 January and 25 December noon to 5pm. Closed Yom Kippur. f10. ☎ (020) 5567100.

Rijksmuseum – ☐ Open daily from 10am to 5pm. Closed 1 January. f15. ☎ (020) 6747047.

Van Gogh Museum – ☐ Closed for renovation until April 1999, then open daily from 10am to 6pm. Closed 1 January. f15. ☎ (020) 5705200.

Stedelijk Museum – ☐ Open daily from 11am to 5pm (March to September from 10am to 4pm). Closed 1 January. f9. ☎ (020) 5732737.

Filmmuseum – Performances: daily at 7pm, 7.30pm, 9.30pm and 10pm. Children's performance on Sundays at 3pm. Closed 1 January, 30 April and 25 December. f12.50. ☎ (020) 5891400.

Hortus Botanicus – April to October: open Mondays to Fridays from 9am to 5pm, weekends and public holidays 11am to 5pm. November to March: Mondays to Fridays from 9am to 4pm, weekends and public holidays 11am to 4pm. Closed 1 January and 25 December. f7.50. ☎ (020) 6259021.

Nationaal Vakbondsmuseum – ☐ Open Tuesdays to Fridays from 11am to 5pm, Sundays 1pm to 5pm. Closed Mondays, Saturdays and public holidays. f5. ☎ (020) 6241166.

Dierentuin Artis – ☐ Open daily from 9am to 5pm. f23. ☎ (020) 5233400.

Tropenmuseum – &. Open Mondays to Fridays from 10am to 5pm, weekends and public holidays noon to 5pm. Closed 1 January, 30 April, 5 May and 25 December. f12.50. ☏ (020) 5688215.

Nederlands Scheepvaart Museum – Open Tuesdays to Sundays from 10am to 5pm; mid-June to mid-September also Mondays from 10am to 5pm. Closed Mondays from mid-September to mid-June, and on 1 January, 30 April and 25 December. f14.50. ☏ (020) 5232222.

New Metropolis – &. Open daily from 10am to 6pm (9pm on Saturdays). f23.50. ☏ (0900) 9191100.

Heineken Brewery – Tours (in English only, over 18s only) Mondays to Fridays at 9.30am and 11am; June to September also at 2.30pm; July and August also on Saturdays at 11am and 2.30pm. Closed Saturdays (except in July and August), Sundays and public holidays (except 31 December). f2. ☏ (020) 5239666.

Excursions

Molen van Sloten – &. Open daily from 10am to 4pm. Closed 1 January, 25 and 26 December. f5. ☏(020) 6690412.

Cobra Museum voor Moderne Kunst &. Open daily (except Mondays) from 11am to 5pm. Closed Mondays, and on 1 January, 30 April and 25 December. f7.50. ☏ (020) 5475050.

Aviodome – April to September: open daily from 10am to 5pm. October to March: open Tuesdays to Fridays from 10am to 5pm, weekends noon to 5pm. Closed Mondays from October to March, and on 1 January, 25 and 31 December. f12.50. ☏(020) 6041521.

APELDOORN 🚉 Stationsstraat 72 – 7311 MH – ☏ (0900) 168 16 36 fax (055) 521 12 90

Veluwsche Stoomtrein – &. Departs mid-July to late August and during autumn half-term, Mondays to Fridays. f13 (single), f19 (return). ☏ (055) 5061989.

Historisch Museum Apeldoorn – &. Open Tuesdays to Saturdays from 10am to 5pm, Sundays and public holidays 1pm to 5pm. Closed Mondays, 1 January, Easter Day, Whit Sunday and 25 December. f2.50. ☏ (055) 5788429.

Apenheul (Berg en Bos) – Open April to June, daily from 10am to 5pm; July and August, daily from 9.30am to 6pm; September and October, daily from 10am to 5pm. Closed November to March. f18. ☏ (055) 3575757.

ARNHEM 🚉 Stationplein 45, 6811 KL – ☏ (0900) 202 40 75 – fax (026) 442 26 44

Boat tours: Depart mid-April to late October. Information from tourist office, ☏ (026) 4426767.

Nederlands Openluchtmuseum – &. Open April to October, daily from 10am to 5pm. Closed November to March. f17.50. ☏ (026) 3576100.

Additional sights

Grote Kerk or Eusebluskerk – Open Tuesdays to Saturdays from 10am to 5pm, Sundays and public holidays noon to 5pm. Closed Mondays. f10. ☏ (026) 4435068.

Historisch Museum Het Burgerweeshuis – Open Mondays to Fridays from 10am to 5pm, weekends and public holidays 11am to 5pm. f5 (ticket also valid for Museum voor Moderne Kunst on same day). ☏ (026) 4426900.

Museum voor Moderne Kunst – Same opening times as Historisch Museum Het Burgerweeshuis. f5 (ticket also valid for Historisch Museum Het Burgerweeshuis on same day). ☏ (026) 4426900.

Burgers' Zoo, Bush, Desert en Safaripark – Open April to September, daily from 9am to 7pm; October to March, daily from 9am to 5pm. f25. ☏ (026) 4424534.

Excursions

Kasteel Rosendael – Guided tours only: mid-April to October, Tuesdays to Saturdays from 10am to 5pm, Sundays and public holidays 1pm to 5pm. Closed Mondays, 30 April, November to mid-April. f8 (f12 including park). ☏(026) 3644645.

Park – Open May to October, Tuesdays to Saturdays from 10am to 5pm, Sundays and public holidays 11am to 5pm. Closed Mondays, 30 April, November to April. f6 (f12 including castle). ☏(026) 3644645.

Veluwezoom visitor centre – Open daily (except Mondays) from 10am to 5pm. Closed Mondays. ☏ (026) 4951023.

Kasteel Middachten – Open July, Wednesdays to Sundays from 1pm to 4pm; early December, noon to 7pm. f12.50 (castle and gardens). ☏(026) 4954998.

Garden – Open mid-May to mid-September, Wednesdays to Sundays from 10.30ar
to 4.30pm. f12.50 (castle and gardens). ☎(026) 4954998.

Airborne Museum – Open Mondays to Saturdays from 11am to 5pm, Sunday
and public holidays noon to 5pm. Closed 1 January and 25 December. f€
☎ (026) 3337710.

Museum voor Natuur- en Wildbeheer – April to October: open Tuesdays to Friday
from 10am to 5pm, weekends and public holidays 1pm to 5pm. November to March
daily (except Mondays) 1pm to 5pm. Closed Mondays, 1 January, 25 an
31 December. f8. ☎ (026) 3390698.

Ouwehands Dierenpark – ♿ Open April to September, daily from 9am t
6pm; October to March, daily from 9am to 5pm. f22. ☎ (0317) 650200.

Cunerakerk – Open July and August, Tuesdays to Fridays from 2pm to 4pm
☎ (0317) 612333 (tourist office).

ASSEN   🚹 Noorderstaete 20 – 9402 XB – ☎ (0592) 37 37 55 – fax (0592) 31 73 0

Drents Museum – Open daily (except Mondays) from 11am to 5pm. Close
Mondays, 1 January and 25 December. f7.50. ☎ (0592) 312741.

Outskirts

Herinneringscentrum Kamp Westerbork – ♿ Open March to November, Monday
to Fridays from 10am to 5pm, weekends and public holidays 1pm to 5pm (fror
11am in July and August); 4 May from 10am to 7pm. Closed during Christma
period. f5. ☎ (0593) 592600.

Excursion

Nationaal Rijtuigmuseum – Open April to October, Tuesdays to Saturdays fror
10am to 5pm, Sundays and public holidays 1pm to 5pm. Closed Mondays and publi
holidays, and from November to March. f6. ☎ (0594) 512260.

Midwolde church – Open Easter Day to autumn half-term, daily from 11am t
12.30pm and 2pm to 5pm; autumn half-term to Easter Day, open Sundays 11ar
to 5pm. f1.

B

BERGEN OP ZOOM   🚹 Beursplein 7 – 4611 JG, ☎ (0164) 26 60 00 fax (0164) 24 60 3

Stadhuis – Open May to September, Tuesdays to Saturdays from 1pm t
4.30pm. Closed Mondays, Sundays and public holidays, October to March. f2
☎ (0164) 251859.

Markiezenhof – Open April to September, daily (except Mondays) from 11am t
5pm; October to March, daily (except Mondays) from 2pm to 5pm. Closed Mondays
1 January, Easter Day and 25 December. f 5. ☎ (0164) 242930.

Excursion

Wouw church – Guided tours only: Thursdays and Fridays from 10am to noon an
2pm to 4pm. ☎ (0165) 303252 (tourist office).

Streekmuseum De Ghulden Roos – Open daily (except Mondays) from 2pm to 5pm
Closed Mondays, 1 January, carnival, Easter Day, Whit Sunday and 25 Decembe
f2.25. ☎ (0165) 536916.

BOLSWARD   🚹 Marktplein 1 – 8701 KG – ☎ (0515) 57 27 27 – fax (0515) 57 77 1

Stadhuis – April to June and September to October: open Mondays from 2pm t
4pm, Tuesdays to Fridays 9am to noon and 2pm to 4pm. July and August: ope
Mondays to Saturdays from 10am to 5pm. Closed weekends (except Saturday
in July and August), public holidays, November to March. f2. ☎ (0515) 578787

Martinikerk – Open May to October, daily from 10am to noon and 2pm to 4pm. Res
of the year by appointment. ☎ (0515) 572274.

Excursion

Menno-Simonskerkje – Open daily from 10am to 4pm by appointment. ☎ (0517
531959.

BOURTANGE

The fortifications may be visited at any time. The museums, exhibitions and slid
show are open from April to October, Mondays to Fridays from 10am to 5pm
weekends 12.30pm to 5pm. Information from Westerwolde tourist office (Bou
tange fortress dept), ☎ (0599) 354600.

BREDA ☒ Willemstraat 17 – 4811 AJ – ☎ (076) 522 24 44 – fax (076) 521 85 30

Grote Kerk or Onze-Lieve-Vrouwekerk – Mid-April to October: open daily from 10am to 5pm. November to mid-April: open Mondays to Fridays from 10am to 5pm. ☎ (076) 5218267.

Organ concerts – *April to October on Friday evenings. Information from the tourist office,* ☎ *(076) 5222444.*

Additional sights

Het Spanjaardsgat Castle – Guided tours only (2hr). Information from Breda tourist office, ☎ (076) 5222444.

Stadhuis – *Open Tuesdays to Fridays from 9am to 4.30 pm.* ☎ *(076) 5294055.*

De Beyerd – Open Tuesdays to Fridays from 10am to 5pm, weekends and public holidays 1pm to 5pm. Closed Mondays, 1 January and 25 December. f6. ☎ (076) 5225025.

Breda's Museum – Scheduled to open in December 1998. Information: ☎ (076) 5223110.

Outskirts

Kasteel Bouvigne – ♿ The castle itself is not open to the public. The gardens are open on Mondays to Fridays from 9am to 4pm, and closed at weekends and on public holidays. f1. ☎ (076) 5222444.

Excursions

Volkssterrenwacht Simon Stevin – ♿ May, June, September and October: open Tuesdays to Sundays from 10am to 5pm, Thursday, Friday and Saturday evenings 7.30pm to 10pm. July and August: open Tuesdays to Saturdays from 10am to 5pm, Sundays noon to 5pm, Thursday, Friday and Saturday evenings from 7.30pm to 10pm. November to April: open Wednesdays and weekends from noon to 5pm, Friday and Saturday evenings from 7.30pm to 10pm. Closed Mondays, 1 January and 25 December. f12.50. ☎ (0165) 502439.

Nederlands Zouavenmuseum – May to September: open Tuesdays, Thursdays and the 1st and 3rd Sundays of the month, from 2pm to 5pm. October to April: open Tuesdays and the 1st Sunday of the month, from 2pm to 5pm. Closed on public holidays. f2.50. ☎ (0165) 313448.

Prinsenhof or Mauritshuis – May to September: open Mondays to Fridays from 9.30am to 4.30pm, weekends 1pm to 4pm. October to April: open Mondays to Fridays from 9.30am to 4.30pm. f2. ☎ (0168) 476055 (tourist office).

Nationaal Automobielmuseum – ♿ Open Easter Day to October, Tuesdays to Saturdays from 10am to 5pm, Sundays 11am to 5pm. Closed Mondays, and from November to Good Friday. f16. ☎ (0162) 585400.

Boat tour: reservations required. Information: ☎ (078) 6211311.

BRIELLE ☒ Markt 1 – 3231 AH – ☎ (0181) 47 54 75 – fax (0181) 47 54 70

Historisch Museum Den Briel – April to October: open Tuesdays to Fridays from 10am to 5pm, Saturdays 10am to 4pm, Sundays 1pm to 5pm. November to March: open Tuesdays to Fridays from 1pm to 5pm, Saturdays from 10am to 4pm. Closed Mondays, public holidays, and Sundays from November to March. f4. ☎ (0181) 475477.

Grote Kerk or St.-Catharijnekerk – Open May to September, daily. Rest of the year by appointment, ☎ (0181) 475475 (tourist office).

BULB FIELDS See KEUKENHOF

D

DELFT ☒ Markt 83-85 – 2611 GS – ☎ (015) 212 61 00 – fax (015) 215 86 95

Nieuwe Kerk – April to October: open daily (except Sundays after noon) from 9am to 6pm. November to March: open daily (except Sundays after noon) from 11am to 4pm. f3. Closed Sundays after noon. ☎ (015) 2123025.

Tower – ♿ Same opening times as church.

Museum Paul Tetar van Elven – Open mid-April to October, Tuesdays to Saturdays from 1pm to 5pm. Closed Mondays, Sundays, and from November to mid-April. f3.50. ☎ (015) 2124206.

Legermuseum – ♿ Open Tuesdays to Saturdays from 10am to 5pm, Sundays and public holidays noon to 5pm. Closed Mondays, 1 January, Easter Day, Whit Sunday, 25 December. f6. ☎ (015) 2150500.

DELFT

Prinsenhof – Open Tuesdays to Saturdays from 10am to 5pm, Sundays and public holidays 1pm to 5pm. Closed Mondays, 1 January and 25 December. f5 ☎ (015) 2602358.

Oude Kerk – Closed for restoration until late 1999. ☎ (015) 2123015.

Cultuurtuin voor technische gewassen – Open Mondays to Fridays from 8.30am to 5pm, Saturdays 10am to 3pm. Closed Sundays and public holidays ☎ (015) 2782356.

Techniek Museum Delft – Open Tuesdays to Saturdays from 10am to 5pm Sundays noon to 5pm. Closed Mondays, 1 January and 25 December. f5 ☎ (015) 2138311.

Museum Lambert van Meerten – Open Tuesdays to Saturdays from 10am to 5pm Sundays and public holidays 1pm to 5pm. Closed Mondays, 1 January and 25 December. f3.50. ☎ (015) 2602358.

Volkenkundig Museum "Nusantara" – ‰ Same opening times as Museum Lambert van Meerten. ☎ (015) 2602358.

DELTA

WaterLand Neeltje Jans – ‰ Open April to October, daily from 10am to 5pm November to March, Wednesdays to Sundays from 10am to 5pm. Closed Mondays and Tuesdays from November to March, 25 December. f20. ☎ (0111) 652702.

The Zeelandbrug, linking Zierikzee and Noord-Beveland

Slot Moermond – Guided tours only: July and August, Thursdays at 7pm, Saturdays at 2.30pm. f1.50. ☎ (0111) 460360.

St.-Nicolaaskerk – Open Whitsun to August, Mondays to Saturdays from 1.30pm to 4.30 pm. ☎ (0111) 691719.

DEVENTER   🛈 Keizerstraat 22 – 7411 HH; ☎ (0570) 61 31 00 – fax (0570) 64 33 30

Boat tours – Summer only. Information: Rederij Scheers, Worp 39, ☎(085° 229439 and Rederij Eureka, Bolwerksweg 1, ☎ (0570) 643151.

Historisch Museum De Waag – ‰ Open Tuesdays to Saturdays from 10am to 5pm Sundays and public holidays 1pm to 5pm. Closed Mondays, Easter Day, Whit Sunday 25 December. f5. ☎ (0570) 693780.

Speelgoed- en Blikmuseum – Same opening times as Historisch Museum De Waag ☎ (0570) 693786.

Stadhuis – Open Mondays to Fridays from 9am to 5pm. Closed weekends and public holidays. ☎ (0570) 613100 (tourist office).

Grote Kerk or St.-Lebuïnuskerk – Open Mondays to Saturdays from 11am to 5pm ☎ (0570) 612548.

Carillon and organ concerts – *Fridays from 10am to 11am, Saturdays 2pm to 3pm.*

Tower – *Open July and August, Mondays to Saturdays from 1pm to 5pm. Closed Sundays and public holidays. f2.* ☎*(0570) 612548.*

Additional sight

Atheneumbibliotheek – Open Mondays from 1pm to 6pm, Tuesdays and Thursdays 11am to 8pm, Wednesdays 11am to 6pm, Fridays 11am to 5pm, Saturdays 11am to 3pm. Closed Sundays and public holidays. ☏ (0570) 693887.

Excursion

Natuurdiorama Holterberg – April to October: open Mondays to Saturdays 9.30am to 5.30pm, Sundays and public holidays 11am to 5.30pm. November to March: open Sundays and daily during school holidays, 1pm to 5pm. f7.50. ☏ (0548) 377777.

DOESBURG   ∎ Kerkstraat 6 – 6981 CM – ☏ (0313) 47 90 88 – fax (0313) 47 19 86

Boat trips – April to September, Mondays to Saturdays from 2pm to 5pm. Closed Sundays and public holidays. ☏ (0313) 479088 (tourist office).

Grote Kerk or Martinikerk – Open April to September, Mondays to Saturdays from 2pm to 5pm. ☏ (0313) 479088 (tourist office).

Streekmuseum De Roode Tooren – Open Tuesdays to Fridays from 10am to noon and 1.30pm to 4.30pm, Saturdays 1.30pm to 4.30pm; July and August also on Sundays from 1.30pm to 4.30pm. Closed Mondays, Sundays (except in July and August), 1 January, Easter Day, Whit Sunday and 25 December. ☏ (0313) 474265.

Doesburgsch Mosterd- en Azijnmuseum – ♿ April to December: open Mondays to Fridays from 10am to 5pm, Saturdays 11am to 4pm. January to March: open Tuesdays to Fridays from 10am to 5pm, Saturdays 11am to 4pm. Closed Mondays from January to March, Sundays, 1 January, 30 April, Easter Day, 25 December. f2. ☏ (0313) 472230.

Excursion

Huis Bergh – Guided tours only. June and September: daily at 2pm and 3pm. July and August: Mondays to Fridays 11am to 3pm, Saturdays at 2pm and 3pm, Sundays at 1pm and 3pm. October to May: Sundays at 2pm and 3pm. Closed 1 January, carnival, 24, 25 and 31 December. f8.50. ☏ (0314) 661281.

DOKKUM   ∎ Op de Fetze 13 – 9101 LE – ☏ (0519) 29 38 00 – fax (0519) 29 80 15

Museum Het Admiraliteitshuis – April to September: open Tuesdays to Saturdays from 10am to 5pm, Sundays (July and August only) from 2pm to 5pm. October to March: Tuesdays to Saturdays 2pm to 5pm. Closed Mondays, Sundays (except in July and August), 1 January, 30 April, 25 December. f3.50. ☏ (0519) 293134.

Grote Kerk or St.-Martinuskerk – Guided tours only: July and August, Wednesday afternoons and Friday evenings. Contact the coster: ☏(0519) 292065 or ☏ (0519) 293440.

DOORN   ∎ Dorpsstraat 4 – 3941 JM – ☏ (0343) 41 20 15

Huis Doorn – Mid-March to October: open Tuesdays to Saturdays and on public holidays from 10am to 5pm, Sundays 1pm to 5pm. November to mid-March: open Tuesdays to Sundays 1pm to 5pm. Closed Mondays, 1 January and 25 December. f7.50. ☏ (0343) 412244.

DORDRECHT   ∎ Stationsweg 1 – 3311 JW – ☏(078) 613 28 00 – fax (078) 613 17 83

Boat trips – Information and reservations: Bezoekerscentrum 'De Hollandsche Biesbosch', Baanhoekweg 53, 3313 LP Dordrecht, ☏ (078) 6211311.

Grote Kerk or O.-L.-Vrouwekerk – Open April to October, Tuesdays to Saturdays from 10.30am to 4.30pm, Sundays and public holidays from noon to 4pm; first and third Sundays in November and December from 2pm to 4pm. ☏ (078) 6511338.

Carillon – All year: Fridays 11am to noon, Saturdays 2.30pm to 3.30pm; July and August, Thursdays 8pm to 9pm.

Organ concerts – May to September, Wednesdays at 8pm; mid-June to mid-September, Wednesdays from 3.30pm to 4pm. ☏ (078) 6144660.

Tower – Open April to October, Tuesdays to Saturdays from 10.30am to 4.30pm, Sundays and public holidays noon to 4pm; July and August also Mondays noon to 4pm; November to March, weekends 1pm to 4pm. f2. ☏ (078) 6511338.

Museum Mr. Simon van Gijn – Closed for rebuilding until January 2000. ☏ (078) 6133793.

Additional sights

Dordrechts Museum – Open daily (except Mondays) from 11am to 5pm. Closed Mondays, 1 January and 25 December. f7.50. ☏ (078) 6482148.

E

EDAM   🏛 Damplein 1 - 1135 BK - ☎ (0299) 31 51 52 - fax (0299) 37 42 3⬤

Edams Museum - Open April to October, Tuesdays to Saturdays from 10am t⬤
4.30pm, Sundays and public holidays 1.30pm to 4.30pm. Closed Mondays, Novem⬤
ber to March. f3.50. ☎ (0299) 372644.

Kaaswaag - ♿ Open April to September, daily from 10am to 5pm. Closed Octobe⬤
to March. ☎ (0299) 372842.

Grote Kerk or St.-Nicolaaskerk - Open April to September, daily from 2pm t⬤
4.30pm. Closed October to March. ☎ (0299) 371727 (tourist office).

EINDHOVEN   🏛 Stationsplein 17 - 5611 AC - ☎ (0900) 11 22 363 fax (040) 243 31 3⬤

Stedelijk Van Abbemuseum - ♿ Temporary address: Entr'acte, Vonderweg 1
Open daily (except Mondays) from 11am to 5pm. Closed Mondays, 1 January an⬤
25 December. f6. ☎ (040) 2755275.

Museum Kempenland - Open Tuesdays to Sundays from 1pm to 5pm. Close⬤
Mondays, 1 January, Easter Day and 25 December. f6. ☎ (040) 2529093.

Prehistorisch Openluchtmuseum Eindhoven - Open daily from 10am to 5pm⬤
Closed 1 January and 31 December. f5. ☎ (040) 2522281.

Excursion

Helmond castle (museum) - Open Tuesdays to Fridays from 10am to 5pm, weekend⬤
and public holidays 2pm to 5pm. Closed Mondays, 1 January, carnival, 25 December
f3.50. ☎ (0492) 547475.

Beiaard- en Natuurmuseum Asten - Open Tuesdays to Fridays from 9.30am t⬤
5pm, Saturdays to Mondays 1pm to 5pm. Closed 1 January, carnival, 25 December
f7. ☎ (0493) 691865.

De Groote Peel, National Park - Open daily from sunrise to sunset. ☎ (0495⬤
641497.

Bezoekerscentrum Mijl op Zeven - ♿ March, April, September and October: ope⬤
Tuesdays to Sundays from 10am to 5pm. May to August: open daily from 10am t⬤
5pm. November to February: open Sundays from 12noon to 5pm. ☎ (0495) 641497⬤

EMMEN   🏛 Marktplein 9 - 7811 AM - ☎ (0591) 61 30 00 - fax (0591) 64 41 0⬤

Noorder Dierenpark - ♿ Open daily from 9am. f25. ☎ (0591) 618800.

Excursions

Gemeentemuseum "Drenthe's Veste" - Open April to September, Tuesdays t⬤
Saturdays from 11am to 5pm. Closed Mondays, Sundays and public holidays, an⬤
from October to March. f3. ☎ (0524) 516225.

ENKHUIZEN   🏛 Tussen Twee Havens 1 - 1601 EM; ☎ (0228) 31 31 64 fax (0228) 31 55 3⬤

Boat to Enkhuizen - Three crossings a day (90min) from mid-June to mi⬤
September, Mondays to Saturdays. Information: ☎(0527) 683407.

Boat trips - Leave from Spoorhaven for Stavoren three times a day. Informatio⬤
from ☎ (0228) 313164.

Westerkerk or St.-Gomaruskerk - Closed for restoration.

Drommedaris - Open daily from 1pm to 12.30am (2am at weekends). ☎ (0228⬤
312076.

Zuiderzeemuseum:

Binnenmuseum - ♿ Open daily from 10am to 5pm (to 7pm in July and August). Close⬤
1 January and 25 December. f7.50. ☎ (0228) 318260.

Buitenmuseum - Open April to October daily from 10am to 5pm (7pm in July an⬤
August). Free guided tour: daily from 2pm to 3pm (also at 4.30pm in July an⬤
August). Closed November to March. f17.50. ☎ (0228) 318260.

Zuider Kerk or St.-Pancraskerk - By appointment only. ☎(0228) 314819.

ENSCHEDE   🏛 Oude Markt 31 - 7511 GB - ☎ (053) 432 32 00 - fax (053) 430 41 ⬤

Rijksmuseum Twenthe - ♿ Open Tuesdays to Sundays from 11am to 5pm. Close⬤
Mondays, 1 January. f7.50. ☎ (053) 4358675.

Museum Jannink - ♿ Open Tuesdays to Fridays from 10am to 5pm, weekends an⬤
public holidays 1pm to 5pm. Closed Mondays, 1 January, Easter Day, 30 April,
May, 25 and 31 December. f3. ☎ (053) 4319093.

Natuurmuseum - Same opening times as Museum Jannink. f3. ☎ (053) 432340⬤

Excursion

St.-Plechelmusbasiliek – Guided tours only, by appointment. Information from the tourist office, ☎ (0541) 512808.

Het Palthe Huis – Open Tuesdays to Fridays from 10am to 5pm, weekends 2pm to 5pm. Closed Mondays, Easter Day and 25 December. f3.50. ☎ (0541) 513482.

Kasteel Singraven – Guided tours only (1hr): Easter to October, Tuesdays to Fridays at 11am, 2pm and 3pm, Saturdays for groups only. Closed Mondays, Sundays and public holidays, November to Easter. f9. ☎ (0541) 351906.

Watermill – Open Easter to October, Tuesdays to Saturdays 1pm to 4pm. Closed Mondays, Sundays and public holidays and from November to Easter. f3. ☎ (0541) 351906.

Kerk van de H.H. Simon and Judas (Church of St Simon and St Judas) – Open Sundays. ☎ (0541) 293335.

Openluchtmuseum Los Hoes – February to December: open Mondays from noon to 5pm, Tuesdays to Sundays 10am to 5pm. Closed January. f4.50. ☎ (0541) 293099.

Kasteel Twickel: gardens and park – Open mid-May to October, Mondays to Fridays from 11am to 4.30pm. Closed weekends, and from November to mid-May. f7.50. ☎ (074) 3762596.

Zoutmuseum – ♿ April to October: open Mondays to Fridays from 11am to 5pm, weekends 2pm to 5pm. November to March: open Mondays to Fridays and Sundays from 2pm to 5pm. Closed public holidays and Saturdays from November to March. f5. ☎ (074) 3764546.

F

FLEVOLAND

Walibi-Flevo – April to June: open daily from 10am to 5pm (to 6pm on Sundays). July and August: open daily from 10am to 6pm. September and October: open Tuesdays to Sundays from 10am to 5pm. Closed November to March. f32.50. ☎ (0321) 329991.

Nieuw Land Poldermuseum – ♿ Open Mondays to Fridays from 10am to 5pm, weekends and public holidays 11.30 to 5pm. Closed 1 January and 25 December. f8.50. ☎ (0320) 260799.

Batavia dock – Open mid-June to August, daily from 10am to 8pm; September to mid-June, daily from 10am to 5pm. Closed 1 January and 25 December. f17.50. ☎ (0320) 261409.

FRANEKER ⓘ Voorstraat 51 – 8801 LA – ☎ (0900) 919 19 99 – fax (0517) 14 51 76

Stadhuis – Open Mondays to Fridays from 2pm to 5pm. Closed weekends and public holidays. ☎ (0517) 380480.

Planetarium – Open Tuesdays to Saturdays from 10am to 5pm; May to mid-September also on Mondays and Sundays from 1pm to 5pm. Closed Mondays and Sundays from mid-September to April. f5. ☎ (0517) 393070.

Museum 't Coopmanshûs – Open Tuesdays to Saturdays from 10am to 5pm; April to September also on Sundays from 1pm to 5pm. Closed Mondays, and on Sundays from October to March, 1 January, 25 December. f2.75. ☎ (0517) 392192.

G

GIETHOORN ⓘ Beulakerweg 114a – 8355 AL – ☎ (0521) 36 12 48 fax (0521) 36 22 81

Tour of the village – Information from Giethoorn tourist office, ☎ (0521) 361248.

GOES ⓘ Stationsplein 3 – 4461 HP – ☎ (0113) 25 24 20 – fax (0113) 25 13 50

Steam-operated tram – Departs May and June: Sundays at 11am and 2pm. July and August: Sundays to Fridays at 11am and 2pm. September and October: Sundays at 2pm. f20 1st class, f15 2nd class. ☎ (0113) 270705.

Grote Kerk or Maria Magdalenakerk – *Open daily (except Sunday) from 9am to 12noon and 1pm to 6pm.* ☎ (0113) 242938.

Organ concerts – *June to August, Mondays to Saturdays at 11am and 3pm, Sundays at 10am and noon.* ☎ (0113) 233452.

Excursion

Dutch Reformed Church – Open Mondays to Saturdays 9am to 11.30am and 1.30pm to 5pm. Closed Sundays and public holidays. ☎ (0113) 342938.

GORINCHEM ☶ Grote Markt 17 – 4201 EB – ☎ (0183) 63 15 25 fax (0183) 63 40 40

Gorcums Museum – &. Open Tuesdays to Saturdays from 10am to 5pm, Sundays 11am to 5pm (October to March from 1pm). Closed Mondays and public holidays. f3.☎ (0183) 632821.

Grote Kerk or St.-Maartenskerk: *tower* – *Open July to mid-August, Mondays from 10am to noon, also on Easter Monday and Whit Monday. f2.50.* ☎*(0183) 631525 (tourist office).*

Excursions

Nationaal Glasmuseum – Open Tuesdays to Fridays from 10am to 5pm, weekends and public holidays 1pm to 5pm. Closed Mondays, 1 January and 25 December. f5. ☎ (0345) 612714.

Slot Loevestein – April to mid-November: open Mondays from 11am to 5.30pm, Tuesdays to Sundays from 10am to 5.30pm. Mid-November to March: open weekends only, 11am to 5.30pm. Closed 1 January, 24, 25 and 31 December. f7.50. ☎(0183) 447171.

GOUDA ☶ Markt 27 – 2801 JJ – ☎ (0182) 51 36 66 – fax (0182) 58 32 10

Boat trips – Depart: July and August, Wednesdays to Saturdays at 10.45am and 1.45pm. f15. ☎ (0182) 513666 (tourist office).

Cheese and craft market – June to August, Thursdays from 10am to 12.30pm. ☎ (0182) 513666 (tourist office).

Stadhuis – Open Mondays to Fridays from 9am to 4.30pm, Saturdays 11am to 3pm. Closed Sundays. f1. ☎ (0182) 588758.

Kaasexposeum – Open April to October, Tuesdays to Fridays from 10am to 5pm, weekends and public holidays 1pm to 5pm. Closed Mondays, and from November to March. f5. ☎ (0182) 529996.

St.-Janskerk – Open March to October, Mondays to Saturdays from 9am to 5pm; November to February, Mondays to Saturdays 10am to 4pm. Closed Sundays, 1 January, 25 and 26 December. f3. ☎ (0182) 512684.

Museum Het Catharina Gasthuis – Open Mondays to Saturdays from 10am to 5pm, Sundays and public holidays noon to 5pm. Closed 1 January and 25 December. f4.50 (also valid for Museum De Moriaan). ☎ (0182) 588440.

Additional sights

Museum De Moriaan – Open Mondays to Fridays from 10am to 5pm, Saturdays 10am to 12.30pm and 1.30pm to 5pm, Sundays and public holidays noon to 5pm. Closed 1 January and 25 December. f4.50 (ticket also valid for Museum Het Catharina Gasthuis). ☎ (0182) 588440.

Excursions

Stadsmuseum – Open Tuesdays to Fridays from 1pm to 5pm, weekends 1pm to 4pm. Closed Mondays, 1 January, Easter Day, 30 April and 25 December. f3. ☎ (0348) 431797.

Nederlands Goud-, Zilver- and Klokkenmuseum – May to September: open Mondays from 1.30pm to 5pm, Tuesdays to Fridays 9am to 5pm, Saturdays 10am to 3pm. October to April: open Tuesdays to Fridays from 10am to noon and 2pm to 4pm, Saturdays 10am to 3pm. Closed Mondays (except from May to September), Sundays, 1 January, 25 and 26 December. f4.50. ☎(0182) 385009.

GRONINGEN ☶ Gedempte Kattendiep 6 – 9711 PN – ☎ (0900) 202 30 50 fax (050) 311 02 58 – www.vvvgroningen.n

Martinikerk – June to September: open Mondays to Saturdays from noon to 5pm. Easter to May and September to early November: open Saturdays noon to 5pm. Closed Sundays, and from early November to Easter Day. f1. ☎ (050) 3111277.

Martinitoren (tower) – April to June: open daily from noon to 4.30pm. July to September: open daily from 11am to 4.30pm. October to March: open weekends, public holidays and school holidays only, from noon to 4.30pm. f2.50. ☎ (050) 3135713.

Additional sights

Noordelijk Scheepvaartmuseum – Open Tuesdays to Sundays from 10am to 5pm. Closed Mondays, 1 January, 30 April, 28 August and 25 December. f6. ☎ (050) 3122202.

Niemeyer Tabaksmuseum – Same opening times as Noordelijk Scheepvaart Museum.

Groninger Museum – Open daily (except Mondays) from 10am to 5pm. Closed Mondays, 1 January and 25 December. f10. ☎ (0900) 8212132 (tourist office) or ☎ (050) 3666555.

Outskirts

Hortus Haren/Het Verborgen Rijk van Ming – ♿ Open daily from 9am to 5pm. f15. ☎ (050) 5370053.

Excursions

Nederlands Hervormde Kerk – Open April to October, Mondays to Saturdays from 10am to 5pm, and all year on Sundays from 1pm to 5pm. f3.50. ☎ (050) 4032109 or ☎ (050) 4031965.

Petruskerk – Open daily. ☎ (0595) 571677.

EXPOZEE exhibition – Open daily from 10am to 5pm. f6.50. ☎ (0519) 349045.

Garmerwolde bell tower – To view, contact H.Winters, Dorpsweg 62, ☎ (050) 3023921.

Loppersum church – Open Mondays to Saturdays from 9am to 5pm. ☎ (0596) 628014.

Zeerijp church – Open daily. ☎ (0596) 571826.

Krewerd church – Open daily from 10am to 5pm. ☎ (0596) 622347.

Boat trips – By appointment. Information from the tourist office: ☎ (0596) 618104.

Bierum church – Open daily from 9am to 11.30am and 12.30pm to 5pm. ☎ (0596) 591539.

Uithuizermeeden church – See board at tower entrance for information.

Hervormde Kerk – Open May to September, daily (except Mondays) 1.30pm to 4.30pm. Closed Mondays, November to April. ☎ (0299) 671979 (tourist office).

Stichting Museum 1939-1945 – Open April to September, daily from 9am to 6pm. f7.50. ☎ (0595) 434100.

H

Den HAAG ◪ Kon. Julianaplein 30- 2595 AA – ☎ (0900) 340 350 51 fax (070) 347 21 02

Binnenhof visitors' centre – Open daily (except Sunday) from 10am to 4pm. Closed Sundays and public holidays. ☎ (070) 3646144.

Ridderzaal, Eerste Kamer, Tweede Kamer – Guided tours only (45min): daily (except Sundays) from 10am to 4pm. Closed Sundays and public holidays, 14 and 15 September. f6. ☎ (070) 3646144.

Exhibition – Same opening times, entrance free.

Mauritshuis – ♿ Open Tuesdays to Saturdays from 10am to 5pm, Sundays and public holidays 11am to 5pm. Closed Mondays. f12.50. ☎ (070) 3023435.

Haags Historisch Museum – Open Tuesdays to Fridays from 11am to 5pm, week-ends and public holidays noon to 5pm. Closed Mondays. f6. ☎ (070) 3646940.

Museum Bredius – Open Tuesdays to Sundays noon to 5pm. Closed Mondays and public holidays. f6. ☎ (070) 3620729.

Paleis Lange Voorhout – ♿ Open daily (except Mondays) from 11am to 5pm. Closed Mondays, between exhibitions, 1 January, and 25 December. f10. ☎ (070) 3381120.

Vaals-Hervormde kerk – Not open to the public.

Museum de Gevangenpoort – Guided tours only: Tuesdays to Fridays from 10am to 4pm (hourly), weekends 1pm to 4pm (hourly). Closed Mondays, 1 January, 25 and 26 December. f6. ☎ (070) 3460861.

Galerij Prins Willem V – Open Tuesdays to Sundays from 11am to 4pm. Closed Mondays, 1 January and 25 December. f2.50. ☎ (070) 3023435.

Grote Kerk or St.-Jacob-skerk - *Open July and August, Mondays to Fridays 11am to 4pm; rest of the year by appointment.*

Panorama Mesdag - Open Mondays to Saturdays from 10am to 5pm, Sundays and public holidays noon to 5pm. Closed 25 December. f6. ☎ (070) 3106665.

Museum Mesdag - ♿ Open Tuesdays to Sundays from noon to 5pm. Closed Mondays, 1 January and 25 December. f5. ☎ (070) 3621434.

Vredespaleis - Open Mondays to Fridays from 10am to 4pm (to 3pm from October to April). f5. Closed weekends and public holidays. ☎ (070) 3024137.

Gemeentemuseum Den Haag - ♿ Open daily (except Mondays) from 10am to 5pm. Closed Mondays, 1 January and 25 December. f10. ☎ (070) 3381120.

Museon - ♿ Open Tuesdays to Fridays from 10am to 5pm, weekends and public holidays noon to 5pm. Closed Mondays, 1 January and 25 December. f10. ☎ (070) 3381305.

Omniversum - ♿ Open Tuesdays and Wednesdays from 10am to 5pm; Thursdays to Sundays and on public holidays and during school holidays from 10am to 9pm. Closed Mondays. f17.50. ☎ (070) 3545454.

Madurodam - ♿ April to June: open daily from 9am to 8pm. July and August: open daily from 9am to 10pm. September to March: open daily from 9am to 5pm. f19.50. ☎ (070) 3553900.

Museum van het Boek/Museum Meermanno-Westreenianum - Open Tuesdays to Fridays from 11am to 5pm, weekends and public holidays noon to 5pm. Closed Mondays, 1 January and 25 December. f3.50. ☎ (070) 3462700.

Museum Beelden aan Zee - ♿ Open Tuesdays to Sundays from 11am to 5pm. Closed Mondays, 1 January, 25 and 26 December. f6. ☎(070) 3585857.

Sea Life Scheveningen - Open daily from 10am to 6pm; July and August, daily from 10am to 8pm. f15. ☎(070) 3542100.

Excursions

Duinrell theme park - Open early April to October, daily from 10am to 5pm (to 6pm in July and August). Closed November to early April. f26 (includes Tikibad). ☎ (070) 5155155.

Tikibad - Early April to October: open daily from 10am to 10pm. November to early April: open Mondays and Fridays to Sundays from 10am to 10pm, Tuesdays and Wednesdays 2pm to 10pm. Closed Thursdays from November to early March and second half of November. f26 (includes amusement park). ☎ (070) 5155160.

Huygensmuseum - Open weekends from 1pm to 5pm. Closed Mondays to Fridays, 1 January and 25 December. f2.50. ☎ (070) 3872311.

Auctions - Mondays to Fridays (except Thursdays) from 8am to 10am. Closed Thursdays, weekends and public holidays. f4. ☎ (0174) 633333.

HAARLEM   🛈 Stationsplein 1 - 2011 LR - ☎ (0900) 616 16 00 - fax (023) 534 05 3

Grote Kerk or St.-Bavokerk - Open Mondays to Saturdays from 10am to 4pm. Closed Sundays. ☎ (023) 5324399.

Organ concerts - *Mid-May to October, Tuesdays 8.15pm to 9.15pm; July to October also on Thursdays 3pm to 4pm.*

Vishal – ᕳ Same opening times as Frans Halsmuseum. Entrance free. ☏ (023) 5326856.

Vleeshal – ᕳ Same opening times as Frans Halsmuseum. f4.50. ☏ (023) 5115775.

Verweyhal – Same opening times as Frans Halsmuseum.

Stadhuis – Open Mondays to Fridays from 9am to 4pm. Closed weekends and public holidays. ☏ (023) 5113158.

Frans Halsmuseum – ᕳ Open Mondays to Saturdays 11am to 5pm, Sundays and public holidays 1pm to 5pm. Closed 1 January and 25 December. f8. ☏ (023) 5115775.

Teylers Museum – Open Tuesdays to Saturdays from 10am to 5pm, Sundays and public holidays noon to 5pm. Closed Mondays, 1 January and 25 December. f7.50. ☏ (023) 5319010.

Historisch Museum – Open Tuesdays to Saturdays from 12noon to 5pm, Sundays 1pm to 5pm. Closed Mondays, 1 January, 25, 26 and 30 December. ☏ (023) 5422427.

Kathedrale Basiliek St.-Bavo – Open April to September and during school holidays, Mondays to Fridays from 10am to 4pm, Saturdays from 10am to 3pm, Sundays 1pm to 3pm. ☏ (023) 5325690.

Outskirts

Museum De Cruquius – ᕳ Open March to October, Mondays to Fridays from 10am to 5pm, weekends and public holidays 11am to 5pm. Closed November to February. f6. ☏ (023) 5285704.

Stoomgemaal Halfweg – Open April to September, Wednesdays and Thursdays 1pm to 4pm, Saturdays from 10am to 4pm. Closed November to March. f4. ☏ (020) 4974396.

HARDERWIJK 🛈 Havendam 58 - 3841 AA - ☏ (0341) 42 66 66 - fax (0341) 42 77 13

Boat tours – April to mid-September, Sundays and public holidays. f8. Information from Rederij Flevo. ☏ (0341) 412598.

Dolfinarium – ᕳ Open late February to October, daily from 10am to 6pm. Closed November to late February. f29.50. ☏ (0341) 467400.

Veluws Museum – Open Mondays to Fridays from 10am to 5pm, Saturdays 1pm to 4pm. Closed Sundays and public holidays. f3.50. ☏ (0341) 414468.

Grote Kerk – Open mid-May to mid-September, Mondays to Fridays. Closed mid-September to mid-May. ☏ (0341) 426666 (tourist office).

Excursion

Vischpoort – Open June to August, Mondays from 2pm to 4.30pm, Tuesdays to Fridays from 10am to noon and 1pm to 4.30pm. Closed weekends and public holidays, and from September to May. f3. ☏ (0525) 681341.

Gemeentemuseum – April to June and September to October: open Mondays from 2pm to 5pm, Tuesdays to Fridays from 10am to noon and 2pm to 5pm. July and August: open Mondays from 2pm to 5pm, Tuesdays to Fridays from 10am to 5pm. October to March: open Tuesdays to Fridays from 10am to noon and 2pm to 5pm. Closed weekends, public holidays, Mondays from October to March. f3. ☏ (0525) 681341.

St.-Nicolaaskerk – June: open Mondays to Fridays 1.30pm to 4.30pm. July and August: open Mondays from 1.30pm to 4.30pm, Tuesdays to Fridays from 10am to noon and 1.30pm to 4.30pm. Closed weekends, and from September to May. ☏ (0525) 681520 (tourist office).

Boat trips – ᕳ Depart May to September, Tuesdays to Saturdays every hour from 10am to 5pm. f6. ☏ (0341) 414159 or (0341) 415762.

HARLINGEN 🛈 Voorstraat 34 - 8861 BL - ☏(0900) 919 19 99 fax (0517) 41 51 76

Gemeentemuseum Het Hannemahuis – April to June and mid-September to October: open Mondays to Fridays from 1.30pm to 5pm. July to mid-September: open Tuesdays to Saturdays from 10am to 5pm, Sundays and public holidays 1.30pm to 5pm. Closed Mondays in summer, November to March, Easter Day and Whit Sunday. f2.50. ☏ (0517) 413658.

HEERENVEEN 🛈 Van Kleffenslaan 6 - 8442 CW - ☎ (0513) 62 55 55 fax (0513) 65 06 0

Oranjewoud and Oranjestein – Open some weekends in July and August. Information from the tourist office. ☎ (0513) 625555.

HEERLEN 🛈 Honigmanstraat 100 - 6411 LM - ☎ (045) 571 62 00 - fax (045) 571 83 8

Thermenmuseum – ♿ Open Tuesdays to Fridays from 10am to 5pm, weekends and public holidays 2pm to 5pm. Closed Mondays, 1 January, carnival, 25 December. f5 ☎ (045) 5604581.

Excursion

Industrion – ☎ Open Tuesdays to Sundays from 10am to 5pm. Closed Mondays 1 January, carnival and 25 December. f8. ☎ (045) 5670809.

Abdij Rolduc – Open daily (guided tours available) from 10am to 5pm. ☎ (045 5466888.

Den HELDER 🛈 Bernhardplein 18 - 1781 HH - ☎ (0223) 62 55 44 fax (0223) 61 48 8

Marinemuseum – ♿ Open Tuesdays to Fridays from 10am to 5pm, weekends and public holidays 1pm to 4.30pm; also Mondays in June to August from 1pm to 5pm Closed Mondays (except June to August), 1 January and 25 December. f7.50 ☎ (0223) 657534.

Nationaal Reddingmuseum "Dorus Rijkers" – ♿ Open Mondays to Saturdays from 10am to 5pm, Sundays and public holidays 1pm to 5pm. Closed 25 December. f5 ☎ (0223) 618320.

Fort Kijkduin – Open daily from 10am to 6pm. Guided tours at 11am, 1pm and 3pm f12.50 (Includes tour and aquarium). ☎ (0223) 612366.

's-HERTOGENBOSCH 🛈 Markt 77 - 5211 JX - ☎ (0900) 11 22 33
fax (073) 612 89 3

St.-Janskathedraal – Open daily from 10am to 4.30pm.

Additional sights

Stadhuis – Open Mondays from 11am to 5.30pm, Tuesdays to Fridays 9am to 5.30pm, Saturdays 9am to 4pm; May to September also on Sundays from 11am to 3pm. Guided tour: Thursdays at 7pm, Saturdays at 2.30pm. Closed public holidays and Sundays from October to April. ☎ (073) 6135098.

Noordbrabants Museum – Open Tuesdays to Fridays from 10am to 5pm, weekends noon to 5pm. Closed Mondays, 1 January, carnival and 25 December. f10 ☎ (073) 6877800.

Museum Slager – ♿ Open Tuesdays to Fridays and Sundays from 2pm to 5pm Closed Mondays, Saturdays and public holidays. f5. ☎ (073) 6133216.

Museum Het Kruithuis – Closed for restoration. Scheduled to re-open in 2001 Information: ☎ (073) 6122188.

Boat trips on the Binnendieze – May to late October, Tuesdays to Sundays 11am to 5pm, Wednesdays 2pm to 5pm. Closed late October to April. f8 ☎ (073) 6122334.

Excursions

Kasteel Heeswijk – Closed for restoration. ☎ (0413) 292024.

Meierijsche Museumboerderij – March to November: open weekends and public holidays from 2pm to 5pm. April to October: also open on Wednesdays from 2pm to 5pm. Closed December to February. f2.50. ☎ (0413) 291546.

Land van Ooit – Open late April to mid-September, daily from 10am to 5pm mid-September to mid-October, weekends 10am to 5pm; second half of October daily 10am to 5pm. Closed November to late April. f24.50. ☎ (0416) 377775.

Nederlands Leder- en Schoenenmuseum – ♿ Open Tuesdays to Fridays from 10am to 5pm, weekends noon to 4pm. Closed Mondays and public holidays. f5. ☎ (0416 332738.

De Efteling – ♿ Open April to October, daily from 10am to 6pm; July and August daily from 10am to 9pm. f35. ☎ (0416) 288111.

Maarten van Rossummuseum – Open Tuesdays to Fridays from 10am to 12.30pm and 1.30pm to 4.30pm, Saturdays (except from October to March) and Sundays 2pm to 4.30pm. Closed Mondays, and Saturdays from October to March. f3 ☎ (0418) 512617.

Stadhuis: carillon – First Thursday in each month, 12.30-1.30pm. ☎ (0146) 662234.

Autotron Rosmalen – ♿ Open Easter Day to mid-October, daily from 10am to 5pm (to 6pm in July and August). Closed mid-October to Easter Day. f19.50. ☎ (073) 5219050.

HILVERSUM
🚉 Noordse Bosje 1 – 1211 BD – ☎ (035) 624 17 51

Goois Museum – ♿ Open Tuesdays to Sundays from 1pm to 5pm. Closed Mondays, 1 January, 30 April and 25 December. f3. ☎ (035) 6292826.

Singer museum – Open Tuesdays to Saturdays from 11am to 5pm, Sundays and public holidays noon to 5pm. Closed Mondays, 1 January, 30 April and 25 December. ☎ (035) 5315656.

Muiderslot – Guided tours only (50min). April to October: Mondays to Fridays from 10am to 5pm, weekends 1pm to 5pm. November to March: weekends only, 1pm to 4pm. Closed 1 January and 25 December. f7.50. ☎ (0294) 261325.

HINDELOOPEN

Museum Hidde Nijland Stichting – Open March to October, Mondays to Saturdays from 10am to 5pm, Sundays and public holidays 1.30pm to 5pm. Closed November to February. f3.50. ☎ (0514) 521420.

Het Eerste Friese Schaatsmuseum – Open Mondays to Saturdays from 10am to 6pm, Sundays 1pm to 5pm. f2.50. ☎ (0514) 521683.

De HOGE VELUWE

Park – April: open daily from 8am to 8pm. May: open daily from 8am to 9pm. June to August: open daily from 8am to 10pm. September: open daily from 9am to 8pm. October: open daily from 9am to 7pm. November to March: open daily from 9am to 5pm. f8.50. ☎ (0318) 591627.

Visitor centre – Open daily from 10am to 5pm. ☎ (0318) 591627.

Kröller-Müller Museum – ♿ Open daily (except Mondays) from 10am to 5pm. Closed Mondays (except public holidays) and 1 January. f7. ☎ (0318) 591241.

Sculpture garden and sculpture park – Open April to October, daily (except Mondays) from 10am to 4.30pm. Closed Mondays (except public holidays). f7. ☎ (0318) 591241.

Additional sights

Museonder – Same opening times as visitor centre. ☎ (0318) 591627.

Jachtslot St.-Hubertus – Guided tours only (25 min). April to October: daily every half-hour between 11am and noon and between 2pm and 4.30pm. July and August: also at 1pm and 1.30pm. November to March: Mondays to Fridays at 2pm and 3pm. ☎ (0318) 591627.

Excursions

Nederlands Tegelmuseum – ♿ Open Tuesdays to Fridays from 10am to 12.30pm and 1pm to 5pm, weekends and public holidays 1pm to 5pm. Closed Mondays, 1 January and 25 December. f6. ☎ (0318) 591519.

HOORN
🚉 Veemarkt 4 – 1621 JC – ☎ (0229) 21 83 43 – fax (0229) 21 50 23

Steam tram – Departs: Easter Day to autumn half-term and during Christmas period, Tuesdays to Sundays 9.30am to 5.30pm; July and August also on Mondays from 9.30am to 5.30pm. f14 (single), f22.75 (return). ☎ (0229) 214862.

Westfries Museum – Open Mondays to Fridays from 11am to 5pm, weekends and public holidays 2pm to 5pm. Closed 1 January and 25 December. f5. ☎ (0229) 280022.

Museum van de Twintigste Eeuw – ♿ Open Tuesdays to Sundays from 10am to 5pm. Closed Mondays, 1 January, 30 April, 25 and 26 December. f5. ☎ (0229) 214001.

HULST
🚉 Grote Markt 19 – 4561 EA – ☎ (0114) 38 92 99

Streekmuseum De Vier Ambachten – Open Easter Day to October, daily from 2pm to 5pm. Closed November to Easter Day. f2.50. ☎ (0114) 320692.

HUNEBEDDEN

Nationaal Hunebedden Infocentrum – Open February to December, Mondays to Fridays from 10am to 5pm, weekends and public holidays 1pm to 5pm. Closed January and 25 December. ☎ (0599) 236374.

I-K

IJSSELMEER

Kazemattenmuseum Kornwerderzand – Open May to September, Wednesdays and Saturdays from 10am to 5pm. Closed October to April. f5. ☎ (0517) 579453.

KAMPEN
🔲 Botermarkt 5 – 8261 GR – ☎ (038) 331 35 00 – fax (038) 332 89 00

Boat trips – From Kampen: mid-June to mid-September. Information from the tourist office, ☎ (038) 3313500.

Oude Raadhuis – Open Mondays to Thursdays from 11am to noon and 2pm to 4pm; April to September also on Saturdays from 2pm to 5pm. Closed Fridays, Sundays and public holidays. f1.50. ☎ (038) 3317361.

Nieuwe Toren – Open May to mid-September, Wednesdays and Saturdays 2pm to 5pm; July and August also on Fridays from 2pm to 5pm Closed on public holidays. f1.50. ☎ (038) 3392966.

Stedelijk Museum – February to mid-June: open Tuesdays to Saturdays from 11am to 12.30pm and 1.30pm to 5pm. Mid-June to mid-September: open Tuesdays to Saturdays from 11am to 5pm, Sundays 1pm to 5pm. Mid-September to December: open Tuesdays to Saturdays from 11am to 12.30pm and 1.30pm to 5pm. Closed Mondays, Sundays from mid-September to mid-June, January, Whit Sunday, 25, 26 and 31 December. f3. ☎ (038) 3317361.

St.-Nicolaaskerk or Bovenkerk – Open Easter Day to early September, Mondays and Tuesdays from 1pm to 5pm, Wednesdays to Fridays from 10am to 5pm. ☎ (038) 3313608.

Organ concerts – June to September, Thursdays at 8pm; July and August, Saturdays from 3pm to 4.30pm. ☎ (038) 3313608.

KEUKENHOF and BULB FIELDS

Keukenhof National Flower Exhibition – ♿ Open late March to late May, daily from 8am to 7.30pm. f18. Closed late May to late March. Special summer exhibition is being held in 1999, from mid-August to mid-September. ☎ (0252) 465555.

Flights – Mondays to Saturdays 9am to 6pm, Sundays and public holidays from 10am to 5pm. No flights on 1 January or 25 December. From f50. ☎ (010) 4157855.

Excursion through the Bulb fields

Museum de Zwarte Tulp – ♿ Open daily (except Mondays) from 1pm to 5pm. Closed Mondays, 1 January, last Thursday in September, 25, 26 and 31 December. f4. ☎ (252) 417900.

Den Hartogh Ford Museum – ♿ April and May: open Tuesdays to Sundays from 10am to 5pm. June to March: open Wednesdays to Sundays from 10am to 5pm. Closed Mondays, 1 January, 30 April, 25 to 31 December. f15. ☎ (0252) 518118.

L

LEEUWARDEN
🔲 Stationsplein 1 – 8911 AC – ☎ (0900) 202 40 60 fax (058) 215 35 93

Fries Museum/Verzetsmuseum – ♿ Open Mondays to Saturdays from 11am to 5pm, Sundays and public holidays 1pm to 5pm. Closed 1 January and 25 December. f7.50. ☎ (058) 2123001.

Grote Kerk or Jacobijnerkerk – Open June to August, Tuesdays to Fridays from 2pm to 4pm. ☎ (058) 2128313.

Organ concerts – *July and August, Wednesdays at 8pm and Fridays at 12.30pm.*

Fries Natuurmuseum – ♿ Open Tuesdays to Saturdays from 10am to 5pm, Sundays and public holidays 1pm to 5pm. Closed Mondays, 1 January and 25 December. f5. ☎ (058) 2129085.

Museum Het Princessehof, Nederlands Keramiek Museum – Open Mondays to Saturdays from 10am to 5pm, Sundays and public holidays 2pm to 5pm. Closed 1 January and 25 December. f5.50. ☎ (058) 2127438.

Oldehove - Open May to September, Mondays to Saturdays from 2pm to 5pm. Closed Sundays and October to April. f2.50. ☎ (0900) 2024060 (tourist office).

Pier Pander Museum - Open April to September, Tuesdays to Saturdays 2pm to 5pm. Closed Mondays, Sundays and public holidays, October to March. ☎ (058) 2127438.

Additional sights

Poptaslot - Guided tours only (1hr). April, May, September and October: Mondays to Fridays at 2.30pm. June: Mondays to Fridays at 11am, 2pm and 3pm. July and August: Mondays to Saturdays from 11am to 5pm. Closed Sundays, and from November to March. f6. ☎ (058) 2541231.

Otterpark Aqualutra - Open April to October, daily from 9.30am to 5.30pm; November to March, daily from 10.30am to 4.30pm. f9.50. ☎ (0511) 431214.

"Uilenbord", Frisian farmhouse

Excursions

Tinsumageest Church - Open Mondays to Saturdays from 9am to noon and 1pm to 6pm; closed Sundays and public holidays. ☎ (0511) 423399.

Fogelsangh State - Open May to September, Tuesdays to Saturdays from 10am to noon and 1pm to 5pm, Sundays and public holidays 1pm to 5pm. Closed Mondays, and from October to April. f3. ☎ (0511) 441970.

Kollum church - View by appointment. ☎ (0511) 451530.

Oogebeintum church - Open April to October, Tuesdays to Saturdays from 10am to 5pm, Sundays noon to 5pm. ☎ (0518) 411703.

LEIDEN   🛈 Stationsplein 210 - 2312 AR - ☎ (0900) 222 23 33 fax (071) 512 53 18 - www.leiden.nl

Rijksmuseum voor Volkenkunde - ♿ Open Tuesdays to Fridays from 10am to 5pm, weekends and public holidays noon to 5pm. Closed Mondays, 1 January, 3 October and 25 December. f10. ☎ (071) 5168800.

Molen de Valk - Open Tuesdays to Saturdays from 10am to 5pm, Sundays and public holidays 1pm to 5pm. Closed Mondays, 1 January, 3 October and 25 December. f5. ☎ (071) 5165353.

Stedelijk Museum De Lakenhal - ♿ Open Tuesdays to Fridays from 10am to 5pm, weekends and public holidays noon to 5pm. Closed Mondays, 1 January, 3 October and 25 December. f5. ☎ (071) 5165360.

Rijksmuseum van Oudheden - ♿ Open Tuesdays to Fridays from 10am to 5pm, weekends and public holidays noon to 5pm. Closed Mondays, 1 January, 3 October and 25 December. f7. ☎ (071) 5163163.

Hortus Botanicus - Open Mondays to Saturdays from 9am to 5pm, Sundays and public holidays 10am to 5pm. Closed Saturdays from October to March, 1 January, 3 October and 25 December. f5. ☎ (071) 5277249.

Pieterskerk - Open daily 1.30pm to 4pm. Closed during services, and on 3 October and 31 December. ☎ (071) 5124319.

Additional sights

Museum Boerhaave - ♿ Open Tuesdays to Saturdays from 10am to 5pm, Sundays and public holidays noon to 5pm. Closed Mondays, 1 January and 3 October. f5. ☎ (071) 5214224.

LEIDEN

Pilgrim Fathers Documentatiecentrum – Open Mondays to Fridays 9.30am t⦁ 5pm, Saturdays 9am to 12.15pm. Closed Sundays and public holidays, 3 October ☎ (071) 5120191.

Nationaal Natuurhistorisch Museum Naturalis – ♿ Open Tuesdays to Sunday from noon to 6pm; public holidays and school holidays, daily from 10am to 6pm. Closed Mondays except during school holidays, and on 1 January and 25 December f12.50. ☎ (071) 5687600.

Excursions

Avifauna – Open daily from 9am to 6pm. f12.50. ☎ (0172) 487575.

Archeon – May to June and September to October: open daily (except Mondays) from 10am to 5pm. July and August: open daily from 10am to 6pm. Closed November to April. f20 (includes meal). Opening times may vary; check latest details o⦁ ☎ (0172) 447744.

Noordwijk Space Expo – Open daily (except Mondays) from 10am to 5pm. Als⦁ open on Mondays during school holidays from 10am to 5pm, and on 5, 24 an⦁ 31 December from 10am to 3pm. Closed Mondays (except as above), and o⦁ 1 January and 25 December. f13.50. ☎ (071) 3646446.

Het LOO

Park – ♿ Open daily (except Mondays) from 10am to 5pm. Closed Mondays and 2⦁ December. f12.50. ☎ (055) 5772400.

Stables, palace, gardens (tour) – ♿ Same opening times as park. f12.50. ☎ (055⦁ 5772400.

Concerts – Last Friday of every month at 8.15pm. Reservations: ☎ (055) 5772448

M

MAASTRICHT   🛈 Het Dinghuis, Kleine Staat 1 – 6211 ED – ☎ (043) 325 21 2⦁
fax (043) 321 37 4⦁

Spaans Gouvernement – Guided tours: Wednesdays to Fridays and first weeken⦁ in the month, at 2pm, 3pm and 4pm; 26 December from 2pm to 5pm. Close⦁ Mondays, Tuesdays, weekends and public holidays. f5. ☎ (043) 3211327.

St.-Servaasbasiliek: treasury – Enter via Vrijthof. April to November: open dai⦁ from 10am to 5pm (to 6pm in July and August). December to March: open daily fro⦁ 10am to 4pm. Closed 1 January, carnival and 25 December. f4. ☎ (043) 325212⦁ (tourist office).

Onze Lieve Vrouwebasiliek – Open daily from 8am to 5pm. ☎ (043) 3251851

Treasury – Open Easter Day to autumn half-term, Mondays to Saturdays from 10.3⦁ to 5pm, Sundays 12.30pm to 4.30pm. f3.50. ☎ (043) 3251851.

Bonnefantenmuseum – ♿ Open Tuesdays to Sundays from 11am to 5pm. Close⦁ Mondays, 1 January, carnival weekend and 25 December. f10. ☎ (043) 329019⦁

Additional sights

Kazematten – Guided tours only (1hr): Sundays and public holidays at 2pm; Ju⦁ and August at 12.30pm and 2pm; during school holidays, daily at 2pm. f5.5⦁ ☎ (043) 3252121.

Fort St.-Pieter – Guided tours only (1hr): June to October, Sundays at 3.15pm⦁ public holidays and school holidays, daily at 3.15pm. f5.50. ☎ (043) 3252121.

Marl caves: northern tunnel system – Guided tours only (1hr). April to June an⦁ September to October: daily at 12.30pm, 2pm and 3.30pm. July and August: dai⦁ 10.45am to 3.45pm. November to March: Wednesdays and Fridays at 2pn⦁ weekends at 12.30pm and 2pm. During Christmas period: daily at 2pm. f5.5⦁ ☎ (043) 3252121.

Zonneberg tunnel system – Guided tours only (1hr). Late March to late April an⦁ first half of September: daily at 12.45pm (except Sunday), 1.45pm and 2.45pn⦁ May to mid-September: Mondays to Saturdays from 10.45 am to 3.45pm (departin⦁ every hour), Sundays 1.45pm to 3.45pm (every hour). October to mid-Decembe⦁ Sundays at 2.45pm. Autumn half-term: daily at 1.45pm (2.45pm on Sundays⦁ Closed mid-December to late March. f5.50. ☎ (043) 3252121.

Outskirts

Afrika-Centrum – April to October: open Mondays to Fridays from 1.30pm to 5pm, Sundays and public holidays 2pm to 5pm. November to March: open Sundays only, from 2pm to 5pm, or by appointment. Closed Saturdays, and from November to March (except Sundays), 1 January, carnival, Easter Day, Whit Sunday and 25 December. f5. ☎ (043) 4071226 or ☎ (043) 4071277.

Nederlands Wijnmuseum – Open Mondays to Fridays from 9.30am to 5pm, Saturdays 10.30am to 4pm. Closed Sundays. f6 (includes glass of wine). ☎ (043) 4071206.

Excursions

Archeologiemuseum, Stein – ⅃ Open Wednesdays and Fridays from 9am to noon and 2pm to 5pm, Sundays and public holidays 2pm to 5pm. Closed Easter Day, Whit Sunday and 25 December. f3. ☎ (046) 4338919.

Grote Kerk or St.-Petruskerk – Open June to August, Mondays to Fridays from 2pm to 4pm. ☎ (046) 4524144 (tourist office).

St.-Amelbergakerk – Open May to October, Tuesdays and Sundays from 2pm to 5pm. ☎ (046) 4494618 (tourist office).

MARKEN

Some houses on the harbour are open to the public.

Marker Museum – ⅃ Open Easter Day to October, Mondays to Saturdays from 10am to 5pm, Sundays noon to 4pm. Closed November to Easter Day. f4. ☎ (0299) 601904.

MEDEMBLIK ☐ Stationsgebouw, Dam 2 – 1671 AW – ☎ (0227) 54 28 52

Kasteel Radboud – Open mid-May to mid-September, Mondays to Saturdays from 10am to 5pm; also Sundays and public holidays all year, from 2pm to 5pm. Closed 1 January and 25 December. f3.50. ☎ (0227) 541960.

Nederlands Stoommachinemuseum – Open Easter Day to autumn half-term, Wednesdays to Saturdays from 10am to 5pm, Sundays noon to 5pm. The machines operate on one weekend in each month during this period. Closed Mondays, Tuesdays, autumn half-term to Easter Day. f5. ☎ (0227) 544732.

MENKEMABORG

Castle – April to September: open daily from 10am to 12noon and 1pm to 5pm. October to December, February and March: open daily (except Mondays) from 10am to noon and 1pm to 4pm. Closed Mondays from October to March, and during January. f5. ☎ (0595) 431970.

MIDDELBURG ☐ Nieuwe Burg 40– 4331 AH – ☎ (0118) 65 99 00 fax (0118) 65 99 40

Stadhuis – Guided tours only (45 min): April to October, Mondays to Saturdays from 11am to 5pm, Sundays noon to 5pm. Closed November to March. f4. ☎ (0118) 675452.

Historama Middelburg – Open April to October, Mondays to Saturdays from 11am to 5pm, Sundays noon to 5pm. Closed November to March. f6. ☎ (0118) 616448.

Abbey churches – Open May to autumn half-term, daily from 10am to 5pm. ☎ (0118) 613596.

Lange Jan – Open April to October, Mondays to Saturdays from 11am to 5pm, Sundays noon to 5pm. Closed November to March. f3. ☎ (0118) 675450.

Zeeuws Museum – Open Mondays to Saturdays from 11am to 5pm, Sundays noon to 5pm. Closed 1 January and 25 December. f8. ☎ (0118) 626655.

Additional sights

Miniatuur Walcheren – ⅃ Open April to October, daily from 10am to 5pm. Closed November to March. f11. ☎ (0118) 612525.

NAARDEN ☐ Adr. Dorstmanplein 1b, 1411 RC – ☎ (035) 694 28 36 fax (035) 694 34 24

Stadhuis – Open April to September, Mondays to Saturdays from 1.30pm to 4.30pm. Closed Sundays and public holidays, and from October to March. ☎ (035) 6957811.

Grote Kerk – Same opening times as Comenius Museum. ☎ (035) 6949873.

NAARDEN

Comenius Museum – April to October: open Tuesdays to Saturdays from 10am to 5pm, Sundays and public holidays noon to 5pm. November to March: open Tuesdays to Sundays from 1pm to 4pm. Closed Mondays, 1 January, 25 and 31 December. f4.50. ☎ (035) 6943045.

Comenius Mausoleum – Same opening times as Comenius Museum.

Nederlands Vestingmuseum – April to mid-June, September to October: open Tuesdays to Fridays from 10.30am to 5pm, weekends noon to 5pm. Mid-June to August: Mondays to Fridays from 10.30 to 5pm, weekends noon to 5pm. November to March: Sundays from noon to 5pm. Closed 1 January, 25 and 31 December. f10. ☎ (035) 6945459.

NIJMEGEN ☑ St.-Jorisstraat 72 – 6511 TD – ☎ (0900) 112 23 44 – fax (024) 360 14 29

Boat trips – July and August only. Information: Rederij Tonissen, ☎ (024) 3233285.

St.-Stevenskerk – Open mid-June to August, Tuesdays to Saturdays from noon to 6pm. Closed September to mid-June. f1. ☎ (024) 3292607.

Organ and carillon concerts – Tuesdays at 8.30pm.

Stadhuis – Guided tours only, on request. Closed weekends and public holidays. f2.50. ☎ (024) 3292403.

Museum Het Valkhof – Scheduled to open in 1999. Information: ☎ (024) 3608805

Nationaal Fietsmuseum Velorama – Open Mondays to Saturdays from 10am to 5pm, Sundays and public holidays 11am to 5pm. Closed 1 January and 25 December. f6. ☎ (024) 3225851.

Additional sights

Bijbels Openluchtmuseum Heilig Land Stichting – Open mid-March to October daily 9am to 5.30pm. Closed November to mid-March. f12.50. ☎ (024) 3823110

Bevrijdingsmuseum 1944 Rijk van Nijmegen – Open Mondays to Saturdays from 10am to 5pm, Sundays and public holidays noon to 5pm. Closed 1 January and 25 December. f7.50. ☎ (024) 3974404.

Afrika Museum – April to October: open Mondays to Fridays from 10am to 5pm, weekends and public holidays 11am to 5pm. November to March: Mondays to Fridays from 10am to 5pm, weekends and public holidays from 1pm to 5pm. Closed 1 January and 25 December. f10. ☎ (024) 6842044.

Excursions

Doornenburg castle – Guided tours only (1hr). Easter Day to early November Sundays at 1.30pm, 2.30pm and 3.30pm (public holidays from 10.30am). July and August: Tuesdays to Thursdays at 11am, 2.30pm and 3.30pm, Fridays and Saturdays at 2pm and 3.30pm. During school holidays: Tuesdays to Saturdays at 2pm and 3.30pm. f6. ☎ (0481) 421456.

NOORDOOSTPOLDER

Water tower – Information from Emmeloord tourist office, ☎ (0527) 612000.

Museum Schokland – ♿ April to October: open Tuesdays to Sundays from 11am to 5pm (also Mondays in July and August). November to March: open weekend from 11am to 5pm. Closed Mondays, 1 January and 25 December. f4.50. ☎ (0527) 251396.

NUENEN

Van Gogh Documentatiecentrum – Open Mondays to Fridays from 8.30am to 12.30pm and 1.30pm to 4pm. Closed weekends and public holidays. f1.50. ☎ (040) 2631668.

R

ROERMOND ☑ Kraanpoort 1 – 6041 EG – ☎ (0900) 202 55 88 – fax (0475) 33 50 6

Onze Lieve Vrouwe Munsterkerk – Open Fridays from 2pm to 5pm, Saturday 12.30 to 5pm. ☎ (0475) 333205 (tourist office).

Kathedrale kerk – Open April to November, daily from 2pm to 5pm. ☎ (0475) 333205 (tourist office).

Excursion

Thorn Abbey Church – March: open daily from 12noon to 4pm. April to October: open Mondays to Fridays from 10am to 5pm, Saturdays 10am to 4pm, Sunday 11.30am to 5pm. November to February: open weekends from 12noon to 4pm. f2.50. ☎ (0475) 562555.

Stadhuis – Guided tours only (45min), by appointment. ☎ (010) 4172459.

Carillon concerts – Tuesdays from noon to 1pm.

Grote Kerk or St.-Laurenskerk – Open Tuesdays to Saturdays from 10am to 4pm. ☎ (010) 4131989.

Historisch Museum Het Schielandshuis – Open Tuesdays to Fridays from 10am to 5pm, weekends and public holidays 11am to 5pm. Closed Mondays, 1 January, 30 April and 25 December. f6. ☎ (010) 2176767.

Museum Boijmans Van Beuningen – Closed for renovation until September 2000. Temporary exhibitions of items from the collection are being held in the Kunsthal. Information: ☎ (010) 4419475.

Nederlands Architectuurinstituut – Open Tuesdays to Saturdays from 10am to 5pm, Sundays and public holidays 11am to 5pm. Closed Mondays, 1 January, 30 April and 25 December. f7.50. ☎ (010) 4401200.

Chabotmuseum – Open Tuesdays to Fridays from 11am to 4.30pm, Saturdays 11am to 5pm, Sundays noon to 5pm. Closed Mondays. f6.50. ☎ (010) 4363713.

Kunsthal – Open Tuesdays to Saturdays from 10am to 5pm, Sundays and public holidays 11am to 5pm. Closed Mondays. f10. ☎ (010) 4400300.

Maritiem Museum "Prins Hendrik" – ♿ Open Tuesdays to Saturdays from 10am to 5pm, Sundays and public holidays 11am to 5pm; July and August also Mondays from 10am to 5pm. Closed Mondays (except in July and August), 1 January, 30 April and 25 December. f6. ☎ (010) 4132680.

Cube apartments (apartment open to the public) – March to December: open daily from 11am to 5pm. January and February: open Fridays to Sundays from 11am to 5pm. f3.50. ☎ (010) 4142285.

Museum Schepen uit Verre Landen – Open Tuesdays to Fridays from 10am to 4pm, weekends noon to 5pm. Closed Mondays and public holidays. f5. ☎ (010) 4138351.

Museum "De Dubbelde Palmboom" – Open Tuesdays to Fridays from 10am to 5pm, weekends and public holidays 11am to 5pm. Closed Mondays, 1 January, 30 April and 25 December. f6. ☎ (010) 2176767.

Zakkendragershuisje – Open Tuesdays to Saturdays from 10am to 5pm, Sundays and public holidays 11am to 5pm. Closed Mondays, 1 January and 30 April. ☎ (010) 4772664.

Additional sights

Euromast – April to September: open daily from 10am to 7pm. July and August: open daily (except Mondays) from 10am to 10.30pm. October to March: open daily from 10am to 5pm. f15. ☎ (010) 4364811.

Museum voor Volkenkunde – Closed for renovation until October 2000. Information: ☎ (010) 4112201.

Diergaarde Blijdorp – ♿ Summer: open daily from 9am to 6pm. Winter: open daily from 9am to 5pm. f22.50. ☎ (010) 4431495.

De Ster windmill – April to November: open Tuesdays and Wednesdays from 9am to 4pm. May to September: open on the first Saturday of the month. December to March: open Wednesdays from 9am to 4pm. ☎ (010) 4526287.

Short harbour tour (1hr 15min) – April to September: departs daily from 9.30am to 5pm. March and October: departs daily from 10am to 4pm. November to February: departs daily from 11am to 3.30pm. f15.50. ☎ (010) 2759988.

Longer tour of the port (2hr 15min) – Departs June to August, daily at 10am and 12.30pm. f24. ☎ (010) 2759988.

Europoort tour (6hr 30min). Departs July and August, Tuesdays and Thursdays at 10.30am (returns around 5pm). f40. ☎ (010) 2759988.

Excursions

Kinderdijk windmills – Open April to September, daily from 9.30am to 5.30pm. Closed October to March. f3. ☎ (078) 6132800 (tourist office).

Boat tour – May to September, daily from 10am to 5pm. Information from Rederij Vos & Zoon, ☎ (078) 6912482.

Nederwaard windmill – Same opening times as Kinderdijk windmill. ☎ (078) 3915179.

S

SCHIEDAM   🄸 Buitenhavenweg 9 - 3113 BC - ☎ (010) 473 30 00 fax (010) 473 66 95

Stedelijk Museum – Open Tuesdays to Saturdays from 11am to 5pm, Sundays and public holidays 12.30 pm to 5pm. Closed Mondays, 1 January and 25 December. f3. ☎ (010) 2463666.

Nederlands Gedistilleerd Museum De Gekroonde Bransketel – Open Tuesdays to Saturdays from 11am to 5pm, Sundays and public holidays 12.30pm to 5pm. Closed Mondays, 1 January and 25 December. f7.50 (includes tasting). ☎ (010) 4261291.

Nederlands Malend Korenmolenmuseum – Open Tuesdays to Saturdays from 11am to 5pm, Sundays and public holidays 12.30 to 5pm. Closed Mondays, 1 January and 25 December. f3.50. ☎ (010) 4267675.

SLUIS   🄸 St-Annastraat 15 - 4524 JB - ☎ (0117) 46 17 00 - fax (0117) 46 26 84

Stadhuis – May to October: open Whit Sunday, Ascension Day, and Sundays from 2pm to 5pm. July and August: open daily from 1pm to 5pm. Closed November to April. f2.50. ☎ (0117) 461700 (tourist office).

Molen de Brak – Open daily (except Fridays out of season) from 1pm to 5pm. Closed 1 January, last two weeks of January, 25 and 26 December. f2.50. ☎ (0117) 461250.

Excursions

Streekmuseum West-Zeeuws-Vlaanderen – Open Tuesdays to Fridays from 10am to noon and 1pm to 5pm, Saturdays 1pm to 5pm. Closed Mondays, Sundays and public holidays. f2. ☎ (0117) 301200.

Breskens-Vlissingen ferry – Leaves daily every half-hour, Sundays every hour. Further information: ☎ (0118) 465905.

SNEEK   🄸 Marktstraat 18 - 8601 CV - ☎ (0515) 41 40 96 - fax (0515) 42 37 03

Stadhuis – Guided tours only (30min): July to early August, Mondays to Fridays from 2pm to 4pm. Closed weekends and public holidays, and from early August to June. ☎ (0515) 485371.

Fries Scheepvaart Museum en Oudheidkamer – Open Mondays to Saturdays from 10am to 5pm, Sundays and public holidays noon to 5pm. Closed 1 January, Easter Day, Whit Sunday and 25 December. f3. ☎ (0515) 414057.

Exmorra museum – Open April to October, daily from 10am to 5pm. Closed November to March. f3.50. ☎ (0515) 575681.

Old farmhouse – &. Open April to October, daily from 10am to 5pm. Closed November to March. f7. ☎ (0515) 5756 81.

Fries Aardewerkmuseum "De Waag" – April to October: open Mondays to Saturdays from 10am to 5pm, Sundays and public holidays 1.30pm to 5pm November to March: open Mondays to Fridays from 10am to noon and 1pm to 4pm Closed weekends from November to March, and on 1 January, 25 and 26 December f3. ☎ (0515) 231422.

Tichelaars Aardewerk- en Tegelfabriek – Open Mondays to Fridays from 9am to 5.30pm, Saturdays from 10am to 5pm, public holidays from 10am to 4pm. Closed Sundays, 1 January, 25 and 26 December. f4. ☎ (0515) 231341.

Ferwoude workshop – Open April to October, daily from 10am to 5pm. Closed November to March. f3.50. ☎ (0515) 575681.

Museum Joure – May to October: open Mondays to Fridays from 10am to 5pm, weekends 2pm to 5pm; November to April: open Mondays to Fridays from 10am to 5pm, Sundays 2pm to 5pm. Closed Saturdays (except May to October), 1 January Easter Day, Whit Sunday and 25 December. f4. ☎ (0513) 412283.

Wieuwerd crypt – Open April to October, daily (except Sunday) from 9am to 11.30am and 1pm to 4.30pm. Closed Sundays, and from November to March ☎ (058) 2501475.

Bozum church – Open from Easter to mid-October, Mondays to Fridays ☎ (0515) 521383.

STADSKANAAL

Excursions

Museum-Klooster Ter Apel – April to October: open Mondays to Saturdays from 10am to 5pm, Sundays 1pm to 5pm. November to March: open Tuesdays to Saturdays from 10am to 5pm, Sundays 1pm to 5pm. Closed Mondays from November to March. f6. ☎ (0599) 581370.

T

TIEL

Boerenwagenmuseum – Open May to September, daily (except Mondays) from 1pm to 5pm. Closed Mondays, and from October to April. f3.50. ☎ (0344) 571431.

TILBURG ⊟ Stadhuisplein 128 - 5038 TC - ☎ (013) 535 11 35 - fax (013) 535 37 95

Noordbrabants Natuurmuseum and Scryption – ♿ Open Tuesdays to Fridays from 10am to 5pm, weekends 1pm to 5pm. Closed Mondays, 1 January, Easter Day, 30 April and 25 December. f7. ☎ (013) 5353935 (Natuurmuseum) and ☎ (013) 5800821 (Scryption).

De Pont – Open daily (except Mondays) from 11am to 5pm. Closed Mondays. f5. ☎ (013) 5438300.

Nederlands Textielmuseum – ♿ Open Tuesdays to Fridays from 10am to 5pm, weekends noon to 5pm. Closed Mondays and public holidays. f7.50. ☎ (013) 5367475.

Excursions

Safari park – January and December: open daily from 10am to 4pm. February and November: open daily from 10am to 4.30pm. March to June, September and October: open daily from 10am to 5pm. July and August: open daily from 10am to 5pm. f22.50. ☎ (013) 5360035.

Speelland – Late April to late June: open daily from 10am to 5pm. July to early September: open daily from 10am to 6pm. Closed early September to late April. f9.50. ☎ (013) 5360032.

U

UTRECHT ⊟ Vredenburg 90 - 3511 BD - ☎ (0900) 414 14 14 fax (030) 233 14 17 - www.tref.nl/utrecht/VVV

Domtoren – Guided tours only (1hr). April to October: Mondays to Fridays from 10am to 5pm, weekends and public holidays noon to 5pm. November to March: weekends and public holidays from noon to 5pm. Closed Mondays to Fridays from November to March. f5.50. ☎ (030) 2864540.

Domkerk – May to September: open Mondays to Fridays from 10am to 5pm, Saturdays 10am to 3.30pm, Sundays 2pm to 4pm. October to April: open daily from 11am to 4pm. ☎ (030) 2310403.

Nationaal Museum van Speelklok tot Pierement – ♿ Open Tuesdays to Saturdays from 10am to 5pm, Sundays and public holidays noon to 5pm. Closed Mondays, 1 January, 30 April and 25 December. f9. ☎ (030) 2312789.

Museum Catharijneconvent – Open Tuesdays to Fridays from 10am to 5pm, weekends and public holidays 11am to 5pm. Closed Mondays and 1 January. f7. ☎ (030) 2317296.

X. Richer/HOA QUI

Universiteitsmuseum – Open Tuesdays to Fridays from 10am to 5pm, weekends and public holidays 1pm to 5pm. Closed Mondays, 1 January, Easter Day, 30 April and 25 December. f7.50. ☎ (030) 2538007.

Centraal Museum – Closed for renovation until late 1999. Information ☎ (030) 2362362.

Nederlands Spoorwegmuseum – ✦ Open Tuesdays to Fridays from 10am to 5pm, Sundays 11.30 to 5pm. Closed Mondays and public holidays. f13.50 ☎ (030) 2306206.

Other sights

Waterleidingmuseum – April to mid-November: open Tuesdays to Fridays and Sundays from 1.30pm to 5pm, Saturdays 11am to 4pm. Mid-November to March: open Wednesdays from 1.30pm to 5pm. Closed Mondays and public holidays. f2.50 ☎ (030) 2487211.

Moluks Historisch Museum – Open daily (except Mondays) from 1pm to 5pm. Closed Mondays, 1 January, Easter Day, 25 April and 25 December. f4.50 ☎ (030) 2367116.

Rietveld Schröderhuis – Guided tours only (1hr): Wednesdays to Saturdays 11am to 3.30pm, Sundays and public holidays 12.30pm to 3.30pm. Closed Mondays, Tuesdays, 1 January, 30 April and 25 December. f9. Reservations: ☎ (030) 2362310.

Excursions

Kasteel Sypesteyn – Guided tours only (1hr). April and October: weekends and public holidays from noon to 5pm. May to September: Tuesdays to Fridays from 10am to 5pm, weekends and public holidays noon to 5pm. Closed Mondays and November to March. f10. ☎ (035) 5823208.

Kasteel De Haar – March to May and mid-October to mid-November: open Tuesdays to Sundays from 1pm to 4pm. June to mid-August: open Mondays to Fridays from 11am to 4pm, weekends 1pm to 4pm. Mid-November to February: open Sundays from 1pm to 4pm. Closed mid-August to mid-October. f15. ☎ (030) 6773804.

Slot Zuylen – Guided tours only (1hr). Mid-March to mid-May, mid-September to mid-November: Saturdays from 2pm to 4pm, Sundays from 1pm to 4pm. Mid-May to mid-September: Tuesdays to Thursdays from 11am to 4pm, Saturdays 2pm to 4pm, Sundays 1pm to 4pm. Closed Mondays and Fridays, and from mid-November to mid-March. f8. ☎ (030) 2440255.

V

VALKENBURG AAN DE GEUL   🖪 Th. Dorrenplein 5 – 6301 DV – ☎ (0900) 92 22 fax (043) 609 86 08

Castle ruins – Open April to October, daily from 10.30am to 4.30pm (to 6pm in July and August); November to March, open daily from 10.30am to 4pm. f3.75 ☎ (043) 6090110.

Steenkolenmijn Valkenburg – Open April to October, daily from 10am to 5pm. November to March, weekends and public holidays from 2pm to 4pm. Closed Mondays to Fridays from October to March, 1 January, carnival and 25 December. f10. ☎ (043) 6012460.

Gemeentegrot – ✦ Guided tours only, on foot (1hr) or by miniature train (30min). November to March: on foot, Mondays to Fridays at 2pm, weekends and public holidays at 10.30am, noon, 2pm and 3.30pm; by train, weekends and public holidays at 11.15pm, 12.30pm, 2pm, 3pm and 4pm. April to June, September and October: on foot, daily from 10.30 to 4pm; by train, daily from 11am to 4.30pm. July and August: on foot, daily from 10am to 5pm; by train, daily from 11am to 5pm. Closed 1 January, carnival and 25 December. f5.25 (on foot), f6.75 (train). ☎ (043) 6012271.

Fluweelengrot – Guided tours only (1hr). November to Easter Day: Mondays to Fridays at noon and 1.30pm, weekends and during school holidays from 11am to 3pm. Easter Day to June, September and October: daily from 11am to 4pm. July and August: daily from 10am to 5pm and at 8.30pm. Closed 1 January, carnival and 25 December. f7.75. ☎ (043) 6090110.

Wilhelminatoren – Easter Day to September: open daily from 10am to 6pm. October to November and March to Easter Day: weekends and public holidays from 1pm to 5pm. Closed December to February. f2. ☎ (043) 6090609.

Roman catacombs – Guided tours only (50min). April to October: daily from 10am to 5pm. November to March: weekends at 2pm. Closed November to March (except weekends). f7.50. ☎ (043) 6012554.

Streekmuseum – Open daily (except Mondays) from 10am to 5pm. Closed Mondays, 1 January, Easter Day and 25 December. f3. ☎ (043) 6016394.

Boudewijntoren – Open April to October, daily from 10am to 6pm. f5. ☎ (043) 3065200.

🚺 Oudestraat 28 - 4351 AV – ☎ (0118) 50 13 65 – fax (0118) 50 17 92

Schotse Huizen – Open April to October, Mondays to Saturdays from noon to 5pm, Sundays 1pm to 5pm. Closed November to March, 30 April, Ascension Day and Whit Sunday. f5. ☎ (0118) 501365 (tourist office).

Oude Stadhuis – Open June to September, Mondays to Saturdays from noon to 5pm. Closed Sundays and public holidays, and from October to May. f2. ☎ (0118) 501365 (tourist office).

Carillon concerts – *June to September, Thursdays from 3pm to 4pm and Saturdays 7pm to 8pm.* ☎ *(0118) 501365 (tourist office).*

Grote Kerke or O.-L.-Vrouwekerk – Open April to October, Mondays to Saturdays from 10am to 5pm, Sundays 1pm to 5pm. Closed November to March. f5. ☎ (0118) 501365 (tourist office).

🚺 Koninginneplein 2 - 5911 KK – ☎ (077) 354 38 00 – fax (077) 320 77 70

Boat trips – Wednesdays to Sundays from 8.30 to 5pm. Information: Rederij Het Veerhuis, Schoor 1, ☎ (0475) 591318.

St.-Martinuskerk – Open daily from 9am to noon and 2pm to 4pm. ☎ (077) 3512439.

Limburgs Museum – Closed for renovation until mid-2000. ☎ (077) 3522112.

Museum van Bommel-van Dam – Open Tuesdays to Fridays from 10am to 4.30pm, weekends 2pm to 5pm. Closed Mondays and public holidays. f3.50. ☎ (077) 3513457.

Excursion

Missiemuseum Steyl – ♿ Late March to late October: open Tuesdays to Saturdays from 10am to 5pm, Sundays and public holidays 1pm to 5pm. Late October to late March: open daily (except Mondays) from 1pm to 5pm. Closed Mondays, 1 January, Good Friday and 25 December. f3.50. ☎ (077) 3768294.

Botanische tuin Jochum-Hof – ♿ Open April to October, daily from 1pm to 5pm. Closed November to March. f4. ☎ (077) 3733020.

Arcen Castle gardens – Open April to 2 November, daily from 10am to 6pm; Christmas period, daily from 11am to 6pm. Closed from 3 November to the Christmas period, and from January to March. f18. ☎ (077) 4731882.

🚺 Grote Markt 23 - 5801 BL – ☎ (0478) 51 05 05 – fax (0478) 51 27 36

St.-Petrus Bandenkerk – Open April to October, daily (except Sunday) from 2pm to 4pm. ☎ (0478) 510505.

Excursion

Nederlands Nationaal Oorlogs- en Verzetsmuseum – ♿ June to August: open daily from 9.30am to 6pm. September to May; open daily from 10am to 5pm. Closed 1 January, 24, 25 and 31 December. f11. ☎ (0478) 641820.

🚺 Nieuwendijk 15 - 4381 BV – ☎ (0118) 41 23 45 fax (0118) 41 74 26

Boat trips – In July and August. Information from the tourist office, ☎ (0118) 412345.

Maritiem Attractiecentrum Het Arsenaal – ♿ January to March: open Wednesdays to Sundays from 10am to 7pm. April to October and during school holidays: open daily from 10am to 8pm. November and December: open Tuesdays to Sundays from 10am to 7pm. Closed 1 January, 25 December and 31 December. f16. ☎ (0118) 411463.

Stedelijk Museum – Open Mondays to Fridays from 10am to 5pm, weekends from 1pm to 5pm. Closed 1 January, 25 and 26 December. f2.50. ☎ (0118) 412498.

Reptielenzoo Iguana – June to September: open Tuesdays, Wednesdays, Fridays and Saturdays from 10am to 12.30pm and 2pm to 5.30pm, Mondays, Thursdays and Sundays 2pm to 5.30pm. October to May: open daily from 2pm to 5.30pm. Closed 1 January and 25 December. f9.50. ☎ (0118) 417219.

🚺 Zeestraat 37 - 1131 ZD – ☎ (0299) 36 37 47 – fax (0299) 36 84 84

Volendams Museum – Open mid-March to mid-October, daily from 10am to 5pm. Closed mid-October to mid-March. f3.50. ☎ (0299) 369258.

W

De WADDENEILANDEN

Guided walks across the mudflats – Early April to late October (weather permitting). Information and bookings: Wadloopcentrum Pieterburen, PB 1, 9968 ZG Pieterburen, ☏ (0595) 528300, or Dijkstra Wadlooptochten, Hoofdstraat 118, 9968 AH Peterburen, ☏ (0595) 528345.

AMELAND

Ferry – From Holwerd. Departure times vary; check Wagenborg Passagiersdiensten recorded information on ☏ (0519) 542001. Crossing lasts about 45min. Reservations and other information: ☏ (0519) 546111. f19.65 (return), f133.70 (car).

Natuurcentrum Ameland (Nes) – ♿ January to March and autumn half-term to the Christmas holidays: Wednesdays to Saturdays from 1pm to 5pm (spring half-term: Mondays to Fridays from 10am to noon and 1pm to 5pm, Saturdays 1pm to 5pm). April to June and September to autumn half-term: daily from 10am to noon and 1pm to 5pm (weekends 1pm to 5pm only). July and August: daily from 10am to 5pm and 7pm to 9pm (except weekends). Christmas holidays: daily from 10am to noon and 1pm to 5pm (weekends and public holidays 1pm to 5pm only). f4.25. ☏ (0519) 542737.

Landbouw en Juttersmuseum Swartwoude (Buren) – Mid-November to March: open Wednesdays to Saturdays from 1.30pm to 5pm. April to June: Mondays to Fridays from 10am to noon and 1pm to 5pm, weekends 1.30pm to 5pm. July and August: daily from 10am to 5pm, Wednesdays also 7pm to 9pm. September to mid-November: Mondays to Fridays from 10am to noon and 1pm to 5pm, weekends 1.30pm to 5pm. f4. ☏ (0519) 542845.

Cultuur-Historisch Museum Sorgdrager (Hollum) – November to March: open Wednesdays to Saturdays 1.30pm to 5pm. April to June and September to October: Mondays to Fridays from 10am to noon and 1pm to 5pm, weekends 1.30pm to 5pm. July and August: daily from 10am to 5pm, Tuesdays also 7pm to 9pm. Christmas and Easter holidays: Mondays to Fridays from 10am to noon and 1pm to 5pm, weekends 1.30pm to 5pm. f4. ☏ (0519) 554477.

Reddingsmuseum AbrahamFock (Hollum) – ♿ January to March and November to December: Mondays to Fridays from 1.30pm to 5pm. April to June and September to October: open daily from 10am to noon and 1.30pm to 5pm (weekends 1.30pm to 5pm only). Closed public holidays. f3.50. ☏ (0519) 554243.

Ameland Lifeboat (Hollum) – Demonstrations are given eight to ten times a year. Contact the museum for information. ☏ (0519) 554243.

SCHIERMONNIKOOG

Ferry – From Lauwersoog. Departure times vary; call Wagenborg Passagiersdiensten recorded information line on ☏ (0519) 349079. The crossing takes about 45min, and cars are not allowed on the island. Reservations and other information: ☏ (0519) 349050. f19.30 (return).

Visitor centre – April to autumn half-term and during the Christmas holidays: open Mondays to Saturdays from 10am to noon and 1.30pm to 5.30pm. Rest of the year: open Saturdays from 1.30pm to 5.30pm. ☏ (0519) 531641.

TERSCHELLING

Ferry – From Harlingen. Departure times vary; call the Rederij Doeksen recorded information line on ☏ (0562) 442770 (ferry) or ☏ (0562) 443220 (express service). The ferry crossing takes about 1hr 30min, and the express service 45min. Reservations and other information: ☏ (0562) 446111. f41.25 (return), f21.50 (car).

Terschelling Museum 't Behouden Huys (West-Terschelling) – April to mid-June: open Mondays to Fridays from 10am to 5pm. Second half of June and in September: open Mondays to Fridays from 10am to 5pm, Saturdays 1pm to 5pm. July and August: open Mondays to Fridays from 10am to 5pm, weekends 1pm to 5pm. October and during school holidays: open Mondays to Fridays from 10am to 5pm. Closed November to March. f5. ☏ (0562) 442389.

Centrum voor natuur en landschap (West-Terschelling) – ♿ April to October: open Mondays to Fridays from 9am to 5pm, and weekends, public holidays and school holidays from 2pm to 5pm. Closed November to March, Easter Day and Whit Sunday. f7.50. ☏ (0562) 442390.

De Boschplaat – Open (limited access) from mid-March to mid-August. Motor vehicles not allowed. Haycart tours: contact the tourist office, Willem Barentszkade 19a, ☏ (0562) 443000.

TEXEL

Ferry – From Den Helder. Departure times vary; call the TESO recorded information line on ☎ (0222) 369691. The crossing takes about 20min; reservations not accepted. For more information, ☎ (0222) 369692. f10 (return), f48.50 (car).

Nature reserves – Guided tours: contact EcoMare or the tourist office. Boots and binoculars recommended. Limited access during nesting season.

EcoMare (De Koog) – Open Mondays to Saturdays from 9am to 5pm, also Sundays (except January to March) and public holidays from 9am to 5pm. Closed Sundays from January to March, 1 January and 25 December. f12.50. ☎ (0222) 317741.

Salt water ponds (seal feeding times) – 11am and 3pm.

Oudheidkamer (Den Burg) – Open April to October and during Christmas holidays, Mondays to Fridays from 10am to 12.30pm and 1.30pm to 3.30pm. f3.50. ☎ (0222) 313135.

Maritiem en Jutters Museum (Oudeschild) – Open Tuesdays to Sundays from 10am to 5pm; July and August daily from 10am to 5pm. Closed Mondays (except in July and August). f8. ☎ (0222) 314956.

Agrarisch en Wagen Museum (De Waal) – Open mid-March to autumn half-term, Mondays from 1.30pm to 5pm, Tuesdays to Fridays from 10am to 5pm. Saturdays from 10am to 4pm. Sundays and public holidays from 2pm to 4pm. Closed from after autumn half-term until mid-March. f5. ☎ (0222) 312951.

VLIELAND

Ferry – From Harlingen or Terschelling (May to September only, 30min). Departure times vary; call Rederij Doeksen recorded information line on ☎ (0562) 442969 (ferry boat) or ☎ (0562) 443220 (express service). The ferry boat crossing takes about one and half hours, and the express service about 45min. Cars are not allowed on the island. Reservations and other information: ☎ (0562) 446111. f37.50 (return).

Museum Tromp's Huys – ♿ April to October: open Wednesdays and weekends from 2pm to 5pm; during school holidays, daily from 2pm to 5pm. November to March: open Wednesdays from 2pm to 5pm. Closed 1 January, Easter Day, Whit Sunday and 25 December. f5. ☎ (0562) 451600.

De Noordwester – ♿ April to September: open daily (except Sundays) from 2pm to 5pm. July and August: open daily (except Sundays) from 10am to noon and 2pm to 5pm. October to March: open Wednesdays and Saturdays from 2pm to 5pm, Sundays 1pm to 4pm. f5. Closed 1 January and 25 December. ☎ (0562) 451700.

Church – Guided tours only; by appointment. ☎ (0562) 451669.

WORKUM 🖸 Noard 5 – 8711 AA – ☎ (0515) 54 13 00 – fax (0515) 54 36 05

St.-Gertrudiskerk – Open Easter Day to October, daily (except Sunday) from 11am to 5pm. Closed November to Easter Day. ☎ (0515) 541976.

Warkums Erfskip – Open April to October, Tuesdays to Fridays from 10am to 5pm, Saturdays to Mondays 1pm to 5pm. Closed November to March. ☎ (0515) 543155.

Jopie Huisman Museum – April to October: open Mondays to Saturdays from 10am to 5pm, Sundays 1pm to 5pm. March, November and public holidays: open daily from 1pm to 5pm. Closed December to February. f5. ☎ (0515) 543131.

Z

ZAANSTREEK 🖸 Gedempte Gracht 76 – 1506 CJ – ☎ (075) 616 22 21 fax (075) 670 53 81
– valley.interact.nl/zaanseschans

Boat tours – ♿ April to October: Tuesdays to Sundays from 11am to 4pm (every hour on the hour). July and August: daily from 10am to 5pm. f8. ☎ (075) 6146762.

Klompenmakerij – ♿ Open March to October, daily from 8am to 6pm; November to March, daily from 9am to 5pm. ☎ (075) 6177121.

Bakkerijmuseum – Open Tuesdays to Sundays from 10am to 5pm; July and August daily from 10am to 5pm. Closed Mondays (except in July and August). f1.50. ☎ (075) 6173522.

Kaasmakerij Catharina Hoeve – Open March to October, daily from 8am to 6pm; November to February, daily from 8.30am to 5pm. ☎ (075) 6215820.

Het Noorderhuis – Open March to November, daily from 10am to 5pm; December to February, weekends from 10am to 5pm. f1.50. ☎ (075) 6173237.

Museumwinkel Albert Heijn – Open March to October, daily from 10am to 1pm and 2pm to 5pm; November to February, weekends from 11am to 1pm and 2pm to 4pm. ☎ (075) 6169619.

Klokkenmuseum – Open March to November, daily from 10am to 5pm; December to February, weekends from noon to 4.30pm. f5. ☎ (075) 6179769.

Pewter workshop – Open April to December, daily from 10am to 5pm; January to March, daily from 11am to 4pm. Closed 25 December. ☎ (075) 6176204.

De Poelenburg – Open on the second Saturday of every month, from 2pm to 5pm. f4. ☎ (075) 6215148.

Verfmolen De Kat – Open April to October, daily from 9am to 5pm. Closed November to March. f4. ☎ (075) 6210477.

Oilmolen De Zoeker – Open mid-March to September, daily from 9.30am to 4.30pm. Closed October to mid-March. f4. ☎ (075) 6287942.

Additional sights

Zaans Historisch Museum – Open Tuesdays to Fridays and Sundays from 1pm to 5pm. Closed Mondays, Saturdays, 1 January, Easter Day, Whit Sunday and 25 December. f2.50. ☎ (075) 6217626.

Molenmuseum – June to September: open Tuesdays to Fridays from 11am to 5pm, Saturdays 2pm to 5pm, Sundays and public holidays 1pm to 5pm. October to April: open Tuesdays to Fridays from 10am to noon and 1pm to 5pm, Saturdays 2pm to 5pm, Sundays and public holidays 1pm to 5pm. Closed Mondays. f4.50. ☎ (075) 6288968.

Czaar-Peterhuisje – April to October: open Tuesdays to Fridays from 10am to 1pm and 2pm to 5pm. November to March: open weekends from 1.30pm to 5pm. Closed Mondays and public holidays. f2.50. ☎ (075) 6160390.

ZIERIKZEE ☒ Meelstraat 4 – 4301 EC – ☎ (0111) 41 24 50

Boat trips – July and August, Mondays to Thursdays. Information: Rederij Gebhard. ☎ (010) 2650296.

Maritiem Museum – Open April to October, Mondays to Saturdays from 10am to 5pm, Sundays noon to 5pm. Closed November to March (except during school holidays), 1 January, 25 December. f4. ☎ (0111) 454464.

Stadhuis: carillon – Thursdays from 10.30am to 11.30am. ☎ (0111) 454464.

Stadhuismuseum – Open May to October, Mondays to Saturdays from 10am to 5pm, Sundays noon to 5pm. Closed November to April. f4. ☎ (0111) 454464.

St.-Lievensmonstertoren – Open Mondays to Saturdays from 11am to 4pm, Sundays and public holidays noon to 4pm. f2. ☎ (0111) 412450 (tourist office).

ZUTPHEN ☒ Stationsplein 39 – 7201 MH – ☎ (0900) 269 28 88 fax (0575) 51 79 28

St.-Walburgskerk – Open May to September, Mondays to Fridays. ☎ (0575) 514178.

Museum Henriette Polak – Open Tuesdays to Fridays from 11am to 5pm, weekends 1.30pm to 5pm. Closed Mondays, 1 January, Easter Day, Whit Sunday and 25 December. f5. ☎ (0575) 516878.

Wijndragerstoren: carillon – Thursdays and Saturdays from 11am to noon.

Stedelijk Museum – ♿ Open Tuesdays to Fridays from 11am to 5pm, weekends 1.30pm to 5pm. Closed Mondays, 1 January, Easter Day, Whit Sunday and 25 December. f5. ☎ (0575) 516878.

Excursions

Grolsch Museum – May to August: open Mondays to Fridays from 9am to 12.30pm and 1.30pm to 5pm, Saturdays 9am to 4pm. September to April: Mondays to Fridays 10am to 12.30pm and 1pm to 5pm, Saturdays 10am to 12.30pm. Closed Mondays and public holidays. f4. ☎ (0544) 461247.

Stedelijk Museum Zwolle – Open Tuesdays to Saturdays from 10am to 5pm, Sundays 1pm to 5pm. Closed Mondays, 1 January, Easter Day, Whit Sunday and 25 December. f5. ☎ (038) 4214650.

Grote Kerk or St.-Michaëlskerk – Open July to September, Tuesdays to Fridays from 11am to 4.30pm, Saturdays 1.30pm to 4.30pm. Closed Sundays, and from October to June. ☎ (038) 4535913.

Stadhuis – Guided tours only: Mondays to Fridays from 8.15am to 5pm. Closed weekends. ☎ (038) 4989111.

Museum De Stadshof – Open Tuesdays to Fridays from 10am to 5pm, weekends and public holidays 1pm to 5pm. Closed Mondays, 1 January, Easter Day, 30 April, Whit Sunday, 25 and 31 December. f5. ☎ (038) 4232647.

Ecodrome – Easter Day to October: open daily from 10am to 5pm. November to December: open Tuesdays to Sundays from 10am to 5pm. January to Easter Day: open Tuesdays to Saturdays from 10am to 5pm, Sundays 1pm to 5pm. Closed 1 January. f13.50. ☎ (038) 4215050.

Stedelijk Museum Zwolle - Painted chest

J. P. Lescourret/PIX

Index

Haarlem *Noord-Holland* .... Towns, sights and tourist regions followed by the name of the province

Rembrandt .... People, historical events, artistic styles and local terms covered in the text

Mauritshuis .... Sights in important towns

Individual sights (mountains, lakes, dams, abbeys castles etc) are indexed under their own names.

A

T

S

U

V

W

Y

Z

Notes

Manufacture Française des Pneumatiques Michelin

Société en commandite par actions au capital de 2 000 000 000 de francs
Place des Carmes-Déchaux – 63000 Clermont-Ferrand (France)
R.C.S. Clermont-Fd B 855 200 507

© *Michelin et Cie, Propriétaires-éditeurs, 1997*

Dépôt légal mai 1997 – ISBN 2-06-157402-5 – ISSN 0763-1383
No part of this publication may be reproduced in any form
without the prior permission of the publisher.
Printed in the EU 06-99/3

Compogravure : MAURY Imprimeur S.A., Malesherbes
Impression et brochage : AUBIN Imprimeur, Ligugé

Route planning made *Simple*

internet
http://www.michelin-travel.com

MICHELIN

Michelin Green Guide Collection

France

- Alsace, Lorraine, Champagne
- Atlantic Coast
- Auvergne, Rhône Valley
- Brittany
- Burgundy, Jura
- Châteaux of the Loire
- Dordogne, Berry, Limousin
- French Alps
- French Riviera
- Normandy
- Northern France and the Paris Region
- Paris
- Provence
- Pyrenees, Languedoc, Tarn Gorges

World

- Austria
- Belgium, Luxembourg
- Berlin
- Brussels
- California
- Canada
- Chicago
- Europe
- Florida
- France
- Germany
- Great Britain
- Greece
- Ireland
- Italy
- London
- Mexico, Guatemala, Belize
- Netherlands
- New England
- New York, New Jersey, Pennsylvania
- New York City
- Portugal
- Quebec
- Rome
- San Francisco
- Scandinavia, Finland
- Scotland
- Sicily
- Spain
- Switzerland
- Tuscany
- Venice
- Vienna
- Wales
- Washington DC
- The West Country of England